AF795978

Hand Book of Synthetic Detergents with Formulations

Written By

EIRI Board of Consultants & Engineers

4449, Nai Sarak, Main Road, Delhi - 110006 (India)
Ph: +91-11-23918117, 23916431, 45120361, 23947058, 64727385
* E-Mail: eiribooks@yahoo.com & eiriprojects@gmail.com
*Website: www.eiriindia.org & www.industrialprojects.in

PRINTED & PUBLISHED BY

ENGINEERS INDIA RESEARCH INSTITUTE

4449, Nai Sarak, Main Road, Delhi - 110006 (India)

Ph: +91-11-23918117, 23916431, 45120361, 23947058, 64727385

* E-Mail: eiribooks@yahoo.com & eiriprojects@gmail.com

*Website: www.eiriindia.org & www.industrialprojects.in

Distributors:

EIRI Project Consultants and Publishers
Roop Nagar, Delhi-110007
and
Industrial Technologies, India
Nai Sarak, Delhi-110006

© Copyrights Reserved by Sudhir Gupta, Delhi

ISBN: 9788186732434

2nd Edition

Printed in New Delhi (INDIA)

The book is sold subject to the condition that it shall not, by way or trade or otherwise, be lent, resold, hired out, or otherwise circulated without the publisher's prior written consent, in any form of binding or cover other than in which it is published/compiled and without a similar consent including this condition being imposed on the subsequent purchaser and without limiting the rights under copyrights reserved above, no part of this publication may be reproduced, stored in or introduced into a retrieval system, or transmitted in any form or by any means (electronic, mechanical, photocopying or otherwise), without the written prior permission of both the copyright owner and above-mentioned publisher of this book. While the book has been prepared carefully, yet the publisher, printer and compiler do not hold any responsibility on the subject of the book. All disputes regarding this book are Subject to Delhi Jurisdiction only.

₹ 975/-

Printed & Published by Sudhir Gupta for "Engineers India Research Institute", 4449 Nai Sarak, Main Road, New Delhi -110006

Hand Book of
Synthetic Detergents with Formulations

OTHER RELATED BOOKS

Textile, Garments, Dyeing

01 Modern Technology Of Bleaching, Dyeing, Printing & Finishing Of Textiles
02 Technology Of Textiles (Spinning & Weaving, Dyeing, Scouring, Drying, Printing and Bleaching)
03 Garments Manufacturing Technology

Chemical/ Dyes/ Petrochemicals/ Lubricant/ Electroplating

01 Small Medium & Large Chemical Industries
02 Industrial Chemicals Technology HB.
03 Modern Technology of Organic & Inorganic Chemicals
04 Hand Book of Electroplating Anodizing & Surface Finishing Technology
05 Hand Book of Agro Chemical Industries
06 Technology of Synthetic Dyes, Pigments Intermediates
07 Petrochemicals, Lubricants, Greases & Petroleum Refining
08 Hand Book of Lubricants, Greases & Petrochemicals Technology

Paint, Varnish, Solvents, Coating & Lacquers, Powder Coating

01 Paint Pigment Varnish & Lacquer Manufg.
02 Paint Varnish Solvents & Coating Technology
03 Paint, Pigment, Solvent, Coating Emulsion, Paint Additives & Formulations
04 Technology Of Coating, Resins, Pigments & Inks Industries
05 Manufacturing Technology & Formulations Hand Book On Thinners, Putty, Wall & Industrial Finishes And Synthetic Resins
06 Technology of Synthetic Resins and Emulsion Polymers
07 Technology of Paints and Coatings with Formulations
08 Powder Coating Technology Hand Book

Gums, Adhesives and Sealants

01 Technology Of Gums, Adhesives & Sealants With Formulations
02 H.B. Of Adhesives With Their Formulaes
03 Adhesives Technology & Formulations Hand Book (Hand Book of Adhesives)
04 Technology of Glue and Adhesives with Adhesives Bonding and Formulations

Textile Auxiliaries & Chemicals

01 Textile Auxiliaries And Chemicals With Processes and Formulations
02 Technology of Textile Chemicals with Formulations
03 Modern Technology of Textile Auxiliary and Chemicals with Formulations
04 Textile Processing Chemicals, Enzymes, Dye Fixing Agents and other Finishes with P.P.

Plastic/Polymer Process, Compounding, Injection Moulding, Rotational Moulding, Plastic Film, Fibre Glass, Plastic Waste Recycling, Moulds, Pet & Resins Industries

01 Moulds Design & Processing Hand Book
02 Hand Book Of Plastic Materials & Processing Technology
03 Injection Moulding Of Plastics
04 Plastic Processing and Packaging Industries
05 Plastic Waste Recycling Technology
06 Technology Of Plastic Films
07 Rotational Moulding Technology Hand Book
08 Plastic Compounding, Master Batches, Pet & Other Plastics
09 Synthetic Resins Technology With Formulations
10 Technology Of PVC Compounding And Its Applications
11 HB of Polymer And Plastic Technology
12 Hand Book Of Fibre Glass Moulding
13 Technology of Reinforced Plastics
14 Plastic Additives Technology Hand Book
15 Technology of Pet Bottles, Preform and Pet Recycling
16 Modern Technology of Extrusion & Extruded Products
17 Technology of Synthetic Resins & Emulsion Polymers
18 Technology of Plastic Additives with Processes and Packaging
19 Technology of Disposable Medical Products

Cosmetic (Synthetic & Herbal)

01 Cosmetics Processes & Formulations
02 Herbal Cosmetics & Beauty Products With Formulations
03 Profitable Small Scale Manufacture Of Cosmetics (Synthetic & Herbal)
04 Hand Book Of Synthetic & Herbal Cosmetics (How to Make Beauty Products)
05 Technology Of Herbal Cosmetics & Toiletries Products With Formulae

Soaps & Detergents

01 Household Soap. Toilet Soap & Other Soap
02 Profitable Small Scale Manufacture Of Soaps & Detergents
03 Synthetic Detergents With Formulations
04 Modern Technology of Acid Slurry, Surfactants, Soap and Detergents with Formulae
05 Manufacture of Washing Soap, Toilet Soap, Detergents, Liquid Soap & Deter-gents and Perfumes with Formulations

* E-Mail: eiribooks@yahoo.com & eiriprojects@gmail.com
*Website: www.eiriindia.org & www.industrialprojects.in

PREFACE

You may well ask why soap, which served well for so many years, was eventually displaced. Soaps are cheap and they are manufactured from a renewable source, whereas many of the synthetic detergents are made from petrochemicals. Soaps are also biodegradable; that is, they are readily broken down by bacteria, and thus they do not pollute rivers. However, due to their gelling properties, soaps do have a greater tendency to clog sewerage reticulation systems than synthetic detergents. The grease trap of a non-sewered house was often laden with soap. But the most important reason for the displacement of soap is the fact that, when a carboxylic acid soap is used in hard water, precipitation occurs. The calcium and magnesium ions, which give hardness to the water, form insoluble salts with the fatty acid in soap and a curd-like precipitate occurs and settles, of course, on what ever is being washed. By using a large excess of soap, it is possible to redisperse the precipitate, but it is extremely sticky and difficult to move. This problem with soap can be demonstrated by a simple experiment in which a concentrated solution of hard-water salts is added to a 0.1% solution of soap and also to a 0.1% solution of synthetic surfactant. The soap precipitates, but the synthetic surfactant remains clear because it's salts are water soluble.

You may live in an area where the water is extremely soft. But calcium and magnesium ions are present in the dirt that you wash out of your clothes, so that some precipitation still occurs if soap is used, and gradually deposits are built up in the fabric.

Synthetic detergents dissolve or tend to dissolve in water or other solvents. To enable them to do this, they require distinct chemical characteristics. Hydrophilic (water loving) groupings in their molecular structure, and hydrophobic (water hating) groupings, help the detergent in it's "detergency" action.

This detergency depends on the balance of the molecular weight of the hydrophobic to the hydrophilic portion. This is called the HLB value, and can range from 1 upwards. HLB is Hydrophilic-Lypophilic Balance. As the 0HLB value increases, the product can tend towards being a paste or solid. The lower number HLB values tend to be less water soluble, and more oil soluble. The higher the HLB the more water soluble the product.

Mixtures of low and high HLB detergents produce good detergents to handle oil, fat and grease, the higher HLB detergent helps solubilise the less water soluble, low HLB detergent into an aqueous system.

The Book 'Hand Book of Synthetic Detergents with Formulations' covers Principle Groups of Synthetic Detergents, Manufacturing Technologies with Formulae to produce Detergents. The main chapters of the book are Groups of Synthetic Detergents, Synthesis of Detergents, Manufacture of Finished Detergents, Formulation and Application of Detergents, Perfuming of Soaps and Detergents, Testing of Soaps and Detergents, Manufacturing of Herbal Synthetic Detergents, Detergent Bars, Herbal Liquid and Paste Detergents, Acid Slurry By Manual Process, Anionic Detergents, Detergent Washing Powder (Arial Type), Blue Detergent Powder, Cleaning Powder, Laundry and Dry Cleaners, Liquid Toilet Cleaners (Harpik Type), Acid Slurry (L.A.B.), Nerol Laundry Soap, Liquid Detergents for Wool, Laundry for Clothes Washing, Nirma Type Detergent Powder, Non-Ionic Liquid Detergents, Detergent Paste (Textile Grade), Washing and Laundry Soap, Zeolite-A (Detergent Grade), Detergent Powder Plants- Dry Mix Process, Laundry Soap, Bath Toilet Soap Finishing Line, Detergent Cake Plants, Suppliers of Raw Materials, Suppliers of Plant and Machinery, Present Manufacturers, Packaging Addresses,

Hope, the book will undoubtedly help the new entrepreneurs as well as well established industrialists.

EIRI Board of Consultants & Engineers

Contents and Subject Index

Multiple Project Reports in CD-Roms

01 92 New Lucrative Project Reports In Cd
02. 45 Infotech/It, Hospitality, Hospital, College, School & Club
03. 23 Profitable Construction Projects
04. 56 Agro Based & Food Processing Projects
05. 52 Food, Dairy, Bakery, Confectionery & Snacks Foods
06. 45 New Chemicals & Allied Project Reports
07. 100 Profitable Plastic, Polymers & Allied Projects
08. 44 Textile, Garments, Hosiery & Allied Products In Cd
09. 23 Dairy Farming (Buffalo & Jersey Cow, Dairy Products & Other Milk Processing Ind.
10. 42 Paper, Pulp & Paper Converting Products Reports
11. 31 Essential Oils, Perfumes, Flavours & Aromatic Compounds
12. 28 Surgical And Disposable Medical Projects
13. 36 Profitable Printing & Allied Projects Reports
14. 63 Profitable Packaging & Allied Project Reports
15. 99 Profitable Printing & Packaging
16. 42 Electroplating, Anodizing & Allied Projects
17. 31 Profitable Plantation & Cultivation Projects
18. 55 Profitable Products From Agro And Other Industrial Wastes
19. 35 Profitable Gums, Adhesives, Sealants And Resins Projects
20. 54 Paint, Varnish, Solvents, Lacquers, Resins, Enamel, Pigments, Thinners & Powder (54 Project Reports In Cd)
21 43 Iron, Steel, Casting, Fabrication, Wire Drawing & Rolling Mills Projects
22. 26 New Educational Projects (Schools, Colleges, Training/ Management Institute, Hostels Etc.)
23. 12 Mosquitoes Preventive Projects (Coils, Mats, Liquids, Agarbatti, Nets, Spray Etc.)
24. 21 Bakery And Allied Products
25. 67 Rubber And Rubber Goods Industries
26. 37 Aluminium And Aluminium Based Industries
27. 14 Potato And Potato Based Industries
28. 50 Electrical, Electronics And Computer Based Industries
29. 52 Cosmetics (Herbal & Synthetics) Technology Projects (52 Project Reports)
30. 10 Molasses Based Lucrative Projects
31. 24 Fruits/Veg. & Allied Food Dehydration Projects

ENGINEERS INDIA RESEARCH INSTITUTE

4449 Nai Sarak, Main Road, Delhi - 110006 (INDIA)

Ph : 91- 11- 23916431, 23918117, 45120361, 64727385, 23947058

E-Mail : eiriprojects@gmail.com Website: www.eiriindia.org

Chapter	Page No.

PROCESS TECHNOLOGY BOOKS BY EIRI

Mineral And Minerals

01 Hand Book Of Minerals And Minerals Based Industries

Rubber Chemicals, Compound & Rubber Industries

01 Rubber Chemicals & Processing Industries
02 Modern Rubber Chemicals, Compounds & Rubber Goods Technology
03 Technology Of Rubber & Rubber Goods Industries

Ayurvedic & Herbal Medicines

01 Ayurvedic & Herbal Medicines With Formulaes
02 Hand Book Of Ayurvedic Medicines With Formulations (A Complete Hand Book Of Ayurvedic & Herbal Medicines)

Steel & Stainless Steel, Non Ferrous Metals, Metal Extraction, Rolling Mill & Steel Wire

01 Modern Technology of Non Ferrous Metals & Metal Extraction
02 Processing Technology of Steels and Stainless Steels
03 Modern Technology of Rolling Mill, Billets, Steel Wire, Galvanized Sheet, Forging & Castings
04 Manufacturing Technology of Non-Ferrous Metal Products

Wood, Veneer, Plywood, Particle, Board, Fibreboard, Bamboo & Forest Products

01 Modern Technology Of Wood, Veneer, Plywood, Particle Board, Fibreboard, Bamboo & Forest Products

Products form Waste

01 Technology Of Products From Wastes Industrial, Agriculture, Medical, Municipality, Organic & Biological

ENGINEERS INDIA RESEARCH INSTITUTE
4449 Nai Sarak, Main Road, Delhi - 110006 (INDIA)
Ph : 91- 11- 23916431, 23918117, 45120361, 64727385, 23947058
E-Mail : eiriprojects@gmail.com Website: www.eiriindia.org

Chapter - 1

GROUPS OF SYNTHETIC DETERGENTS

INTRODUCTION

Synthetic detergents, like soap, are materials which dissolve or tend to dissolve in water and in non-aqueous materials under certain conditions. To achieve this double tendency, these materials include two distinct groupings in their molecular structure. One, which is easily soluble in water, is called the *hydrophilic groups*, and the other, which on its own would be insoluble in water, is known as the *hydrophobic group.*

The hydrophilic group is usually, although not always, added synthetically to a hydrophobic material in order to produce a compound which is soluble in water. However, this solubilisation does not necessarily always produce a detergent, since detergency depends on the balance (ratio) of the molecular weight of the hydrophobic portion to that of the hydrophilic portion.

As an illustration, consider the material dodecane, $C_{12}H_{26}$. This is completely insoluble in water. If an OH group is substituted for one of the terminal hydrogens, the new material $C_{11}H_{25}CH_2OH$ lauryl alcohol, is still practically insoluble, but a tendency to solubility has arisen. If now this lauryl alcohol is sulphated to

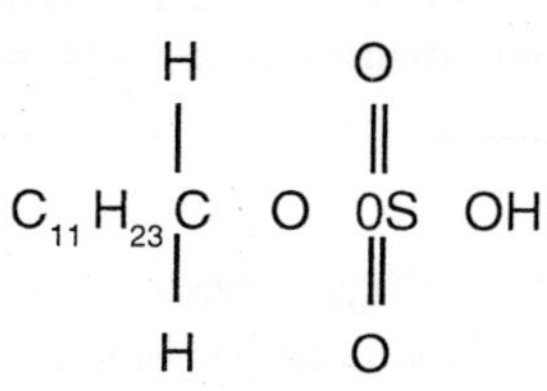

we have a material which is completely miscible in water in all proportions, ignoring, for the sake of development of this theme, hydrolysis which will occur when dissolving the acid product. If this sulphuric ester is neutralised with a caustic alkali, ammonia, or organic amines, the material becomes completely soluble in water and in this instance is a very good detergent.

If, instead of sulphating the lauryl alcohol, it is treated with, say, ten molecules of ethylene oxide :

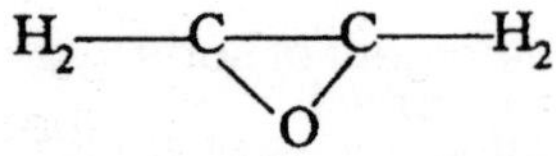

we obtain the material:

$$C_{11}H_{23}CH_2{-}O{-}CH_2{-}CH_2(OCH_2CH_2)_8{-}OCH_2CH_2OH$$

This material is again completely water-soluble and a good detergent. If only five or as much as twenty molecules of ethylene oxide had been used, the detergency would fall off, although the materials would still be water-soluble. If less than five molecules of ethylene oxide had been used, the product would be insoluble.

To return to the lauryl alcohol, if it were to be oxidised to lauric acid, that is the original dodecane, with a carboxyl group replacing the terminal CH_3 group, the material is still practically insoluble in water, but if this acid is neutralised with caustic alkalis or certain selected organic amines, the product is again water-soluble, being, in fact, a soap. In this instance it is a moderately good detergent, but if the original chain length had been say 18 carbons, the detergency would be greatly improved. This demonstrates what was pointed out above, i.e., that the hydrophile/hydrophobe balance is important for optimum detergency.

It should be noted that in the previous paragraph no mention was made of neutralisation with alkaline earths. This illustrates one of the failings of soaps. With the magnesium and calcium salts which are normally present in hard water, soaps form an insoluble scum which lowers the efficiency of the soap. This is a basic defect of the carboxyl group and detergents are so designed that this carboxyl grouping is replaced by something else which does not behave adversely in the presence of salts of calcium and magnesium.

To continue with our analogy of dodecane as the starting material, this in itself can be sulphonated by sulphoxidation to dodecane sulphonic acid :

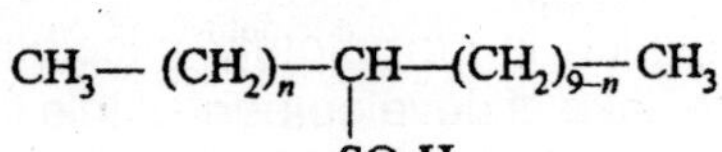

which is miscible with water. When this is neutralised with caustic alkalis, selected alkaline earths or organic amines, solutions in water are obtained which are detergents.

Now if the dodecane were to be chlorinated and then reacted with trimethylamine the compound obtained is lauryl trimethylammonium chloride :-

$$C_{12}H_{23}\overset{+}{N}(CH_3)_3Cl^-$$

again soluble in water and a detergent of sorts.

Finally, if by a rather complicated series of condensations, dodecyl beta alanine :

$$C_{12}H_{25}NHC_2H_4COOH$$

is produced, this is soluble in water, even without neutralisation of the carboxyl group, and also has detergent properties.

Thus, in every example we have discussed, a solubilising group has been added to the dodecane. This group or grouping is hydrophilic, while the original dodecane is hydrophobic, and in every case the resultant product is a detergent which is available on the world market. In practice dodecane itself is not often used as a starting material, very few, if any, of the reactions discussed are as simple as shown. The discussion illustrate how an insoluble hydrophobe can be solubilised and converted into a detergent with varying qualities and reactions are shown schematically in Fig. 3.1. In addition, this diagram includes another very important reaction which reaction consists of chlorinating the dodecane, coupling this product with benzene by means of the well-known Friedel-Crafts reaction, and then sulphonating it to dodecyl benzene sulphonic acid. This process not only provides the most important detergent on the market but is also one of the few cases when dodecane can be used as the starting material.

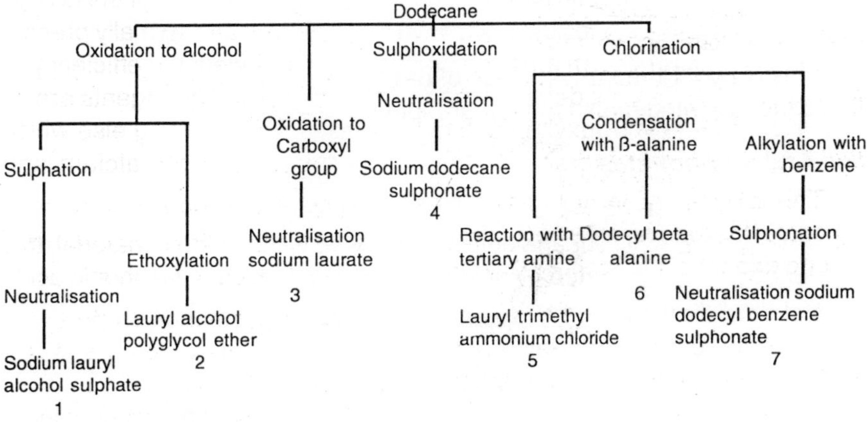

Fig. 3.1. Hypothetical illustration of how dedecane can be solubilised and converted into a detergent with varying qualities.

From the figure it will be noticed that end products 1,3,4 and 7 are all acidic and need to be neutralised with a base before being used. No. 5 is a basic material which in the process of manufacture is produced as the chloride (i.e., it is in effect neutralised with hydrochloric acid) and No. 2 needs no neutralisation at all. If the molecular structure of compound No. 6, for which we have taken as an example dodecyl beta alanine, is examined, it will be noted that it contains both a carboxyl (acid) and an amine (basic) group. The carboxyl group can be neutralised with an alkali, or by the amine group from an adjacent molecule. Similarly, the amine group can be neutralised by a strong acid, such as hydrochloric acid, or by the carboxyl group from an adjacent molecule.

CLASSIFICATION

There are four main classes of detergent: anionic, cationic, non-ionic, and amphoteric.

Anionic detergents are compounds in which the detergency is vested in the anion, which has to be neutralised with an alkaline or basic material before the full detergency is developed. In *cationic detergents* the detergency is in the cation, and although in the manufacturing process no neutralisation takes place, the material is in effect neutralised by a strong acid. *Non-ionic detergents* contain no ionic constituents, as their name implies, and *amphoteric detergents* include both acidic and basic groups in the same molecule.

Anionic Detergents

This is by far the largest class of detergents. The anionic detergents fall into the following main types of grouping:

Alkyl Aryl Sulphonates

This is by far the largest group in general use, since dodecyl benzene sulphonate, the leading member of the group, either as the propylene tetramer benzene or as the linear alkyl benzene.

Not only are the alkyl aryl sulphonates outstanding in their properties as detergents, but they are also based on raw materials which are less difficult to obtain and less expensive than the raw materials on which the other types of detergents are based. The main source of alkyl aryl sulphonates the petroleum industry.

PROCESS TECHNOLOGY BOOKS BY EIRI

Chemical/ Dyes/ Petrochemicals/ Lubricant/ Electroplating

01 Small Medium & Large Chemical Industries
02 Industrial Chemicals Technology Hand Book
03 Modern Technology of Organic & Inorganic Chemicals
04 Hand Book of Electroplating Anodizing & Surface Finishing Technology
05 Hand Book of Agro Chemical Industries (Insecticides & Pesticides)
06 Technology of Synthetic Dyes, Pigments Intermediates
07 Petrochemicals, Lubricants, Greases & Petroleum Refining
08 Hand Book of Lubricants, Greases & Petrochemicals Technology

Gums, Adhesives and Sealants

01 Technology Of Gums, Adhesives & Sealants With Formulations
02 Hand Book Of Adhesives With Their Formulae
03 Adhesives Technology & Formulations Hand Book

Small Scale Industries/ Stationery/Paper/ Inks/ Candles & Export Business

01 Start Your Own Export Business (How To Export)
02 Start Your Own Small Business And Industry
03 Candle Making Processes & Formulations Hand Book
04 Stationery, Paper Converting & Packaging Industries
05 Modern Inks Formulations & Manufacturing Industries
06 Profitable Businesses To Start For Entrepreneurs
07 Modern Small & Cottage Scale Industries
08 Profitable Small Cottage Tiny & Home Industries

Bio Fuel & Bioprocessing

01 Technology Of Bio-Fules (Ethanol & Biodiesel)
02 Modern Technology Of Bioprocessing

ENGINEERS INDIA RESEARCH INSTITUTE

4449 Nai Sarak, Main Road, Delhi - 110006 (INDIA)
Ph : 91- 11- 23916431, 23918117, 45120361, 64727385, 23947058
E-Mail : eiriprojects@gmail.com Website: www.eiriindia.org

Chapter - 1

GROUPS OF SYNTHETIC DETERGENTS

INTRODUCTION

Synthetic detergents, like soap, are materials which dissolve or tend to dissolve in water and in non-aqueous materials under certain conditions. To achieve this double tendency, these materials include two distinct groupings in their molecular structure. One, which is easily soluble in water, is called the *hydrophilic groups*, and the other, which on its own would be insoluble in water, is known as the *hydrophobic group.*

The hydrophilic group is usually, although not always, added synthetically to a hydrophobic material in order to produce a compound which is soluble in water. However, this solubilisation does not necessarily always produce a detergent, since detergency depends on the balance (ratio) of the molecular weight of the hydrophobic portion to that of the hydrophilic portion.

As an illustration, consider the material dodecane, $C_{12}H_{26}$. This is completely insoluble in water. If an OH group is substituted for one of the terminal hydrogens, the new material $C_{11}H_{25}CH_2OH$ lauryl alcohol, is still practically insoluble, but a tendency to solubility has arisen. If now this lauryl alcohol is sulphated to

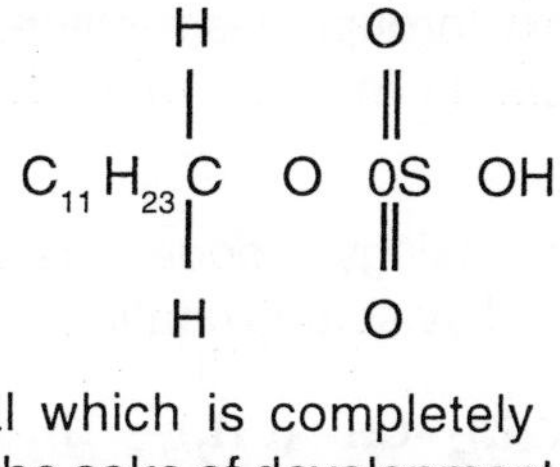

we have a material which is completely miscible in water in all proportions, ignoring, for the sake of development of this theme, hydrolysis which will occur when dissolving the acid product. If this sulphuric ester is neutralised with a caustic alkali, ammonia, or organic amines, the material becomes completely soluble in water and in this instance is a very good detergent.

If, instead of sulphating the lauryl alcohol, it is treated with, say, ten molecules of ethylene oxide :

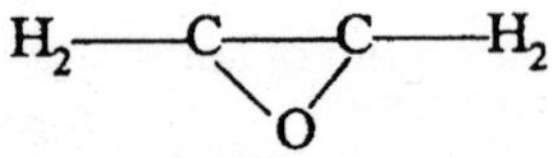

we obtain the material:

$C_{11}H_{23}CH_2–O–CH_2–CH_2(OCH_2CH_2)_8–OCH_2CH_2OH$

This material is again completely water-soluble and a good detergent. If only five or as much as twenty molecules of ethylene oxide had been used, the detergency would fall off, although the materials would still be water-soluble. If less than five molecules of ethylene oxide had been used, the product would be insoluble.

To return to the lauryl alcohol, if it were to be oxidised to lauric acid, that is the original dodecane, with a carboxyl group replacing the terminal CH_3 group, the material is still practically insoluble in water, but if this acid is neutralised with caustic alkalis or certain selected organic amines, the product is again water-soluble, being, in fact, a soap. In this instance it is a moderately good detergent, but if the original chain length had been say 18 carbons, the detergency would be greatly improved. This demonstrates what was pointed out above, i.e., that the hydrophile/hydrophobe balance is important for optimum detergency.

It should be noted that in the previous paragraph no mention was made of neutralisation with alkaline earths. This illustrates one of the failings of soaps. With the magnesium and calcium salts which are normally present in hard water, soaps form an insoluble scum which lowers the efficiency of the soap. This is a basic defect of the carboxyl group and detergents are so designed that this carboxyl grouping is replaced by something else which does not behave adversely in the presence of salts of calcium and magnesium.

To continue with our analogy of dodecane as the starting material, this in itself can be sulphonated by sulphoxidation to dodecane sulphonic acid :

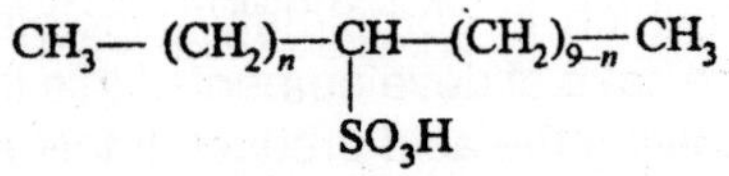

which is miscible with water. When this is neutralised with caustic alkalis, selected alkaline earths or organic amines, solutions in water are obtained which are detergents.

Now if the dodecane were to be chlorinated and then reacted with trimethylamine the compound obtained is lauryl trimethylammonium chloride :-

$$C_{12}H_{23}\overset{+}{N}(CH_3)_3Cl^-$$

again soluble in water and a detergent of sorts.

Finally, if by a rather complicated series of condensations, dodecyl beta alanine :

$$C_{12}H_{25}NHC_2H_4COOH$$

is produced, this is soluble in water, even without neutralisation of the carboxyl group, and also has detergent properties.

Thus, in every example we have discussed, a solubilising group has been added to the dodecane. This group or grouping is hydrophilic, while the original dodecane is hydrophobic, and in every case the resultant product is a detergent which is available on the world market. In practice dodecane itself is not often used as a starting material, very few, if any, of the reactions discussed are as simple as shown. The discussion illustrate how an insoluble hydrophobe can be solubilised and converted into a detergent with varying qualities and reactions are shown schematically in Fig. 3.1. In addition, this diagram includes another very important reaction which reaction consists of chlorinating the dodecane, coupling this product with benzene by means of the well-known Friedel-Crafts reaction, and then sulphonating it to dodecyl benzene sulphonic acid. This process not only provides the most important detergent on the market but is also one of the few cases when dodecane can be used as the starting material.

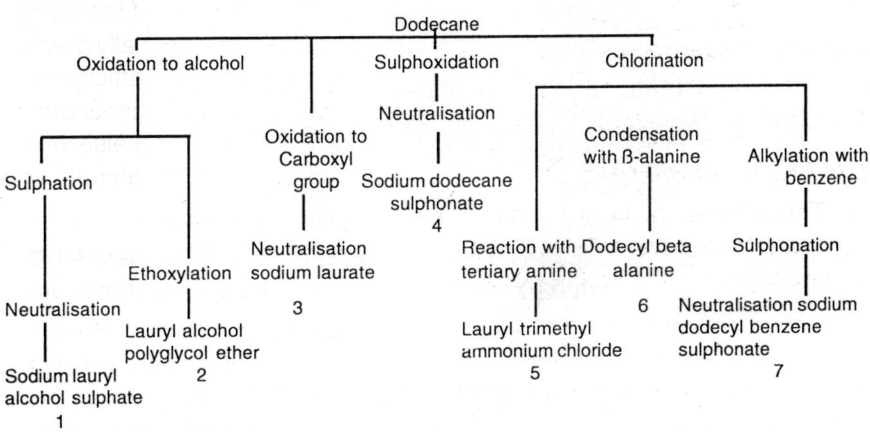

Fig. 3.1. Hypothetical illustration of how dedecane can be solubilised and converted into a detergent with varying qualities.

From the figure it will be noticed that end products 1,3,4 and 7 are all acidic and need to be neutralised with a base before being used. No. 5 is a basic material which in the process of manufacture is produced as the chloride (i.e., it is in effect neutralised with hydrochloric acid) and No. 2 needs no neutralisation at all. If the molecular structure of compound No. 6, for which we have taken as an example dodecyl beta alanine, is examined, it will be noted that it contains both a carboxyl (acid) and an amine (basic) group. The carboxyl group can be neutralised with an alkali, or by the amine group from an adjacent molecule. Similarly, the amine group can be neutralised by a strong acid, such as hydrochloric acid, or by the carboxyl group from an adjacent molecule.

CLASSIFICATION

There are four main classes of detergent: anionic, cationic, non-ionic, and amphoteric.

Anionic detergents are compounds in which the detergency is vested in the anion, which has to be neutralised with an alkaline or basic material before the full detergency is developed. In *cationic detergents* the detergency is in the cation, and although in the manufacturing process no neutralisation takes place, the material is in effect neutralised by a strong acid. *Non-ionic detergents* contain no ionic constituents, as their name implies, and *amphoteric detergents* include both acidic and basic groups in the same molecule.

Anionic Detergents

This is by far the largest class of detergents. The anionic detergents fall into the following main types of grouping:

Alkyl Aryl Sulphonates

This is by far the largest group in general use, since dodecyl benzene sulphonate, the leading member of the group, either as the propylene tetramer benzene or as the linear alkyl benzene.

Not only are the alkyl aryl sulphonates outstanding in their properties as detergents, but they are also based on raw materials which are less difficult to obtain and less expensive than the raw materials on which the other types of detergents are based. The main source of alkyl aryl sulphonates is the petroleum industry.

As the name implies, these products are based on aromatic compounds combined with an aliphatic chain bound to the aromatic nucleus. Taking as an example the most important type of alkyl aryl condensate, dodecyl benzene, this has the following structural formula :

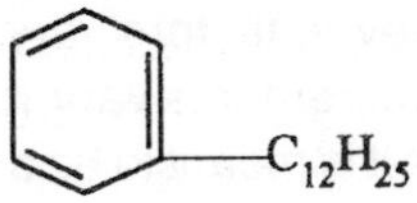

whether the side chain is branched or linear.

This compound may be obtained by condensing benzene with a monochlorinated aliphatic chain having about 12 carbon atoms, by the Friedel-Crafts reaction, usually with anhydrous aluminium chloride as catalyst. The source of the aliphatic chain is either a special cut from straight-chain petroleum, for which purpose the petroleum from Pennsylvania is especially suitable, or a synthetic hydrocarbon chain obtained by condensing a lower molecular aliphatic hydrocarbon (generally propylene, which is condensed to its tetramer). This may be coupled with benzene without any previous chlorination.

The aromatic nucleus is usually benzene, but occasionally it is naphthalene, toluene, xylene, or even phenol. When naphthalene is used, the side chain can be as low as propyl. However, the sulphonated product is not suitable as a detergent, because of the low-molecular-weight side chains on the naphthalene nucleus. Nevertheless, by increasing the length of the side chain the detergent properties are increased.

To achieve the full hydrophile/hydrophobe balance when the lower homologues are used as the side chain, two members are necessary. Thus propyl naphthalene sulphonate is unsuitable either as a wetting agent or detergent. Dipropyl naphthalene sulphonate begins to show some wetting properties. Dibutyl naphthalene sulphonate is considerably better than butyl naphthalene sulphonate and, in fact, has fairly good detergent properties. Mono capryl naphthalene sulphonate is a very good detergent. With a side chain over C_{10}, however, the solubility of the alkyl naphthalene sulphonates starts falling off.

Thus, as the molecular weight of the side chain increases, it is necessary to limit the final product to one side chain. Conversely, if the size of the aromatic nucleus is decreased, it is necessary to increase the length of the side chain. As a rough guide, nonyl naphthalene sulphonate is equivalent to dodecyl benzene sulphonate. Thus it can be generalised that, as the side chain on the aromatic nucleus increases, the solubility decreases, and the detergency reaches a maximum and then starts decreasing. In practice, dodecyl benzene sulphonate was found to have the best balance of characteristics.

As stated above, the dodecyl benzene sulphonate seems to give the best all-round performance. However, factors vary in different parts of the world, and also conditions and requirements vary. It should be stressed that when we discuss dodecyl benzene it is meant to be a material whose average molecular structure suggests something close to dodecyl benzene: that is a product with an average molecular weight of the order of 246. This does not, in fact, indicate that the product is exactly that. In fact, if the base material is 'propylene tetramer', the propylene itself could have had small amounts of ethylene and butylene present as adulterants, and when this is polymerised to the tetramer appreciable amounts of the trimer and pentamer of each of these ingredients can also be produced as well as possible copolymers of two or three of each of the ingredients. Many combinations are now possible and each has several possible stereo-isomers, and when all of these are coupled to benzene, coupling is then possible at many different points of the side chain; so one can appreciate that the total possible amounts of isomes and homologues are enormous. With the switch to linear alkylates, the alkyl portion is less varied, and can be in the range C_{11} to C_{15}.

It is therefore becoming standard practice to refine the raw alkylate to one product with an average molecular weight in the range of 233–45 and to another with the average molecular weight in the range 257–65, the exact figure depending on the manufacturer and his possible sales of the alternate product. The first is called commercially dodecyl benzene and the second sometimes tridecyl benzene. Tridecyl benzene sulphonate, in general, has better detergency and foams better in soft water, whereas dodecyl benzene has a lower cloud point and viscosity in liquid formulations. At approximately 180–200 ppm water hardness, the difference in detergency falls away

Although the branched and the linear alkylates are both usually dodecyl benzene, it has been common to call the sulphonated branched product ABS and the linear one LAS.

With the changeover to linear alkyl benzene certain changes were observed. In this case as the alkyl portion is straight-chained it has no substantial amount of isomers but again contains homologues. When coupled with benzene, isomers arise in that the coupling can be at any of the positions between 2-phenyl and 6-phenyl, and it has been found that detergency is dependent on the position of the phenyl group. It has been suggested that for optimum light-duty detergency, linear alkyl benzene should have a mean chain distribution of lower than 12, the molecular weight should be in the range 231–41 and it should contain 15–25 per cent 2-phenyl isomers. For heavy-duty formulations they suggest a mean chain distribution of higher than 13, a molecular weight range of 258–66, the 2-phenyl content to be less than 20 per cent and the 5- and 6-phenyl content to be at least 40 per cent.

In the refining of the alkylate a certain amount of polyalkyl benzene is left as 'bottoms' in the still. This is a highly complex mixture of materials with an average molecular weight of 300 or more and on sulphonation it in turn yields a product which is a very good emulsifier, but poor detergent.

Three principal ways to use LAS and ABS are open to the manufacturer of cleaning materials :

(1) He may produce his end product from basic detergent raw materials, such as dodecyl benzene, by sulphonation processes and finishing processes requiring rather high initial investment, but giving him the widest scope for developing a complete range of cleaning materials.

(2) He may use a detergent material that has already been sulphonated, the sulphonic acid. This method still provides a fairly wide scope for development and avoids the necessity of erecting an expensive sulphonation plant which can only be operated by skilled labour and under expert chemical supervision.

(3) He may purchase ready sulphonated and neutralised detergents in a highly concentrated form, either as a paste-slurry or in the form of spray-dried, or drum-dried, powder or flakes. This material has than only to be diluted to obtain liquid products, etc., or be mixed with suitable builders to provide products ready to be marketed. The last-mentioned way of simply mixing detergent concentrates is the least expensive, from capital cost but also the least interesting, and does not, in fact, constitute a genuine manufacturing process. By careful selection of those materials with which he compounds the detergent concentrates, quite interesting and valuable cleaning materials may be obtained. This will become clearer during the description of the composition of cleaning materials.

Long-Chain (Fatty) Alcohol Sulphates

More recently, alcohols have been produced by the Ziegler process, a growth reaction using ethylene and trialkyl aluminium. This process yields even-numbered alcohols (those produced from natural fatty acids are invariably even-numbered); any desired length of chain can be produced, and the alcohol can also be blended in proportions not found in nature. Thus myristic alcohol (C_{14}) is not a great supply from natural sources, but can be manufactured is unlimited quantities by this process. Despite the fact that the Ziegler alcohols have to a large extent replaced the lower (C_{12}) natural alcohols, the higher ones (C_{18}) made from tallow are not necessarily more expensive. Several household and industrial detergents have been based either wholly or partially on sulphated tallow alcohols for many years and at the moment it is not clear whether synthetic or tallow alcohols are being used. Also included in this group are the OXO alcohols.

The OXO alcohols, being made by a hydroformylation reaction using an olefine and CO, are mixtures of both even and odd numbered alcohols with some side branching. Catalysts are now being used which limit the branching to 25 per cent 2-methyl to give a structure :

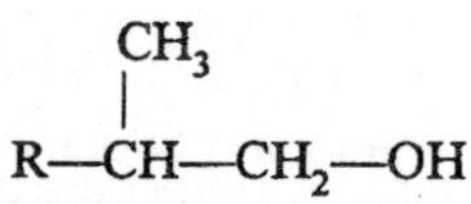

There was a misapprehension that this side-branched alcohol is a secondary alcohol but as can be seen from the above structure it is an isoalcohol.

OXO-type alcohols are both ethoxylated and sulphated. It must be pointed out that some manufacturers use a type of process which does give some secondary alcohols :

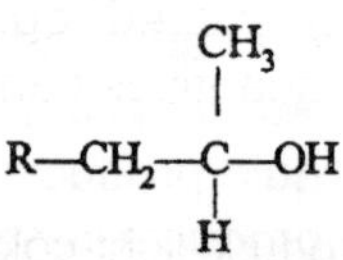

and these are not readily sulphated.

Many of the large 'soapers' are now using in their heavy-duty washing powders both LABS and a high molecular (C_{12}-C_{18}) alcohol sulphate. This is achieved relatively easily by a firm which does its own sulphonation, not so easily by a firm that has to buy its detergent raw materials.

Despite the fact the sulphate bond –C–O–SO_3 is not as stable as the sulphonate bond –C–S–O_3, the stability of the alcohol sulphates is sufficient for all normal purposes, and there is not much to choose between the detergency of, say, cetyl alcohol sulphate and dodecyl benzene sulphonate.

Sulphonated Olefins

The first commercial sulphonation of olefins with SO_3 involved the use of an SO_3-organo compound complex, either produced separately or in *situ*. Nowadays best results are obtained by sulphonating with uncomplexed diluted SO_3 in a film reactor.

The reaction between alpha olefins and SO_3 is not straightforward, mixtures of alkene sulphonic acids, sultones, alkene disulphonic acids and sultone sulphonic acids might be formed. The sultones need to be hydrolysed (saponified) to produce hydroxysulphonic acids. The materials sold under the name AOS are all therefore neutralised, usually with soda, and consist of mixtures of :

$R{-}CH{=}CHCH_2SO_3Na$ and $R{-}CHOH(CH_2)_nSO_3Na$

where n can be both 2 and 3.

Despite what was said above about internal olefins, it is claimed that the presence of internal olefins together with alpha olefins gives an AOS with syngergistically improved detergency over pure alpha olefin sulphonates.

AOS has not yet made great strides in the heavy duty laundry field but is being used successfully for light duty detergents, hand dishwashing, shampoos, bubble baths and synthetic soap bars.

There is also controversy about skin sensitising by materials containing AOS. One party to the dispute maintains that after twenty years of commercial use no ill effects have been noted, whereas the other party states that if hypochlorite bleaching is used together with the alkaline hydrolysis, traces of sultones in ppb quantities can remain and cause this skin sensitisation.

The newer film reactors which produce light-coloured olefin sulphonates without bleaching are therefore the answer.

Sulphated Monoglycerides

These were a moderate success, but, being based on fats, which are expensive and in short supply, they were quickly superseded by the cheaper alkyl benzene sulphonates. Quite apart from the economic aspect, the sulphated monoglycerides do not lend themselves easily to the manufacture of suitable powder products, although they are still being used occasionally in light-duty liquid formulations. Because of their sensitivity to alkaline hydrolysis, no real advantage is seen for them.

Sulphated Ethers

Non-ionic detergents of the ethylene oxide condensate type, are in general excellent detergents. They have two disadvantages, however, in that they produce weak or unstable foams and although completely soluble in water, they exhibit 'invert solubility' in that they are more soluble in cold than in hot water. Thus when solutions of non-ionics are heated, at certain temperatures the solution becomes cloudy and in the limiting instance can separate into two phases. Fatty alcohol sulphates on the other hand are high foamers but their sodium salts do not produce clear solutions unless in very low concentrations. To produce clear solutions of fatty alcohol sulphates, recourse must be made to cations other than sodium with concomitant difficulties.

If a fatty alcohol is ethoxylated the ether produced still has an –OH group at the end able to be sulphated. This class of ether sulphates has become the fastest-growing group of anionic detergents. In practice the alcohol is not ethoxylated to the degree where it becomes it itself a detergent; only two to four molecules of ethylene oxide are added and the unsulphated material is still water-insoluble. The material is then sulphated by chlorosulphonic acid, or SO_3 and neutralised normally by caustic soda.

The sodium salts of these ether sulphates have very low cloud points even in relatively high concentrations. In addition, their wetting properties are lower than other anionic detergents, while their foaming properties are considerably higher, making them excellent raw materials for hair shampoo, and in combination with other anionic or non-ionic detergents, they are being used more and more for household dishwashing. They are used to increase the detergency of liquid detergents based on alkyl benzene sulphonate or n-paraffin sulphonates. Generally 20 per cent of the total active matter is replaced by sulphated ethers.

Lightly ethoxylated alkyl phenols are also being sulphated. In this case, however, the molecule contains two possible points of attack. The terminal –OH group can be sulphated and the benzene ring can be sulphonated. As the hydrophilic group in this class of product is the 'ethoxy sulphate' it is desirable that sulphation and no ring sulphonation takes place. A complete exclusion of ring formation can only be achieved by the use of sulphamic acid, which, however, produces simultaneously with the sulphation the ammonium salt. The use of SO_3 can under the best of conditions give a mixture of 20 per cent ring sulphonate but if great care is not taken disulphation, i.e., sulphation of the –OH group and also sulphonation of the ring of the same molecule, can occur. Alkyl phenol either sulphates have been recommended as bases for toilet preparations but their main use is as components of light duty household detergent liquids, and for emulsion polymerisation.

These lightly ethoxylated alcohols are more complex mixtures than one would consider at first glance. The ethylene oxide content is only a mean and for these low values appreciable portions of the alcohol will remain unethoxylated (25 per cent when 2 moles EO are added, 18 per cent for 3 moles), thus the sulphated product will have alcohol sulphate as well. Figures can vary for different manufacturers so nominal ethylene oxide from two manufacturers will not necessarily have the same properties, not taking into account that the basic alcohols might also vary in their micro-composition. Ethoxylation of alkyl phenols follows a different path, all the phenol is ethoxylated before multiple ethoxylation starts.

Sulphosuccinates

Materials of excellent detergency can be obtained by condensing a hydrophobe containing an –OH group with maleic anhydride :

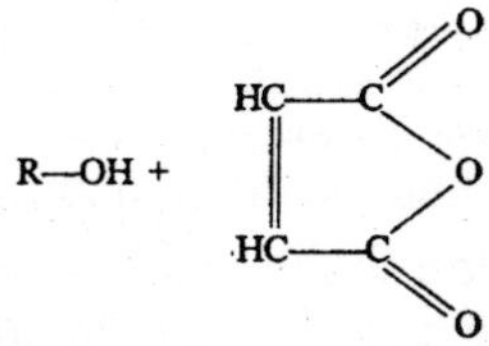

to produce the half-ester :

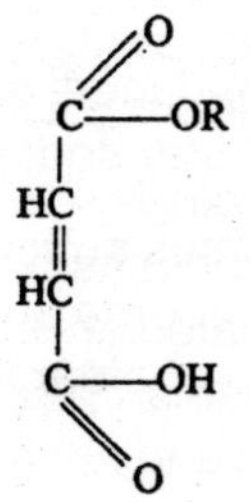

and reacting this with sodium sulphite or bisulphite to produce the sulphosuccinate :

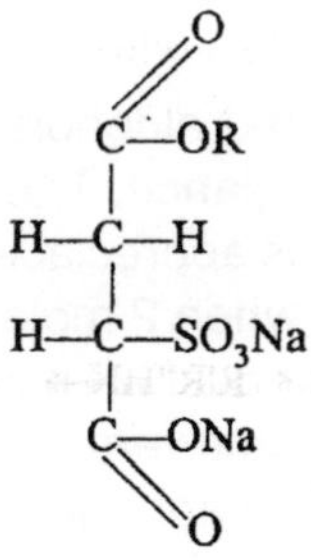

Sulphosuccinates, depending of course on the choice of the R-group, are excellent high-foaming detergents and ideally suited for toilet preparations as they are non-irritating to the skin.

This is a process which does not require large capital outlays and allows the small or medium sized manufacturer to do his own synthesis. The choice of the hydrophobe is wide, it can be an alcohol, a lightly ethoxylated alcohol or an alkanolamide (which also has a terminal –OH)or a mixture of any of the possible variations of these. The maleic anhydride (the common choice but other unsaturated anhydrides can be used) can be reacted with 1 mol of the (mixture of) hydrophobe(s) to produce the half (or mono-) ester or with two molecules to produce the di-ester. In the case of the di-ester the properties of the finished sulphosuccinate are more wetting than detergent and they are used for industrial purposes. The halfesters are excellent high-foaming detergents, mild to the skin and ideally suited for toilet preparations.

If the di-ester is produced, the sulphonation is performed with sodium bisulphite; for the half-ester sodium sulphite is used.

The sulphosuccinates suffer from one disadvantage, their solubility is not good (depending of course on the choice of hydrophobe). This does not allow of the preparation of clear liquids if the concentration is over 10 per cent active matter.

Solubility can be increased by using monoethanolamine sulphite in place of sodium sulphite. This monoethanolamine sulphite is not an article of commerce but can readily be manufactured by passing SO_2 into a solution of monoethanolamine in water to form either the bisulphite or sulphite as required :

$$HOC_2H_5NH_2 + SO_2 + H_2O \rightarrow HOC_2H_5NH_3SO_3H$$

$$2HOC_2H_5NH_2 + SO_2 + H_2O \rightarrow (HOC_2H_5NH_3)_2SO_3$$

Allied to the sulphosuccinates are the sulphosuccinamates, where the maleic anhydride is reacted with a primary or secondary amine :

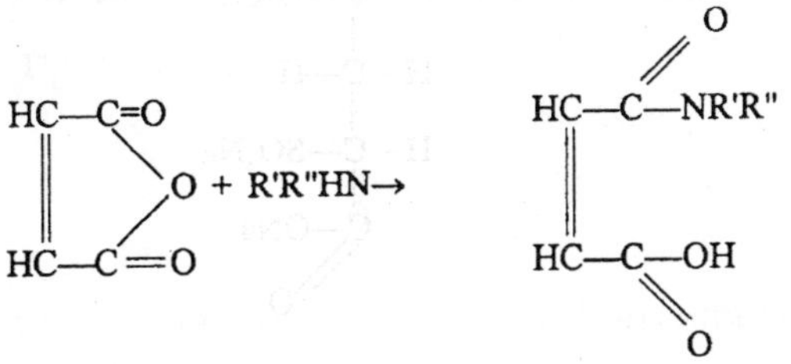

Maleic acid amide or
maleamic acid

The second carboxyl group can also be amidised to form the di-amide or it can be esterified with an alcohol, ethoxylated alcohol, alkanolamide, etc., to produce the mixed ester-amide.

These are again sulphonated in the usual way, using either sulphite or bisulphite.

The possibilities of all the possible variations of the sulphosuccinamates have not yet been fully explored but they are said to be even kinder to the skin than the normal sulphosuccinates.

Sulphonated Methyl Esters

In considering the aforementioned ad following detergent raw materials, it will be noted that the vast majority are from petrochemical sources.

Fats and oil are self-replenishing and attention is being paid to their use as detergent intermediates. Alcohol sulphates are one such product and now attention is being drawn to sulphonated methyl esters.

They are already being used in powders and a surprising spin-off was noted in that the material has the ability to sequester calcium and magnesium ions, even in the presence of soap, without the use of phosphates.

The methyl esters need to be a high quality with a minimum of double bonds, indicating the use of refined coconut or hydrogenated tallow as starting materials. Production of methyl esters will be discussed later.

The sulphonation reaction is considered to be :

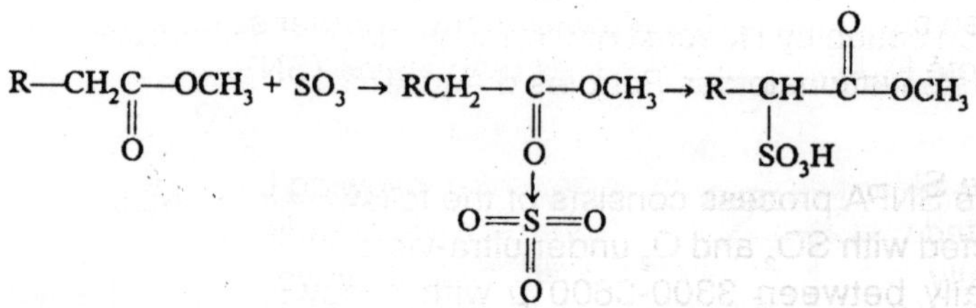

that is, an intermediate complex is formed and this rearranges to the sulphonate.

There are two competing reactions. If double bonds are present, an olefin type of sulphonation will occur, particularly as that rate of reaction is considerably faster than the methyl ester sulphonation. It is, therefore, necessary to produce the methyl esters from material with very low iodine values. The second reaction is a double sulphonation of the easter which on neutralisation produces a disodium sulphocarboxylate, a sodium carboxylate and sodium methyl sulphate.

Fortunately the second reaction can be controlled by sulphonating conditions. However, on neutralising the sulphonated methyl ester neutralisation conditions must be such that no ester hydrolysis (saponification) occurs.

Alkane sulphonates

They were made according to the Reed reaction by chloro-sulphonation of petroleum fractions, but were quickly superseded by sulphoxidation and by alkyl benzenes when these appeared in commercial quantities. When the problem of biodegradation of propylene tetramer dodecyl benzene arose. Thus a new process for sulphonating straight-chain alkane fractions, which uses gamma rays from a cobalt-60 source was developed. The method of synthesis is not straightforward but appears to be the initial formation of a peroxy-sulphonate as an intermediate, and this acts as an initiator for the sulphonation reaction.

Gamma irradiation has been replaced by the less dangerous ultra-violet irradiation system. It is very important that the n-paraffins used are practically free from aromatics or alkyl aromatics, whose presence retards the reaction. The removal of aromatics and alkyl aromatics is best accomplished when the n-paraffins obtained by the molecular sieve process are treated with SO_3 converter gas.

In Europe three large production units for the sulphoxidation process have been set up by Hoechst of Germany. Another sulphoxidation plant by the Société Nationale des Petroles d'Aquitaine (SNPA) is now at planning stage.

The SNPA process consists of the following basic steps: n-paraffins are reacted with SO_2 and O_2 under ultra-violet radiation with a wavelength essentially between 3300-3600 μ with a power level of several kW. Unfortunately, at the same time as paraffin sulphonate is formed, SO_2 reacts with O_2 and H_2O to form H_2SO_4. The overall reaction can be written as follows:

$$RH + 2SO_2 + O_2 + H_2O \rightarrow RSO_3H + H_2SO_4$$

where RH represents *n*-paraffin and RSO_3H the sulphonation product on a secondary carbon. Operating temperature and pressure are close to ambient/

The next step is to remove the sulphuric acid and some dissolved SO_2 from the mixture of paraffin sulphonate and unreacted paraffin (the latter to be recycled). SNPA has developed its own separation process which used a solvent or solvent mixture of a 'slightly polar nature' with alcohol of at least five carbon atoms. No exact details of the SNPA process have yet been revealed. A flowsheet attached to the article, however, shows the basic principle. The paraffin sulphonate is neutralised with NaOH and the product marketed in the form of a 30 or 60 per cent past.

The detergency of alkane sulphonates is very similar to that of LABS. Stability against hardness and biodegradability are even better. Liquid detergents based on alkane sulphonates are being manufactured in combination with ether sulphates, where the ether sulphate constitutes 20 per cent of the active matter. Powders have not been produced so easily by spray-drying detergents solely based on a high percentage of alkane sulphonates because the material is soft and somewhat hygroscopic. This, however, can be overcome by the use of sodium toluene sulphonate and by the addition of colloidal silica.

Another method of producing alkane sulphonates is by the bisulphite addition to alpha olefins. This is a well-known reaction but until recent years complete reaction of the olefin was not attained, necessitating extraction of the unreacted olefin.

Recently in a latest process in which the olefin, the bisulphite solution and an initiator are all reacted together in the presence of a water-miscible organic solvent, which is eventually stripped off. Yields are close to 100 per cent based on the olefin.

Phosphate Esters

A series of interesting and highly specialised detergents are the phosphate esters.

Two phosphating reagents can be used, P_2O_3 and polyphosphoric acid. If one takes as an analogy sulphonation with oleum, where oleum is considered to be SO_3 dissolved (or loosely combined) with H_2SO_4, we have the same phenomenon.

P_2O_5 when dissolved in phosphoric acid (or in a dearth of water) gives the complex phosphoric acid :

$$4H_3PO_4 + P_2O_5 \longrightarrow 3H_4P_2O_7$$

In this reaction we have shown the production of pyrophosphoric acid, but of course in practive higher condensed acids are also produced and commercial polyphosphoric acid is sold as 115 per cent (calculated as orthophosphoric acid).

The reactions between an alcohol and polyphosphoric acid are :

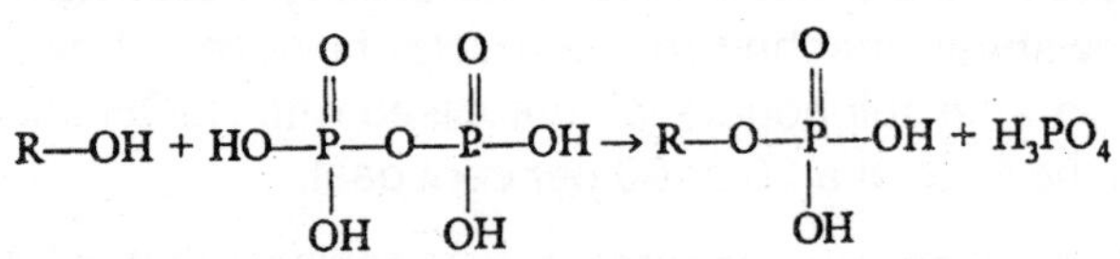

or

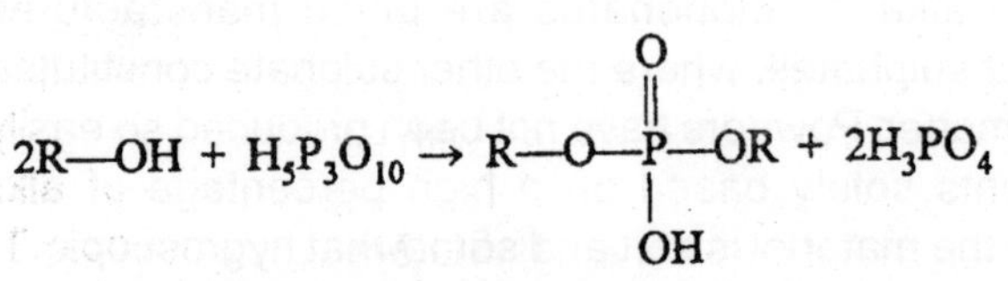

Thus both mono- and di-esters are formed and also free phosphoric acid.

Conditions can be varied but as a general rule when using 115 per cent polyphosphoric acid two-thirds mono- and one-third di-ester are formed. The free phosphoric acid is not normally removed from the ester.

When using P_2O_5 as the phosphating agent the reaction is different :

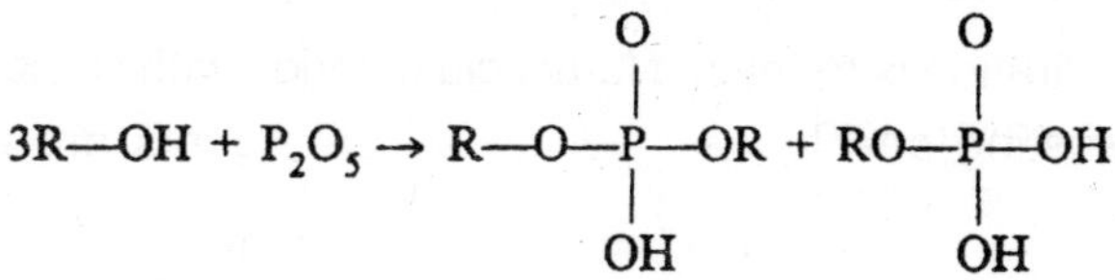

and yields equimolecular amounts of di- and mono-esters and no phosphoric acid (in practice a small amount of orthophosphoric acid is always formed).

Depending on the choice of the hydrophobic portion and the phosphating reagent, the possibility of varying the properties of phosphate esters is enormous.

Theoretically any compound containing reactive —OH can be phosphated. More often than not ethoxylates rather than pure alcohols are used. These ethoxylates need not necessarily be the lightly ethoxylated one as used for ether sulphates, the true detergent grades, both alcohol and alkyl phenol based, are often used. Also if low molecular weight materials, not necessarily water-insoluble, are phosphated, wetting agents and good hydrotropes are obtained.

The phosphate ester possess good detergency, especially on hard surfaces, are low foamers with good acid and alkali stability, and are biodegradable. They find application in metal cleaning and plating, and since they are very soluble in organic solvents they are used in combination with solvents as dry-cleaning detergents, for hard surface cleaning and as agricultural emulsifiers.

Alkyl Isethionates

These are made by reacting ethylene oxide with sodium bisulphite :

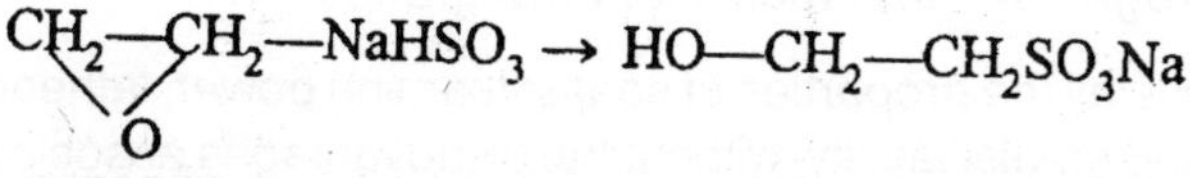

This sodium isethionate is then dried and the —OH group is esterified with a fatty acid.

Alkyl isethionates, which are gentle to the human skin, have been used successfully in synthetic toilet soap bars and for hair shampoos.

Acyl Sarcosides

Early attempts to improve soap were based on the principle of adding hydrophilic groups to the carboxylic acid. One of the first poducts of this type, and a rather successful one, was acyl sarcoside, in which an amido linkage is interspersed between the carboxyl group and the hydrophilic radical.

A method of proporation is to react a fatty acid chloride with N-methyl glycine (sarcosine), an amino acid :

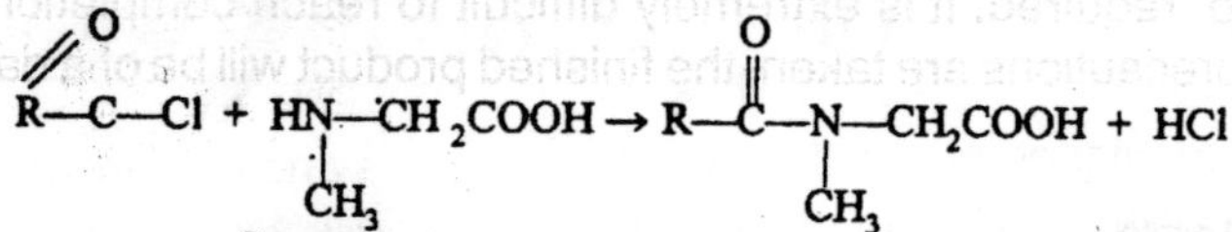

Sarcosine

The reaction is normally carried out in alkaline solution so the sodium salt is naturally produced together with salt as a by-product.

The sarcosides are gentle to the skin and are affected considerably less than carboxylates by hard water ions. They are used for personal care products, as dyeing aids and for textile finishing.

Alkyl Taurides

Allied to, but somewhat different from, sarcosides, the taurides are manufactured by a somewhat similar process. Taurine (amino ethane sulphonic acid) or methyl taurine are reacted with a fatty acid chloride :

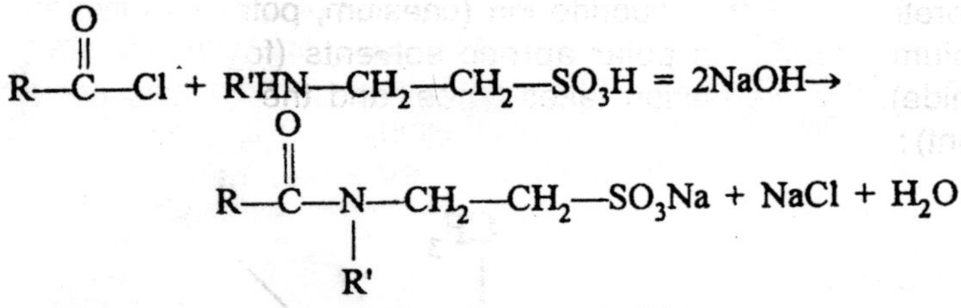

where R' can be hydrogen or either methyl or ethyl groups.

The taurates have all the properties of soaps: foaming power, lathering, kindness to the skin and emulsifiability, without the disadvantages associated with carboxylates. They are used in synthetic toilet 'soaps', in personal care items, in textile finishing and in agricultural wettable powders.

It will be noted that the last two items are manufactured from fatty acid chlorides, with the production of salt, whereas the alkyl isethionates are shown to be made from fatty acids without any salt as a by-product.

Alkyl isethionates can also be made by reacting a fatty acid chloride with sodium isethionate in alkaline solution with the production of salt.

Conversely, the taurides and sarcosides can also be made by reacting a fatty acid with the anhydrous, molten sodium salt of taurine or sarcosine.

The difference between the two routes is that using the fatty acid chloride the reaction is done in a water solution at a temperature below the boiling point and goes to completion quite easily. Sodium chloride is formed. Using the fatty acid route, no sodium chloride is formed but temperatures over 200° C are required. It is extremely difficult to reach completion and unless special precautions are taken, the finished product will be of a darkish colour.

Fluoro Surfactants

A new development in the surface active field is fluoro chemicals, which are at the moment very expensive but have unique properties :

(a) They lower surface tension of aqueous systems to 2.0 N m^2 (most detergents give a surface tension in the range of 2.8-3.1 N m^{-2}).

(b) They are effective in concentrations of the order of 0.01 per cent.

(c) They show surface activities in organic systems.

(d) They are chemically stable in hostile environments.

Most modern methods of manufacture involve reacting tetrafluorethylene with a fluoride ion (caesium, potassium or tetra alkyl ammonium fluoride) in polar aprotic solvents (for example dimethyl formamide). Polymerisation takes place, and the pentamer (the most abundant) :

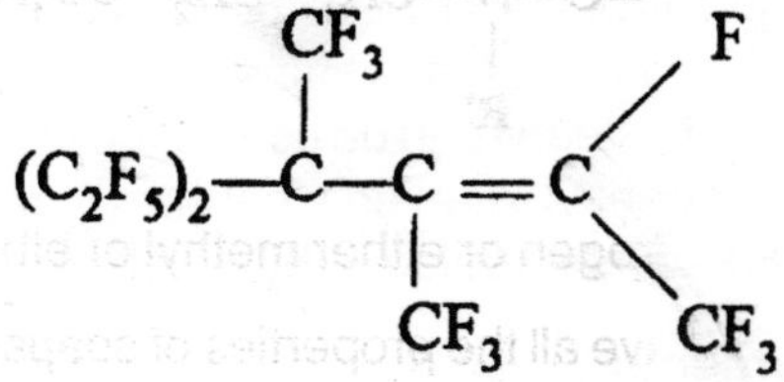

is used for further synthesis.

This pentamer is coupled with phenol :

$$(C_2F_5)_2CF_3CC(CF_3):C(CF_3)F + C_6H_5OH \longrightarrow (C_2F_5)_2CF_3CC(CF_3): C(CF_3)OC_6H_5 + HF$$

This phenol group can be sulphonated to give an anionic detergent; also it may be chlorosulphonated to give the sulphonyl chloride, then treated with *N'N'*-dimethylpropanediamine to give a tertiary amine and then quarternarised with methyl iodide to produce a cationic detergent. The tertiary amine can also be reacted with propiolactone to produce an amphoteric surfactant.

Non-ionic fluorosurfactants can also be made from these phenyl compounds or else by reacting the pentamer with ethylene oxide condensates and rearrangement of the molecule (with the removal of one molecule of HF).

Cationic Detergents

The cationic detergents are of relatively limited interest to the cleaning materials manufacturer. Compared with the anionic and non-ionic detergents their detergency is relatively poor.

The term cationic detergents is somewhat of a misnomer. These materials do exhibit surface active properties but are seldom used in cleaning formulations. Their detergency is relatively poor and the cost high. The principal uses for cationic detergents are as germicides, fabric softeners and specialised emulsifiers. Anionic and cationic detergents are mutually incompatible, as the anion and cation precipitate each other.

These cationic detergents are almost invariably amino compounds and the most effective of the group are the quaternary ammonium salts, with one long chain attached to the nitrogen nucleus, or quaternary pyridine based salts. Here the possible permutations are again enormous. For example, cetyl trimethylammonium chloride, which is a typical normal quaternary ammonium salt, can also appear as the bromide and then, instead of the cetyl group, any of the long chains available both from fatty or synthetic sources from lauryl to stearyl can be used. One methyl group can be replaced by another cetyl or benzyl (or even a naphthyl) radical and then one or all of the methyl groups can be replaced by an ethyl group and so forth.

Non-ionic Detergents

In discussing anionics we mentioned that most of the anionic detergents are sulphonates or sulphates of one sort or another. Similarly, the vast majority of all non-ionic detergents are condensation products of ethylene oxide with a hydrophobe.

This hydrophobe is invariably a high-molecular-weight material with an active hydrogen atom, and the non-ionic material can be one of four main reaction products :

Fatty alcohol and alkyl phenol condensates

The reaction proceeds thus :

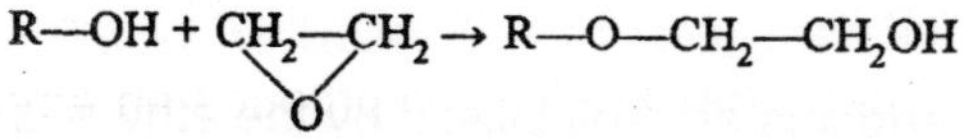

Reaction of one molecule of ethylene oxide is not sufficient to produce a water-soluble detergent product and the reaction is continued :

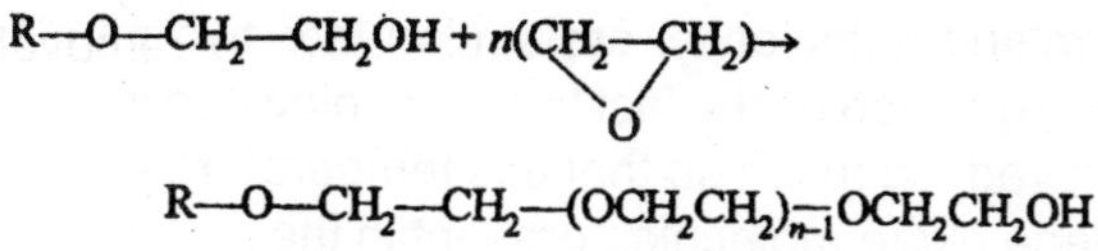

It will be noted that an ether linkage is obtained. Since this linkage is basically a strong one, the material is not subject to hydrolysis and, as there is no possibility of ionisation, it is not affected by metallic ions. In general for an average hydrophobe when *n* is approximately 6, the product becomes water-soluble and starts assuming detergent qualities.

The above reaction can be continued indefinitely, but, in practice, optimum detergency is found in the range of 10–15 molecules of ethylene oxide per molecule of fatty alcohol. The source of the alcohol varies greatly, but natural, ZIEGLER and OXO alcohols of various molecular weights are being used and up to 50 molecules of ethylene oxide are being added.

Although chemically very different from fatty alcohols, the alkyl phenols behave in exactly the same manner as the fatty alcohols. Here again the choice of one particular alkyl phenol (or naphthol) is quite wide, but the preference usually falls on nonyl (sometimes octyl) phenol. With 4 molecules of ethylene oxide, nonyl phenol is still completely insoluble in water; at 6-7 molecules it is completely soluble in water at room temperature; at 8-12 molecules it exhibits excellent detergency.

Two further variations are now also being used, dodecyl phenol ethoxylate for certain agricultural emulsifiers and dinonyl phenol ethoxylate (where problems of non-ionic biodegradation have not yet arisen) as low or non-foaming ingredients of household washing machine powders.

Up to now, the alkyl phenol ethylene oxide condensates have been the most widely produced non-ionic detergent. However, with the recent international preoccupation with biodegradation they have fallen into slight disfavour and fatty alcohol ethylene oxides condensates are gaining. The situation is not completely clear because of conflicting claims as to the biodegradability of the alkyl phenols (which by virtue of their method of manufacture are branched chain), largely because there is not at present an internationally accepted method for chemical determination of non-ionics in micro quantities.

These ethylene oxide adducts are solubilised by the ethylene oxide units forming hydrates with water. Compared with all other materials which dissolve in water, these products show an apparent anomaly: their solutions are completely clear in the cold, but when heated they become turbid and, if the temperature is raised sufficiently, separation into two phases can even take place. This is explained by the fact that at an elevated temperature the hydrates are destroyed; so much so that this temperature is a function of the amount of ethylene oxide molecules present in the molecule.

It should again be stressed that, although the number of molecules of ethylene oxide present is considered a basic property of the material, this number is only an average, and if, say, there are 10 molecules stated to be present, the actual molecular configuration can vary from 4 to 15.

With the advent of polyester fibres for use in clothing and bedding, the use of a non-ionic constituent in laundering increased tremendously as it was found non-ionics will remove soil from these fibres better than the hitherto used anionics, but most laundry powders or liquids use a combination of the two.

With the latest trend to 'cold water' washing a further discovery has been made. As stated above the ethylene oxide distribution follows a Poisson curve around the mean. It has now been found that if 'peaked' ethoxylates are used the performance in cold water is improved.

Normal ethoxylation is done with an alkaline catalyst, usually KOH, sometimes K_2CO_3 or sodium methylate. These give the normal distribution of condensations. Kravetz has indicated that these peaked narrow range ethoxylates are produced commercially in two ways. The first way is to distil off the more volatile elements of the condensate, in which case if the alcohols are the base material the unethoxylated alcohol and the 1 or 2 mol products are 'topped'. The topped portion being returned for further processing. The distribution of a normal and topped ethoxylate is indicated in Fig. 3.2.

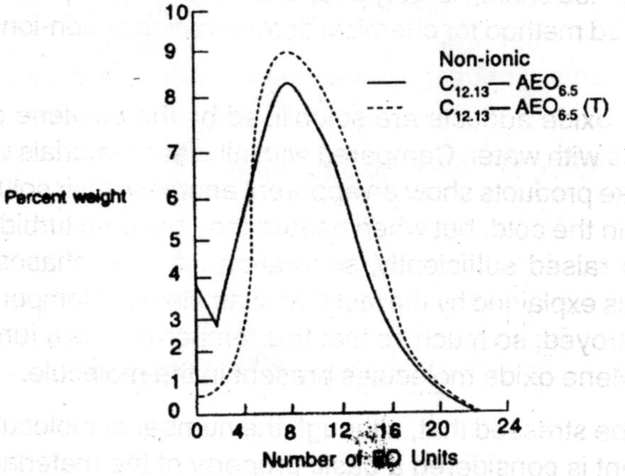

Fig. 3.2 EOD of conventional versus narrow range ethoxylate.

Fatty Acid Condensates

Another type of non-ionic can be prepared by reacting fatty acids with ethylene oxide. This is the same type of reaction :

$$R\text{—}COOH + n(CH_2OCH_2) \rightarrow$$

$$R\text{—}\overset{\overset{\displaystyle O}{\|}}{C}\text{—}O\text{—}CH_2\text{—}CH_2\text{—}(OCH_2CH_2)_{n-2}\text{—}OCH_2\text{—}CH_2OH$$

A second method of manufacture is by the esterification of a fatty acid with a polyethylene glycol, $HOCH_2(CH_2OCH_2)_nCH_2OH$. The difference in these two methods is that the polyethylene glycol has two —OH groups, so that unless very specific catalytic control is taken, non-ionic esters made by esterification will always have a certain proportion of di-esters. This is not necessarily a disadvantage, but makes the esterification ester different from the ethoxylation ester.

Being esters, these materials have one drawback that non-ionics in general do not suffer from. Non-ionic detergents are not in general affected by metallic ions, acids or alkalis and their functions as detergents are only marred by the way these extraneous ions in the water affect the physical properties of the water itself. However, the fatty acid ethylene oxide condensates are readily hydrolysed by acids or alkaline solutions to their component fatty acid and to polyethylene glycol. Thus in strong alkaline solutions these materials are no better than the soap of the fatty acid from which they were made, and in strong acid solution they are ineffectual. However, as components in household detergent powders, they do perform quite well.

Condensation of ethylene oxide with an amine

Two reaction products are possible :

$$R\text{—}NH_2 + n(CH_2OCH_2) \rightarrow$$

$$R\text{—}NH\text{—}CH_2\text{—}CH_2(OCH_2CH_2)_{n-2}OCH_2\text{—}CH_2OH$$

or

$$R\text{—}NH_2 + 2n(CH_2OCH_2) \rightarrow$$

$$R\text{—}N\begin{cases} CH_2CH_2(OCH_2CH_2)_{n-2}OCH_2\text{—}CH_2OH \\ CH_2\text{—}CH_2(OCH_2CH_2)_{n-2}OCH_2\text{—}CH_2OH \end{cases}$$

In the case of the second reaction, the end product is shown as being symmetrical, but it need not be, and can again be a mixture of many homologues and isomers. Other than specialised items, this class of non-ionic has not been used to a large extent in cleaning compositions. It should be noted, however, that these materials in acid solution can exhibit cationic characteristics, whereas in neutral or alkaline solutions they are non-ionic.

Condensation of ethylene oxide with an amide

We shall later describe the alkylolamine type of products. These are basically amides of an alkylolamine and a fatty acid. Certain members of this class exhibit detergency and others do not. To convert the non-detergent materials into detergents, they can be condensed with ethylene oxide :

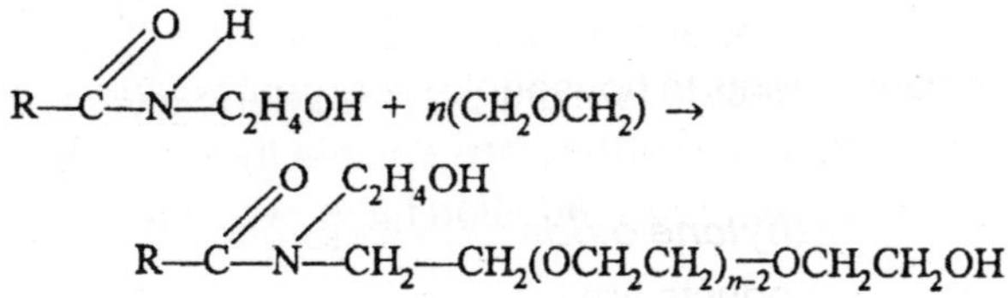

or

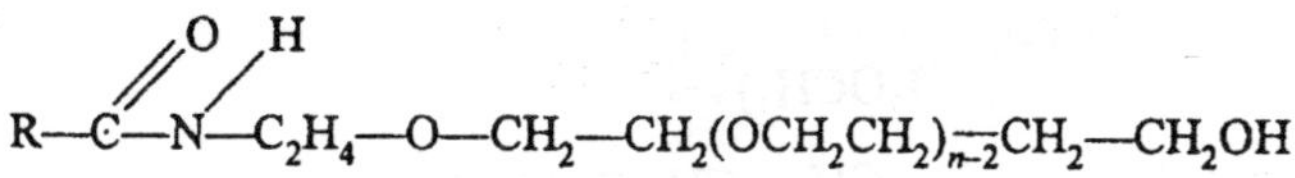

or

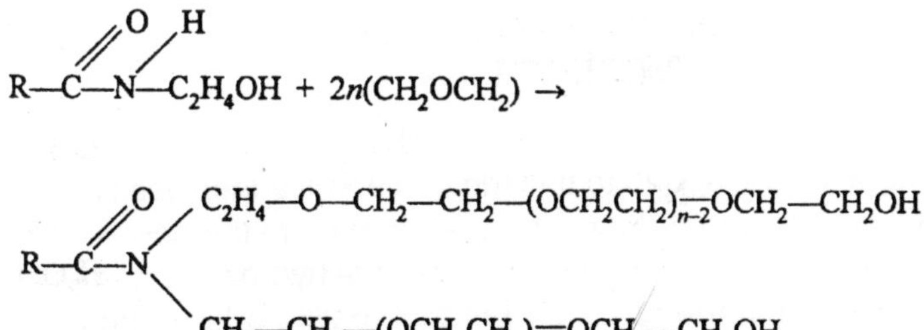

Again, the last reaction product is shown to have the ethylene oxide equally divided between the two possible directions, but there is no absolute reason for this. The ethylene oxide is divided at random in the two directions; also, any amount of either of the first two reaction products may be present. The alkylolamines are themselves complex mixtures and not as simple as shown above, so that an alkylolamide condensed with ethylene oxide consists of many components.

Block polymers

As a general rule glycols are water-soluble. Polyethylene glycols (produced by the ethoxylation of ethylene glycol) are also completely water-soluble, the lower molecular weight members of the class are described as infinitely soluble and at a molecular weight of 10,000 specifications state the solubility to be of the order of 50 per cent.

Polypropylene glycol behaves somewhat differently. The glycol itself and the lower condensation products are miscible in all proportions with water. Thus at molecular weight 400 the solubility is still infinite. Above 400 it starts falling off; polypropylene glycol of molecular weight 900 has a solubility in water of 1 per cent and this becomes even lower as the molecular weight rises.

These high-molecular-weight polypropylene glycols can be classed and serve as hydrophobes (they are soluble in or mix with oils, aromatic and paraffinic solvents) and in addition have two terminal —OH groups :

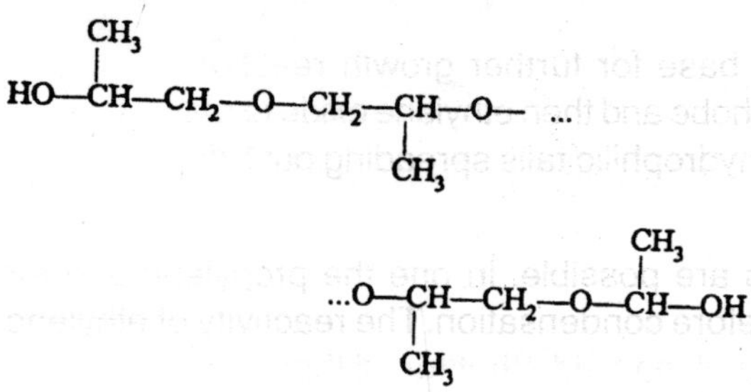

Ethylene oxide, added to this molecule, will attach itself at random to either —OH group and then again at random on to the new —OH groups formed. The ethylene oxide chains serve as the hydrophilic portion. Surface activity is attained in the resultant product, called a block polymer, when the ethylene oxide added has reached a definite ratio to the starting hydrophobe.

Block polymers can be and made with a wide range of hydrophobic/hydrophilic ratios and molecular weights to give surfactants 'tailor-made' to specific physico-chemical requirements.

Several modifications of the basic block have been developed. One is the 'inverse' type in which the propylene oxide is condensed on to the preformed polyethylene glycol. Here the hydrophilic portion is in the centre of the molecule with hydrophobic tails emerging.

All these materials need an initiator—a core on to which the initial charge of either propylene or ethylene oxide can be attached. In the two examples given above the initiators can be propylene or dipropylene glycol or ethylene or diethylene glycol, all four of which have two reactive —OH groups, Initiators with more reactive hydrogens are also used. On occasion these initiators are condensed with formaldehyde to give a bigger, more compact core with several hydrogen nuclei. One of the more interesting products used ethylene diamine to which four molecules of propylene (sometimes ethylene) oxide are condensed :

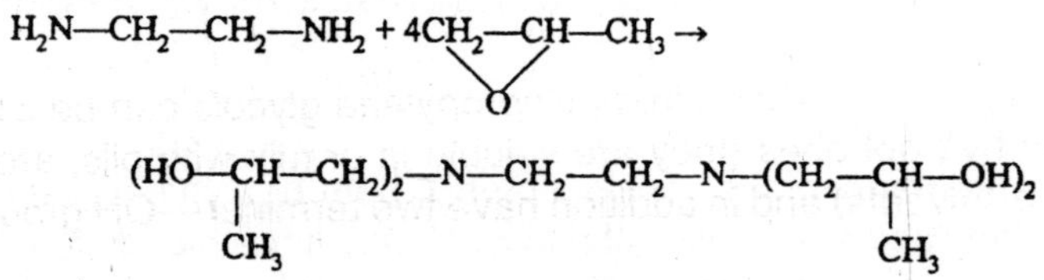

This serves as a base for further growth reactions with propylene oxide to form the hydrophobe and then ethylene oxide to make the surfactant. The molecule has four hydrophilic tails spreading out from the hydrophobe in the shape of an X.

Further variations are possible. In one the propylene and ethylene oxides are pre-mixed before condensation. The reactivity of ethylene oxide is nine times that of propylene oxide, but for all that random distribution of the two is obtained. In another, propylene oxide and ethylene oxide are added alternately to the chains.

It can be seen that the possible permutations and combinations are enormous to give an extremely wide spectrum of properties. Block polymers are manufactured for use in a large variety of processes and products from defoamers and de-emulsifiers through wetting agents, emulsifiers and cosmetics to laundry detergents. One particular use where they have proved very successful is in automatic dishwashing powders where foam is unacceptable.

Sucrose esters

These are products which have had their ups and downs in the detergent world. A future is being predicted for sucrose esters, particularly when production costs can be brought into line with other detergent raw materials.

Production is based on the original Foster D. Snell method which reacts sucrose with a fatty acid ester (methyl stearate) in dimethyl formamide solution. Mono- or di-esters can be formed, depending on the original ratio of reactants. The mono-esters are suited to detergent use.

Recently a new technique has been developed which works with a large excess of sugar, and uses potassium carbonate as a catalyst, operating at 90°C at a pressure between 9.3 and 13.3 kPa. Unreacted sugar is precipitated from the reaction solution by the addition of toluene.

Recently a new method has been developed in which the sucrose is dissolved in propylene glycol and the methyl ester emulsified into this solution. The glycol is distilled off and in the distillation process transesterification takes place. This process eliminates the use of expensive and poisonous solvents used hitherto.

Sorbitan esters

Sorbitol and mannitol (its stereo-isomer), both hexahydric alcohols, can react with fatty acids (usually in the form of fatty acyl chlorides) to form the mono-, di-, tri, ..., hexa- esters, but these products have not attained great commercial importance.

When sorbitol (or mannitol) is heated with a maximum of four molecules of a fatty acid to a temperature of close to 200°C in the presence of an acid catalyst, esters and an internal ether are formed. In the case of the mono-ester the product could be :

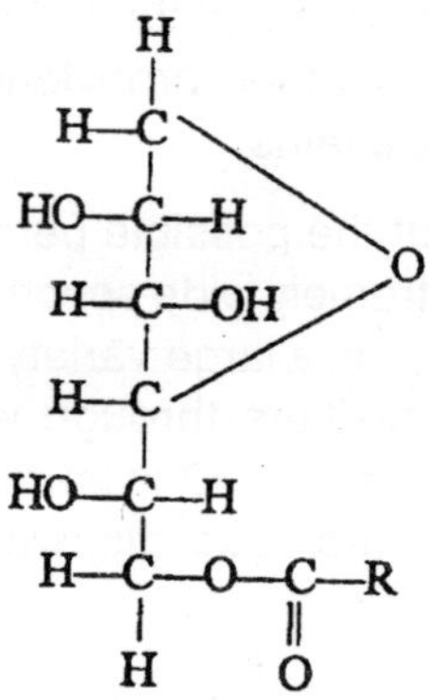

called sorbitan ester. These are water-insoluble, oil-soluble and useful as water-in-oil emulsifiers in the food, pharmaceutical and cosmetic industries. Except for sorbitol hexa-ester or sorbitan tetra-ester they all have at least one reactive hydrogen derived from an –OH group. Ethylene oxide is coupled to these hydrogens to make the material more hydrophilic and in the ultimate water-soluble.

Ethoxylated sorbitan esters are available in varying degrees of esterification, ethoxylation and with different fatty acid tails. They are valuable emulsifiers for cosmetics and polishes, in the food industry, and for specialised treating purposes in the paper, textile and plastics industries. As emulsifiers they behave differently from the conventional non-ionics because of the distribution of the hydrophilic chains. Vary rarely is the ethylene oxide attached to one —OH group only. The molecule has thus several (relatively) short ethylene oxide chains rather than one long one, making it more compact.

Alkylolamides

Another group of synthetic detergents which falls into the non-ionic category is the fatty acid alkylolamides. These are made by reacting fatty acids with alkylolamines :

$$R{-}\overset{\displaystyle O}{\overset{\|}{C}}{-}OH + H{-}\overset{\displaystyle H}{\overset{|}{N}}{-}C_2H_4OH \rightarrow R{-}\overset{\displaystyle O}{\overset{\|}{C}}{-}\overset{\displaystyle H}{\overset{|}{N}}{-}C_2H_4OH + H_2O$$

The reaction outlined above is between a fatty acid and a monoethanolamine. This has no detergent properties nor is it soluble to any great extent in water. The uses of this type of compound will be dealt with below.

However, if certain fatty acids are reacted with a di-alkylolamine as above, and if the amide formed is then reacted with a further molecule of the di-alkylolamine, the resultant product becomes water-soluble and has detergent properties.

The materials commonly used for this condensation are lauric acid, myristic acid, coconut fatty acids, palm-kernel fatty acids, and occasionally the fatty acids of vegetable oils with higher molecular weights. The alkylolamines used are generally monoethanolamine and diethanolamine, but the isopropanolamines are also employed.

The alkylolamides are rarely used by themselves as detergents, but as additives to other detergent materials, for example, with dodecyl benzene sulphonates. They act as foam boosters and increase the detergency synergistically, and in liquid products they increase viscosity without increasing the cloud point. They also have the valuable property of acting as skin-protecting agents: whereas detergents in general tend to de-fat the skin, the emollient effect of these alkylolamides helps to overcome this tendency.

A further use of alkanolamides is as an intermediate for the manufacture of sulphosuccinates. The preference is for the monoethanolamide or isopropanolamide of coconut fatty acid.

The thickening effect of alkanolamides on detergents has been demonstrated to be dependent on inorganic salts present as an effect of the inorganic salt on the micelles. Salts need not necessarily be added, they can be present as the neutralisation products of the excess sulphonating agent.

More recently monoethanolamides, especially those derived by reacting a fatty acid methyl ester with monoethanolamine, are further condensed with ethylene oxide. Depending on the type of fatty acid methyl ester and the number of molecules of ethylene oxide, non-ionic surfactants with excellent detergency power may be obtained.

Table 3.1 shows the change in viscosity of a 12 per cent neutralised dodecyl benzene sulphonate solution with the addition of 2 per cent alkylolamide and the foam height of a 0.1 per cent active solution in hard water of 300 ppm at 45°C.

Table 3.1. Effect of the addition of alkylolamides to dodecyl benzene sulphonate solution

Alkylolamide	Viscosity at 25°C (Pa s)	Foam height Immediate	Foam height After 5 minutes
None	0.075	16	15
Coconut momoethanolamide	0.305	18	17
Coconut monoisopropanolamide	0.305	16.5	16
Coconut diglycolamide	0.960	18.5	17
Coconut diethanolamide	0.650	17.5	16
Oleic diethanolamide	0.840	17	17
Coconut di-isopropanolamide	0.360	17	16

Table 3.2 Effect of the addition of ethanolamide on the foaming power of various detergents

		Detergent alone		Detergent with ethanolamide*	
		Foam height at 45°C in hard water			
Type of detergent	Concentration of detergent (%)	Imme-diate (cm)	After 5 minutes (cm)	Imme-diate (cm)	After 5 minutes (cm)
Lauryl alcohol triethanolamine salt	0.02	3.8	1.5	11	9
Lauryl alcohol monoethanolamine salt	0.02	3.0	1.2	10.5	10
Lauryl ether sulphate Lauryl alcohol	0.02	16.0	15.0	15.0	14.5

Contd...........

sodium salt	0.02	5.5	5.0	13.5	12.5
C_{10-14} alcohol sulphate sodium salt	0.02	2.0	1.0	4.0	3.5
Octyl phenol, 10 mols ethylene oxide	0.12	14.0	9.0	17.0	15.5
Nonyl phenol, 10 mols ethylene oxide	0.12	13.5	12.5	15.5	14.5
Octyl phenol, 14 mols ethylene oxide	0.12	15.5	14.5	15.5	15.0
Nonyl phenol, 14 mols ethylene oxide	0.12	16.0	14.5	14.5	14.0
Low foam non-ionic	0.12	1.5	1.5	2.0	2.0

* The ethanolamide was added at the rate of 20 per cent of the active matter.

Table 3.2 indicates the increase in foaming power of various detergents at low concentrations when coconut diethanolamide is added. It will be noted that the effect is very marked for alcohol sulphates, the ether sulphates are hardly affected, and the effect on non-ionic detergents varies.

Fatty Amine Oxides

A further type of non-ionic detergent is the group known as fatty amine oxides. These again offer many different possibilities, but basically they are made by treating tertiary amines with hydrogen peroxide. For our purposes, those amines which contain at least one long-chain group, usually from a fat source, are detergents. Two typical reactions are shown :

$$C_{12}H_{25}(CH_3)_2N + H_2O_2 \rightarrow C_{12}H_{25}-N(CH_3)_2 \rightarrow O + H_2O$$

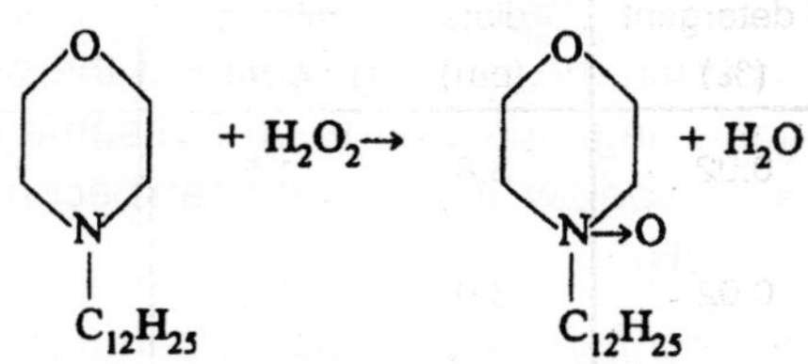

Again these two representative types include the dodecyl grouping.

These amine oxides are in themselves good detergents, but their main use is as foam boosters, viscosity increasers, and skin-protecting agents in liquid detergents. They are sticky materials and are not suggested for incorporation into powdered materials.

Their foam-boosting ability has been compared with lauric diethanolamide in Table 3.3. The method was to wash soiled plates in water of 125 ppm hardness at 46–49°C till the foam disappeared, with a 0.0125 per cent solution of the following formulation :

Sodium linear alkyl benzene sulphonate	18
Sodium lauryl ether sulphate	12
Foam stabiliser	x
Water	to 100

From the table, it appears that the fatty amine oxides are as effective as the alkylolamides as foam boosters, but in smaller concentrations.

Table 3.3. Comparison of foam-boosting ability between amine oxides and lauric diethanolamide.

Foam stabiliser	x	Plates washed to foam end-point
Dimethyl cocoamide oxide	0.48	26
Dimethyl hydrogenated tallowamide oxide	0.48	26
Dimethyl hexadecylamine oxide	0.48	27
Bis (2-hydroxyethyl) stearylamine oxide	0.60	20
Lauric diethanolamide	1.5	25

Amphoterics and Zwitterionics

This class of material contains in the same molecule both an anionic and a cationic group. The amphoterics are usually manufactured so that the anionic (carboxylate or sulphate/sulphonate) group is neutralised by Na and the cationic (quaternary ammonium) has associated with it, depending on the pH, an hydroxyl or chloride anion.

Zwitterionics also contain the same groups but the positive electric charge is neutralised by the negative charge on the same or an adjacent molecule. As will be explained below amphoterics can become zwitterionics under certain conditions of pH.

The chemistry of the syntheses is smothered in trade secrets. One route to the manufacture of amphoterics is the condensation of a fatty acid with a substituted ethylene diamine :

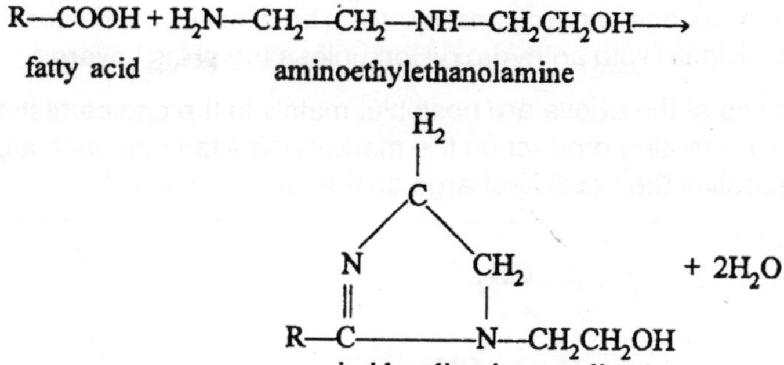

imidazoline intermediate

Cyclosation has taken place to form the imidazoline. This is not the complete picture as some esterification can occur. This imidazoline is now both quaternarised and given an anionic group. The common reactant for this is sodium chloracetate in strongly alkaline solution to produce :

either

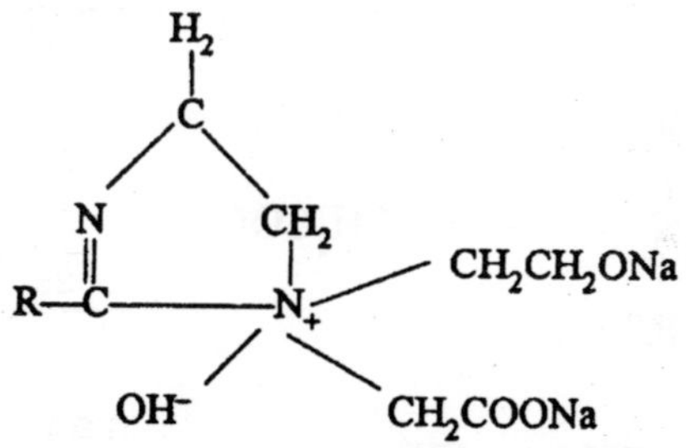

or

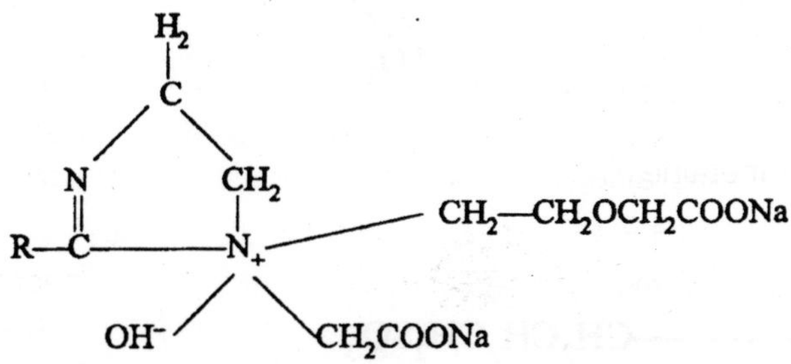

It will be noted that in the first example the caustic soda reacts with the –OH group to produce an alcoholate (in addition to the quaternarisation)

and in the second example further chloracetate has reacted with this group to give an ether linkage and a dicarboxylate. In both instances the quaternary N will be associated with an hydroxyl ion unless the pH is lowered.

Variations of the above are possible, mainly in the choice of the fatty acid, but an interesting product on the market has a fatty alcohol sulphate anion to neutralise the positive charge on the quaternary N:

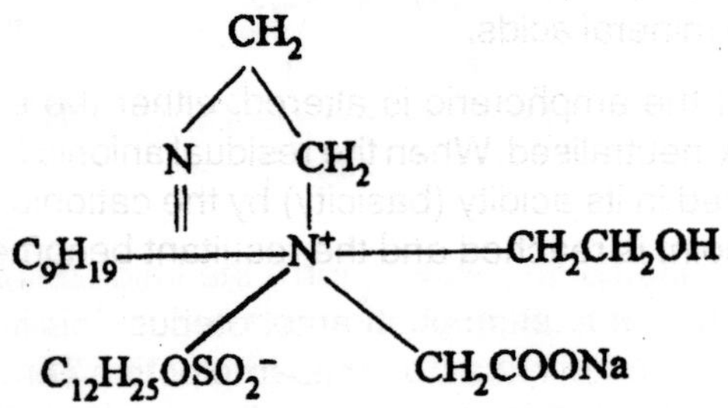

One method of manufacturing zwitterions is to react a tertiary fatty amine with either chloracetic acid to produce the betaine

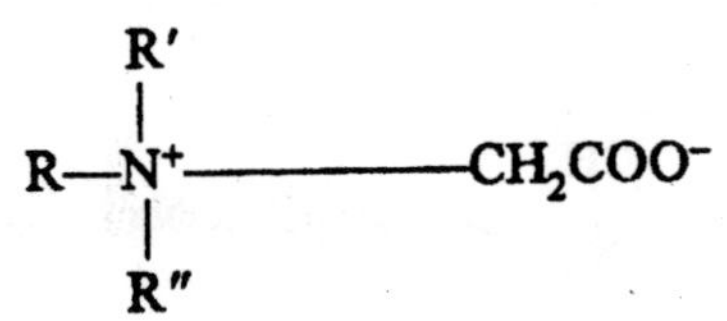

or with propane sultone

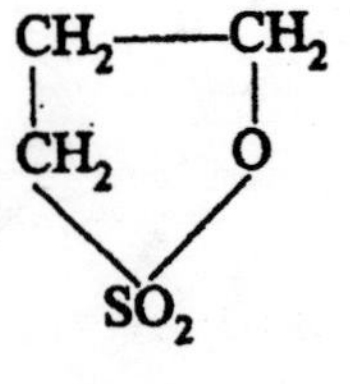

to form the sulphobetaine :

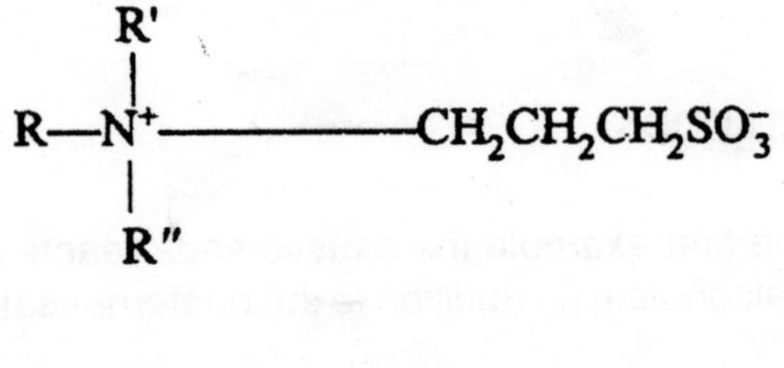

Sultones can also be reacted with imidazolines to form the corresponding sulphonate.

Ammonia is a relatively weak base and when converted to an amine the basicity is weakened further, a primary amine being however a stronger base than a tertiary. Also the longer the chain on the N nucleus, the weaker the basic quality of the amine.

Carboxylic acids are weak acids, the higher the molecular weight, the weaker the acid. Sulphonic acids and sulphuric esters are strong acids, comparable with mineral acids.

If the pH of the amphoteric is altered, either the anionic or cationic portion is partially neutralised. When the residual anionic (or cationic) radical is exactly balanced in its acidity (basicity) by the cationic (anionic) portion, the iso-electric point is reached and the resultant becomes a zwitterion.

To summarize, in acid solution amphoterics behave as cationics, in alkaline solution as anionics and at the iso-electric point the behaviour is between the two extremes.

Amphoterics are used in cosmetics, textile and metal cleaners and as fabric softeners. They have excellent compatibility with inorganic salts, acids and bases. Advantage is taken of the zwitteion/pH effect to promote a desired characteristic. For example, at the iso-electric point they are almost completely non-irritating to the skin and eyes, indicating the use in baby shampoos and skin cleaners.

We list below some amphoterics which are available on the world markets :

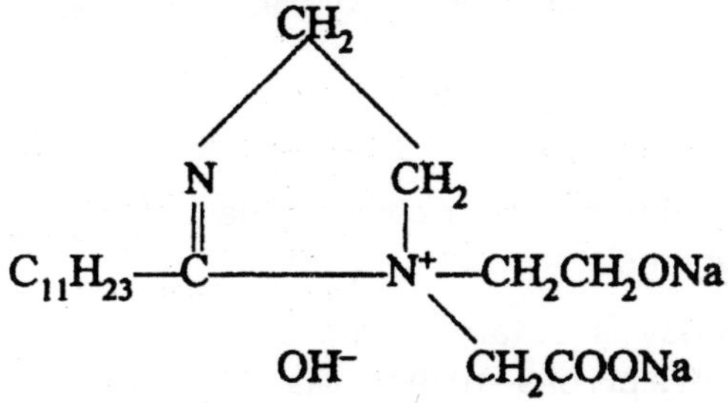

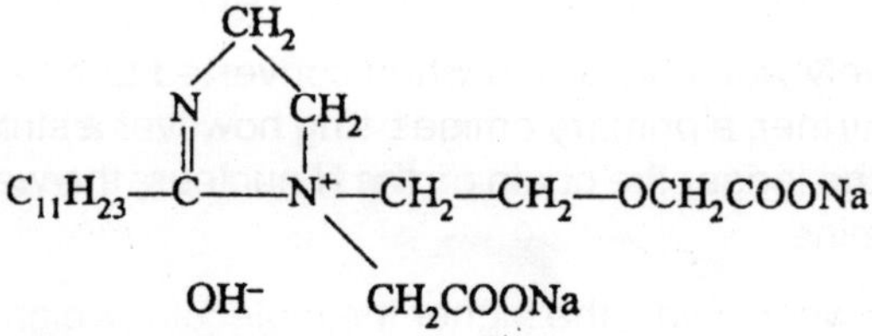

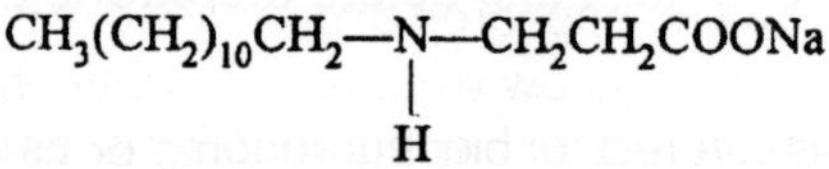

Derivatives of the basic betaine structure can be:

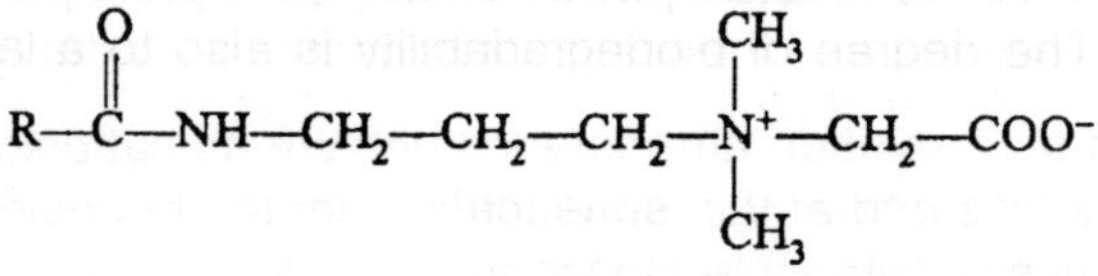

Alkylamidopropylbetaine

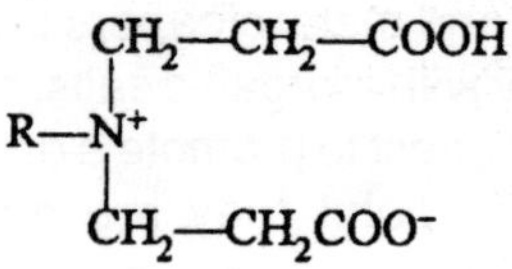

Alkylimidodipropionate

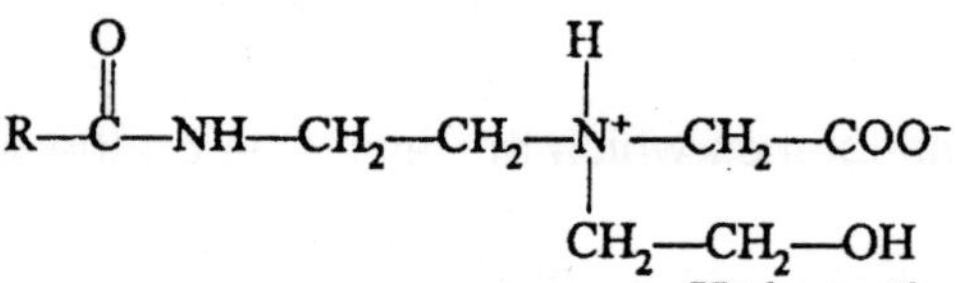

Hydroxyethyl-alkylamidoethylglycinate

The chain length of the R group being of course dependent on the fatty amine or acid used in the synthesis.

The optimum detergency is obtained with only one long-chain component and at a pH of 7. At a pH of 9–10 there is a considerable drop in detergency. In acid solutions these amphoteric compounds are mainly cationic and in alkaline solutions they behave as anionic detergents. Depending on the type of 'cationic' radical being used they may be incompatible with anionic detergents in acid solution but they are all compatible with cationic and non-ionic detergents.

Some of the amphoterics give very excellent foam, which makes them suitable for foam cleaners which are to work at a neutral pH, such as hair shampoos and rug shampoos.

A very useful property of the amphoterics is that they are stable in highly acid solutions, and have thus found use in acid cleaners based on hydrofluoric acid.

BIODEGRADABILITY

With legislation or agreements having appeared or appearing in many countries, it is important for the chemist to know whether a material he is using or intends using is biodegradable. A test for biodegradability is usually beyond the means of even a well-equipped laboratory as found in most detergent factories, and reliance must be placed on accepted principles or manufacturers' advice. The degree of biodegradability is also to a large extent dependent on the method of test.

As a general rule we can, however, state that it has been found that straight-chain materials are biodegradable. Hence soaps, linear alkyl benzene sulphonates, olefin sulphonates, alkane sulphonates, fatty alcohol and ALFOL sulphates, ether sulphates, sucrose esters, alcohol phosphates and fatty alkanolamides are all sufficiently biodegradable for all standards laid down by legislation or agreements. The position of non-ionic detergents of the ethylene oxide condensate type is obscure. Various claims for the biodegradability of alkyl phenol ethylene oxide condensates have been made but not substantiated. It appears that fatty alcohol and *ziegler ethoxylates* are biodegradable but this falls somewhat with increasing amounts of ethylene oxide. Some OXO alcohol sulphates and ethoxylates appear to be biodegradable but this again is dependent on the degree of branching.

Chapter - 2

SYNTHESIS OF DETERGENTS

INTRODUCTION

In this chapter descriptions of industrial processes for the synthesis of detergents are discussed. Sulphonation with sulphuric acid or oleum of various free sulphurtrioxide strength plays an important role in synthesis. The advantages by using sulphur trioixe for sulphonation is the additional assets that its oxygen content is low compared with vapourised liquid sulphur trioxide, where air acts as a carrier gas. The synthesis of these materials can be done with relatively simple equipment a glasslined or stainless steel reactor equipped with a dual purpose heating/cooling jacket or stainless steel dissolving tank.

RAW MATERIALS FOR ANIONIC SYNTHETIC DETERGENTS

Fatty Alcohols, Natural and Synthetic

The process used for the reduction of the glyceride to the alcohol (it also works on esters) iss reduction by metallic sodium in the presence of a reducing (hydrogen donating) lower alcohol.

The reaction can be written :

$$RCOOR' + 4Na + 2R''OH \rightarrow RCH_2ONa + R'ONa + 2R''ONa$$

and the sodium alcoholates are then hydrolysed with water and fractionated. The reducing alcohols can be butanol, cyclohexanol or 4methyl-2-pentanol. The use of metallic sodium requires that all the reactants be completely anhydrous.

The reduction is only on the ester linkage and all double bonds originally present remain intact.

With the development of high pressure hydrogenation in the organic process industry and its application to the 'oil-hardening' process for natural oils, attention is directed to the conversion of fats and oils by this means. Catalysts and process conditions are rapidly developed and the sodium reduction process fell into disfavour.

High-pressure hydrogenation was originally carried in batch processing units. More recently, however, continuous plants have been introduced. Such plants may use fats, fatty acids or preferably methyl esters. Pressure is high, between 30 and 32 MPa, and the temperature is between 300 and 320°C. Earlier, somewhat lower pressures but even higher temperatures had been used. However, for product quality it is better to use a higher pressure and a lower temperature for the reaction. In this way residence time is reduced to a minimum and the temperature not higher than 320°C maximum. The catalyst is usually copper chromite, sometimes promoted by cadmium or cerium compounds. The catalyst is well dispersed in the fatty acids or methyl ester, and dosed by dosing pump into the reaction system proportionally to the required hydrogen. Sometimes it is recommended to pre-mix the catalyst with a fraction of the fatty alcohol obtained in the process. As can be seen from the flow diagram (Fig. 9.1) part of the spent catalyst is recycled and fresh catalyst added.

Typical process data are as follows :

For 1000 kg tallow fatty alcohol from distilled tallow fatty acids :

1060 kg distilled fatty acids

5–8 kg catalyst

hydrogen 270 m^3

Cooling water 50m^3

electricity 350 kWh

yeild 94 per cent calculated on the fatty acids

The figures will vary slightly for coconut fatty acids or their methyl ester owing to their lower molecular weight. They would require somewhat more hydrogen and also slightly more electricity, steam and cooling water. Approximately 25–30 per cent more for coconut fatty acid, some 20 per cent more for coconut methyl ester. The yield would be 92.5 per cent calculated on distilled coconut fatty acids.

During the hydrogenation process, the unsaturated fatty acids are transformed into saturated fatty acids of the same molecular weight, and, of course, the amount of hydrogen consumed will be correspondingly higher for unsaturated fatty acids than for saturated fatty acids or their methyl esters.

By altering the process conditions somewhat and using a selective catalyst (Al_2O_3/CdO/Cr_2O_3) the double bonds present can be retained in the final alcohol. The chemical reaction for high-pressure reduction of fats and oils, or 'hydrogenolysis', as it is often called, is as follows :

$$R{-}\overset{\overset{\displaystyle O}{\|}}{C}{-}OH + 2H_2 \rightarrow RCH_2OH + H_2O$$

The equation and heatof reaction for fatty acid esters of lower alcohols and triglyceride hydrogenation. (The heat of reaction is for the hydrogenation of the COOR group only and not for the transformation of unsaturated double bounds in case unsaturated feedstock is used) are given as under :

$$R_1COOR_2 + 2H_2 \rightarrow R_1CH_2OH + R_2OH \qquad \Delta H_R \approx -500 \text{ kJ}$$

$$\begin{array}{l} CH_2OCOR \\ | \\ CHOCOR \\ | \\ CH_2OCOR \end{array} + 8H_2 \rightarrow \begin{array}{l} CH_3 \\ | \\ CHOH \\ | \\ CH_3 \end{array} + 3RCH_2OH + 2H_2O \qquad \Delta H_R \approx -105 \text{ kJ}$$

Virtually all plants for the production of alcohols by high-pressure hydrogenation use as starting materials the methyl esters. These have now become an important intermediate in the industry for at least two further processes.

Fig. 9.1. shows a detailed flow sheet for high-pressure hydrogenation. During past, the plants using both OXO and Ziegler chemistry came on stream to manufacture synthetic alcohols. These were based on petroleum and with the low price of crude oil at the time, synthetically produced alcohols quickly surpassed natural alcohols in volume.

In essence, the OXO process uses an olefin, carbon monoxide and hydrogen as the raw materials to form an aldehyde with one carbon more than was originally present in the olefin thus :

$$R{-}CH = CH_2 + CO + H_2 \xrightarrow[\text{high pressure}]{\text{catalyst}} \begin{array}{l} R{-}CH_2{-}CH_2{-}CHO \\ \quad\text{or} \\ R{-}CH_2{-}\underset{\displaystyle CH_3}{\underset{|}{CH}}{-}CHO \end{array}$$

and this aldehyde is then reduced to an alcohol.

As mentioned above, the alcohol produced contains one carbon more than the original olefin, and thus does not make OXO alcohols comparable with the alcohols produced from natural sources as these are always even-numbered carbon chains, and also the OXO alcohol need not necessarily be straight-chained.

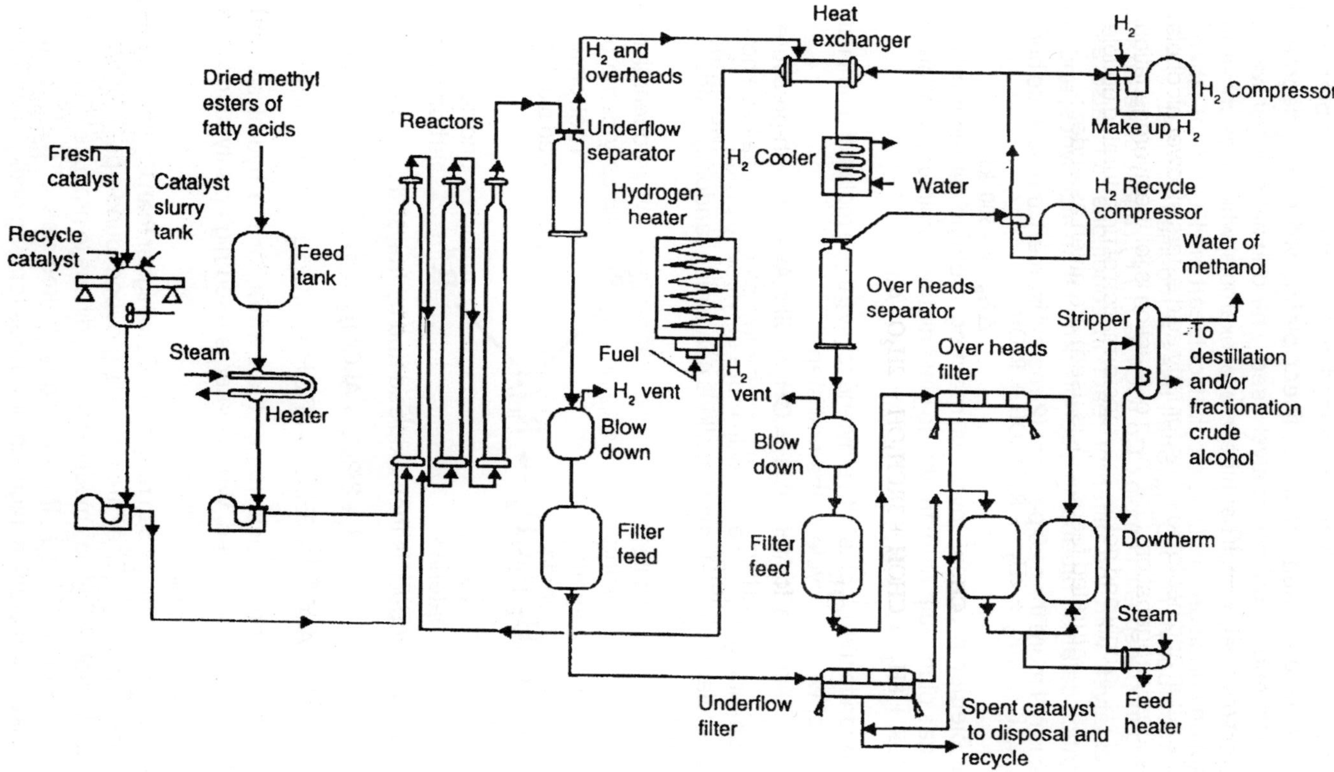

Fig. 9.1. Flow chart for high-pressure hydrogenolysis to obtain fatty alcohols from natural fats.

Normal alcohol are always produced by this process, but branched olefins will give branched products, linear olefins wili give a degree of branching, depending on the catalyst used. The original catalyst was an oilsoluble salt of cobalt (cobalt naphthenate for example) which was converted in the reaction conditions firstly to dicobalt octacarbonyl, $Co_2(CO)_8$, then to cobalt hydrocarbonyl, $HCo(CO)_4$, Shell uses a modified catalyst, cobalt-carbonyl-organophosphate complex, $Co_2(CO)_6[(C_4H_9)_2P]_2$, again formed *in situ*, and this catalyst, with the different reaction conditions acts also as a hydrogenation catalyst, producing alcohols rather than aldehydes, and the branching is not more than 20 per cent (2-methyl isomer), the balance being linear alcohols.

The Ziegler process, involves reacting metallic aluminium with hydrogen gas plus aluminium triethyl to yield diethylaluminium hydride:

$$Al + 3/2H_2 + 2Et_3Al \rightarrow 3Et_2AlH$$

The hydride then reacts with ethylene to give three moles of aluminium triethyl, two of which recycle to the first step:

$$3Et_2AlH + CH_2 = CH_2 \rightarrow 3Et_3Al$$

The remaining triethyl reacts with more ethylene to produce a mixture of high-molecular-weight aluminium alkyls containing randomly distributed alkyl groups :

$$Et_3Al + nCH_2 = CH_2 \rightarrow R.Al\begin{matrix} \diagup R' \\ \diagdown R'' \end{matrix}$$

This 'growth product' is then oxidised and hydrolysed :

$$AlR_3 + 3/2O_2 \rightarrow Al(OR)_3$$

$$Al(OR)_3 + 3H_2O \rightarrow 3ROH + Al(OH)_3$$

Ethyl uses sulphuric acid rather than water for the hydrolysis and aluminium sulphate is formed. When water is used high purity alumina is obtained.

The alcohols produced can range fom C_6 to higher than C_{20}, depending on the process conditions. They are normally grouped round a peak following a Poison distribution. Ethyl has modified the conditions to produce 'controlled peaking'. It is surmised that the company makes use of the fact that aluminium alkyls can crack at high temperatures forming dialkyl aluminium and an alpha olefin. These olefins are sepaated into high and low boiling fractions, the lower fraction is sent upstream for further growth and the higher fraction to another reactor for 'transalkylation', both reactors contacting the incoming streams of olefin with aluminium trialkyl. A narrower chain distribution of the final alcohol mixture is thus obtained. Table 9.1 shows a comparison of the distribution of alcohols produced by the normal Ziegler type plant and the Ethyl modification.

Table - 9.1

Comparison of alcohol distribution from two types of Ziegler production units.

Carbon length	Normal distribution	Ethyl controlled peaking
6	9.6	1.4
8	16.9	3.2
10	20.7	7.7
12	19.4	34.5
14	15.1	26.3
16	9.8	1.7
18	5.3	8.9
20	3.2	1.3

Reaction conditions can be controlled to shift the peak higher or lower, and the C_{14} alcohol (not very abundant in nature) can be produced at will. The alcohols in the C_{12} to C_{20} range are the important ones for the industry, the lower fractions have other uses–solvents, plasticisers, etc. Very seldom is a pure alcohol used as a detergent intermediate, blends are quite sufficient. It has been found that a blend of a (relatively) low-molecular-weight alcohol sulphate or ethoxylate with a higher molecular weight one can have synergistic effects.

In the East European countries petroleum is oxidised to fatty acids and then reduced to alcohols. These alcohols are straight-chain random secondary, not suitable for sulphonation but can be ethoxylated to non-ionic detergents.

The fatty alcohols, either natural or fully synthetic, are used for three main synthetic detergent process.

(i) Alcohol sulphates

$$CH_3(CH_2)_nCH_2OSO_3^-Na^+$$

(ii) Alcohol ethoxylates

$$CH_3(CH_2)_nCH_2O(CH_2CH_2O)_mCH_2CH_2OH$$

(iii) Alcohol ether sulphates

$$CH_3(CH_2)_nCH_2O(CH_2CH_2O)_mCH_2CH_2OSO_3^-Na^+$$

Table 9.2, 9.3, 9.4 and 9.5 give the specifications of commercial fatty alcohols produced by high-pressure hydrogenation of natural fats and oils, and of selected Ziegler alcohols.

Table 9.2.

Properties of typical commercial fatty alcohols derived from oils and fats.

Name	Number of C-atom	Iodine number	Solidification point °C	Boiling range °C/ 101 kPa	Hydroxyl number
Lauryl alcohol wide-range type	C_{10}–C_{18}	Less than 0.5	17-21	220-320	275-85
Lauryl alcohol	C_{12}–C_{16}	Less than 0.5	18-22	240-320	280-5
Lauryl alcohol c.80% C_{12}	C_{12}–C_{14}	Less than 0.5	17-23	255-85	283-93
Myristyl alcohol c 95% C_{14}	C_{14}	Less than 0.5	36-38	280-95	25-62
Cetyl alcohol c. 95% C_{16}	C_{16}	Less than 0.	4-49	31-30	225-35
Stearyl alcohol c. 95% C_{18}	C_{18}	Less than 0.5	55-57	340-55	203-10
Tallow fatty alcohol	C_{14}–C_{18}	Less than 0.5	48-52	120-90	210-20
Oleyl-cetyl alcohol mixture	Mainly C_{18} saturated and unsaturated	45-120*	4-35*	310-5	200-20

* The more unsaturated the mixture, the higher the iodine value and the lower the solidification point.

The alpha olefins are reacted with dry hydrogen bromide in the presence of peroxides or ultra-violet light to give the primary alkyl bromides, which are then converted to an ester through metal-halide catalysed reaction with organic acid. The ester is then hydrolysed with superheated steam to yield the corresponding primary alcohols. The process has the advantage that anhydrous hydrogen bromide produced in the esterification and the organic acid can both be recycled. The Ziegler process consumes expensive compounds such as tri-butyl aluminium and boron hydride, while the OXO process for the production of secondary alcohols uses a cobalt catalyst over which olefins are passed in the presence of carbon monoxide and hydrogen.

Higher alcohols made by the Ziegler and modified OXO processes have one characteristic which make them particularly useful in detergent manufacture: both anionics and non-ionics produced from them are easily degraded by the bacteria flora in normal sewage treatment plants.

Table - 9.3

Properties of pure fatty alcohols

Name of alcohol	Formula	Mol. weight	Melting point °C	Boiling-point/ Boiling range °C	Hydroxyl number
Decanol	$C_{10}H_{21}OH$	158	7	231 (101.1 kPa)	355
Undecanol	$C_{11}H_{23}OH$	172	14	131 (1.98 kPa)	326
Dodecanol (lauryl alcohol)	$C_{12}H_{25}OH$	186	24	135-7 (1.33 kPa)	301
Tridecanol	$C_{13}G_{27}OH$	200	30	155 (1.73 kPa)	280
Tetradecanol (myristic alcohol)	$C_{14}H_{22}OH$	214	38	159-61 (1.33 kPa)	262
Pentadecanol	$C_{15}H_{31}OH$	228	44		246
Hexadecanol (palmitic alcohol or cetyl alcohol)	$C_{16}H_{31}OH$	242	49	179-82 (1.9 kPa)	232
Heptadecanol	$C_{17}H_{35}OH$	256	54		219
Octadecanol (stearyl alcohol)	$C_{18}H_{37}OH$	270	58	202 (1.33 kPa)	208
Octadecanol (oleyl alcohol)	$C_{18}H_{35}OH$	268	15–16	177–83 (0.40 kPa)	209

Olefins

Olefins are required as intermediates for three kinds of detergent materials, alpha olefins for the OXO process and for sulphonation, and internal olefins as alkylation reagents for alkylbenzene and alkyl phenol.

Alpha olefins

Cracking of hydrocarbons to produce lighter fractions has been practised for many decades, both by catalytic and thermal processes. For the production of alpha olefins thermal cracking is preferred. The main reaction can be shown :

$$C_nH_{2n+2} \rightarrow C_{n'}H_{2n'} + C_{n''}H_{2n''+2}$$

where $n'+n'' = n$ and n'' is a low integer.

Table 9.4

Typical composition and properties of selected alfol alcohol blends

	Alfol 1014 CDC	Alfol 1214	Alfol 1412	Alfol 1216	Alfol 1218 DCBA	Alfol 1618
Individua! alcohol content %						
C_{10}	31	0.6	0.6	0.3	0.7	–
C_{12}	37	55	38	64	39	–
C_{14}	31	44	60	24	30	1.0
C_{16}	0.8	0.9	1.9	11	18	58
C_{18}	–	–	–	tr.	11	39
C_{20}	–	–	–	–	0.7	2.4
Colour APHA max	0	30	20	30	30	40
Density 22/22°C	0.834	0.836	0.839	0.840	0.840	0.814*
Freezing point °C		22	23	20	21	46
Average molecular weight	184	198	203	198	211	253
Flash point PMCC °C	121	129	132	129	135	163
Hydroxyl number	302	277	272	276	260	215
Iodine number	0.07	0.1	0.1	0.1	0.2	0.9

* Density at 60/4°C.

A linear paraffin will produce a linear olefin. Several side reactions are possible but a highly refined paraffin wax will yield 80-90 per cent alpha olefins with a small amount of branched olefins, some internal and diolefins.

The refined wax is pre-heated, mixed with steam (to avoid coking) and fed to a cracking furnace at a temperature of about 550°C under pressure two to four times atmospheric. A low residence time is necessary (about 10 seconds), this maximises alpha olefin production, and cracking conversion is kept low (20-40 per cent per pass).

Table - 9.5

Typical composition and properties of selected epal blends

	Epal 12/8	Epal 1214	Epal 1218	Epal 1416	Epal 1418	Epal 1618
Individual alcohol content %						
C_{10}	0.1	–	0.3	–	–	–
C_{12}	86	66	48	0.3	0.7	–
C_{14}	13	27	20	62	35	1.5
C_{16}	0.01	7	17	36	40	47
C_{18}	–	–	14	1.4	23	50
C_{20}	–	–	0.3	–	0.8	2
Colour APHA max	5	5	5	5	5	5
Density	0.831*	0.831*	0.834*	0.825+	0.825+	0.819+
Iodine value	0.02	0.02	0.34	0.2	0.4	1.0
Hydroxyl number	297	283	266	250	235	219
Average molecular weight	189	198	211	224	239	256
Flash point PMCC °C	137	137	125	143	149	202
Freezing point °C	20	22	25	37	42	46

* At 25°C.

† At 40°C.

‡ At 50°C.

The vapour exiting from the furnace is quenched with water and the uncondensed vapour is separated from the liquid in a flash tower. These vapours are then fractionated to remove the (unwanted) lighter fraction and distilled into the various commercial cuts.

The quenched liquid is recycled to the cracker. The light fraction contains ethylene, propylene and butylene, and needs to be disposed of economically, possibly with a link to a lower olefin plant.

The specifications for linear alpha olefins of wax origin indicate that the branched alpha olefin content is fractional, internal olefins can be from 1-5 to 10 per cent, di-olefins upto 4 per cent, saturates upto 4 per cent with fractional amounts of aromatics. If it is desired to sulphonate wax-cracked olefins, the exact composition should be considered as some of the extraneous constituents can adversely affect the quality of the sulphonate. The olefins will of course have both even and odd numbered carbon chains.

As mentioned in describing the Ethyl modification of the Ziegler process for the manufacture of alcohols, olefins can also be produced by this growth reaction. After the aluminium alkyl has grown to the required length, the temperature is raised and a low molecular-weight olefin (ethylene) is added. The ethylene replaces an alkyl from the aluminium trialkyl, yielding an alpha olefin.

Olefins produced by this method are of even numbered carbon lengths. Table 9.6 indicates the typical values for detergent grade olefins produced by ethyl. It will be noted that for the higher molecular weight products the amount of branched terminal olefins is high. Despite this the sulphonated alpha olefin produced from the olefin biodegrades at a faster rate than LAS.

Table - 9.6

Typical composition and properties of selected ethyl alpha olefins

	Tetra decene-1	Hexa decene-1	Octa decene-1	C12-14	C14-16	C16-18
Carbon no.						
C_{10}	–	–	–	0.3	–	–
C_{12}	2	–	–	62	1	–
C_{14}	96	2	–	36	65	1
C_{16}	2	97.5	18	1.2	33	55
C_{18}	–	0.5	81	–	1	36
C_{20}	–	–	1	–	–	8
Mono-olefin %	99.6	99.1	98.9	99.6	99.6	99.2

Cont ...

Paraffin %	0.4	0.9	1.1	0.4	0.4	0.8
Olefin isomers mol %						
Linear terminal	81	72	59	87	76	63
Branched terminal	14	21	35	9	19	29
Linear internal	5	7	6	4	5	8
Colour APHA	---------------- All less than ------------					
Density 20°C	0.760	0.780	0.788	0.764	0.776	0.787
Flash point °C	107	128	143	81	113	135
Boiling range °C						
IBP	245	276	298	216	245	285
FBP	250	283	316	250	279	316

Linear Internal Olefins

Internal olefins are one of the preferred feedstocks for the alkylation of benzene as these are random in nature. It has been pointed out that the presence of 2– and 3–phenyl alkanes impairs the detersive effects of the final sulphonate, whereas by increasing the 5–, 6– and 7– isomers the detergency is increased. Internal olefins can also theoretically be used as feedstock for OXO alcohol production but here the alpha type is preferred.

Kerosene is the normal base material but the term is very loose as refineries produce to physical rather than to chemical constants. The chemical characteristics depend on the crude being used, but a kerosene with a median boiling point of 220°C will contain upto 25 per cent normal paraffins of C_{11} to C_{16} chain length, with aromatics, iso-paraffins and cyclic naphthenes. If substantially free of olefins, this kerosene is suitable for processing. The absence of olefins is necessary as the dehydrogenation step will convert to any olefin present to the undesirable di-olefin. The feedstock needs to be hydrotreated to remove any impurities which would impair the catalyst used in subsequent operations. Depending on the molecular weight required of the final linear alkylate, the hydrotreated kerosene is first fractionated to either $C_{10}-C_{13}$ or $C_{11}-C_{14}$ fractions or any other ranges the market calls for.

Normal paraffins are then separated by selective adsorption processes:

Urea has the property of adsorbing to itself straight-chain hydrcarbons with at least 7 carbon atoms in the molecule. It is suggested that the mechanism is that the urea molecules wrap themselves round the hydrocarbon molecule in a hexagonal spiral and these spirals form channels which can accommodate straight-chain molecules but not he branched ones.

In practice urea can adsorb some 30 per cent of its own weight of hydrocarbon.

An activator is necessarfy for this action to take place. Suitable activators are methanol and the lower ketones.

The procedure basically is to add the kerosene to the solution of the urea in the activator with stirring. The hydrocarbon/urea complex crystallises (the reaction is not instantaneous), when it is filtered, washed with a short-chain raraffin solvent (less than 7 carbons) and the n-paraffin is released from the complex by hot water.

Variations of this basic method are the use of continuous processes and decomposition of the complex by non-aqueous solvents. Many patents have been granted for these variations.

These normal paraffins can now be used for alkylation (via chlorination) or be dehydrogenated to internal olefins, also as the alkylation reagent. Dehydrogenation of the paraffin to an internal olefin is an endothermic, catalytic process.

In brief, the process involves passing the vapourised feedstock, together with recycle, through a fixed bed reactor where only part of the paraffin is dehydrogenated to linear mono-olefins. Hydrogen is produced as a by product, and the olefin/paraffin mixture is separated from light materials by fractionation. The olefins are separated from the unreacted paraffins by selective solvents, the paraffin being fed back to recycle. If the olefin is to be used for alkylation, this final separation need not be too thorough as the paraffin can act as a diluent in the reaction and can easily be separated after the alkylation, then recycled. Alkylation units therefore normally start with an olefin-unit, if not with a linear paraffin unit.

The catalyst is the important point in this operation and new and efficient ones have been developed capable of working for long periods without the need for regeneration.

Normal Paraffins

For the production of linear internal olefins, normal paraffins are required. When paraffins are required as feedstock for the production of alkane sulhonates, the aromatic content needs to be brought down to below 50 ppm, otherwise undesirble side reactions will occur in the sulphoxidation process.

The removal of aromatics can be accomplished by two methods, hydrogenation, when they are converted to cycloparaffins, which remain in the liquid and do not increase the n-paraffin content, or by sulphonation and removal as the sulphonic acid.

Alkyl Benzene

Among the many different synthetic detergents the alkyl aryl sulphonates are the most important. There are many impotant reasons for this. Not only are the alkyl aryl slphonates outstanding in their properties as detergents, but they are also based on raw materials which are easier to obtain and cheaper than those on which the other types of detergents are based.

The main source of alkyl aryl sulphonates is the petroleum industry, but before going into details about raw materials and methods of manufacture, it will be convenient to deal with their chemical structure.

As the name implies, these products are based on aromaic compounds combined with an aliphatic chain bound to the aromatic nucleus. Thus, dodecyl benzene, which is the most important type of alkyl aryl condensate, has the following structural formula:

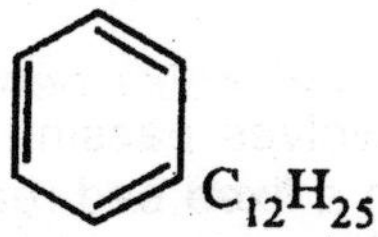

The nature of the propylene polymerisation is such that the tetramer (also the trimer when used) has a branched chain. When the problems with biodegradation arose the cause was quickly pinpointed to this branched chain structure and it was proved that linear alkyl benezene sulphonates (LAS) are biodegradable. The propylene tetramer type is still manufactured for use in countries which have not as yet legislated against it and for specialised purposes such as agricultural emulsifiers, where the problems of re-formulating, both administrative and technical, are great.

The chemistry of the alkylation is represented by the equations:

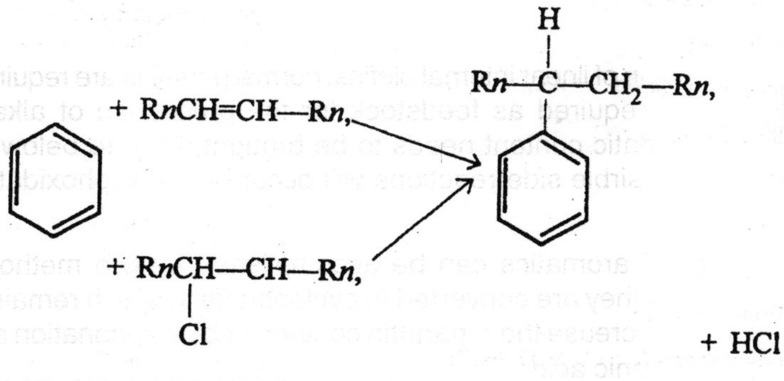

Certain side reactions can and do take place; dimerisation of the olefin, alkylation of this dimer, di-alkylation of the benzene, possibly di-phenylation of the olefin or chlorparaffin and cyclo-alkylation of the benzene. Thus in the reactor together with the alkylbenzene, we can find diphenyl alkane, di-alkylbenzene, di (alkylbenzene), all in the ortho- or para-positions:

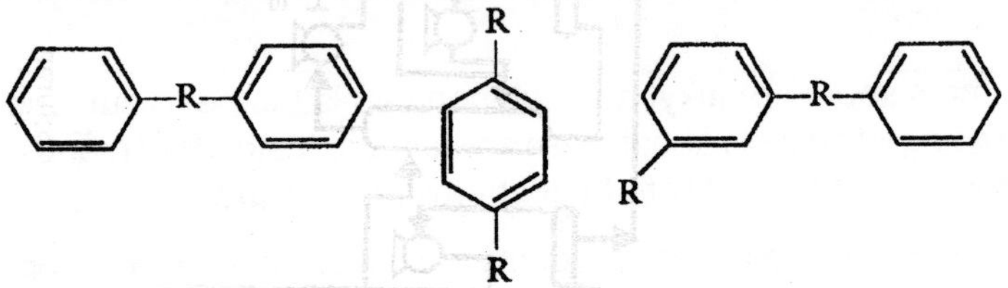

and also alkylbenzene with a side chain consisting of the dimer of the olefin. Although we have mentioned mainly the reactions of an olefin, the 'heavy alkylate' from chlorparaffin alkylation is surprisingly similar to that of the olefin based product.

The typical properties of linear alkyl benzene are given in Table 9.7.

Table 9.7

Typical properties of linear alkyl benzene (LAB)

Bromine	0.02
Saybolt colour	+ 30
Alkyl benzene content	97.4%
Doctor test	Negative
Unsulphonatable matter	1.0%
Water	0.1%
Specific gravity 15°C	0.8612
Refractive index $n_D 20$	1.4837
Flash point	138°C
Average molecular weight	240
Distillation range °C	
IBP	281
50 vol %	290
EP	309
2-Phenyl isomer	20%
Biodegradability (ASTM D-2667)	> 95%

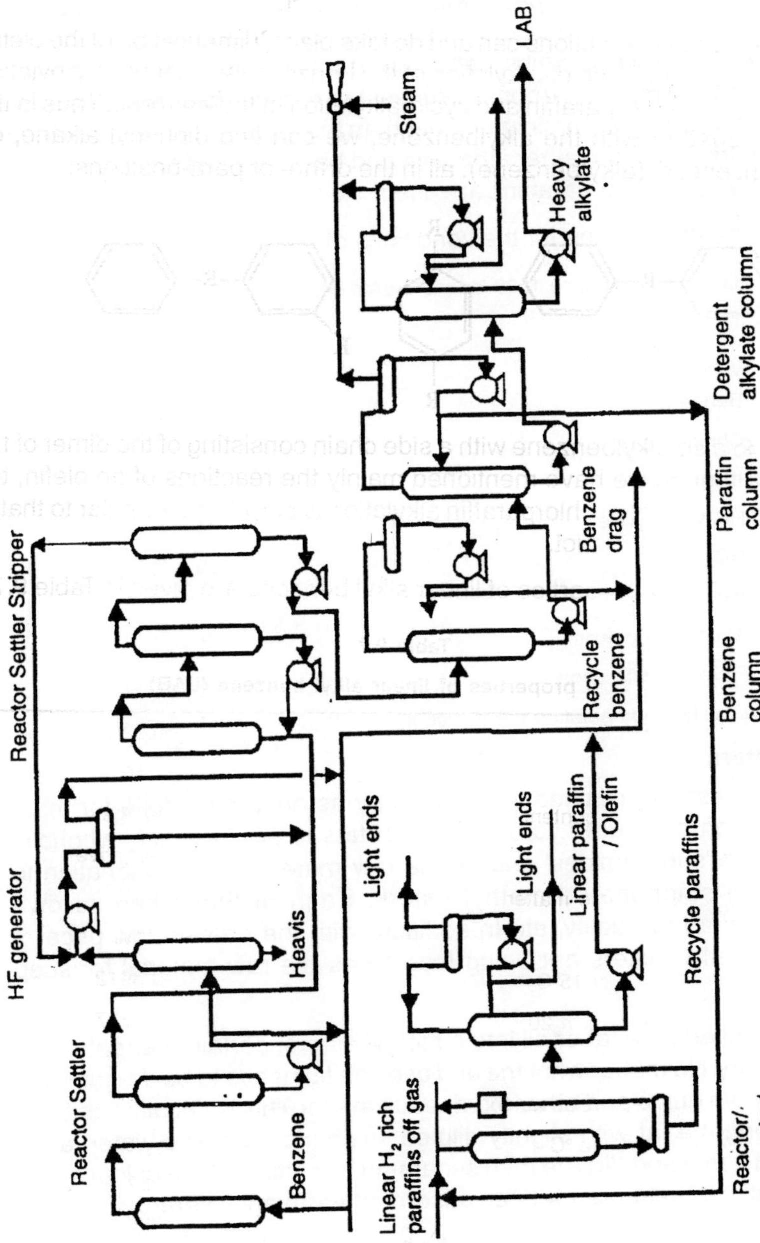

Fig. 9.2. Production of linear alkyl benzene schematic flow (UOP process).

The paraffinic (C_{12-14} petroleum fraction) the HCl is recovered during the dehydrochlorination process, in the Rheinpreussen process HCl from the monochlorinated paraffinc petroleum fraction (or a synthetic paraffin fraction from the Fischer-Tropsch process) is recovered during alkylation. The idea of using pure aluminium rather than the hygroscopic and corrosive aluminium trichloride is rather attractive and has become fairly universal in the industry when chlorparaffins are used.

The material balane for the conditions of reaction is given as :

	kg
Raw materials to produce 1000 kg linear alkyl benzene :	
n-paraffin	76
Benzene	359
Chlorine gas	368
By-products produced :	
Heavy alkylate	81
HCl	365
Chemicals used :	
Aluminium powder	1
Flake caustic soda	5
Caustic soda solution (50 per cent)	74

Methyl Esters

Methyl esters are used in the industry as an intermediate for three purposes, high-pressure hydrogenation of fats to produce fatty alcohols, production of 'superamides' and as the raw material for sulphonation to produce the sulphonated methyl esters. Each of these has its own requirements as to quality, etc In addition, with the present low price of methanol, methyl esters aer being mooted as the raw material for soap production.

For converting a fat or oil into a methyl esters, certain pretreatments are necessary. No matter what the end use, the fat needs to be de-gummed to remove both gums and other extraneous matter This is usually achieved by contacting the fat with slightly diluted sulphuric acid. The water, acid, coagulated gums and dirt are then separated by settling. If the colour of the fat is poor it is then treated with an absorbent earth and filtered.

For sulphonation the fat needs to be hydrogenaed or to have an intrinsic low iodine value. The hydrogenation is of the normal fat hardening kind, not as described in the production of alcohols, i.e., using a nickel catalyst at mopderate pressure. For the preparation of alkanolamides the fat is not normally hydrogenated unless special properties are sought.

Thirdly, the free fatty acid in the oil must be reduced to less than 0.4 acid value as the presence of the fatty acids will react with and impair the performance of the catalyst. The free fatty acid reduction can be achieved by one of the conventional methods used in the production of edible oils, using a caustic wash or steam distillation under vacuum.

An alternative method of reducing free fatty acid for methylester production is by pre-esterification of the ffa with methanol thus transforming the ffa into methylesters prior to the transesterification process.

Pre-esterification may either be carried out in a simple batch process or, alternatively, in a continuous system under pressure.

Distillation of excess methanol required for esterification, is a simple operation; methanol for esterification of fatty acids needs not to be completely anhydrous, as for the transesterification process, and a simpler rectification may be carried out independently from the recirculation system in the transesterification unit.

The classical ester-interchange alcoholysis reaction occurs when pre-refined or pre-esterified oils and fats are reacted with anhydrous methanol in the presence of an alkaline catalyst. In order to obtain maximum conversion into methylesters, the following conditions have to be maintained: the fat and oil must be degummed and deacidified to reduce the acid value below 0.4. Methanol must be anhydrous (max. 0.3 water).

The catalyst of choice is sodium methylate. The catalyst originally used is dry NaOH or KOH, dissolved in methanol.

During extensive laboratory and pilot work, a conversion rate as good as with sodium methylate, when a conversion rate or at least 95 per cent could easily be obtained, provided the sodium methylate was fresh and the methanol practically anhydrous.

Sodium methylate powder should however immediately be dissolved in methanol as a stock solution, otherwise it very quickly absorbs water and even CO_2 from the air, thereby reducing its efficiency as a catalyst.

Two alternatives exist to separate the glycerine layer set free after completion of the interchange reaction. One is the classical method, namely to separate it from the reaction mixture in the form of crude glycerine containing the soap formed by the catalyst, some methylesters and methanol.

This glycerine layer then undergoes a prerefining step: distilling off methanol, splitting the soap with acid and separating the fatty acids and some methylester on top of a glycerine solution slightly diluted with water to give a prerefined glycerine of about 70 per cent concentration, which can of course easily be brought upto a higher concentration.

The alternative method to separate glycerine is as follows: after the transesterification reaction is terminated, excess anhydrous methanol is distilled, and recovered for recirculation from the total reaction mixture containing methylester, glycerine, soap formed by the catalyst and some small percentage of unconverted triglyceride, at about 70° C. A low temperature is recommended in order to prevent any reverse reaction of methylester with glycerine. The last traces of methanol are then stripped off preferably under reduced pressure.

When all the methanol has been removed from the reaction mixture, about 3 per cent water containing sufficient acid to neutralise any free sodium methylate and to split the soap formed, is added.

Glycerine separates rapidly from the methylester in the form of an about 70 per cent glycerine solution. The sodium salt content of the glycerine solution, either sodium sulphate or chloride, is less than the salt content of crude glycerine obtained from soap spent-lye.

Organic matter, too, is less. The methylester may be washed free from last traces of glycerine and salt by again adding about 3 per cent water. This rinse is again made up with acid and used for the next process batch.

Obviously, when using this system for glycerine recovery, the methylester contains a small percentage of free fatty acid (ffa) from the split soap. However, when the methylester is used for alkanolamide production or for soap, the presence on ffa does not represent a disadvantage. Only when the methylester has to undergo distillation and the distilled methylester is marketed as a commodity, the acid value has to be reduced to a low level below 1.

This can easily be accomplished by conventional alkali or carbonate neutralisation, a process which is not much more dificult, than washing the methyl ester free from glycerine and soap in the conventional process.

Alternatively, it was found that, on neutralising the ffa with monoethanolamine prior to distillation, no foam problems occur and no highly viscous sticky bottom fraction is obtained. The modified method of separating glycerine is especially attractive, when transesterification is carried out continuously. Fig. 9.3 shows a batch system for transesterification.

The components, fats and oils, sodium methylate stock solution in methanol, and methanol are introduced, by automatic batching, into the reactor. The reaction mixture is kept boiling under reflux at about 70° C for about two hours, when conversion of triglyceride into methyl ester reaches 95 per cent for tallow and even 97 per cent for cocount or palmkernel oil. Subseqent processing steps have already been described.

In the continuous process, Fig. 9.4 which can also be carried out under pressure, residence time is considerably reduced; the components are dosed by triple-head dosing pump, the fat or oil passes through a preheater, so as to give a temperature of the total mixture, catalyst stock solution, methanol and fat of about 70° C in the static mixer.

From there the reaction mixture enters the reactor. The temperature is above 70° C when the alcoholysis is carried out at atmospheric pressure, and higher when carried out under pressure.

Correlation between temperature and pressure is, e.g., 3.4 bar at 100° C, 10.4 bar at 140° C. From a practical constructional and operational point of view, operation at 3.7 Bar at a temperature around 120° C would be preferable.

From the reaction column, the reaction mixture enters the distillation column for distilling off the excess anhydrous methanol for recirculation via the surge tank.

Splitting off the soap, separation of glycerine and washing are generally performed discontinuously. It may be mentioned that the batch and the continuous transesterification processes should be able to use the two alternate methods separating the glycerine.

SULPHONATION OF DETERGENT RAW MATERIALS

Sulphonation and sulphation are the most important processes for the production of anionic detergents, which, as we have seen, are by far the most important synthetic detergents. In recent years sulphonation processes have been developed which have revolutionised the detergent industry. Sulphonation and sulphation with acids, such as sulphuric acid, oleum of various concentrations, and chlorosulphonic acid, is now being replaced by methods which use gaseous SO_3, obtained either by vapourisation of liquid stabilised SO_3 (sulphuric acid anhydride) or directly as converter gas from a contact sulphuric acid plant. However, sulphonation with acids is still widely practised, so that a description of the more conventional acid-sulphonation processes will also be given in this chapter.

The Inorganic Raw Materials for Sulphonation

A precondition for properly carrying out sulphonation is the knowledge of the inorganic raw materials. We will therefore give a short description of the most important inorganic acid raw materials used in detergent sulphonation processes. (In this context we consider liquid SO_3—i.e., sulphuric acid anhydride—as an acid, too. We will also give the properties of sulphur since this is the starting material for the most modern sulphonation process.)

Sulphuric Acid and Oleum (Fuming Sulphuric Acid)

The oldest, and still widely used, acid in the detergent industry is sulphuric acid and oleum of various strengths. The chemical formula of sulphuric acid is H_2SO_4, molecular weight 98.08. For sulphonation processes either the so-called monohydrate of 98/99 per cent acid strength is used, or oleum, i.e., sulphuric acid with various percentages of free SO_3 dissolved. The physical properties of more dilute sulphuric acid are of interest for the practical man in the detergent industry, as he might well encounter dilute sulphuric acid in the form of so-called 'spent acid' and in acid cleaners.

The tables show that, especially at a percentage between 97 and 100 per cent sulphuric acid, there is a curious irregularity in density. The specific gravity of an acid of 97 and 98 per cent is identical, and the density of an acid of 99 and 100 per cent strength is practically the same as that of an acid of 94—95 per cent strength. This fact is of great practical importance, because it makes determination of acid strength by simple hydrometer reading impossible within this range of concentration, which unfortunately is the most important concentration range for acid sulphonation proceses. There are other physical control methods for the determination of acid strength in the range of 93—100 per cent, such as the measurement of conductivity and 'heat of dilution'. Incidentally, these physical methods have been worked out for the control of SO_2 absorption and air-drying in the classical contact sulphuric acid production processes.

Table - 9.8

Properties of Sulphuric Acid

Degrees baume	Specific gravity 60'F	% sulphuric acid H_2SO_4	Weight of 1 Imp gal in ib av	Normal boiling-point °C	Freezing (melting)-point °C
0	1.0000	0.00	10.011	100.0	00.0
1	1.0069	1.02	10.079	100.1	–0.39
2	1.0140	2.08	10.150	100.3	–0.83
3	1.0211	3.13	10.222	100.4	–1.28
4	1.0284	4.21	10.295	100.6	–1.72
5	1.0357	5.28	10.369	100.8	–2.22

Cont ...

1. Fatty materials tank
2. Methyl alcohol tank
3. Interesterification reactor
4. Settling vessel
5. Methylester collecting tank
6. Glycerine collecting tank
7. Methylester transfer pump
8,9. Methanol evaporator
10. Glycerine transfer pump
11,12. Methanol flash evaporator
13. Glycerine transfer pump
14. Soap splittling vessel
15. Settling vessel
16. Methanol condenser
17. Condensed methanol collecting drum
18. Vacuum pump

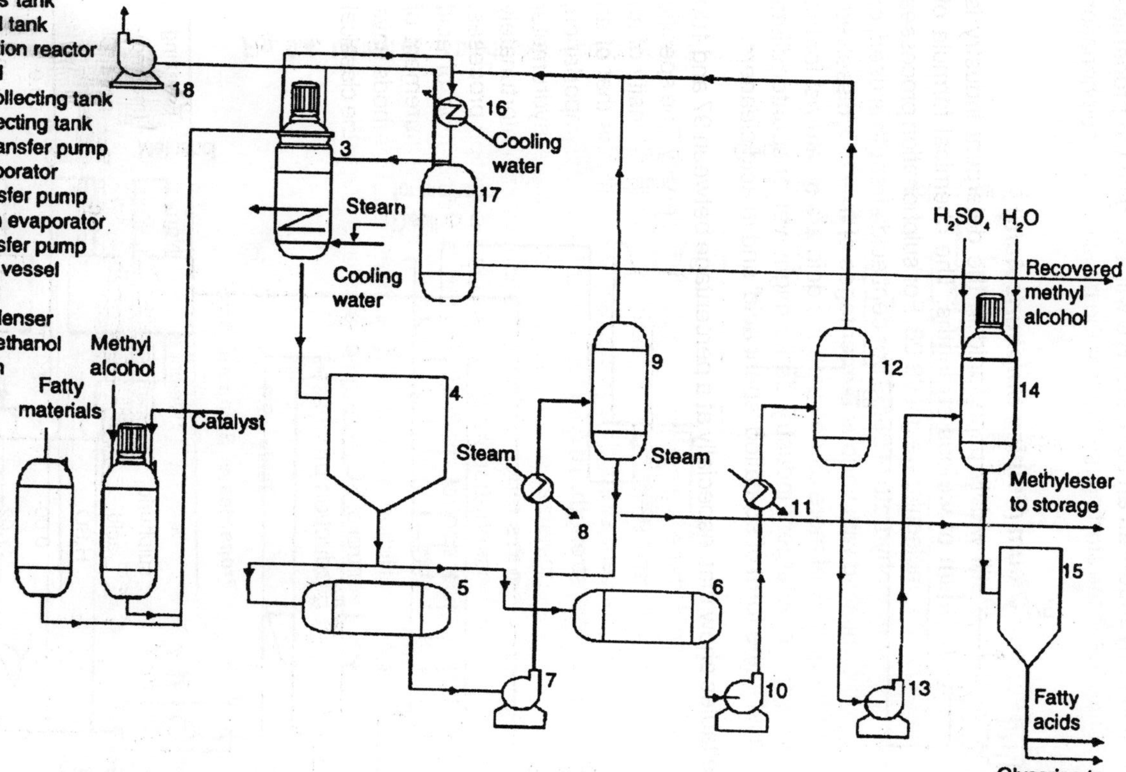

Fig. 9.3. Ester interchange process—batch process.

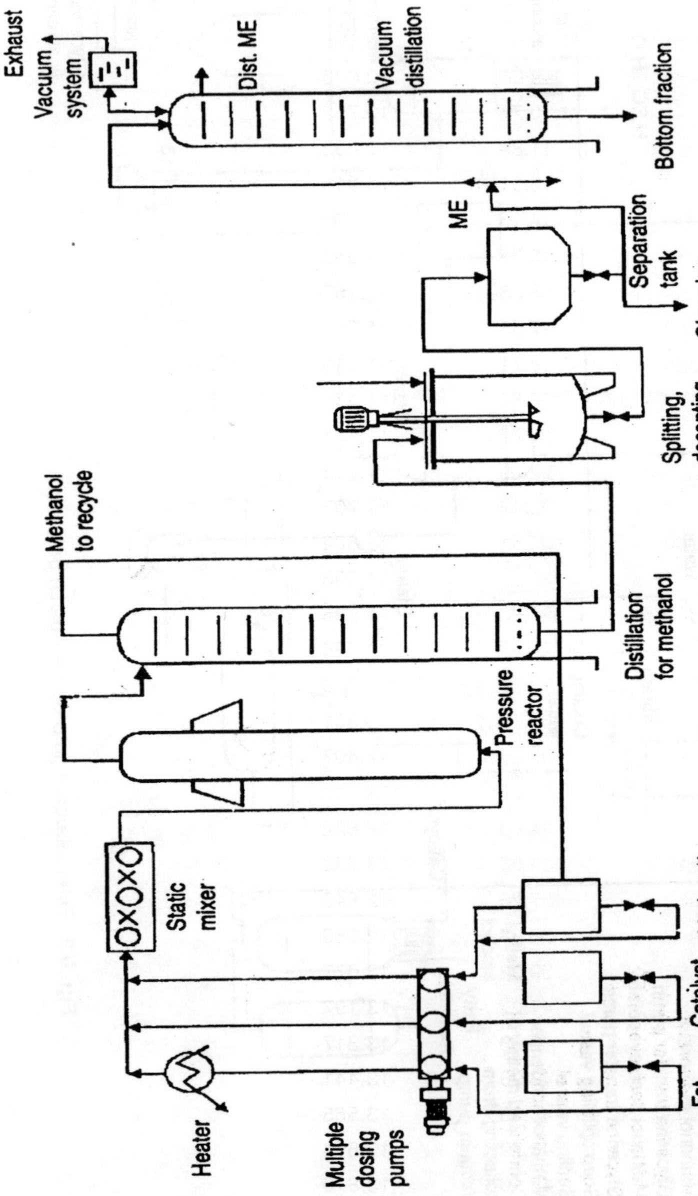

Fig. 9.4. Methyl ester production—continuous system.

6	1.0432	6.37	10.443	100.9	–2.77
7	1.0507	7.45	10.517	101.1	–3.44
8	1.0584	8.55	10.595	101.3	–4.11
9	1.0662	9.66	10.673	101.5	–4.72
10	1.0741	10.77	10.752	101.7	–5.39
11	1.0821	11.89	10.832	101.9	–7.00
12	1.0902	13.01	10.915	102.2	–7.00
13	1.0985	14.13	10.996	102.4	–7.94
14	1.1069	15.25	11.082	102.7	–8.72
15	1.1154	16.38	11.167	102.9	–10.00
16	1.1240	17.53	11.251	103.2	–11.11
17	1.1328	18.71	11.340	103.6	–12.28
18	1.1417	19.89	11.430	103.9	–13.61
19	1.1508	21.07	11.521	104.3	–15.33
20	1.1600	22.25	11.612	104.7	–17.22
21	1.1694	23.43	11.707	105.1	–19.17
22	1.1789	24.61	11.802	105.8	–21.39
23	1.1885	25.81	11.898	105.8	–23.94
24	1.1983	27.03	11.996	106.3	–26.67
25	1.2083	28.28	12.096	106.8	–29.94
26	1.2185	29.53	12.198	107.3	–33.33
27	1.2288	30.79	12.301	107.9	–37.56
28	1.2393	32.05	12.407	108.6	–42.39
29	1.2500	33.33	12.513	109.2	–48.50
30	1.2609	34.63	12.622	110.0	–56.39
31	1.2719	35.93	12.732	110.9	–61.50
32	1.2832	37.26	12.845	111.8	–59.56
33	1.2946	38.58	12.959	112.7	–57.78
34	1.3063	39.92	13.077	113.6	–56.27
35	1.3182	41.27	13.197	114.6	–54.72
36	1.3303	42.63	13.317	115.7	–42.50
37	1.3426	43.99	13.441	116.9	–49.44
38	1.3551	45.35	13.565	118.2	–45.88
39	1.3679	46.72	13.694	119.7	–42.22
40	1.3810	48.10	13.819	121.2	–39.00
41	1.3942	49.47	13.952	158.3	–36.10
42	1.4078	50.87	14.087	124.6	–33.70
43	1.4216	52.26	14.226	126.4	–31.90

44	1.4356	53.66	14.365	128.6	–30.40
45	1.4500	55.07	14.510	130.08	–29.40
46	1.4646	56.48	14.656	133.1	–28.50
47	1.4796	57.90	14.806	135.8	–28.40
48	1.4948	59.32	14.958	138.4	–28.80
49	1.5104	60.75	15.114	141.4	–31.90
50	1.5263	62.18	15.274	144.4	–31.90
51	1.5426	63.66	15.437	147.8	–34.20
52	1.5591	65.13	15.601	151.1	–36.80
53	1.5761	66.63	15.772	155.0	–38.20
54	1.5934	68.13	15.944	159.2	– 39.70
55	1.6111	69.65	16.121	163.6	–42.80
56	1.6292	71.17	16.302	168.3	– 40.40
57	1.6477	72.75	16.488	174.1	–39.70
58	1.6667	74.36	16.678	179.7	–33.60
59	1.6860	75.99	16.872	186.3	–22.80
60	1.7059	77.67	17.071	193.1	–11.40
61	1.7262	79.43	17.273	200.6	–1.50
62	1.7470	81.30	17.482	208.6	–4.20
63	1.7683	83.34	17.695	218.8	7.60
64	1.7901	85.66	17.914	230.7	7.10
64¼	1.7957	86.33	17.969	234.2	6.10
64½	1.8012	87.04	18.024	238.1	4.40
64¾	1.8068	87.81	18.080	2,13.4	2.20
65	1.8125	88.65	18.138	247.2	–0.40
65¼	1.8182	89.55	18.194	252.2	–4.20
65½	1.8239	90.60	18.252	258.9	–9.40
65¾	1.8297	91.80	18.310	268.3	–16.40
66	1.8354	93.19	18.366	279.4	–29.40

Table 9.9.

Properties of Oleum. (Free $S0_3$ total $S0_3$ and equivalent H_2SO_4).

% free sulphur trioxide SO_3	% actual sulphuric acid H_2SO_4	@/0 total sulphur trioxide SO_3	% equivalent sulphtiric acid H_2SO_4	0/@ free sulphur trioxide SO_3	% actual sulpburic o@cid H_2SO_4	0/10 total sulphur tiioxide SO_3	% quivalent sulphuric acid H_2SO_4
0	100	81.63	100.00	21	79	85.49	104.73
1	99	81.82	100.23	22	78	85.67	104.95

2	98	82.00	100.45	23	77	85.86	105.18
3	97	82.18	100.68	24	76	86.04	105.40
4	96	82.37	too.90	25	75	86.22	105.63
5	95	82.55	101.13	26	74	86.41	105.85
6	94	82.73	101.35	27	73	86@59	106.08
7	93	82.92	101.58	28	72	86.78	106.30
8	92	83.10	101.80	29	71	86.96	106.53
9	91	83.29	102.03	30	70	87.14	106.75
10	90	83.47	102.25	31	69	87.33	106.98
11	89	83.65	102.48	32	68	87.51	107.20
12	88	83.84	102.70	33	67	87.69	107.43
13	87	84.02	102.93	34	66	87.88	107.65
14	86	84.20	103.15	35	65	88.06	107.88
15	85	84.39	103.38	36	64	88.24	108.10
16	84	84.57	103.60	37	63	88.43	108.33
17	83	84.75	103.81	38	62	88.61	108.55
18	82	84.94	104.05	39	61	88.80	108.78
19	81	85.12	104.28	40	60	88.98	109.00
20	80	85.31	104.50	41	59	89.16	109.23
42	58	89.35	109.45	72	28	94.86	116.20
43	57	89.53	109.68	73	27	95.04	116.43
44	56	89.71	109.90	74	26	95.22	*116.65*
45	*55*	89.90	110.13	75	25	95.41	116.88
46	54	90.08	110.35	76	24	95.59	117.10
47	*53*	90.27	110.58	77	23	95.78	117.33
48	52	90.45	110.80	78	22	95.96	117.55
49	51	90.63	111.03	79	21	96.14	117.78
50	*50*	90.82	111.25	80	20	96.33	118.00
51	49	91.00	111.48	81	19	96.51	118.23
52	48	91.18	111.70	82	18	96.69	118.45
53	47	91.37	111.93	83	17	96.88	118.68
54	46	91.55	112:15	84	16	97.06	118.90
55	45	91.73	112.38	85	15	97.25	119.13
56	44	91.92	112.60	86	14	97.43	119.35
57	43	92.10	112.83	87	13	97.61	119.58
58	42	92.29	113.05	88	12	97.79	119.80
59	41	92.47	113.28	89	11	97.98	120.03
60	40	92.65	113.50	90	10	98-16	120.25

61	39	92.84	113.73	91	9	98.35	120.48
62	38	93.02	113.95	92	8	98.53	120.70
63	37	93.20	114.18	93	7	98.71	120.93
64	36	93.39	114.40	94	6	98.90	121.15
65		93.57	114.63	95	5	99.08	121.38

Fig. 9.5 showing the freezing point of concentrated sulphuric acid and oleum, again demonstrates another irregularity of great practical importance in handling oleum at various strengths, especially during the colder months. For sulphonation of detergent raw materials, mainly alkyl benzene, grades of oleum with 10–22 per cent freeSO_2 are used. It is thus of interest to note that it is within this range of free $S0_3$ that the greatest irregularity in the freezing temperature occurs. 100 per cent H_2SO_4 has a relatively high freezing point, whereas an oleum of 15–20 per cent has a relatively low freezing point. Oleum with 60 per cent free $S0_3$ and a rather low freezing point serves as a source of So_3 in some detergent sulphonation processes.

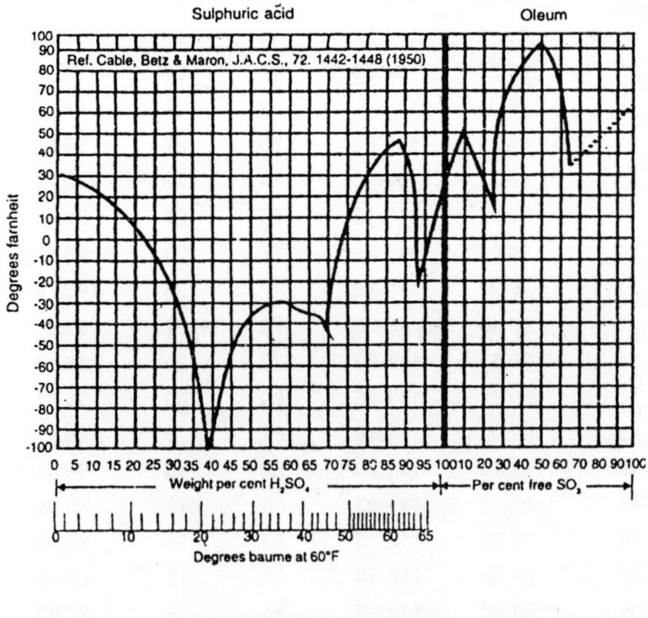

We emphasize, however, that in many countries explicit regulations exist for the safe handling, storage, etc., of sulphuric acid and oleum. These regulations should be carefully studied and followed by anybody starting a sulphonation plant.

Storage areas should have facilities for drainage and for the washing down of spills with water. Major spills of acid should not be discharged into a sewer, or washed into a sewer or river until they have been neutralised. Where convenient, the use of crushed limestone as a foundation under storage tank areas is considered good practice since it both provides good natural drainage and neutralises the spills before they are discharged into the sewer.

Storage tanks should be equipped with vents of such size as to maintain the tanks at atmospheric pressure. Metal catwalks should be provided for working on top of tanks.

Drums should be stored with the plugs up. The plugs should be loosened upon receipt and every week thereafter, or more frequently depending upon the weather, to release the internal pressure created by the evolution of hydrogen.

Although sulphuric acid is not inflammable, it should not be stored near organic materials, nitrates, carbides, chlorates and metal powders. Contact of high concentrations of sulphuric acid with these materials may cause ignition.

Sulphuric acid in drums, tank cars and metal storage tanks evolves hydrogen. Therefore open lights, flames and spark-producing tools should not be permitted near such containers.

Heating of storage tanks or storage areas is necessary for certain strengths of acid which freeze at common winter temperatures.

Sulphuric acid, like any other corrosive liquid, is dangerous when improperly handled. However, if suitable precautionary steps are taken, proper handling procedures followed, and adequate protective equipment wom, there is relatively little danger in working with this chemical.

The storage of sulphuric acid in bulk storage tanks, and piping it directly to process, is by far the easiest and safest way to handle the acid. This not only results in a considerable saving of space, but eliminates the hazards involved in lifting, transporting and discharging of drums and carboys. With properly designed and maintained equipment, handling hazards are reduced to a minimum.

Before being moved, drums should be inspected for loose plugs, for leakage and for bulging. To remove drum plugs, a pipe wrench or a plug wrench with a long handle should be used. The plug should be turned very slowly for one full turn, and accumulated pressure should then be permitted to vent itself After the hydrogen is released, the plug may be further loosened and removed.

Drums of sulphuric acid should be emptied by gravity, using a faucet or safety siphon. A pump may also be used. Air pressure should never be used. Since the drums may contain hydrogen gas, they should never be struck with a spark-producing tool.

Employees should wear face shields and rubber gloves when opening drums.

For all practical purposes the dilution of sulphuric acid and/or oleum with water should not be carried out in a detergent plant. There is a strong exothermic reaction, and as a general rule one should never add water to acid. Dilution of acid is a process step during sulphonation, and will be described later in this chapter. (The elimination of spillages has already been mentioned.)

The handling of sulptiuric acid and/or oleum as well as of 'spent acid' presents a corrosion problem, too.

Liquid sulphur trioxide (SO_3)

Appearance and colour:	Clear to slightly turbid liquid. 30-50 APHA
Assay:	99.5 per cent So_3
Boiling point:	44.8°C
Freezing point:	16.8°C
Density at 20'C:	1.922 g/ml
Heat of reaction with water:	1.096 kJ/g
Vapour pressure (mm of mercury)	25°C 265
	50°C 950
	75°C 3000

Sulphur trioxide in the vapour form always exists as the monomer, but when cooled below its boiling point, in the presence of minute traces of moisture or even on standing for any length of time, it can polymerise to liquid and solid polymers. Thus liquid So_3 can only be transported or used in its stabilised form.

Stabilised liquid sulphur trioxide is chemically the gamma form of $S0_3$. The alpha and beta forms are solids having a higher melting point. Since transformation between these three forms of sulphur trioxide can result in formation of the solid varieties, stabilised liquid $S0_3$ (gamma) ,which is protected against the formation of high melting-point solids by the addition of stabilisers such as borates or sulphonic acids, is the preferred sulph (on) ating agent.

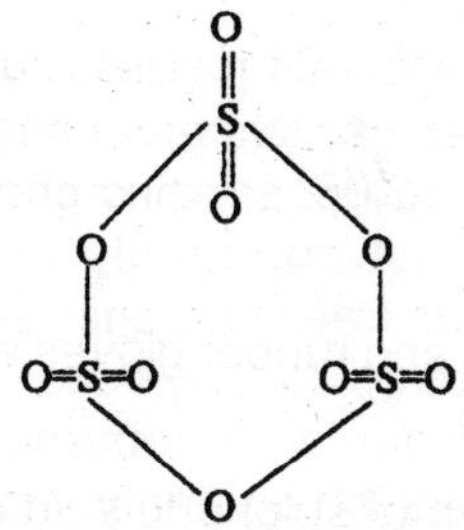

Gamma form of sulphur trioxide (Trimer)

In the detergent industry, liquid SO_3 is not used directly in its liquid form as a sulphonation agent, but mainly in its vapourised form strongly diluted with dry inert air. It must be mentioned that liquid SO_3 is also used as a liquid sulphonation agent diluted with undercooled liquid SO_2.

Sulphur trioxide from Oleum Stripping

In areas where liquid SO_3 is not readily available (there are stringent restrictions on the marine transport of this type of material), and where for some reason or another a sulphur burning plant is not to be established, SO_3 can be obtained by the stripping of oleum —60 per cent oleum is preferred although 25 per cent can be used.

The method is to distil the oleum, condense the evolved SO_3 gas into a storage vessel and add a stabiliser. Continuous evolution of SO_3 to feed into a reactor cannot be employed because as the SO_3 is removed from the oleum, the rate of evolution will fall, and a constant supply of SO_3 can never be maintained.

The liquid SO_3 thus formed needs to be treated as described above, i.e., to be vapourised prior to feeding into the reactor (s). When the oleum concentration falls to 20 per cent, distillation is discontinued. This 20 per cent oleuin has to be disposed of, usually by returning to the sulphuric acid manufacturer for enrichment.

Another possibility is to blow dried, heated air through the liquid, possibly in a heated column, thus obtaining directly, diluted SO_3 gas for sulphonation. To maintain an accurate and constant gas flow, the concentration of SO_3 in the evolved gas should be monitored with a feedback to control the air supply.

As can be seen, problems of corrosion and handling will be enormous, and the plant is in essence two plants, one for vapourisation and the other for treatment of the liquid SO_3. These factors should it,fluence the potential manufacturer to install a sulphur burning plant.

Sulphur

As already mentioned, sulphur is an important raw material for the most modern sulphonation method, which applies converter gas for direct sulphonation of detergent raw materials. It is this process which will be described in much detail later in this chapter. For this process elementary, technically sulphur of high purity (atom wt 32.06, specific gravity 2.03) is required. Three types of sulphur are most commonly used. Crude, run-of-mine 'bright' 99.5 per cent pure sulphur, free of arsenic, selenium and tellurium. Refined sulphur, which is an elemental sulphur produced by distilling crude sulphur, of not less than 99.8 per cent purity. Free-burning, available in lumps or cast sticks. A more recently available variety is the socalled 'gas-sulphur' which is obtained from natural gas or petroleumrefining processes. These types of sulphur solidify at about 114.5°C.

For practical purposes, data on the viscosity of liquid sulphur are important. As will be seen later, an exact pumping of liquid sulphur by dosing pump is the basis of the modern sulphonation process with converter gas, The pumping is best carried out at the lowest viscosity, i.e., 150–155°C (302-311°F). In this connection it must be mentioned that carbonaceous and hydrocarbon impurities tend to cause 'sticking valves' in the dosing pump.

The advantage of sulphur as basic inorganic raw material for sulphonation is obvious indeed. It is safe, to handle, practically non-toxic and non-corrosive to the skin. (Irritation of ocular conjunctivate and the mucous membranes of the respiratory organs may occur.) What has to be taken into account, however, is its inflammability. Even so, for all practical purposes of sulphonation, solid sulphur would not have to be ground in a mill, which would represent a certain ignition hazard. Storage of solid sulphur should exclude humidity and ignition hazards. Solid sulphur has to be molten in steam-jacketed vessels.

Chlorosulphonic Acid

This acid is still widely used in the detergent industry for the sulphonation of fatty alcohols, ethylene' oxide condensation products, etc. For alkyl benzene it cannot be used, as in the presence of an aromatic ring structure sulpho-chlorination would occur, whereas in all other sulphation procedures using chlorosulphonic acid free hydrochloric acid (HCl) in gaseous form is evolved during the sulphation reaction and has to be absorbed in water, to give liquid HCl of various strengths.

Physical and chemical properties

Chemical formula:	$ClSO_2OH$
Molecular weight:	116.53
Colour:	Colourless
MP :	– 80.0°C

BP :	151-5°C at 101.75 kPa
Solubility :	Decomposes in water, decomposes in alcohol, insoluble in CS_2
Index of refraction nD :	1.437 at 14°C
Specific gravity :	1.787 at 25°C
Specific heat :	1.18 J/g, °C, 15°C to 80°C
Heat of vapourisation :	406 kJ/kg
Heat of formation (from elements) :	597.1 kJ/mol
Viscosity :	2.5 mPa s at 30°C
Inflammability :	Non-flammable, but may cause ignition of combustible materials on contact. In contact with metals hydrogen gas is formed which can be very explosive in certain mixtures with air.

The physical data listed summarise the bulk of information available on chlorosulphonic acid and are adequate for many engineering calculations. Additional data on a good commercial grade acid are :

Appearance :	Pale yellow liquid
Assay $ClSO_3H$:	99.4 per cent
Iron–Fe):	< 5.0 ppm
Free SO_3:	0.40 per cent

For handling chlorosulphonic acid it is advisable again to ask the supplier for detailed safety data, and also about materials of construction, etc.

Sulphamic Acid

HSO_3NH_2 (also called amido-sulphonic acid) is occasionally used commercially for specialised sulphonations. It is non-corrosive and the plant required is relatively simple. Alcohol and phenol ethoxylates have been sulphated by sulphamic acid, although results with linear alcohols have not been successful.

Compared to other methods of sulphation, this process is rather expensive. Materials sulphated with sulphamic acid are neutralised naturally to the ammonium salt :

$$R—O—CH_2—CH_2—OH + HSO_3NH_2 \rightarrow R—O—CH_2—CH_2—O—SO_3NH_4$$

In general, the fact that the material is neutralised with ammonia is usually no detriment, but if the final formulation has a pH of over 8, a smell of ammonia will develop. The ammonium cation can then be replaced by adding the stoichiometric amount of caustic soda solution and heating to 100°C, when the ammonia will be distilled off.

SULPHONATION WITH SULPHURIC ACID AND/OR OLEUM

Sulphonation with sulphuric acid and/or oleum of various free SO_3 strengths is still widely carried out in the detergent industry. The sulphonation with acid is mainly used for the sulphonation of alkylate, either ABS or LABS. The procedure of sulplionation is described in detail in publications issued by the producers of alkylate.

The chemical reaction is as follows :

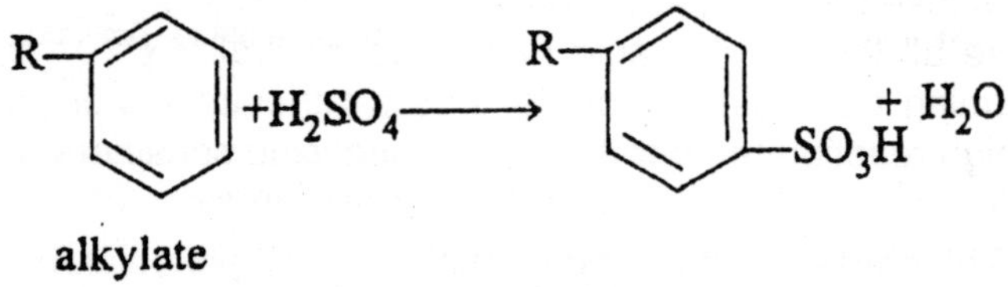

As is to be seen, water is set free by the reaction. The presence of water retards the sulphonation reaction, or even prevents it altogether. This is the reason why either a very large surplus of H_2SO_4 or a lesser surplus of oleum ($H_2SO_4 + SO_3$) is required to bring the reaction to completion.

Because alkyl benzene is produced to precise specifications, the detergent manufacturer can work out sulphonation procedures for detergent alkylates from various sources, without changing process conditions which, once established, have become standard procedures for an established sulphonation set-up. This does not mean, however, that there are no differences in quality among detergent alkylates of various provenances, Another important point must be mentioned: that sulphonation procedures vary to a certain extent depending on whether straight-chain alkylate or PT alkylate is used. In the following we will give a description of a batch sulphonation process of alkylate.

For sulphonation, a glass-lined (or stainless) jacketed vessel with an anchor type agitator of *c* 120 rpm is suitable. During sulphonation, optimum temperature is maintained by cooling, with water through the jacket. In hot climates it may be necessary to augment the cooling effect by a refrigeration system and/or a side-arm heat exchanger through which the reaction mass is recirculated by means of a gear pump. The pipes through which the reaction mass is circulated should be of stainless (type 316) steel. It is our opinion that in all cases where the batch size is above 1000 kg a side-arm heat exchanger should be installed.

For acid sulphonation the following process variables are decisive for the quality of the finished product :

1. Acid strength (and, of course, purity of acid, colour, etc.).
2. Ratio alkylate/acid.
3. Sulphonation temperature and time of acid addition.
4. Digestion time and temperature.

After the actual sulphonation step the separation of spent acid (i.e., the greater part of surplus acid) has to be accomplished. Sulphonation without subsequent spent-acid separation is rarely carried out, because in this case all the surplus acid has to be neutralised with caustic soda, transforming it to sodium sulphate. This is rather uneconomical and, owing to the high reaction temperature for neutralising considerable amounts of free sulphuric acid, special precautions are required to keep neutralisation temperatures under control. We will therefore describe a sulphonation process with subsequent spent-acid separation.

Table 9.10 shows the variables in sulphonation for various acid strengths.

This table should serve as a guide. In practice, some variations will be necessary, e.g., when sulphonating with 98 per cent acid, it might be advisable to warm the alkylate to *c* 40°C, in order to start the reaction smoothly. Otherwise, when starting at too low a temperature, the reaction might not begin until a very large amount of acid is added, and then it might be quite sudden, with an excessive amount of heat which might cause the reaction to get out of control. Anyway, it is a good rule to follow. Reaction should start immediately with the addition of acid, so that the time of acid addition and cooling together keep the reaction well within the range of optimum conditions. Naturally the reaction temperature also has an effect on the ratio alkylate/acid. Saving on acid generally means a sulpbonation temperature at the upper limit. Furthermore it may often be preferable not to aim at too complete a degree of sulphonation, and to be satisfied with, say 1.2–1.5 per cent of unsulphonated oil calculated on 100 per cent active matter, rather than 0.8 per cent, which would require more acid, higher temperature, longer ageing time, etc. This would result in a product of poorer colour and odour properties–on the whole a disadvantage that might not be warranted by a decrease of unsulphonated content from 1.5 to 0.8 per cent. With straight-chain alkylate, the reaction conditions are very much the same as for PT alkylate; however, the reaction temperatures should generally be about 5°C lower at the end of the reaction than those given for PT alkylate.

Table - 9.10

Acid sulphonation conditions

Acid strength	Ratio alkylate/acid	Reaction temperature (°C)	Digestion time (°C)
20–22% SO_3 oleum	1:1.1 (min. 1:1)	30 until half of acid addition 45° at the end	2 h at 40–45°
12–14% SO_3 oleum	1:1.2 (min. 1:1.1)	45° half, 55° end	2 h at 50–55°
100% H_2SO_4	1:1.5	50° half, 55° end	2 h at 55–60°
98% H_2SO_4	1:1.65 (min. 1:1.55)	45° half, 55° end	2 h at 50–55°

Now to the separation of spent acid. As a rule of thumb, 10 per cent of water calculated on the total of alkylate plus acid are added to obtain a good spent-acid separation. The water is added as it is, or in the form of crushed ice (not too large lumps of ice, in order to prevent damage to the sulphonation equipment). Under no circumstances should the temperature rise above 60°C, when all the water has been added. Separation takes about six to eight hours, and the resulting spent acid has a 'strength of 70–80 per cent. In case the sulphonic acid is to be used for the production of liquid detergents, where freedom of electrolytes is of great importance, a modified 'double-wash' spent-acid separation is recommended.

As previously mentioned, sulphuric acid and/or oleum sulphonation is still used in the detergent industry, mainly for the sulphonation of alkyl benzenes, PT benzene, or straight-chain alkylates. It is not suitable for the production of fatty alcohol sulphates, or for the sulphation of fatty alcohol and/or alkyl phenol ethoxylates.

SULPHONATION WITH SULPHUR TRIOXIDE

The greatest advance in sulphonation technique in recent years is the use of SO_3 as sulphonating agent, made possible by the commercial availability of this material. Whereas sulphuric acid and/or oleum is mainly used for the sulphonation of alkyl benzene, and chlorosulphonic acid is only suitable for detergent raw materials where an OH group is present, SO_3 is suitable for practically all types of detergent raw materials.

The reaction with So_3 takes place without formation of water (see above). The following equation clearly shows this :

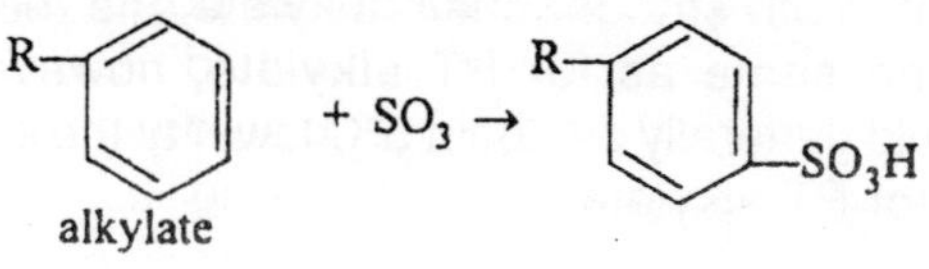

One hydrogen wanders from the aromatic ring to form SO_3H, sulphonic acid.

As SO_3 is a vigorous sulphonating and dehydrating medium, on occasion certain side reactions take place :

(a) Formation of anhydride

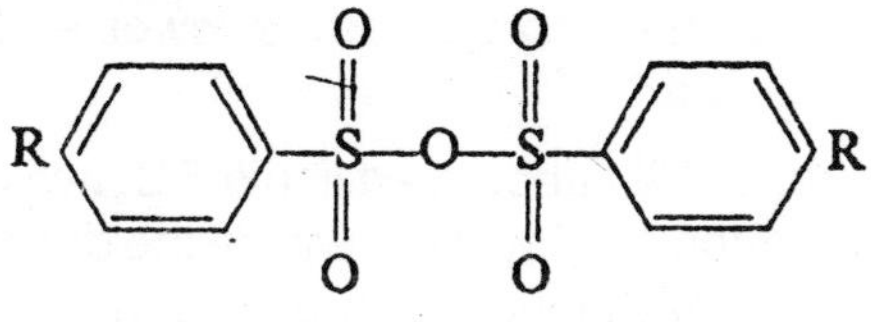

(b) Formation of sulphone (not to be confused with sultone)

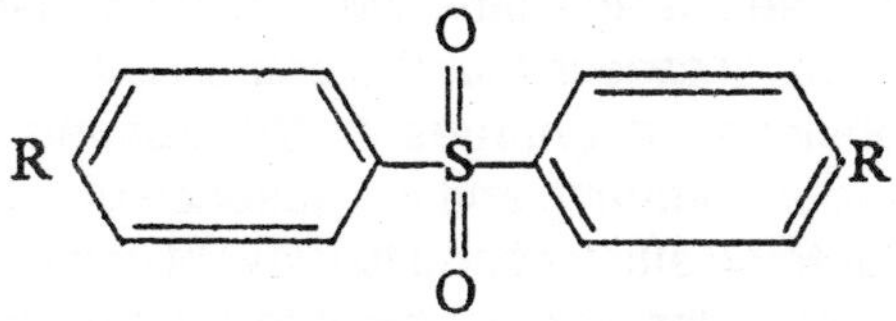

In practice either or both of these materials can be formed in small quantities, usually less than 1 per cent of the total mass.

Various methods of hydrolysing these two products have been patented, all consisting of adding small quantities of water, dilute alkali, aromatic solvents or alcohols to destroy either the anhydride or the sulphone.

It can be seen that the anhydride hydrolyses to two molecules of sulphonic acid, whereas the sulphone produces one molecule of sulphonic acid and one of alkyl benzene on hydrolysis.

For fatty alcohols the reaction is as follows :

$$RCH_2OH + SO_3 \rightarrow RCH_2OSO_3H$$

Again, a hydrogen wanders to the So_3 to form the acid sulphate which in the case of fatty alcohols has to be neutralised immediately to prevent hydrolysis.

The most widely accepted method of using liquid So_3 as sulphonating agent is to employ it in its vapourised form diluted with inert carrier gas, mostly dry air, to give a dilute So_3 gas stream of 7–12 per cent (vol) SO_3 Naturally the carrier gas must be as dry as possible, otherwise the SO_3 would react to give H_2SO_4 fumes which would cause poor quality of the finished product. Vapourisation of SO_3 and air-drying is an essential part of process equipment in sulphonation plants using liquid SO_3. (Air-drying units are also essential components in SO_3-sulphonation plants starting with elementary sulphur. Producers of liquid SO_3 generally give advice on the proper type of vapouriser to be used. Usually, the liquid SO_3 is fed by dosing pump (e.g., Teflon-lined pumps) into the electrically heated vapouriser, so that not much liquid SO_3 enters at a time, and vapourisation is aided by the stream of dry air passing through the vapouriser. Often the equipment is designed as a film vapouriser, so that at the lower end, the .sump', the stabiliser collects as a liquid.

For the air-dilution of the vapourised liquid SO_3 two principal methods may be used : (a) a 'once-through' system, where the dry air used for dilution of the SO_3 passes from the sulphonation unit to vent; and (b) a 'closed' system, where the air leaving the sulphonation unit is recircled to the SO_3 vapouriser. The advantage of the first method is that no droplets and fumes recycle to the vapouriser, which otherwise might cause serious colour deterioration. The disadvantage is that the entire dilution air must be dried all the time. The obvious advantages of the second method are the elimination of continuous air drying and the absence of exhaust fumes from the vent. But, in order to be efficient and to prevent colour deterioration, an extremely efficient mist-collector must be inserted between the vent from the sulphonation unit and the vapouriser. In a closed system, nitrogen may be used as the carrier gas, which otherwise would be.too expensive, but has the advantage of being completely inert.

The actual sulphonation technique with vapourised liquid SO_3 is the same as with converter gas from a sulphur-burning unit. However, sulphonation with liquid SO_3 has the advantage that such a plant may be operated on a daily shift basis, whereas a plant based on sulphur burning and conversion to SO_3 is only economical when operated continuously, or at least on a weekly basis. Some sulphonation plants using dilute SO_3 vapour obtain the SO_3 by stripping it from 60 per cent SO_3 oleum.

This method of obtaining vapourised sulphur trioxide diluted to about 7-10 per cent in dry air may seem to be unduly complicated in view of the fact that the converter gas which enters the sulphur trioxide absorber in any contact sulphuric acid plant has the same percentage of gas as one wishes to obtain by vapourisation of the liquid. However, upto now, there have been good reasons why converter gas has not been so widely used as a direct sulphonating agent. For instance, it may happen that the industry wanting to use converter gas from a sulphuric acid plant is not situated near a contact plant. Furthermore, it is not always economically advisable for the industry producing sulphonated materials to become dependent on a sulphuric acid plant. Technically, it is not a simple matter to use 'split-off' converter gas from a sulphuric acid plant, mainly because of the difficulty of measuring exactly the amount of sulphur trioxide taken from the cooler to be used in the sulphonation process.

To control the actual amount of sulphur trioxide, one must know the volume of converter gas at constant temperature and the concentration within a very narrow range. This does not appear to be too difficult, but in practice it is not a simple matter. For many sulphonation processes the amount of sulphur trioxide used must be accurately measured to within ±1 per cent, as any greater variations will lead to either over- or undersulphonated material. In the case of detergent alkylate, this would mean a product with too much unsulphonated matter or with an unacceptable dark colour. With fatty alcohols it is even more dangerous, as inaccurate addition of sulphur trioxide might even lead to a reversal of the sulphonation reaction.

However, methods for controlling the degree of sulphonation have been worked out, which automatically record the amount of unsulphonated material, and by feedback adjust the flow of alkylate to the sulphonation plant. This method of control might overcome the difficulties in working with 'split-off' converter gas.

It is only with those sulphonation processes where accuracy is less important that the use of 'split-off' converter gas is a relatively easy matter. Thus, white oil and highly refined kerosene can be produced by treating the appropriate petroleum fraction with converter gas either in a continuous or discontinuous process.

The possibility of designing a plant to produce sulphur trioxide on a small scale, where all the sulphur trioxide from the converter is cooled and used for the sulphonation of detergent raw material. To do this, certain conditions had to be fulfilled. First of all, to ensure a constant dosing of sulphur into the system, a metering pump was used. Then, in order to have the sulphur transformed into a constant amount of dry sulphur trioxide, the air used for burning the sulphur in the sulphurburner had to be completely dry, as otherwise stilphuric acid would be formed by the reaction with the water present. Drying of air was therefore carried out in a silica-gel drying unit, which brought the humidity down to about 0.5 g/m^3 air. If a still higher degree of drying is required, it is possible to carry out a kind of 'threshold drying' by having the silica-gel-dried air pass through a molecular sieve system, which brings the final humidity down to as little as 0.05 g/m^3 air.

A more efficient method to reach a very low dew point is by precooling the air to about 5°C, condensing and then removing the bulk of the moisture present. The silica gel, operating at a lower temperature works better and the final dew point of the air can be –.30°C or even –60°C.

A simple method of controlling the efficiency of the drying unit is to use the Draeger system of gas detection. The method is to draw by means of a hand pump, a constant volume of air through the appropriate Draeger tube and the concentration of moisture is read off. For more exact determinations special instrumental methods are available.

The same principle can be applied to the measurement of the SO_2 content of the exhaust gas leaving the sulphonators. Determination of SO_2 gives an indication of the original degree of convertion and also is important from the point of view of air pollution.

As already mentioned, the sulphur fed into the sulphur-burner in a converter-gas plant must also be measured very exactly. Furthermore, it was found in practice that the sulphur-burner used should preferentially be so designed that the sulphur is not sprayed under pressure through a nozzle into the burner, but flows through a relatively large orifice. Such a design is less liable to irregularities because of the clogging of the nozzle, and there is also the advantage that the pump is not working against a high pressure.

The sulphur used in small converter plants should be of high quality.

SULPHONATION PROCESSES

In addition to the advantages previously mentioned, the use of sulphur trioxide for sulphonation, generated as described, has the additional asset that its oxygen content is low compared with vapourised liquid sulphur trioxide, where air acts as the carrier gas. In the production of the trioxide direct from sulphur, about half of the oxygen in the air is used for conversion. This reduction in the amount of oxygen in the sulphur trioxide gas stream eliminates side effects often encountered with vapourised gas. Furthermore, the traces of sulphur dioxide in converter gas are also beneficial in this respect.

Sulphonation was carried out semi-continuously in two small sulphonating vessels of about 250 litres capacity. The unit consumes 1000 kg sulphur/24 hour, and this produces 2400 kg of sulphur trioxide (as 7-8 volume per cent converter gas), i.e., enough for about 7500 kg alkyl benzene/24 hour.

Some 175 kg (200 litres) of alkyl benzene are charged into one of two sulphonation vessels and sulphur trioxide admitted. Sulphonation requires about 60 min and, while the reaction is proceeding in one vessel, ageing is taking place in the other. After ageing, which takes about 15 min, a small amount of water or NaOH solution is added, and the alkyl benzene sulphonic acid is either run to storage or immediately converted to the neutralised AB-sulphonate. The small amount of water (about 2–3 per cent in the sulphonate mixture) helps to prevent 'anhydride-sulphonate' formation and keeps the colour of the AB-sulphonic acid stable, even on prolonged storage in mild steel drums or tanks. By introducing a time control and autoinatic-operated valves, etc., the semi-continuous sulphonation system can be converted to a continuous process.

The Sulphurex process Fig. 9.6 represents a further development. Here both the sulphur and the detergent raw material are metered into the system in the requisite proportions

After being cooled, the So_3 gas stream passes into the sulphonators at about 50°C. These consist of two or more reactors-different in number and size depending on the capacity of the plant. The SO_3 gas stream enters the reactors in parallel, with the major portion entering the first reactor and the minimum portion entering the last reactor. This proportioning of the SO_3 gas into the various reactors is done automatically and requires no attention from the operator.

The alkyl benzene (or any other material to be sulphonated or sulphated) essentially passes through a series of reactors in cascade, but because of the 'free oil' controller, a small amount is proportioned into the last reactor, since it is this quantity which is varied according to the completion of reaction.

Special high-speed turbine mixers disperse the So_3 gas and the alkyl .benzene with a high degree of efficiency, which prevents and local overheating of the reactants. Inside the reactor are precisely located cooling coils and baffles which immediately remove the large amount of heat released during the reaction.

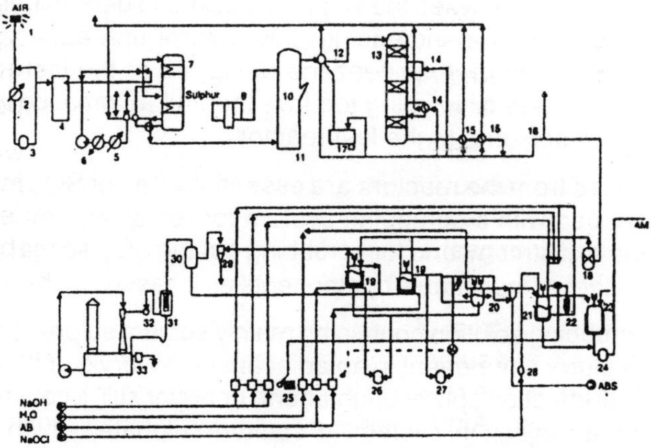

1. Air filter
2. Pre-cooling unit
3. Blower
4. Air cooling unit
5. Silica gel regeneration unit
6. Fan
7. Silica gel air driers
8. Sulphur melter
9. Filter
10. Proportining pump
11. Sulphur combustion Furnace
12. SO_3 cooler
13. Converter
14. Intermediate coolers
15. SO_3 coolers
16. Cooling fan
17. Pre-heating furnace
18. Filter
19. Sulphonators
20. Digestor
21. Neutraliser
22. pH control group
23. Final homogenising unit
24. Active matter transfer pump
25. Raw material proportioning pumps
26. Start-up pump
27. Free oil control group
28. Bleaching proportioning pump
29. Cyclone
30. Filter
31. SO_3 filter
32. Exhaust gas fan
33. Gas scrubber

Fig. 9.6. Flow diagram of Ballestra sulphurex process.

The temperatures normally used for various raw materials are :

(a) for the usual types of alkyl benzene (branched or straight-chained)

Sulphonators : 50°C

Digestion: 55°C

Neutralisation 45°C

(b) for lauryl alcohol :

Sulphonators 35°C

Neutralisation 45°C

(c) for tallow alcohol :

Sulpbonators 55°C

Neutralisation: 50°C

(d) for C_{14}–C_{18} Ziegler alcohols :

Suipbonators 50°C

Neutralisation 45°C

After the sulphonators, the main stream of sulphonic acid passes on to the digestion vessel, where it is held, to allow the reaction to go to completion. A side portion of this stream is directed to a patented device which automatically analyses the sulphonic acid and determines its 'free oil' content. If the free oil is increasing, this control unit automatically cuts down on the quantity of alkyl benzene being fed to the last reactor, and conversely, if the free oil is going too low, the unit automatically increases the flow of alkyl benzene to the last reactor.

The gases from the reactors are essentially free of SO_3. However, the plant is equipped with a scrubbing system for removing any SO_3 gas that may be in the exit stream, and for scrubbing out the SO_2, so that the exhaust gas is free of these undesirable components as it passes to the atmosphere.

The scrubbing solution containing mainly sodium sulphite may be used directly as a slurry component in an adjacent spray-dryig unit (sulphite has no detrimental effect on optical brighteners) or better still, it could be oxidised by a special air injection system to sodium sulphate, which again may safely be used as a slurry component, or in case no spray-drying unit is near the sulphonation unit, be discharged to the sewer. The scrubbing system is efficient enough to absorb the SO_2 so that the exhaust gas exits with as little as 5 ppm SO_2.

After the digestion vessel the sulphonic acid stream can be passed into another small reactor where water or NaOH solution can be added if desired. This unit is to take care of any anhydride formation that may occur.

Of course, no water or NaOH solution is used during the sulphation of the fatty alcohols. Because of the combination of reactors it is very easy to perform co-sulphonation-sulphation reactions and produce a high-quality product.

The sulphonic acid then passes on to the neutraliser, where caustic soda and water are continuously added to give a white paste containing the desired percentage of active ingredient. An automatic pH control unit controls the addition of caustic by sending a signal to the controller which varies the stroke of the proportioning pump of the neutralising agent by means of a servomotor.

The neutralised paste overflows into a storage tank, where it is continuously homogenised. From here it is pumped to any further processing operations, such as spray-drying, liquid production, etc.

It is important to note that after the sulphonators no transfer pumps are required. The reactants and acid flow from vessel to vessel by gravity. Operation and control of this plant are extremely precise and yet simple. One operator runs the entire plant-sulphur-burning, conversion, and sulphonation.

Neutralisation of sulphonated products can be an important operation, particularly for materials other than alkyl benzene sulphonates made by SO_3 sulphonation. If oleum sulphonation is used, the sulphonic acid contains both free sulphuric acid and water, rendering it corrosive. Unless special storage conditions are observed the acid material will both corrode iron and darken on standing. Neither of these restrictions applies to SO_3 suiphonated alkyl benzenes, they can be stored and transported in mild steel with no deleterious effects. For all that even the SO_3 sulphonated variety is often neutralised immediately after sulphonation.

Alcohol sulphates and alcohol ether sulphates need to be neutralised immediately, otherwise, in acid medium, the sulphuric ester will split to its original components (the reverse of the sulphation reaction).Olefin sulphonates need to be hydrolysed in addition to neutralisation. Sulphonated methyl esters need special treatment to prevent (or minimise) ester saponification in an alkaline medium.

For all the above reasons, the system of double step neutralisation has been developed recently has been developed, which eliminates the local concentrations of acid or water (or alkali), preventing hydrolysis of the ester group, or the formation of highly viscous hydrated lumps which dissolve slowly, causing pH drift. If hydrolysis were to occur, free sulphuric acid and free oil are formed. Free oil increases the unsulphonated portion of the finished paste, free sulphuric acid requires considerably more neutralising agent which can increase both the costs and the amount of inorganic salts present. Increase of free acid (even for a short period) can cause corrosion problems to the equipment and this is enhanced if, as is sometimes the case, bleaching agents are added during the neutralisation step. The plant is also so designed that the temperature of the paste is kept within reasonable limits.

To overcome all these problems, the Neutrex system neutralises 90 per cent of the incoming material in the first of two reactors, equipped with specially designed low speed impellers, which mix and homogenise. The heat of neutralisation is removed in this vessel. The remaining 10 per cent is fed into the second (larger) mixer and this mixes with the incoming neutralised paste from the first. The neutralising base which can be any of the alkaline materials commonly used is accurately dosed with linked pH control. The mass in the second neutraliser is kept at a temperature such that it can be easily transported further.

This unit can be coupled to any SO_3 sulphonation system, and by using this system the hitherto difficult to produce 70 per cent alcohol ether sulphates can easily be made.

Comparison of oleum and sulphurex processes

	Oleum process	Sulphurex processes
Sulphonating agent	Oleum	Sulphur
–characteristics	Corrosive liquid	Inert powder
–supply	Tanks, drums	In bulk (powder)
–storage	Tanks, drums	In bulk (powder)
Sulphonic acid purification	Washing and separation	No purification required
By-products	Dark 70% spent sulphuric acid	No by-products
Products storage	Lead-lined tanks	Mild steel tanks

For the production of 100 kg of 100 per cent active material from 72.5 kg alkyl benzene, the acid sulphonation process requires 75 kg of oleum, while the Sulphurex process consumes 10.5 kg of sulphur.

Only one man per shift is needed to operate the 'switch-over' and the Sulphurex processes. A sulphur-trioxide absorption tower is not essential for warming up and cooling down the unit. While the unit is being brought into equilibrium, the converter gas of irregular composition may be absorbed, for example, in alkyl benzene.

To use the converter-gas plant for the sulphonation of other compounds, such as toluene, xylene, etc., some modifications are necessary. Thus, for sulphonating low-boiling aromatic compounds, special cooling condensers have to be provided, to prevent undue losses by carrying over of unsulphonated product. By special modification of the sulphonation process on the basis of the 'dominant bath' system for low-boiling aromatics, a less expensive condensing system is obtained.

It is also possible to co-sulphonate toluene or xylene in conjunction with detergent alkylate, to give the proper proportion of hydrotrope or anticaking agent in the finished detergent.

Production of toluene sulphonates with oleum or SO_3 is rather costly, so the price of separately bought toluene sulphonate is higher than the price of AB-S. Since only a small percentage of toluene sulphonate is used (5–10 per cent calculated on AB-S used), it would be worth while to co-sulphonate toluene with the alkylate. The main difficulty encountered here is the low boiling point and high volatility of toluene. There is danger of ,carry-over' of the toluene with the inert gas stream leaving the system through the exhaust, before the toluene is sulphonated completely in the system. This leads to losses, unpleasant exhaust problems, and danger of ignition; problems which can be overcome in the laboratory by adding condensers and scrubbers to the sulphonation unit, but which are costly and difficult to set up on a plant scale. A different approach is used. The toluene is fed into the sulphonation system (in this case a 'switch-over' system) via the side-arm heat exchanger. Once the alkylate is sulphonated, toluene is fed into the suction line of the circulation pump for the side-arm heat exchanger in a ratio corresponding to the feed of So_3 entering the system. The toluene is thus pre-mixed with the AB-sulphonic acid in the circulation pump and heat exchanger, and then further mixed into the 'dominant bath' of the AB-S in the sulphonation system. No losses occur, and the toluene can be properly co-sulphonated. (The same principle can, with modifications, be applied to the fully continuous system.) If an automatic control system is not available, or if it is desired to control the system from time to time, the unsulphonated toluene can be controlled by a quick and simple technique: a sample of the AB-sulphonic acid is with-drawn and heated under an infrared drying balance. Weight losses during five minutes give the amount of unsulphonated toluene, since neither AB-sulphonic acid nor toluenesulphonic acid is volatile enough to disturb this quick test.Of course the same technique applied to co-sulphonation of cumene or xylene.

Practical test runs on a large scale have been made in a Sulphurex plant in which the standard Sulphurex set-up was used. Sulphonation in the first vessels was carried to about 85-90 per cent, and toluene was fed by the second dosing pump into the last sulphonation vessel, where the practically fully sulphonated AB-S (or for that matter fatty alcohol sulphate) was used as the 'dominant bath' for the toluene to be co-sulphonated. No special mixing pump was required in this case. Adjustment of the automatic instrument for sulphonatioii control can easily be made.

Recently there has been an increased interest in α-sulpho-fatty-acid methyl ester. They form useful components for many types of powder detergents, and are also used as components for syndet bars and syndet/ soap combinations. They can be produced by sulphonating methyl esters of coco fatty acids, stearic and palmitic fatty acids. It is important for the quality and colour of the sulphonated end product, that the methyl esters should have a low iodine value, i.e., below 0.5.

With the introduction of large-scale SO_3 sulphonation which, as we have stated, revolutionised the industry, considerable work has been done on improving the process both to produce higher quality materials and to adapt the procedure to allow of the sulphonation of the hitherto hard to sulphonate hydrophobes.

Sulphonation units for detergent production based on the falling film reactor are now being almost universally supplied to the exclusion of all other types, as these have proved to be able to cope with practically all the base materials except of course paraffin sulphonates.

Basically these units use a film of the material to be sulphated/ sulphonated, injected on to the wall(s) of a vertical tube or series of tubes (bundle type). The SO_3 is fed concurrently into the centre of the space. The reaction takes place on the surface of the tube(s) and the heat of reaction is dissipated through the walls of the conduit.

As the reaction is almost instantaneous, and as the film is flowing downwards continuously, and as 70–80 per cent of the SO_3 is consumed in the first third of the reactor, the sulph (on) ated material does not remain in contact with a large concentration of SO_3 for any length of time.

The advantages of the failing film reactor are :

1. Contact time of already sulphonated material with SO_3 is minimal.
2. Low residence time, thus acid sensitive materials (alcohol, alcoholether sulphates) can be transported rapidly to the neutralising section.
3. Relative flow rates and dilution of the SO_3 can be adjusted so that olefins, which react very vigorously, are contacted with dilute SO_3 for a relatively short time, on the one hand, and slow reacting materials, such as methyl esters, can have their residence time increased, on the other hand.

The problems in designing the reactor are :

1. Maintaining a constant uniform film of the organic feed on the walls.

2. Metering almost stoichiometric quantities of organic feed and accurately diluted SO_3.
3. Dissipating the heat of reaction but not at such a rate that the already sulph(on)ated material becomes a viscous mass and ceases to flow.
4. Controlling the velocity of the gas stream so that the organic feed is not carried over as a mist or the lower boiling components are not volatilised.
5. Having and maintaining a uniform small diameter (or aperture) as this increases the contact between the SO_3 and the feed.

The Ballestra Multitube Film Reactor consists of a vertical bundle of long, small-daimeter tubes.

The liquid film, which forms inside the tubes, comes into contact with the gaseous reactant. The length and diameter of each tube is so dimensioned as to provide the optimum product quality performance.

The most interesting feature of the Ballestra reactor is the simple way in which the exact reactants ratio is maintained in all the tubes.

The automatic adjustment of the reactants in each of the tubes is the result of the geometric design of the reactor itself and is completely independent of the actual number of tubes. It is a simple matter, therefore, to scale up the reactor to meet any production capacity requirement. All that is required is to increase the number of reaction tubes.

Fig. 9.7 illustrates the principle of the reactor. The SO_3 gas enters at the top of the reactor and then flows, without restriction,into each of the parallel-mounted reactor tubes. The liquid is uniformly distributed, by means of a simple concentric slot, over the inner walls of each tube.

The concentric slot permits the same amount of liquid to be fed to each tube. A difference of about 20 per cent between each tube is permissible, and the correct amount of gas is automatically fed to each tube, due to the aforementioned geometric design of the reactor.

The special patented feature of the reactor is that the required molar ratio between the reactants in each tube is self-adjusting and, furtheremore, is close to the preset ratio of the total liquid to the total gas flow rates in each of the tubes. The total gaseous reactant is fed to the reactor at the proper rate and at the proper concentration. The total liquid reactant is pumped to the reactor by means of the proportioning pump.

The flow of gas and liquid inside the reactor is parallel, with the liquid phase forming the film on the inner surface of each tube and the gas flowing through the tubes at very high speed. The outsides of the tubes, the shell

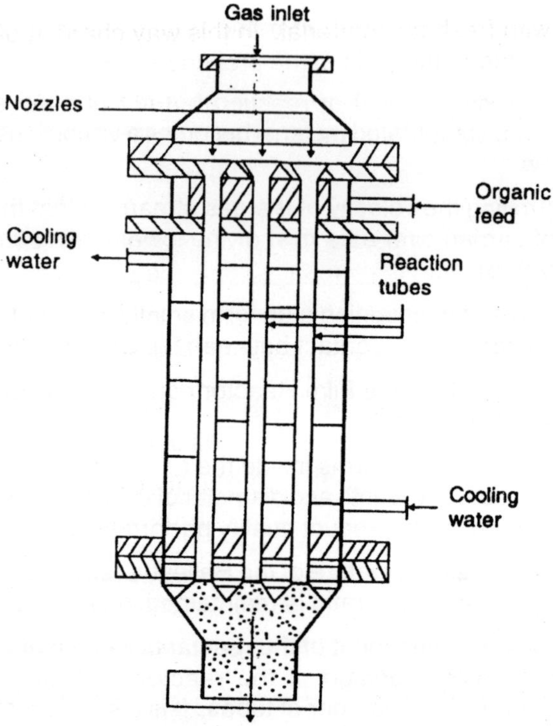

Fig. 9.7. Ballestra multitube film reactor.

side, are provided with cooling to ensure correct reaction temperature. The reaction takes place at a very high rate, with about 70 to 80 per cent of conversion occurring in the first third of the reactor.

Each individual tube, being fed at a particular average rate of liquid flow which is different from the next, has a correspondingly different film thickness and viscosity profile. This contributes to the self-adjustment of the gas-to-liquid mol ratios to the optimum average values, since the flow of gas in each tube then is directly proportional to the flow of liquid itself. The sulphonated liquid and exhaust gas leaving the reactor enter the gas separation vessel.

The separated exhaust gas is sent to the cleaning, electrostatic precipitation and scrubbing section and then released to the atmosphere. The liquid remaining in the separation vessel is transferred by pump to the neutralisation section.

Should the flow of liquid to the reactor be interrupted for any reason, an independently powered stand-by emergency system takes over and purges the reactor with fresh raw material. In this way charring of sections of the reactor due to stagnant liquid in the presence of So_3 is avoided.

Fig. 9.8 shows the flow sheet for the complete sulphonation process. All data are shown on a control panel detailing the complete process. Operation can be by push-button or computer.

Different feedstocks require differing concentrations of SO_3 in the gas stream. These can range from 2 to 7 volume per cent. The air-drying section is therefore dimensioned to supply the requisite dilution of dry air.

A combination of the film reactor and sulphonation under vacuum and liquid SO_3 is vapourised under vacuum and this vacuum is maintained throughout the whole system till the sulphonated material is discharged. The organic feed is fed into a specially designed egg-shaped reactor by a rotor to form a thin film on the internal wall of the egg.

These patentees claim that all the feedstocks normally used as detergent raw material intermediates can be sulph(on)ated by this unit. Advantages are that no air-drying or gas-liquid separation is necessary, considerably reducing both capital costs and space required.

Film reactor plants are being used to sulphonate all types of conventional detergent materials. They are, however, not suitable for co-sulphonating volatile materials, such as toluene, xylene, or cumene. They have found great success in the sulphonation of α-olefines which are playing an increasing part in detergent formulations and which hitherto had required very special methods of sulphonation.

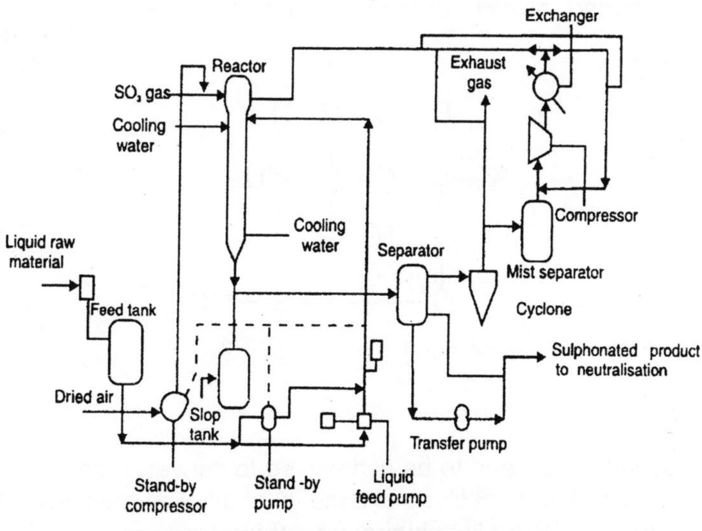

Fig. 9.8. Ballestra's film sulphonation system.

Alpha Olefin Sulphonates (AOS)

The sulphonation of α-olefins produces in approximately equimolar proportions :

(a) 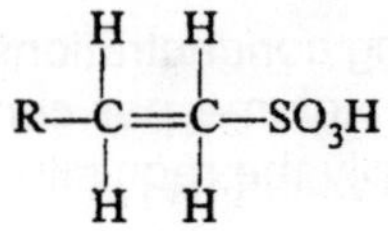

Alkene sulphonate

(b) 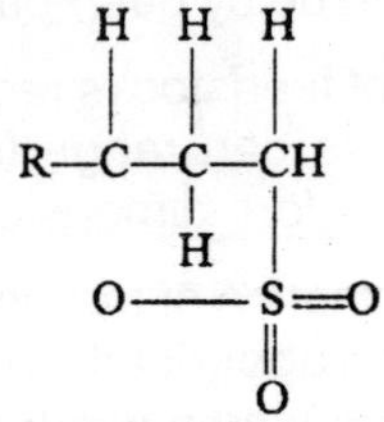

Alkyl sultone

with minute amounts of

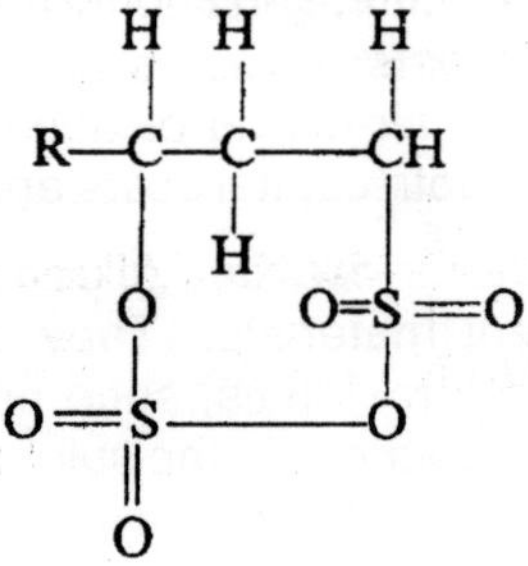

Alkyl disultone

The sultone shown is the 1,2-alkyl sultone but this is not the only one that can be formed. More often than not equal quantities of the 1,2- and 1,3 sultones :

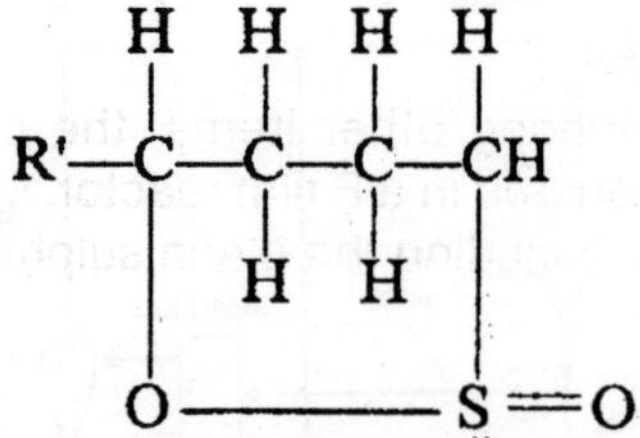

are formed.

These sultones need to be hydrolysed to convert them to detergent active materials. This hydrolysis is done in an alkaline medium, when the ring opens to form the sodium hydroxy sulphonate :

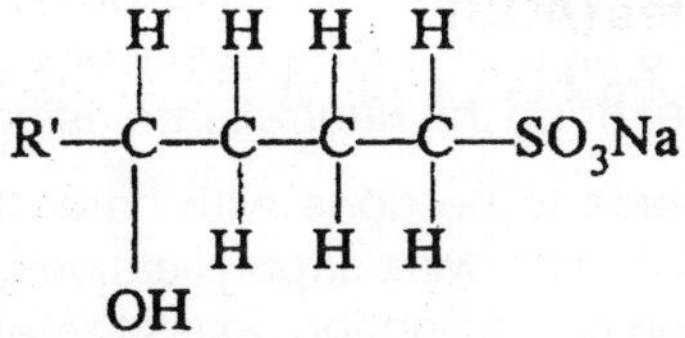

b-Hydroxy sulphonate is an undesirable product of this hydrolysis as it is not soluble in water, giving a hazy solution. Fortunately the 1,2- sultone from which it is formed is thermodynamically unstable, and will isomerise to the 1,3- or 1,4-sultone on standing. This isomerisation takes only a matter of minutes so that sulphonation/neutralisation/ hydrolysis conditions need to be arranged so that there is a 'hold' period between the sulphonation on the one hand and the neutralisation and hydrolysis on the other.

Formation of disultones is dependent on sulphonating conditions, excess of SO_3 and temperature, and should be kept as low as possible. The disultone on hydrolysis forms

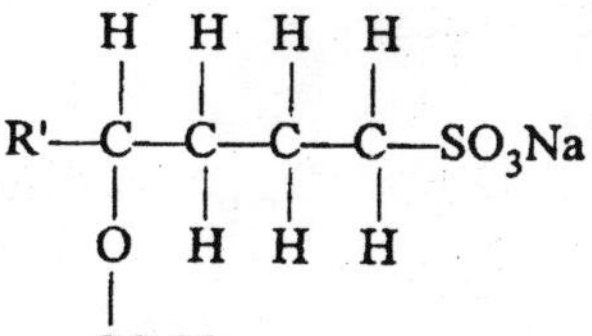

Alkane sulphato-sulphonate

As stated the a-olefin plants are almost invariably of the falling film type and must have neutralisation/hydrolysis units coupled to them.

α-Olefin sulphonates have not been accepted as universally as their initial proponents hoped, mainly because the chemistry is somewhat different from normal sulphonation.

Table 9.11 shows. among other items, the colour of unbleached detergent materials sulphonated in a F film reactor. It can be seen that the colour of all the materials, including the olefin sulphonate, is such that no bleaching is required.

Methyl Ester Sulphonates

The basic chemistry of the sulphonation of methyl esters of fatty acids has been touched on as has their method of preparation. The chemistry is not completely elucidated but appears to be the rapid formation of the complex, which can be termed a 'sulpho-anhydride' and this rearranges (relatively) slowly to the sulphoiiic acid.

It is evident that suiphonation is best done in a film reactor, requires an excess of SO_3, a relatively high temperature and a holding period to allow the intermediate complex to rearrange to the true sulphonic acid. Colour of the sulphonate will be high but this is easily bleached, either on the acid material using peroxide, or on the neutralisate using hypochlorite.

Neutralisation needs to be done with care, the pH, even localised, should not rise above 8.5, otherwise saponification of the ester might occurs The Neutrex double step neutralisation unit is therefore an ideal solution to the after-treatment of the sulphonic acid.

Table - 9.11

Production characteristics of materials sulphonated in a Ballestra Sulphurex F film reactor

Material	Neutralised material			On 100% material		Klett
	Am %	Uns %	Na_2SO_4	Uns %	Na_2SO_4	colour*
LABS	–	–	–	0.8	0.9†	25
Lauryl alcohol sulphate sodium salt natural or synthetic	35	0.3	0.5	0.9	1.4	7
Lauryl ether sulphate3 mol EO-sodium salt	30	0.3	0.4	1.0	1.3	15
Alcohol C_{16-18} sodium salt	25	0.65	0.4	2.6	1.6	60
α-Olefin sulphonate sodium salt	40	0.72	0.56	1.8	1.4	70

* On 5 per cent AM solution, 40 mm cell, # 42 filter, Unbleached products.

† Free sulphuric acid.

Heavy Alkylate Sulphonates

The heavy alkylate produced as the 'bottoms' in the alkylation of benzene is sulphonated by either oleum or SO_3 to produce synthetic petroleum sulphonates, not to be confused with paraffin sulphonates. Natural petroleum sulphonates are produced as by-products in the production of white oils, and the 'synthetic' variety is almost identical functionally, although not chemically.

As already mentioned, the heavy alkylates are complex mixtures but all the constituents of the mixture contain an aromatic ring, coupled to alkyl, alkyl-aromatic, other aromatic or cyclic nuclei in the ortho- or parapositions. Sulphonation of alkyl benzene is almost invariably at the paraposition, so if the para- position is blocked, sulphonation in the orthoposition is not feasible due to steric hindrance.

Heavy alkylates can therefore be only partially sulphonated and commercial products normally contain 60-70 per cent sulphonated matter.

Sulphonation is best achieved by SO_3 plus a non-reactive paraffinic solvent (boiling range *c* 210–230ºC) to facilitate the separation of any oilinsoluble acid sludge. The unsulphonated and unsulphonateable portion acts as a solvent for the neutralised material allowing neutralisation to be done with concentrated caustic soda or alkaline earth hydroxide slurries. The small amount of water introduced and produced in the neutralisation process can either be left in the material or distilled off if the specifications require.

The sodium salts of the heavy alkylate sulphonates are used as emulsifiers, wetting agents and dry-cleaning additives.

The alkaline earth salts (calcium, barium and magnesium) are used in lubricants and greases and their 'over-based' varieties as rust preventatives. Over-basing is achieved by adding surplus hydroxide or carbonate to the neutralise in such a way that the base remains in colloidal suspension.

Sulphonation with Chlorosulphonic Acid

Chlorosulphonic acid is widely used for the sulphonation of fatty alcohols, fatty alcohol-ethoxylates, alkylphenol-ethoxylates, and related detergent raw materials with OH groups available for the attachment of an SO_3H group. The reaction of lauryl alcohol with chloro-sulphonic acid illustrates the chemistry involved :

$$C_{12}H_{25}OH + ClSO_3H = C_{12}H_{25}O—So_3 + HCl$$

The hydrogen chloride must be absorbed to give a 30 per cent HCl solution as a by-product. One can well consider the HCl in the formula of chlorosulphonic acid as a kind of 'carrier gas' present as liquid bound to $S0_3$, and set free during the sulphonation reaction. Whereas sulphonation with $S0_3$ within an inert carrier gas consists of a gas/liquid reaction, sulphonation with chlorosulplionic acid is a liquid/liquid reaction, with liberation of HCl.

Sulphonation with chlorosulphonic acid requires special corrosion-procf equipment, either glass-lined steel or all-glass, the latter especially suitable for small-batch-size sulphonation. The HCl-absorber, too, is built either of glass-lined steel or is all-glass. Some firms use glass-lined steel reactors and all-glass Hcl-absorbers. A typical batch sulphonation process of lauryl alcohol is carried out as follows :

250 kg lauryl alcohol are charged into the glass-lined reaction vessel. 156 kg chlorosulphonic acid (the calculated stoichiometric amount of the laurv] alcohol used) are added slowly with cooling. The reaction temperature is kept at an optimum of 25°C (not exceeding 30°C). 47 kg HCl gas are set free and have to be absorbed to 30 per cent HCl acid solution. (Some small amounts of HCl remain dissolved in the acid sulphonate and form a neutral chloride with the neutralisation agent.) If NaOH is used as the neutralisation agent, *c* 85 kg NaOH are required. Generally, the resulting 359 kg of acid lauryl-alcohol-sulphate are run into a crushed ice/water mixture *c* 1000 kg, while the NaOH is run into the neutralisation vessel (as 255 kg 38^0 Be NaOH), keeping a small excess of NaOH, so that the mixture is always at a slightly alkaline pH. This prevents splitting off of the sulphuric acid by hydrolysis of the O–SO_3H group, which would rapidly occur at an acid pH in the presence of water. Neutralisation should be carried out as quickly as possible after the sulphonation process step; otherwise hydrolysis will occur, even in the absence of water.

The slurry (*c* 35 per cent active matter) is adjusted to a pH of 7.7–8.0, and is then stable on storage. Good mixing during neutralisation is very important to prevent agglomeration of acid sulphonate, which again would lead to hydrolysis and a high unsulphonated alcohol content in the finished paste. Any bleaching required is carried out with sodium hypo-chlorite at a near neutral pH. Neutralisation with ethanolamines is also often practised, and this method, and neutralisation with ammonia, is, in fact, less critical: the mixture remains liquid and agglomeration of acid sulphonate does not occur so frequently. The heat of neutralisation is more easily dissipated than in the case of caustic soda neutralisation.

In sulphating ethers (and to a lesser extent alcohols) with chlorosulphonic acid, the HCl liberated in the initial stages of the reaction dissolves exothermically in the reaction mass, and in the second stage is displaced from solution together with the fresh portion of HCi being formed. The evolution of this double quantity of gas in the second stage of the reaction causes troublesome foam.

This foam formation, in continuous process particularly, can be overcome by arranging the flow of the liberated HCl on the one hand, and the incoming alcohol or ether on the other hand in such a manner that the evolved HCl is allowed to flow upwards through an absorption tower, down which the incoming alcohol or ether is allowed to trickle. This saturates the unsulphated material with HCl and does not allow any further HCl to dissolve during the reaction process. To a large extent this eliminates foaming in the case of alcohols but when ethers are being sulphated, in addition to the above arrangement it is necessary to dissolve in the unsulphated ether about 40 ppm of an anhydrous, oil-soluble, silicone antifoam. With these precautions, although a certain amount of foaming takes place, the foam formation remains within reasonable limits.

It is interesting to note that in the sulphation of ethers with SO_3, the same troublesome foam is encountered due to the large excess of air or other inert gas. Addition of silicone will prevent undue foam formation. In So_3 film sulphonation systems this trouble does not occur.

Commercial specifications of various anionic detergents produced by the several sulphonation methods are given below, where the first comparison made is between commercial sodium alkyl benzene sulphonate pastes produced by either oleum or sulphuric acid sulphonation with spent-acid separation and those produced by SO3 sulphoiiation (either with vapourised SO_3 or directly will, converter gas).

Anionic detergents	By acid sulponation %	By SO_3 sulphonation %
Sodium alkyl benzene sulphonate	50	50
Unsulphated free oil	0.5	0.5
Sodium sulphate	7.5	0.8
Water to make	100	100
Colour	White	White

Typical specifications for converter-gas-derived AB-sulphonic acid are as follows :

	Dodecyl benzene sulphonic acid	Tridecyl alkylate sulphonic acidt
Active detergent matter calculated as the sodium salt	100% ± 1%	100% ± 1%
–calculated as sulphonic acid with molecular weight 325	94% ± 1%	94% ± 1%
Unsulphonated free oil (calculated on 100% am)	1.7% max	1.7% max
Acid number	182–7 mg KOH/g	174 –81 mg KOH/g

† Specifications for sulphonic acid produced with converter gas from straight-chain' alkylates have principally the same data, depending on the molecular weight of the alkylate, generally either the range of PT alkylate or of tridecyl benzene. Heat of neutralisation with NaOH is about 45 cal/g.

Not all sulph(on)ated materials are made using either oleum or SO_3. Sulphamic acid can be used for special applications, sulphosuccinates and sulphosuccinamates are made using sulphite addition and alkanes are sulphonated' using SO_2 and oxygen.

Sulphation by Means of Sulphamic Acid

A method of sulphating alcohols and ethoxylates is by the use of sulphamic acid. The acid is quite expensive so the final cost of the finished product will be high compared to conventional methods of sulphation, but against this must be balanced the fact that no large investment in plant is needed.

The plant for sulphamation is relatively simple; all that is required is a closed stainless steel reactor with stirring, heating and cooling arrangements and a coil for the introduction of a nitrogen purge.

The reaction of sulphamic acid with an—OH group is :

$$—CH_2OH + H_2NSO_3H \rightarrow —CH_2—O—SO_3H + NH3$$

$$—CH_2—O—SO_3H + NH_3 \rightarrow —CH_2—O—SO_3NH_4$$

Thus the ammonia liberated immediately neutralises the sulphuric ester produced and an ammonium salt is formed. Sulphàmic acid is particularly useful in sulphonating alkyl phenol ethers as in this case the aromatic ring is not attacked, whereas with SO_3 and chlorosulphonic acid upto 20 per cent ring sulphonation takes place.

It is not considered that ring sulphation detracts from the quality of the finished product, but the two types of sulphates (the ring has a sulphonate group) will be different. If 20 per cent ring sulphonation occurs, an equivalent amount of the terminal-OH will remain unsulphated (assuming stoichiometric quantities are used). This molecule will therefore be somewhat more, hydrophilic than the non-ring sulphonated material. Recentally a process has been developed in which all types of alcohols and alcohol ethoxylates can be sulphated using this acid.

The procedure is relatively simple but varies for different materials. In principle the material being sulphated is charged into the reactor, the stirrer started and 1.05 mol of sulphamic acid, which should be finely divided, is fed in rapidly. The rate of stirring and rate of feed of the sulphamic acid should be such that the powder is well dispersed throughout the mass of the material. When all the sulphamic acid has been added, the lid of the reactor is closed and nitrogen is passed through the vessel to purge all the air. Simultaneously the reactor is heated to 110°C rapidly and kept at 110-

115°C for 1½ hours. After this period the reaction mass is cooled rapidly to 70°C and dropped into water or a mixture of water and alcohol, the amounts depending on the final concentration required and the viscosity of the finished sulphate'. pH is then adjusted with ammonia to 6.5 to 7.

Sulphosuccinates and Sulphosuccinamates

Synthesis of these materials can be done with relatively simple equipment, a glass-lined or stainless steel reactor equipped with a dual purpose heating/cooling jacket and a stainless steel dissolving tank.

The choice of hydrophobe is wide, it can be any of the long-chain alcohols (natural or synthetic), long-chain primary amines (if a succinamate is to be made) or an alkanolamide or a mixture of any of these.

For this reason hard and fast rules as to quantities cannot be given but it is essential for the manufacture that the (average) molecular weight be known.

For alcohols and alkanolamides, the molecular weight can be obtained from suppliers' specifications or it can be calculated from the hydroxyl number by the formula :

$$\text{Molecular weight of monoalcohol} = \frac{56{,}100}{\text{Hydroxyl Number}}$$

The hydroxyl number if not available can be determined by standard Procedures on the mixture. If an alkanolamide is being analysed for hydroxyl number, the natural alkalinity present will affect the result but as this alkalinity can also be a factor in the coupling to the maleic anhydride, no correction need be made.

For amines the hydroxyl procedure will also give a result for molecular (or equivalent) weight but a simpler method is to determine the base number by titrating in alcoholic solution with acid using bromcresol green indicator.

The hydrophobe, which needs to be practically anhydrous, is charged into the reactor and heated to 60–70°C. Heating is now stopped and maleic anhydride in the proportion of 1.04 moles of the anhydride calculated on the hydrophobe, is added slowly. Maleic anhydride is normally supplied as lenses or flakes and the heat required to melt roughly balances the heat of reaction of the esterification. The'rate of addition of the anhydride is adjusted so that the temperature remains within the range 60–70°C.

Concurrently with this the sodium sulphite or bisulphite is dissolved in water to make an approximately 25 per cent solution. The sulphite should be freshly prepared and free of thiosulphite. If monoethanolamine sulphite is to be used, prepare a solution of 8 per cent monoethanolamine in water and bubble in approximately half its weight of SO_2, for the sulphite, and an equal weight for the bisulphite. Completeness of the reaction can be checked by alkalinity and iodine titrations.

In every case the amount of sulphite salt should be the molar equivalent of the amount of maleic anhydride used. For determining these figures we give the molecular weights of the reactants :

Maleic anhydride	91.1
Maleic acid	134.1
Na_2SO_3	126.1
$Na_2SO_3 . 7H_2O$	252.2
$Na_2S_2O_5$ (the anhydrous form of sodium bisulphite)	190.1 (equivalent weight 95.05)
Monoethanolamine sulphite	187.0
Monoethanolamine bisulphite	126.6

When all the maleic anhydride has been added, maintain a temperature of 60–70°C for 1 hour and check acidity. Figures for acidity should be set as a standard based on laboratory work, because if the half-ester is being produced this also gives an acid reaction in addition to the unreacted maleic anhydride. For the di-ester only maleic acid will react if no half-ester is formed concurrently.

Once the reaction is found to be complete, the maleic ester (or amide) is transferred by gravity or pump to the solution tank containing the sulpliite solution. Stirring is continued for 1 hour without further heating till the residual sulphite content has fallen to below 0.5 per cent (checked by iodimetric titration). Surplus sulphite is then destroyed by adding peroxide. This procedure produces a paste of 40—45 per cent active matter.

Alkane (Paraffin) Sulphonates

This croup of anionic detergents. initially obtained by sulpho-chlorination under ultra-violet irradiation. The reaction involved is as follows :

$$R_1{\cdot}CH_2{\cdot}R_2 + SO_2 + Cl_2 \rightarrow \underset{\displaystyle SO_2Cl}{\underset{|}{R_1{\cdot}CH{\cdot}R_2}} + HCl$$

The source of the paraffins being the coal hydrogenation process. This process is carried out in special reactors undei the influence of ultra-violet rays. The next step is saponification oil' the chlorosulphonate by treatment with NaOH :

$$R_1.\underset{\displaystyle SO_2Cl}{\underset{|}{CH}}.R_2 + 2NaOH \rightarrow R_1.\underset{\displaystyle SO_3Na}{\underset{|}{CH}}.R_2 + NaCl + H_2O$$

In brief, water and n-paraffin (which needs to be specialty purified, are fed into a photochemical reactor equipped with lamps emitting ultraviolet radiation of wavelength between 3300 and 3600 Å. Sulphur dioxide and oxygen are introduced with vigorous agitation.

In another process sulphur is burnt in oxygen to produce the correct ratio of SO_2 to O_2 for sulphoxidation. Separation of the sulphoxidised paraffin from by-product dilute sulphuric acid is performed by extraction with hexanol.

The paraffin for the Ato process is n-paraffin from the appropriate petroleum fraction separated from the iso-paraffins by molecular sieve. It has to be practically free of aromatics the presence of which would severely inhibit the sulphoxidation reaction.

Pressure and temperature in the reactor are close to ambient. As the reaction proceeds, a portion of the reaction mass is withdrawn to be replaced by fresh or recycled reactants.

The outflow is passed to a decanter and consists of sulphonic'acid, n-paraffins, dissolved So_2, water and sulphuric acid. This is separated into two phases, n-paraffins which are recycled to the top of the reactor, and a sulphonic/sulphuric acid mixture.

The aqueous phase is degassed and passed to the solvent extraction unit, where it is mixed with an alcohol of at least five carbon atoms. This again separates into two phases, sulphonic acid/solvent and a sulphuric acid solution in water of about 25 per cent acid.

The sulphuric acid solution can be either neutralised to sodium sulphate (for captive use) or after concentration sent to a sulphuric acid/fertiliser plant,

The organic phase is neutralised with caustic soda and contains sodium alkane sulphonate, solvent, water and unreacted paraffm. The water and solvent are stripped off under vacuum and finally the unreacted paraffin is distilled off and recycled.

A flow sheet for the complete process is shown in Fig. 9.9

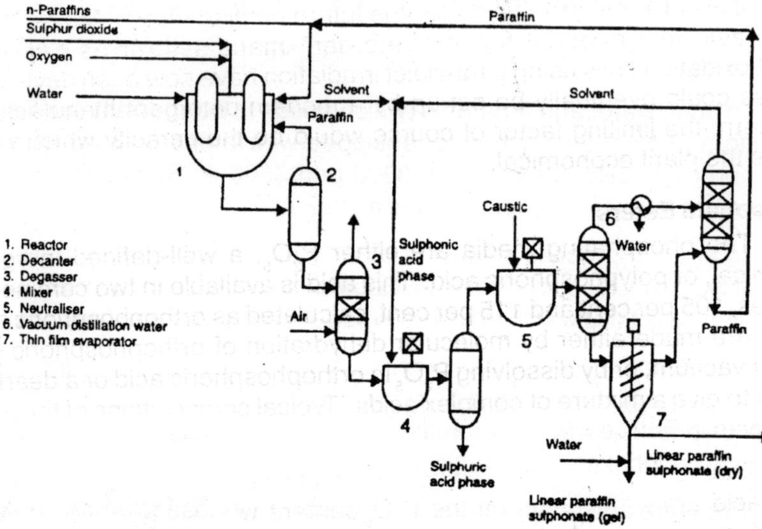

Fig. 9.9. Process for making linear paraffin sulphonate detergent.

To produce 1000 kg active matter the plant uses the following raw materials :

n-Paraffins	675 kg
SO_2	410 kg
Oxygen	110 kg
Caustic soda (100%)	145 kg
Process water	1865 kg
and utilities :	
Cooling water	310 m3
Steam	2000 kg
Power	0.65 k WH
Fuel	215,000 kcal

As far as the detergent processor is concerned it would be better if future development would lead to a change in the raw material for sulphonation (either straight-chain alkylates or synthetic fatty alcohols) rather than in the production of ready-sulphonated material supplied by giant concerns, which leaves nothing to the detergent industry but the last stages of processing: spray-dryin and compounding. Producers of primary raw materials for anionic deterrents have recently begun to give special attention to this requirement, and are now supplying manufacturers with new raw materials rather than finished products.

It is quite conceivable that in the future purified n-paraffins may forrn the basic raw material for the detergent manufacturer as packaged sulphoxidation units using ultra-violet irradiation have now been developed. These could eventually be set up by a modem detergent manufacturing concern; the limiting factor of course would be the caracity which would make the plant economical.

Phosphate Esters

The phosphating media are either P_2O_5, a well-defined inorganic chemical, or polyphosphoric acid. This acid is available in two commercial grades, 105 per cent and 115 per cent, calculated as orthophosphoric acid. They are made either by molecular dehydration of orthophosphoric acid under vacuum, or by dissolving P_2O_5 in orthophosphoric acid or a dearth of water to give a mixture of complex acids. Typical compositions of the acids are given in Table 9.12.

The variations in the composition and the viscosity of the 115 per cent acid are dependent' on the P_2O_5 content which differs for different manufacturers. Handling of this polyphosphoric acid at ambient temperatures is difficult and the containers should be heated over 50°C for efficient flowing or pumping. It is also to be noted that these acids are hygroscopic. Absorp tion of water tends to hydrolyse the complex acids to orthophosphoric acid rapidly.

Table - 9.12

Composition of polyphosphoric acids.

	105% acid	115% acid
Orthophosphoric acid (H_3PO_4)	49–54	3–5
Pyrophosphoric acid (H_4PO_7)	41–42	9–16
Triphosphoric acid ($H_5P_3O_{10}$)	5–8	10–17
Tetraphosphoric acid ($H_6P_4O_{13}$)	0–1	11–16
Higher acids	–	46–67
Total P_2O_5%	76	83.5–84.5
Density g/cm³	1.92	2.06
Viscosity at 25°C Pa s	0.8	30–60
at 100°C Pa s	0.035	0.5–1.7

The favoured acid for phosphating is the 115 per cent acid but for very special reactions the 105 per cent acid suffices.

NON-IONIC DETERGENTS

Ethylene and Propylene Derivatives

The most important non-ionic detergents are those obtained by reacting various hydrophobic groups with ethylene-oxide or propylene oxide. It is essential that any compounds to be condensed, with either ethylene oxide or propylene oxide, should contain a suitably reactive group, and Table 9.13 shows the principal types of reaction involved.

Before describing the various groups of compounds for condensing, it will be useful to outline the processes for making ethylene oxide and propylene oxide. Ethylene oxide is produced, either by reacting ethylene with hypodhlorite followed by hydrolysis with calcium hydroxide or by direct oxidation of ethylene with oxygen. It is essentially a two-stage process, in which ethylene is first chlorohydrinated and then hydrolysed with calcium hydroxide. The reactions may be represented by the following equations :

$$CH_2 : CH_2 + HOCl \longrightarrow CH_2ClCH_2OH$$

$$2CH_2ClCH_2OH + Ca(OH)_2 \longrightarrow 2\underbrace{O\ .\ CH_2.\ CH_2} + CaCl_2 + 2H_2O$$

Ethylene dichloride, CH_2ClCH_2Cl and beta-beta'-dichloroethyl ether, $O(C_2H_4Cl)_2$ are produced by side reactions.

This process is presently of historical interest only.

In the newer process, ethylene reacts with oxygen or air at temperatures between 220 and 300°C over a silver catalyst at elevated pressure.

The reaction involved is as follows :

$$H_2C = CH_2 + \tfrac{1}{2}O_2 \ \mathrm{R}\ H_2C\underset{\diagdown\, O\, \diagup}{\text{——}}CH_2$$

A competing reaction which can take place is :

$$CH_2{=}CH_2 + 3O_2 \rightarrow 2CO_2 + 2H_2O$$

This obviously reduces the yield but modern technology has settled on reaction parameters to minimise this reaction. In modern plants the yield is 70–72 per cent, thus 100 kg ethylene oxide will produce approximately 100 kg ethylene oxide.

Initially the conditions were that a mixture of 3–5 volume per cent ethylene in air was fed into a tubular reactor with a fixed bed supported silver catalyst at a pressure of 10–20 bar with a temperature of 220–280°C. Selectivity is highly sensitive to temperature, dropping as temperature rises. The reaction is highly exothermic and temperature control is maintained by heat exchangers with a circulating heat transfer agent.

Table - 9.13

Preparation of non-ionic surfactants from ethylene oxide.

Hydrophobic portion	Product

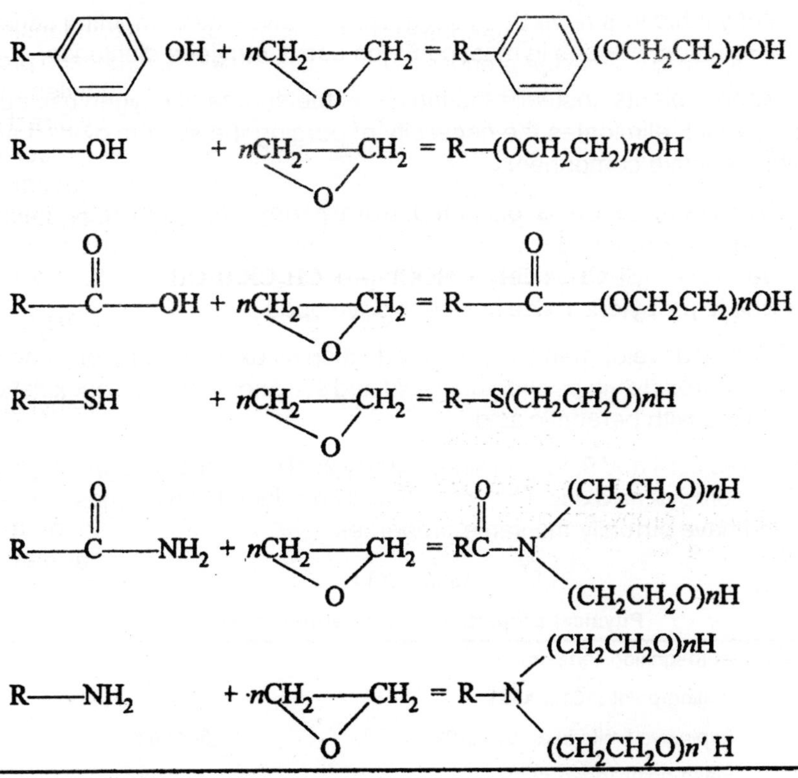

n and *n'* = the number of ethylene molecules

The gas leaving the reactor is cooled by another heat exchanger, and scrubbed by water to retain the ethylene oxide produced. The waste gas, containing unreacted ethylene is then split, part is fed back as recycle to the reactor and part is passed through a second reactor for further reaction. Ethylene oxide is then stripped from the water solution and condensed.

Many inhibitors have been suggested to lower the competing carbon dioxide reaction, the one in most common use is ethylene dichloride.

Modern plants, instead of using air as the source of oxygen use pure oxygen, which eliminates the necessity of purging the system of inert and possibly reactive components.

Propylene oxide is obtained from propylene generally via its chlorohydrin by reacting it with hypochlorite similar to the Wurtz reaction described for ethylene oxide. A recent process for the direct oxidation of propylene to propylene oxide has been developed.

Further developments are the production by oxidation of propylene by hydrogen peroxide via perpropionic acid and still another by the epoxidation of propylene with peracetic acid.

Tables 9.14 and 9.15 give selected physical properties of pure ethylene oxide and propylene oxide. The commercially produced compounds are very pure and have virtually the same properties.

Table - 9.14

Physical properties of pure ethylene oxide.

Auto-ignition temperature	571°C
Boiling-point (101.1 kPa)	10.7°C
Explosive limits in air by vol %	3–100%
Flash-point (open cup)	< –17.8°C
Heat of vapourisation (101.1 kPa)	569.4 J/g
Molecular weight	44.05
Refractive index (8.4°C)	1.3599
Solubility in water, weight % (20°C)	Complete
Specific gravity 20/20°C	0.8711
Specific heat, liquid (0°C)	0.44
Vapour pressure (20°C)	146.0 kPa
Viscosity (0°C)	0.32 mPa s
Density (20°C)	870 kg/M^2

Table - 9.15

Physical properties of pure propylene oxide.

Boiling-point (101.1 kPa)	34.1°C
Explosive limits in air by vol %	2.1–38.5%
Flash-point (open cup)	– 37.2° C
Freezing-point	– 104°C
Heat of vapourisation (101.1 kPa)	372.6 kJ/kg
Molecular weight	58.08
Refractive index, n_D (20°C)	1.3657
Solubility in water, weight % (20°C)	12.5
Specific gravity 20/20°C	0.8305
Specific heat, kJ kg^{-1} K^{-1} (20°C)	2.1304
Vapour pressure (20°C)	60.5 kPa
Viscosity (20°C)	0.33 mPa s
Density (20°C)	8.29 kg/m'

The handling and storage of ethylene oxide and propylene oxide, as well as their reactions, must be carried out with the utmost caution. When starting a plant where ethylene and/or propylene oxide is used it is advisable to contact the supplier for details of safety precautions, and to follow these instructions conscientiously. An outline of these precautions will be given later, when we describe propylene oxide reactions.

We will now describe some of the compounds that constitute the hydrophobic portion of Surface active ethylene oxide compounds. We will confine ourselves to three main groups : (a) fatty acids; (b) fatty alcohols; and (c) alkyl phenols.

Fatty acids react with ethylene oxide to form esters. The same product can theoretically be formed by the esterification of the fatty acid with the appropriate polyethylene glycol, but in practice some di-ester is formed.

Table 9.16 shows the properties of fatty acids (representative commercial products) suitable. for reaction with either ethylene oxide or propylene oxide, and also for reaction with alkylolamines. The properties of fatty alcohols, natural and synthetic, have already been described.

Alkyl phenol ethylene oxide condensation products still comprise a substantial proportion of the total world production of non-ionic detergents. This in spite of the fact that the alkyl phenol ethoxylates, obtained from polymerised propylene or butylene, represent a similar sewage problem to that caused by anionic detergents derived from PT benzene; less serious, however, owing to their low foam property.

The most important alkyl phenols are C_8 to C_{12} phenols. They are obtained by alkylation of phenol with the corresponding olefins. The olefins are the dimeric or trimeric polymers of propylene or butylene or their mixture.

Table - 9.16

Properties of fatty acids

	Titre °c	Acid value	Saponification value	Iodine value	Unsaponifiable %
Lauric acid 94/96%	39–41	279–84	279–84	max 0.5	0.5
Lauric acid 98/100%	43–43.6	279–82	279–82	max 0.2	0.2
Dist. stripped coconut oil fatty acid	25–28	250-60	252-62	8–14	0.5
Dist. stripped palm-kemel oil fatty acid	23–27	.250-60	250-60	16–22	1.0
Myristic acid 94/96%	50–53	244–54	245-55	max 1.0	0.5
Myristic acid 98/100%	51–54	244–54	245-55	max 1.0	0.5
Palmitic acid 94/96%	60–61	215–25	215-25	max 2.0	0.5
Palmitic acid 98/100%	61–62	219–24	219-24	max 2.0	0.5
Stearic acid 94/96%	64–66	195–8	196–9	1–3	1.5
Stearic acid 98/100%	66–68	195–9	196-200	max 2.0	1.5
Stearine single pressed	52-53	207–11	207–11	8–10	0.5
Stearine double pressed	53–54	208–11	208–11	5-8	0.5
Stearine triple pressed	54–56	207–11	207–11	1.5-5	max 0.5
Dist. tallow fatty acid	39–43	204–8	205–9	53–57	max 1.5
Oleine light coloured	7–10	186–204	188–206	85–92	2–6
Dist. palm oil fatty acid	42–46	207-13	209–15	44–54	max 1.5
Dist. refined tall oil light coloured	–	188–93	190–5	155–65	1.5–2.2
Tall oil refined	–	163–8	165–7C	153–67	7–8

Table 9.17 gives the properties of three of the most important alkyl phenols for the production of surface active ethylene oxide condensates.

Before discussing laboratory and industrial ethoxylation processes, a general remark must be made on the hydrophobe/hydrophile balance of ethylene oxide and propylene oxide condensates: the higher the molecular weight of the hydrophobe component, the more moles of ethylene oxide (or propylene oxide) are needed to produce water-soluble condensates. Conversely, the lower the molecular weight, the smaller the number of moles required to obtain a water-soluble product. For the purpose of producing non-ionic detergents, it is generally desirable that the products be easily soluble in water. For the production of non-ionic emulsifying agents, on the other hand, a certain affinity to the oil phase is preferable. Thus, to condense the hydrophobe component, fewer moles of ethylene oxide will be needed.

As has been mentioned, the production of ethylene and propylene oxide condensates requires a great deal of experience and it is thus advisable to study the reaction of ethoxylation on a laboratory scale. We give details of a laboratory synthesis of alcohol ethoxylates and alkyl phenol ethoxylates.

Quantities of about a pound are readily made in the laboratory by the following procedure : A 1–litre four-necked flask, fitted with a water-cooled stirrer, condenser, thermometer, and gas-dispersion thimble is connected through two 500 ml safety bottles to a graduate containing white oil and a manifold connected to low-pressure nitrogen and a tank of ethylene oxide (Fig. 9.10). 200 g (1.00 mol) of tridecyl alcohol is charged to the flask followed by 0.4 to 0.5 g of powdered sodium hydroxide. The flask, thermometer, gas disperser, and contents are weighed. A slow stream of nitrogen is started through the alcohol and the temperature raised to 150–160°C by means of a glass-insulated heating mantle. Ethylene oxide gas is admitted to the manifold and allowed to escape momentarily to the atmosphere through the three-way stopcock. The three-way stopcock is then turned to vent the nitrogen to the atmosphere and the ethylene oxide is simultaneously introduced into the flask. The operation should be carried out in a well-ventilated hood and away from naked flames.

Absorption takes place immediately, with a rise in temperature. The ethylene oxide rate is increased to the point where an occasional bubble of ethylene oxide escapes through the white oil. 'ne temperature is permitted to rise to 180–220° C, and is maintained within this range until the required amount of ethylene oxide has been absorbed. For trial purposes, between 8.5 and 10 moles of ethylene oxide per mole of alcohol is suitable. This is equivalent to an absorption of 374–440 g of ethylene oxide. Approximately three to six hours are required to absorb the above quantities.

In shutting down, the ethylene oxide is vented to the air, and the nitrogen is turned into the flask and a slow stream maintained until all of the ethylene oxide has been purged from the system. The flask and contents are weighed to determine the ethylene oxide absorption.

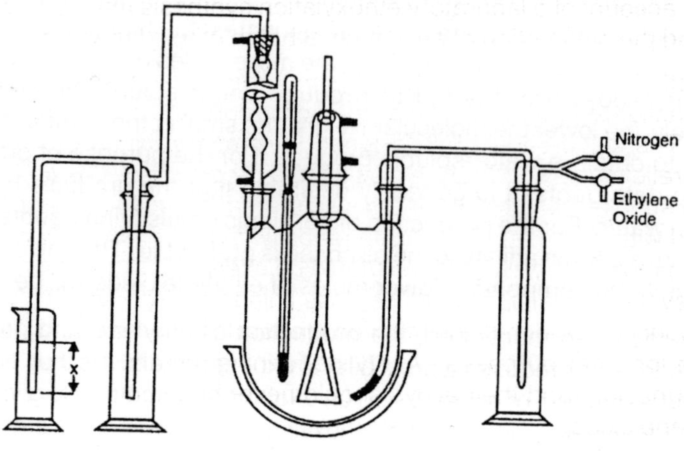

x= Hydrostatic head equivalent to 2.5 Cm Hg

Fig. 9.10. Laboratory ethoxylation plant.

When the desired quantity of ethylene oxide has been absorbed, the free alkali is neutralised with either 30 per cent sulphuric acid or glacial acetic acid to a phenotplithalein end point (external indicator). Ten grams of decolourising carbon are then added and the mixture stirred and heated at, 100°C for 15 minutes. The mixture is filtered through a Buchner funnel using a small amount of a filter-aid on the paper as a precoat in order to ensure a bright filtrate. The small amount of water resulting from neutralisation can be permitted to remain, or may be stripped from the product by heating under reduced pressure.

Another example is for the ethoxylation of I mole C_{12} lauryl alcohol (either natural or synthetic) with 4 moles of ethylene oxide :

Lauryl alcohol C_{12}	186 g (1 mol)
Ethylene oxide	176 g (4 mol)
NaOH powdered	0.6 g

Proceed as described for tridecyl alcohol ethoxylate, including the same purification method.

Finally an example for the ethoxylation of nonylphenol with 9.5 moles ethylene oxide :

Nonylphenol	215 g (1 mol)
Ethylene oxide	418 g (9.5 mol)
NaOH powdered	0.7 g

The same procedure is used.

This account of a laboratory ethoxylation synthesis makes it easier to understand the description of an industrial batch ethoxylation plant.

An ethylene oxide kettle should have provisions for maintaining the desired reaction temperatures. Heating-cooling coils and a jacket are usually suitable. The kettle should be designed for predetermined pressures. A pressure-relief valve and rupture disc should be provided. A suitable vent should be supplied which will vent to a safe area through a flame arrester. The speed with which ethylene oxide reacts with other materials depends on intimate mixing; therefore, care should be exercised in the choice of the agitation system. Stainless steel or glass linings are recommended if the quality, especially colour, of the reaction product is important. Carbon steel is suitable for other purposes. Acetylide-forining metals such as copper, silver, magnesium and their alloys should never be.used in direct contact with ethylene oxide.

Heating of the charge can be accomplished with steam or some other heat-transfer medium. Cooling water should be available to remove heat of reaction, for emergency cooling, and for routine cooling of the finished product preparatory to removing it from the kettle. Precautions should be taken to avoid overcooling the reaction mass and thus allowing the accumulation of unreacted ethylene oxide in the kettle. With an excess of unreacted ethylene oxide in the vessel, the reaction could proceed with explosive violence. The inert gas, preferably nitrogen or methane, used to purge the system should be free of impurities such as oxygen, ammonia, hydrogen sulphide and acetylene. Prior to purging with an inert gas, vacuum equipment must be used to remove most of the air. Suitable facilities should be provided as required for introducing the charge materials, cooling water and inert gas. Automatic shut-off of ethylene oxide feed should be available for activation by : (1) drop in temperature below that at which the reaction rate is enough to consume the ethylene oxide being introduced; or (2.) rise in pressure or temperature above that which has been determined as safe for the design of the equipment.

An intermediate ethylene oxide charge tank, located between the reaction kettle and ethylene oxide storage tank, should be available to serve as a work tank and to prevent the backflow of catalyst from the reactor to the ethylene oxide storage vessel. The work tank might also be used as a volumetric or weighing tank.Ethylene oxide transfer lines to process equipment should contain at least one check valve. Adequate storage facilities should be available for the other reactants and the product. Processing equipment and transfer lines should be thoroughly cleaned, leak tested and purged free of air before being placed in service. The equipment and transfer lines should be electrically bonded and grounded. Explosion-proof motors and spark-proof tools should be used.

The catalyst and oxide accepter are charged to the kettle. The charge is purged free of oxygen and brought to the temperature at which the reaction may be initiated. Ethylene oxide is cautiously added to the kettle. A temperature rise will indicate that the reaction has begun, at which point the ethylene oxide feed rate may be increased to the desired level, but never to a rate greater than that at which it is being consumed. The build-up of unreacted ethylene oxide in the vessel must be carefully avoided. Most ethylene oxide reactions take place in the temperature range of 120–200°C and in the pressure range of 205–410 kPa.

In general, ethylene oxide reartions are exothermic in nature, giving up about 80 kJ/mol of ethylene oxide reacted. This heat of reaction must be removed. Overcooling may result in stopping the reaction and allow accumulation of unreacted ethylene oxide in the vessel. The reaction may then resume and proceed with explosive violence.

After the predetermined amount of ethylene oxide has been added, flow to the kettle is stopped. The temperature of the kettle is held for a time to allow the last of the ethylene oxide to react, as indicated by a gradual drop in pressure. When the pressure is steady, the product is cooled, treated where necessary and removed from the kettle. Minimal moisture content of reactants is essential, otherwise side reaction with the formation of polyethylene glycol occurs.

Completely enclosed explosion-proof magnetic mixers, without a stuffing-box, are very much to be recommend as agitators for the reactor.Furthermore, it is our experience that the safety of the set-up is greatly increased by a side-arm heat exchanger. Reaction time and reagent flow should be similar to the laboratory procedure, so that the process on a plant scale is, in fact, an upscaled laboratory process. Many ethylene oxide (and propylenq oxide) condensation products and the processes for their production are subject to patents in various countries. Thus it is always advisable to study the patent situation carefully, before starting with the production of ethylene oxide and/or propylene oxide condensation products.

It must be mentioned that the condensation reaction may be carried out in a continuous 'run-through' pressure tube reactor. Such a system employs, e.g., an 'in line' mixing system (without moving parts). The reactants are fed in proper proportion into the tube reactor by means of dosing pumps. Heat control-and thus control of reaction-is, in fact, easier than for a batch reactor system. The quantity of reaction mixture in the continuous reactor is relatively small; and the safety of such a system is to a certain extent easier to guarantee than for a batch system. When using a continuous system, the NaOH catalyst is pre-mixed with the alcohol or alkyl phenol respectively, to be condensed with ethylene oxide or propylene oxide. The refining step with acid and active carbon can be carried out after the continuous condensation reaction is accomplished, either in a subsequent batch refining and filtering system or on a continuous basis.

In a commercial plant for the production of ethylene oxide adducts the production of 2500 kg of C16—C_{18} alcohol natural or synthetic with 25 mol ethylene oxide condensed requires :

C_{16}—C_{18} alcohol	1250 kg
Ethylene oxide	1250 kg
Steam	150 kg
Nitrogen	5–6m^3
Cooling water at 15–20°C	16 m^3
Electricity	45 kW

Operation of the plant is as follows (refer to Fig. 9.11).

A preset amount of material to be reacted with ethylene oxide and/or propylene oxide by the RP programming system together with the catalyst is fed into the process unit through line 1. (The amount of catalyst is generally less than that usually introduced in a conventional ethoxylation plant, and this has a beneficial effect on the colour and purity of the end product.) After the starting material and catalyst have been introduced, the unit is set under vacuum, heating begins through F 1, and the recirculation through circulation pump PC 1 is set into operation. The mixture flows again into the upper part of SA 1, the gas-liquid contactor, and the desirable temperature is maintained by F 2. During this phase of operation the material is de-aerated and de-humidified. This operation is carried out in a very short period of time. Low residual moisture is essential to prevent any undesirable side reactions, e.g., the formation of polyglycols and irregularity in the formation of the ethylene oxide and/or propylene oxide chain. Quick nitrogen injection and venting is then carried out; some nitrogen pressure is left in the system, and the actual condensation reaction starts by feeding the preset (RP programming system) amount of ethylene and/or propylene oxide into the pre-treated starting material and catalyst. Recirculation through circulation pump PC I into the gas-liquid SA I is carried out and the heat of reaction removed by the cooling heat exchanger F 2. In some cases it is desirable to pass the cooling medium, either water or a diathermic fluid, through a refrigeration system in a closed circuit.

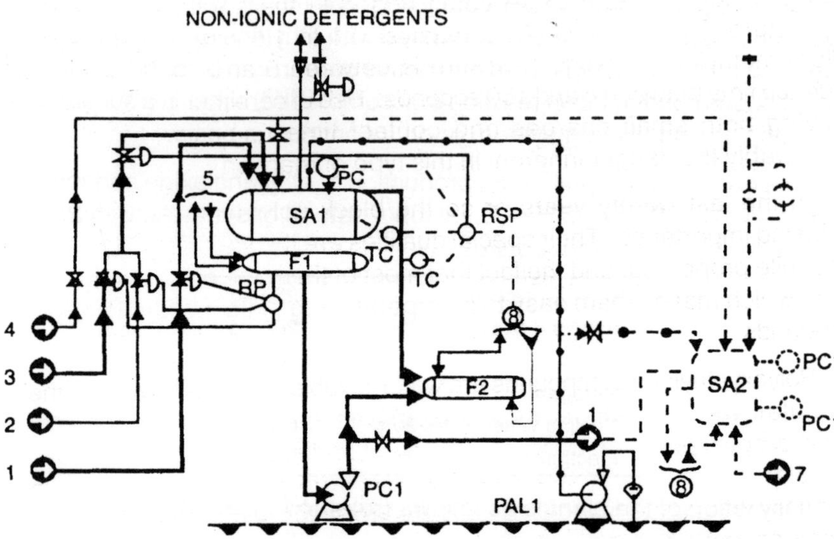

1. Basic raw material (eg alkylphenol or fatty alcohol)
2. Ethylene oxide from storage
3. Propylene oxide from storage
4. Nitrogen for purging and pressurising
5. Heat transfer fluid for reaction start-up
6. Cooling circuit
7. End product discharge
8. Cooling-water for final cooling of product

SA 1. Special 'Pressindustria' gas liquid contactor

RSP. Automatic reaction rate governing system.

RP. Automatic programming system (formula preset system)

SA 2. Cooler (optional) for reaction product

PAL 1. Vacuum pump

PC 1. Process circulation pump

F2. Heat-exchanger for reaction heat control

F 1. Heater for reaction start-up

Fig. 9.11. Pressindustria plant for the manufacture of ethylene oxide adducts.

An automatic control system regulates the flow of ethylene oxide and/or propylene oxide in relation to the temperature of the reaction mixture. This feedback system guarantees a constant reaction rate and constant temperature which accounts for uniform quality of the end product. The end product is cooled down by the F 2 cooling system and by the optional additional cooling vessel SA 2. No bleaching of the end product is required.

In small pilot plant for the continuous production of ethylene oxide the reactor is in two parts, the first reactor working at a temperature between 170 and 240°C giving a condensate of molecular ratio 1:1 to 1:6, and the balance of the ethylene oxide being added in the second reactor at a temperature of 240–360°C. As a catalyst 0.1 to 1.5 per cent sodium as sodium methylate is used. Pressure is between 5 and 10 MPa and the residence time between 8 and 150 seconds. Use of continuous type reactors involving both small charges and contact time can obviously lessen considerably the danger inherent in this type of reaction.

In the last twenty years or so the block polymers have assumed increasing importance. Their special qualities are the variable hydrophobe/hydrophile properties, and the fact that most of them are produced as solid flakes, which makes them easy to incorporate, e.g., into powder detergent compounds.

Polyoxyethylene compounds are water-soluble-no matter how high their molecular weight. For many years it was generally assumed that polyoxypropylene compounds would also be water-soluble. However, at a molecular weight of about 800-900, polyoxypropylene glycols become essentially water-insoluble. As the molecular weight of this chain increases it becomes more hydrophobic.

If, however, water-soluble polyoxyethylene groups are added to both ends of the water-insoluble polyoxypropylene chain, a complete series of new block polymers with highly desirable surface active properties can be obtained.

These block polymers are prepared by adding propylene oxide to the two hydroxyl groups of a propylene glycol nucleus. The resulting hydrophobic base can be made to any controlled length varying from 800 to many thousands in molecular weight.

By adding ethylene oxide to both ends of this hydrophobic base, it is possible to put polyoxyethylene hydrophilic groups on the ends of the molecule. These hydrophilic groups are controlled in length to constitute anywhere from 10 to 80 per cent of the final molecule. The simplified structure can be represented as :

$$HO(CH_2{-}CH_2{-}O)_a(\underset{\displaystyle CH_3}{\underset{|}{CH_2}}{-}CH_2{-}O)_b(CH_2{-}CH_2{-}O)_cH$$

If the hydrophobe portion of a normal non-ionic is calculated it will be found to be of the order of 30–40 per cent of the finished product. Block polymers are produced by (usually) propoxylating and then ethoxylating on to an initiator. This initiator is seldom 5 per cent, usually ½–1 per cent of the final product. It can be seen that in batch process it will be extremely difficult

Table 9.17. Properties of three important alkyl phenols for the production of surface active ethylene oxide condensates.

	Octylphenyl	Nonylphenol	Dodecylphenyl
Formula	C_8H_{17} 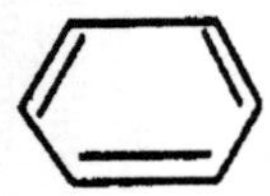 —OH	C_9H_{19} 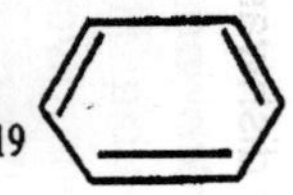 —OH	$C_{12}H_{25}$  —OH
Molecular weight (theoretical)	206.2	220.2	262.2
Molecular weight of commercial products	200–7	221–4	262–7
Appearance	Yellowish crystalline mass	Colourless to yellowish oil	Yellowish oil
Density 30°/4°	–	0.93–0.95	0.92–0.94
Distillation range at 101.1 kPa	280–95°C	290–315°C	330–35°C

to start the process with such a small amount of material in the reactor. It is common practice to produce a 'precursor', of the initiator with a definite portion of (say) propylene oxide. This precursor is then stored till required and the requisite amount(s) of ethylene and/or propylene oxides are added.

The newest development in the non-ionic detergent field is the extralow-foam products. As has been mentioned, ethylene oxide condensates, especially with a short ethylene oxide chain (4-5 mol), produce poor foam but for all that the amount of foam generated in certain operations can still be a hindrance.

Modified non-ionics, usually made by coupling an alkyl group to the terminal –OH, are now available and are used in household powders for foam sensitive machines and more particularly for dishwashing machine powders which also contain active chlorine, as the blocking of the terminal –OH reduces the tendency for degradation of the material producing the active chlorine.

Block polymers specially designed to give no (not low) foam are available and these are being used successfully in automatic dishwashing machine detergents, both liquid and powdered.

Fatty Acid Alkanolamides

This important class of non-ionic detergents is derived by condensing alkanolamine with fatty acids. These are the so-called fatty acid alkanolamides.

Alkanolamines combine readily with loiig-chain fatty acids, such as oleic and stearic acids, to give neutral alkanolamine soaps.

$$HOCHRCH_2NH_2 + C_{17}H_{35}COOH ® HOCHRCH_2NH_2 . HOOCC_{17}H_{35}$$

This neutralisation reaction takes place at room temperature. The products are waxy, non-crystalline materials which have widespread commercial application as emulsifiers.

At elevated temperatures (140–160°C) n-alkylol amides are the chief products formed by reacting mono- and dialkanolamines with fatty acids in a 1: 1 ratio.

$$HOCHRCH_2NH_2 + R'COOH \rightarrow HOCHRCH_2NH{-}\overset{\overset{O}{\|}}{C}{-}R' + H_2O$$

0

At the same time, significant quantities of amine esters and amide esters are formed by side reactions involving the hydroxyl moiety.

$$\mathrm{HOCHRCH_2NH_2 + R'COOH \rightarrow H_2NCH_2CHROOCR' + H_2O}$$

$$\mathrm{HOCHRCH_2NH{-}\overset{\overset{\displaystyle O}{\|}}{C}{-}R' + R''COOH \rightarrow R''COOCHRCH_2NH{-}\overset{\overset{\displaystyle O}{\|}}{C}{-}R' + H_2O}$$

In addition, when dialkanolamines are the starting materials, small amounts of amine diesters and amide diesters result.

$$\mathrm{(HOCHRCH_2)_2NH + 2R'COOH \rightarrow HN(CH_2CHROOCR')_2 + 2H_2O}$$

$$\mathrm{(HOCHRCH_2)_2N{-}\overset{\overset{\displaystyle O}{\|}}{C}{-}R' + 2R''COOH \rightarrow (R''COOCHRCH_2)_2{-}N{-}\overset{\overset{\displaystyle O}{\|}}{C}{-}R' + 2H_2O}$$

When diethanolamine is the starting dialkanolamine, some morpholine and some piperazine derivatives are also obtained.

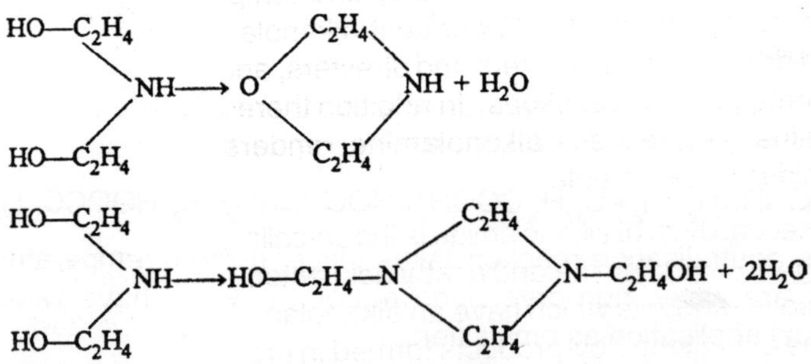

Reaction of dialkanolamines with fatty acids in a 2:1 ratio at 140–160°C gives a second major type of alkanolamide. These products, in contrast to the 1:1 alkanolamides, display aqueous solubility. In composition, they are complex mixtures which comprise n-alkylol amides, amine esters and diesters, plus a considerable percentage of unreacted dialkanolamine. This latter constituent chiefly accounts for the aqueous solubility of the 2:1 dialkanolamide.

Both the 1:1 and the 2:1 alkanolamides are of commercial importance as detergents and detergent additives.

An improved process comprised mixing an ester of an aromatic or aliphatic carboxylic acid with an alkanolamine, adding an alkali metal alkoxide catalyst and heating the mixture to 100°C at atmospheric or above atmospheric pressures.

A continuous process for making fatty alkanolamides in a thin-film reactor. The reaction involved condensation of a methyl ester of a fatty acid with a mono- or dialkanolamine, in the presence of an alkali metal, alkali metal'alkoxide, or alkali metal amide catalyst. A short contact time in the reactor produces a high purity alkanolamide.

More recently another process for making high purity alkanotamides has been developed. A fatty acid is first reacted with an excess of alkanolamine, forming amine arid amide esters in addition to the intended unsubstituted alkanolamide. In a second step involving an alkali metal catalyst, the amine and amide esters are converted to the unsubstituted alkanolamide.

Also a process of making high-purity alkanolamides by condensing a dialkanolamine with a fatty triglyceride, then adding phosphoric acid to remove the excess amine and most of the glycerine by-product.

There are two types of alkanolamide products. The first is the Kritchevsky-type liquid product, made by reacting an alkanolamine with a fatty acid or fatty acid derivative at elevated temperatures in a 2:1 ratio. Such a product contains 60–70 per cent alkanolamide, plus some amine esters and di-esters, amide esters and di-esters, and piperazine derivatives that are formed by side reactions. In addition there is significant unreacted alkanolamine. This excess alkanolamine renders the Kritchevsky-type alkanolamides water soluble.

The second type of alkanolamide is the so-called 'super' amide, prepared by reacting an alkanolamine and a fatty acid ester in a 1:1 ratio. These are generally solid products which have an alkanolamide content above 90 per cent. Some of the same by-products formed in preparing 2:1 alkanolamide are likewise formed in preparing super amides, but in much smaller quantities. For this reason, and because they contain only relatively small amounts of free alkanolamine, super amides have poor water-solubility. They are therefore always used in conjunction with a small amount of anionic or non-ionic surfactant which acts as a solubiliser, converting an aqueous alkanolamide dispersion into a viscous, clear solution. The isopropanolamine-based alkanolamides do however show an increased solubility in water over the ethanolamine types.

The starting material for the super amides are the methyl esters of fatty acids.

For the Kritchevsky type of fatty acid diethanolamide no catalyst is needed. The high surplus of diethanolamine (DEA) makes this unnecessary.

One mol lauric acid is reacted with 2 mol DEA in an electrically heated stainless steel reactor fitted with an agitator and a sparger-pipe for the introduction of nitrogen as purging gas. The reaction is carried out at 160°C for 5 h. (Purge nitrogen is introduced when the reaction mass has been heated to about 120°C). The reaction may be controlled by having a water trap and cooler fitted to the reactor, so that the amount of water (1 mot) liberated during the reaction may be measured. Of course, any water present in the DEA must be taken into account. In the same manner other fatty acid diethanolamides can be produced.

'Superamides' are generally prepared by reacting methyl esters of fatty acids with diethanolamine, using sodium methylate as a catalyst.

Recently it has been. found :

1. The optimum mol ratio of DEA to methyl ester is 1.1:1.
2. The optimum temperature is 105°C if the reaction is carried out at atmospheric pressure.
3. There is very little difference in the catalystic effect of sodium methylate between 0.15 and 0.25 per cent, calculated on the batch as a whole and under atmospheric pressure.
4. The undesirable amine and amide esters are not stable in sodium methylate catalysed reactions and if formed will revert to the amide.

All the above parameters yielded an amide content verging on 90 per cent. To produce over 90 per cent it was found that a reduced pressure (4 kPa) and temperature (60°C) with 0.75 per cent catalyst were necessary.

The temperatures are all above the boiling point of methanol which is liberated by the reaction. The plant needs to be equipped with condensing units to recover the methanol for recycle.

From infra-red studies of the superamide it is found that on allowing the material to stand for a month or so at room temperature, there was a considerable drop in ester content with a corresponding rise in the amide, despite the fact that superamides are solid at room temperature.

To produce high quality superamides it is suggested to hasten this post-reaction by keeping the finished amide at 50°C for 3–4 hours when the bulk of the esters will have reverted to the amide.

It has been found that in producing monoethanolamides, a surplus of monoethanolamine is useful. This reduces reaction time, and improves the quality and odour of the end product. The surplus amine is stripped at the end of the reaction under reduced pressure- In general, operating under reduced pressure, especially towards the end of the Condensation, was found to be of advantage.

In Fig. 9.12 shows the commercial production of alkanolamides, using methyl esters. This process produces the 'superamides'. If the older types are to be produced, the methyl ester is simply replaced by the equivalent fatty acid or neutral fat.

The monoethanolamides and monoisopropanolamides of fatty acids are very easy to manufacture. The production process consists in simply heating stoichiometric amounts of fatty acids or neutral fats with monoalkanolamine at about 160°C for 2–3 hours.

If neutral fats (glycerides) are used, the glycerine liberated will remain in the final product, lowering its setting point. This will also add to the emolient effect of the finished formulation.

The monoethanolamides and monoisopropanolamides are waxlike substances, practically insoluble in water, but solubilised by another hydrophilic anionic or non-ionic detergent. Table 9.18 gives the setting points and main uses of various monoethanolamides and monoisopropanolamides. These types of detergents are generally marketed in the form of flakes produced by running the molten products over chilling rolls fitted with doctor blades for scraping off the flakes.

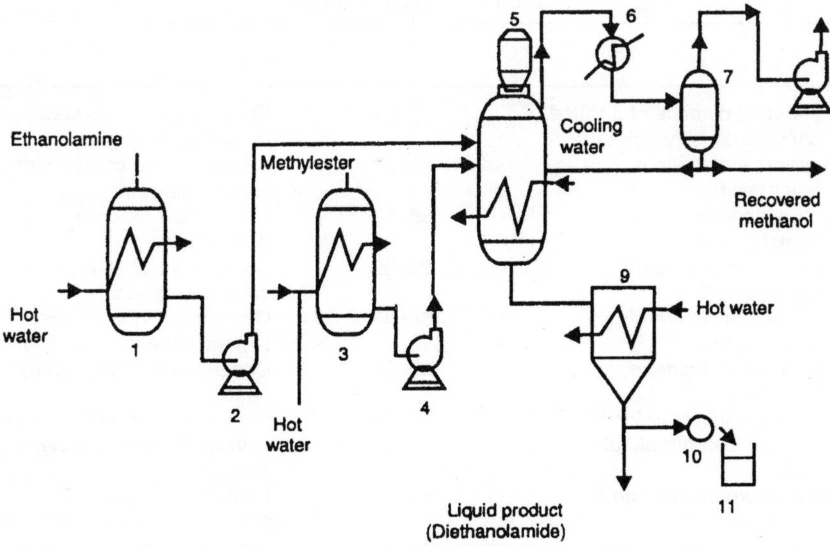

1. Ethanolamine tank
2. Ethanolamine charging pump
3. Methylester tank
4. Methylester charging pump
5. Reactor (monoethanolamide)
6. Condenser
7. Vacuum drum
8. Vacuum pump
9. Surge tank
10. Cooled flaking drum
11. Flaked product

Fig.9.12. Plant for the production of normal and super alkylolamides.

It will be noted from the table that the isopropanolamides show a lower setting point than the monoethanolamides of the same fatty acids.

CATIONIC DETERGENTS

A very good description of the principle of manufacture and the use of these detergents is given as under :

Cationic Surtace Active Agents

Cationic surface active agents contain a long-chain cation which is responsible for their surface active properties. They are marketed in solid form or as pastes or in aqueous solution. Important examples include :

Amine acetates $[R.NH_3]O_2C.CH_3$(R = 8 – 18 carbon atoms).

Alkyl trimethyl ammonium chlorides $[R.N(CH_3)_3]Cl$ (R = 8–18 carbon atoms).

Table - 9.18

Setting-point and main uses of various monoethanolamides and monoisopropanolamides.

	Setting-point °C	Main use
Monoethanolamide of distilled coconut oil fatty acids	72–74	Perfume and foam stabiliser in syndet toilet bars
Monoethanolamide of lauric acid	80–82	As above and component of liquid detergents
Monoethanolamide of myristic acid	88–89	Component of liquid detergents
Monoethanolamide of palmitic acid	90–93	Component of powdered and solid detergents
Monoethanolamide of stearic acid	88–92	Component in toilet soap and syndet bars
Monoethanolamide of oleic acid	59–62	Component of detergent pastes
Monoisopropanolamide of distilled coconut oil fatty acid	46–50	Increases viscosity and foam stability of liquid and paste detergents
Monoisopropanolamide of lauric acid	54–58	Perfume stabiliser, 'feel improver' in syndet toilet bars.

Dialkyl dimethyl ammonium chlorides $[R_2N(CH_3)_2]Cl$ (R = 8–18 carbon atoms)

Alkyl pyridinium chlorides and bromides, e.g., (R = 12-18 carbon atoms)

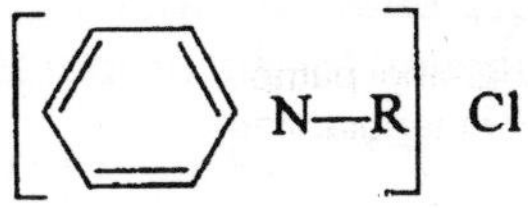

Lauryl dimethyl benzyl ammonium chloride

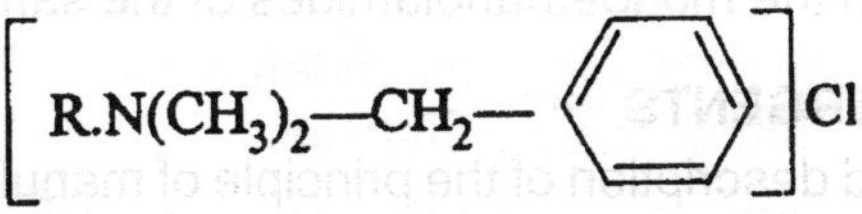

Amine acetates are produced by neutralising fatty amines with acetic acid, and are water-soluble. Quaternary ammonium compounds are normally prepared by one of four methods, viz, exhaustive alkylation of a primary or secondary fatty amine, alkylation of a low-molecular-weight tertiary amine with a fatty alkyl halide, alkylation of a tertiary fatty amine or by treating a tertiary amine or its salt with an epoxide.

In the detergent industry the main use of cationic detergents is for fabric softeners. For this purpose quaternary ammonium compounds derived from hydrogenated tallow are used; distearyl dimethyl ammonium chloride is preferred in Europe while in the USA distearyl dimethyl ammonium sulphate is also used. Although called 'distearyl' the tallow molecule contains an appreciable quantity of palmitic (C_{16}) acid and also, depending on the degree of hydrogenation, a proportion of oleyl amine (as the quaternary compound) might also be present.

Starting materials are either the fatty acid or alcohol, both of which are converted to the secondary (sometimes primary) amine.

If fatty acids are used they are reacted with ammonia successively to the ammonium salt of the fatty acid, dehydrated to the amide and again dehydrated to the nitrile :

$$R{-}COOH \rightarrow R{-}COONH_4 \rightarrow R{-}CONH2 \rightarrow R{-}C \equiv N$$

This nitrile is then reduced (hydrogenated) to form as required the primary secondary amine :

$$R{-}C \equiv N + 4H_2 \rightarrow (R{-}CH_2NH_2$$

or

$$2R{-}C \equiv N + 2H_2 \rightarrow (R{-}CH_2)_2NH + NH_3$$

If an alcohol is to be the starting material, it is reacted with anonia gas in the presence of a catalyst, when the nitrogen atom replaces the reactive hydrogen. The reaction for the preparation of a secondary amine is

$$2ROH + NH3 \rightarrow R_2NH + 2H_2O$$

The primary or secondary amine can then be methylated with formaldehyde to the tertiary amine, an example of the reaction being

$$2R_2NH + 3HCHO \rightarrow 2R_2CH_3N + CO_2 + H_2O$$

or the primary or secondary amines undergo exhaustive methylation with methyl chloride according to the equations :

$$RH2N + 3CH_3Cl \longrightarrow R(CH_3)_3N^+Cl^- + 2HCl$$

$$R_2HN + 2CH_3Cl \longrightarrow R_2(CH_3)_2N{+}Cl^- + HCl$$

In both instances HCl is formed and as the reaction cannot go to completion in an acid medium, it is necessary to provide a scavenger for the acid produced. Industrially sodium or potassium carbonates are used in a polar medium such as water or alcohol and at a temperature between 60 and 95°C under slight pressure.

Tertiary amines can also be methylated as above, but they are often reacted with dimethyl sulphate :

$$2R_3N+(CH_3O)_2SO_2 \square\square\square\square \rightarrow 2R_3CH\text{-}_3N^+SO_4^=$$

forming the quaternary ammonium sulphate.

The same reaction can be employed on secondary amines to add two methyl groups, producing for example a di-alkyl dimethyl ammonium sulphate.

Cationic surface active agents have wetting, foaming, and emulsifting properties. They are not, however, good detergents, being substantive to solids. Most of their applications are in fields where non-ionic detergents cannot be used and depend on this substantiveness to solid surfaces, whilst others arise from their excellent germicidal properties (all have high phenol coefficients). Amine acetates are used to eliminate the normal static electrical charges on resins and plastics, as collectors and frothers for a variety of minerals, e.g., mica, phosphates, lead ores, etc., as emulsifying agents, as bactericides, and for other purposes. Alkyl trimethyl and dialkyl dimethyl ammonium chlorides are used as antistatic agents for plastics, as softening agents for textiles, as germicides, as flotation agents for the separation of certain minerals from low-grade ores, and for other purposes. The dialkyl dimethyl compounds are in addition used for emulsifying oils into water, as corrosion inhibitors, and as mould inhibitors. Cetyl trimethylammonium bromide is used as a skin-sterilising agent, for cleansing wounds, and as a hospital disinfectant. Alkyl pyridinium chlorides and bromides and alkyl dimethyl benzyl ammonium chlorides are used in the textile industry for a varietv of purposes (e.g., as antistatic and lubricating aids, in dyeing processes, and for stripping vat and azo dyes, in finishing processes, as germicidal and mildew-retarding agents); in the leather industry as bactericides and dye fixatives; as sterilising agents for plant and equipment in food production and catering, brewing, and allied industries; in medicine; in the paper industry to control moulds and slime and as assistants in dyeing.

Amphoteric detergents

Amphoteric detergents are speciality detergents, which find application mainly in the field of cosmetics.

Chapter - 3

MANUFACTURE OF FINISHED DETERGENTS

INTRODUCTION

Any substance that reduces the surface tension of water; specifically, a surface-active agent which concentrates at oil-water interfaces., exerts emulsifying action, and thus aids in removing soils. The older and still widely used types are the common sodium soaps of fatty acids, which are relatively weak. The much stronger synthetic detergents are classed as anionic, cationic, or nonionic, depending on their mode of chemical action. The latter functions by a hydrogen bonding mechanism. The most widely used group comprises linear alkyl sulphonates (LAS), often aided by "builders". LAS are preferable to alkyl benzene sulphonates (ABS), because they are readily decomposed by microorganisms (biodegradable). LAS are straight-chain compounds having ten or more carbon atoms in the chain; the branched-chains characteristic of ABS resist decomposition; these have been largely replaced by LAS because of water pollution.

POWDER DETERGENTS

The bulk of detergent materials are eventually converted into powders by one process or another. The problem in the production of powders is that all active detergent materials, with only a few exceptions, are not in themselves solids. It is, therefore, necessary to combine them with the builders and filling materials in such a way that the finished powder does not tend to cake or lump and remains dry to the touch. For each detergent raw material there is a limit of active material that can be incorporated into a powder, and the method of production of the powder also limits its active matter.

The principal methods of producing powders are :

(a) Absorption of a liquid detergent on to inorganic salts.

(b) Simultaneous absorption and neutralisation of a sulphonic acid by soda ash.

(c) Dry mixing of previously dried concentrated detergents with the other powder ingredients.

(d) Spray-drying.

(e) A combination of spray-drying with one of the other above alternatives.

(f) Drum-drying.

Simple Absorption

This method is the most limited in application, and the amount of active material that it is possible to incorporate into the finished powder depends on the physical form of the active ingredient. If the detergent is available in the form of a water solution, containing not more than 40 per cent active matter (i.e., it is of relatively low viscosity), then 8 per cent active matter calculated on the final powder can easily be incorporated; and with special manipulation, upto 12 per cent car be achieved. If the detergent is in a more concentrated form, for example, a non-ionic detergent, which is usually available in 100 per cent concentration, 15 per cent active matter is usually the practical limit.

The plant required for this method is any one of the conventional bladed powder mixers available, such as ribbon mixers, plough mixers, incorporators, screw mixers'. In recent years several sophisticated powder mixers have been developed and these are finding more and more applications in the absorption process of making detergent powders.

Manufacture of powders by adsorption with a high percentage of active matter depends on the physical structure of the surfactant to be absorbed. A solid non-ionic is obviously no problem at all. In the other extreme, low ethylene oxide non-ionics can cause stickiness. It has been found that a nonyl phenol with 12 EO gives better flow characteristics to the finished powder than does one with only 10 EO.

The physical characteristics or structure of the builders have a marked effect on adsorption. One has to distinguish between the water absorption capacity of the builder, i.e., the water of crystallisation and the adsorptive capacity for organic matter, the surfactant.

In these methods, anhydrous inorganic salts, which can be hydrated, are used, and on the addition of the detergent solution the salts are partially hydrated and the active matter is dispersed with this water of crystallisation.

It is essential that the detergent solution be of very low viscosity and that it contain more water than active matter. However, if low concentrations of active matter are to be incorporated, this condition need not necessarily be fulfilled. In this case, the detergent is merely adsorbed on to the surface of the inorganic material. To obtain the higher concentrations of active matter, it is necessary for the formula to contain a large proportion of soda ash, as it can theoretically absorb as water of crystallisation 170 per cent of its weight of water. This figure is impossible to achieve in practice, as the organic detergent material does not allow the full 10 molecules of water of crystallisation to be formed. The same effect can be achieved by the use of borax either in the anhydrous or pentahydrate forms. Borax is, of course, more expensive than soda ash but has two added advantages in that it is a better builder and can also to a certain extent eliminate stickiness.

As mentioned above, if a 40 per cent active matter solution is used, 8 per cent active matter can easily be incorporated. If, however, the vessel is steam-jacketed, or if the mixing blades are hollow and can be steam-heated, powders containing upto 11 per cent active matter can be produced.

The method of producing powders is to charge the mixer with the dry ingredients, start the mixing, and to pump (or pour) the solution through a jet into the powder slowly while mixing. The rate of addition of the liquid must be adjusted so that the liquid is absorbed as it reaches the surface of the powder; if not, hard crystalline lumps will be formed.

After all the liquid has been added, mixing is continued for at least 15 minutes, and the powder is discharged on to a concrete floor to age for 12-24 hours. If the total amount of liquid is small (not more than 5 per cent) this ageing can be dispensed with, but in general the ageing serves the purpose of allowing the crystals to form and cool. If one of the more sophisticated mixers, mentioned above (especially one with a disintegrating effect) is used, this ageing process and the grinding can often be dispensed with.

By these methods a free-flowing powder, free from lumps, should be obtained; but if any of the original dry ingredients contain an appreciable amount of lumps, it will be necessary to pass the powder through a hammer mill after ageing. This grinding can be obviated by charging the powders into the mixer through a 60-mesh sieve. In this case, the lumps are screened out and can be themselves be milled to recover for use in future batches.

Because this process permits only a limited amount of active matter to be incorporated into the powder, it yields materials with only limited application for household use. However, the process can be used for industrial cleaners where the active-matter requirement is low.

To illustrate this process, we give below one typical formulation which can be used for the washing of stone floors

Formula 1

Floor-washing Compound	
Soda ash	77
Sodium tripolyphosphate	5
Sodium metasilicate pentahydrate	5
ABS-Na (40 per cent active matter)	12
Pine oil	1

The soda ash, phosphate and metasilicate are charged into ',he mixer, the mixing started and the ABS-Na is added slowly with stirring. After all the ABS-NA has been added, the mixing is continued for 15 minutes and the pine oil added. Mixing is continued for a minute or two after the pine oil has been incorporated and the powder discharged on to the floor to age.

Combined Absorption and Neutralisation

The method of neutralisation and absorption is more versatile than that of simple absorption. The process depends on the utilisation of an unneutralised alkyl benzene sulphonic acid, and neutralising it with soda ash which has previously been dry mixed with all the other dry ingredients of the formula. It is immaterial whether this sulphonic acid is of the 90 per cent (oleum or acid sulphonation) or 100 per cent (SO_3 sulphonation) type. If the manufacturer is doing his own sulphonation, it is obviously more economical to use his sulphonic acid without any intermediate manipulation, and if the manufacturer buys his raw detergent material, the use of a substantially anhydrous material will obviously save freight costs on water or other inert filling materials. It should be pointed out that if material other than 100 per cent sulphonic acid is being used, precautions against iron pick-up must be taken in storage and transport.

By this method there is obviously no lower limit to the amount of active material that can be incorporated into the powder, and a product such as Formula I can be manufactured with ease. The upper limit of active matter is generally 20 per cent, but it is possible to achieve as much as 24 per cent. Another advantage of this method is that powders incorporating solvents (solvent detergents) can be manufactured (in this case, however, milling of the powder should be dispensed with). If an attempt were made to manufacture solvent detergents by spray-drying, the solvent would be carried off in the air stream and could also constitute a fire and explosion hazard.

The plant required is the same as that mentioned in the section on absorption, such as plough mixers, ribbon mixers, incorporators and screw mixers, but in this case no heating arrangements are required. Although, theoretically, the powder produced by this process should not need to be ground, in practice a better appearance is obtained if the finished powder is passed through a hammer mill.

Systems combining spray-drying with other forms of preparation, are ancillary units and can also of course be used by themselves for powder production. With all of these specially designed mixers, ageing and grinding can usually be dispensed with. If perborate is to be added, the powder after manufacture can be discharged into a silo, fed on to a conveyor belt on to ,which perborate (and enzymes if required) is directly charged, and thence to a further simple drum-type mixer.

The method of manufacture is as simple as that for the absorption process. The dry materials are charged into the mixing vessel and the mixer started. The sulphonic acid is now poured in slowly while the mixer is running. If 90 per cent sulphonic acid is being used, the acid immediately reacts with the soda ash present to form the sodium salt, and the sulphonic acid should be run in at such a rate that no large unabsorbed excess of the acid is allowed to form. If 100 per cent sulphonic acid, which is more inert, is being used, it will not react so easily with the soda ash, and it can be added fairly fast and the mixer will merely disperse the acid. When the sulphonic acid has been well dispersed, i.e., when there is a uniform brownish-blue discoloration of the powder, 2 per cent of water, based on the final weight of powder, is added. This water renders the sulphonic acid reactive and almost immediately the powder will assume a light-yellow colour without any dark lumps of sulphonic acid. The sodium silicate can now be added, followed by the optical brightener, if the formulation calls for it.

In this reaction of alkyl benzene sulphonic acid with soda ash, no carbon dioxide is liberated, as in every case the formulation is arranged so that at least double the amount of soda ash is present over the stoichiometric amount and the reaction proceeds only as far as :

$$C_6H_4C_{12}H_{25}SO_3H + Na_2CO_3 = C_6H_4C_{12}H_{25}SO_3Na + NaHCO_3$$

Therefore, only one sodium atom of the two in the soda ash is utilised to form the sodium salt of the sulphonic acid and the soda ash is converted to sodium bicarbonate. If this were not the case, the evolution of carbon dioxide would cause the mixture to overflow the vessel. For this reason, when the 100 per cent type of sulphonic acid is used, it is necessary to disperse the acid well, so that no local concentrations are formed before the water is added.

An alternative method has been developed for neutralising sulphonic acid, by using anhydrous sodium metasilicate. The reaction can be written:

$$C_6H_4C_{12}H_{25}SO_3H + 2Na_2SiO_3 \longrightarrow C_6H_4C_{12}H_{25}SO_3Na + Na_2O{:}2SiO_2 + H_2O$$

the metasilicate has neutralised the sulphonic acid and been converted to a colloidal type of silicate, obviating the use of energy intensive liquid or dry forms. The above equation converts the silicate to the 1:2 ratio. As already mentioned, the preferred form can be the ratio 1:2:4. To obtain this form of the colloidal silicate, 3.2 parts of sulphonic acid are reacted with 1 part of anhydrous metasilicate to give a ratio of sodium sulphonate to colloidal silicate of 1:7.

Once the reaction is completed, which in practice should not take more than 30 minutes for a 300-500 kg batch, the powder is discharged on to a concrete floor and allowed to age overnight. After the ageing period, the powder is fed into a hammer mill to break up any lumps and is then ready for packing.

If one of the sophisticated mixers described later, is being used the ageing and grinding can of course be dispensed with.

Powders made by this process will have a cream to light-yellow colour, the exact shade depending on the colour of the sulphonic acid used. If a whiter powder is required, this can be achieved by bleaching it with sodium hypochlorite. When 100 per cent sulphonic acid is used, a 10 per cent solution of sodium hypochlorite is employed instead of the water, and when 90 per cent sulphonic is being used, the sodium hypochlorite is added thus:

The mixer is charged with all the powdered ingredients, except the optical brightening agent, and the mixing started. As soon as the powders are uniformly dispersed, the sulphonic acid (either 90 per cent or 100 per cent) is added. When the sulphonic acid has been well mixed in, the sodium hypochlorite solution, calculated at the rate of 2 per cent on the final weight of powder, is added. This will help to disperse the sulphonic acid, trigger the reaction with the soda ash and simultaneously bleach the powder. The silicate of soda is added after the bleaching is completed.

When sodium hypochlorite is used for bleaching of powders, the optical brightening agents should not be added to the mixing vessel immediately after the neutralisation, as the hypochlorite will attack the dyestuff. If perborate is to be added to the powder, the optical brightener can be incorporated simultaneously with the perborate. If the perborate is not to be added, after the reaction of the sodium hypochlorite has ended, the powder can be qualitatively checked for active chlorine. If this test is negative, the optical brightener can then safely be added. If this test is positive, 50 g of an 'anti-chlor' (sodium thiosulphate, sodium sulphite or sodium bi-sulphite)/ 300 kg batch of powder are added, the mixing continued for 3-5 minutes and then the optical brightener can be added with safety. The qualitative test for chlorine could even be dispensed with and the anti-chlor added as a routine, but one must stress that the anti-chlor can only be added after the powder has been bleached to the required shade, as otherwise it will interrupt the bleaching reaction.

Sodium perborate, if called for in the formulation, cannot be added prior to the ageing or grinding (unless one of the modem powder mixers is used) whether sodium hypochlorite is used or not. If sodium hypochlorite is not used, the perborate will start decomposing when the powder is damp, prior to ageing, if it is introduced initially into the mixing vessel, or it will start decomposing in the hammer mill as a result of the heat of friction in the grinding process. If sodium hypochlorite is used, the hypochlorite and perborate (peroxide) ions are mutually incompatible (so much so that perborate can be used as a rather expensive form of anti-chlor if nothing else is available). Sodium perborate can only be added after the ageing and grinding processes by reintroducing the powder into the mixer and adding the requisite amount of perborate. It is preferable to make use of a separate simple powder mixer for this operation.

The active ingredient by this process need not necessarily be only alkyl benzene sulphonic acid, but this can be mixed with any other active material desired to give special properties. These other materials can be non-ionics of the ethylene oxide condensate type, alkylolamides (the preferred types being lauric acid monoethanolamide or monoisopropanolamide) and even fatty acids to form a soap *in situ.* If the material to be mixed with the sulphonic acid is a solid at room temperature, it should be warmed about 10°C above its melting-point, then added to the sulphonic acid immediately before the addition to the powders. By this method the reaction of the sulphonic acid with the soda ash causes the fatty acid, if used, to be saponified completely and eliminates the need for the presaponification of 'fats or fatty acids prior to their -incorporation into powders of this sort. To obtain this 'auto-saponification' the fatty acid should be of the distilled grade with a maximum of 1½ per cent neutral oil (triglyceride) or unsaponifiable matter present. If neutral oil is present it will not be saponified under these conditions and will tend to make the powder sticky if present in too large quantities.

If solvent detergent powders are to be manufactured, the solvent must be chosen with care for the particular operation involved.

Solvents incorporated in detergent powders made by dry neutralisation should have a boiling range of 125-260°C, such as deodorized kerosine. The finished product should be marketed in metal or other containers non-permeable to vapour, or in high-density polyethylene bags which may be used as liners for jute or paper sacks.

Adjustment of the inlet air temperature will give any desired changes in Δt in a concurrent tower. In a countercurrent installation, adjustment of the inlet air temperature will also change Δt but less so.

A temperature reading even more pertinent to Δt can be taken at the jet. It is general practice to observe the inlet air temperature in the inlet duct immediately prior to its entry into the tower, and the outlet air temperature in the outlet duct at some point between the tower and the exhaust fan. A very important further point of reference is in a plane cutting through the atomisation tower about 60 cm (2 ft) below the plane of the jet. Temperature readings at this point will give an accurate idea of any changes in Δt, and are more sensitive than the inlet air temperature because some heat from the inlet air is dissipated in warming up the dried powder and the walls of the chamber.

A change in Δt does not necessarily mean a change in fuel supply to the furnace.

The temperature of the inlet air can be modified by altering the volume of fuel fed to the furnace. In this case the amount of heat from the furnace is changed, which changes the drying conditions. As an alternative, the volume of air entering the tower may be modified while the amount of fuel remains constant. This does not change the quantity of heat but has a material effect on Δt.

In an installation permitting infinite variations in the rate of feed (in a spinning disc atomiser or by the use of a return flow jet) changes in the feed rate can be used to modify Δt. For instance, by stepping up the rate of feed Δt is increased. Here the total evaporation of water is greater but the amount evaporated from each individual particle is smaller. Product moisture content and therefore density are increased.

By virtue of the design Δt must be smaller in a countercurrent spray-drier than in a concurrent installation. Therefore, as a general rule countercurrent spray-drying will yield heavier powders than concurrent operations.

$$x = \frac{dk\,e^{0.705v}}{2P^{0.375}\sin\frac{1}{2}\sigma}$$

where x = mass median drop size

d = orifice diameter

k = constant

v = kinetic viscosity

P = nozzle pressure

a = spray cone angle

shows the drop diameter to be an inverse function of pressure. The greater the pressure on the nozzle (or the faster the revolutions of a disc) the smaller the drop size. The same amount of material dispersed into more and smaller drops means a larger surface area giving more evaporation and lower residual moisture. Increased evaporation means a lower Δt. This in turn results in less and slower evaporation per droplet and therefore less puffing and greater density. Increasing the pressure on a jet or the revolutions of a disc will increase bulk density.

As will be noted from the above equation, the viscosity of the slurry plays a very important part in the atomisation. The viscosity of the slurry is dependent on the actual formulation (i.e., the types of ingredients), the pH, the degree of hydration of the phosphate, the concentration of solid matter, the amount of material in true solution and in suspension and the temperature. It is suggested that continuous viscosity metering be done with a dynamic viscometer to control any change in slurry structure. It may even be arranged with an automatic alarm if the viscosity changes radically from pre-set conditions.

The amount of residual water retained in the powder is another factor affecting density which is discussed below.

The actual formulation of a product plays an important part in bulk density. Generally, the higher the percentage of active ingredients the lower the bulk density, and the higher the alkaline builder content the higher the bulk density. Sodium sulphate rather surprisingly tends to reduce density. Bulk density is increased by sodium chloride.

Residual moisture

For economic reasons it may be necessary to retain a certain amount of residual water in the powder. As the powder must of necessity be free-flowing, this water can only be present as water of crystallisation and not as surface moisture. Account should also be taken of the fact that certain inorganic salts which have more than one physical form tend to assume the stable form. For example, washing soda crystals Na_2CO_3. $10H_2O$ Will effloresce down to $Na_2CO_3.H_2O$, whereas anhydrous sodium carbonate will take up moisture from the atmosphere to its stable form $Na_2CO_3.H_2O$. Therefore if a formula containing soda ash is spray-dried to be bone dry, the soda ash will tend to absorb moisture up to 17 per cent of its weight. This phenomenon occurs with most inorganic salts used in detergents but it is difficult to give hard and fast rules because, in virtually every case, the problem may be complicated by double and co-crystals. Generally a spray-dried powder containing a fair proportion of inorganic salts can be expected to pick up moisture on storage. Table 10.1 lists some crystalline inorganic salts used as fillers or builders in detergent powders and the percentage of water absorbed by the anhydrous salts to form the stable molecule.

Table 10.1. Percentage of water absorbed by anhydrous salts to form crystals.

	% water absorbed by anhydrous salts	Temperature of instability of crystal
$Na_2B_3O_7.5H_20$	44	-
$Na_2B_4O_7.10H_2O$	89	60
$Na_2CO_3.H_2O$	17	100
$Na_2CO_3.7H_2O$	105	32
$Na_2CO_3.10H_2O$	170	32
$Na_2CO_3NaHCO_3.2H_2O$	17	85
$Na_2HPO_4.7H_2O$	79	-
$Na_3PO_4.10H_2O$	110	-
$Na_3PO_4.12H_2O$	130	100
$Na_4P_2O_7.10H_2O$	67	93
$Na_5P_3O_{10}.6H_2O$	29	-
$Na_2SiO_3.5H_2O$	74	-
$Na_2SiO_3.9H_2O$	133	100
$Na_2SO_4.7H_2O$	89	-
$Na_2SO_4.10H_2O$	126	32.4

Storage conditions determine the rate at which water of crystallisation is taken up. If the powder is packed immediately in 'airtight' containers, the rate of absorption will be comparatively slow. (No container commonly used for packaging powders is truly air-tight). Storage in an atmosphere of fairly high relative humidity will result in fast moisture take-up and a tendency to agglomeration. However, the absorption will be slower the closer the moisture content of the powder is adjusted to that of the stable form. If a powder must be stored in ambient relative humidity exceeding 60 per cent, the risk of lump formation can be minimised by discharging the powder from the spray-tower with at least three-quarters of the stable moisture content. It is economically unsound to dry a powder to I per cent moisture content when the powder must revert to, say, 7 per cent. The operation would be a lot more efficient if the powder were dried to 7 per cent in the first place.

The stable moisture content can be determined only by prolonged storage tests. These call for small samples of the powder to be kept in desiccators designed to expose the samples to varying degrees of relative humidity.

Temperature of the outlet air and product residence time in the tower are the two factors used to control moisture content of the finished powder.

Contrary to general belief the outlet air temperature need not be above 100°C to obtain a desirable product. Spray-driers can work efficiently at temperatures well below 100°C. However, for a bone dry powder the temperature must be in the vicinity of 100°C or near the boiling point of water at the altitude of the particular plant.

To keep water of crystallisation in the finished powder the outlet air temperature must be low and residence in the tower must be extended to permit crystallisation (which has both a time and heat factor) to take place. Some spray-driers are designed to discharge the powder while slightly wet and then to transport it through a pneumatic conveyor or air lift to the packing department. This conveyor system serves a useful purpose by cooling the product and effecting crystallisation (for example $Na_2SO_4.10H_2O$ exists only below 32.4°C; to form the crystal the wet powder must be cooled below this temperature). However, the extra cooling step is not essential. A dry free-flowing powder of 10-15 per cent moisture content can be obtained from the tower without this aid. The amount of water of crystallisation retainable in a powder is determined by the type and quantity of the inorganic salts incorporated in the particular formulation.

Spray-drier manufacturers and operators sometimes do not pay sufficient attention to residence time in the tower. Disadvantages attendant upon excessive time in the chamber have been discussed above. But there are disadvantages also resulting from too short a time in the tower. It is not enough to expose the spray to a quantity of heat sufficient to dry it. The spray must be in contact with the hot air long enough to permit all necessary heat to be transferred. In a countercurrent installation operating at a low outlet temperature the temperature at the point of atomisation will be only a few degrees higher than that of the slurry. Therefore Δt will be small and the rate of heat transfer slow. The residence time in the tower must then be increased. This is a very important point.

Air pressures in spray-drier towers are usually balanced to range between 0 and 5 Pa vacuum water gauge. This is accomplished by means of dampers on either the inlet air duct or exhaust duct, or both. The rate of exhaustion of air plus vapour is adjusted to be either equal to or slightly greater than the rate of ingress of hot air into the chamber. Positive pressure inside the tower is not advisable sine it may cause blowing out of dust. The vacuum in the chamber can be raised, however, quite easily to 125 Pa water gauge provided that the tower is sealed off at its base with a rotary valve or other sealing-discharging device. The increased vacuum will retard the rate of fall of the dried particles and thus extend the residence in the tower. At the same time the higher vacuum will tend to add to the amount of fines produced, the actual increase being dependent on the particle spread of the powder.

Thus if the powder exists slightly wet, this may be remedied by increasing the vacuum in the tower (by opening the outlet air duct slightly). By the same token, if more residual water is required, a drop in outlet temperature (by increasing the rate of feed or decreasing inlet heat) and a higher vacuum in the tower will have the desired effect. Operating variables are tabulated in Table 10.2.

The following range of parameters shows typical tower operation conditions :

Slurry concentration	60-70 per cent
Hot air inlet temperature	300-450°C
Average air velocity	0.3-0.6 m/second
Exhaust air outlet temperature	90-95°C
Powder temperature at outlet	60-70°C
Powder bulk density at outlet	200-400 g/litre
Retained moisture in powder at outlet	2-15 per cent

Stickiness

Slickness is a phenomenon difficult to define but absolutely unacceptable in a spray-dried powder. It may be caused by poor drying or faulty atomisation leaving large particles incompletely dried or by some ingredient or lack thereof in the formulation. Addition of sodium silicate will somewhat improve a slightly sticky powder. However, certain materials tend, *per se,* to yield a sticky product. In -particular the linear alkyl benzene sulphonates yield stickier products than the branched chain materials. This stickiness is usually easily overcome by the addition of one of the hydrotropes, particularly sodium toluene sulphonate. Certain alkylates, for all that and depending on their isomerism, do, when sulphonated, yield powders which remain sticky even when toluene sulphonate is added. This can be overcome by the addition of small percentages of fumed silica or calcium silicate. Magnesium silicate, added either as such or, more commonly, formed *in situ* by the reaction of magnesium sulphate (added as a stabilising agent for perborate) and sodium silicate, also adds to the free flowing properties of problematic powders.

Table 10.2. Effect of variation of operating conditions on powder characteristics.

	Particle spread		Particle size		Bulk density		Water content	
	Incr	Decr	Incr	Decr	Incr	Decr	Incr	Decr
Orifice diameter	+	–	+	–				
Pressure	–	+	–	+	+	+		
Slurry concentration (solids)	+	–	+	–	–	+*		
Active matter			+	–	–	+		
Alkalis			–	+	+	–		
Viscosity			+	–				
Rate of feed			+	–	+	–	+	–
Feed temperature					+	–†		
Δt						–	+†	
Outlet air temperature					–	+	–	‡

\+ Sign indicates increase of the function in the left-hand column, and —— sign the converser

* Within limits.

† These two factors tend to neutralise each other.

‡ In conjunction with increased residence time in the chamber.

Product uniformity

After careful adjustment of all processing variables one may attain all desired characteristics in the product, but this is not enough. For uniform product quality, optimum conditions must be established, maintained and repeated from run to run. Trial runs need to be made to establish the best processing conditions for each individual product and these must be recorded and repeated for each production run. Accurate measuring instruments located at all vital points in the spray-drying installation are absolutely essential. Readings should be made and recorded at frequent intervals or better still the instruments should be of the continuously recording type. A recording instrument will predict a trend which can only be derived from ordinary indicators by very frequent readings and recording of results.

Separation of powder

Separation of the powder from the exhaust air is an integral part of the function performed by a spray-drying installation. Factors pertaining to the sometimes third separation step is performed by external cyclone separators and/or bag filters or by wet scrubbing. The manufacturer is faced with a problem of collecting the resulting fines and using them.

Wet scrubbing

Even the best of cyclones or bag filters do not completely trap all the solid particles entrained in the exhaust air, particularly those of micron size. In addition due to intermittent faulty operation of the tower, the separation system can become overloaded.

The detergent manufacturer has a moral responsibility to ensure that he does not contaminate or pollute the air he discharges, this apart from any legislation which has been or will be enacted.

As dry separation systems are known to pass, at best, a few per cent of the entrained particles, recourse may be made to wet scrubbing, when the solid material is scrubbed out by water. Wet scrubbers can bring the concentration of solid particles in the outgoing air down to 15-25 ppm.

One such scrubber is shown in Fig. 10.3. The water is circulated through the unit until the concentration reaches a predetermined amount, when the solution is pumped to the slurry preparation.

To avoid troublesome foam formation, particularly when the active content is high, a salt or preferably a silicate solution rather than water can be used. If the fuel used for hot air generation contains an appreciable amount of sulphur, caustic soda can also be injected to neutralise acidity.

Use of fines

In some plants detergent fines can be used in the manufacture of scouring powders or other related products. In that case the fines can be collected in bags at regular intervals from the cyclones or filter bags. If no other use can be made of the fines they must be reintroduced into the slurry. Where the slurry is made up continuously this reintroduction should be continuous also. In plants where the slurry is made up in batches, reintroduction of fines simply calls for transporting them from the collecting points to the slurry vessels.

Where a wet scrubber is used the reintroduction of fines is easiest. Water is pumped through the scrubber to form a solution of fines and this solution is recirculated continuously until it reaches a predetermined concentration when it is pumped to the slurry vessel where the primary water must be adjusted accordingly.

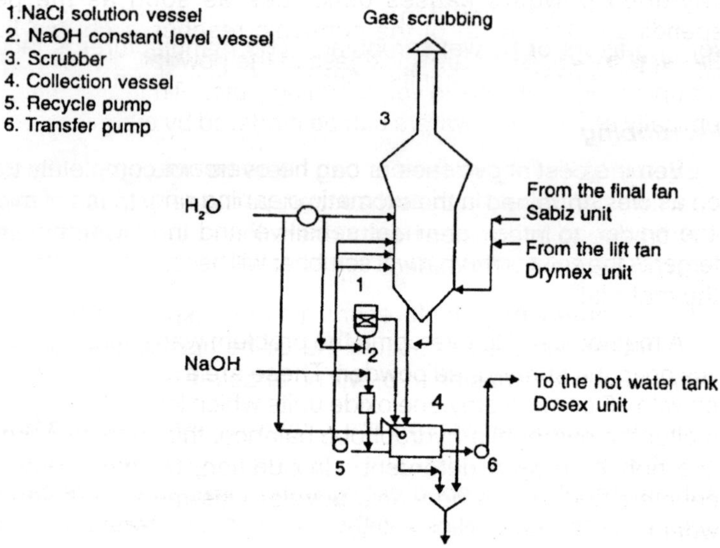

Fig. 10.3. Ballestra wet scrubber system.

Another method (Ballestra system) used is to blow the fines continuously to the top of the tower and to reintroduce them concurrently with the atomised slurry (Fig. 10.2). As they come into contact with the wet atomised slurry they tend to agglomerate with the atomised particles and in this way all the problems of handling fines are disposed of.

There is one prerequisite for the automatic reintroduction of fines into either the slurry or the tower: there must be no soot whatsoever and careful attention must be paid to the accurate adjustment of the furnace. The slightest trace of carbon in the fines will discolour a large amount of powder. Freedom from soot is not easily attained since some of the factors involved are beyond the operator's control. A temporary stoppage of electric current, for instance, can cause soot. An outside use for fines is therefore usually preferable to their reintroduction, if freedom from soot cannot be guaranteed. In a scouring powder for example, a trace of off-colour powder will not affect the appearance or performance of the final product but it is axiomatic that white linen cannot be washed with a powder containing soot.

Combination of Spray-dried and Dry-mixed Powders

The introduction of linear alkyl benzene led to problems of stickiness which were rapidly overcome. Nowadays more and more powders have certain amounts of non-ionic detergents incorporated into them and this is again leading to problems of stickiness. The use of non-ionic detergents in spray-dried powders causes difficulties as soon as the percentage (depending on the type) of the non-ionic reaches a certain figure. The difficulties encountered are stickiness of the powder, clogging of cyclones, build-up on walls of the tower, 'pluming', etc. Thus the development of chemically advanced powders can be hindered by technical problems.

Some of the above factors can be overcome by mechanical means such as wet scrubbers and automatic cleaning rings; but for all that, some of the newer additives are heat sensitive and in using certain non-ionic detergents the solution from a wet scrubber will become black due to scorching of the material.

A method used to overcome the problem was to dose powdered non-ionics on to the spray-dried powder. These are available in various grades, often with 25 or more ethylene oxide units which lower the biodegradability, and alter the hydrophile-hydrophobe balance, thus reducing the efficiency of the non-ionic as a detergent. In addition, technical problems were encountered when the non-ionic powder was mixed with a .spray-dried powder while the latter was still hot.

All of the above problems have been overcome by the use of a combination of dry-mixing and spray-drying techniques. The principle is basically that the alkyl benzene sulphonic acid and the soap (fatty acid) portions of the active matter are spray-dried in the normal way with phosphates, CMC, etc. The non-ionic component, ethanolamide, and other difficult-to-spray constituents are adsorbed on to a portion of the inorganic filler, with or without the use of colloidal or fumed silica in a mixer.

Ballestra 'combex' system

This system consists of a special mixing/dispersing unit in which a powder containing ingredients that are difficult to spray-dry is produced. It has two advantages in that it can be a fully integrated system linked to a spray-drier or can be run separately to make 'heavy powders' and it may be adjusted to produce powders of a granular or fine structure.

This process consists of a dispersion system which distributes the active matter components on to the detergent builders. This very homogeneous dispersion of the surfactants on to the builders is accomplished in a mixer which has specially designed plough type horizontal mixing blades rotating at high speed, and passing very close to the mixer walls. This design guarantees very efficient blending of all the components. In addition, ultra high speed rotating desintegrators are inserted to prevent any lump formation.

In contrast to 'spray-mixing', 'fluid bed', and 'agglomeration' processes, fixation of the active matter components is accomplished by mechanical disintegration of the solid builder material on to which the active matter components are added by means of a rather simple dispersion system. In most spray-mixing systems special high absorption types of builders are used, whereas in a system based on mechanical dispersion and powerful disintegration a much wider variety of builders in normal powder form may be used. The mixing-disintegration unit is of a relatively small size in relation to its output. Loading, discharging and residence times are short. While most spray-mixing systems are designed to obtain powders approaching the structure of spray-dried beads with relatively low density, the system described here aims at a powder with relatively high density, but with a structure to make it adhere strongly to the surface of beads coming from a spray tower.

The mixing unit may be used either for the incorporation of high percentages of non-ionics or for the incorporation of sulphonic acid and/or distilled fatty acids, with or without non-ionics. In this case the LAS and fatty acids are neutralised immediately on contact with the builders. Fatty acids are transformed in a single step operation into soap without leaving any unreacted fatty acids. Certain processing details are to be observed to guarantee the complete neutralisation of LAS and the complete saponification of distilled fatty acids.

This 'dry neutralisation and saponification' is accomplished by using a small percentage of an alkaline aqueous phase (representing only a small fraction of the stoichiometric amount of NaOH) as a kind of accelerator or 'trigger' for the reaction. The aqueous phase, generally only 2-4 per- cent on the total mix, is added at the same time, but not pre-mixed with the surfactant components. To give a general indication of the efficiency of the mixing system: only about 3-4 minutes are required for even distribution of non-reacting non-ionic components on to the builder mix, and about 4-6 minutes for 'reacting' components, i.e., AB sulphonic acid and/or distilled fatty acids. Automatic charge and discharge takes approximately an additional minute or two, depending on the size of the mixing system. The process can be run completely automatically with weighing and dosing similar to continuous slurry preparation.

Depending on the bulk density of the builders used, the amount of the surfactants added, the bulk density of this powder :from the first phase of the process is in the range of 0.6-0.9. The product from this process may be used as such for detergent powders, e.g., washing powders for commercial laundries, metal cleaning detergents, etc. The powder is less dusty than otherwise produced 'heavy powders'. The process may be carried out in such a manner that powders, either with a granular or a finer structure, are produced. The process is flexible enough to produce powders in a wide range of particle size.

The dry-mixed powder can also be fed continuously on to the powder being discharged from the spray drier while it is still hot and the two streams of powder are passed through a slow-acting baffle mixer, a slowly rotating cylinder mixer or by weighing belts. From this mixer the powder is taken to storage or packing.

The entire system is completely co-ordinated and features automatic controls. Being a closed system, there are no problems with dust. Proportions of builders and liquid components, as well as those of the final mixture, are set on the central control panel and may be changed quickly; the density of the final mixtures of 'heavy' powder and beads from the spray-drier is determined more by the low density of the beads than by the high density of 'heavy' powder. Table 10.3 gives some examples of the density of various mixtures of 'heavy' powder with spray-dried beads having a density of 0.3.

Table 10.3. Density of mixed powders made by the combex system.

Density of 'heavy' powder	Density of mixture (proportion of heavy to light powder with a density of 0.3)		
	50:50	40:60	30:70
0.9	0.52	0.43	0.38
0.8	0.45	0.41	0.37
0.7	0.42	0.40	0.36
0.6	0.40	0.39	0.35

The approximate expected density of the resultant mixtures may be calculated as follows :

$$\text{density of mixture} = \frac{100}{\dfrac{a}{d'} + \dfrac{b}{d''}}$$

where a = percentage of heavy powder

b = percentage by weight of beads

d' = density of heavy powder

d'' = density of beads

This does, of course, give only an approximation of the expected density, but may serve as an indication.

Using this method the detergent chemist has a great amount of latitude in formulation and the output of the spray-tower is enhanced.

In certain countries of the world there is a swing away from light density spray-dried powders to medium density powders. Two of the factors influencing this swing are high packaging costs and disposal problems with packages. This combination system can be arranged to produce powders of intermediate bulk density, regardless of whether nonionic detergents are used, by producing a powder and mixing it with a spray-dried powder in a proportion to give the desired formulation and density. This again will vastly increase the production of powder without the necessity of increasing the capacity of the spray-drying plant.

In further development is the alkaline powders are fluidised in a cooled air stream and the liquid components are sprayed on to the fluidised powders by special nozzles. Intimate mixing allows of the production of *expanded granules* by the explosive release of CO_2 from the reaction.

These expanded granules are agglomerated, tooled and aged in a second stage by the use of another turbo-reactor, with or without the addition of further liquid ingredients, from additional nozzles.

If no neutralisation occurs (when only non-ionics are used), agglomeration and granulation can still be achieved by spraying through four different nozzles, using agglomerating agents.

Perfume is added to the cooled powder by a further nozzle.

Patterson-Kelley systems

In this system V-shaped blender (Fig. 10.4) for both powder mixing and liquid/solids blending and agglomeration is used. As can be seen from the drawing, this method achieves a precision blend through a divergent flow and by the intermeshing action when two inclined cylinders combine their flow. Material is rotated close to the axis, reducing power requirement. As the blender rotates, liquid is sprayed into the material through a high-speed liquid dispersion bar located concentric to the trunnion axis. The blades on the bar aerate the material to increase the speed and thoroughness of the blend. Liquid is dispersed through disc apertures in a controlled pattern and extended to all solids throughout the blend.

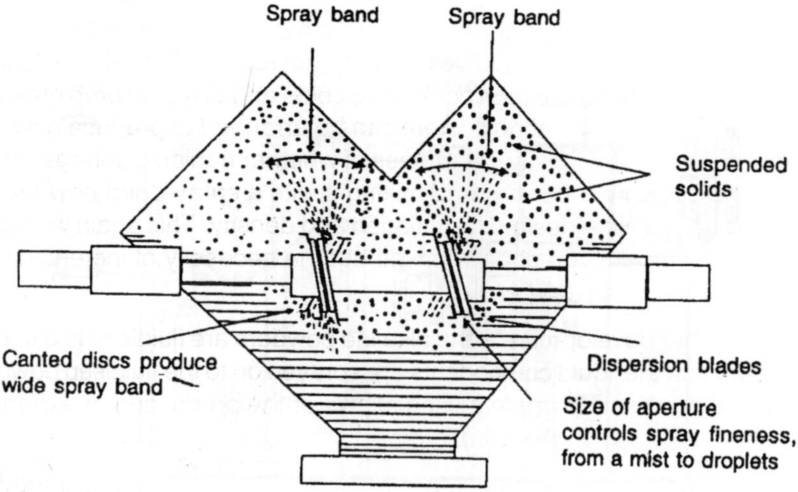

Fig. 10.4. Patterson-Kelley V-shaped blender.

The blender is used for manufacture of detergents by combined neutralisation/absorption processes, for the hydration of sodium tripolyphosphate, and if colloidal sodium silicate solution is added, agglomeration can be achieved.

An improvement of this system is their Cross-Flow Blender, where the two legs of the V are of unequal length, giving unequal displacement in the powder mass in each revolution of the shell, producing an axial exchange from each leg, thus faster blending.

The above two blenders are of the batch type, the solid material needs to be added while the blender is stationary and the machine needs to be stopped for discharge. There is no cooling so if perborate, enzymes and perfume are to be added, this can only be done after ageing and cooling, when the powder needs to be reintroduced into the same or another blender.

A development of this principle of uneven flow is the P-K zig-zag continuous blender shown in Fig. 10.5. The blender combines the action of a rotating, eccentric drum with multiple recycling to produce uniform blends of both solid/solids and liquid/solids materials. The zig-zag completes most blends within two minutes. Two liquids can be added simultaneously.

As the blender revolves, the blended material leaves the drum and flows into the legs, where recycling begins. At each half turn, part of the powder moves forward, part of it backwards within the legs. Splitting, tumbling and merging of the material bring particles into contact with each other to complete the blending.

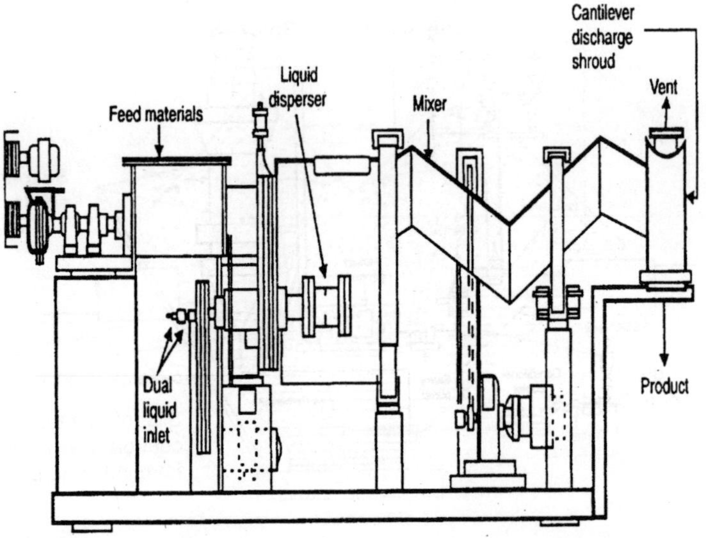

Fig. 10.5. Patterson-Kelley zig-zag continuous blender.

The blender typically recycles thirty parts of material for every part it discharges. Recycling serves as an averaging device to level off short-term feed variations. With each revolution, the machine discharges a uniform quantity of material of constant volume and weight.

This blender can also be combined with a spray-drying plant to increase capacity. STP is hydrated in a zig-zag blender (as shown in Fig. 10.6) mounted in series with a spray tower. The hydrated STP is then passed through a conditioner/cooler. The first part of the conditioner is a fluidised bed which both ages and cools the hydrate, the second part brings the power down to 30°C.

On passing out of the conditioner the material is split into two parts, the smaller part is fed to the crutchers to become part of the spray-dried matrix, while the larger part moves on to the second stage.

The second stage is a second zig-zag blender which is used to combine the spray-dried matrix, the STP hexahydrate and the non-ionic. Perborate, perfume and enzymes can be added at this stage. The non-ionic is dispersed through a liquid dispersion bar, designed for gentle but thorough mixing so

as not to destroy the bead structure of the matrix. The non-ionic acts as a binder to form a soft agglomerate and to prevent segregation. Bulk densities of 410-430 g/litre are obtained.

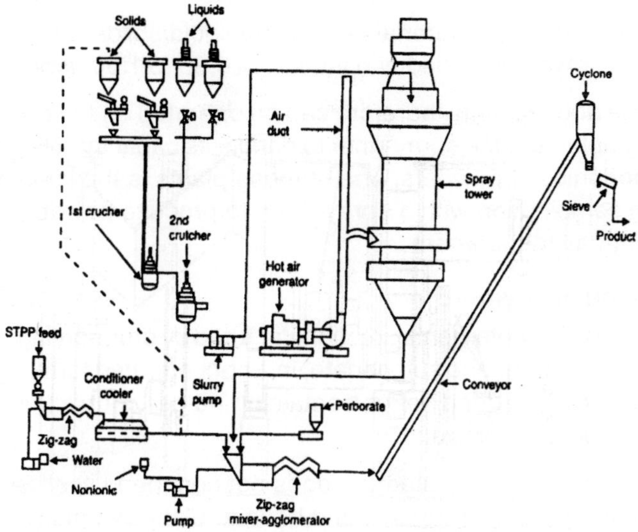

Fig. **10.6.** Patterson-Kelley system for increasing spray-drier capacity.

Anhydro system

In Anhydro fluid-mix system, illustrated in Fig. 10.7, of the mixing, neutralisation and agglomeration take place in a fluid bed reactor. Powders are fed continuously from the day silos one of the other powdered ingredients so that they can be measured efficiently in the volemetric measuring device.

Materials discharged from the silos, after being measured by the volumetric measuring devices at the base of the silos, are transported to the fluid bed by belt conveyors. Liquids are fed into the reactor by metering pump(s) and atomised by compressed air directly on to the bed. The fluid bed reactor consists of a mixing chamber with a fluidised area, fines separating area and a perforated plate for air distribution. The air supply is divided into a number of compartments each with a guiding vane to allow differential fluidisation to take place. The reactor bed outlet is connected to a series of cyclones to separate fines from the exhaust air. The fines separated thus are continuously recycled and agglomerated in the reactor bed. Heat sensitive materials, perborate, enzymes, etc., are added in an area adjacent to the fluidised bed, where the powder has cooled sufficiently.

As no mechanical mixing is used, the fluid-mix reactor can be easily combined with a spray-drying unit, the discharge from the spray-drier being connected to the entrance to the fluidised bed, thus the beads from the tower are combined in the agglomerisation process. Bulk densities, depending on the raw materials used, the liquid/solids ratio and whether spray-dried powder is added can vary from 0.35 to 1.00 g/ml.

All the above plants therefore can be operated on their own or can be used to complement the spray-drier to double its capacity. With the growing use of non-ionics in powders, one of these plants is the ideal solution, by itself or in combination with a spray-drier, to produce powders suitable for the present-day requirements.

Drum-drying of Powders

Occasionally detergents are manufactured by drum-drying. Historically the first dry alkyl benzene sulphonate, in a concentrated form, appeared on the market as drum-dried flakes containing 40 per cent active matter and filled with sodium sulphate.

This process of manufacture does not commend itself, as the flakes produced are not very attractive and have a relatively small surface area. Compared to spray-dried powders, and even to well-made powders from the simultaneous absorption and neutralisation process, drum-dried powders are slow to dissolve in water.

The operation of a drum-drier is expensive (compared with a spray-drier) and there is always the risk of scorching the finished product. Furthermore, unless the drums are made of stainless steel, the detergent slurry will corrode them quickly.

Drum-driers have one advantage over spray-driers in that they can be started and stopped in a relatively short time, allowing for the possibility of short runs.

For the above reasons drum-driers are not normally used for the manufacture of built powders, but when a highly concentrated powder of alkyl benzene sulphonate or fatty alcohol sulphate needs to be made in relatively short runs, drum-drying has a definite economic advantage over spray-drying.

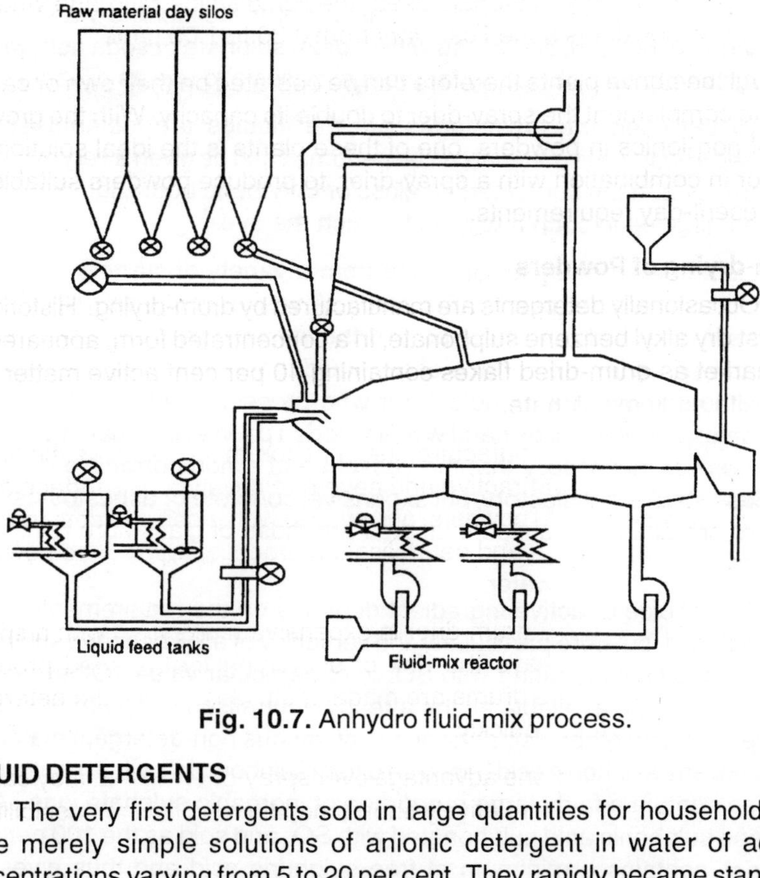

Fig. 10.7. Anhydro fluid-mix process.

LIQUID DETERGENTS

The very first detergents sold in large quantities for household use were merely simple solutions of anionic detergent in water of active concentrations varying from 5 to 20 per cent. They rapidly became standard household requisites for dishwashing and for the washing of fine articles of clothing such as wool and silk. Of recent years, these light-duty detergents have become more sophisticated and liquids (or lotions) have now appeared with builders for heavy-duty washing, both by hand, and more particularly, in household washing machines.

At first glance, it might be considered that liquids are cheaper in raw material costs than powders, as the filler (or diluent) is water rather than soda ash or sodium sulphate. This might hold true for light-duty liquids, but

where the heavy-duty product is to be considered, it is by no means axiomatic. For heavy-duty liquids hydrotropes, potassium rather than sodium salts and ethanolamines need to be used. These in no way add to detergency but increase the price somewhat. However, to offset this plant for liquid production is in no way comparable in cost with powder plants.

The advantages to the manufacturer of liquids are that they can be made in relatively simple plant and also that the diluent is water which costs virtually nothing, compared with sodium sulphate or soda ash, which, although cheap, are obviously far more expensive to use as diluents.

To the user, the advantages are that liquids are instantaneously dispersed in water, the material can be perfumed and be given a very attractive appearance and the containers–a glass or Polythene bottle, for example— can be designed in such a way as to catch the eye.

Liquid detergents can be made from a variety of starting materials, but in every case the plant is the same. A vessel equipped with a slow-speed stirrer is all that is required and the stirrer should be positioned so that it is well under the surface of the liquid, so as not to cause foaming. The authors know of a manufacturer who processes 4.5 m^3 at a time of liquid detergent, stirring by hand with a wooden paddle, in a matter of hours. It is, however, necessary that the vessel be of a non-corrodible material. Stainless steel is satisfactory, but expensive; concrete or asbestos-cement vessels are eminently suitable, and so are those of glass-fibre reinforced plastics.

The choice of active ingredient depends on the requirements of the finished liquid, but here particularly, the versatility of alkyl benzene sulphonic acid made by sulphonating with SO_3 is of particular value. Other anionic raw materials are available as the already neutralised salt, with or without the presence, whether incidental or not, of various non-detergent materials. Alkyl benzene sulphonic acid based on oleum sulphonation, when neutralised, will also contain a fairly large proportion of inorganic sulphate ions. Alkyl benzene sulphonic acid sulphonated with SO_3 and sold as the 100 per cent material, contains a minimum of free sulphuric acid and thus gives the manufacturer the greatest scope in formulation.

This 100 per cent material can be neutralised by any base to give various types of liquids, from low viscosity to gels. The solubility of the alkyl benzene sulphonic acid salt of the alkali metals is opposite to that of the regular order, in that the most soluble of the salts is that of lithium, followed by sodium, with potassium the least soluble. When manufacturing heavy-duty liquid detergents, this must be taken into account if potassium silicate and pyrophosphate are to be used, since the potassium ion of the inorganic filler can precipitate the sulphonic acid ion unless the formulation is carefully controlled.

Table 10 .4 gives the physical properties of 10 per cent solutions of dodecyl benzene sulphonic acid, neutralised by various bases. In every case 100 g of the sulphonic acid was neutralised to pH 7 by the particular base and the final solution made up to I litre.

The figures in Table 10.4 will vary with the type of ABS used, as small amounts of free sulphuric acid in the original material will greatly influence the behaviour of the neutralised salt. Furthermore, these figures were given for propylene tetramer DDBS. Linear DDBS in general has a lower viscosity, both for the alkali and ethanolamine and ethylamine salts, but these figures give a relative idea of the differences according to the base used.

If partial neutralisation of the sulphonic acid is to be done with caustic soda (or potash) as is possible when using the DDBS produced from SO_3 a slight amount of ferrous iron present in the caustic soda can cause unpleasant complications in the final product. (The same holds good for sulphonic acid produced by oleum or sulphuric acid sulphonation and where iron pick-up is possible.) Traces of the ferrous salt of the sulphonic acid will in time precipitate as a black sludge. This can be eliminated by oxidising the ferrous to ferric ions, and is easily accomplished by the use of sodium hypochlorite thus:

All the water necessary for the formulation, together with the caustic soda solution, is run into the vessel. Then 1 per cent of a 10 per cent solution of sodium hypochlorite is added and the solution mixed. The sulphonic acid is now added and mixing continued until all the sulphonic acid has been dissolved, and the solution allowed to stand for at least 20 min. longer to permit the oxidation process to go to completion.

The ethanolamine or other organic basic which is to be used for the completion of the neutralisation is now added, together with all the other additives.

The sodium hypochlorite will have been partially destroyed in the initial oxidation process; then, when the sulphonic acid is added, the excess hypochlorite will completely bleach all the colouring matter if any is present in the sulphonic acid. After this process a small residue of active chlorine will still be present, but this need not be eliminated as it will react with the organic amines to produce a chloramine, which is unstable. The amines will thus reduce the balance of the active chlorine left and render it innocuous. (It is for this reason that sodium hypochlorite cannot be used to bleach amine-containing solutions.)

Table 10.4. Physical properties of ABS solutions neutralised by various bases.

Base	Appearance of sot at 20ºC	Viscosity at 25ºC (Pa S)	Surface tension of 0.1% active material N/m	Foam height of 0.1% active material solution (Ross Miles) Initial cm	After 5 min. cm.
Ammonia	Separates into 2 phases	-	0.0310	17.5	17
NaOH	Clear liq	0.0045	0.0300	18	17
KOH	Gel	0.0285	0.0310	16	15
LiOH	Clear liq	0.0024	0.0310	17	16
Monoethanol-amine	Clear liq	0.0285	0.0310	16.5	15
Diethanolamine	Clear liq	0.0870	0.0300	17.5	16.5
Triethanolamine	Clear liq	0.0635	0.0310	18	17
Morpholine	Gel	0.4350	0.0300	12	11.5
Monoisopropanol-amine	Gel	0.3100	0.0310	15	15
Di-isopropanol-amine	Clear liq	0.3450	0.0300	15	14
Tri-isopropanol-amine	Clear liq	0.0910	0.0310	15	14.5
Mixed Isopropanolamine	Clear liq	0.3750	0.0305	16	15
Diglycolamine	Clear liq	0.1180	0.0310	16	15
Diethyl-ethanolamine	Clear liq	0.3050	0.0320	15	14
Triethylamine	Liquid*	0.1350	0.0320	14	13
Trimethylamine	Liquid*	0.3100	0.0360	13	12
Cyclohexylamine	Liquid*	0.0240	0.0310	6.5	6
Iso-butylamine	Gel*	0.7000	0.0340t	5t	5t
n-Butylamine	Cloudy liq*	0.0078	0.0310	5	4

Cont ....

sec-Butylamine	Gel*.	0.4450	0.0305	5	4
ter-Butylamine	Gel*	0.2250	0.0310	5	4
Diethylamine	Gel*	0.5250	0.0310	12	11
Dimethylamine	Gel* separates	0.1250	0.310	12.5	12

With characteristic smell. t Not completely soluble.

If for any reason it is not possible to use sodium hypochlorite for this oxidation process, the same effect can be achieved by the use of hydrogen peroxide, either as such, or in the form of sodium perborate. It is general practice to add to detergents based on alkyl benzene sulphonic acid one of the alkylolamides as a foam stabiliser, thickening agent and skin-protecting agent. No special procedures are involved. Opacifying agents, especially for solutions based on linear alkyl benzene sulphonates are often used to give the liquid a 'different' appearance. Aqueous dispersions of an alkali insoluble polymer of styrene, substituted styrene, a co-polymer of styrene with acrylamine, PVC or polyvinylidene chloride are used. All these above materials produce an opacity in the liquid which enhances the appearance. Stability and freeze-thaw studies should, however, be made on all trial formulations.

Liquid formulations can be light sensitive. This can however be overcome either by the addition of ultra-violet absorbers or by packing in opaque bottles.

Liquid formulations allow the incorporation of solvents (solvents are however being incorporated successfully in powders). These solvents need not. necessarily be of the water-immiscible type, glycol ethers being examples of excellent fat solvents which are completely water-miscible.

Light-duty liquid detergents can be based on alkyl benzene sulphonic acid, alcohol sulphates non-ionics as such, or sulphated non-ionics, or amphoteric detergents, or combinations of two or more of these materials.

Except when sulphonic acids are used, all the other components are available as concentrated (from 40-100 per cent) neutralised material which needs only to be diluted down to the required activity. With sulphonic acid, however, the manufacturer has the choice of varying his neutralising agent to give his liquid any property he wants, from a low viscosity to a thixotropic gel (Table 10.4).

If non-ionics of the ethylene oxide condensation type are being used in liquid detergents, either alone or in combination, it should be borne in mind that this type of material has a peculiar cloud point, in that it forms a cloudy solution when the temperature is raised and not (as is usually the case) when the temperature is lowered. It is thus important that products should be tested extensively, taking into account the highest possible temperature that the liquid may encounter on storage.

Heavy-duty liquids are coming more and more into use and require special formulation techniques. The problem here is to incorporate into the liquid active matter, sequestering agents, silicates, anti-redeposition and optical brightening agents. To achieve all this and to retain the finished material as a clear liquid with a low cloud point is not easy. If at a moderately high temperature the liquid 'clouds', it is an indication that separation into at least two phases is taking place and each phase will contain different proportions of each of the ingredients.

This problem is best overcome by producing the heavy-duty liquid as a lotion or gel, but this must be formulated so that it will not separate into two phases at the highest ambient temperature to which it may be subjected.

Toilet Preparations

As hair shampoos, shaving creams and bath preparations are all basically detergents, more and more detergent manufacturers are manufacturing either ready-made cosmetic preparations of this type or a concentrate for supply to the cosmetic manufacturer. The alcohol and ether sulphates have proved themselves over the years to be dermatologically safe for this type of preparation.

For hair shampoos the choice depends on the desired physical form of the product. For a cream the sodium slat of one of the fatty alcohol sulphates is recommended. For a liquid an ether sulphate is used or else an ethanolamine salt of a fatty alcohol sulphate. The latter has the disadvantage in that it cannot normally be obtained with as light a colour as the ether sulphate and it also foams less, but this can be enhanced by the use of a foam booster. The pearlescent type of shampoo can use as a base either an ether sulphate or sodium salt of the alcohol sulphate.

In addition to the well-tried sulphated alcohols and ethers, more and more use is being made of the amphoteric detergents as either a portion or all of the active ingredient in shampoos, etc. If they are used as the sole ingredient an additional advantage is that cationic detergents can be incorporated as bactericides.

Perfumes used in shampoos should all be dermatologically tested and in addition preservatives need to be added, as fungi and yeasts grow in detergent solutions. All formulations should be made up to include perfume dyes and preservatives and subjected to extensive storage tests as no hard and fast rule can be laid down for the interaction of the micro constituents. Furthermore, it is best to add a small portion of a chelating agent (0.25 per cent or so) as traces of iron may have an adverse effect on dyes in storage.

Dyes themselves or the constituents of certain dyes have come to be considered health hazards and are now subject to certification for use in toiletries or domestic preparations.

Some basic formulae for shampoos are given below

Formula 4

Cream shampoo

Sodium fatty alcohol (C_{12-14}) sulphate (50% paste)	25
Coconut monoethanolamide	2
Thickening agent	1
Sodium chloride	2
Chelating agent	0.25
Perfume, dye, preservative	qs
Water	to 100

The thickening agent is predissolved or dispersed in a portion of the water in accordance with the manufacturer's instructions. The sodium chloride is added to increase the viscosity if desired.

Formula 5

Liquid Shampoo

Sodium ether sulphate (C_{12-14}, 2 mol ethylene oxide)	
(100% basis)	12.5
Thickening agent	qs
Sodium chloride	2
Perfume, dye, preservative	qs
Chelating agent	0.25
Water	to 100

The thickening agent is added as required because hard and fast rules cannot be given as very often the concentrated ether sulphate contains ethyl alcohol or propylene glycol both of which drastically lower the viscosity.

Formula 6

Liquid Shampoo

Triethanolamine fatty alcohol sulphate	
(40% concentrate)	35
Coconut diethanolamide	3

Chelating agent	0.25
Perfume, dye, preservative	qs
Water	to 100

In place of the triethanolamine salt, the monoethanolamine neutralised fatty alcohol sulphate can be used. This will give a higher viscosity.

A pearlescent effect can be obtained by adding to the paste ethylene glycol stearate, diethylene glycol stearate, polyethylene glycol stearate, magnesium stearate or myristic diethanolamide.

Formula 7

Pearlescent Shampoo

Sodium fatty alcohol sulphate (50% concentrate)	25
Palmitic monoethanolamide	2
Ethylene glycol stearate	1
Chelating agent	0.25
Perfume, dye, preservatives	qs
Water	to 100

The alcohol sulphate, the glycol stearate, the monoethanolamide and the water are charged into the vessel and warmed with gentle stirring until a clear solution free from dispersed particles is obtained. This is then cooled to 50^{0}C and the other ingredients added and passed to packing. When cold the pearlescence will have developed.

Formula 8

Bubble Bath Preparation

Sodium ether sulphate (100% basis)	20
Triethanolamine fatty alcohol sulphate (100% basis)	8
Chelating agent	0.25
Perfume, dye, preservative	qs
Water	to 100

Paste Detergents

In certain parts of the world detergents are used in a finished or semi-finished form as pastes of varying concentrations. Certain detergent raw materials are sold as pastes: for example, the sodium slat of lauryl alcohol sulphate in a concentrated form without any addition of inorganic fillers.

The detergent manufacturer who wishes to manufacture a paste can do so very easily from alkyl benzene sulphonic acid, again either from the 100 per cent or 90 per cent varieties, depending on which is available to him. To produce a snow-white-paste from 90 per cent sulphonic acid can only be achieved if the acid is neutralised immediately after sulphonation, and not stored. The 100 per cent sulphonic acid can produce a snow-white paste even though stored for many months.

The manufacture of the paste can be done in a soap crutcher, or in a specially built neutraliser, equipped with a cooling jacket as shown in Fig. 10.8. The neutralising vessel would preferably be built of stainless steel, but if precautions are taken so that the pH of the paste does not fall below 7 during the process of manufacture, a mild steel vessel can be used.

Because sodium alkyl benzene sulphonates are not completely homogeneous in concentrated solution, especially in the presence of electrolytes, various materials must be used to prevent separation into two phases. This can be done by the use of hydrotropes, small proportions of CMC or alkylolamides. However, hydrotropes will tend to produce thinner pastes and this will mean adding inorganic salts to make them stiffer again, depending, of course, on the requirements of the market. In general, tridecyl benzene sulphonate will produce the stiffest paste; dodecyl benzene sulphonate a paste of medium consistency; and the biodegradable linear alkyl benzene sulphonates, the thinnest pastes. Consistency can again be varied by the addition of inorganic salts. In some countries high concentrations of borax are added to produce a stiff paste.

These inorganic salts can be sodium chloride, sodium sulphate, tetra sodium pyrophosphate or sodium silicate solution, or a combination of these. To achieve a stiff paste, it is very rarely necessary to add more than 3 per cent in total. Sodium chloride is the cheapest and gives the greatest stiffening effect, but is corrosive to iron or steel. Sodium sulphate and tetra sodium pyrophosphate suffer from the disadvantage that in cold weather they might crystallise out from the paste into needle-like crystals, while both the tetra sodium pyrophosphate and the sodium silicate raise the pH of the paste, but add to the detergency. The high pH can be regulated by using some of the sulphonic acid to neutralise a portion of the alkalinity of these materials. In particular, to improve the stability of a paste based on SO_3 sulphonated LAS the 1:3.3 ratio sodium silicate is used for partial neutralisation. Colloidal silica is formed in the neutralisation and it serves as a kind of absorbent skeleton to prevent separation. The LAS is thus neutralised by sodium only, the exact amount of caustic soda being dependent on the acid value of the sulphonic acid and also whether partial neutralisation by an inorganic salt has been done. The acid value will vary not only with the average molecular weight of the alkyl benzene (tridecyl benzene has a lower acid value than dodecyl benzene), but also with the method of manufacture (i.e., oleum, sulphuric acid or SO_3) and finally according to the individual manufacturer.

For this reason, although the acid value is usually expressed as the amount of milligrams of-caustic potash required to neutralise 1g of acid, it is better to consider the acid value as the number of grams of caustic soda required to neutralise 100 g of acid. This can readily be calculated from the internationally accepted acid value by the formula :

$$\text{Acid value in g NaOH / 100 g acid} = \frac{\text{Acid value in mg KOH / g acid}}{14}$$

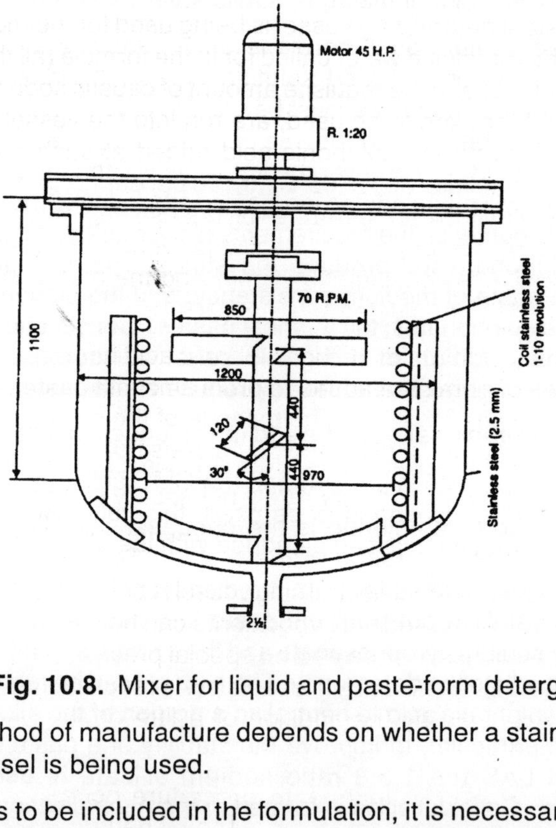

Fig. 10.8. Mixer for liquid and paste-form detergents.

The method of manufacture depends on whether a stainless-steel or mild-steel vessel is being used.

If CMC is to be included in the formulation, it is necessary to dissolve it separately. If a separate mixing vessel with a slow-speed stirrer is available, water to the amount of ten times the weight of the CMC is charged into the container and the CMC poured in slowly with stirring. The stirring is continued until all the lumps of CMC are dispersed, concurrently with the process of the manufacture of the paste. If a mixing vessel is not available, the solution can be made in the same way in a 200 litre drum and the CMC added while stirring with a hand crutcher. This dispersion is best prepared the day before it is required and left to swell and dissolve by itself overnight.

The CMC dispersion, if in contact with iron or steel, will tend to corrode the vessel and also will become discoloured by the rust formed. It is therefore essential to produce this dispersion in a non-corrodible vessel—stainless steel, asbestos cement or steel clad with plastic or rubber. The stirrer itself should also be non-corrodible.

However, some manufacturers are able to achieve rapid wetting, swelling and solution of the CMC in a matter of half an hour by the use of a high speed turbine mixer. The addition of alkali can also help in this dispersion.

If a mild steel neutralizing vessel is being used for the manufacture of the paste, all the remaining water called for in the formula (all the water if no CMC is to be added) and the requisite amount of caustic soda solution, with inorganic salts if they are to be used, are run into the vessel. Mixing and cooling is started and the sulphonic acid added at such a rate that the temperature does not rise above 65°C. (If 100 per cent acid is used the heat of reaction is low and the temperature will not rise very high, provided that an efficient cooling coil or jacket is available. If 90 per cent acid is used, the heat of reaction is considerably higher and the rate of addition of the sulphonic acid must be adjusted.)

When about 80 per cent of the sulphonic acid has been taken up and the paste is still distinctly alkaline, the requisite amount of sodium hypochlorite solution is added and mixed in. The balance of the sulphonic acid is now added, taking care that the pH of the paste does not fall below 7. Mixing is continued until the paste is uniform and the CMC solution (if called for) is added, or, if an alkylolamide is to be used, this can now be put in. If a hydrotrope is employed, this can be added with the sulphonic acid.

When a stainless-steel neutralising vessel is being used, the procedure is similar, except that the sodium hypochlorite can be put in at the beginning with the water and caustic soda and no special precautions need be taken about not passing to the acid pH. If an acid pH is reached, the desired pH of 7.5-8 can be achieved by the addition of a litre or two of caustic soda solution.

A slight variation of this paste procedure occurs when a highly concentrated liquid is required. This is done by neutralising the sulphonic acid with an ethanolamine.

In this instance, the requisite water (which depends on the final concentration desired) and the ethanolamine are charged into the vessel. The sulphonic acid is added slowly with intermittent stirring so as not to generate foam. The reaction is instantaneous. The only precautions that need be observed are to avoid the production of foam and to keep the temperature from rising above 60°C.

Calcium Sulphonates

Although efforts of formulators are concentrated in the direction of neutralising the effects of calcium ions by chelation, the calcium salts of alkyl benzene sulphonic acid play an important role in the production of agricultural emulsifiers because of their solubility in the semi-polar solvents used as diluents for insecticides. The calcium ion, being divalent, yields a sulphonate which has the pictorial formula

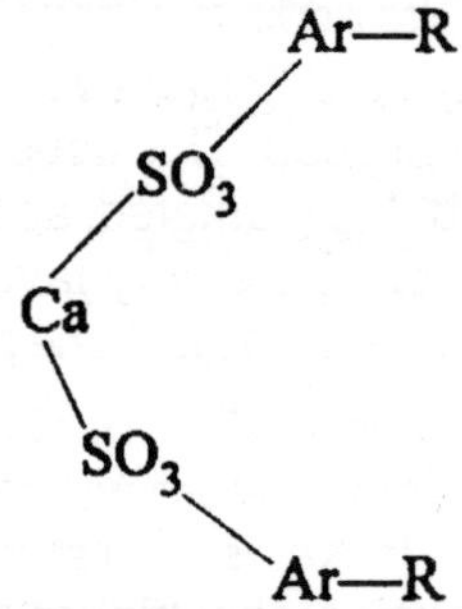

that is, the hydrophilic portion is in the centre of the molecule with two hydrophobic tails. For reasons not readily apparent this allows of spontaneous emulsification, an absolute prerequisite in the field. The sulphonic acid is not necessarily of the same molecular weight as that used in cleaning materials, quite often it can be greater, increasing its oil-solubility. The calcium sulphonate is not the only constituent of these emulsifiers whose formulation is beyond the scope of this volume.

To manufacture calcium sulphonates, good quality SO_3 sulphonated alkyl benzene is essential with an absolute minimum of free sulphuric acid. To attain this completeness of sulphonation is often sacrificed so that (almost) no surplus $S0_3$ is needed for the sulphonation. As can be understood, the presence of free sulphuric acid will produce insoluble calcium sulphate.

The neutralisation is performed with good quality lime in the presence of a polar solvent as-a diluent, and after completion the diluent is distilled off.

SOLID DETERGENTS

Solid detergents are usually manufactured in three forms for the following different applications

(i) toilet cakes;
(ii) household scrubbing;
(iii) 'one-shot' additions to washing machines.

Detergent Toilet Bars

The manufacture of a detergent toilet bar comparable with soap is fraught with many difficulties, and is the subject of many patent applications throughout the world. Not many of these patents have been successfully exploited commercially for technological or economic reasons, or both A few toilet detergent bars have been put on the market, but not all of them have captured the sales that the manufacturers had hoped for.

One hundred per cent of detergent active matter is considerably more expensive than 100 per cent soap. This does not matter when detergents in liquid or powder form are being marketed, as 20-25 per cent active matter in a well-made powder can compete very favourably with a 40-60 per cent fatty acid soap powder. To be sold in the same price range as soap a detergent bar cannot have much more than 40 per cent active matter. If only 40 per cent active matter can be used the mass needs to be filled to 100 per cent with relatively inexpensive materials and this causes the problem. The use of soluble inorganic salts is precluded because the cake will be heavy compared to soap and will tend to effloresce. Talc, although not efflorescent, will again make the cake extremely heavy and hard to the feel.

A detergent used as a soap will tend to defeat the skin overmuch and superfatting' or retarding agents need to be incorporated into the bar.

One of the big disadvantages to overcome is the behaviour of a detergent tablet when wet compared to a soap tablet. When soap is wetted, water is absorbed over the whole surface of the soap and the viscosity of the water-soap mixture drops dramatically and then increases with further dilution to form the viscous 'middle soap'. Thus when a wet tablet of soap is placed in a soap dish this viscous middle phase prevents water from penetrating into the tablet and the soap remains dry inside, the outside surface gradually drying out by evaporation. This middle phase does not occur with detergents and therefore the water in a wet detergent tablet under the same conditions will penetrate right to the centre of the mass, making it soft and slimy.

For all that, synthetic toilet tablets have one very big advantage in that because of the chemistry of synthetic detergents they do not make a scum or leave a ring in the bath tub. A toilet detergent tablet should therefore not be readily soluble or should not disintegrate, and should have the feel of soap when wet; it should lather freely and when stored should not crack or effloresce. Finally, it should be possible to work the mass in normal soap-milling and stamping machinery.

The bulk of these problems have been overcome by the use of a soap/ detergent mixture, but although this improves the physical behaviour of the cake, it does not do away with the disadvantages of soap. Tolerance to hard water can be improved by the addition of lime soap dispersants or even by using them wholly as the synthetic part of the 'combo' soap as it is sometimes called.

There are a few detergent cakes on the market and these are based on sulphated monoglycerides, fatty alcohol sulphates, alkyl isethionates, sulphosuccinates and sulphated fatty acids. Very often the potassium salt is preferred to the sodium because of its better theological properties. To these 'active raw materials are added plasticisers such as fatty alcohols, the phosphate and phthalate esters, alkylolamides, particularly coconut or palmitic mixtures, and polymerised ethylene glycols and binders such as starch and talc.

Manufacture is the subject of many patents and trade secrets, but the process consists of using raw material in as nearly an anhydrous form as is possible to maintain, melting it with plasticisers, adding the binders, and then milling, plodding and stamping in the normal soap-making machinery.

General composition for toilet soap :

Surfactant	30-70%
Plasticiser/binder	10-30%
Filler	10-30%
Additives	0-20%
Water	3-10%

A specific formula can be suggested as under

Coco fatty alcohol sodium sulphate (70—80% AM)	50%
Monoalkanolamide of palmitic/stearic acid derived from either hydrogenated tallow or palm oil methyl ester or fatty acid	20%
White dextrin	30%

The dextrin serves not only as a binder but also as a skin protectant. This formulation contains no insoluble matter.

Household Scrub Bars

Historically, in this field again the first attempts were based on a detergent which had been available as a water solution. Binding the water was done with materials such as bentonite and sodium stearate, i.e., soap produced in *situ.* Because the starting material contained at least as much water as active matter, the final bar or cake contained the same ratio of water to active detergent matter. This limited the amount of active matter that could be incorporated, because the more active matter added, the more water appeared in the final product. Nowadays a bar of this type can be manufactured at concentrations between 20 and 60 per cent, as desired, by the use of alkyl benzene sulphonic acids.

The sulphonic acid is mixed with the dry ingredients in a dough-mixer. A plough-mixer or amalgamator is also suitable provided that the arms and motor are strong enough to withstand the resistance of the material and the neutralising agent is either soda ash or a concentrated caustic soda solution. If caustic soda is used, a percentage of water is automatically added to the material, but the final product can be controlled to have a neutral pH. When soda ash is used (as in the manufacture of powders) a surplus of soda ash needs to be present and it is thus impossible to have a neutral pH. Although a neutral pH is not essential, as it would be for bars meant for toilet use, nevertheless the bar will still come into contact with the hands, and must not be too alkaline. The pH can be lowered by having a large amount of bicarbonate in the formula or by the addition of sodium acid pyrophosphate after the neutralisation has been completed.

After neutralisation, and the addition of any special ingredients, the mass is allowed to age. This ageing process varies with the formulation and further manipulation. If a bar of high active-matter content (60 per cent or so) is being made, the mass should be aged for at least 12 hours. If a low active-matter material (40 per cent) is being manufactured, the mass can be transferred to the next stage immediately. In fact, it is not advisable to allow it to age, as it will set hard and become unworkable. (If by any chance a low active-matter bar has set hard before it can be worked, it is possible to regenerate the plasticity by warming it to 50-60°C in a soap-drying room.)

Low-active concentration bars or tablets are not recommended because they are both inefficient and uneconomical in use. However, in certain of the developing countries it is considered that the unit cost of a bar might be too high if it contains the normal amount of active matter. This is a false consideration because the filling materials as well as the extra manipulations involved all cost money. For all that, bars of 25 per cent active matter or less are being produced.

To make bars of this type filling materials need to be used. Plain water cannot be used alone as this will make the bar too soft. If inorganic salts alone are used the bars become heavy, hard and unattractive in appearance and are also subject to efflorescence on storage. These problems can be partially overcome in various ways.

Paraffin wax at the rate of 2 per cent can be added. The wax needs to be melted separately and poured on the mass while mixing, before the temperature has fallen to 60°C. The addition of the paraffin wax gives a better feel to the tablet and to a certain extent hinders the defatting action of the detergent on the human skin. This skin-protecting action can be enhanced by using a blend of paraffin wax and polyethylene wax. In this instance the polyethylene wax (which has a -melting point of the order of 100°C) needs to be dissolved in the molten paraffin wax. Surprisingly enough, this addition of waxes in no way detracts from the detergency of the bar or tablet.

Another method is to use 5 per cent starch and to include in the basic formula a total of 15 per cent water. After the reaction is completed, the starch is added and the mass heated to a minimum of 80°C to solubilise the starch.

Finally, a combination of both the above methods can be used and also on occasion talc is added to improve the feel of the tablets.

After the requisite ageing period, the mass is passed through a soap mill. In certain factories this milling is dispensed with and the aged mass is fed directly into a plodder. However, the appearance and texture of the finished product is definitely inferior if it is not passed through a mill.

For this reason, we stated above that the period of ageing depends on the further processing. If the mass is to be milled, the ageing period can be shorter, as it is desirable to feed the mass into the mill while it is still very plastic. If no milling is to be done, the mass should be less plastic. In some factories the mass is allowed to set hard, then chipped in a soap-chipper, and then passed into a mill or direct into the plodder.

FABRIC SOFTENERS

The fabric softeners have become a necessary adjunct to washing of clothes particularly when machines are being used.

It was becoming apparent that clothes were coming out of the machine 'hard' to the feel. The wool industry had for years used the term 'handle' to test the feel or softness of the fibres and this in turn was a function of the efficient washing or scouring of the wool.

In the same manner as CMC was introduced to produce whiter washing, fabric softeners filled the gap formed by the 'hardness' of the clothes. The reason for the washing coming out hard is a build-up of salts on the fibres and these salts are deposited in such a manner that they are not easily rinsed away. (It should be remembered that no matter how much chelating or sequestering agents are added to the washing powders or liquids, the final rinse in household washing is with tap, i.e., relatively hard, water.)

Certain quaternary ammonium salts (cationic detergents) and also alkylolamides were found to be effective as additives for the softening of clothes. These softeners are adsorbed on to the fibres from the final rinse and the washing comes out softer, probably due to an interfibre lubricating effect.

In addition to softening, the fabric softeners of the quaternary ammonium type also act as bacteriostats if not bactericides. Finally, with the synthetic materials being used nowadays, a very common occurrence is the build-up of electrostatic charges on the fibres. The softener tends to diminish production of this static electricity.

The common cationic detergents in use are di-tallow di-methyl ammonium chloride (or iodide) (1), alkyl di-methyl aryl ammonium chloride (II) or 2-heptadecyl-l-methyl-l-(2'-stearoylamido-ethyl)-imidazolinium methyl sulphate (III) which are pictured below :

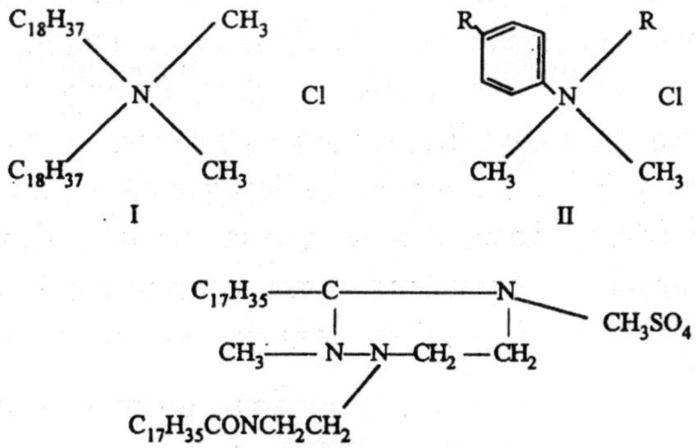

I II

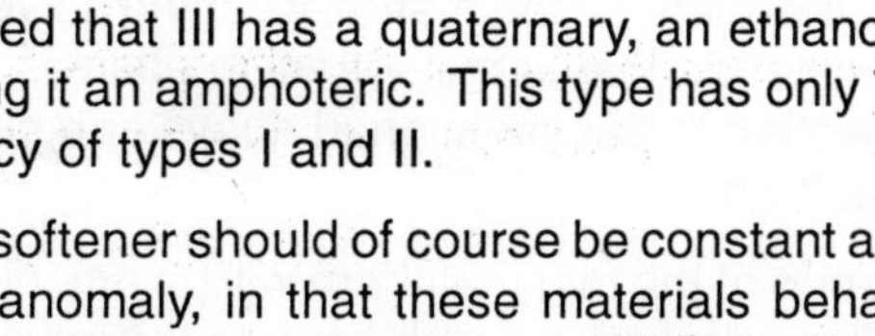

III

It will be observed that III has a quaternary, an ethanolamide and a sulphate group making it an amphoteric. This type has only 70 per cent of the softening efficiency of types I and II.

Viscosity of the softener should of course be constant and here again we come across an anomaly, in that these materials behave differently from other surfactants. If the electrolyte content of the final solution is high the formulation can be almost water-like in its viscosity. If the electrolyte content is very low the solution (dispersion) can be like a jelly. To allow for variations in the hardness of the water supply it is best to use demineralised water for diluting and then control viscosity by addition of electrolyte (sodium chloride or sodium acetate).

These materials are merely dispersed in water to give a convenient concentration so that 0.1 per cent (based on the weight of the clothes) of the softener can be dosed. Thus for a machine taking 5 kg of wash, 5 g of the softener need to be applied. It is therefore advisable to dilute the softener sufficiently so that 5 g (or less for machines taking smaller quantities) of the 100 per cent material can be measured easily.

This concentration is normally in the 5-8 per cent range, but 'concentrated' softeners of double, triple or even greater strengths are available. At the higher concentrations the solubility of the distearyl or ditallow derivatives is poor and the 'dispersion' could separate on storage. To prevent this, recourse to emulsifiers is necessary. Of the emulsifiers suitable for this purpose we mention glycerol monostearate, ethoxylated fatty amines, and fatty alkyl diamines.

Again as the solubility is poor, if too viscous a solution is made, it might not disperse sufficiently in the water during the rinse cycle. For the very concentrated solutions viscosity can be lowered by the addition of small quantities of calcium chloride.

The imidazoline softeners give a thin solution, and the viscosity of this solution can only be increased by using a thickener or by combining them in the ratio of 60:40 or 70:30 with a quaternary softener. This has the added advantage of giving enhanced softening.

As the quaternary ammonium salts are incompatible, with anionic detergents, they obviously cannot be included in the washing powder or liquid formulation and they need to be added to the washing when the anionic detergent used initially has been effectively rinsed away. It has been found that subsequent washing of clothes treated with fabric softener does not tend to neutralise the softener already adsorbed on the fibre; rather softener tends to build up with consecutive washes.

However, there are on the market washing powders and liquids which incorporate a softener, that is the softening effect is achieved in the wash cycle. The objection to this mentioned above can be overcome by one of the following methods :

1. Acceptance of the fact that there will be anionic-cationic interaction. This will neutralise a small part of the anionic component (and incidentally reduce foaming) to form the complex (or salt). This complex is still substantive to the fibres, its softening effect will be diminished but will still produce an anti-static function.

2. Use of only non-ionic material as the active matter.

3. Encapsulation of the cationic with a relatively high melting, water-insoluble material (paraffin wax). The softener then becomes dispersed in the water when the temperature in the wash cycle reaches its maximum after the bulk of the washing has been done. There will of

course be a competing reaction between the anionic on the one hand and adherence to the fibre on the other.

4. Use of a tertiary amine with two fatty acid groups (di-tallow methyl) for example. These materials are negatively charged at normal wash pH and behave as ordinary bases, although not soluble to any extent in water. This insolubility allows them to adhere to the fibres of the cloth. In subsequent rinse cycles the pH will drop to the neutral range and they become converted to cationic material (they have been called crypto-cationic) and exert the softening effect.

A further tendency has arisen to add optical brightening agents to the softening solution. Care must be taken in the selection of the brightening agents as many of them are incompatible with cationic detergents or unstable in solution. It is best to work in close co-operation with the manufacturers when selecting these dyestuffs.

Fabric softeners for the rinse cycle are always perfumed. The type and quantity of perfume should be chosen with care, preferably with the help of an expert perfumer, as a well-formulated softener can leave the clothes with a pleasant, fresh smell even if they are passed through a drier.

The criteria, apart from the germicidal or bacteriostatic properties, that have been suggested for fabric softeners are :

1. Easy dispersion in a final rinse solution,
2. Substantivity to the fabric.
3. Ability to impart softness and fluffiness (handle).
4. Ability to impart good interfibre lubrication without giving a greasy feel.
5. Ability to impart an anti-static effect.
6. The softener must not adversely affect the colour of the fabric (yellowing or greying) and, optionally, should impart a brightening effect.
7. The fabric must be easily re-wettable after treatment.

ABRASIVE CLEANERS

To this class belong the abrasive hand-cleaners and scouring powders for pots and pans as well as cleaners for tiles and bath-tubs. The vast majority are sold as powders or pastes, but bars and liquids are also available.

Powders, pastes and solids are made in much the same way as the nonabrasive product, with the addition of the abrasive material. In liquids, abrasive matter will always tend to settle out, but, to prevent it from compacting, a gelling agent is incorporated. This increases the viscosity, so that the abrasive can easily be re-dispersed when the liquid is shaken to prevent the abrasive from compacting. The choice of abrasive in the above compounds is one of extreme importance in avoiding undue costs and yet giving the abrasiveness desired without scratching. For example, an abrasive used in a wall-cleaner must be softer than one used on windows, one for aluminium ware softer than one for steelware. Usually the manufacturer employs a compromise type of Material. The following materials are listed in order of hardness. Generally, they are used in a size of 200 mesh or finer.

Talc : Hydrous magnesium silicate; very soft; suitable for special scouring agents for tile and porcelain enamel, but not for a general household product.

Diatomaceous earth : Siliceous skeletons of small aquatic plants called diatoms; also called infusorial earth, kieselguhr, tripolite, etc; soft; expensive; not recommended in general household products.

Dolomite and calcite: Natural magnesium carbonate and calcium carbonate.

Marble dust : Calcium carbonate, mild abrasive, commonly used in household cleaners.

Volcanic ash : Sedimentary rock composed of volcanic dust, ash, and cinders; suitable for use in household cleaners. Pumice, also a derivative of volcanic ash, is slightly harder.

Felspar : Mixture of various metal aluminium silicates, chiefly $K_2O.Al_2O.6SiO_2$. Its hardness is just about the equivalent of volcanic ash, and it is usually of a whiter colour, so that it is a very desirable product when available.

Quartz : Crystallised SiO_2. It is harder than pumice and is apt to be abrasive on softer metals such as aluminium and copper. Not recommended where milder abrasives are available.

Sand : Fine grains of disintegrated siliceous rock, chiefly quartz which it resembles m hardness.

In many cases the soap plays a minor role. This fact leads to an interesting development, namely, the use of synthetic detergents to replace soap in the formula.-A product containing 5 per cent soap-will rapidly lose its sudsing value through the precipitation of the soap by the hard water. This destroys the penetrating action necessary to such cleaners. Synthetic detergents such as alkyl benzene sulphates which are not affected by hard water retain this property under all conditions of use.

Abrasive powders or pastes containing about 5-10 per cent active detergents (the DDBS detergents are specially suitable) have been found by the authors to possess excellent detergent and foaming qualities.

Also specifies cleaners which contain vegetable abrasives. For this purpose sawdust, etc., may be used, and it seems that the fact is taken into consideration that these kinds of abrasive are usually less irritating to the skin than the common mineral abrasives, with the exception perhaps of bentonite or colloidal clay.

Again, it must be emphasized that fineness of particle size of the abrasive material, especially if inorganic, is of the greatest importance; otherwise irritation of the skin may be caused.

The strong defatting action of synthetic detergents and their power of penetrating into the skin may lead to dermatitis. However, the irritant effect of synthetic detergents can be counteracted by adding superfatting agents such as lecithin and lanolin, and also alkanolamides, especially those based on vegetable oils with a high content of double unsaturated fatty acids.

Chapter - 4

FORMULATION AND APPLICATION OF DETERGENTS

INTRODUCTION

An attempt has been made in this chapter to incorporate a wide range of formulations giving various process details. The emphasis has been given on the technoeconomic and functional aspects of the ingredients used in such formulation. The chapter also highlights the various industrial and household applications of detergents.

FOAM

At one time the amount of foam formed by a detergent was considered to be a measure of its effectiveness. It is true that foam is formed when surface tension is low, but lowering of surface tension is not always a criterion of detergency because this is in actual fact related to the lowering of interfacial tension.

In certain detergent operations high foam is a definite requirement, in certain cases it is immaterial whether the detergent foams or not, and in other cases foam can be considered a nuisance if not a prohibition to the use of the detergent for a particular operation.

It is obvious that a hair shampoo, shaving cream (other than the brushless type) and bubble bath preparations need to produce copious foam. Dishwashing compounds which are primarily meant for washing by hand in a sink full of water also need to foam copiously but the reason is not so obvious. As the plates are dipped in the solution and washed oil is freed from the surface of the plate and floats to the top of the solution and in time this fatty layer can become appreciably thick. When the plate is withdrawn from the liquid it will pass through this layer last and part of the oil might become redeposited on the surface. It, however, a thick foam is developed in the liquid by the physical actions of washing, the oil will be trapped in the tremendous surface area of the foam and the amount of oil available for redeposition on the plate in its passage out of the solution is greatly reduced. When the foam becomes saturated with -oil it collapses and this is an indication that the solution is no longer suitable for washing. For detergents intended for hand-washing of clothes foam is desirable as a sales-appeal factor.

Commercial and automatic household laundry machines are almost without exception 'foam sensitive'. If the detergent foams unduly the foam overflows on to the floor and also can interfere with the free flow of clothes through the water. In automatic machines the foam can interfere with water level pumps and the proper working of the controls in the machine. A small amount of foam is necessary as this tends to trap dirt particles.

Similarly, dishwashing machines cannot tolerate foam, firstly because again the foam might overflow and also interfere with the pumping of the liquid and secondly, once foam forms, bubbles remain on the dishes and leave spots on drying.

Hard and fast rules cannot be !aid down as certain household washing machines (usually those with a propeller) can tolerate foam, and in dishwashing machines using a propeller a small amount of foam is not harmful, but in the case of those working with jets the smallest trace of foam leaves spots on glassware.

The following rough guidelines for foam:

(a) Anionic detergents in general produce voluminous foam; somewhat less is produced in hard water but foam is always increased with an increase in temperature.

(b) Non-ionic detergents foam considerably less than anionics, but this depends on the type of non-ionic. There are 'low-foam' non-ionics which can be used alone for most operations, while other non-ionics still need 'foam control'. Non-ionics usually foam somewhat less in hot water than in cold.

(c) When soap is added to an anionic detergent, foam is depressed.

(d) Non-ionic detergents do not depress foam of anionics; they can even enhance it.

(e) Alkaline builders in general enhance the foaming power of all types of detergents.

We shall later in this chapter include formulations for both powders and liquids with foam control whereby a foam control agent is added to a ready-made powder.

The patent describes a combination of a white mineral oil, paraffin wax or microcrystalline wax and/or glycerol monostearate with microfine precipitated hydrophobic silica in the proportions:

Mineral oil	80 parts
Paraffin wax or microcrystalline wax and/or glycerol monostearate	2-12 parts
Microfine hydrophobic silica	0.3-1 part

The solid waxes are dissolved in the oil with warming and the silica dispersed in it.

To give a non-foaming detergent, 100 parts of finished powder are sprayed with 1 part of this solution/dispersion.

HOUSEHOLD CLEANING

The days of one bar of soap, which served as a hair shampoo, toilet bar, laundry soap, for general washing and (mixed with sand from the garden) for pot-scouring, have long since passed. Now-a-days, materials are manufactured for special purposes, such as heavy-duty laundering (the washing of cotton goods which by their very nature are usually heavily soiled), fine wash (the laundering of delicate fabrics such as silks, nylons, woollens), general purpose, dishwashing, floor-washing, window-cleaning, tile-cleaning, etc.

Heavy-duty Laundering

Detergents should be formulated with the type of clientele in mind. Again washing habits both personal and for clothes differ greatly in the two continents.

Non-ionics perform better than other detergents on fabrics made from synthetic fibres and also under cold -water conditions. They also find use as 'rubbing agents' for badly soiled collars.

Cotton goods, which are still the bulk of the household wash, require a moderately, high alkalinity. In contact with a solution of a pH of 10 or more, the cellulose fibre swells slightly, allowing the water to penetrate into the fibre and thus loosen adhering dirt.

Household heavy-duty washing powders are generally of two types, for hand washing and for fully automatic washing machines. The hand-washing type of powder requires a copious lather for psychological reasons. Fully automatic washing machines, which have a drum which revolves around a horizontal axis, cannot use a powder with a copious foam. Because of the action of the drum, the foam can spill out of the machine, and also the foam interferes with the action of the automatic floats which adjust the level of the water. However, a small amount of foam is necessary, as some of the dirt is trapped by this foam. For these reasons the powder has to have 'controlled foam'. Semi-automatic machines, i.e., those that have propellers or impellers to do the agitation, or with drums rotating about a vertical axis, can in general, utilize either of the two types of powders.

A formulation for a hand-washing or semi-automatic machine, manufactured by simultaneous absorption and neutralisation, has already been discussed in Chapter 10, Formulae 2 and 3. The addition of sodium perborate is, of course, optional and depends on washing practices in the particular area. We recommend the addition of at least 10 per cent sodium perborate to all laundry powders. In countries where this is not normal practice the addition of sodium perborate might make the powder expensive, but the extra whiteness achieved will compensate for the increased cost.

If the powder is being manufactured by the spray-drying process, the formulation can, if desired, be the same as that given in Formula 2 or 3, but an infinitely better powder can be made by using Formula 1.

Formula 1

Spray-dried heavy-duty, household hand-washing powder

Sodium alkyl benzene sulphonate (or equivalent)	25
Sodium tripolyphosphate	25
CMC (66% basis)	2.5
Sodium silicate (1:2.4 ratio)	15
Optical brightening agent	0.2
Sodium sulphate	32.3

and to this powder after spray-drying add sodium perborate at the rate of

Spray-dried powder	90
Sodium perborate	10

Foam Control

The above formula cannot be used in foam-sensitive washing machines. To overcome the foaming problem several methods of foam control are used.

One is to use a low-foaming non-ionic detergent as the active matter. An alkyl phenol condensed with not more than eight molecules of ethylene oxide will not foam unduly, but the physical characteristics (free-flowing, stickiness) both of spray-dried powders and those made by other methods will suffer when using low ethylene oxide content non-ionics and therefore the amount of active matter it is possible to incorporate in the powder is limited.

A typical powder to be made by either spray-drying or spray-mixing is given in formula 2.

Formula 2

Heavy-duty fully automatic washing machine powder	
Non-ionic detergent (low-foaming)	10
Sodium tripolyphosphate	30
CMC (66% basis)	1.5
Sodium silicate (1:2.4 ratio)	15
Optical brightening agent	0.2
Sodium sulphate (can be partially replaced by soda ash)	43.3

Another trend is to use a moderately high-foaming non-ionic such as isotridecyl alcohol with 15 molecules of ethylene oxide, tallow alcohol or alkyl phenol both with 10-12 molecules of' ethylene oxide. All of these detergents foam quite highly, and to depress the foam a nonyl phenol with 1½ molecules of ethylene oxide is used. The addition of this foam-depressor is critical and if proportions different from the optimum are used the foam is likely to be enhanced. The amount suggested is normally 15 per cent of the total active matter, but this figure should be checked against the particular type of active matter with the exact proportions of builders being used.

Sodium perborate can be added in the same manner as in Formula 9, if the powder is spray-dried. If the powder is manufactured by a spray-mixing process which has arrangements for continuous discharge of the powder, the sodium perborate can be fed continously on to the conveyor belt which receives the discharged powder. If not, the perborate can be incorporated batch-wise in a powder mixer.

To incorporate appreciable quantities of non-ionics into spray-dried powders, recourse must be made to the 'Pluronics', some of which are available as flakes, prills or flakeable solids.

A simpler and cheaper 'controlled foam' powder can be made by the use of a mixture of soap and alkyl benzene sulphonic acid. This will give both lower foam and higher detergency than when either is used alone in comparable proportions. It has been found that the foam is at a minimum when the soap proportion of the total active matter is between 30 and 60 per cent. Outside these limits, foam begins to form. If hard water is prevalent in the area, the detergent/soap ratio should be richer in the synthetic portion. If there is predominantly soft water in the area, more soap can be used if required. A word of caution needs to be, given in the use of soap or soap mixtures in automatic washing machines. Some automatic machines have their heating elements protruding directly into the water, while others have the elements protected by a sleeve, which disperses the initial heat over a greater surface area. If the element is itself immersed in the water, it has been found that in areas of moderate to very hard water, a layer of insoluble limesoap can form on the element, decreasing the efficiency of the heat transfer. This can to a certain extent be eliminated by the inclusion of NTA or EDTA in the formula, but this leads to a further complication in that both NTA and EDTA in the presence of oxidising agents (perborate) and corrosive to copper and zinc. Inhibitors have been developed to minimise this corrosion to an acceptable level.

A powder of this type can be made by the absorption and neutralisation process according to Formula 3.

Formula 3

Low- foaming machine powder for soft-water areas

	Mix together with warming to 45°C	
(a)	LAS (100 per cent)	11.6
	Distilled tallow fatty acid	6.4
In the powder mixer, mix together:		
	Sodium tripolyphospbate	15.0
(b)	Soda ash, light	55.0
	CMC (66% basis)	2.0

When uniform, add (a) with mixing. When the LAS/tallow fatty acid mixture has been dispersed, add immediately in order

Sodium hypochlorite	2.0
Sodium silicate 40%	8.0

This is mixed for a few minutes until the reaction is seen to have been completed, and then discharged for ageing. Next day the powder is ground and recharged to the mixer in the following proportions :

Milled powder from Formula 6	90.0
Sodium perborate	10.0
Optical brightening agent	0.15

and mixed until uniform and then sent to packing.

If one of the mixers (described in Chapter 10) is used the ageing and grinding can of course be dispensed with.

To manufacture the same formula using ready-made soap powder the formulation is:

Formula 4

Low-foaming machine powder for soft-water areas using ready-made soap powder

Mix together:	
Sodium tripolyphosphate	15
Soda ash, light	53.7
CMC (66% basis)	2
add in order :	
LAS (100%)	11.4
Sodium hypochlorite	2
Sodium silicate	8
when the reaction is completed add:	
High titre soap powder 82 per cent fatty acids	7.9

Thereafter proceed as in Formula 3.

The same powder can of course be made by spray-drying, but a vastly superior one can be made in a spray-drier according to Formula 5. Modern tendencies are to manufacture 'ternary' powders, that is, powders having the active matter made up of three constituents, soap," an anionic and a low-foaming non-ionic detergent, a formula -for which is given in Formula 6.

Formulae 5-6

Spray-dried household low-foaming laundry powders

	5	6
Sodium dodecylbenzene sulphonate (100% basis)	15	7
Tallow soap, soda based (100% basis)	10	5
Low-foaming non-ionic detergent	-	7
Sodium tripolyphosphate	15	15
Tetrasodium pyrophosphate	10	10
(optional, can be completely replaced by sodium tripolyphosphate)		
Sodium silicate (anhydrous basis, ratio 1:2.5)	7	7
CMC (66% basis)	2.5	2.5
Optical brightening agent	0.2	0.2
Soda ash	0-20	0-20
Sodium sulphate	to make I 00	

Sodium perborate is added at the rate of 10 per cent (or more if desired) after drying.

In place of tallow soap, the soap of behenic acid (a C_{22} saturated acid) is being used. Sodium behenate in the formulation acts mainly as a foam control agent (a very efficient one) and at a maximum concentration of 2 per cent. The synthetic active agents can then be increased to give a more effective wash, even at low temperatures.

Behenic acid has a high melting point (80°C), therefore special precautions need to be applied for its introduction and saponification.

For dry neutralised powders it is best dissolved in the LAS and the liquid non-ionic (if being used) or a solvent with the aid of heat and the mixture is sprayed hot on to the powders.

For spray-drying it can be dissolved in the LAS, and the mixture kept at a higher than normal temperature in the supply tank. The neutralised paste or slurry, which should also be kept at a higher temperature than normal, will probably have a higher viscosity than normal. Contrary to generally accepted principles, lowering the water content of the slurry slightly will, in this case, also decrease the viscosity. As mentioned in Chapter 10, non-ionics can cause trouble on being spray-dried, pluming and also auto-oxidation.

Pluming can be minimised by the use of the narrow range ethoxylates. Auto-oxidation, which at best can discolour the fines and at worst will discolour the powder, can be inhibited according to a Lever patent by the inclusion of about I per cent of charge transfer agent, two examples of which arc stannic chloride or tetrachlorobenzoquinone. The most efficient methods of incorporation are of course the methods already described. These methods also lend themselves to the incorporation of enzymes, perborate, etc.

Even in areas where there are no restrictions (total or partial) on the use of phosphates, consideration should be given to the use of zeolites, either the zeolite itself or the zeolite/silicate blend. This will have the added advantage, particularly in dry mixed or agglomerated powders, of surface adsorption. The zeolite can adsorb on its surface larger amounts of liquid surfactants than the normal builders are able to, thus drier, more free-flowing powders with higher active matter can be produced.

Where there are bans or restrictions on the use of phosphate, the STP suggested in the formulations can be replaced by mixtures of zeolites on the one hand and NTA or one of the polycarboxylic acids.

Enzymatic laundry powders for automatic washing machines are now being produced in large quantities. It is difficult to give directions as to the amount of enzyme concentrate to add to powder as the concentration of the ,net' enzyme varies from manufacturer to manufacturer, but they give explicit instructions as to usage. Enzymes for washing machine powders are commonly used together with perborate. The enzyme operates while the, temperature of the water is low and it is rapidly inactivated when the temperature reaches 60^{0}C, perborate taking over. Although the manufacturers state that the enzymes are stable to perborate, this stability is only relative and if both enzymes and perborate are included in a powder, it is advisable to increase the enzyme concentration over that normally recommended. Formula 6 with little or no soda ash can serve as a useful base for enzymatic powders.

In all of the above and subsequent formulae which are to be spray-dried,. consideration should be given to the addition of 3-5 per cent of sodium toluene sulphonate. This does not serve the purpose that it does in a liquid detergent. In this instance the function of the toluene sulphonate is twofold: it lowers the viscosity of the slurry, allowing a higher solids content, and also promotes the free-flowing characteristics of the finished powder, particularly when linear alkyl benzene sulphonate is used. Also when powders are made by processes other than spray-drying, the inclusion of toluene sulphonate is essential if linear alkyl-benzene sulphonate is being used.

Heavy-duty liquid detergents are now making headway for household laundering. The problem here is that the solution for efficient laundering needs a certain amount of alkali, sequestering agent and soil-suspending agent. To incorporate sufficient of these with a detergent into a solution which will stay bright and clear is not easy. As a result, new materials are coming on the market specially for this purpose and new techniques are being employed. Many patents for heavy-duty liquids are daily appearing in the literature and as a result the trend is to move away from conventional materials.

The active ingredient can be chosen from one or more of the alkyl benzene sulphonates, olefin sulphonates, paraffin sulphonates or ethylene oxide condensates. For reasons given below the anionic should preferably not be neutralised with a sodium ion, rather potassium or an ethanolamine. This condition cannot always be observed, particularly if paraffin or olefin sulphonates are bought as the already hydrolysed/neutralised solution.

The linear alkyl benzene sulphonates show better solubility in water than do the branched. For the production of liquids the choice should be in the lower register of molecular weight (C_{10-12} rather than C_{11-13}). Again the high 2-phenyl fraction is more suitable for the production of liquids for reasons of solubility. True the detergency is somewhat lower than for the low 2-phenyl isomers, but the production of liquid detergents does require some compromises and the detergency can be enhanced in different Ways.

On this score it should be pointed out that, contrary to expectation, the potassium salt of LAS is not more soluble than the sodium salt; it is less soluble. However, the potassium salts are used on occasion because the inorganic constituents are often potassium salts and to introduce a sodium salt would result in precipitation of the sodium salt of the inorganic compound by double decomposition. This also works the other way in that the potassium ion of the salt could precipitate the LAS. More often than not, however, the LAS is neutralised with an ethanolamine to obviate this problem.

The problem in heavy-duty liquid detergents (HDLD) formulations is-in incorporating the builders into the solution in such a way that the liquid has enough of all the necessary ingredients for efficient washing without detracting from the appearance of the product.

The builders in question are sequestering agents, which are usually phosphates; alkalis, which are invariably silicates; anti-soil redeposition agents (CMC) and optical brighteners.

Spray-dried heavy-duty powders invariably contain sodium tripolyphosphate as the sequestering agent, sometimes with the addition of other sequestering agents. Polyphosphates hydrolyse rapidly in neutral or acid solutions., first to a mixture of ortho- and pyrophosphates, and the pyrophosphates in turn hydrolyse further, albeit at a slower rate, to the simple phosphates. If the pH of the solution is 9 or higher, the hydrolysis of polyphosphates is slow so much so that a solution containing polyphosphate at this pH can be stored for a year at 25°C with no appreciable hydrolysis having taken place.

The solubility of sodium tripolyphosphate in pure water is 15 per cent at room temperature, but this figure will be considerably lower in the presence of other dissolved materials, particularly anionic, due to the common ion effect. The solubility of tetrapotassium pyrophosphate in water is over 60 per cent whereas the corresponding sodium salt is only soluble to the extent of 5 per cent. It is for this reason that tetrapotassium pyrophosphate is often used as a constituent of liquid detergents, however sodium salts need to be excluded almost completely because, due to the common ion effect, tetrasodium pyrophosphate can be precipitated from a solution containing both sodium and potassium ions. Again the use of pyrophosphate is a compromise as it does not have the sequestering and peptizing properties found in the polyphosphates.

Potassium tripolyphosphate, with a solubility in water of 55 per cent, has appeared on the market and this does not suffer from the same defect in that its sodium salt might precipitate due to the increased solubility of its sodium analogue.

Alternatively, phosphates are completely dispensed with and the organic sequestering agents, such as sodium (or potassium) ethylene diamine tetraacetate, or nitrilo triacetate are employed.

The alkali required is obtained from the colloidal silicates. Potassium silicate has been found to be superior to sodium silicate in this respect and silicates act as corrosion inhibitors against the action of phosphates on stainless steels.

However, to get sufficient of all three of the above ingredients into solution is virtually impossible, as the presence of one affects the solubility of the others. For this reason it is necessary to use a hydrotope, i.e., a solvent aid, a product which is itself soluble in the medium and aids in the solution of other products. There are a variety of these, but the most commonly used are potassium (or sodium) xylene, toluene, cumene or ethyl benzene sulphonates. These have to be used in relatively large quantities, of the order of 5-10 per cent of the finished product. They can either be sulphonated (or bought) as such, or else co-sulphated in the correct proportion with the original sulphonate, if the basic detergent is one of the sulphonate types.

Urea, apart from its other uses in the detergent industry, is an efficient hydrotrope, as efficient as the lower alkyl sulphonates. However, it suffers from one disadvantage. If one considers its method of manufacture, the combination of carbon dioxide with ammonia :

$$CO_2 + 2NH_3 \longrightarrow NH_4CONH_2$$

Ammonium carbamate

$$NH_4CO_2NH_2 \longrightarrow NH_2CONH_2 + H_2O$$

Urea

it is conceivable that industrial urea can contain small proportions of unreacted ammonium carbamate. In water solution this can hydrolyse:

$$NH_4CO_2NH_2 + H_2O \longrightarrow (NH_4)_2CO_3$$

to ammonium carbonate. If the solution is alkaline, which it almost invariably is, a smell of ammonia will become apparent, which might be objectionable to some people. Thus if urea is to be considered as the hydrotrope, the purchase specification should stipulate no ammonium carbamate to be present.

Recently potassium salts of lower molecular weight phosphate esters have been developed, specifically as hydrotropes for the production of liquid detergents based on alkyl phenol ethoxylates in admixture with potassium tripolyphosphate. These phosphate esters have a further advantage in that they have detergent or wetting properties in their own right, thus aiding in the washing process, a property which none of the other hydrotropes can claim.

CMC now has to be brought into this solution. It is best incorporated by making a 10 per cent 'solution' separately, when it swells and forms a gel. This swelling and gelling, however, is influenced by ions already in solution and, if present, the CMC in a very short time precipitates out and sinks to the bottom. This problem can be overcome in three ways. One method is to adjust the density of the solution so that it is the same as the density of the precipitated CMC (± 1.37) and the precipitate will therefore not settle. This is achieved by the addition of sodium sulphate or chloride. In another method carboxymethyl cellulose and methyl cellulose are used. Both cellulose compounds tend to precipitate from the solution. By itself, the methyl cellulose would normally rise to the top and the CMC by itself would normally sink to the bottom. By using this pair in equimolar proportions, however, they precipitate, but neither rise nor fall.

With the incorporation of CMC as outlined above, one tends to get an opaque type of suspension. It is felt that once the solution tends to be thick and opaque, it should be made to look like a lotion, and the incorporation of sodium nitrate is said to give a better appearance and easier density control.

If it is decided to dispense with phosphates, one of the organic chelating acids neutralised preferably in this case by monoethanolamine, can be used. Alkalinity can also be obtained by excess monoethanolamine.

In the manufacture of these liquids, very often a sludge of insoluble material settles out. This has been identified as traces of iron contamination in the ingredients or even the water. The addition of l per cent triethanolamine, over and above any base needed for neutralisation will eliminate this sediment.

Finally, it is desirable to incorporate an optical brightener in the solution. This is the least of the producer's problems, as optical brighteners are now available which are stable in water solution. The amount is so small that this has no effect on the solubility of the other materials, nor have they any bearing on the solubility of the dye.

Thus, to summarise, the following formulae could be used as heavy-duty liquid detergents.

Formulae 7, 8, 9, 10

Heavy-duty liquid detergents

	7	8	9	10
Alkyl aryl sulphonic acid (ABS)	10	20	9	12
Diethanolamine	3.6	7.2	3.3	4
Non-ionic (100%)	2	-	3	-
PVP (100%)	0.7	—	-	0.7
$K_4P_2O_7$ (100%)	12	12	10	-
Potassium silicate (100%)	4	3	4	—
Monoethanolamine	-	-	-	3
EDTA			-	5
CMC (100%)		1	1	-
Potassium xylene sulphonate or other hydrotope	5	5	4	4
Optical brightening agent	0.1	0.1	0.1	0.1
Water to	100	100	100	100

All the above formulae are of the medium- to high-foaming type and thus unsuitable for fully automatic washing machines.

A formulation for a heavy-duty liquid detergent with a 'controlled foam' using the normal type of CMC is given in Formula 11

Formula 11

Heavy-duty liquid detergent with 'controlled foam'

Disperse with gentle mixing:	
CMC (66% basis)	2
in water	18
Into a stainless-steel vessel equipped with a slow-speed stirrer charge:	
Distilled coconut oil fatty acid	8
Water	25
Caustic potash (40% solution)	5
Stir and warm gently until the solution attains a clear and homogeneous appearance, then add with stirring in order:	
Non-ionic detergent	4

Cont ....

Monoethanolamine	1.7
LAS	4
NTA or EDTA (acid form)	1
Hydrotrope	8'
Tetrapotassium pyrophosphate or Potassium tripolyphosphate	10
Potassium silicate (40% solution, 1:2.5 mol ratio)	10
Optical brightening agent	0.2

The CMC gel prepared above is now added, mixing continued, and water added to make this solution upto 100.

This will produce a lotion type of liquid. It is not necessary to 'saponify' by boiling, because if all the above directions are adhered to, the coconut fatty acid will be completely neutralised and no free unsaponified oil will be present.

PVP is being used with success in place of the CMC. The PVP is added as a 5 per cent pre-prepared solution, and the water adjusted accordingly. This will produce a clear solution, possibly with a slight haze due to insoluble matter sometimes found in poly- or pyrophosphates.

As mentioned on trace quantities of iron contamination in the raw materials can cause a sludge of ferric hydroxide to separate. This separation is not always immediately visible and an insurance against this is the addition of I per cent triethanolamine to chelate the ferric ions. The iron will still be present in the solution, but inactivated.

Gantrez resins as chelating agents are high-molecular-weight polymers with anhydride rings, which on hydrolysis with water form dibasic acids. Thus for a typical molecular weight of 40,000, the hydrolysed resin can have 250 dibasic acid groups per molecule. These need to be neutralised and in fact the maximum chelating action is attained at a pH of 10 minimum. These acid groups can also be esterified and in our particular field the esterification agent they suggest is a non-ionic detergent, which normally has a terminal—OH group available for reaction with a carboxylic acid. If the major portion of the carboxylic groups is esterified, an insoluble mass is obtained, but if a partial ester is formed (I per cent non-ionic based on the weight of the resin), this serves as a stabilizing agent for non-ionic liquids.

The non-ionic of choice is an alkyl phenol with 15 ethylene oxide units and the procedure is important. A stock solution of the resin is made (medium viscosity). Dissolve in water

Non-ionic	10
Water	890

and raise the temperature to 90ºC. Add slowly with stirring

Resin	100

keeping the temperature at 90ºC, and continue stirring till a clear solution is obtained. (Caution, a large amount of foam might be formed in this esterification.)

A formulation can give excellent results as a heavy duty liquid is

Formulation 12

Water	4.0
Gentrez stock solution	10.0
NaOH (45% solution)	2.0
CMC	0.5
Nonyl phenol 9-ethoxylate	3.5
NaOH (45% solution)	29.0
Potassium silicate (1:3 mol ratio, 36%)	51.0
Optical brightener, dye, perfume	qs

The solution is made at 60ºC, every ingredient to be dissolved completely before the next one is added.

The first addition of caustic soda is to neutralise the Gantrez resin. The second is to convert the silicate to metasilicate. We have found that a mixture of potassium/sodium metasilicate gives better freeze-thaw characteristics than pure sodium metasilicate as recommended by GAF. This can also be reversed, to use potassium hydroxide and sodium silicate to achieve the same purpose.

An interesting and new development in the liquid heavy-duty household laundering field is a liquid containing a mixture of active chlorine and anionic detergent. It had been generally considered that chlorine (derived from sodium hypochlorite) could not be stable in the presence of considerable amounts of organic matter. However, sodium toluene or xylene sulphonates seem to stabilise sodium hypochlorite, and mixtures of sodium hypochlorite with sodium ether sulphates can now be produced with the chlorine reasonably stable for over three months.

Formula 13

Heavy-duty liquid detergent and bleach	
Sodium lauryl ether sulphate (60% concentration)	20
Sodium toluene sulphonate	5
Sodium hypochlorite solution (10% available chlorine)	75

Even better results have been obtained in using one of the range of alkylated diphenyloxide disulphonates of the generic formula

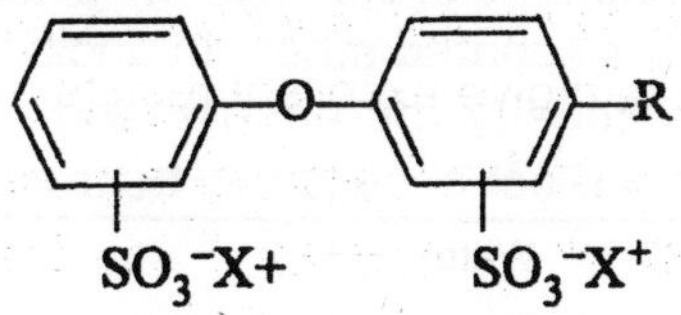

'X' is the sodium ion. This novel surface active material is stable in moderately strong alkali and acid solutions, in the presence of large amounts of inorganic materials and in solutions of oxidising agents.

The high stability of hypochlorite in admixture with di-sulpho-diphenyl type of detergent is due to the inertia against chlorination of the multi-substituted benzene ring, one of the rings being tri-substituted, the other disubstituted.

To achieve maximum stability, it is suggested that the diluted alkylated diphenyloxide disulphonates be heated to 70°C together with 2 per cent of a 12 per cent active chlorine hypochlorite solution, then cooled to 30°C and 20 per cent of a 12 per cent active chlorine hypochlorite solution added. This will give a 2.5 per cent active chlorine solution stable for a reasonable period, when packed in a plastic bottle. For a 6 per cent active detergent solution the formulation could be

Soft water	65.4
Alkylated diphenyloxide disulphonate	13.0
Sodium hypochlorite, 12% active heat to 70°C, then cool to 30°C	1.6
Add sodium hypochlorite, 12% active	20.0

Free alkalinity should then be adjusted by the addition of caustic soda solution to 0.5-1.0 per cent. This free alkalinity, in addition to stabilising the hypochlorite, reacts with the water hardness lowering the pH for maximum disinfecting and bleaching action of the active chlorine.

Light-duty Household Products

In the field of light-duty detergents, or (as it is sometimes called) fine wash, are the materials for washing delicate fabrics such as wool, nylon, silk, etc. Also, in general, this type of detergent is suitable for household dishwashing by hand as well.

Synthetic detergents first took a hold in the household for this purpose, and liquids consisting only of detergents diluted with water very quickly achieved a large sale and large quantities are still being sold. Now-a-days, liquid detergents are more sophisticated than the plain solutions that were originally sold. They can be based on anionic detergents only, usually dodecyl or tridecyl benzene sulphonate, or can utilize a mixture of the above anionics with a non-ionic, or a sulphated ether. In addition to foam boosters, these liquids can have viscosity increasers and cloud-point depressants. Furthermore, they need not necessarily be transparent liquids, but can be opaque lotions.

The concentration of active matter present in a liquid detergent of this type varies from country to country, but an average figure is 12 per cent for the simpler liquids, but this can go upto 40 per cent for the more sophisticated market.

The cloud point of a detergent is an important factor in its sales appeal, as it is axiomatic that no housewife will buy a liquid which tends to deposit a precipitate or to cloud over on storage. Requirements for the actual cloud point will vary from place to place and no hard-and-fast rules can be given. The cloud point naturally obtained from a particular concentration of active matter depends on the type of material used and the method of neutralisation.

In. general, the sodium salt of the alkyl benzene sulphonic acids, at a concentration of 12 per cent active matter, gives a cloud point too high for commercial use. The diethanolamine and triethanolamine salts of the alkyl benzene sulphonic acids give a very low cloud point, lower than is needed generally. -Thus for economic reasons, neutralisation is usually done partially with caustic soda and partially with an ethanolamine.

Among the alkyl benzene sulphonates, all other things being equal, the cloud point of the neutralised solution rises in the following order

(i) Linear dodecyl benzene sulphonate.

(ii) Linear tridecyl benzene sulphonate.

(iii) Branched dodecyl benzene sulphonate.

(iv) Branched tridecyl benzene sulphonate.

The viscosity of the final solution, all other things being again equal, rises in the same order.

In addition to the above factors, the method of sulphonation is important, since on this method depends the amount of free sulphuric acid present. When neutralised, the acid produces inorganic sulphates, both of which raise the cloud point and the viscosity. SO_3 sulphonated material will give the lowest free sulphuric acid present; and normal oleum sulphonation will produce the highest. (The figure is normally as high as 7-8 per cent).

The factors involved in producing an, acceptable liquid detergent are therefore dependent on:

(i) The type of alkyl benzene sulphonate.

(ii) The method of manufacture of this sulphonate.

(iii) Whether any other active material is used.

To take an average case, if conventional dodecyl benzene, sulphonated with SO_3, is to be used as the base material for the manufacture of a 12 per cent liquid, a cloud point of below 5°C can be obtained by neutralising half of the active matter with caustic soda and the other half with diethanolamine or triethanolamine. From Table 10.4, Chapter 3, it will be seen that neutralisation with diethanolamine will give a slightly higher viscosity than if neutralisation had been done with triethanolamine. Diethanolamine is a solid, except in very hot climates, and therefore is more difficult to handle. On the other hand, when alkyl benzene sulphonates are wholly or partially neutralised with triethanolamine, which is a liquid, a buffer is formed at a pH of approximately 6. To pass this buffer, it is necessary to use a large excess of base. To preserve a low cloud point, it is not advisable to use too much caustic soda to overcome this buffer, so a fair excess of triethanolamine must therefore be used. The manufacturer must consequently consider the disadvantages involved in handling diethanolamine against the extra cost of triethanolamine.

If in the examples of alkyl benzene sulphonates given above, one of the sulphonates which normally gives a low cloud point were to be used to maintain the same cloud point level, the proportion of caustic soda can be raised and that of the ethanolamine correspondingly reduced.

Furthermore, if an acid sulphonated material is used as the base material, the proportion of ethanolamine needs to be raised considerably (and the caustic soda to be lowered) to maintain the low cloud point.

If it is required to raise the viscosity of the solution, a simple but limited method is the addition of an inorganic salt, like sodium sulphate or sodium chloride. This is limited in that it raises the cloud point. A better and more efficient method of increasing the viscosity is the use of an alkylolamide, preferably a diethanolamide.

Because of the various factors involved in the formulation of a liquid, it is not possible to describe formulations for all possible permutations and combinations.

Formula 14 gives a basic formula to be used as a starting-point. The manufacturer is advised to modify this according to the conditions he requires and the materials available to him.

Formula 14

Light-duty household liquid detergent	
LAS (SO_3 sulphonate)	10
Triethanolamine	2
Caustic soda (45% solution)	1.7
Sodium hypochlorite (10% solution)	0.6
Lauric acid diethanolamide	1
Sodium sulphate	1
Water	83.7

Full and detailed instructions on the method of production of this solution are given in Chapter 3.

An opaque lotion type of liquid can be made (taking into account the same factors as mentioned above) from Formula 15.

Formula 15

Lotion-type light-duty liquid detergent	
LAS	19.5
Monoethanolamine	4
Lauric acid monoethanolamide	1.5
Sodium hypochlorite (10% solution)	0.6
Sodium sulphate	0.9
Water	73.5

In this case the dodecyl benzene sulphonic acid, the sodium sulphate and the water are mixed in the neutralisation vessel, the sodium hypochlorite added and mixing continued for at least 20 min. The lauric acid monoethanolamide, being solid, is best dissolved in the monoethanolamine with heating. The mixture of the two is then added to the vessel, after the bleaching has if necessary been completed. If an opaque solution is required an opacifier can be added. The product can now be dyed and perfumed.

To manufacture a liquid from an alkyl benzene sulphonate neutralised only with caustic soda (in practice, a concentrated paste of the sodium sulphonate is used as the starting material), a low cloud point can be achieved by the addition of urea. With the sodium sulphonate, however, urea lowers the viscosity considerably. Addition of a fatty acid dialkylolamide will restore the viscosity.

Modem tendencies are to use both stronger solutions and mixtures of active matter. One of the main uses for light-duty liquid detergents is hand dishwashing, and for this particular application foam is important other than from the point of view of sales appeal. Grease released from the dishes floats to the top of the washing solution and forms an oily film which can be redeposited on the plate when it is withdrawn from the sink after having been washed. Due to the enormous surface area in a foam, this grease is held in a thin, easily rinsable film on the bubbles, preventing redeposition. When the foam collapses due to saturation with oil, the solution is considered to be exhausted and methods of test for the efficiency of dishwashing liquids are based on this foam collapse.

Ether sulphates, both of the alcohol and alkyl phenol types are finding more and more use as constituents of dishwashing liquids. If the ammonium salt of the alkyl phenol type is used care must be taken not to raise the pH of the final liquid over 8 or otherwise a smell of ammonia will appear. If a high pH is desired without the ammonia smell, the ammonium ether sulphates can be heated with a stoichiometric amount of caustic soda until the ammonia is distilled off. Alternatively an 'ammoniated' cleaner, which has some sales appeal, can be made at the high pH.

The choice of the type of ether sulphate is rather wide, as the base material can be any one of the alcohols available on the market or any of the alkyl phenols and then again the amount of ethylene oxide can be varied from between 1.7-4 molecules per molecule. Recently viscosity and foam height with different alcohols and different degrees of ethoxylation has been investigated and it is found that the best foamers are a C_{12-14} alcohol with 2 molecules of ethylene oxide. Another important fact in the make-up of the ether sulphate is the amount of polyethylene glycol present. It has also been found that relatively large (of the order of 3 per cent) amounts of polyethylene glycol can act as a solvent or 'thinner' on the final sulphate to reduce the viscosity of the solution.

As the wetting properties of ether sulphates are low they are not recommended as dishwashing agents alone, rather in conjunction with nonionic or other anionic detergents.

Alcohol sulphates, neutralised with ethanolamines can, of course, be used alone, or with an alkylolamide as a foam booster. It is interesting to note that alkylolamides have no effect on the foaming properties of ether sulphates. Some typical basic formulations are given in formulae 16-20.

Formulae 16-20

Light-duty liquid detergents

	16	17	18	19	20
LAS (SO3 sulphonated)	I 0	15	20	12	-
Caustic soda (40% solution)	3.2	3.2	3.2	3.2	-
Triethanolamine	-	2.2	4.4	9	-
Sodium alcohol ether sulphate (100% basis)	-	3	3	-	-
Ethanolamine alcohol sulphate (100% basis)	-	-	-	-	24
Coconut diethanolamide*	2	1	1	-	2
Sodium sulphate or chloride	qs	qs	qs	qs	qs
Dye, perfume	qs	qs	qs	qs	qs
Water	to make 100				

* The ethanolamide might contain some free ethanolamine, in which case this can be used as a partial neutralising agent for The LAS, reducing the amount of NaOH or triethanolamine.

It will be observed that the first and fourth formulations are relatively cheap, the others more sophisticated.

SO_3 sulphonated LAS can be considered the work-horse of liquid detergent formulations. It is good practice, when mixtures of LAS with alcohol or ether sulphates are used, to ensure that the LAS is neutralised completely before the sulphate is introduced into the reactor. This will eliminate hydrolysis of the acid -unstable sulphates. To facilitate formulation the following data show the alkali requirement of a typical LAS.

100 kg LAS requires for complete neutralisation

12.8 kg NaOH (100%)

18.8 kg KOH (100%)

45.5 kg triethanolamine

33.6 kg diethanolamine

19.7 kg monoethanolamine.

The inorganic salts are included only if it is desired to increase the viscosity. The diethanolamide acts as a viscosity booster but particularly where the ether sulphates are included coconut monoethanolamide will be more effective. To incorporate the monoethanolamide, the solution is merely warmed to 60°C with mixing, when all the monoethanolamide will melt and dissolve and will not be thrown out of solution on cooling.

Household fine-wash detergents are, of course, not limited to liquids. They can be made as spray-dried powders, sometimes only with 20-30 per cent active matter and the balance sodium sulphate as the inert filler, but more often than not they include sodium tripolyphosphate, some silicate, occasionally CMC, and an optical brightening agent, substantive to the fibres for which the powder is being used. The phosphate, of course, helps in the detergency, and the silicate acts in this case as a corrosion inhibitor. Here, the action of the CMC is not as pronounced as it is on cottons, but on woollen fabrics it does aid in preventing redeposition, and as these powders are meant for hand-washing, it does tend to give a protective colloidal action on the skin.

A powder of this type can be manufactured as detailed in Formula 21.

Formula 21

Household fine-wash spray-dried powder

	Minimum	Maximum
Sodium alkyl benzene sulphonate	10	25
Sodium tripolyphosphate	15	25
Sodium silicate (preferably 1:3 ratio) anhydrous	3	5
CMC (100%)	0	1
Lauric acid monoethanolamide	0	2.5
Optical brightening agent	0.2	0.2
Sodium sulphate	Balance	

By virtue of the nature of manufacture, fine-wash powders of this type cannot be made by the absorption methods, as the surplus of soda ash will prove detrimental to the operation of the powder. However, a dry-mixed type of powder can easily be made to Formula 21, using as a base a concentrated powder of about 60 per cent active matter.

In certain parts of the world, neutral pastes of sodium alkyl benzene sulphonate are sold also for fine-wash purposes. These pastes vary in concentration between 20 per cent and 50 per cent active matter. The consistency of the paste varies with the ingredients and the method of manufacture of the alkyl benzene sulphonic acid. Stiffer pastes are obtained with tridecyl benzene sulphonic acid, sulphonated with oleum; and the softest paste is linear dodecyl benzene sulphonic acid, sulphonated with SO_3 gas.

The alkyl benzene sulphonates have limited solubility in water. They, however, can absorb water to form a natural paste. If the amount of water present in above that which can naturally be absorbed, the mass will separate into two phases on standing: a concentrated phase of alkyl benzene sulphonate on top and a weak solution of alkyl benzene sulphonate and inorganic salts at the bottom. The concentration of the sodium alkyl benzene sulphonate in the upper phase varies with the material, but is of the order of

55 per cent active matter, This means that pastes of 55 per cent can be manufactured with no special additions. If lower concentrations are required, it is necessary to add certain ingredients to prevent this separation. Materials that can be used are: hydrotropes, which will make the final paste thinner in consistency, so that stiffening materials have again to be added; alkylolamides, which have the added advantages of foam boosting and skin protection (these pastes are to be used by hand); and CMC. Both the CMC and the alkylolamides tend to increase the viscosity of the mass in such a way that separation cannot take place.

If only CMC is used as the thickening agent, a general rule is to manufacture the paste to a 55 per cent concentration and then to add sufficient of a 10 per cent CMC solution in water to bring the concentration down to the required amount. Sodium sulphate is then added to increase the consistency.

A 40 per cent active paste, using both conventional dodecyl benzene and linear dodecyl benzene sulphonic acids, both sulphonated by SO_3 gas, is given in Formula. 22.

Formula 22

40 per cent detergent paste

ABS (100%)	40
Caustic soda (45% solution)	11.4
Sodium sulphate	2
Sodium hypochlorite solution	0.6
Water	29.3
{ CMC	1.7 }
{ Water	15 }

This paste may be reduced to 30 per cent by increasing CMC to 2.5 or 3.5 per cent and adding water.

General Purpose Detergents

Powders of this type are the most popular for household use. They are not harshly alkaline, and contain relatively large quantities of both active matter and' sodium tripolyphosphate. These achieve the action on cottons without the addition of further alkalis, and the alkalinity naturally present from the phosphate does not harm delicate fabrics.

By virtue of their formulation these powders are truly general-purpose and can be used for virtually every household job. They suffer from the disadvantage, however, of being unsuitable for fully automatic household washing machines, as, in general, they foam too much.

A generally accepted formula for this type of powder to be manufactured by a spray-drier is given in Formula 23.

Formula 23

Spray-dried general-purpose powder

Active matter as alkyl benzene sulphonic acid neutralised with caustic soda	25
Sodium toluene sulphonate*	2.5
Lauric monoethanolamide	3
Sodium tripolyphosphate	30
Sodium silicate (1:2 ratio) anhydrous	10
CMC (100% basis)	2
Optical brightening agent	0.2
Sodium sulphate	27.3

If sodium perborate is to be added, we suggest that 2 per cent of the sodium sulphate be replaced by magnesium sulphate on any anhydrous basis. This magnesium sulphate is added to the slurry prior to spray-drying.

A general-purpose powder can be made by the absorption and mixing process as well, but in this case, due to the limitations of the process, the active matter is limited. The formulation suggested is given in Formula 24.

Formula 24

General-purpose powder

Dodecyl benzene sulphonic acid	18
Sodium tripolyphosphate	25
Sodium silicate (1:2 ratio) 40% solution	5
CMC (100% basis)	5
Sodium bicarbonate	28
Soda ash	20
Optical brightening agent	0.15
Water (or sodium hypochlorite solution)	2

As in Formula 24, the same remarks apply regarding the addition of sodium perborate. If this is to be introduced, it is suggested that the sodium bicarbonate be lowered to 25 per cent and 3 per cent magnesium sulphate crystals added. If sodium hypochlorite is used to bleach the powder and if sodium perborate is to be incorporated.

A general-purpose powder can be manufactured by dry-mixing according to Formula 25.

Formula 25

General-purpose powder

60% alkyl benzene sulphonate powder containing silicate	45
Sodium tripolyphosphate	30
CMC (100% basis)	2
Optical brightening agent	0.2
Sodium sulphate	22.8

Here, if sodium perborate is to be used, no special precautions need to be taken and it can, of course, be added initially with all the other ingredients.

In all the formulations given hitherto, we have included relatively large amounts of sodium tripolyphosphate, this despite the fact that in certain countries there is a complete or partial ban on the use of phosphates. To date no 'plug-in' replacement for this excellent builder has been developed.

Where this is a partial ban, the above formulations to include STP up to the limit allowed and to add a zeolite to make up the difference is suggested. Where there is a total ban, the available alternatives must be considered; increasing the silicate, use of NTA, use of zeolite (the zeolite/silicate cocrystal mentioned might be eminently suitable), or one of the polymers specially mooted for this purpose. The final formulation will probably be a combination of any two or more of the above.

For fully automatic, front-loading household washing machines, foam control needs to be applied. This can be by the use of soap as for heavy duty powders, but infinitely better performance will be attained if the ternary mixture of the anionic/non-ionic/soap is used. With the new processes and mixing equipment for the inclusion of non.-ionics into powders, there need be no practical limits to the formulation.

Choice of Non-ionic

As can be appreciated from the descriptions of the possible non-ionic surfactants, the choice is wide and often confusing. Much work has been done on the optimisation of the molecule. It is true that the results cannot be compared directly because of the different substrates, but the results are revealing.

The results can be summarised :

1. From the work on hard-surface cleaning it appears that linear alcohols with a low molecular weight and containing 50 per cent ethylene oxide (average chain length 8.6 carbons with 3.1 moles EO) in a relatively

high concentration (5 per cent), are better in cleaning efficiency for grease, wax and particulate soil than the molecules containing C_{10} and higher chain lengths with the appropriate amount of ethylene oxide to maintain the balance.

This can be explained by the fact that the low-molecular-weight hydrophobe acts as a solvent and this was confirmed by adding a glycol ether when no improvement of soil removal was noted.

2. For low dilutions of the surfactant the optimum chain length was shifted to the C_{8-10} range. Under these conditions of dilution the hydrophobe can no longer act as a solvent and performance was dependent solely on the surface active effect.

3. Comparison of the low carbon number ethoxylated alcohols with a built formulation containing nonyl phenol with 9½ EO units again showed a better performance for the low-molecular-weight alcohol ethoxylates.

4. By comparing the performance of a linear primary alcohol ethoxylate, a linear secondary alcohol ethoxylate, both of approximately C_{13} average chain lengths, and a branched octyl phenol ethoxylate, each with varying amounts of ethylane oxide and for both cotton and cotton/polyester blends.

5. The results show that 7-9 EO units on each give optimum performance for sebum, oil and clay removal on the blend but for sebum removal from pure cotton 12-15 EO was superior.

Recent investigations confirms the above in that and thus short-chain non-ionics are better in removing water repellent soils.

The above facts and figures do not take into account the added complications of the presence of anionic detergents and builders but they do indicate a trend.

From the above it appears that any of the commercially available nonionic types with approximately 8 EO units will give good all round performance. For powders, for technological considerations, the choice of non-ionic has been in a somewhat higher register hitherto.

With the development of systems for incorporation of non-ionics into powders without spray-drying the problems associated with making powders using these (relatively) low-molecular-weight materials no longer apply.

The use of this type of non-ionic in liquids will tend to give a low cloud point but this can be overcome by the judicious use of co-solvents and hydrotropes.

The term cloud point can be somewhat confusing. Normally it is the temperature at which a cloud forms on cooling. This demonstrates the lowest temperature at which a liquid can be stored and still remain clear. When applied to non-ionic solutions it indicates the temperature at which the -solution becomes cloudy on heating, at this temperature the solution separates into two phases, one of which will be richer in non-ionic than the other.

Concentrated Powders

A new approach to the manufacture of powders is what is called the ½ or ¼ cup concentrates, where a minimum of inert filler, if any at all, is used. A patent by Colgate describes the technology for the production of these powders.

In brief the process is to mix STP with water and sodium silicate in a crutcher to allow the STP to hydrate to its hexahydrate, then to add a further quantity of STP and water under conditions that this second addition does not hydrate and to spray-dry the mix. To the spray-dried beads nonionic detergent is added in a special mixer.

The details are :

Mix together	
STP	14.5
Sodium silicate (1:2.4 ratio, 50% solution)	15.2
Deionized water	21.0
Maintain this slurry at 60°C for hydration and then raise the temperature to approximately 90°C, add	
STP	28.3
Deionized water	21.0

At this higher temperature no hydration takes place. This slurry is then spray-dried to a bead containing 10% moisture, with a bulk density of ±0.55 g/ml.

The finished beads are then sprayed, either continuously or batch-wise with a non-ionic, of the alcohol ethoxylate type mixed with minor ingredients; optical brighteners, dye, perfume, etc. The finished powder has a bulk density of 0.68 g/ml and contains :

Base bead	78.0
Non-ionic	19.7
Minor ingredients	2.3

The granules are attractive and dustless and a further claim by the patentors is that they are sufficiently pourable to be packed in a transparent specially designed bottle.

Further embodiments of the patent include adding fillers other than STP to the hydrated STP. No mention of the inclusion of CMC is made but it is envisaged that it could quite easily be added to the slurry prior to spray-drying.

Cold Water Washing

Generally all washing is done at the boil or near it. With the advent of synthetic fibres wash temperatures came down drastically and now in an attempt at energy conservation householders are beginning to use cold water only, for washing of clothes.

The industry is facing and meeting the challenge, and a challenge it is because the highly complicated washing process requires, among other things, energy to break the bond of the dirt to the substrate. This energy can come from lowering of the interfacial tension, the mechanical energy imparted by the motor of the machine and from heat.

For cold washing the thermal energy needs to be replaced, and one method is by increasing the amount of active matter in solution and using more non-ionics which are better for soil removal from synthetics. On studying the parameters involved in cold washing with non-ionics. The conclusions can be summarised as under :

1. Non-polar soils are difficult to remove from polyester/cotton fabrics at low temperatures, thus the inherent detergency needs to be enhanced.

2. Optimum detergency for this system is found with non-ionic mixtures which have cloud points in the range of 15-25°C below the wash temperature.

   This is explained by the fact that a surfactant-rich pseudo-phase separates at temperatures above the cloud point. This can be considered to be globules of concentrated surfactant which are attracted to the soil.

3. Low cloud points were obtained by blending lightly ethoxylated alcohol or unethoxylated alcohol with a normal detergent non-ionic.

A blend of 3 mol ethoxylated alcohol with an 8 mol non-ionic to gives a cloud point close to O°C enhanced the mineral oil detergency of the 8 mol alcohol ethoxylate by 50 per cent and a blend of a 9 mol non-ionic with decanol, again to give a cloud point close to zero enhanced the detergency of the alcohol-9 ethoxylate by 20 per cent.

As can be seen from the foregoing, possibilities of formulating are varied and later in this chapter we also discuss solvent powder detergents. The actual formulations to be used depend on many factors, mainly the materials easily available and the trends in the area where the powder is to be sold. The above statement also holds good for liquids.

To sum up we give in Tables 11.1 and 11.2 formulations which can be used as starting points for the manufacture of both dry-mixed and spray-dried powders. These formulations do not necessarily parallel those already described in the text, but do give an indication of what is being made.

Table 11.1. Typical formulations for powders produced by dry neutralisation.

	All purpose non-machine	All purpose machine	Light-duty hand	Heavy-duty non-machine	Heavy-duty machine	Solvent powder
LAS	14-15	5	15	12-15	5	5
Dist. fatty acids	-	4	-	-	4	3
Non-ionic	2-3	67	2	-	4	3
STP	30	30	20	15	20	20
Metasilicate ($5H_2O$) or spray-dried disilicate	3	3	-	5-6	5-6	5
Soda ash	15-20	15-20	20 max	to 100	to 100	to 100
Sodium bicarbonate	-	-	30	-	-	-
Sodium sulphate	to 100	to I 00	to 100	-	-	-
cmc	2	2	-	1.5	1.5	1.5
Optical brightener	0.2	0.2	0.2	0.2	0.2	0.2
Perborate	I 0	1.0	-	I 0	1.0	-
Enzymes as300,000DU	-	0.5	-	0.5	-	
Perfume	qs	qs	qs	qs	qs	qs
NaOH (30% solution)	2-3	2-3	2-3	2-3	2-3	2-3
Solvent deodorized kerosine	-	-	-	-	-	4

Table 11.2. Typical formulations for powders produced by spray-drying.

	Heavy-duty hand	All-purpose cold water hand	Heavy-duty machine	Light-duty hand
LAS (Na salt)	12	16	6	18
Non-ionic	3	4	4	2
Soap or distilled fatty acids	-	-	6	-
cmc	2	3	2	2
Sodium silicate 1:2.45 ratio (100% basis)	3	3	4	-
Soda ash	10	10	-	-
STP	30	35	30	15
$MgSO_4$	1.5	-	1.5	-
Optical brightener	0.15	0.15	0.15	0.1
Na_2So_4	22	28	30	60.1
Perborate	15	-	15	—
Sodium toluene sulphonate	1	1	1	1
Perfume	qs	qs	qs	qs
Enzymes		-	0.5-0.8	
Residual moisture (approx.)	10	5	10	5

Note

1. Part or all of the LAS can be replaced by sulphonated methyl esters.
2. Perfumes for this type of powder should be of low volatility and added after spray drying
3. All the above formulations lend themselves to production by the combined systems.

Hard-surface Cleaners

A new development in both the household and the institutional cleaning fields in the all-purpose liquid meant specifically for hard-surface cleaning-by hard surfaces are meant those surfaces that cannot be immersed in a bath or basin for cleaning, and the operation needs to be done *in situ*.

These cleaners are usually liquid, alkaline and often contain solvents. Their purpose is to clean grease, mud, and atmospheric grime from walls, doors, glass, tiles, etc. Alkalinity can be derived from alkaline salts, or ammonia (occasionally caustic soda or potash) can be added. The solvent is added because it has been found that oil stains, although theoretically saponifiable by the alkali, cannot always be removed without it. This solvent needs to be soluble in water (unless an emulsion is to be made), reasonably odourless, non-toxic, with a fairly high flash-point and last but not least, a good fat solvent. The glycol ethers, in particular ethylene glycol monobutyl ether or dipropylene glycol methyl ether answer to all the above requirements admirably. Silicates are added both to buffer the alkalinity and to minimise corrosion on metallic surfaces. A typical formulation is

Formula 26

Hard-surface cleaner

Sodium alkyl benzene sulphonate (100% basis)	15
EDTA sodium salt	4
Ammonia (100% basis) (optional)	5
Butyl cellosolve	7
Sodium silicate (1:2 ratio, 100% basis)	3
Water	to 100

It goes without saying that if ammonia is to be added the solution cannot be used on copper surfaces.

A generalised formulation which is becoming popular in household use is:

Formula 27

Syndet	5-8 wt %
Hydrotrope	6
Alkali	5
Dipropylene glycol methyl ether	4
Pine oil	2
Water	Balance

The syndet can be non-foaming (non-ionic) or medium foaming (LAS) or high foaming (mixture of LAS and ether sulphate). The alkali can be ammonia, trisodium phosphate, tetrasodium pyrophosphate or sodium silicate, or one of the organic amines such as monoethanolamine. If organic alkine salts are not used the hydrotrope can be dispensed with. It is necessary to use softened water for this formulation as otherwise the hardness salts will precipitate or form a haze due to the high pH.

A particular instance of hard-surface cleaning is the oven cleaner. The above formula will theoretically clean ovens, but as grease is normally heavily encrusted on the surfaces of ovens more alkalinity than that provided in this formula is needed. A typical formula could be:

Formula 28

Hard-surface cleaner

Alkyl benzene sulphonate, sodium salt	4
Phosphoric acid (85%)	4.5
Caustic potash (100%) or monoethanolamine	9
Tetrapotassium pyrophosphate	4.5
Ethylene glycol monobutyl ether	6
Isopropyl alcohol	2
Sodium silicate 1:2 ratio (100%)	2
Water	68

It will be noted that the amount of caustic potash suggested is in excess of that required to neutralise the phosphoric acid, the surplus is needed to provide alkalinity. In the above formula the glycol ether is not completely soluble but the isopropyl alcohol acts as a coupling agent. Contrary to general belief, isopropyl alcohol is in itself a good fat solvent.

For certain institutional purposes it might be necessary or desirable to produce an oven cleaner as a paste or viscous liquid so that it will not drain down vertical surfaces. Formulae 34 and 35 can be modified by the addition of either a thickening agent or colloidal silica. If a viscous liquid is to be made it can be conveniently packed as an aerosol. The following formula for an aerosol oven cleaner is suggested

Formula 29

Aerosol oven cleaner

Veegum-T	1.5
Ammonia solution	6
1, 1, 1-Trichlorethane	18
Water	24
Ethanol	7.5
Tergitol	18
Propellant:	
Dichlorodifluoromethane	17.5
Dichlorotetrafluoroethane	7.5

A low temperature oven cleaner has been described in a patent where mannitol or sorbitol is used for alcoholysis of the fat deposited, with sodium or potassium bicarbonate as the alcoholysis catalyst and salts of low molecular weight organic acids to esterify the alcoholysis product. The formulation is as under:

Formula 30

Sorbitol	2-5
Potassium bicarbonate	0.1-4.0
Eutectic mixture of	
Sodium acetate	
Lithium acetate	1-5
Potassium acetate	
Thickener	qs
Precipitated chalk	20-30
Wetting agent	qs

The eutectic mixture is to lower the melting point of the salts to allow them to react easily. Other salts recommended could be sodium tartrate, Rochelle salt or sodium glycolate.

Machine Dishwashing

Until a few years ago household dishwashing was done by using one of the fine-wash or general-purpose formulations mentioned above. Of recent years the household dishwashing machine has come into popular use and this has requirements of its own. The mechanical cleaning action is done by means of jets of water. These jets are produced by a high-pressure pump or by the whipping action of a fast revolving propeller. In either case it is essential to the operation of the machine that the detergent added be completely non-foaming (and not even with a 'controlled foam' as in household laundry).

Non-ionics, in general, foam considerably less than anionics, but even they do foam slightly, so the amount of detergent is therefore kept to a minimum and the cleaning effect is achieved by the use of alkalis and phosphates. Almost completely non-foaming non-ionics have now been developed by blocking the terminal —OH group. One of the common methods is to add a methyl group to the terminal —OH. If, for example, a non-ionic is to be made by the esterfication of a polyethylene glycol and a fatty acid, instead of the polyethylene glycol a methoxy-polyethylene glycol is used. Another method is to condense to the finished non-ionic detergent a further molecule of butylene oxide. The formulation also depends to a very great extent on the type of water being used. Household water-softeners are only now beginning to appear on the market; so the formula must take into account whether the water being used is soft, moderately hard or hard.

For soft-water areas, soda ash, besides being cheap, can provide a portion of the alkalinity, but in moderately hard and hard water the soda ash will leave a scum of calcium carbonate on crockery and cutlery.

For moderately hard water tetrasodium pyrophosphate can be used to give both detergency and alkalinity, but for hard water sodium tripolyphosphate in combination with strong alkalis must be employed.

Most dishwashing machines have a drying cycle as well as the rinsing cycles, or at least dishes are left hot and the last traces of moisture on them dry very quickly on contact with the air. It is, therefore necessary to provide for the last traces of water to drain from the dishes in a uniform film to avoid water spots, particularly on glassware.

This effect can be achieved by incorporating solvents or an organic chlorine-releasing compound into the powder. Chlorine-releasing materials react with non-ionic detergents and it has been found that these powders work very successfully without any detergent at all. If, however, it is desired to incorporate a detergent, a very small amount of non-ionic detergent can be used. In another method in which non-ionic detergents can be incorporated into these powders in the presence of chlorine releasing agents. It recommends the low-foam modified non-ionic detergents mentioned above. This detergent, at the rate of 1-2 per cent based on the final weight, is pre-mixed with the most alkaline ingredient present (anhydrous metasilicate), the tripolyphosphate added next and then the other ingredients and finally the chlorine-releasing compound.

Highly alkaline materials such as metasilicate can affect the over-glaze on delicate china and cause 'crazing' of the glaze. This can be eliminated by the incorporation of boric acid (not more than 5 per cent), sodium aluminate (2 per cent) or zinc salts in the formula.

Since these powders usually contain large amounts of sodium metasilicate, they are not normally made by spray-drying, as there is a limit to the amount of sodium metasilicate (which is hygroscopic) which can be incorporated into a spray-dried powder. They are produced instead, by a mixing and absorption technique.

To make these powders dustless, granulation techniques are used. The powders and the non-ionic detergent are mixed as described above, without the chlorine-releasing material. On to this mixture a small amount of waterglass is sprayed in a mixer with a revolving or tumbling action, when the waterglass glues the particles together and the revolving action gives them a spherical shape. The chlorine-containing material is then added.

A formula suitable for use in soft-water areas is given in formula 31.

Formula 31

Machine dish-washing powder for soft-water areas

Tetrasodium pyrophosphate	49
Sodium metasilicate anhydrous	25
Soda ash	22.5
Sodium dichloro-iso-cyanurate (60% available chlorine)	1.5-4.5
Non-ionic detergent, e.g., nonyl-phenol 9 mol ethox	2

This formulation is also suitable for dishwashing machines used in catering establishments.

Because of the small amount of detergent involved, it is not necessary to use any special procedure for the incorporation of the active matter. The easiest method is to blend- in with the other powders a concentrated detergent powder. Alternatively, any other already prepared detergent powder can be used as the source of the active matter and due allowance must then be made for the other ingredients in this powder.

Where the water is moderately hard the product should be made according to Formula 32.

Formula 32

Machine dish-washing powder for moderately hard-water areas

Tetrasodium pyrophosphates	60
Sodium metasilicate anhydrous	38
Trichloro-iso-cyanuric acid	1-3.5
Non-ionic detergent	1

For very hard-water areas the following formulation will be suitable:

Formula 33

Machine dish-washing powder for hard-water areas

Sodium tripolyphosphate	50
Sodium metasilicate pentahydrate	25
Trisodium phosphate anhydrous	15
Non-ionic detergent	3
Hexylene glycol	2
Isopropyl alcohol	1.5
Water	3.5

The liquids are pre-mixed, and then the powders are charged into the mixer and the liquid sprayed on to the powders while mixing.

For institutional machine dishwashing the tendency is to move away from powders to liquids as these can be dosed either continuously or in accordance with pre-set requirements based on electronic controls.

Liquid for dishwashing machines can be formulated with either a non-ionic component or active chlorine, but not both.

Alkalinity is obtained from caustic alkali (soda or potash) with the addition of the corresponding silicate, together with a condensed phosphate. The same problems of common ion effect occur as described for (heavy duty liquid detergent (HDLD) thus a basic formula could be:

Formula 34

Tetrapotassium pyrophosphate	15
Potassium silicate (1:2 mol ratio, 40% solution)	8
Potassium hydroxide (45%)	10
Soft water	67

Potassium tripolyphosphate, if available, would obviously give vastly' improved performance.

To this solution is added a per cent of a non-foaming non-ionic or 2 per cent active chlorine. The chlorine in this instance can be added by direct injection of chlorine gas to form potassium hypochlorite in the solution.

Abrasive-type Cleaners

The most popular household abrasive cleaners are scouring powders. These are usually dry mixes of all of the ingredients. A typical formulation is given in Formula 35.

Formula 35

Household scouring powder

Abrasive	87
Soda ash	5
60% concentrated detergent powder	8
If desired, this can also be manufactured from sulphonic acid by mixing together:	
Abrasive (powdered calcite or marble)	85
Soda ash	7
then adding in the mixer:	
100% alkyl benzene sulphonic acid (ABS)	5
and water	3

If this scouring powder is to contain active chlorine, as is becoming the fashion now, it is advisable not to use soda ash, as concentrated organic-chlorine-releasing materials are not in general stable in the presence of soda ash, except for the potassium salt of trichloro-iso-cyanuric acid.

Alkalinity can be obtained by anhydrous sodium tripolyphosphate or tetrasodium pyrophosphate. To avoid introducing moisture into the powder, the active matter can best be put in by the use of an already made detergent powder, not necessarily a concentrated one. A chlorine containing powder is best packed in plastic containers.

A suggested formulation is Formula 36 which is a chlorine-containing household scouring powder.

Formula 36

Chlorine-containing detergent scouring powder	
Detergent powder containing 20% active matter (without soda ash)	15
Tetrasodium pyrophosphate	5
Abrasive	79
Trichloro-iso-cyanuric acid	1

Where a spray-drier is being operated, Formula 36 is a useful outlet for the cyclone fines produced by the spray-drier.

A scouring liquid can be made according to Formula 37.

Formula 37

Household scouring liquid	
Disperse	
Bentonite	5
in water	25
Add 12% active ready-made liquid detergent	35
and dissolve in the liquid:	
Sodium metasilicate pentahydrate or water-glass	3
and then disperse in this solution:	
Abrasive	32

Special suspending agents suitable for this type of product are now available. These prevent settling of the abrasives.

Miscellaneous Household Cleaners

Window cleaners of the gentle abrasive type, using whiting, were once popular. These have now been superseded by liquids, like those of Formula 38.

Formula 38

Household window-cleaning liquid	
Active detergent matter	0.25-0.5
Isopropyl alcohol	15-35
Water	to 1 00
Dye	as required.

Formula 39

Floor cleaner	
Active detergent matter	2-5
Isopropyl alcohol	8-15
Pine oil	1-2
Water	to I 00

Commercial Laundering

In commercial laundering, powders are used which do not foam and which are in general more alkaline than household powders. Most commercial laundries use soft water, and we suggest to the detergent manufacturer that if he supplies washing powders to a laundry which does not use soft (or softened) water, he should make every effort to convince his customer that it is essential for him to use it.

Laundry powders can be made both by spray-drying and by absorption and neutralisation. The two formulations below have been used with success in commercial laundries.

Formula 40

Spray-dried industrial laundry powder		
Alkyl benzene sulphonic acid	20	Neutralised with
Distilled tallow fatty acid	15	NaOH to sodium salts
Tetrasodium pyrophosphate	15	
Sodium metasilicate	15	
CMC (100% basis)	2	
Optical brightening agent	0.15	
Soda ash	33	

Formula 41

Industrial laundry powder not spray-dried	
Alkyl benzene sulphonic acid	11
Distilled tallow fatty acid	7
Tetrasodium pyrophosphate	10
Sodium metasilicate pentahydrate	7
CMC (100% basis)	1.8
Optical brightening agent	0.1
Soda ash	61.1
Water	

Many laundries carry out a pre-wash at a lower temperature. One of the above powders can be added to the pre-wash, but a more effective method is to use for the pre-wash a solvent detergent.

Solvent Detergents

It is not too difficult to combine non-ionics with solvents, but anionics are not easy to combine, especially those of the alkyl aryl sulphonate type, as most of these are insoluble, or only slightly soluble, in most non-polar solvents such as kerosene or deodorised kerosene which, of course, are generally the least expensive ones.

Detergents often serve only as emulsifying agents for the solvents, and not so much as detergent or cleaning agents. Emulsifiable insecticide concentrates, for example, are based on a solution of the emulsifying agent within the insecticide solvent mixture, forming a clear stable solution which, on dilution, gives a milky white emulsion with water. Here the emulsifying agent is very often a non-ionic detergent acting as an emulsifier, rather than as a detergent proper. However, we are more concerned with solvent-detergent combinations, in which the detergent acts both as an emulsifying agent for the solvent, and as a detergent in its own right.

In detergent-solvent combinations, the job of the solvent is to dissolve grease and similar oily dirt. The function of the detergent is to act as a penetrating and wetting agent and as an emulsifying agent for carrying off solvent after it has dissolved the oil or grease from the material to be cleaned, but it also keeps solid dirt particles in suspension. In many cleaning operations the detergent, by its surface activity alone, is simply not powerful enough to loosen dirt which is kept strongly, attached to the surface by oily or resinous matter. This is very often encountered in metal-cleaning, or during the laundering of oily overalls. On the other hand, it is often impossible for a solvent alone to develop its full dissolving power where the oily matter is covered by solid crusts of insoluble matter. This is the case in the decarbonising operations carried out on the working parts of internal combustion engines. It is the combination of surface activity plus solvent power which makes solvent-detergents so useful in widely different fields of application.

The most easily produced type of solvent-detergent is a combination of non-ionic detergent with solvents. Very often a simple mixing of solvents with detergents is sufficient to obtain a clear, stable product, which generally forms milky emulsions in water. However, not all non-ionics are soluble in any proportion in any solvent. Very often they are only slightly soluble in non-polar solvents of the aliphatic type. Here it is necessary to use so-called 'co-solvents', together with the non-polar aliphatic solvent, to give the desired results.

The subject of solvency is of the greatest importance in working out effective products. By giving concrete examples, it will be made clear how important this type of solvent is in formulating high-grade products.

Generally speaking, the non-ionic detergents are more easily soluble in solvents than most anionic detergents. It is, nevertheless, quite incorrect to assume that they are soluble in all kinds of solvents. Thus, for example, a condensation product of nonyl phenol with 9-10 moles ethylene oxide is readily soluble in chlorinated solvents, xylene, benzene, and in most polar solvents; it is, however, only slightly soluble in kerosene and white spirit and even less so in dearomatised (deodorised) kerosene. To increase the degreasing power Of trichlorethylene, it is possible to add a certain percentage of non-ionic, e.g., 3-5 per cent, to the solvent. Furthermore, a stable solution of trichlorethylene may be produced by dissolving 10-15 per cent of non-ionic in trichlorethylene. On dilution of the clear solution with water, a milky-white emulsion will be obtained. In order to prevent corrosion due to free hydrochloric acid, an addition of about 0.5 per cent monoethanolamine to the composition is advisable.

Chlorinated solvents should be used with caution preferably they should be used in closed systems, where the solvent is distilled, condensed and recycled, such as in dry cleaning and closed metal degreasing systems. The low heat of vaporisation of these chlorinated solvents (210 J/g for perchlorethylene) and non-inflammability are distinct advantages.

As already pointed out, most non-ionic detergents are soluble in aromatic solvents and by dissolving 10 per cent in xylene and diluting the clear xylene solution with water, stable milky white emulsions may be obtained which are very useful for metal-degreasing compounds. Aromatic solvents may serve as co-solvents for dissolving non-ionic in aliphatic non-polar solvents such as dearomatised kerosene and white spirit. To obtain clear solution, a proportion of about 30-40 per cent of aromatic solvents is necessary, e.g., 10 parts non-ionic; 30 parts aromatic solvent; 60 parts kerosene.

Formula 42

Detergent-solvent combination	
Nonyl phenol 9 EO	30 parts
Isopropanol	20 parts
Xylene	50 parts

Formula 43

Detergent-solvent combination	
Nonyl phenol 9 EO	30 parts
Methylethylketone	35 parts
Deodorised kerosene	50 parts

Mix the materials in the order given. A clear solution is obtained which becomes blue-white opalescent when diluted with water (hard or soft). Nonylphenol-9-ethox, behaves similarly to octyl phenol ethoxylates.

For the internal degreasing of motors, etc., such combinations with nonionic detergents and solvents should prove very useful, possibly in combination with flushing oils. Even in the unlikely event of solvent-detergent remaining in the engine, practically no danger of subsequent corrosion should exist, because of the complete volatility of the products of combustion, which are hardly any more corrosive than the combustion products of motor fuels. It would even be possible to formulate an 'internal' decarboniser on the basis of anionic detergents (AB sulphonic acid neutralised with alkanolamine or alkylamine), which does not leave any residues in the engine. Here again, an entire field for further research is open.

Another non-ionic detergent useful for formulating solvent-detergents is alkylolamide. Experiments with this compound (which is a condensation product of ethanolamine with fatty acids) have yielded very efficient solvent-detergents. However, the wetting power of alkylolamide is somewhat lower than that of water-soluble alkyl phenol or fatty alcohol ethoxylates.

A special solvent-detergent combination of interest is one which gives a clear solution of kerosene in water according to Formula 44.

Formula 44

Kerosene water solution

Coconut fatty acid diethanolamide	20
Kerosene	20
Water	20

On dilution with soft or hard water, all these products given very stable solvent emulsions of good detergent power.

The alkyl benzene sulphonic acids can also be used as the basis of solvent-detergent combinations.

It is essential to start operations with the unneutralised sulphonic acid. SO_3 sulphonated sulphonic acids, because they contain minimal amounts of inorganic acids, can quite easily be incorporated into these combinations, but oleum sulphonated dodecyl benzene, if treated as described below, can also be turned into an acceptable solvent-detergent.

Formula 45

Solvent-detergent combination

Mix together :	
SO_3 produced alkyl benzene sulphonic	
acid (ABS)	50 parts
Kerosene	50 parts
Aromatic solvent	25 parts
Then slowly add:	
Caustic soda solution (38° Be)	17-18 parts
After cooling to about 50°C add:	
Isopropanol	10 parts
Pine oil	2 parts

A clear liquid is obtained, which at low temperatures becomes gel-like.

A small amount of water from both the water of solution of the caustic soda and the water produced by neutralisation, will be present. If a completely anhydrous material is required, the lower amines, isopropyl or butyl, can be used for neutralisation. Care should be exercised in their use as they are volatile, toxic and inflammable.

The product is completely soluble in soft water, somewhat turbid in hard water, and is completely soluble in organic solvents. It is almost completely soluble in non-polar paraffinic solvents, such as kerosene, petrol, etc. By diluting the solvent-detergent with solvents, e.g., 1:10 with white spirit or kerosene, a solvent-emulsion concentrate is formed which gives very stable emulsions on dilution with water. This is important for metal-degreasing operations.

It is interesting to note that the wetting power of the ABS detergents is practically unaffected if only aromatic and polar solvents are used, and only slightly affected when non-polar paraffin solvents are present. In all cases, sinking time as measured by the Draves test is not greater than 25s at a concentration of 0.1 per cent active detergent matter in distilled water.

A completely anhydrous solvent-detergent can be manufactured from SO_3 sulphonated LAS according to Formula 46.

Formula 46

Solvent-detergent based on 100 per cent ABS (SO_3 produced)

Kerosene	35
ABS (100% basis)	35
Monoethanolamine	15
Trichlorethylene	13
Pine oil	2

All the ingredients, except for the trichlorethylene, are merely mixed together until uniform. When the liquid has cooled to below 50°C, the trichlorethylene is added and the pH adjusted to 8 by using monoethanolamine. This pH was found to be advisable as the trichlorethylene might release traces of hydrochloric acid and the surplus monoethanolamine will absorb this. Trichlorethylene may be replaced by higher boiling perchlorethylene. Formula 50 is an excellent general-purpose combination and can be used for adding to the pre-wash in laundering, as an additive for dry-cleaning fluids, and for degreasing of engine parts, etc.

One of the most important uses of solvent-detergents is as a dry-cleaning aid. The purpose of the dry-cleaning detergent is a multiple one, to increase the effectiveness of the solvent in dissolving solvent-soluble spots and stains, to aid in the removal of water-soluble stains by dispersing or solubilising a small percentage of water in the solvent, and to increase the dispersion of these water-soluble stains in this water. To achieve this effect generally a combination of non-ionic and anionic detergents is used together with a coupling agent. For example,

Formula 47

Dry-cleaning detergent

Nonyl phenol-9 ethylene oxide	40
Propylene glycol	17
Butyl cellosolve	3
Monoethanolamine	7
Alkyl benzene sulphonic acid	33
(SO_3 sulphonated to minimise inorganic salts)	

All the ingredients are mixed together and the pH (tested at a dilution of 1:10 in water) is adjusted to between 7 and 8 with small additions of either monoethanolamine or sulphonic acid.

This is added to the dry-cleaning solvent at the rate of 1-1½ per cent with or without the addition of small quantities of water.

If a readily dispersible product is required, the above formula can be diluted 1:1 with a dry-cleaning solvent (for example, perchlorethylene) and is then used at the rate of 2-3 per cent based on the volume of the solvent in the machine.

Although dodecyl benzene sulphonic acid gives excellent results in the above formulations, even better results are obtainable by replacing the ABS with heavy alkylate-sulphonic acid, which has a higher molecular weight and renders the sulphonate more oil soluble. Of course, with a higher molecular weight, the acid value will obviously be lower. The amount of alkali in the above formulations should, therefore, be correspondingly reduced. (This is best determined by the acid value of the heavy alkylate sulphonic acid.)

CARPET AND UPHOLSTERY CLEANERS

Fabric cleaners of this type differ in their operation from other detergent materials in that it is usually very difficult to rinse the material being cleaned. To overcome this, methods of cleaning have been developed where a solution of the detergent is applied to the carpet by 'shampooing' to form copious foam, or a foam is formed first and the carpet sponged with this foam. In either instance the combination of the detergency of the cleaner and the mechanical energy applied lifts and holds the dirt in the foam.

The foam, having very thin walls and enormous surface area dries relatively quickly into brittle particles of dust and this dust is either vacuum cleaned or brushed away.

Initial formulations for these carpet shampoos were normal light-duty detergents with the addition of tetrasodium pyrophosphate, its function being both to increase detergency and to make the dried residue more brittle. A suitable detergent material which is also in itself fairly brittle when dehydrated is the sodium or magnesium salt of one of the fatty alcohol sulphates. Some formulae also called for the incorporation of a solvent but with the newer fabrics and rubberised bases being used, the solvent should be chosen with care or left out.

These formulations were not, however, the complete answer to the problem. A portion of the active matter became absorbed into the fibre and when dried this left a deposit which tended to attract dirt. Carpets cleaned in this manner became soiled very quickly.

This problem has been overcome by using more crystalline detergents as the base. Such detergents are the half ester of sodium sulphosuccinates used alone or in admixture with fatty alcohol sulphates. The lithium salt of fatty alcohol sulphate for this specific purpose are used. The detergent then absorbed on the fibre is more brittle and when dried will shatter and can easily be brushed away. Another line of attack is to add colloidal silica to the formula to produce the same effect.

TEXTILE DRESSING

Detergents of the anionic type have to a large extent replaced soap in the scouring of wool and cotton. The main factor involved is that anionic detergents do not precipitate their lime and magnesia salts on to the fibres, and thus give a better 'handle' to the finished goods.

As textile processing is a complex process, the detergent manufacturer can only be called upon to supply a concentrated detergent; the various alkalis, phosphates or solvents are added by the textile processer himself This concentrated detergent is usually manufactured by agreement between the textile scourer and the detergent manufacturer. Fatty alcohol sulphate pastes, neutralised immediately after sulphation, are as often used as are alkyl benzene sulphonate pastes. Depending on the requirements of the textile mill, the alkyl benzene sulphonate can be a concentrated paste neutralised only with caustic soda, or a semi-liquid paste neutralised with ethanolamine. A typical formula can be

Formula 48

Textile scouring paste

Alkyl benzene sulphonic acid (ABS 100%)	375
Diethanolamine	130
Water	495

The ingredients are mixed together and the final pH adjusted according to the buyer's requirements.

On occasion, especially for degumming, detergents compounded with pine oil are preferred for textile scouring, particularly of wools.

We suggest the following formulation

Formula 49

Textile degumming detergent paste

Pine oil	250
Alkyl benzene sulphonic acid (ABS 100%)	280
Diethanolamine	97
Water	373

Mercerising

Cotton cloth is treated for anti-shrink properties by dipping in a concentrated (of the order of 12-18 per cent) caustic soda solution. To allow the solution to penetrate well and evenly into the fibres a detergent or rather a wetting agent is necessary. The bulk of detergents are either not soluble or not effective (or both) in strong caustic soda solutions. A commonly used wetting agent for this purpose is the sodium salt of sulphated 2-ethyl hexanol. By itself it is not completely effective but if blended with 10 per cent each of the unsulphated 2-ethyl hexanol and butanol, the material soluble in caustic soda solutions, the solution remains stable and the wetting properties are greatly enhanced. Ethoxylated glycosides (moderate to high foaming) and the low-molecular-weight phosphate esters (low foaming) are also used for this purpose. Another possibility, which has not yet been exploited commercially, is SO_3 sulphonated olefins.

FOOD AND DAIRY INDUSTRIES

As with any food industry, dairies require spotless cleanliness to prevent spoilage, and sterilisation against bacterial contamination. The tolerance for residual bacteria is, however, lower for dairies than for other food industries, as in this case bacteria can cause the milk to turn sour. A further complication is the presence of high amounts of lime salts in the milk.

Many plants use strong alkalis only for cleaning, and sterilisation is achieved by steam. These materials have their limitations, as can be seen from Table 11.3, detailing the properties of various alkalis for dairies.

It will be noticed that no one material supplies all the requirements. Chlorinated trisodium phosphate adds a sterilising action. For this reason it is often desirable to combine several of these alkalis to produce a blended material which will provide all the requirements. The addition of a detergent greatly enhances the performance of these alkalis, but in certain processes foaming will interfere with the operation. Even low-foaming non-ionics foam slightly, and the use of detergents is thus sometimes excluded. Formulae 50-52 give some typical formulations for food- and dairy-cleaning alkaline detergents.

Formula 50-52

Food and dairy alkaline detergent cleaner

	Non-foaming	*Medium foam*	*High foam*
	50	51	52
Trisodium phosphate	15	-	10
Sodium carbonate	10	39	35
Sodium metasilicate Pentahydrate	40	20	20
Tetrasodium pyrophosphate	-	40	-
Sodium tripolyphosphate	35	-	30
Non-ionic detergent	-	1	-
Concentrated anionic detergent powder	-	-	5

Table 11.3. Alkalis for dairy cleaners.

Agent	Wetting power	Solution of heat-deposited milk solids	Emulsification of fats	Buffering power	Rinse-ability	Water-softening properties	Corrosive action
Caustic soda	Poor	Very good	Poor	Poor	Poor	Good	strong
Carbonates	Poor	Good	Fair	Poor	Fair	Good	Weak
Trisodium phosphate	Good	Poor	Fair	Good	Good	Good	Weak
Orthosilicate	Good	Good	Very good	Very good	Fair	Fair	Strong
Metasilicate	Good	Good	Good	Fair	Fair	Fair	Weak
Sesquisilicate	Good	Good	Fair	Good	Fair	Fair	Medium
Chlorinated trisodium phosphate	Good	Fair	Fair	Good	Good	Good	Medium

To produce a powder that simultaneously sterilises and cleans, the metasilicates must be of the anhydrous variety, and soda ash and non-ionic detergents should not be used. Subject to the above conditions, sufficient organic-chlorine-bearing materials can be added to the above formulation to give, say, 3 per cent active chlorine in the finished powder.

For bottle-washing in the food industry the pH required is very high. Sodium gluconate should be added for its sequestering action.

Formula 52

Bottle-washing compound

Caustic soda flakes	55
Sodium metasilicate	20
Soda ash	17
Sodium gluconate	5
60% anionic detergent concentrate	3

In addition to the above alkaline cleaning materials, in the dairy industry it is necessary as a routine to give the pipelines, etc., an acid wash to dissolve milkstone deposited on the walls.

Very often concentrated hydrochloric acid is used. This is very corrosive and although the dairy plant is invariably stainless steel it is advisable to add an inhibitor. Nitric acid is also used on occasion. Although nitric acid is both a strong acid and on oxidising agent, sight must not be lost of the fact that the original stainless steels were developed to withstand this acid, so no inhibitor is necessary. Both these acids are unpleasant to handle and environmentally unsound, therefore, to overcome these difficulties less corrosive materials have been developed.

Combinations of lactic acid with acid-resistant detergents have found application. So, also, have combinations of phosphoric, citric, and tartaric acid with acid-resistant detergents. The most recent development in this important field is the application of sulphamic acid. This has the structural formula

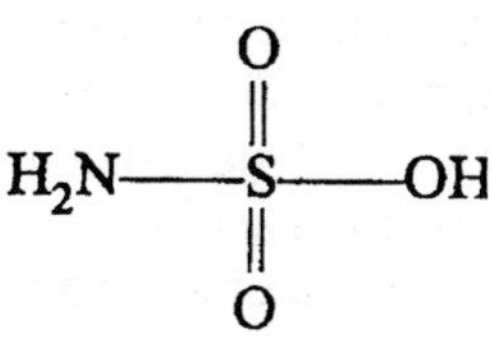

It is the half amide of sulphuric acid.

Molecular weight 97.09

Specific gravity 2.03

The following advantages of sulphamic acid are enumerated.

1. Its crystalline, non-volatile nature, which makes it easy, safe and economical to handle, and eliminates the evolution of objectionable fumes when solutions are needed.
2. Its strong acid character gives the 'bite' necessary for the removal of deposits.
3. All salts of sulphamic acid (e.g., calcium, magnesium, iron) are readily soluble in water. Hence, adequate dissolving and thorough rinsing of scale is assured. Further, it is expected that less sulphamic acid is needed than other commonly used acids.
4. In spite of its strong acid character, dilute sulphamic acid solutions are not unduly corrosive to dairy equipment.
5. It is simpler and less hazardous in handling.

The following five general steps are recommended for cleaning heat-transfer equipment and vats, using sulphamic acid:

1. Thoroughly rinse or flush the equipment with warm water until the water is no longer milky.
2. Prepare an adequate quantity of sulphamic acid solution of 0.2-2 per cent concentration (1.6-16 kg/m^3), heat the solution to 65-70°C, and circulate for 10-30 minutes. Because of the many variables in equipment, composition of deposits and preferred cleaning practices, precise recommendations suitable for all cleaning applications cannot be given, The above ranges of concentration, temperature and time have developed from experience and should cover most situations.
3. Rinse thoroughly with warm water.
4. Flush the equipment with a cleaning and neutralising solution consisting of 15-85 g of trisodium phosphate or other alkaline-type detergent compound for each gallon of water. The alkaline treatment should consist of approximately the same concentration, temperature and time as used with the sulphamic acid cleaning solution.
5. Rinse the equipment again with warm water.

In the case of some stubborn or fat-containing deposits which tend to be water-repellent, it is sometimes advantageous to use a small amount of a wetting agent along with the sulphamic acid, so as to enhance the rate at which it penetrates and attacks the material to be moved. Alkyl benzene sulphonic acid is suitable for this purpose.

Since uninhibited sulphamic acid is rather corrosive to ordinary steel and cast iron, it is wise to provide a separate pump for circulating solutions if existing pumps have ferrous metal parts in contact with the fluid.

On conducting experiments with 100 per cent dodecyl benzene sulphonic acid to clean milkstone. The calcium salts of DDBS are dispersible in water and therefore the acid should be suitable. However the 100 per cent acid dissolves with difficulty in water in low concentrations. It was found that the addition of 10 per cent xylene sulphonic acid to the 100 per cent DDBS rendered the mixture very easily soluble. A 5 per cent solution of this mixture dissolves the milkstone readily and the surplus is easily rinsed away.

DETERGENT SANITISERS

The halogens have long been known to be effective germicides, and chlorinated trisodium phosphate is used pretty effectively to clean and disinfect milking equipment.

Mere also has been a tendency in the past years tc use bromine as such for disinfection but it has no real advantage over chlorine and is much less pleasant to handle.

Iodine is now gaining considerably in this field, particularly combinations of iodine with non-ionic surfactants.

These products called iodophors with a 1-3 per cent iodine content are active against bacteria at a concentration of 0.012-0.025 g/litre and it has been found that maximum activity is obtained in an acid environment.

The iodophors are prepared by mixing nonylphenol adducts containing at least 8 mol ethylene oxide or ethoxylated propylene glycols with 20-25 per cent iodine and heating this mixture to 50-60°C. Care should be taken with ventilation as iodine sublimes, even at room temperatures. Under these conditions 75 per cent of the iodine combines chemically with the nonylphenol ethoxylate.

Typical formulae 53, 54 are given below.

Formula 53 and Formula 54

	53	54
	%	%
20% available iodine in nonylphenol ethoxylate	8.75	8.75
Phosphoric acid (75%)	8.00	0.60
Nonylphenol + 30 mol ethylene oxide	5.00	5.00
Water	78.25	85.65

METAL CLEANERS

The cleaning of metals is done with either acid or alkaline materials. The acid treatment is meant for the removal of rust and other products of corrosion, and for the solution of 'scale'. This is a very wide term and includes both the layer of insoluble heavy metal salts precipitated on the walls and tubes of steam boilers, and also the layer of oxides (as opposed to rust) formed on steel surfaces under certain conditions of heating. The alkaline treatment is for the removal of grease, oil, paint and foreign matter, and is also necessary as a preliminary treatment prior to pickling (acid treatment) to remove the film of oil which at best will hinder the pickling acid in its work and at worst -will only allow this acid to work in patches, producing an uneven finish.

Scale removal by pickling calls for cleaning compounds (which are added to help the acid to penetrate and give a uniform finish) that will resist the strong acids used in pickling processes. Generally, detergents' without any special additions of builders are used in these cases. However, it is of great advantage to use detergents in conjunction with 'inhibitors' which prevent (or retard) the, attack of the pickling acid on the metal itself. The detergent has not much inhibiting effect, but its wetting action is apt to prevent pitting to a certain extent—a very important reason for using detergents in the pickling bath. The most suitable detergents are the alkyl benzene sulphonates, but certain petroleum sulphonates or heavy alkylate sulphonates may also be used with advantage. In these instances it is not necessary to neutralise the sulphonic acids, merely to add the material to the bath. If, however, a ready-neutralised material is all that is available, this can be used. These detergents need to be highly acid-resistant and to stand up to severe conditions, such as a 5 per cent sulphuric acid solution at 70°C. The amount of detergent to be added to the bath is on the average between 0.1 and 0.2 per cent, calculated as active detergent matter.

As inhibitors, phenylthiourea and thiourea are very effective. They are solid substances which can be compounded with powdered detergents to increase the rapidity of the pickling effect (in this case a neutralised concentrated detergent powder is used), and to prevent excessive corrosion of the metal proper. The amount of corrosion inhibitor required is 0.01 to 0.05 per cent, based on the sulphuric acid content of the pickling bath. If the concentration of the active detergent in the bath is of the order of 0. I per cent, it follows that the compounding of an effective pickling bath is not very difficult. An example would be: a concentrated detergent powder containing 40 per cent active dodecyl benzene sulphonate is mixed with 10 per cent of its weight of phenylthiourea or thiourea. This mixture is added to the pickling bath in the proportion of 0.25-0.5 per cent. An alkyl aryl sulphonate of the alkyl naphthalene type was effective in concentrations of 0.1 per cent, both as an inhibitor and a wetting agent.

The following inhibitors were also found to be effective in sulphuric acid pickling baths:

Butyl sulphide, *o*-tolylthiourea, *p*-tolylthiourea, butyl disulphide, amyl mercaptan, ethyl selenide, propyl sulphide, butyl-methyl-sulphide, butyl mercaptan, p-thiocresol, iso-butyl-mercaptan, trianyl amine, *m*-thiocresol, trihexylamine, ethyl sulphide, phenyl morpholine, ethyl mercaptan, formaldehyde, methyl sulphide, 2-thionaphthol, crotonaldehyde. (This is only a selection from a list of more than a hundred compounds listed.)

In the past types of inhibitors especially suitable for acid cleaners, such as cleaners for automobile cooling systems, etc., have been developed, such as alkyl-substituted thioureas, diethyl- and dibutylthiourea, on to the market. These are suitable for use with 10 per cent hydrochloric acid solutions in concentrations as low as 0.05 per cent. Other type of acid inhibitors, are based on rosin amine derivatives, namely polyoxyethylated dehydroabeitylamines. These inhibitors were found to be effective in the range of 0.05-0.2 per cent in hydrochloric acid.

The effect of inhibitors in conjunction with surface-active agents is of great importance when removing water scale from steel pipes with hyrdrochloric acid. Again it was found that thiourea and phenylthiourea are very effective inhibitors whose effect is strongly enhanced by the use of detergents. A further line of research is the use of surface active agents in conjunction with corrosion inhibitors, such as sodium chromate, in brine solutions, calcium chloride refrigeration solutions and in automobile radiators.

For automobile cooling systems, acid mixtures are often used to remove hard and adherent scale. The effect of these mixtures is often greatly increased by the addition of detergents, which help in the penetration and removal of grease and oil which may have entered the cooling system and which prevent the acid cleaners from exerting their full effect on the scale. Mixtures of the solid acids, such as oxalic acid or sulphamic acid, and acid salts such as sodium bisulphate, may be improved by the addition of DDB sulphonate powders. The following formula is a suggestion for such a product:

Formula 55

Acid cleaner for water-cooling systems

Oxalic acid	80
Sodium bisulphate	10
Concentrated detergent 40 per cent active	10

The concentrated detergent can be either dodecyl benzene sulphonate or an acid-resistant petroleum sulphonate.

Aluminium is often cleaned and brightened by acid solutions containing hydrofluoric acid. One of the few detergents found to be compatible with this highly corrosive acid is an amphoteric of the dicarboxyethylated derivative of cocoimidazoline. A formulation suggested found to be effective is:

Formula 56

Miranol conc.	5
Glycol ether	6
Phosphoric acid (85%)	38
Hydrofluoric acid (70%)	8
EDTA	1
Water	42

Although -this is called a cleaner, it actually removes the oxides on the surface thus giving a brightening effect. This solution should be used after an alkaline wash to remove the surface film of dirt and oil. Aluminium is attacked by alkali, but silicates effectively inhibit this attack.

Besides the acid-type metal cleaners described above, metals are cleaned in strongly alkaline solutions to remove grease, oil and foreign matter prior to plating, painting, enamelling or other protective treatments used nowadays.

The method of removing this foreign matter determines the composition of the alkaline cleaner. It is obvious that if a spray method is to be used the cleaning solution cannot foam. The principal methods of alkaline metal treatment are soaking, spraying and electrolytic, or combinations of two of these processes. In the soaking process, the cleaning effect is obtained by the high concentration of the detergent, and also a possible circulation of the solution by a pump. The spray process adds mechanical energy from the jet to aid in the removal of the dirt. The electrolytic process produces the cleanest surface because of the scrubbing action of the gases evolved and the attraction of the electrically charged dirt particles by the electrodes.

In addition to the types of cleaning process used, the type of metal to be cleaned influences the choice of formulation of the detergent. No detergent can do the universal job of cleaning every surface, and various formulations for different types of metals and also the different cleaning processes are given in Formulae 57-71.

In these formulae, mention is made of sodium resinate, which is saponified tall oil, obtained as a by-product in the paper industry. This soap is relatively cheap and in addition has good emulsification properties for oil. As its detergency is poor, it is invariably used in conjunction with a detergent. We suggest that the same emulsification can be achieved by the use of a sulphonated heavy alkylate. The formulae also call for alkyl aryl sodium sulphonate. This is meant to be a concentrated powder containing 40 per cent sodium dodecyl benzene sulphonate. If another concentration is available the proportion should be varied accordingly.

MISCELLANEOUS CLEANERS

Lavatory Cleaner

The universal ingredient of lavatory cleaners is sodium bisulphate ($NaHSO_4$, technically called nitre cake). The most popular lavatory cleaner is based on this compound. Caking of sodium bisulphate can easily be overcome by adding to the ground salt some 0.5-1 per cent pine oil or a mixture of pine oil and kerosene. This also largely prevents corrosion of the metal containers in which these products may be marketed. (Recently, high density Polythene containers have been adopted in many European countries. These are completely unaffected by lavatory-cleaning compounds.)

The cleaning effect can be improved by adding to the sodium bisulphate not only the 0.5-1.0 per cent pine oil, but also approximately I per cent alkyl benzene sulphonic acid.

In the last few years liquid toilet bowl cleaners have appeared in market. These are packed in specially designed plastic bottles so that they can be dispensed on to the inner, invisible, rim of the toilet pan. These liquids are acid, either mineral or organic acids being the acidic component, contain relatively large amounts of surfactants, are dyed and perfumed and have medium viscosity. A typical representative formulation is given as under :

Formula 72

Non-ionic detergent	11.0
Hydrochloric acid (33%)	10.0
Phosphoric acid (85%)	10.0
Perfume	0.2
Water	68.8

Due to the acidity of the solution, the non-ionics need to be chosen with care and are usually a blend of alkyl phenol ethoxylates of both short and long chains. The perfume needs to be matched to the formulation to render it stable under acid conditions.

Formula No. 57-71

Alkaline metal cleaning compounds

	Aluminium		Copper			Copper-plate	Iron and steel			Magnesium			Zinc	
	Soak	Spray	Soak	Spray	Electro-lytic	Electro-lytic	Soak	Spray	Electro-lytic	Soak	Spray	Soak	Spray	Electro-lytic
	Composition of cleaners, % by weight													
Builders														
Sodium hydroxide, ground	–	–	20	15	15	55	20	15	15	20	20	–	15	15
Sodium carbonate, dense	–	–	18	–	–	8	18	29	8½	18	29	–	–	–
Sodium bicarbonate	21	24	–	34	34	–	–	–	–	–	–	–	35	34
Sodium tripolyphosphate	30	30	–	–	10	–	20	20	10	20	20	90	10	10
Tetrasodium pyrophosphate	–	–	20	10	–	10	–	–	–	–	–	–	–	–
Sodium metasilicate, anhydrous	45	45	30	40	40	25	30	30	25	30	30	–	40	40
Surface-active (wetting) agents)														
Sodium resinate	–	–	5	–	–	–	5	–	–	1	–	5	–	–
Alkyl aryl sodium sulphonate	3	–	5	–	–	–	5	–	–	5	–	5	–	–
Alkyl aryl polyether alcohol	–	–	2	–	–	1	2	–	–	2	–	–	–	–
Nonionic high in ethylene oxide	1	1	–	1	1	1	–	1	½	–	1	–	–	–
	Other conditions													
Operating temperature of solution °F	70	70	80	75	70	80	95	75	80	95	75	80	75	80
Concentration of cleaner, kg/m^3 H_2O	25	6	50	6	50	50	50	6	50	50	6	25	6	37

A viscous lavatory cleaner with both sanitizing and deodorizing effects may be produced by using LAS (So_3 sulphonated) and pine oil as its two components

Formula 73

LAS (acid form)	100
Pine oil	50-70
Water	150

The LAS and the pine oil are mixed and the water added immediately to prevent reaction of the sulphonic acid with the pine oil.

The water and/or the pine oil are varied to produce the desired viscosity. An oily liquid with lower viscosity but faster dispersibility in water is obtained by adding 10 to 20 parts isopropanol.

Hand Cleansers

The manufacture of hand cleanser is similar to that of other abrasive cleaners. Thus a hand soap in paste form may be produced according to Formula 74

Formula 74

Hand cleanser

40% sodium ABS paste	130 parts
Bentonite	150 parts
Fine sand	200 parts
Sodium carbonate	10 parts

Or it can be manufactured by using as the base a detergent paste according to Formula 75.

Formula 75

Detergent hand cleanser

40-50% sodium alkyl benzene sulphonate paste	100 parts
Bentonite	30 parts
Abrasive powder	200 parts
Sodium carbonate	10 parts

The solid materials are incorporated into the soft soap or paste. Some water may need to be added to regulate consistency.

A hand cleanser in powder form may be produced with Formula 76.

Formula 76

Hand cleanser in powder form	
Pure powdered soap or concentrated detergent powder	26 parts
Abrasive material	70 parts
Borax	4 parts

Some of the abrasive material may be replaced by vegetable abrasives, sawdust, etc.

A special hand-cleansing compound containing approximately 75 per cent borax and 25 per cent of dry soap was found by the laboratories to possess desirable fungicidal properties, and yet to be so mild in its action on the skin as to reduce any tendency to dermatitis. The borax is in finely granulated form, so that, when mixed with dry, powdered soap, gumming or caking is avoided. The product is described as a good cleanser, and will effectively, and without the use of waste, remove dirt from hands. The borax is not merely a diluent for the soap. Its hardness of two makes it even softer than chalk; it is readily soluble, and its abrasive action is only temporary, as the sharp edges of the grains become blunted almost immediately. It has detergent and water-softening properties of its own and it is a mild alkaline salt possessing the characteristic properties of imparting to a soap solution a pH value lower than that of soap alone.

Waterless Hand Cleansers

This type of hand cleanser is specially suitable for motorists, for removing oil, grease and grime after changing tyres or doing repairs while on the road. We confine ourselves to giving some formulae which we have worked out and found suitable for the purpose. The formula 77 especially useful to motorists for removing oil, paint, tar, etc., from the hands.

Formula 77

Waterless hand cleanser	
Stearic acid and/or 100% alkyl benzene sulphonic acid	25
Lanolin and/or lecithin	15
are dissolved in :	
Deodorized kerosene	350

The mixture is kept at a temperature of about 70°C.

To this solution the following mixture, having the same temperature of 70°C, is added

Triethanolamine	25
Water	95

Stir constantly until the mixture is cold

3.5 parts of pine oil is recommended as a cheap perfume and disinfectant.

Formula 78

Waterless hand cleanser

White mineral oil	40.5
Oleic acid	10.5
Non-ionic detergent	6.0
Propylene glycol	5.0
Triethanolamine	2.6
Morpholine	1.0
Water	34,4

Formula 79

Waterless hand cleanser

Deodorized kerosene	42.8
Lanoline	0.9
Oleic acid	5.9
Cetyl alcohol	0.4
Triethanolamine	2.9
Propylene glycol	2.7
Sodium lauryl alcohol sulphate	1.4
Water	43.0

It is suggested not to add abrasives to this type of waterless hand cleanser, because they cannot be completely wiped off the hands after use and are likely to choke the pores and thereby irritate the skin. If, for very heavy-duty waterless cleansers, an abrasive cannot be dispensed with, only the softest kinds, such as whiting, bole, kaolin, etc., should be used, and in the instructions for use it should be recommended to wash the hands with soap and water as soon after the application of the cleaner as possible. Neither halogenated solvents nor aromatic solvents should be used.

Chapter - 5

PERFUMING OF SOAPS AND DETERGENTS

INTRODUCTION

The terms 'fragrance' and 'perfume' are synonymous and are used interchangeably throughout the perfumery and cosmetics industries. This will also be so throughout this chapter. Fragrance (or perfume) is a blend of two or more materials characterised by having olfactive properties, and is incorporated into a preparation with the intention of imparting specific odours characteristics to that preparation. Very occasionally, the fragrance may consist of one raw material only.

The most important function of the perfume is usually to impart a pleasant and suitable odour to the product into which it is to be incorporated. It is the job of the creative and evaluation teams to define the terms 'pleasant' and 'suitable' for each particular brief that is received. The perfume may also be required to perform other roles in the product, which may take priority over, or be additional to the primary role of imparting odour.

Most soap products have a mild but detectable odour, which is derived from the raw materials in the formulation. Although this 'base' odour is usually inoffensive, it can detract from the overall aesthetic character of the product and should at least be 'masked'. This can be effectively achieved by the use of a suitable fragrance. Very pungent bases, such as permanent-wave lotions, are almost impossible to mask, even with the strongest of perfumes.

The role of the perfume in these products is therefore to produce as pleasant an odour as possible, and this can often be attained by harmonising the fragrance with the base odour.

Fragrances can be designed to give subliminal support to a particular product. For example, a fragrance may appear to make a shampoo wash the hair more cleanly, a perfumed night cream may seem more nutritional to the skin, or a perfumed body spray may appear to impart all-over freshness, all-day. In other words, the perfume may have the role of apparently enhancing product performance.

Some fragrance materials have antimicrobial activity, particularly against bacteria. Both bacteriostatic and bacteriocidal properties are evident. Consequently, fragrance blends often take on the antimicrobial activity of some of the individual components. Fragrances that have spicy and herbal notes usually exhibit some antibacterial activity owing to the presence of phenols such as eugenol (from clove oil), and thymol and carvacrol (from thyme oil). Consequently, the fragrance may also have the role of assisting the preservative system and even in extreme cases, of replacing the preservative system altogether. Similarly, the fragrance may assist a bacteriocide/bacteriostat in its effect on the skin's microflora (reducing body odour) or may be required to carry this attribute of the finished product on its own.

TYPES OF PERFUMES

The cost of soap is determined largely by the perfume. A perfect sample should be strong without being harsh and should retain its fragrance right up to the last thin wafer in use. The stability in the presence of alkali of the aromatic substances in any compound is of importance, as also any change in colour which they may effect in the soap after manufacture. Successful soap perfuming therefore requires a knowledge of the durability of each individual raw material when in contact with the soap and any of its constituent impurities. One or 2 per cent of compounded perfume, spread through a large and non-volatile mass has to yield an odour suggestive of the finer alcoholic perfumes in which the solvent plays an important part in determining the delicacy of the finished odour. While alcohol develops the finer ingredients of a perfume, soap on the contrary modifies the odour to such an extent as to often make it unrecognisable in the absence of correct blending. Raw materials listed in the odour classification under basic notes play an important part in solving this problem, and the durability of a perfume in soap largely depends upon their correct selection. Natural oils and resins are often the key, and if price will allow they should be used liberally. Some makers rely upon a very small range of raw materials, and in consequence their products lack variety. Many of the newer synthetics have proved of great value in soap perfumery, but in all cases, before adoption, experiment is necessary. For this purpose a miniature mill and plodder are used. To save expense, however, many chemists use an ordinary mincing machine, and after passing the perfumed ribbons through two or three times, pound them into a mass in a mortar, and stand aside under ordinary commercial conditions for three months. At the end of this time the durability of any perfume compound can be well judged. To facilitate choice a list of substances with their properties are discussed. The stability and keeping qualities are indicated as follows—*very good, A; good, B; weak, C; poor, D.* These are al' that are necessary for the standard lines of soap, but may be added to when the creation of a new bouquet is desired:

Ajowan oil will replace thyme oil. It is stronger and imparts a pleasing freshness *(A)*.

Almond oil, bitter, useful in acacia and fancy compounds, generally replaced by benzaldehyde, free from chlorine.(*C*).

Ambergris tincture, not often used excepting in very high-class soaps, generally replaced by labdanum *(B)*.

Amyl cinnamic aldehyde, useful in jasmin soaps and very persistent.(*B*).

Amyl salicylate, very good in trefle compounds and quite strong and lasting in use.(*A*).

Aniseed oil, very powerful. Use traces only.(*B*).

Anisic aldehyde, excellent in May blossom and acacia compounds. About 10 per cent sufficient.(*A*).

Atlas cedarwood oil, excellent in acacia, mimosa, santal, and violet. Very strong and lasting. Resinoid also good in fern and chypre.(*A*).

Basil oil, indispensable for mignonette, but requires to be well blended(*B*).

Bay oil, sometimes used in place of clove oil.(*B*).

Benzaldehyde, cheap and useful in almond soaps, traces in fancy compounds yield pleasing results.(*C*).

Benzoin, used as a resinoid and also as a tincture made with industrial methylated spirit, inclined to darken soaps.(*B*).

Benzyl acetate, 5 or 10 per cent will give a refreshing and sweet odour to most soaps, useful in jasmin and orange blossom when blended with petitgrain oil.(*B*).

Benzyl alcohol, weak and faintly balsamic, useful as a diluent.(*C*).

Benzyl benzoate, a good solvent for musk xylene.(*A*).

Benzylidene acetone, useful in the sweet-pea type, blends well with bromstyrole for cheap bouquets. Owing to its irritating effect on the skin, should be used with care.(*B*).

Bergamot oil, very good, often replaced by lemon oil.(*A*).

Beta naphthol ethers, very powerful, but require to be well blended, otherwise coarse. Use in moderation.(*A*).

Bois de rose oil, indispensable in all flower compounds, much improves Bourbon geranium.(*A*).

Bornyl acetate, the base of all pine perfumes, useful in lavender compounds.(*A*).

Bromstyrole, very powerful and stable, good hyacinth base.(*A*).

Cananga oil, useful in violet and santalwood, not very strong and lacks body.(*D*).

Caraway oil, an indispensable constituent in brown windsor. Rather fleeting.(*B*).

Cassia oil, base for all brown windsors, good blender in bouquets, and should not be overlooked in some rose compounds. Causes darkening.(*A*).

Castoreum tincture, excellent and cheap substitute for musk.(*A*). Cedarwood oil, strong and persistent, good basis for violets.(*A*). Cinnamic alcohol, weak but good hyacinth base.(*C*).

Cinnamic aldehyde, occasionally used to replace cassia oil.(*A*).

Cinnamon leaf oil, good substitute for clove oil, darkens in soap.(*C*).

Citral, sometimes used as a substitute for lemon oil.(*B*).

Citronella oils. Both Java and Ceylon very largely employed in all forms of cheap soap compounds, Ceylon frequently preferred and not always on account of its lower cost-very strong.(*A*).

Citronellol, useful in rose compounds.(*B*).

Citronellyl esters, useful as modifiers and blenders.(*C*).

Civet tincture, made with industrial spirit, often replaced by synthetic civets based on phenylacetic acid and skatole.(*A*).

Clove oil, much used for imparting a pleasant sweetness to compounds and indispensable in carnation, darkens rapidly.(*A*).

Copaiba resin (balsam), good fixative.(*A*).

Coumarin, very good in all compounds, not forgetting lavender. Gives a yellowish tinge in time.(*A*).

Para-cresol methyl ether, very strong and stable. Use only about 1 per cent.(*A*).

Diphenyl methane and oxide, very strong and stable, substitutes for geranium oil.(*A*).

Ethyl cinnamate, very powerful and balsamic.(*B*).

Eucalyptus oil, traces useful in fern compounds, much used in medicated soaps.(*A*).

Eugenol, good in carnation, but darkens less than clove.(*B*).

Fennel oil, very useful, requires moderation.(*C*).

Geraniol, stable in rose and other compounds.(*A*).

Geranium oils, both Algerian and Bourbon indispensable, latter rather coarse, equal parts of each give best results, used in rose and all bouquets.(*A*).

Geranyl acetate, excellent in rose and lavender.(*C*).

Ginger-grass oil, very good, but requires to be well blended.(*B*).

Guaiac-wood oil, an excellent base for all compounds.(*A*).

Heliotropin, only permissible in coloured soaps, odour good, and indispensable in heliotropes.(*A*).

Hydroxy-citronellal. Use the residues—quite stable and persistent.(*C*).

Ionone, unpurified 100 per cent or residues will yield good results., about 20 per cent sufficient in violets, less in bouquets.(*B*).

Iso-butyl esters, good modifiers and blenders, rather weak excepting the phenylacetate and salicylate.(*B*).

Iso-eugenol, excellent in carnation but darkens rapidly, colours the soaps containing it.(*B*).

Labdanum, very persistent in small quantities, will replace ambergris, good in lavender.(*A*).

Lavender oil, useless alone, must be strengthened and well blended, oakmoss excellent for the purpose, also rose-mary, thyme, and borneol.(*B*).

Lavender oil, spike, powerful and very good in lavenders, ferns, etc.(*A*).

Lemon-grass oil, basis of all verbenas. Modify with bois de rose or palmarosa—turns the soap yellowish.(*C*).

Lemon oil, inclined to darken slightly. Ten per cent will make a marked difference to many compounds, indispensable in Cologne soaps, but must be well fixed to retard oxidation of terpenes.(*C*).

Linalol. Better use bois de rose oil.(*A*).

Linalyl acetate, good, but better to use bergamot oil.(*B*).

Methyl acetophenone, must be used in small quantities and requires well blending, useful in acacias and mimosas.(*A*).

Methyl anthranilate, very cheap and strong, but inclined to darken.(*A*).

Methyl benzoate, very strong and stable.(*A*).

Methyl cinnamate, better than ethyl ester, small quantities give an amber note.(*A*).

Methyl heptine carbonate, traces sometimes used in violets, sharp at first but softens after a few days.(*C*).

Methyl salicylate, used in chypre and fern soaps.(*B*).

Mirbane oil. Don't use it.(*B*).

Musk ambrette, about 2 per cent is excellent, more gives a sickly sweetness. Residues are good and cheaper.(*A*).

Musk tincture, seldom employed.(*B*).

Musk xylene, very useful, but make sure it is all dissolved, otherwise the soap will be spotty—turns yellowish in time.(*A*).

Nutmeg oil, used occasionally in lavender compounds.(*D*).

Oakmoss, excellent in lavender and fern, much used in fancy bouquets, very persistent. The green resin is good enough for all purposes.(*A*).

Orange oil, excellent sweetener but must be well fixed, inclined to darken.(*C*).

Orris oil concrete, much used in violets, but often replaced with the oleo-resin Or resin extracted from the spent rhizomes. Industrial tinctures of this material useful.(*B*).

Palmarosa oil, good and stable, useful in rose and similar compounds. (*A*).

Patchouli oil, very good and stable, more than 10 per cent becomes unpleasant, much less generally enough, useless in rancid bases.(*A*).

Pepper oil, traces employed in fancy bouquets and carnation compounds.(*B*).

Peppermint oil, traces are useful for developing other odours.(*A*).

Peru balsam, imparts warmth, darkens in time.(*A*).

Petitgrain oil, good in many compounds, but turns yellowish in time, often used for predominating note in glycerine and cucumber and Cologne soaps. Very durable.(*B*).

Phenylacetic aldehyde, not very valuable in soap, better use bromstyrole.(*D*).

Phenylethyl alcohol, useful in all flower compounds.(*A*).

Phenylethyl esters, good blenders, rather weak.(*B*).

Rhodinol, excellent in rose and other compounds, usually too expensive. Use Bourbon Geranium.(*A*).

Rosemary oil, good and stable, imparts freshness, useful in many compounds, especially lavender.(*A*).

Safrole, much used in cheap soaps.(*A*).

Sandalwood oil, excellent blender in violets and roses, requires to be developed in santal soaps.(*A*).

Sassafras oil, indispensable in chypre.(*A*).

Spearmint, powerful at first but evanescent.(*C*).

Storax, the best all-round resinous fixative.(*A*).

Terpineol, often the only perfume in cheap soaps, excels rather as a basis on which to build fanciful odours. Use 10 per cent or thereabouts very stable and strong.(*A*).

Terpinyl esters, fair blenders, but not so stable.(*B*).

Thyme oil, excellent for imparting freshness to all kinds of soap compounds, antiseptic value good.(*A*).

Tolu balsam, good fixative, but inclined to darken.(*B*).

Vanillin, traces useful in fancy bouquets, turns the soap yellowish.(*B*).

Vetivert oil, small quantities are most persistent, good in violets.(*A*).

Flower oils are only used in the highest priced soaps. They yield excellent results. A cheaper jasmin is made at Grasse by distilling the flowers with cedarwood oil. This product is of considerable value. Mimosa absolute should not be overlooked since it is fairly cheap.

MATCHING A PERFUME

Matching a perfume of known composition requires experiment and is often necessary when a toilet soap is included in any series of cosmetic products. As will be readily understood it would be impossible, from a pecuniary point of view, to use a first-class compound in soaps. From another point of view it would be equally unsatisfactory, since some of the ingredients might undergo decomposition, cause discolouration, or generally upset the finished odour to such an extent as to make it unrecognisable. A formula therefore requires very careful examination and analysis. Those ingredients which are known to be stable and not too dear are allowed to remain although the quantities may have to be adjusted. The others are eliminated but replaced with raw materials having similar odours. Other substances may have to be added to diffuse the perfume. The most important point is to choose the right combination of basic notes and add just sufficient to regulate the volatility of the perfume. There are, of course, many essential oils having distinctive odours which at the same time act in this way as for instance, vetivert and santal in violets; patchouli and guaiac-wood in roses. These are often more stable than synthetics but, nevertheless, gum-resins in liberal quantity are imperative constituents. The soap perfumer's stand-by is styrax, but this is by no means the only one of value, almost all the resinous substances are excellent and many useful variations can be made with them. It should be noted that it is useless to judge the odour of a soap compound by the usual methods. The perfume must be incorporated in the soap by milling and the finished tablet left on one side for three months. The experiments leading up to this stage may be carried out with a mincing machine.

In order to indicate the lines upon which matching may be conducted an example of violet will be examined. A good quality compound for general use in perfumery will be approximately as follows

Formula 1

500	Ionone alpha (1)	500
80	Orris oil, concrete (2)	80
50	Heliotropin (3)	50
150	Bergamot oil (4)	150
30	Ylang-ylang oil, Manila (5)	30
40	Sandalwood oil (6)	40
30	Violet leaf absolute (7)	30
25	Cassie absolute (8)	25
50	Jasmin absolute (9)	50
1	Aldehyde C_{12} (10)	1
25	Rose otto, Bulgarian (11)	25
20	Benzoin R. (12).	20
1001		1001

This formula would be adjusted as follows

Replace I with ionone 100 per cent for soaps and reduce the quantity: Replace 2 with orris oleo-resin and reduce, only when costs compel: Retain 3 and 4: Replace 5 with cananga oil and increase: Increase 6: Replace 7 with methyl heptine carbonate and reduce: Omit 8: Replace 9 with benzyl acetate or inexpensive jasmin compound: Omit 10: Replace 11 with Algerian geranium oil and increase: Retain 12: To strengthen and diffuse add cedarwood, clove, and vetivert oils, terpineol and musk xylene or residues.

The formula for the violet soap compound having a similar odour to the above would therefore read (Formula 1a)

Formula 1(a)

Ionone, 100 per cent for soaps	200
Orris oleo-resin	80
Heliotropin	50
Bergamot oil	150
Cananga oil	50
Sandalwood oil	60
Methyl heptine carbonate	1
Benzyl acetate	50
Algerian geranium oil	40
Benzoin R.	20
Cedarwood oil	130
Clove oil	20
Vetivert oil	30
Musk residues	50
Terpineol	70
	1001

In making violet soaps some manufacturers add palm millings which emit a violet-like odour. Others add powdered orris-roots, but the use of the oleo resin dispenses with the necessity.

Formulation of Perfumes in Soap Compounds

Two examples of each of the principal toilet soap perfumes will now be given. The first and better quality one being based where possible largely upon essential oils, and the second and cheaper more particularly upon synthetics. They are all workable and are capable of endless modification to suit individual tastes. By applying the principles outlined above it will be quite easy to further cheapen the compound as desired. With a view to assisting the experimenter in the choice of raw materials for odours of specific type, the more important components are enumerated in accordance with the classification of odours (Formula 2)

Formula 2

Acacia soap (Based on essential oils)

Rosewood	100
Methyl acetophenone	20
Petitgrain para	200
Terpineol	50
Bergamot	50
Methyl cinnamate	20
Cananga	40
Anisic aldehyde	200
Methyl anthranilate	50
Clove	20
Geranium, African	50
Methyl naphthyl ketone	50
Santal	50
Tolu balsam	30
Vetivert	40
Musk xylene	30
	1000

Formula 3

Acacia soap (Based upon synthetics)

Rosewood	50
Petitgrain para	100
Bromstyrole	20
Terpineol	100
Geraniol, Java	100
Cedarwood	100
Methyl cinnamate	20
Cananga	40
Anisic aldehyde	200
Ionone	50
Methyl anthranilate	50
Clove	20
Methyl naphthyl ketone	50
Styrax resin	70
Musk xylene	- 30
	1000

Formula 4

Almond soap

Benzaldehyde	400
Rosewood	150
Clove	100
Geranium, African	50
Orris resin	70
Peru balsam	100
Santal	100
Musk xylene	30
	1000

Formula 5

Amber soap

Rosewood	150
Phenyl ethyl alcohol	50
Bergamot	150
Amyl salicylate	100
Geranium, Bourbon	40
Castoreum absolute	10
Coumarin	100
Labdanum resin	200
Musk xylene	30
Oakmoss	20
Phenyl acetic acid	50
Resin (styrax)	100
	1000

Formula 6

Cedarwood

Santal	150
Bromstyrole	10
Cananga	100
Terpineol	100
Methyl ionone	150
Cedarwood	250

Geranium, Bourbon	100
Vetivert	30
Orris resin	60
Heliotropin	50
	1000

Formula 7

Carnation soap

Amyl salicylate	100
Geraniol, Java	100
Eugenol	450
Geranium, African	50
Cassia	30
Orris resin	50
Iso-eugenol	70
Musk xylene	30
Pepper	20
Peru balsam	—100
	1000

Formula 8

Chypre soap

Bergamot	400
Methyl ionone	100
Geranium, African	100
Civet absolute	5
Orris resin	50
Castoreum absolute	5
Coumarin	50
Musk xylene	30
Oakmoss	50
Patchouli	30
Santal	80
Peru balsam	100
	1000

Formula 9

Cologne soap

Petitgrain para	200
Lavender	50
Bergamot	200
Lemon	150
Lemongrass	50
Methyl anthranilate	40
Rosemary	60
Geranium. African	100
Citral	100
Methyl naphtha] ketone	50
	1000

Formula 10

Heliotrope soap

Benzaldehyde	10
Benzyl acetate	40
Bromstyrole	10
Phenyl ethyl alcohol	90
Geraniol, Java	100
Sweet orange	50
Heliotropin	300
Anisic aldehyde	50
lonone	50
Benzoin resin	100
Musk xylene	50
Peru balsam	100
Vanillin	50
	1000

Formula 11

Herb

Thyme, red	100
Rosemary	100
Lavender, spike	200
Fennel	50

Spearmint	50
Geranium, bourbon	300
Cassia	50
Clove	100
Camomile	50
	1000

Formula 12

Herb compound	500
Citronella, Java	100
Terpineol	300
Rosewood	100
	1000

Formula 13

Bergamot	200
Rosewood	200
Geranium, Algerian	100
Miel compound	100
Amyl cinnamic aldehyde	50
Civet absolute	10
Peru balsam	60
Musk xylene	30
Phenylethyl alcohol	150
Terpineol	100
	1000

Formula 14

Honey

Citronella	450
Lemon	200
Cinnamon leaf	100
Bay	50
Iso-butyl phenylacetate	20
Phenylethyl alcohol	100
Phenylacetic acid	30
Musk residues	50
	1000

Formula 15

Hyacinth soap

Benzyl acetate	200
Rosewood	200
Bromstyrole	50
Phenyl ethyl alcohol	100
Methyl cinnamate	30
Cananga	50
Ionone	50
Clove	70
Geranium	50
Galbanum resin	50
Amyl cinnamic aldehyde	50
Styrax resin	100
	1000

Formula 16

Jasmin soap

Benzyl acetate	200
Rosewood	100
Petitgrain para	80
Phenyl ethyl alcohol	100
Bergamot	100
Amyl salicylate	70
Sweet orange	25
Cananga	100
Clove	50
Civet absolute	3
Orris resin	50
Undecalactone	2
Amyl cinnamic aldehyde	40
Liquidambar resin	50
Musk xylene	30
	1000

Formula 17

Jasmin *(Another formula)*

Benzyl acetate	200
Rosewood	200
Terpineol	100
Petitgrain para	150
Amyl salicylate	50
Cananga	50
Ionone	50
Methyl anthranilate	50
Clove	20
Amyl cinnamic aldehyde	50
Musk xylene	30
Resin (styrax)	50
	1000

Formula 18

Lavender soap

Bergamot	70
Geraniol, Java	50
White thyme	20
Spike lavender	100
Lavender	130
Rosemary	100
Clove	10
Orris resin	30
Benzoin resin	70
Coumarin	50
Musk xylene	30
Oakmoss	30
Patchouli	10
Santal	30
	1000

Formula 19

Lily soap

Benzyl acetate	50
Rosewood	200
Terpineol	200
Citronellol	200
Bergamot	100
Cananga	50
Heliotropin	50
Ionone	30
Hydroxy citronellal	100
Cyclamen aldehyde	10
Amyl cinnamic aldehyde	20
Coumarin	10
Styrax resin	- 80
	1000

Formula 20

Musk

Musk ambrette	20
Musk ketone	30
Vetivert	40
Santal	100
Methyl ionone	200
Liquidambar resin	70
Bergamot	100
Geranium, Bourbon	200
Musk extract, 3 per cent	100
Civet absolute	5
Castoreum absolute	5
Terpineol	100
Cassia oil	-30
	1000

Formula 21

Palm and olive oils

Palm compound	500
Terpineol	200
Lavender, spike	300
	1000

Formula 22

Frose soap

Citronellol	200
Phenyl ethyl alcohol	200
Geraniol palmarosa	200
Verbena	20
Ionone	50
Clove	10
Geranium, African	150
Orris resin	50
Musk xylene	30
Santal	50
Trichlor phenyl methyl carbinyl acetate	30
Vetivert	10
	1000

Formula 23

Santal soap

Rosewood	100
Geraniol, Java	100
Clove	30
Geranium, African	50
Orris resin	50
Coumarin	70
Musk zylene	30
Patchouli	20
Peru balsam	100
Santal	400
Vetivert	*50*
	1000

Formula 24

Violet soap

Rosewood	100
Bergamot	150
Methyl heptine carbonate	10
Cananga	40
Methyl Ionone	300
Mimosa absolute	20
Anisic aldehyde	30
Ionone	200
Orris resin	50
Iso-eugenol	10
Musk xylene	30
Styrax resin	30
Vetivert	30
	1000

Antiseptic and Medicated Soaps

Antiseptic and medicated soaps are made up with all kinds of medicaments, such as iodoform, thymol, phenol, betanaphthol, sulphur, etc. Many of the essential oils used in perfuming the soaps are highly antiseptic.

Perfuming Boxes

When packing wrapped soap it is advisable to spray the boxes with perfume—an example of which is given

Formula 25

Violet soap

Bergamot oil	30
Geranium oil, Algerian	40
Rose, synthetic	30
Jasmin, synthetic	10
Tuberose, synthetic	20
Oakmoss	5
Benzyl cinnamate	20
Coumarin	20
Musk ambrette	10
Tincture of civet, 3 per cent	100
Tincture of benzoin, 10 per cent	715
	1000

Chapter - 6

TESTING OF SOAPS AND DETERGENTS

INTRODUCTION

For a practical and realistic evaluation of quality of soap and detergents, performance test constitute the ideal yardstick. Thus the need of the testing is to prove performance that is material has to pass through various specifications in a process. Physico-chemical analysis alone is not adequate. This chapter highlights current practices followed during testing from time to time to improve their precision and accuracy,

TEST METHODS

Few methods for measurement of physico-chemical properties of surface active agents have been adopted by various industries. Since there are upwards of a thousand available surface active agents whose claims of activity widely overlap, for choice oil the best agent for a given purpose it is necessary that all their properties be recognised and selection made accordingly. Certainly if an agent is not stable to hard water is resembles soap, and must possess other properties sufficiently different from soap to make it competitive. Screening tests can save much effort and can increase the general knowledge of utility when properly used. The tests described have been used successfully for years and cover the general properties of synthetics which make them industrially useful.

An over simplified statement of the detergent process indicates that it is the removal of soil (matter out of place) from a surface in some medium, generally through the application of mechanical force, and most frequently in the presence of a substance which may lower the adherence of the soil to the surface, then maintain the soil in suspension so that it can be rinsed or flushed away. When it is considered that the medium in which the cleansing can take place may be aqueous, nonaqueous, or mixed, that the force applied may be of almost any kind, and that the surfaces and soils to be separated are legion, then the real complexity of the detergency picture becomes apparent. Since some surfaces may be satisfactorily cleaned in one or more media using a wide variety of cleaning agents on any of them, a choice must be made which will prove economically satisfactory. When all these factors are recognised it may not appear so unusual that no accord has been reached as to recognised testing methods.

The most effective method, and the most reasonable one, is to perform the laboratory screening tests, meanwhile building up a fund of data to be correlated with practice, progressing as soon as feasible to a semi- or full-scale trial under practical conditions of operation. Regardless of verbal expression to the contrary, this is the procedure most generally followed.

STATISTICAL PRESENTATION OF DATA

Knowledge of the reliability of results obtained in any test is necessary. Frequently this is accomplished simply by comparison with standard samples.. Certainly the use of samples of known characteristics for comparison purposes is highly desirable but this method lacks precision. In the presentation of data the ASTM Manual on Quality Control of Materials is a useful reference.

In the operation of a test method it should be realised that the error of the average obtained is inversely proportional to the square root of the number of observations made. This simply means that in order to improve upon the information obtained, the method must either be improved to reduce variables which are recognised as resulting in lack of control, or the number of replicate samples must be increased. However this can be carried to extremes when it is recalled that the average of four observations reduces the error of the average only to half that of the single observation. Likewise that the average of 16 samples or observations has 1/4 the error of the single observation. It quickly becomes apparent that for minimisation of effort that the test method itself should be more rigidly controlled if this is possible.

The minimum data which should be presented in recording experimental results is the mean ($\bar{X}$), the standard deviation (σ), the number of observations (n) and sometimes the range. From these data it is a relatively simple matter to compare results and certainly offers much over no statistical data of any kind, as a means for ascertaining the reliability of the experimental work.

Having developed the experimental data, the next question that will arise is whether samples which have been tested actually differ. It is suggested that a rough approximation of the differences between two mean values can be obtained by applying the twice standard error criterion to the data. In other words, if the difference between two mean values is equal to, or greater than twice the larger standard error, the chances are roughly 95 out of 100 that the two samples are different. This is a useful and reliable method when more than six replicate samples have been used in the observation of the mean value. However, for less than this number of replications the approximation becomes even more rough. The significance level between the difference of two mean values can be ascertained more accurately by several methods which presents the factors for calculating 90, 95, and 99% confidence limits for averages which includes the number of observations from 4 up to 25 and greater. These values were computed from Fisher's table of "t". Application of this method will indicate for these several levels of confidence whether the differences between observed mean values are real.

Still a further method is use of Student's *t* for the comparison of two means. The calculations used are given below

$$t = \frac{\overline{X} - \overline{X}'}{\sigma} \sqrt{\frac{n_1 \times n_2}{n_1 + n_2}}$$

where

$$s^2 = \frac{\left[S(x'^2) - \frac{(S(x'^2))}{n_2} + S(x^2) - \frac{(S(x))^2}{n_1} \right]}{n_1 + n_2 - 2}$$

Although these calculations may look rather Formidable they actually are relatively simple and straight forward. Having calculated $(O^{-2}$ it is possible to enter student's table of *t* for the number of degrees of freedom observed, to determine the significance of the difference between two means.

In analytical work it is generally assumed that the reproducibility of data should lie within the 99.25% range. In other words, the chances of being in error should be extremely small. However, in tests such as those described here, where control of many factors is very difficult, the significance level may be considerably broader. Whether this is a 95 or 90% level of significance depends upon the number of samples used, the reproducibility of the method, and the judgment of the operator. Obviously the significance level should be as high as possible, without, as previously suggested, increasing the number of observations too extensively.

Radioactive Tracer Technic

As a new medium, this technic offers possibilities for the investigation of the quantitative characteristics of a system not readily susceptible to other methods. It also makes possible the estimation of extremely minute amounts of materials. Other uses for the radioactive tracer technic lie in the calibration of other methods of examination and in some instances can be used in certain industrial applications for estimation of quality or quantity.

There are two general classifications in the detergent industry to which this method has been applied. One is in estimating the surface active characteristics of agents and the other has been applied to metal cleaning processes. In the former investigation, synthetic agents were synthesized containing a radioactive isotope and the orientation of these at solution-air interfaces measured. The adsorption or relative solubility of ordinarily insoluble salts of surface active agents was measured using a radioactive calcium salt as the insolubilising agent. In the metal cleaning application tagged hydrophobic materials such as stearic acid were used in the soiling medium and the ease of removal from metal surfaces was measured.

Health hazards in the use of radioactive materials must always be considered and it was this that ruled against the use of graphitised carbon 14 as a constituent of a graphite soil for fabric.

In general the radioactive tracer technique would appear to be a most useful tool where the sensitivity of a method is to be determined or for which the usual methods of investigation fail. It currently appears that for the detergent industry, the radioactive tracer technic will find its greatest use in research rather than in regular control operations.

Water Hardness

The water hardness values chosen were for both soft and hard areas in order that detergents might be evaluated for use under the extremes of operating conditions ordinarily encountered. The water itself is comprised of Ca and Mg salts in the ratio of 60 to 40. There are those who object correctly that many synthetic detergents are more affected by the Ca in the water than by the Mg ions, hence that the ratio of Ca in the water should be increased. Others will criticise the range of water hardnesses chosen. The obvious answer to both criticisms is that a really effective agent will be only mildly affected by either type of water hardness, and that at any rate a full investigation of the characteristics of a material will include concentration-water hardness curves for a range up to 1,000 ppm. The present method has successfully served the purpose of screening potential detergents :

2000 ppm. water

Ratio of Ca: Mg of 60:40 is 29.6 g. $MgSO_4 \cdot 7H_2O$, 26.4 g. $CaCl_2 . 2H_2O$

Dissolve separately in distilled water and make up to 15 litres. Dilution to hardness desired :

$$\frac{\text{No. of ml. wanted x hardness}}{2000} = \text{(A) ml. of 2000 ppm. water to use}$$

Make (A) up to volume wanted with distilled water.

SCREENING TESTS

With so many available agents it is desirable to use screening tests to minimise the effort involved in running laborious detergency evaluation, since there are frequently other factors involved which may aid in, controlling their application. Frequently the conditions which either precede or follow a deterging or cleansing operation, or the chemicals with which they may come into contact may control the type of agent which may be used.

It frequently is necessary that the agent to be used in a plant must not only be an effective detergent, but must perform several other additional functions. For example, it may be necessary that the detergent be an excellent wetting agent, must have high effectiveness for promoting emulsion formation, or if not completely rinsed from the fabric may beneficially aid in rewetting that fabric satisfactorily.

The tests which follow are designed to differentiate between the characteristics of surface active agents so that suitable selection may be made. These tests can frequently be initiated prior to wash testing to save much time and effort. The discussion which accompanies each test will further suggest some of the applications for these or other similar materials and reasons for choice.

Acid Stability

A surface-active agent chemically unaffected by acid has many potential uses. Soap is not useful under these conditions since it is decomposed, forming inactive, and many times obnoxious, oily or waxy fatty acids. In the textile industry, the acid-stable agents are used among, other purposes for acid-dyeing operations and in carbonising baths. The metal trades utilise them in pickling and electroplating baths, and they may even be used in the acidisation of oil

Chemical stability may vary markedly among the available agents. Esters may be stable to slight acid concentrations for some time, but increase in acid concentration, temperature, or time of exposure may induce decomposition. Sulphonic acid types of agents generally are quite stable to acids, but sulphonic acid separation may be mistaken for decomposition.

One possible method for evaluating these agents is to add a known excess of acid to a given solution of the agent, boil under reflux, then back titrate, thus quantitatively measuring any change. This method, while quantitative, does not provide acid concentrations of the degree many times encountered in industry. Consequently the qualitative method later described has given adequate results.

The other agents may therefore be used in acid media of considerable strength, but a further elimination would be required by evaluation under conditions approaching actual use as closely as possible. Combinations of tests such as acid stability, surface-tension measurements in acid media, and stability to metallic ions under acid conditions may prove adequate means for comparison of several otherwise almost identical materials.

Acid stability test method

Apparatus .- 250 ml wide-mouth extraction flasks, Allihn condensers, four-bulb, Porous plate fragments.

Procedure : Transfer 100 ml of a solution containing 1.0 g. of agent to a 250 ml. wide-mouth extraction flask and add a piece of porous plate to prevent bumping. Attach condenser.

Bring to the boil and record appearance.

Add 0.1 per cent (1 ml. of 10 per cent) sulphuric acid and boil 15 min. Record appearance. Lack of stability is exhibited by turbidity, separation of an oil, and loss of lathering power.

If no change occurs or the change is minor, add acid to provide I per cent acidity (0.5 ml. of concentrated sulphuric acid) through the condenser. Boil for 15 min. and again record appearance.

If no change occurs, or the change is minor, add acid to provide 3 per cent acidity (1.0 ml. of concentrated sulphuric) and boil a further 15 min. period.

If the product is still stable add sufficient acid for 10 per cent concentration (6.5 ml. concentrated sulphuric). Again boil 15 min. If no change occurs record this fact and discontinue test. At this acid concentration there may be a separation of oil which may perhaps be sulphonic acid insoluble at the conditions prevailing. Dilute with an equal volume of water and agitate vigorously to determine whether foaming power has been destroyed. If separated sulphonic acid has resulted this test indicates its stability but relative insolubility.

Record as "stable," "partially decomposed," or "decomposed" at the acid concentrations indicated.

Alkali Stability and Solubility in Caustic Soda Solutions

Although soap is chemically stable to alkali, it may be salted out and loses its effectiveness whenever a sufficiently high caustic alkali concentration is reached. Consequently, there is a definite place for an alkali-soluble surface-active agent. Perhaps the outstanding use for an agent of this type is in mercerisation, but surface-active agents are also used in the manufacture of viscose yam. There are many other processes where lower alkalinity values are used in which fully soluble, active agents may be effective. It is obvious, however, that such agents must not be subject to decomposition, so that a suitable test may serve to screen out those agents most likely to successful application under the foregoing conditions of usage.

A second test of a more quantitative nature is used to determine the approximate solubility of the wetting agent in sodium hydroxide solutions, while saponification determinations may be made if the materials are of saponifiable nature and such quantitative data may prove necessary.

Few materials are fully soluble in 25 per cent caustic soda solutions, but in many cases such an agent is most desirable, so that an adequate screening test or tests may materially simplify practical testing.

The low surface tension of the more dilute solutions of surface-active agent in dilute alkali are to be expected, but what actually is desired is surface tension lowering even in concentrated alkali, as shown by Areskap 100. However, lowered effectiveness of even this compound may be expected at caustic soda concentrations in excess of 21.6 per cent, or Areskap concentrations greater than 0.8 per cent at 21.6 per cent NaOH solution.

Test method—alkali stability

Apparatus : 250 ml. wide-mouth extraction flasks, Allihn condensers, four-bulb, Porous plate fragments.

Procedure : Dissolve 1.0 g. of sample in 74 ml. of water. Add 25.0 g. of sodium hydroxide (c.p.) and a small piece of porous plate and swirl to dissolve the sodium hydroxide. Record appearance of system after sodium hydroxide is dissolved.

Boil under reflux for 13 min. and again record appearance which most generally will be a salting-out effect.

Cool the contents of the flask. Decant the solution through a fluted filter.

Transfer the insoluble agent from the paper to a beaker containing 25 ml. of distilled water. Add 3 drops of methyl orange indicator solution, stir and titrate with dilute acid to a faintly acid end point.

Stir thoroughly, heat to boil, permit to cool to room temperature, and note separation of oil. If oil separates under these conditions, and material has proven unstable to dilute acid, record the material as being "unstable." If the insoluble material completely dissolves in acidified solution and shows no separation, consider the product as "stable."

Test method—solubility

Apparatus : l-litre Erlenmeyer flask, Dispensing burette.

Reagents .- Solution sodium hydroxide, c.p., 30 g. per 100 g. of solution.

Procedure : Dissolve 1.0 g. agent in 9.0 g. distilled water, add 90 g. of 30 per cent sodium hydroxide solution and transfer to a l-litre Erlenmeyer flask. Rinse the beaker in which the solution was prepared into the flask with small increments of distilled water. Continue the addition of distilled water either until the solution becomes clear and free from undissolved particles, or when 900 ml. of water have been added.

The surface tension of the resultant solution is measured at 25-1C.

Calculations

$$\text{Percentage Agent} = \frac{1.0}{\text{wt. water (g.)} + 100 \text{ g.}} \times 100$$

$$\text{Percentage NaOH} = \frac{27.0}{\text{wt. water (g.)} + 100 \text{ g.}} \times 100$$

Stability toward Metallic Ions

Water solubility of the metallic salts of surface-active agents will greatly influence their ultimate application. First, these agents must be stable to the calcium and magnesium ions of hard water, since one of the factors unfavourable to soap is its ready formation of insoluble, sticky lime and magnesia soaps. In textile processing many operations require the use of acids, as for example, in dyeing, and metal from equipment may be dissolved, so that in this case the agent must not only be a good wetting agent but must be chemically stable both to acid and metallic salts incidentally formed. In carbonising wool a wetting agent may find considerable usage, but must be stable to acid or to a combination of acid and aluminium salts. For scouring pulled wool, a detergent is required which is stable to lime salts. Other agents may be useful in metal salt solutions as in electroplating, pickling or soldering fluxes. Although the foregoing is but a partial list of uses where metallic salts are encountered, it should be evident that knowledge of solubility of the metallic salts of the surface-active agent should be available.

There are two general methods for obtaining these solubility data: One is to prepare the salts by metathesis or other process and determine their solubility; the other is to add the metallic ion in question to a solution of the agent and determine the point at which a given maximum degree of turbidity is obtained, where lathering ceases, or both. 'There are advantages to both methods. The preparation of the pure compound permits accurate measurement of values, but experience with metallic soaps, for example, has shown that the solubility characteristics are entirely different after drying than they are in solution or dispersion, prior to drying. Furthermore, attempted preparation of a salt will present an entirely different problem from one in which the metallic ion represents a small portion of the system. Casual contamination in many cases will give vastly different results from an attempt to measure the solubility of the salt in water, since the pH value of the solution will have profound effect upon degree of solubility.

The specific metallic ions are chosen for this test for the following reasons:

(a) Calcium and magnesium because they are responsible for water hardness.

(b) Copper and nickel because of possible contamination from processing equipment.

(c) Aluminium and iron salts because they readily form insoluble salts and any agent stable to them should prove useful for many purposes.

(d) Barium was chosen because sulphates and even sulphonates are precipitated or become turbid in its presence.

(e) Heavy metal salts because they are represented by lead contamination.

(f) Zinc salts since they are somewhat amphoteric in nature and are present in certain processing baths.

(g) Other salts or varying concentrations at varying pH values may advantageously be evaluated, but their applications are more specific.

Test method

Sample : 1.0 per cent solution in distilled water.

Metallic Salt Solutions: 1.0 per cent solutions (dry weight basis) of the following c.p. salts are used

Salt	Weight for I per cent (dry basis) g. per I 00 ml.
$CaCl_2.2H_2O$	1.327
$MgSO_4.7H_2O$	2.048

Cont .....

$CuSO_4.5H_2O$	1.564
$Al_2(SO_4)_3.18H_2O$	1.948
$BaCl_2.2H_2O$	1.173
$Fe_2(SO_4)_3.xH_2O$	-
$Pb(NO_3)_2$	1.000
$ZnSO_4.7H_2O$	1.781
$Ni(NO_3)_2.6H_2O$	1.591

Dissolve the required amount of salt in water, cool if necessary, and make up to volume.

Equipment : 50 ml. Erlenmeyer flasks, Mohr measuring pipettes.

Procedure : Transfer 10 ml. volumes of I per cent surface-active agent solution to each of nine Erlenmeyer flasks.

Add solution of metallic salt dropwise from a Mohr measuring pipette to the solution of surface-active agent until the solution becomes turbid or precipitation is noted. Record the volume of metallic salt solution used, and heat the flask containing the mixture to the boil. If the solution becomes clear, add additional metallic salt: (*a*) Until 10 ml. of metallic salt solution has been added. (*b*) Terminate the test when the addition of metallic salt causes no further precipitation or when lather no longer is formed.

The total volume of metallic salt solution used to attain the end point is recorded.

Calculation : Metallic ion stability = volume metallic ion solution x 10.

Surface and Interfacial Tension Values and Spreading Coefficient

Potential detergent and wetting action may be ascertained by measurement of surface and interfacial tension. In general, the greater the ability to reduce surface tension and to lower the interfacial tension between oil and water, for example, the more useful the composition may be for producing desired effects under actual conditions of usage. These measurements have a practical application since dilution effect and quality may thus be indicated. The activity of certain baths, as for example electroplating baths, in which a surface-active "anti-pitting" agent has been used, may be controlled by use of these methods.

Surface-tension measurements generally refer to the liquid-air interface, while interfacial tensions refer to interfaces such as liquid-liquid or solid-liquid. Since these interfaces are so interrelated, it is difficult to discuss them separately, but an attempt will be made to do so as a means for simplification.

Surface tension

(a) Capillary height or pressure.

(b) Drop weight.

(c) Maximum bubble pressure.

(d) Capillary waves.

(e) Vibrating jet.

(f) Drop height.

(g) Drop-shape.

(h) Maximum pressure in drops.

(i) Method of Sentis (capillary tube hanging drop and measurement of meniscus height in tube above drop).

(j) Ring method.

Interfacial tension

Wetting of liquid by a liquid, or solid by a liquid may be estimated by several methods. The solid-liquid interface may be measured by several techniques which require estimation of the angle of contact

(a) Pressure of displacement.

(b) Horizontal plate.

(c) Vertical bar.

(d) Deposited film.

Liquid-liquid interfaces may be determined by several methods

(a) Stalagmometer.

(b) Drop weight (Millard)

(c) Ring

(d) Ripple.

The facility with which a solution may wet another surface, whether solid or liquid, may have considerable influence upon subsequent operations. Cleaning or dyeing a fibre, wetting a metal surface or foliage, and formation of emulsions all are dependent upon optimum interfacial tension properties.

The lower the surface and interfacial tensions of a system, the better the chance of forming an emulsion or wetting a given surface. Cupples has applied these data to foliage wetting by utilising the measurement of surface tension against air and against mineral oil. The spreading coefficient (SC) of a system may be calculated as follows :

SC = surface tension oil - (surface tension solution
+ interfacial tension)
(1)

The more positive the value obtained, the greater the spreading value of a system. Consequently, the possible utility of the wetting agent for insecticidal sprays may be predicted as an emulsifier for mineral or other oil, or as a means for wetting oiled soiled surfaces.

In general, the du Nouy instrument may most satisfactorily be used for liquid-liquid systems. One instrument may furthermore be used for the determination of both surface and interfacial tensions. For control purposes, the dial reading after calibration may be adequate, but if highest accuracy is desired, ring corrections have been developed.

Surface Active Agents

Since surface activity is increased by this addition, the term "builder" for added sodium sulphate is warranted, and this effect may be attributed at least in part to orientation of the surface-active agent at the interfaces involved.

The generally high surface activity of these agents upon dilution indicates their potential utility for the wide variety of uses open to surface-active agents. Those materials with most highly positive spreading coefficients are potentially useful as inseetidical spreading agents and are most likely to be good emulsifying agents.

Test Method

Apparatus .- Either the precision (surface tension) or interfacial tensiometers may be used.

Calibration :

(a) Level the tensiometer.

(b) Adjust the torsion wire until it is taut.

(c) Adjust vernier of scale to zero.

(d) Adjust platinum ring.

(e) Place piece of paper on ring and adjust until index level of arm is opposite reference line of mirror (thus compensating for weight of paper).

(f) Place weights totalling 600 mg. on paper platform.

(g) Turn adjusting head (controlling dial reading) until the index level of the arm is opposite the reference line of mirror. Record dial reading to 0.10 division.

(h) Calculate scale reading as follows : Weight added to ring (m) = 0.600 g. Mean circumference of ring (L) = 4.00 cm. Acceleration of gravity *(G)* = 980.3 cm. per sq. sec. (at Chicago)

$$Y = \frac{MG}{2L} = \frac{0.600 \times 980.3}{2 \times 4.00} = 73.52 \text{ dynes per cm.}$$

For the interfacial tensiometer substitute the pertinent values in the above equation.

(i) If the recorded value is greater than the calculated value of h, shorten the torsion arm, or lengthen it if the recorded value is less.

(j) Repeat the calibration procedure, readjusting to the zero position after each change of torsion arm length until the dial reading corresponds to the calculated value.

(k) Adjust the dial reading to zero, remove the weights and the paper platform and readjust so that the torsion arm indicator is in alignment with the reference line of the mirror.

Precautions :

(a) The wire of the ring should lie in one plane, be horizontal, and round.

(b) The vessel holding the liquid should be large enough so that curvature of the free surface shall have no effect upon the shape of the liquid column raised by the ring.

(c) The liquid surface should be free from motion.

(d) The ring should be only very slowly raised.

(e) There should be no evaporation or coating of the surface.

Procedure : Prepare 1.0 per cent solutions of the agents in distilled water. Retain a portion of dilution. Determine surface tension by averaging four measurements. The reading is taken at the point where the film breaks, while every effort is made to maintain the torsion arm indicator exactly opposite the reference line of the mirror. The interfacial tension measurement is made by immersing the ring in the aqueous layer, then carefully flowing a sufficient depth of layer of paraffin oil (Nujol) over the aqueous surface that the inverted V of the ring shall at all times during the measurement be immersed in the oil. The measurement is carefully made, since extremely low interfacial tensions are hard to discern, and in some instances no more than one measurement may be made because of preferential wetting of the ring by the oil. The results are averaged and recorded.

The ring is cleaned between determinations by immersion in turn in carbon tetrachloride and dilute hydrochloric acid solution followed by flaming.

Similar readings are obtained for 0.25 per cent solutions of the agents, and 0.0625 per cent solutions.

Corrections for surface tension measurements may be made by reference to calibration curves or to the data developed by Harkins and Jordan (4) or Zuidema and Waters (7) for interfacial measurements.

Lime Soap Dispersion

The synthetic surface-active agents will themselves form calcium and magnesium salts of varying degrees of solubility, and highly effective compounds will exhibit exceptional tolerance for these ions. A possible use for these agents is in combination with soda soap as a dispersant for subsequently formed insoluble soaps. This lime soap dispersing action has been put to use in the war effort since both the Army and Navy use certain synthetics in combination with soap in their all-purpose or sea-water detergents. A further possibility is that these synthetics may be used to cleanse lime soap-containing garments, since these soaps may readily be removed either by solubilising them or removing them by peptisation or emulsification. In such cases high washing temperatures will have important effect upon degree of removal by the synthetic. Two possible conditions may thus be encountered : (1) presence of large amounts of insoluble soap; (2) presence of' relatively light films, of insoluble soap. Laboratory test conditions should be chosen which will duplicate the most severe conditions which will be encountered, so that relatively large amounts of lime soap should be present in the test medium.

Nonlathering agents may also be useful for lime soap dispersion (phosphates) but in cases where soap is actually regenerated, by exchange of ions to form a soluble calcium or magnesium complex, a lesser amount of lime soap should be used or formed in situ, and the solution should be titrated with the regenerating agent to permanent lather.

Test, Method

Reagents : 2.3 per cent sodium oleate (dry weight). Either pure sodium oleate or oleate flake soap.

0.34 per cent $CaCl_2$ solution.

0.2 N HCl.

Methyl orange-xylene cyanole indicator solution (Eastman No. 2216). 10 per cent volume solution of auxiliary agent under investigation.

Procedure :

(a) Add 1-ml. increments of auxiliary or dispersing agent up to 8 ml. to separate 20 ml. volumes of 2.3 per cent soap solution in 125 ml.

flasks. The solutions are then shaken and to them are added 25 ml. of 0.34 per cent calcium chloride solution. Heat for 15 min. on a water bath, then suction filter through a prepared No. 4 Whatman paper on a Gooch crucible. The flask and crucible are then washed with three 10 ml. portions of distilled water. If complete filtration is impossible with 8 ml. of auxiliary agent, this fact is recorded without further examination.

(b) The filtered solutions are titrated with 0.2 N HCl to the xylol-cyanole end point which is gray in colour. A blank for each agent comprising 20 ml. of soap solution, 25 ml. of calcium chloride solution, and the volume of auxiliary agent required, are titrated without filtration. When the filtered test sample has a titration value practically equal to that of the blank, the volume of auxiliary agent required to produce complete dispersion is recorded.

(c) The results are expressed as centigrams of auxiliary agent required to disperse 45.5 mg. of calcium oleate formed. One millilitre of auxiliary agent is equal to a dispersion number of 10.

Calculation : Dispersion number = ml. auxiliary agent x 10.

Practical Wetting Tests

Since the usual surface and interfacial tension measurements limit the systems under investigation to liquid-air, liquid-liquid, or liquid-solid, more practical systems may prove useful in evaluation. In these systems capillarity may be a sufficient criterion of suitability, and the height to which the solution rises in a strip of fabric or paper may provide adequate comparisons. In these cases the interfaces involved may be liquid-solid-air-oil, but other materials may further complicate the picture.

Generally Draves-Clarkson skein test and the canvas disk method are used. The canvas disk test can readily be used under conditions not suited to the use of skeins.

Regardless of what test surface is used, standardisation of the test is necessary. With skein preparation wetting times will vary for a given weight of skein with humidity, spool, tension on the skein winder, and age of yarn or variation from lot to lot. The canvas used may age to give progressively slower wetting times as the finishing agents become progressively more water repellent. In fact, whenever *any fibre, yarn* or fabric is used, steps should be taken to standardise against a stable wetting agent under a given set of conditions, and this standardisation made periodically, to save embarrassment. The Draves-Clarkson and canvas disk tests have in their favour simplicity of operation, minimum of equipment, and adequate reproducibility. Both methods are subject to variation in the standard fabric or yarn used in the determination, either as a result of aging or actual variation in the character of the manufactured article. They furthermore have been most widely used, and evaluation data on either basis are available from the literature. Either method provides data which, under careful control, can be used for the evaluation of comparative wetting efficiency, but their values are not directly comparable.

Test method : Draves-Clarkson test

Equipment : 500 ml. graduate.

Hook or sinker, 1.50 g. in weight (of No. 12B. and S. gage copper: with ¼-in. hood opening

Anchor, 20 g. in weight.

Skeins : A 5.0 g. skein of two-ply (70/2 combed peeler yarn) is prepared such that an 18-in. loop can be formed. The yarn may best be standardised against a standard sample of wetting agent, adjusting the weight of skein to yield a specific wetting time.

Wetting Test :

(a) Prepare 500 ml. of 1.0 per cent test solution.

(b) Transfer 250 ml. of 1.0 per cent solution to a 600 ml. beaker, add 250 ml. distilled water and adjust the temperature to 25 ± I C.

(c) Transfer the temperature-adjusted 0.50 per cent solution to a 500 ml. graduate.

(d) Attach the hool or sinker to the 18-in. loop, hold the skein in the middle and cut the end opposite the hook.

(e) Transfer the hook, anchor, and skein to the graduate of solution and dip the hook into the solution until the surface is just touched, then drop the skein and start the stopwatch simultaneously.

(f) The sinking time is attained when the skein sinks, and the hook just reaches the level of the anchor, at which time the stopwatch again is snapped.

(g) Repeat steps d, e, and f until five replicate skeins have been tested, using the same solution throughout.

(h) In a manner similar to step c, prepare an 0.25, 0.125, 0.0625 or further dilution until a wetting time in one dilution of + 180 sec. is attained for two replicate skeins. The test is then terminated.

(i) The mean values for each dilution shall then be reported.

Note : This test is applicable to acid, alkaline, or saline conditions.

Canvas disk test method

Equipment : Vernon duck.

Steel die, I in. in diameter.

Carbon filter tube of 75 mm. stem and 38 mm. inside top diameter. 600 ml. Griffin beaker with spout.

Disks: The disks may best be cut using a 1-in. steel die. Cut the disks on a smooth, hardwood surface. The disks for use must be flat and free from rough edges and ravelings. Cut the disks from the fabric area bounded by I in. within either side of the selvedge.

Wetting Test :

(a) Transfer 500 ml. of test solution at 25 ± 1 C. to a 600 ml. beaker.

(b) Drop the flat canvas disk into the funnel and quickly invert and immerse in the test solution.

(c) Start the timer as soon as the disk enters the solution. The individual test is considered as terminated when the disk first begins to sink.

(d) Four replicate tests shall be made for each dilution tested.

(e) The average results shall be reported as seconds wetting time for each of the concentrations tested, which shall be 0.5, 0.25, 0.125, 0,0625 or further dilution until the disks give wetting times greater than 180 sec., at which point the test shall be terminated.

Note : This test is applicable to acid, alkaline, or saline conditions.

The test equipment should be so aligned that a disk held horizontally by the filter tube should be I in. below the surface of the liquid.

Rewetting Test

It frequently is desirable to know whether the agent in question is suitable for rewetting purposes since this may be an important factor in its choice for subsequent processing.

Briefly, this test consists of applying the solution of rewetting agent by means of dipping in a bath and running through squeeze rolls (a pair of regular hand wringer rolls will prove satisfactory). Good impregnation is obtained by running two ends (i.e. opposite end of tape fed through wringer first) at a sufficiently high roll pressure to give a 100% weight pick-up. The test strips are then either air or oven force-dried and allowed to condition over night. The next morning the rewetting times are run in much the same manner as wetting times. Though pretested, the tape has been found to vary from lot to lot, and drying conditions have been found to alter the rewetting times considerably so that it is necessary to run a standard agent for comparison with the experimental sample.

Test Method

Equipment : Stopwatch. 500 ml. graduate, Hook, 1.00 g., Anchor, 40 g., Distance hook to anchor, 20 mm., Tape, length 9 in., width 1¼ in, Laboratory padder or wringer rolls.

Impregnation : A 21 in. length of tape (sufficient to allow for shrinkage and trimming) is required for duplicate determinations at each concentration of surface active agent.

An initial bath concentration of 0.0625% is suggested, though this may be adjusted to double or half this concentration, depending upon effectiveness in speed of wetting.

The bath temperature is adjusted to 70^{0}C.

The tape is run through the padder or wringer twice, reversing ends at 200, pounds pressure (20 lb. pressure/inch face). Adjustment of add-on or solution pick-up is made for 100% weight increase of tape.

The tape is oven-dried 10 minutes at 105 C. or dried overnight and conditioned overnight in either case at 70^{0}F. and 65% R.H.

Rewetting time :

(a) The 500 ml. graduate is filled with water at the required temperature. (A fresh portion of water is used for each test to avoid contamination by surfactant)-

(b) The hook is inserted through the tape about ¼ in. from one end on the centre line.

(c) The tape is held by the free end so that the anchor and bottom hook are just submerged in the liquid in the graduate.

(d) The tape is dropped and the stopwatch is started when the anchor strikes the bottom of the graduate.

(e) When the hook and tape start to sink at a constant rate the sinking time (rewetting time) is reached and the watch is stopped.

Lather Values

The relative lathering action of surface-active agents is obviously important with detergents and wetting agents used largely for their foaming action. Soap, as the time-recognised detergent, foams profusely in soft water or even in hard water if a sufficient amount is present to overcome both water hardness and the insoluble soap formed. As a consequence, foam is now considered a requisite to detergent action. Many detergent adjuncts, which are detergents in their own right, produce no foam. These adjuvants are the alkaline salts such as the carbonates, silicates, borates, and phosphates. The fact that these materials did not foam disproved the theory that foam was useful as a measure of detergency, but the volume of foam formed is still a very valuable property of surface-active materials. Ability to foam at extreme dilution or under adverse conditions may be an important factor in application, Wetting agents have been used in the wash water of conditioning systems to remove foreign substances, but excessive foam would be a liability rather than an asset.

Many methods for measuring foaming characteristics of compositions have been devised. From the consideration of equipment involved they may be classified as follows

(a) Bubble cylinder.

(b) Manual manipulation of closed container.

(c) Capillary under constant pressure.

(d) Solution drop, open cylinder.

(e) Mechanical agitation in closed vessel.

(f) Single bubble.

The subject, of foams is a complicated one, but for many purposes a measurement of foam height will suffice as a means for preliminary comparison. The method often used in the absence of other equipment is to shake a volume of solution in a stoppered graduate in a standard manner, and measure the foam formed. This method provides only a rough estimate. Since a variation of ± 15 per cent is about the best that may be expected under carefully controlled conditions.

The most satisfactory method for the evaluation of foaming agents is that developed by Ross and Miles. This test is easy to make, the equipment made according to ASTM specifications is commercially available and relatively inexpensive, outside variables are reduced to a minimum, and reproducibility is good. Figs. 12.1 and 12.2 give the necessary specifications which must be checked against the equipment as supplied. Careful evaluation will require tests over a range of concentrations and temperatures.

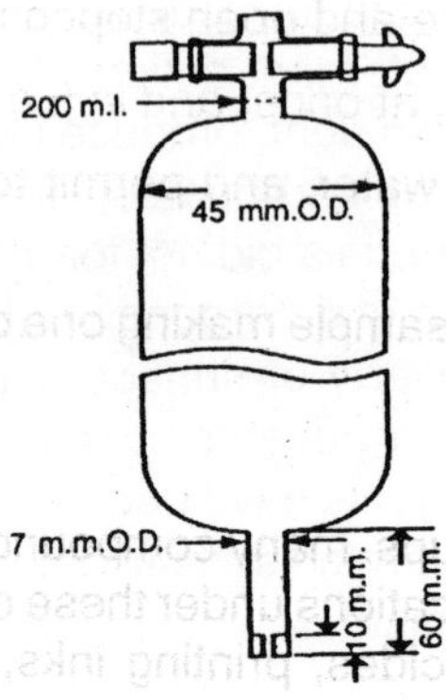

Fig. 14.1. Ross-Miles lather test foam pipette.

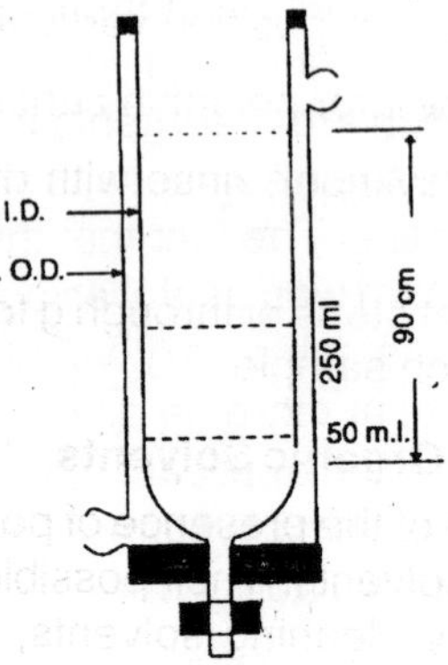

Fig. 14.2. Ross-Miles lather test foam receiver.

The anionic synthetic detergents will form salts of varying degrees of solubility and these will foam to greater or lesser extent. Consequently, hard water (calcium or magnesium ions) will have more or less effect upon the lather of the sodium salts. In some cases, the calcium and magnesium ions may depress foam formation, in others foam may be increased, while in still others no change will be observed.

Test method : Ross-Miles pour foam test

Apparatus: Level cylinder so that drops fall vertically into centre of liquid at bottom of cylinder.

Solution Preparation

(a) Dissolve sample in distilled water at double the concentration desired by bringing to the boil then cooling to 25°C.

(b) Make back to weight with distilled water for loss by evaporation.

(c) Dilute to correct concentration by using water at 25°C of double the hardness or strength finally required.

Procedure :

(a) Start circulation pump on column to maintain temperature at 25 0.2°C.

(b) Rinse cylinder walls with distilled water, drain 10 min. and close stopcock.

(c) Age solution for 10 min. in constant temperature both at 25 ± 0.2°C.

(d) Wet down walls of cylinder with 50 ml. of test solution by washing walls in circular motion with 50 ml. pipette of solution.

(e) Immediately transfer 200 ml. of test solution to tipped pipette. Insert in holder in position vertical to base and open stopcock.

(f) Record later height in centimeters, at once, and in 5 min.

(g) Drain cylinder, rinse with distilled water, and permit to drain for 10 min.

(h) Repeat steps of through g for next sample making one determination for each sample.

Solubility—Organic Solvents

In spite of the presence of polar groups, many compounds are soluble in nonpolar solvents. Their possible applications under these conditions are in paints, dry cleaning solvents, insecticides, printing inks, and as self-emulsifying agents.

Since the surface active agent generally is added to produce some given effect, it is not necessary that solubility be determined under conditions of greatest accuracy: Small amounts of agent are generally sufficient or must be maintained. It is therefore felt that the accuracy of the method used is entirely adequate.

Only the pure materials are evaluated for this purpose, since even traces of inorganic salts or of water will reduce actual or apparent solubility.

Other solvents may be used in this test when further information is desired, although chlorinated hydrocarbons, a polar solvent, and a hydrocarbon are represented.

Test Method

Sample Weight : 0.50 g.

Equipment .- 16-oz. glass stoppered bottles dispensing burettes.

Temperature : 25 ± 3°C.

Solvents : Transfer 0.50 g. of sample to the glass-stoppered bottle. Add 1.0 mi. of solvent, shake thoroughly, and determine whether solution has taken place. Continue adding increments of solvent, either until solution is effected, or until 450 ml. of solvent has been added.

Calculation :

$$\text{Percentage solubility} = \frac{0.50}{\text{vol. solvent} \times \text{sp. gr.}} \times 100$$

COTTON WASHING

Through the process of forming fibre into yarn arid into fabric, and prior to conversion into garments, rigorous cleaning schedules are followed which require considerable amounts of detergents. When of sufficiently high tensile strength characteristics, those fibres and fabrics which can withstand the cleaning process most satisfactorily will be chosen for the hardest wear. Cotton still retains its historic leadership even though the synthetic fibres are gaining much favour. Indeed several of the synthetic fibres are simply cellulose which has been treated to provide fibres differing from the original cotton in luster, evenness of character, and offering opportunities for styling that cotton does not provide. Cotton as well as many of the fabrics made from these fibres can be washed repeatedly, wear well, and retain their dimensional stability. These are the fibres which are washed most often and their cleansing represents the large outlet for cleansing agents.

The controversy as to whether an applied soil should simulate a "real" soil or be a synthetic one continues. Practically speaking, the soil and its method of application and the laboratory machine used in washing are minor factors so long as they remain constant, provided that the data so obtained can be correlated with practice. Advancement from the laboratory to the practical scale for proof of utility is a "must" and should proceed as soon as laboratory data are convincing.

Water Hardness

In general, most detergents become less effective when water hardness increases. Certain of the anionic type synthetics are improved in detergency in the presence of moderate amounts of calcium and magnesium salts but excesses render the surface active agent totally ineffective or at least reduce effectiveness in cleansing action. Calcium is the ion which causes most difficulty. Nonionics are generally only slightly affected by water hardness.

Exactly what ratio of calcium to magnesium to use and what shall be the water hardness for detergent testing are factors which must be decided. Many investigators have used a ratio of calcium to magnesium of 60 to 40 while others have increased the ratio or have excluded magnesium entirely. Regardless of the ratio used it is desirable that the detergency test be made over a range of water hardnesses, and if this is done, and the range is sufficiently extended, the effect of having used only calcium as the hardening ion will have been equivalated.

A standardised water hardness is desirable and one which can be made in a stock solution for dilution purposes should be used. For general screening purposes hardness levels of 50 and 300 ppm. have been used successfully. First and most important, they demonstrate the comparative effectiveness of a detergent when subjected to hard water usage; and second they represent levels of practical significance. A 50 ppm. level probably represents the maximum (with exceptions) for the large population areas, while the 300 ppm. hardness is one frequently approached in hard water areas.

Because of test discrepancy, suspected inaccuracy in preparation of standard water, or necessity for analysis of unknown water, it is valuable to have several test methods available. Both of the following have been used successfully : Langelier method or the Versenate method. The former is a variation of the soap titration method, and the latter a calorimetric titration procedure. The APHA soap titration method is still useful, but in inexperienced hands can prove misleading and takes longer to perform than either of the foregoing methods.

Machines

When a decision has been reached as to the manner in which mechanical action shall be applied in the washing operation, the machine should then be designed so that all of the other factors involved in the washing operation can be controlled. It should be obvious that mechanical action is applied in the washing operation and depending upon the fibre and fabric, and the state of manufacture, the application of mechanical "elbow grease" may be varied.

A very short review of some of the operations in washing (scouring or cleansing) may indicate why some of the types of washing machines have been developed. In the manufacture of textile fibres there are many points where cleansing must be performed before subsequent processing can be properly controlled. In the cotton mill raw cotton is mechanically cleaned of burrs and extraneous matter and formed into yarn which is then woven into a fabric. Before this fabric can be further processed it must be kiered, which is simply removal of the cotton wax and lignin-like materials inherent to the cotton; then it is bleached and further processed. Following the dyeing operation it generally is necessary to "soap off' or scour for final finishing. Washing of fabrics in the home may take many forms. It may be simple hand washing or it may be accomplished with any one of several different types of washing machines, either manually or automatically operated. Here the detergent is selected with a view to providing the greatest soil removal for the amount of mechanical energy applied to the fabric in scrubbing and removing the closely adherent soil.

Many laboratory machines have been designed which provide control of operating conditions for the evaluation of detergents, most of them varying in the method of applying force to the cleaning operation. Generally the evaluation of a washing machine, as contrasted with detergent testing, will be accomplished on a full scale basis.

Standard Cotton Soil Fabric Preparation

The requirements for a standard soiled fabric are

The fabric should be uniform.

The soiling operation should provide the same initial amount of soil, and the same removal value for any given detergent under identical conditions of cleansing.

The soil removal values should be reproducible, preferably of analytical accuracy.

The effect of aging should be minimised.

The method for determination of soil removal or retention should be reproducible, preferably quickly accomplished, and closely correlated with actual practice.

The process of preparing a standardised soil fabric may be subdivided as follows: fabric, desizing of fabric, soil, soiling machine, wash test machine, wash test method, storage, evaluation of washed swatches, soiled fabric testing, statistical data.

Fabric choice

Indian Head fabric is a plain weave sheeting, has a thread count of 48 x 54, is available in several widths, and has a weight of 5 ounces to the square yard. To minimise the desizing problem, purchase is made on specification requiring from the manufacturer a scoured, bleached, dried, but unmercerized or otherwise finished grade. This meant that chemical change or deposition of chemicals liable to change the surface reactivity of the fabric were eliminated since a mercerized or chemically treated surface is much more reactive than one not so treated.

Desizing

For purposes of uniformity all sizing should be removed. Variation in fabric characteristics resulting from small scale operation led to desizing in a 25 x 25 in. pony wash wheel.

Soil

A test solid generally will comprise a binding agent and a material which permits quantitative estimation of removal and which in itself may be a natural soil. Since soot is a common soiling agent and certainly lends itself to reflectance measurement against a white fabric, it is not unusual that carbon in some form should be used. Carbon will vary widely in composition depending upon its method of manufacture. Some may be very finely divided, others coarse, and the particle size distribution may vary widely. Some carbons may be predominantly oil-dispersible and others water-dispersible, but apparently satisfactory results have been obtained using either type.

Oildag concentrate has been used satisfactorily for at least 12 years and is comprised of colloidal graphite and apparently an oil-soluble dispersing agent, dispersed in mineral oil. This forms relatively stable dispersions in nonaqueous solvents. So long as the code number which appears on the Oildag package is specified, satisfactory reproducibility by the manufacturer has been noted. The binding agent for the graphite may be chosen from a wide variety of agents, but preferred is a vegetable oil such as Wesson oil, though Mazola oil can be substituted for it. Others have used lard, tallow, or other natural oils. Yet others have used mineral oils because they are not readily susceptible to atmospheric oxidation. Wesson oil was chosen because when it was properly aged or cured on the fabric, it made the graphite much more difficult to remove than did mineral oil, giving a satisfactory spread in soil removal. The difficulty in the use of an oxidizable oil however is that the degree of oxidation must be controlled and the storage conditions maintained at an optimum to prevent further oxidation.

The medium to be used for dispersion of the carbon and oil is obviously important. In some systems graphite or carbon is deposited upon the fabric in water, loose carbon removed, and the soiled fabric either used as such or the dried fabric impregnated additionally with an oil. Water is a safe and inexpensive medium for soil application, but the fabric must be treated to remove wrinkles and loose carbon. Choice of a chlorinated solvent may be preferable to a naphtha solvent wherever fire hazard is involved, though the latter is less expensive and relatively nontoxic.

A technical grade of carbon tetrachloride has been used and while there is no evidence that inhibitors added to the carbon tetrachloride may affect oxidation, this is a possibility which has not been explored.

The soiling solution (or suspension) used has the following composition

5.0	grams Wesson oil
10.0	grams Oildag concentrate (Acheson Colloids Corp.)
12.0	litres carbon tetrachloride (Dowelene, Dow Chemical Co.)

The amounts of Wesson oil and Oildag are weighed to the accuracy indicated, and the carbon tetrachloride measured from a two-litre graduate. Care is taken to disperse the Wesson oil and Oildag thoroughly during dilution.

Soiling machine

'The soiling operation is important, and to insure reproducibility of application it is general practice to use a machine of some sort. Generally a chlorinated solvent or hydrocarbon is used as a means for uniformly applying them to the fabric. The machine was developed from an initially hand operated heated tube to the presence equipment. Since moisture as dew deposited on the fabric (as a result of solvent volatilisation) has such a marked effect upon soil characteristics, the machine was designed to minimise the effect of condensed moisture by raising the dewpoint.

Soil storage

The ideal soiled test fabric should be completely stable toward ageing or storage. The soil described continues to age over a considerable period of time, but to minimise this effect it was found that ordinary mechanical refrigeration during storage of the soiled cloth in a dry atmosphere will prevent change in soil removal characteristics over a period of a month. All of the usual methods for inhibiting oxidation such as vacuum, absence of light, inert atmosphere, desiccator, etc. (and other than the use of an inhibitor) were evaluated in arriving at the most desirable storage conditions noted above.

Evaluation of washed swatches

Since the soil is designed to permit a spread of results from original soil to original white (which seldom if-even is attained), and since this is what the eye sees, regardless of actual weight percentage soil distribution, a photometric method for soil removal evaluation is indicated. Other investigators prefer the measurement of soil removed from the fabric and held in suspension in the solution, essentially disregarding the fabric as a means for evaluation of removal. This latter method utilises the photometer, reading transmittance against a curve for removal, but possible turbidity of detergent in solution interferes, and somewhat narrows the utility of this method.

Standardisation of Solid Fabric Testing

Since every load of samples includes at least one standard detergent product, for many years it was considered sufficient simply to use the soiled fabric as it was cured or artificially aged and without preliminary evaluation. Apparently this is the general method followed by a large proportion of the investigators reporting detergency data.

In an attempt to improve reproducibility each roll of soiled fabric is tested immediately after preparation and without further treatment. There are variations from roll to roll as evidenced through the use of the standard detergent sample. Having ascertained the degree of soil removal immediately after soiling, and knowing the degree of retentivity of soil desired, the freshly produced fabric is then baked in a circulatory oven in festooned form for periods of time which experience indicates will provide adequate resistance to removal. After baking, the soiled fabric is again tested under standard conditions to be certain that specified control has been attained.

COTTON WASH TEST METHODS

The wash test method chosen will depend to a considerable extent upon the soiled test fabric and the washing machine available. Depending upon the mechanical energy expended in the washing operation, a soiled fabric may be of single or multiple wash characteristics.

Frequently, a soiled fabric designed for one type of operation will be found useful for others, and the influence of the washing machine will be minimised.

Having decided that the fabric may prove satisfactory with the available washing machine, a decision will be made as to whether a single or multiple washing operation shall be followed. Home laundering may encompass pre-wash and wash operations; a single wash; and single or multiple rinse procedures. Power laundries follow a multiple suds, multiple rinse procedure. Which procedure is chosen will be arbitrary, since the laboratory machine used frequently cannot be compared exactly with a full scale washer.

Next the duration of the wash period must be decided. It should be long enough that stabilised conditions of soil removal can be attained, but not so long that unnatural redeposition of soil can occur. For laboratory work where many samples must be screened under a variety of concentrations and water hardnesses, the shorter the washing period (within reason) the greater will be the work output.

Whether the rinse shall be by machine or by hand, and whether the test pieces shall be wrung out by hand or by using wringer rolls will depend upon the degree of stability of soil removal. Certainly, if the rinse removes considerably further amounts of soil, this should be done under controlled conditions and not haphazardly, and the rinse will be by machine. However, if the soil removed in the rinse is negligible, a simple hand-rinsing is indicated to save time and effort. The same argument is applicable to hand vs. roll wringing of swatches, but in either case the rinse water should be as well removed as possible to prevent possible migration of soil or retained discoloration.

Drying of the washed swatches is important. Migration frequently may occur when the test pieces are laid out flat or hung on a line and permitted to dry overnight. Forced hot air drying in either vertical or horizontal position is therefore indicated.

Deter-Meter Test Method

Dynamics. General testing, 120 cycles/minute. 50 min. amplitude. No. 2 impact surface spacing. 5 minute wash time.

Concentrations. At three chosen levels.

Temperature. 120, 140 160°F.

Replicate Tests. Three, using fresh swatches in each. Where a relatively large number of concentrations or temperatures are involved two swatches at each point are suggested.

Sensitiveness of Test Method Ability is claimed to distinguish between concentrations which differ as little as 0.01% with a single swatch at each concentration.

Conventional Washer Method

The water capacity of machine with an 8-pound load (or other recommended load) is determined for calculation of detergent requirement. The load is weighed into the machine and should consist of normally soiled, fast-coloured or white garments.

Test Cloth Preparation. Each load contains, in addition to the soiled garments, five 5 x 6 inch swatches of standard soiled fabric marked for identification.

Charging the Washer.

(a) The machine is filled to the predetermined level with water at 120°F.

(b) The detergent is added with the agitator in motion to permit rapid solution.

(c) The 8-pound weighed load is added.

(d) The load is washed for 10 minutes.

(e) The garments are then wrung into a stationary tub of 9 gallons of water of the same hardness as the wash, at 100 ± 5°F.

(f) A hand rinse is administered in the water of step (e) by thoroughly moving the garments up and down in the water.

(g) The rinsed garments are wrung into the machine filled with 17 gallons of fresh water of the hardness in use at 100 ± 5°F.

(h) A machine rinse is made for 5 minutes,

(i) The garments are wrung from the rinse.

Drying the Washed Swatches. The soil swatches are removed and pressed dry at a low iron temperature in a flat work ironer.

Practical Wash Tests

For complete assurance that any developed detergent composition is satisfactory for the purpose designed, it is necessary that the product at least be pilot-plant tested. Satisfactory screening on a full scale with home washer and on a pilot scale with a pony washer for commercial laundering has been the rule.

Home laundering

If after completion of the small scale bench testing of the detergent an apparently satisfactory product has been developed, it is then reasonable that the sample be evaluated under conditions which at least approximate those for large scale use. For the home washing machine this means that a load of fabric of about a maximum of 9 lbs. dry weight (dependent upon machine capacity) will be required. Obviously a mechanical set-up for the supply of water of the proper temperature and hardness is necessary. Quite satisfactory results have been obtained with several types of home washing machines.

Sea Water Detergency Tests

A sea water detergent should be soluble in this medium, and should exert reasonable soil removal characteristics. Any detergent which can be operated successfully in this medium can probably be used in the hardest of waters. This led to a combination of tallow soap, as a binder, and alkyl benzene sulphonate as the active detergent ingredient.

Detergency methods

These methods can be made to exactly duplicate fresh water tests with the possible exception that a final fresh (distilled) water rinse may be used. In laboratory as well as power laundry trials this rinse will remove some of the stiffness from the fabric without markedly increasing soil removal: for garments it is feasible aboard ship and greatly improves the wearer's personal comfort.

A synthetic sea water used and successfully applied to evaluation either in laboratory machines or the 25-pound capacity pony wash wheel follows:

1.60 g.	$CaCl_2.2H_2O$
11-00 g.	$MgCl_2.6H_2O$
4.00g.	Na_2SO_4 anhydrous
25.00 g.	NaCl

Dissolve in 500-700 ml. of distilled water then make up to I litre.

Concentration. For laboratory evaluation it may be desirable to cover a range of sample concentrations such as 0.10, 0.20, and 0.40%. For power laundry work the several materials used successfully have been used at near normal power laundry concentrations of near 0.1%.

Redeposition

Soap is relatively effective in preventing redeposition of soil once it has been removed from the fabric, but this property is not a "built-in" attribute to most synthetic detergents. It is generally understood that the synthetic detergents are less colloidal in character than soaps, and consequently lack certain properties of which this is one. Certain soaps may likewise be lacking in these redeposition-preventing characteristics, but these are not the soaps generally used in commercial work.

Even though the individual factor or factors involved in preventing redeposition have not been isolated, it is possible to measure the effectiveness of detergent compositions in preventing this occurrence. It has long been recognised that some detergent type materials may remove soil from a fabric and then redeposit it in such a form that the washed fabric is darker than the original before immersion in the test solution. It is this redeposition of soil particles under conditions of high soil, adverse temperature conditions, low solution volume and low detergent concentration that promotes graying of fabrics.

It has been recognised that synthetic detergents were deficient in preventing redeposition of soil and developed sodium carboxymethyl cellulose to remedy this shortcoming. This is one of the very few materials for use with synthetic detergents which prevent redeposition of loosened soil. So extensive now is the use of CMC that almost without exception, there are no synthetic detergents on the market which do not contain this compound in greater or lesser proportion.

General methods

The evaluation of redeposition in washing compositions, and of agents potentially useful for this purpose, can be accomplished by two general methods. In one case a sample of soiled fabric for the wash test is accompanied by a swatch of white fabric, and the net detergency or the soil redeposition measured photometrically after a proper washing period. The second and preferred method is to add a known amount of soiling agent to the detergent solution, add a swatch of white fabric, then determine the reflectance of the swatch after washing. The second method permits better control of amount of soil used than the first, and is generally under better statistical control.

Redeposition test procedure

Launder-Ometer. In duplicate swatches per sample. *Time of Wash.* 20 minutes.

Temperature. 140 ± 2°F.

Water 300 ppm. hardness unless otherwise noted.

Fabric. Indian Head Permanent Finish as received. Cut into swatches 6 x 5 inches and mark for identification.

Standard Value. This is obtained by making 6 or 8 readings on the Hunter Reflectometer on swatches taken at random from those to be used in test. This standard value is repeated for each separate test.

Solution Preparation. Make 200 ml. of 0.2% concentration as follows: Weigh 0.4 g. of sample and dissolve in 100 ml. of water of desired hardness. After sample is dissolved, add 2 ml. of 10% Aquadag suspension and 98 ml. of water of same water hardness. If excessive heating is required to dissolve sample, enough water should be added to maintain total volume at 200 ml.

Preheating. The solutions are preheated on a hot plate to 60°C. They are then transferred to jars in the preheating tray on Launder-Ometer, each jar to contain 100 ml. of solution and 10 rubber balls.

Washing. After all solutions have been transferred to the preheating tray, the test swatches are transferred to them. The jars are at once tightly capped, tested for leaks and placed in the Launder-Ometer.

Blotting. At the end of the 20-minutes wash period, the jars are removed from the Launder-Ometer and the contents poured into a strainer. Each duplicate set of swatches is removed before another set is poured into the strainer. The swatches *without being squeezed,* are placed between filter papers (or paper towels). The papers are then placed between glass plates and a 5 or 6 lb, weight applied for one minute.

Rinsing. While the wash is running, the rinse is prepared. Water of the same hardness is heated on the hot plate to 60°C and 100 ml. is transferred to each jar. 10 rubber balls are included in the rinse. After all swatches have been blotted they are placed in the jars for rinsing. The jars are tightly capped and tested for leaks as before, and then placed in the Launder-Ometer and run for 5 minutes. At the end of the rinse period the swatches are removed, as before and blotted.

Drying. The swatches are then either air or preferably oven dried, and the reflectance measured on the Hunter Reflectometer.

Record of Values. Standardise the Hunter instrument and record the reflectance values for each swatch and average them.

Redeposition Index

$$\frac{\text{Reflectance after treatment}}{\text{Reflectance of white watches}} \times 100 = \text{Redeposition index}$$

Standard Sample. A standard comparison sample of known quality is desirable, and should be included with each wash load.

WOOL WASHING

Detergents and their evaluation, or the evaluation of cleansing methods are important throughout the processing of wool, from the scouring of raw wool, back washing, wash-off after dyeing or fulling to the cleansing of soiled garments after the wool has been fabricated and worn. This may be simplified to: raw wool scouring, in-process scouring, and finished fabric cleansing.

Raw Wool Scouring

The first requirement in the treatment of raw wool is mechanical removal of the dirt and extraneous matter by a simple opening and beating or picking operation. Following this, the raw wool is generally carried through what is known as a train of scouring bowls which vary in number. Since wool is sensitive to mechanical action in the scouring operation, the agitation involved in the wool scouring train is mild and accomplished by rakes which simply pull the mass of raw wool through each of the bowls between a nip, sometimes rinsed between bowls, passing into the next bowl in the train. In general these bowls consist of a steep bowl where the greatest portion of the dirt is removed and where some of the fatty acids are saponified (by soda ash, a desirable sodium bicarbonate content being built up). The second bowl consists of a detergent-builder mixture, either soap and soda ash (or modified soda) or synthetic detergent and soda ash. The next bowl may either be a final rinse bowl in simpler operations, or is a second soap-detergent bath of lower concentration, followed by one or two water rinses. Temperatures of scour and rinse are carefully controlled and seldom exceed 130°F.

Laboratory evaluation of raw wool scouring is difficult unless a satisfactory sample of raw wool of the type expected to be used in the plant is available. To satisfy this requirement a quantitative method for the evaluation of wool-scouring detergents has been developed by using small skeins of wool-in-the-grease (in this case carpet yarn), the use of a laboratory bowl (beaker) scouring train and determination of the point at which the bath became exhausted or lost its effectiveness in the removal of the grease (as determined by solvent extraction of the skeins and determination of residual grease content). The method is reasonably reproducible from laboratory to laboratory and has the decided advantage that it closely approximates plant scouring conditions using wool which might actually be encountered. This method has been used successfully in the evaluation of surface active agents for this purpose, and detergents tested in the laboratory by this method have been taken directly to the mill and have met successful acceptance.

Continuous scouring of raw grease wool

This specification covers a method for the laboratory evaluation of continuous wool scouring. It is adaptable to the comparison of detergents, builders, and other chemical factors in the scouring operation; and also to the study of mechanical and other control variables, such as temperature, the number of bowls, immersion time, etc.

A standard apparatus and set of operating conditions are specified for purposes of calibration. Beyond that, conditions and apparatus may be varied in accordance with the desires of the operator to study any particular system which may exist in his own plant.

The criterion for scouring effectiveness is the extent of grease removal. Extraction is done by agitating the scoured and dried wool specimens in a piston and cylinder system while immersed in carbon tetrachloride. An aliquot sample of the carbon tetrachloride is then evaporated in a tared aluminium cup on an infrared dryer to determine the grease residue

In-Process Scouring

The Detergency Comparator for the evaluation of detergents on woollen and worsted materials is used.

The Detergency Comparator is constructed of stainless steel and has a thermostatically controlled, electrically-heated outer water bath, and the solution may be circulated by means of an electric pump to further insure close temperature control. Stepped pulleys are used for speed selection and it has Hyear-covered nip rolls (3 inch diameter), driven take-off rolls, baffles to prevent suds from cross-contaminating the detergent solutions under test and suds boxes with piping arrangements to permit the expressed liquor to be returned to the main washing tank either by cascading or bypassing through the pipe drains or to be drained off into the waste line. The adjustable pot eyes help to prevent the formation of hard creases in the knitted tubing samples. The rinsing process is controlled using a reservoir fitted with calipered openings and a valve for close control.

The Detergency Comparator is said to be the only device that will compare detergents under the conditions of high concentration and low bath ratio similar to those obtained in good plant practice.

1. **Soiled Suspension.** The composition recommended follows commercial grease oil 50% (by wt.); refined mineral oil 50% (by wt.).

   To one gallon of the oil blend was added ½ pound of Bear Brand Lamp Black (Monsanto). This was mixed thoroughly before use.

2. **Soiled Fabric Preparation.** The mixture of oil and lamp black was applied to worsted top sliver during the first drawing operation so as to deposit 5.0 to 5.5% oil on the stock. The worsted stock was then drawn and spun to 2/40's count and 1.75 inch wide knitted tubing was prepared (2 yards long weighing 40 grams).

3. **AATCC Detergency Comparator Test Method.** This method of test is applicable to the evaluation of detergents on woollen and worsted material. It provides an ideal method for classification without conducting costly, time-consuming plant runs.

Finished Fabric Scouring

In comparison with cotton, much less effort has been spent on the standardisation of a test method for wool. The soil or soils vary, but in general are similar to those used for cotton. The fabric chosen should be scoured, in the grey, neutral, and as free from adsorbed soap or synthetic detergent as possible. The laboratory washing machines can be the same as those used for cotton, the wash temperature being adjusted to a level to prevent excessive felting.

Wash test method

Soiled Fabric Preparation. The fabric is Botany Worsted Mills, Style 404, prescoured.

The proportions for the soiling ingredients are

Edible tallow	2.0	g.
Nujol	6.0	g.
Grinders	0.125	g.
Lamp black		

These ingredients are mixed in the Waring Blender then passed through a homogeniser. To 8.125 g. of the homogenised mixture add 4 litres carbon tetrachloride and mix thoroughly.

Using the soiling machine a 7 inch width of fabric 22 feet long, is passed six times through the soiling bath and machine until a reflectance of 28.32% is obtained. This soil is baked one hour at 90°C.

WASHING PROCEDURES FOR OTHER FIBRES

The increasing number of new fibres and mixtures of them with cotton or wool may change some of the practical washing procedures mainly as to temperatures used, but laboratory wash test procedures described in Section 12.3 and 12.4 are applicable.

Dry Cleaning

Dry cleaning establishments are as numerous as power laundries and indeed both are frequently maintained.

The effect of the moisture regain and the relative humidity of the air in the cleaning operation, and of added moisture in certain instances has marked effect upon both soil removal and soil redeposition. It has been found that when the relative humidity is lower than 40% that 1.5-3.0% water, added on the weight of the fabric, will reduce soil redeposition. It has been investigated that of a variety of detergents tested, certain ones were more susceptible to the addition of moisture or to relative humidity conditions than others. Thus it was found that both Stoddard solvent and tri-chloroethylene were beneficiated in preventing redeposition, when the garments were preconditioned, or when water was added to the cleaning solution.

Evaluation can consist either of redeposition or soil removal, or both. In any event, the effect of preconditioning the fabric or of adding water to the cleaning medium must be considered.

Shampoos

Since the materials which may be used in the production of shampoos are legion, it might be expected that fairly well defined methods would exist for their evaluation. The reverse is true, however, since the cleansing of the scalp is a rather difficult process to control. Generally the evaluation of shampoos has been performed either through experienced operators in beauty parlors or by the panel technique.

One of the important factors in a shampoo is the abundance and stability of the lather formed, and this phase of the evaluation can be performed in the laboratory and separately from the actual cleansing operation. A recent innovation for detergency evaluation has been the use of a variation of the raw would scouring technique.

Detergency method

Fabric. Wool yarn "in-the-grease" is used for this test. A small skein about 4 inches from end to end when stretched is prepared from a 20 foot length of yarn and will weigh between 4.5 and 5 grams.

Detergent Solution. A sample of detergent weighing 0.50 g. (100% basis) is dissolved in 200 ml. of water (hardness selected). The solution is adjusted to 38°C.

Procedure

(1) Accurately weight the skein of wool yarn.

(2) Transfer to a 500 ml. Erlenmeyer flask containing the temperature-adjusted detergent solution and stopper.

(3) Slowly invert flask back and forth 50 times per minute for 4 minutes.

(4) Remove skein and either hand or wringer-squeeze to remove excess solution.

(5) Drain and rinse flask, add 100 ml. of water of hardness in use at 38°C and add the squeezed skein of yarn.

(6) Rinse by shaking for 2 minutes in same manner as before.

(7) Remove wool, squeeze as before and repeat rinse as above for I minute.

(8) Remove wool, squeeze to remove water and dry in an oven at 45°C.

(9) During drying of scoured yarn accurately weigh two 400 ml. extraction flasks and a second skein of wool yarn.

(10) Place washed sample and unwashed control in separate extraction thimbles and reflux each with 200 ml. of petroleum ether to remove residual grease.

(11) Remove solvent in hood over a steam bath and dry to constant weight. (this generally will take one hour).

Calculation. For the *control :*

$$\frac{(\text{wt. flask} = \text{contents}) - \text{wt. empty flask}}{\text{wt. of wool sample}} \times 100$$

% grease content

For the *scoured wool* sample :

$$\frac{\text{grease content of control} - \text{grease content scoured sample}}{\text{grease content of control}} \times 100$$

= % grease removal by detergent.

Lather - Shampoo

This method is a tentative standard for the American Society for Testing Materials, D- 1 173, Method of Test for Foaming Properties of Surface-Active Agents.

Use of soiling agents in combination with the foaming agents under test is not convenient with the Ross-Miles test equipment because it is so difficult to clean. Consequently other methods for estimation of foam volume and stability in the presence of soils must be devised. Moderately successful results have been obtained using a simple stirrer agitation method in a graduated, temperature controlled vessel, to which may be added successive increments of a chosen soil such as lanolin, mineral or vegetable oil.

HARD SURFACE CLEANING

Hard surfaces as contrasted with soft, or textile surfaces, exhibit several differences which strongly affect detergency operations. In general, hard surfaces have a comparatively restricted surface area, though still of considerable dimensions when closely examined.

Metal Cleaning

A metal surface offers a number of conveniences in the estimation of soil removal. Though it may seem perfectly flat, when observed microscopically may contain a tremendous number of pores or hills. Many of the metals are chemically reactive and either oxidize rapidly, presenting an adsorptive surface, or can react preferentially to provide chemisorbed surfaces as with adsorbed corrosion inhibitors, etc. Another factor which may have influenced the extensive investigation in this field is the tremendous tonnages of metal processed.

Performance tests

The main performance test is effectiveness of soil removal under actual (or simulated) conditions of use. However, there are many individual factors which can be measured and when properly used can be made excellent supplements to detergency testing. The more generally investigated performance tests are :

pH and titration values

Colloidal properties

Water softening

Conductivity

Solvent action

Surface and interfacial tension measurements Emulsification

Rinsability

Stability under conditions of usage.,

A very short review will indicate the variety of metal cleaning processes:

Wiping (by hand or machine)

Brushing (by hand or machine)

Sand blasting

Tumbling

Hydraulic spraying

Steam gun spraying

Dipping in still tank

Machine washing

Electrolytic cleaning (anodie or cathodic)

Continuous acid or alkaline dip

Vapour degreasing

Solvent degreasing.

To this may be added:

Emulsion degreasing : (1) Organic solvent containing oil soluble emulsifying agent. (2) Organic solvent containing oil-soluble emulsifying agent mixed with kerosene and solvent to form emulsion.

Diphase cleaning

The main general types of cleaning, however, may be reduced to the following:

Soak tank cleaning

Mechanical tank or spray cleaning

Electrolytic cleaning (anodie, cathodic, alternate current)

Solvent or vapour degreasing

Emulsion degreasing

Diphase cleaning.

Surfaces

Cleaning of metals represents the entire gamut of pure metals and alloys. All must be cleaned to a greater or lesser extent for either processing or for use as a finished product. The chemical reactivity of the surfaces to form either oxide coatings or reactions with components of corrosion inhibiting compositions or cleaning compounds, may greatly influence the effectiveness of the compositions used and of the finished product. Lard oil which has a stronger bond of attachment for metal than mineral oil, is readily removed by the addition of surface active agents in contrast with mineral oil which is not. Presence or absence of oxide film is an important factor in the ease with which oil may be removed, since this probably depends upon the bond between the oil and the metal surface. The effect of freshly pickled surfaces in increasing the attraction of the oil for the metal is an important one and is most marked with mineral oils. In contrast, fatty oils containing considerable amounts of free fatty acid are more strongly adsorbed by the oxide films. Condition of the metal as it is to be worked in the plant will be the controlling factor in metal cleaning operations.

Soils

The variety of soils encountered in the cleaning of metals is numerous. Generally, however, they are comprised of fatty or mineral oils, debris from previous processing, corrosion inhibitors, drawing compounds and the like. These oils act as entraining agents for solids which may be oxides or simply debris picked up in the processing operation.

Machines for removal

Probably the simplest device which is used in the metal cleaning industry is the so-called soak tank method of cleaning. This may be manually or mechanically operated and in either event is strongly dependent upon the temperature of the bath and the degree of agitation (with steam, air or pump) to provide the desired amount of mechanical action.

Laboratory machines for duplicating the results obtained in plant machines are simple and are frequently quite representative of what can be done in the plant, particularly when samples of the actual soiled surface can be cleaned with the material expected to be used. Generally the simple soak bath is used in laboratory evaluation but spraying operations may be set up with spray nozzles and pumps which simulate plant application. A device which agitates the article to be cleaned in the soak bath has been suggested. Whichever piece of machinery is used for laboratory evaluation is not as important as control of the surface prior to, and subsequent to, the cleaning operation and full recognition of the desired state of cleanliness is important for maximum economy.

Sample

The size and shape of the panel to be soiled and cleaned can vary at will. Disks one inch in diameter to panels 6 x 6 inches or more have been used. The shape of the panel can likewise vary, some being perforated at two points on one edge so that when held at an angle they drain from a corner, while still another was shaped like a flat spearhead so that drainage can be made to take place from the tip.

Estimation of soil removal

In general, either a metal surface is clean or it is not, and any degree between these two extremes may be considered unsatisfactory. In effect, this is a "go," "no go" type procedure,. However, for the estimation of the effectiveness of' cleaning agents in the laboratory it is desirable that satisfactory quantitative methods be available. Historically the water-break method is the one which has provide most satisfactory. It can be made in the plant as well as in the laboratory, and is indicative of general cleanliness. In either case, maximum advantage is obtained by an acid dip prior to evaluation of the degree of soil removal. An obvious method of attack is to submit the cleaned sample to *solvent extraction* and to weigh the oil or soil which is removed. In cases where almost complete cleanliness has been obtained, sensitivity of this test is obviously dependent upon technic and a sufficiently sensitive weighing device. The *radioactive trace technic* has been used in the evaluation of metal cleaning compositions and likewise for the evaluation of the several methods available to determine the cleanliness of cleaned metal surfaces. The *copper dip method* has been used for the estimation of the cleanliness of surfaces which are to be electroplated. The adherence and the brightness of the copper coating which results from dipping the cleaned ferrous metal in an acid copper sulphate solution is indicative of the quality of electroplate to be expected. *The fluorescent dye method* depends upon the inclusion of an ultraviolet sensitive fluorescing material combined with the oil used as a soiling agent. This has certain advantages for pictorial evaluation of data but is not entirely satisfactory as a quantitative method for estimation.

Dishwashing

The cleansing of dishes has been investigated with one or more objectives which are: deposition of hard water film, soil removal, bacteriological cleanliness, and washing machine design and efficiency.

Frequently several of these factors can be combined and a clear over-all conception of the effectiveness of the detergent solution or of the machine design can be obtained. Mahlmann and his co-workers in a number of different publications. It has been found that for bacteriological cleanliness a temperature of not less than 170°F. in the wash and rinse will generally provide the desired bactericidal action. Consequently the temperature of wash and of the abundance of the supply of wash water to a mechanical washing machine is most important.

Prior to the introduction of polyphosphates there was considerable difficulty in the deposition of an insoluble hard water film upon glassware which was most unsightly and could potentially harbor bacteria and the soil particles. It has been found that the inclusion of polyphosphates in the washing composition is most beneficial in reducing hard water precipitate and deposition. The essentials of a test for dish washing evaluation are comprised of the following

Soil

In evaluating the removal of these soils it generally is necessary that a tracer compound of one sort or another be added with the expectation that it will be removed in the same ratio as the soil itself and thus can be used as a device to measure the soil retained on the surface. Agents which have been used for this purpose are lamp black, India Ink, a combination of printing ink and linseed oil, a test organism suspension, and also ferric chloride.

The most recent thinking on this general subject is that the method for deposition of the soil is important to the extent that the viscosity of the soil medium should be adjusted and the soil applied in some given and reproducible manner.

Measurement of soil retention (or removal)

A number of different photometers, calorimeters and glossimeters are available on the market and it seems hardly necessary that a special design of equipment now be developed. Obviously if the desire is to ascertain bacteriological cleanliness, a properly standardised plating technique will be used and several of these have been described.

Machines for washing

Most of the small scale laboratory devices for evaluation of washing efficiency have been based on the use of microscope slides and either an agitating, rocking or rotating device in which these slides are held while immersed and moved by mechanical action in the bath to provide soil removal.

MISCELLANEOUS TESTS

There are several tests which may prove useful in the further evaluation of compounds to be market tested. Most synthetic detergents are deficient in the ability to suspend soil once it is removed from a fabric surface. The redeposition method will indicate the comparative ability of a composition to prevent this graying, effect. A compound almost universally used for this purpose is carboxymethylcellulose, and it might be thought that its isolation from the detergent composition and its analysis would prove the most effective method for estimation. Such is not the case even though methods of analysis exist, and the redeposition characteristics will be fully as revealing as an analytical procedure. Furthermore, though there are a few other compounds which possess this same power to prevent redeposition, analysis means little when measure of comparative effectiveness is desired.

Another useful addition to the detergent field, and used both in soaps and synthetic detergents, is the fluorescent dye. These are also called brightening or "bleaching" agents. The best criterion of effectiveness again is a direct comparison, under use conditions of either competitive detergents or competitive dyes. While not actually increasing detergency or soil removal, the effect is as if increased cleanliness had occurred and is especially evident in actual practice over a sequence of washings.

Determination of pH can be very helpful, but unless properly executed, can be most misleading. This determination should be a routine operation.

A product, before introduction to the market, should be as free from possibility of harm to equipment as possible. Corrosion of metal, glass or vitreous enamel surfaces can cause many complaints and even result in rejection of a product. The methods chosen cover aluminium and vitreous enamel surfaces.

Brightening Agents

These compounds are colourless to the eye but are excited by ultraviolet light, fluorescing blue. They have been termed "bleaching" agents because they are so effective in converting daylight ultraviolet to visual, making white fabric appear bleached or brightened in comparison with one not so treated. Brightening is a better term since colours are also increased in intensity as well.

The most generally used dyes are chosen for their substantivity to cellulosic fabrics, though some less generally used are available which exhaust onto wool rather than cellulose. Depending upon chemical structure, these dyes will fluoresce as a reddish blue or preferably as a brilliant, almost true blue colour.

Choice of brightening agent will depend upon the hue of the dye, the degree of substantivity or exhaustion from the bath, stability toward excess untraviolet illumination, stability toward bleaching compositions, buildup of colour and cost. A reddish blue fluorescence may not have the intensity of a dye giving a deep blue. Unless the dye is evenly adsorbed in a short time, and essentially quantitatively, it may fail under adverse conditions of operation or in the small amounts used. Some dyes will "sunburn" when exposed continuously to ultraviolet, producing an undesirable visual colour. Other dyes may be oxidised to undesirable visual "off" colours by the common bleaching agents. Early experience with these agents in repeated washings resulted in "off' shades of pink built up by adsorption on the fabric. The evidence of the effectiveness of well selected brightening agents is so clear that a detergent manufacturer can hardly afford not to use them, especially as they are used in such minor percentages.

The evaluation of these dyes can be complicated or relatively simple, depending upon the size of the detergent operation, and upon the accuracy and sensitivity of the method chosen. Certainly a dye manufacturer can afford a complicated evaluation method if it will either control his operation or permit development of better, more effective agents. The detergent manufacturer is interested in producing maximum effectiveness at minimum cost of dye and of process control and the method which follows has proved quite adequate.

Evaluation

Machine. Launder-Ometer, or Terg-O-Tometer, set at 345⁰ rotation and 117 half-cycles per minute.

Fabric. Desized Indian Head or white terry cloth towelling, 8 x 9 inch size.

Temperature. 120⁰F.

Detergent concentration. 0.25%

Volume of solution. 1 000 mi. Terg-0-Tometer. 200 ml. Launder-Ometer.

Time of wash. 10 minutes.

Time of Rinse. 5 minutes.

Procedure

(1) Wash for 10 minutes.

(2) Remove swatches, run through hand wringer.

(3) Rinse for 5 minutes.

(4) Remove swatches, ran through hand wringer.

(5) Oven dry.

Number of washes. Selection of fabric swatch size will make it possible to remove a portion after every wash or alternatively after the fifth and tenth was periods.

These same tests Can be performed in varying water hardnesses with various fabrics, and in the presence of commercial bleaching agents in the amounts recommended by the bleach manufacturer. If temperature of wash water or rinse is important, tests can be made to cover a range to indicate effectiveness of the agent.

pH Determination

The pH values of soaps, alkalies, and detergents are valuable indications useful in application. It should be recalled that soaps, as "neutral" salts of fatty acids, have pH values much higher than organic sulphates or sulphonates. Should soap pH values fall in a range lower than those for the normal salts, difficulty in the way of reduced detergency or actual deposition of insoluble fatty acids may be expected. The surface active sulphate or sulphonates may be finished off at pH values over a considerable range, but they generally closely approach pH 7 as the normal salts.

"Building" of soaps or synthetic detergents with alkaline salts frequently is accomplished to conform to some predetermined pH level dependent upon the sensitivity of the product or equipment with which they are to be used. Most built soap or synthetics to come into contact with the hands are maintained at levels below pH 10.5 since otherwise they may cause excessive skin irritation. This buffering ability to maintain a given level is most readily ascertained using a combination of pH and titration methods.

Colorimetric methods for pH determination can be most useful, but for precise estimation the electrometric method is to be preferred. Simplified apparatus is available for electrometric measurement, largely with the glass electrode which may be operated from line current or from batteries and may be secured for versatility of measurement in different media.

The first item to recall in making pH measurements is that distilled water unless freshly boiled may absorb much carbon dioxide from the air and will then have a quite acid value. Freshly boiled distilled water is indicated for the measurement of pH values for detergent solutions since the synthetic detergents are frequently poorly buffered. The fact is that very many of the neutral or sodium sulphate-built detergents will simply assume the pH of the water used in the test. Attempts to obtain check pH values between laboratories may frequently fail unless this precaution of using freshly boiled distilled water is observed.

The second item of importance is to standardise the pH meter with appropriate standard buffer solutions using the proper glass electrode for the pH range and temperature used.

The American Society for Testing Materials Specification E-70 is a tentative method for Determination of the pH of aqueous Solutions of Soaps and Detergents with the glass electrode and gives specific data for the proper use of this equipment.

Proposed method of test for pH of aqueous solutions of soaps and detergents

Scope. This method covers procedures for the preparation of aqeuous solutions of soaps and detergents and for the determination of their pH.

Sampling. The material shall be sampled in accordance with the Standard Methods of Sampling and Chemical Analysis of Soaps and Soap

Products, or the Standard Methods of Sampling and Chemical Analysis of Alkaline Detergents, whichever is applicable.

Reagent, Distilled Water Distilled water shall be boiled thoroughly, or purged with CO_2-free air, to remove CO_2 and shall be protected with soda-lime or soda-asbestos (Ascarite) while cooling and in storage. The pH of this water shall be between 6.2 and 7.2 at 25°C. The residue on evaporation, when heated at 105°C for I hr., shall not be more than 0.5 mg. per litre.

Preparation of solutions. Weigh I ± 0.001 g. of the soap or detergent and transfer to a I -liter volumetric flask. Partially fill the flask with distilled water and agitate until the sample is completely dissolved. Adjust the temperature of the solution and the distilled water to 25 ± 0.5°C. and fill to the calibration mark with distilled water. Stopper the flask, mix thoroughly, and allow the solution to stand at a temperature of 25°C. for 2 hours prior to measuring the pH.

Determination of pH. Measure the pH of the solution as directed in the Tentative Method for Determination of the pH of Aqueous Solutions with the Glass Electrode (A.S.T.M. Designation: E-70). Use the "low sodium-error" glass electrodes for solutions having pH values higher than 9. Use type I or type II meters.

Corrosion

Detergent compositions are designed for many purposes, but one thing they should *not* do, is to cause corrosion or remove protective coatings. Dishwashing compositions should rot remove decorative decals or overglazes, nor should they cause corrosion of silverware or of the machines in which they may be used. Washing machine detergents should not cause corrosion of metal parts of the machine, nor remove vitreous enamel or damage organic finishes. The machine designer and the metallurgist can do much to eliminate complaint, but because detergent compositions contain alkaline builder salts and are generally very effective electrolytes, they must be suitably inhibited to minimise attack.

Aluminium is a metal commonly found in machines and is rather easily attacked by either acid or alkaline media, but can be protected through the use of silicates in alkaline compositions. Chrome or nickel plating, when available and well deposited, prove quite satisfactory but when skimped are quickly removed. Substitute platings frequently are less resistant and may even cause electrolytic corrosion with rapid removal and complaint. This latter difficulty can be alleviated by sound metallurgy, but in any event, the less corrosion caused by the detergent, the better the washer.

Polyphosphates have been shown to remove vitreous enamel under conditions of high temperature and high concentration, but even this corrosion can be controlled. In this same category would be removal of ceramic overglaze from chinaware. Complaints from organic finishes originate from wear, brittleness, crazing or impact, with exposure of base metal to electrolytes; however under normal conditions they are unaffected by detergents.

Corrosion and corrosion inhibition studies can be carried out using the following two methods as applied to metal or to ceramic surfaces.

Chapter 7

MANUFACTURING OF HERBAL SYNTHETIC DETERGENTS

The formulation of herbal based detergent powders is indeed a challenging task in the Indian context. Since it must take into account the purchasing power of different sections of the population while offering a good detergency. A variety of detergents. Varying widely in price and performance characteristics produced by, the small-scale as well as by the organised sector are being marketed. In general, the small-scale sector produces detergent powders by the dry mix route whereas the organised sector produces the bulk of the powder by the spray drying route although in recent times the latter are also following the dry mix route for some of the powder detergents. Heavy duty liquid detergents have not yet become popular because of price constraints.

PERFORMANCE CRITERIA

The formulation of a detergent powder normally takes into account the following factors.

1. The washing habits
2. The quality of water used for washing used for washing (iron content, hardness).
3. The nature and extent of soiling
4. White vs. coloured clothes
5. Facilities available for manufacture (dry mix vs. spray drying route).
6. Safety and pleasant 'in use' qualities
7. Pleasing colour, odour and flow characteristics
8. Long shelf life
9. Pricing

1. Washing habits

The normal practice is to dissolve the powder in warm or hot water, soak the clothes for some time, squeeze and rinse, Profuse lather is a chief requirement in this case. For use in washing machines, low foam detergents are preferred.

2. Quality of water

In India, the hardness of water varies widely and the detergent powder must incorporate a water softener in the formulation, either for precipitating calcium and magnesium salts or for chelating them.

3. Soiling

In India the extent of soiling is fairly severe, especially in large cities, which necessitates the formulation of heavy duty detergents. Soil mainly comprises collar and under arm stains, caused by dirt/particulates/sweat/oily matter and also from atmospheric pollution that settle on the main body of the clothes.

4. White vs. coloured clothes

In spite of good intentions, white and coloured clothes are seldom washed separately with the result that no separate formulation exists for the whites and coloured. Added complications some times result from the running of colours and their deposition on other coloured or white garments being washed together.

5. Manufacturing facilities

The spray drying route for detergent powder is capital and energy intensive. Therefore, this route is mainly followed by the organised sectro. On the other hand the small-scale or cottage sector follows the 'dry-mix' route since hardly any capital equipment other than pots and pans is required. Formulation by the dry-mix route is far more flexible and as a result in small-scale sector the bulk of the detergent powders are of this type. Efforts are however now being made by the organised sector to produce dry mixed powder for reducing costs and possibly for improving efficacy.

6. Safety and pleasant 'in-use' qualities

The advantage of spray dried powder is that the powder is more uniform and dissolves in water easily. The powder is also generally kinder to the skin as compared to powders produced by the dry mix route which have higher soda ash levels responsible for skin irritation on prolonged contact.

7. Colour, odour and flow characteristics

The flow characteristics of spray dried powder are generally superior to those of dry-mix powders. The former can however give rise to dust in handling if the moisture content is not kept under control. Colour and odour of powders manufactured by both the routes are comparable.

8. Shelf life

With moisture proof packaging, the product is generally well protected and remains satisfactory for several months.

9. Pricing

Pricing is a function of formulation, packaging and government incentives if any. There is such a keen competition between the small-scale and organised sector that latter has been compelled to re-align some of their formulations in order not to be widely different from those adopted by the small scale sector.

Formulation Requirements

For maximum cost effectiveness, conventional detergent powder should be optimised to match user requirements and brand positioning. Two criteria for formula optimisation are :

1. Alkalinity
2. Good building and adequate levels of active matter

In any organised study, it is necessary to employ a computer modelling technique using formulation details and wash solution data, and matching them with two criteria viz. free calcium and micellar active concentrations. A control formulation serves as a standard for comparison of results.

1. Alkalinity

The pH should be maintained at a level of 10 to 11 throughout the wash. This ensures maximum Calcium-STPP binding leading to good detergency.

2. Good building and active matter

In good building, the STPP level and pH (up to 11) must give low free Ca^{++} so as to produce good detergency and oil suspension (anti-redeposition). The AD level should be adequate to give high micellar active concentration in solution leading to good foaming and detergency.

The most cost effective way of introducing reserve alkalinity into a product is sodium carbonate. No other equally cost effective alternative buffering agent is available.

Approach to Product Formulation

The ingredients commonly used in the formulation of a good grade powder, their level of usage, technical benefits, and key variables are given in Table 4.1

Item Nos. 3 and 4 are used selectively under Indian conditions by the organised sector. A few typical formulations (Nos. 1-4) used by the organised sector are listed in Table 4.2 along with two others (Nos. 5 and 6) that are similar to those followed by small-scale manufacturers.

Table 4.1

	Ingredient	*Usual level %*	*Technical benefit*	*Key variable*
1.	Active Detergent	18-20	Soil removal, foaming, all temperatures	Actual concentration in wash
2.	Phosphate	22-32	Softens water by binding Ca, Mg	'Free'level of Ca
4.	Perborate	10	Oxidative bleaching, removal of Chromophoric stain at over 60 °C	Concentration of H_2O_2 in the wash
5.	Enzyme	1	Removes protein stain at less than 50 °C.	Total integrated enzyme active conc. x Time at given wash temperature.
5.	S CMC	1.3% @ 50% active	Prevents soil redeposition on fabric	Amount of adsorbed SCMC on cotton.
6.	Fluorescer	0.2-0.4	Increased whiteness and brightness of white cotton fabric	Quantity of fluoresper present in the wash in relation to total cotton load.

Table 4.2

Non Soapy Detergent Powder Formulations

	1	2	3	4	5	6
AD	20	20	18	20	10	12
STPP (Castor Oil)	22	25	25	32	5	—
Sod. Sil, Alk, (anhy)	10	10	11	8	5	5
Soda ash	10	7.5	8	—	45	50
Soap Stock (50%)	1	2	2	1	—	—
Na_2SO_4	25	23	19	24	20	20
Photine C	0.2	0.3	0.3	0.3	0.1	0.1
Colour	0.06	0.08	0.08	0.04	0.05	0.05
Perfume	0.10	0.10	0.10	0.10	0.10	0.10
NaCl	—	—	—	1.0	5.0	4.00
Moisture norganics etc.	100	100	100	100	100	100

Formulations Nos. 5 and 6 are similar to those employed by the small-scale industry and are definitely more affordable for the common man. The formulations listed are applicable to hand washing situations. For washing machines, a low lathering tailor-made product is used. A fo:mulation involving the use of 10% non-ionic component such as tallow alcohol 10 EO, or one with, 14% LABS, 5% soap and 1% non-ionic component gives a low lather. This product is preferred as a washing machine-detergent to prevent lather overflowing from the machine during the washing operation.

Production Procedure

Manufacture of detergent products involves the following principal operations and processes as shown in the flowsheet of Fig. 13.

1. Manufacture of linear Alkyl Benzene Sulphonate (LAB Sulphonate).
2. Manufacture of Coconut Oil. Tallow Derived Alcohol Sulphates.
3. Mixing the above two, Sulphonate and Sulphates in appropriate proportions.
4. Neutralization of the mixture with requisite quantity of sodium Hydroxide solution to make Surfactants.
5. Mixing Surfactants with builders, fillers, additives in their precalculated proportions.
6. Drying in spray dryer for desired granularsize with the help of size separating units. Cyclone separator, sieve screening etc.
7. Cooling the products.
8. Perfuming.
9. Packing.

In smaller units, detergent manufacturing process may start from procurement off LAB and coconut oil fatty alcohols. Actual chemical processes to be performed are sulphonation and sulphation and then other finishing operations are performed as mentioned above.

Further smaller units (cootage industries) may start from procurement of LAB sulphonic acid and fatty alcohol sulphates (acid slurries). Only neutralization of acid slurry in the chemical process to be performed. Other finishing operations are to be done as described before.

FORMULATIONS OF SYNTHETIC DETERGENT POWDERS
A TYPICAL BATCH OF FINISHED PRODUCT
(A GOOD QUALITY HOUSEHOLD DETERGENT GRANULES)

For 1000 kg. yield

Surfactants	**kg.**
LAB sulphonic acid	75
(86 percent active matter	
Fatty alcohol sulphate	75
(High active)	
NaoH (98 percent)	25 used as 20% solution
Builders	
Sodium tripolyphosphate	400
Trisodium phosphate	75
Soda ash	275
Sodium silicate (40 percent)	80
Additives	
Sodium carboxy methyl cellulose	15
Fluorescent dye, perfume	
and pigment (if desired)	3
Water (process) requirement	500
Final moisture content	33

A TYPICAL BATCH USING ACID SLURRY OF UNSEPARATED SPENT ACID

For 1000 kg. of finished detergent

Surfactant	**kg.**
LAB acid slurry	450
NaOH (98%)	60
	Used as 20
	Percent solution.
Builders	
Sodium tripolyphosphate	455
Trisodium phosphate	55
Soda ash	182
Sodium bicarbonate	20
Sodium silicate (40%)	90

Additives	
Sodium carboxy methyl cellulose	15
Other miscellaneous additives	3
(brightener, tarnish inhibitor,	
perfumes, dye etc.)	
Water (process)	450
Final moisture content after drying	10

Detergent Powder Prepared Without Using Spray Dryer (High Bulk Density)

Household detergent powder marketed by numerous small scale producers follow this method of simple neutralization and mixing of various ingredients. The final product requires no drying.

A TYPICAL FORMULATION OF HOUSEHOLD DETERGENT POWDER

For 1000 kg. finished product	Kg.
LAB acid slurry, 84 percent	180
soda ash	360
Sodium silicate, 40 percent	65
Sodium bicarbonate	57
Triosodiumphosphate	75
Sodium tripolyphosphate	300
Carboxy methyl cellulose	30
Other additives silica jell,	8
still bene dye, bleaching agent perfume	
Water (dry dissolved in water)	30

Procedure

The neutralization of surfactant is made by soda ash instead of NaOH solution in ribbon blender (Fig. 17).

Soda ash is first taken in the ribbon blender. Then acid slurry in which, dye dissolved in 30 *kg* of water is already admixed: is added slowly while blending operation is on. Slow addition is necessary to allow generated CO_2 gas to dissipate and to keep the temperature controlled under 80°C. After addition of acid slurry is complete, other ingredients are added one after another according to the sequence as listed in the formulation.

At the end of mixing the product is sieved to separate the fines and small quality of over sized particles. The oversized may be ground and admixed with the product. The fines are reused in the next batch. The finished detergent is then packed.

This type of products have high bulk density.

All the builders and addtives may not be perfectly blended.

As mentioned above, the product contains good percentage of fines and some oversized particles. Fines may be allowed to remain as it is in the finished product. But bigger sized products are slower in dissolving and hence they have less acceptability in the market.

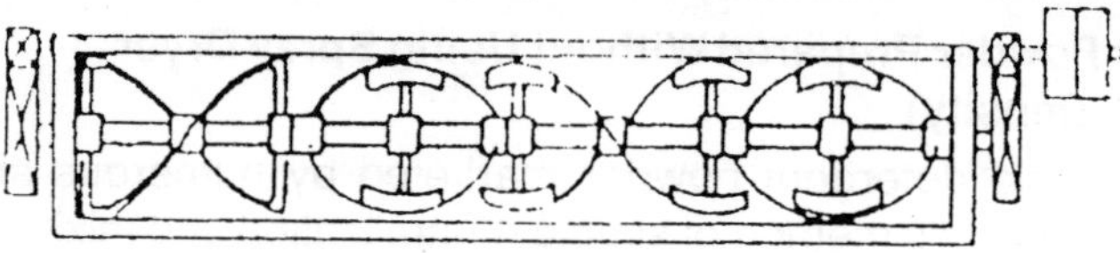

Fig. 17. Ribbon Blender

Foam Regulation

For surfactants to work for cleansing efficiently while these are used in washing machine regulation of foam is necessary. This is done by combining anionic surfactant with non ionic surfactant or anionic surfactant with soap (anionic). Ethylene oxide condensates of fatty alcohols such as lauryl ethoxylate (described) later are low foam producers. With increase in the number of carbon atoms of saturated fatty acids of C_{20}-C_{24} carbon atoms are good foam inhibitors.

Other foam inhibitors are higher fatty acid amides, alifatic carboxylic acid esters containing at least C_{18} carbon atoms in one or in both acid and alcohol chain and n-alkylated aminotriazine.

Typical Suds Regulated Surfactant Compounds

1. Combining anionic with nonionic

Sodium LAB sulphonate	75 parts
Lauryl ethoxylate	25 parts

Lauryl ethoxylate formed by following reaction.

$$Ch_3(CH_2)_{10}CH_2OH + 8CH_2 — CH_2 \rightarrow CH_3(CH_2)_{10}(OCH_2CH_2)_8OH$$

Lauryl alcohol	Ethylene oxide	Lauryl ethoxylate of 8 moles ethylene oxide

2. Combining anionic with soap

Sodium LAB sulphonate	14 parts
Tallow fatty acid soaps	7 parts

General Formulations for Industrial Detergent Powder

	Light Duty Parts	Heavy Duty Parts
Sodium LAB SULPHONATE	15.00	9.00
Lauryl Ethoxylate (castor oil)	5.00	3.00
Sodium tripolyphosphate (coconut oil)	25.00	40.00
Sodium sulphate	40.00	10.00
Soda ash	5.00	20.00
Sodium metasilicate penta hydrate	5.00	10.00
Soapstock	1.50	1.80
Fluoroscent dye	0.05	0.05
Tarnish inhibitor	-	0.05
Perfume	0.10	0.10
Other ingredients	0.35	-
Water	3.00	6.00

Woollen Piece Goods Scouring Preparation

For woollen piece goods or worsted piece goods scouring detergent formulations: sodium chloride is the essential builder.

A combination of sodium chloride with lauryl alcohol polyethoxylate nonionic or sodium chloride with ammonium LAB sulphonate anionic scours mineral oil very well even at temperature as low as 26°C. These formulations found greatest acceptability in piece goods scouring.

Formulation with anionic and soap as active surfactants

Light Dury

	Parts
Sodium LAB sulphonate	16.00
Palm oil fatty acid soap	8.00
Sodium tripolyphospahte	15.00
Tetrasodium pyrophosphate (castor oil)	5.00
Sodium sulphate	30.00
Soda ash	7.00
Sodium bicarbonate	5.00
Sodium metasilicate pentahydrate	7.00
Soapstock	1.75
Optical whitener	0.10
Tarnish inhibitor	0.10
Perfume	0.05
Water	5.00

To select the basic ingredients in formulating finished detergent granules for servicing specific type of duty, quantitative range of each chemicals for different types of duty, as recommended, are given below. One may select the quantity from among the range and formulate the product to serve desired purpose.

Ingredients In Wt Percent	Types Light Duty High Foaming	Heavy Duty High Foaming	Heavy Dury High Foaming
Surfactants with foam regulators	20-35	20-35	7-18
Sodium tripolyphosphate/ tetrasodium pyrophosphate	5-30	35-55	35-55
Sodium sulphate	25-60	8-15	0-25
Soda ash	0-5	0-5	5-25
Other ingredients; CMC, Perfume, Dye etc.	1-7	6-2	5-10
Water	3-7	3-10	

Machine Dish Washing Powder

	For Soft Water Parts	For Hard Water Parts
Sodium LAB sulphonate	4.00	-
Nonionic surfactant	2.00	4.00
Hexylene glycol	-	3.00
Soda ash	24.00	-
Tetrasodium pyro phosphate	40.00	-
Sodium tripolyphosphate	-	50.00
Sodium metasilicate	20.00	24.00
Trisodium phosphate	-	15.00
Sodium sulphate	5.00	-
Potassium dichloroisocyanurate (50 percent active chlorine)	1.30	-
Tarnish inhibitor	0.10	0.50
Perfume	0.10	0.10
Water	3.40	3.40

Scouring Powders Including Kitchen Cleaners

Under this category fall the kitchen cleaners in household and similar cleaners in industry for cleaning of utensils, dishes, china ware, metallic surfaces, floors etc.

The function of these powders are to remove highly adhering soil (oils, greases, dirt, stain etc.) by abrasion and to keep the loosen dirt in suspension which are to be cleansed away by rinse.

To achieve this, various abrasive powders are incorporated in the detergent formulations.

Abrasives

Abrasive powders are selected on the consideration of following requisites.

1. Hardness of them should be less than the hardness of surfaces to be scoured, so that no scratch is produced on the clean surfaces.
2. These are to be chemically inert.
3. They should not impairs in the free flowing nature of detergent powders.

Fulfilling the above properties, the abrasive powders used for scouring preparations are described below:

Pumice: A highly porous rock, usually contains 60-75 percent SiO_2 and 10-20 percent Al_2O_3. Insoluble in water and not attached by acids. Available as coarse, medium and fine powdered form.

Feldspar : General name for a group of potassium, sodium, calcium, barium, aluminium silicate usually potassium alumino silicate minerals. Available as coarse, medium and fine powders.

Kieselguhr : Soft bulky solid (mild abrasive) composed of skeletons of small aquatic plants and contains 88 percent silica. Available as powder. Insoluble in acids, soluble in strong alkalis, absorbs 1.5 to 4 times its weight to water and also has high oil absorption capacity.

Bentonite : A colloidal clay (aluminium silicate). There are two varieties- Sodium bentonite has highly swelling in water and calcium bentonite has negligible welling capacity. Available as light to cream coloured powder.

Marble Dust : A metamorphic form of calcium carbonate usually containing iron and other minerals. Available as perfectly whit coarse, medium powder.

Valcanic Ash : Igneous rock deposit by volcanic eruption containing lava.

Cleasing powders apart from its abrasive property should have good emulsifying, good foaming characteristics.

To meet all these requisties the formulations are necessarily made with other ingredients taken from following chemicals.

Surfactants

This types of cleansing powders usually contain abound 3 percent of synthetic surfactants (100 percent active) as soap (anhydrous powder). The surfactants used are generally sodium LAB sulphonate, fatty alcohol sulphates, polyglycol ethers and x to some extent quaternary ammonium compounds (good germicidal, antistatics, lubricating properties, less detergency and this cationics cannot be used in combination with anionic surfactants, can be used if desired in combination with nonionic surfactants).

Other Chemicals

These are Sodium tripolyphosphate, (castor oil based)

Tetrasodium pyrophosphate, (linseed oil based)

Foam stabilizer like Red Turkey oil Perfume having appeal for disinfection (generally pine oil).

Soap Powder

Though synthetic surfactants are mostly used as organic active matter in formulating kitchen or floor cleaners, soap powders from cotton seed oil are also used as surface active agent in this type of cleaners. 10 to 15 percent or more of anhydrous soap is used in a formula.

Typical Formulations of Household Cleansing Powder (Kitchen cleaner)

Formula -1

	kg.
Sodium LAB sulphonate	6.0
Feldspar	60.0
Kieselguhr	5.0
Lime juice	5.0
Soda ash	10.0
Sodium metasilicate (Cotton seed oil)	3.0
Sodium sulphate	8.0
Benzotriazole	0.5
PVM/MA	0.1
Perfume	0.1
Water	2.3

Formula -2

	kg.
Sodium LAB sulphonate	6.0
Kieselguhr	55.0
Bentonite	5.0
Pumice powder	5.0
Lime juice	5.0
Soda ash	6.0
Sodium metasilicate	7.0
Sodium sulphate	8.0
Soap stock (Cotton seed oil)	0.3
PVM/MA	0.2
Perfume	0.1
Water	2.4

Formula -3

	parts
Sodium LAB sulphonate	2.5
Soda ash	10.0
Soap powder from cotton seed oil	7.5
Marble dust	70.0
Trisodium phosphate	5.0
Other Chemicals (foam stabilizer, perfume)	2.0
Water	3.0

Formula -4

	Parts
Anhydrous soap powder	15
Soda ash	10
Sodium metasilicate	10
Pumice stone (fine powder)	60
Other chemicals	2
ternish inhibitor, foamstabilizer, perfume etc.	
Water	3

Formula -5

	parts
Synthetic surfactant powder	2
Soap powder (cotton seed oil)	12
Soda ash	10
Marble dust	70
Other chemicals; perfume etc.	2
Water	2

Manufacturing Process

All the ingredients of the scouring powder are to be well mixed preferably in a ribbon type powder mixer. If trisodium phosphate or soda ash are found to be in lump form then these are to be ground first before mixing. After finishing the mixing operation the product is finally sieved through 100 mesh sieve and packed.

Soap powder is to be mixed in dry condition. If that soap is wet the soda ash may be added to absorb moisture from soap.

Formula -1

Floor Washing Compound

Soda ash	77 parts
Sodium tripolyphoshate*	5 parts
Sodium metasilicate pentahydrate (Caster Oil)	5 parts
Sodium deodecyl benzene sulfonate	12 parts
(40% active matter slurry)	
Pine oil, colour	1 part

*If sodium tripolyphosphate is not available or is too costly to be incorporated, a mixture of sodium triphosphate and tripolyphosphate or triphosphate alone may be used.

The soda ash, phosphate and metasilicate are charged into a ribbon blender, the mixing is started and neutralized acid slurry is added slowly with stirring. After all the slurry is added, the mixing is continued for another 15 minutes and a concentrated solution of colour then added; mixing is continued for another five minutes till a product of homogenous colour is obtained. The powder is then left for drying in sun or on the floor and when it is sufficiently dry for packing, it is again placed in the mixer and the pine oil is sprayed on it and it is then packed for sale.

Formula -2

Heavy-duty Household Washing Powder

Soda ash	58 parts
CMC (66% active)	2 parts
Sodium Tripolyphosphate (castor oil)	15 parts
Dodecyl benzene sulfonic acid (87%)	20 parts
Water	2 parts
Sodium silicate (40% acid)	5 parts
Perfume, colour	1 parts

Charge and mix the first three ingredients in a ribbon blender and then slowly add the fourth ingredient with continuous mixing: when it is well dispersed add water and continue mixing till the colour of the powder changes from brownish yellow to yellowish white. Now add sodium silicate and colour. Dry this paste in a drum dryer or under the sun and after drying, grind it in a ball mill and add the perfume in the ribbon blender containing the ground powder. Mix and pack for sale.

Formula -3

White Household Heavy-duty Washing Powder

Soda ash	57 parts
CMC	2 parts
Sodium tripolyphosphate (cotton seed oil)	15 parts
Dodecyl benzene Sulfonic acid (87%)	20 parts
Sodium hypochlorite solution	2 parts
Sodium silicate (54% soln.)	5 parts

Prepare as indicated for formula (2): add sodium hypochlorite solution in the end of mixing and before drying or grinding.

Formula -4

Spray-dried Heavy-duty Household Hand-washing Powder

Sodium dodecyl benzene sulfonate	25 parts
Sodium tripolyphosphate (Linseed oil)	15 parts
Tetrasodium pyrophosphate	10 parts
CMC (66% basis)	2.5 parts
Sodium metasilicate (anhydrous)	15 parts
Optical brightening agent	0.2 parts
Sodium sulfate	32.7 parts
Sodium perborate	5.0 parts
Colour and perfume	1.0 parts

Prepare as described in the text.

Formula -5

Household Spray-dried Powder

Sodium alkylbenzene sulfonate	10-25 parts
Sodium tripolyphosphate (cotton seed oil)	15-25 parts
Sodium Silicate (1:3) anhydrous	3-5 parts
CMC (100%)	0-1 parts
Lauric acid monoethanolamide	0-25 parts
Optical brightening agent, colour, perfume	0.5-1.0 parts
Sodium Sulfate	Balance

Prepare as described in the text.

Formula -6

General-purpose Spray-dried Powder

Sodium dodecyl benzene sulfonate	25 parts
Sodium toluene sulfonate	2.5 parts
Lauric monethanolamide	3 parts
Sodium tripolyphosphate (coconut oil)	30 parts
Sodium silicate (1:2), anhydrous	10 parts
CMC (100% basis)	2 parts
Optical brightening agent, colour and perfume	1 parts
Sodium sulfate	25 parts
Sodium perborate	10 parts

Prepare as described in the text.

Formula -7

General Purpose Powder

Dodecyl benzene sulfonic acid	18 parts
Sodium tripolyphosphate (coconut oil)	25 parts
Sodium Silicate (1:2) (40% Soln.)	5 parts
CMC (100% basis)	2 parts
Sodium bicarbonate	28 parts
Soda ash	20 parts
Sodium hypochlorite soln.	2 parts
Optical brightening agent and perfume	0.5 parts

Prepare by combined neutralization and absorption method as discussed in the text.

Formula -8

High-foam Food/Dairy Detergent Cleaner

Trisodium phosphate	10 parts
Sodium carbonate	35 parts
Sodium metasilicate pentahydrate	20 parts
Sodium tripolyphospahte (coconut oil)	30 parts
Sodium dodecyl benzene sulfonate (solid)	5 parts

Dry, mix, grind and pack.

Formula -9

Heavy-duty Detergent Powder

Soda ash	50 parts
Trisodium polyphosphate	2.5 parts
Alkylbenzene sulfonic acid	15 parts
Sodium hypochlorite soln. (10% Cl_2)	2.5 parts
Sodium silicate (1:2)	5 parts
Soapstock	2 parts
Optical dye	0.5 parts

Formula -10

Light-duty Detergent Powder

Soda ash	10 parts
Trisodium polyphosphate	40 parts
Alkylbenzene sulfonic acid	18 parts
Sodium hybochlorite soln. (10% Cl_2)	2.5 parts
Sodium sulfate	20 parts
Sodium bicarbonate	10 parts
Micronised silica	2.5 parts
Soap stock	2 parts
Optical dye	0.05 parts

Formula -11

General Formula for Detergent Powders

Sodium dodecyl benezene Sulfonate	20-25 parts
Foam booster	0-2 parts
Sodium perborate	4-9 parts

Sodium silicate (1:2)	6-11 parts
Sodium tripolyphosphate	22-35 parts
Soda ash	0-2 parts
Sodium sulfate	14-20 parts
Optical brightener, colour, perfume and CMC	0-3 parts

Formula -12

Spray-dried Enzyme Detergent

Sodium dodecyl benzene sulfonate	20 parts
Sodium tripolyphosphate (cotton seed oil)	20 parts
CMC (60%)	2.5 parts
Sodium silicate	8.5 parts
Sodium sulfate	0.15 parts
Optical bleaching agent	38.5 parts
Sodium sulfate	8.85 parts
Borax or sodium bicarbonate	0.5 parts
Colour, perfume	q.s.
Enzyme	1 part

Formula -13

Medium-Foam Detergent Powder

sodium dodecyl benzene sulfonate	0-15 parts
Lauric monoalkanolamide	0-3 parts
Tetrasodium pyrophosphate (cotton seed oil)	0-10 parts
Sodium tripolyphospahte	40 parts
Sodium metasilicate	5 parts
Sodium sulfate (anhydrous)	35 parts
CMC	1 part
Perfume and colour	1 part
Optical dye	0.03 parts

Formula -14

Glass rinsing Sanitizer

Trichloromelamine	20 parts
Monosodium dihydrogen phoshate (L.O.)	68 parts
Sodium dodecyl benzene sulfonate	12 parts

Formula -15

Industrial Sanitary Cleaner

Sodium/Potassium dichloroisocyanurate	8.4-33.3 parts
Sodium tripolyphosphate (Linseed oil)	30-40 parts
Sodium dodecyl benzene sulfonate	0-2 parts
Sodium sulfate	Balance

Formula -16

General Cleaning compound

Light soda ash, anhyd.	42-49 parts
Tetrasodium pyrophosphate, anhyd.	23-28 parts
Trisodium phosphate, anhyd. (linseed oil)	8-10 parts
Sodium metasilicate pentahydrate	6-8 parts
Sodium dodecyl benzene sulfonate	4-5 parts

Formula -17

Diswashing Compound

Trisodium phosphate	10 parts
Sodium tripolyphosphate (Linseed oil)	25 parts
Sodium sesquicarbonate	25 parts
Borax	5 parts
Sodium metasilicate	25 parts
Sodium alkylbenzene sulfonate (40%)	10 parts

Formula -18

Heavy-duty Detergent

Sodium dodecyl benzene sulfonate	20 parts
Sodium tripolyphosphate (Castor oil)	50 parts
Sodium metasilicate pentahydrate	5 parts
Carboxy methyl cellulose	0.8 parts
Optical brightener	0.1 parts
Sodium sulfate	Balance

Formula -19

Household Laundry Bleach

Sodium/Potassium dichloroiso cyanorate	8.5-11.9 parts
Sodium tripolyphosphate (Castor oil)	10-40 parts
Alkylaryl sulfonate	0-3 parts
Sodium metasilicate anhyd	1-5 parts
Optical brightening agent	0.1 parts
Sodium Sulfate	Balance

Formula -20
Low Sudsing Detergent Powder

Sodium tripolyphosphate (Linseed oil)	30-40 parts
Sodium metasilicate (anhyd.)	7-9 parts
Sodium perborate	10 parts
Sodium dodecyl benzene sulfonate	15-20 parts
Soap stock	0.5-1.0 part
Optical brightener	0.05-0.1 part
Sodium sulfate	Balance

Formula -21
Hand Laundering Powder

Sodium tripolyphosphate (Linseed oil)	25-40 parts
Sodium dodecyl benzene sulfonate (40%)	15-30 parts
Sodium perborate	2-5 parts
Lauroyl diethanolamide	2-4 parts
Carboxy methyl cellulose	0.5-1.0 part
Optical brightener	0.05-0.1 part

Sodium Sesquicarbonate or Borax — Balance

Formula -22
Plastic-ware Destaining Compounds

Sodium tripolyphosphate (L.O.)	30 parts	25 parts
Sodium perborate	10 parts	9 parts
Sodium metasilicate (anhyd.)	25 parts	17 parts
Soda ash	32 parts	14 parts
Sodium sesquicarbonate	32 parts	32 parts
Epsom salt	2 parts	2 parts
Sodium dodecyl benzene sulfonate	1 part	1 part

Formula -23
Magic Dip Bleach

Sodium perborate	65 parts
Sodium silicate	5 parts
sodium tripolyphosphate	25 parts
Sodium carbonate	1 part
Sodium alkylaryl sulfonate	4 parts

Formula -24

Purex Bleach

Tetrasodium Pyrophosphate (Linseed oil)	10 parts
Calcium hypochlorite	8 parts
Sodium chloride	25 parts
Sodium sulfate	55 parts
Sodium alkylaryl sulfonate	2 parts

Formula -25

All-purpose Metal Cleaning Compound

Sodium sulfate (anhyd.)	15 parts
Sodium metasilicate	40 parts
Sodium sesquicarbonate	35 parts
Tetrasodium pyrophosphate (Linseed oil)	4 parts
Oxalic acid	4 parts
Sodium alkylbenzene sulfonate	2 parts

Standards

The Indian Standards Institutions has laid down standards for synthetic detergents for both household (IS : 4955-1948) and industrial use (IS : 4956-1968). the first prescribes the requirements and methods of sampling and test for anionic detergents base predominantly on alkylaryl sulfonates. It also prescribes packing and marking requirements. The second standard gives indentical details for similar type of detergents used for industrial purpose, which are divided into three types based on physical form. viz. , powder, paste and liquid. The requirements of household and industrial powder detergents are as follows.

	Composion	Household	Industrial
(1)	Moisture and Volatile Matter content at 105°C, % by wt, max.	15	8
(2)	Active ingredient, % by wt, min.	18	40
(3)	Matter insoluble in alcohol, % by wt. max.	70	50
(4)	Phosphates (expressed as sodium tripolyphosphate), % by wt. of matter insoluble in alcohol, min.	40	
(5)	pH of 1% solution (w/v) at 30°C	9-11	7-9
(6)	Non-detergent organic matter, % by wt. max.	1.0	1.0
(7)	Matter insoluble in water, % by wt, max.	0.5	0.5

Chapter 8

DETERGENT BARS

INTRODUCTION

The detergent bar (also called non-soapy detergent (NSD) bar or detergent cake) was first introduced into the market in the late sixties by the organised sector s a natural corollary to the existence of washing soap cakes. The prices of indigenous soap making oils were increasing rapidly while the price of alkylate was attractive in comparison to the level of usage in bars. Weight for weight, synthetic detergents were 1½ to 2 times more efficient than soaps especially in hard water. Taking these factors into account and using a process similar to the toilet soap finishing line, a processing route for detergent bars was developed indigenously. In view of the heavy costs involved in setting up the plant, the production of detergent bars has largely been confined to the organised sector.

Detergent bars constitute about 30% of the 14 lakh tonnes of synthetic detergents made in the country annually. The small scale sector has now also successfully entered the manufacturing scene. The synthetic detergents bar industry has a bright future since, this offers a more visible alternative both for the producer as well as the consumer, as compared to the manufacture of brown powder.

Requirements of a Detergent Bar

The requirements of a detergent bar are:

1. The bar must have superior detergency as compared to washing soaps with a pH maintained around 9-10 during washing.
2. The colour must be attractive.
3. The bar must have a soft yet firm texture.
4. The bar must have a density as close as possible to that of washing soap.
5. The bar must not undergo undesirable changes in storage.
6. The bar must produce copious lather, must not wear fast or become soggy with use.

7. The bar must be pleasantly perfumed and the perfume stability must be assured.
8. In brief, the bar must provide all the attributes and more, as compared to washing soaps.

It was soon realised that the development of an acceptable bar posed one of the most daunting challenges to chemists, chemical engineers and chemical technologists. Research for the removal of some of the deficiencies such as sogginess during use is underway and considerable success has already been achieved.

NSD Bar Vs. Soap

The fundamental difference between a soap and an NSD bar is that while soap comprises a single major organic component i.e. the soap itself, the NSD bar is a heterogeneous mixture of organic and inorganic components compacted into a bar.

While soap behaves in a set pattern and it is easier to process soap chips into the finished product, this is not so in the case of the NSD bar. With every minor change in formulation arising from cost control measures, the processing of the NSD bar can vary. The variation in the density and the size of the bar for the same weight can result in a host of problems. Therefore the formulation and processing of the NSD bar require continuous attention.

In addition, the high degree of wear and tear of the equipments, heat generated during processing, need for weathering of the bar for imparting hardness, and labour intensive-operations are other problems.

The storage and in-use behavior of an NSD bar is vastly different from that of washing soap. While soap tends to lose weight in storage, the NSD bar gains weight. Since the NSD bar is a heterogeneous mass comprising some water soluble ingredients, there is a need to minimise the *in-use* contact time with water because prolonged contact could leach out the soluble ingredients, resulting in sogginess and eventual high rate of wear.

Users of the NSD bar have to learn to use the bar in such a way that soggy appearance of the bar is discouraged. This is done by minimising the contact time for rubbing the bar against the clothes, wiping the bar free of water after use and leaving it in a dry state before the next use. For the same reason, the fluted design of the NSD bar has been specially chosen for minimising the contact area with standard soap dishes.

Another undesirable phenomenon that is observed when the NSD bar is left to dry, is a powdery or spotted appearance on the surface. This is basically a function of the formulation and if the otherwise satisfactory, this may be ignored. It is however necessary to formulate the bar in such a manner that the build up of insoluble matter on the fabric is minimised.

A common problem with the blue coloured NSD bar is the staining of fabrics. This can be controlled by minimising the usage of colour, improving the quality of other ingredients and resorting to a correct order of addition of the ingredients in the mixer. This step is less critical in the case of soaps since a very small quantity of colour is used.

The perfumes of NSD bars are generally stable since, unlike soaps, the detergent bars are virtually not susceptible to oxidative rancidity.

Components of Detergent Bars

The main objective of the formulation is to be able to produce a bar which meets all the listed in section 4.6.2 requirements. It should feel like soap while maintaining an overall price-performance advantage over soap. All the additives that have been considered from time to time are discussed below.

1. Active detergent

Initially, while the NSD bar was in a development stage, AD in the range of 30-40% was being considered. High AD bars proved to be too soft. Over a period of time because of the rising price of alkylates, the AD level has been steadily brought down to about 20% in good grade bars. Some manufacturers have brought it down further to 10-12.5 as a cost reduction measure and for offering the product at competitive prices.

The AD originally comprised the sodium salt of dodecyl benzene sulphonic acid but over the years for reasons of poor biodegradability the AD is now based on linear alkyl benzene and is fully biodegradable.

While dodecyl benzene sulphonic acid was more viscous and generally darker in colour it required a bleaching step. The LAB sulphonic acid is less viscous, more easily sulphonated and has a lighter colour without bleaching. From the point of view of the bar and lathering properties for the same AD, the DOB based AD has an edge over LAB.

The active detergent is obtained as an acid slurry and is neutralised *in situ* in a heavy duty mixer with a mixture of soda ash and caustic soda. Soda ash as such can also be used as neutralising agent but it is necessary to finely grind the material and sieve it before use for preventing the appearance of white specks in the finished bar.

2. Sodium tripolyphosphate

The importance of sodium tripolyphosphate (STPP) as a sequestrated and builder in NSD formulations is well known. However, its usage is being severely restricted in developed countries since it is said to be a major contributor to a process called *eutrophication* of lakes, rivers and ponds when spent wash water containing detergents and STPP enter them. Eutrophication ultimately leads to increased biological oxygen demand (BOD) in such waters affecting aquatic life.

In India although the *eutrophication* problem does not appear to be serious, there is an increasing trend to reduce the level of usage of STPP in detergent bar formulations because of price considerations.

Thus from an original level of 25 to 35% in the sixties and seventies the current trend is to reduce the level to 2-16% or even eliminate it altogether, the price factor outweighing the pollution aspect.

Regarding the grade to be used, the fast hydrating variety with a glycerine temperature rise of a minimum of 15°C is preferred from the point of view of the firmness of the bar.

3. Talc

Talc is cheap filler that is freely used in NSD bars, the level depending mainly on cost considerations. A usage level of 10-15% is common. Talc occurs in various degrees of whiteness the price being directly proportional to the whiteness. It is used as a fine powder after passing it through a 200 mesh screen.

4. Starch

Starch is used as binder at a level of 5-10% or less depending on the rest of the formulation. Usage of starch in not a must if more economical substitutes are available.

5. China clay

China clay is a from of hydrated aluminium silicate which is obtained as a mineral. It is treated for the removal of impurities such as iron compounds, sand, mica etc. and is used as a very fine powder.

China clay serves the purpose of a binder and is used to the extent of 10-15% in the formulation as a fine powder passing through 200 mesh.

6. Calcite

Calcite is a widely used filler at levels ranging from 10 to 30%. It helps to reduce cost while being compatible with the formulation. The cheaper NSD bars have higher levels of calcite. The material is used as a fine powder which passes the 200 mesh test.

7. Soda ash

Soda ash is used both as a neutralising agent for sulphonic acid as well as a builder instead of STPP. Usually soda ash is used for neutralising sulphonic acid, the excess being retained in the product as a builder. The extent of the excess soda ash depends on the formulation and is in the range of 10-20%.

8. Sodium sulphate

Sodium sulphate is produced *in situ* during the neutralisation of sulphonic acid in the mixer. It is usually not included as an external additive since it does not serve any useful purpose and cheaper substitutes offer a price advantage.

9. Sodium silicate

Alkaline silicate of soda is sometimes used since it acts as a synergist in detergency. It has a mild buffering, chelating and anti-soil redeposition action.

The materials is obtained as a thick liquid with about 45% solid content and is directly added to the mixer.

Sodium silicate helps to harden the bar when used in con-junction with either aluminium or magnesium sulphate.

10. Coconut mono ethanolamide

Earlier, up to 2% of coconut mono ethanolamide was included (CMEA) in NSD bar formulations but presently it is not being used. CMEA is a lather booster but it is very expensive.

11. Soapstock

Soapstock (SS) acts as an anti-soil redeposition agent and it was earlier used in NSD bar formulations. Currently its usage has been discontinued since controlled trials have shown that it could be dispensed with in NSD bars but not in powders.

12. Dicalcium phosphate

Dicalcium phosphate (DCP) has been used in bar formulations to the extent of upto 5% but its continued usage has not found favour because of the availability of alternative cost effective substitutes.

13. Rosin

Rosin had been used in the form of magnesium rosinate as a binder and lather booster but was not favoured in the formulation since the advantages were not commensurate with its high price.

14. Titanium dioxide

Anatase grade of titanium dioxide (TiO_2) is used as an opacifier in detergent bar formulations and its usage varies from 0.1% to 0.3% depending on the desired end result. Titanium dioxide contributes to a bright colour by masking the colour of other ingredients by its opacifying action.

15. Colour

The most popular colour for detergent bars is blue and the colouring matter that is more commonly used is a water-dispersible blue pigment called Phthalocyanine blue.

The objective should be to produce the best result with minimum colour usage so as to prevent possibilities of staining of the fabrics during washing.

If a fluorescer (optical brightener) is used in the formulation, the blue colour must be added as the last ingredient in the mixer, since it may acquire a greenish tinge in direct contact with the fluorescer if added together.

16. Fluorescer

A common fluorescer (optical brightener) that is incorporated into the bar for fabric brightening is 'Photin C'. The level of usage varies from nil to 0.3% depending on the product desired and the cost of production. In high grade detergent bars, the fluorescer is an essential ingredient.

17. Perfume

Perfume is an important ingredient in NSD bar formulations. Its usage varies from 0.05% to 0.2% based on price considerations.

The perfume itself comprises a limited number of stable ingredients. As already stated, once incorporated, the perfume remains quite stable in an NSD bar.

18. Water

Usually water does not constitute a separate ingredient in NSD bar formulations. Water is derived from raw materials in a free and combined state, from reactions such as neutralisation of sulphonic acid or as a medium of dispersing minor ingredients such as colour.

The moisture content of an NSD bar is usually in the range of 9% to 11%.

Processing of NSD Bars

The process technology of NSD bars has undergone changes since its inception. Without going into the details of the evolutionary process changes which have given satisfactory results, the present method is described below :

Handling of Raw Materials

The raw materials can be broadly categorised as solids (powders) and liquids. The liquids are acid slurry (active detergent base), liquid caustic soda, sodium silicate, and colour solution. Acid slurry is stored in storage tanks and transferred to batch tanks located above the mixer. Liquid caustic and silicate are handled similarly. The colour solution is prepared in a small tank fitted with a stirrer and is volumetrically dispensed by a measuring mug.

The powdery materials are received in bags in a free flowing and fine state and are stacked neatly on a platform above the mixer.

Processing

The processing unit comprises a heavy duty mixer, screw conveyor, pre-plodder, final plodder, rotary cutter, pneumatic stamper and wrapping machine. The mixer used is a heavy duty, Sigma type with double Z type arms, lined with stainless steel, and fitted with a water jacket either for cooling or heating. The original mixers were of the tilting type with top discharge. These have now been replaced by bottom discharge versions.

The neutralising agents are first dropped into the mixer followed by the sulphonic acid slurry while mixing. Other ingredients are added in a pre-determined sequence under continuous mixing, taking the usual precaution of separating additives such as colour and fluorescer, and silicate and aluminium/magnesium sulphate.

When all the ingredients have been added and after sufficient mixing time(10 minutes) has been allowed to obtain a homogeneous mass, the material is discharge into the hopper of a multi-screw conveyor.

The function of the multi-screw conveyor is to convey the mass from the mixer at a regulated rate to the pre-plodder. There are four screws arranged in parallel which push the mixed mass through openings in the casing and as the mass emerges, it is cut to smaller sizes by a rotary cutter fitted to the end of the screw conveyor and fed to a conveyor for feeding pre-plodders arranged below. The pre-plodder feeds the final plodders which are maintained under vacuum. The final plodder can be either a single head or double head type depending on whether it is intended to extrude a single bar or two bars. Twin worm Plodders are used for a positive extrusion of the bar. The plodder barrels are provided with a chilled water jacket for the removal of heat generated during the plodding process. The *nozzle* of the plodder is heated electrically for imparting a high degree of polish to the emerging bar. The bar is automatically cut into smaller lengths by as in-line rotary cutter. The cut bars are further cut into tablets on an in-line wire cutter, stamped

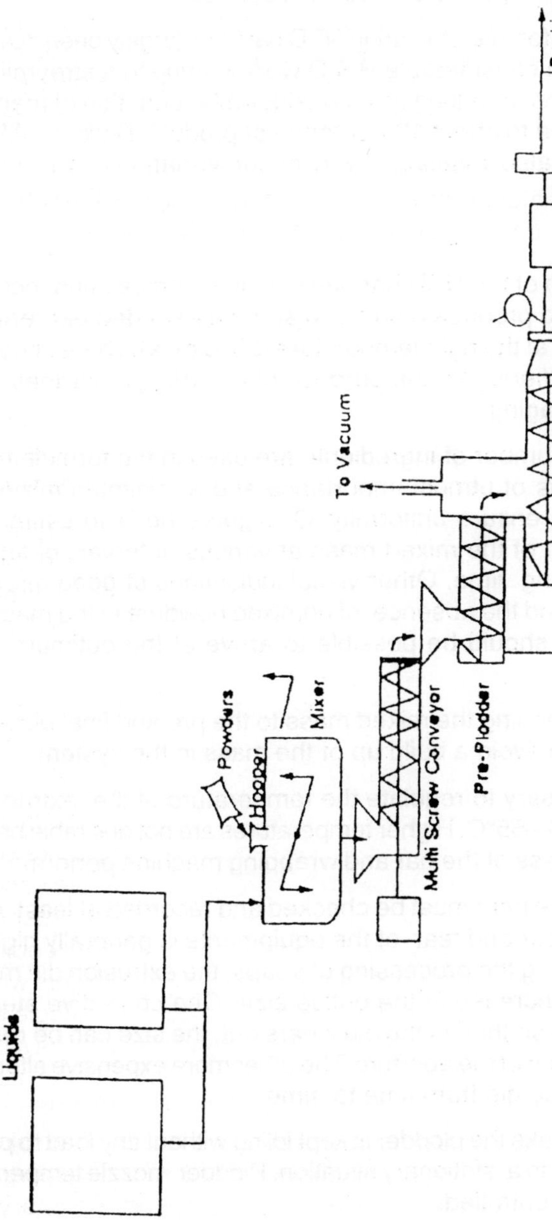

Fig. 4.18 Flow sheet of NSD bar processing

by an in-line pneumatic stamper, and fed directly to a Rose type of wrapping machine that uses a polythene coated wrapper reel.

The technology for manufacturing NSD bars has largely been developed indigenously through considerable R & D work leading to a streamlining of the various operations, resulting in a considerable reduction of man hours from say 60 per tonne to about 10 per tonne of product. Ballestra/Mazzoni turnkey plants are also available with minor variations in processing techniques.

Process Control

The formulation of the NSD bar has to suit the processing technique, the objective being to produce a firm and smooth extruded bar emerging from the final plodder at the right temperature (55°C max). There should also be no need for *weathering* for the purpose of imparting a hardness to the product prior to packaging.

Since a large number of ingredients are used in the formulation, the efficiency of mixing is of utmost importance and a minimum mixing time needs to be fixed to ensure uniformity. One guideline is to estimate the active matter content of the mixed mass at various intervals of time and fix the minimum mixing time. Other visual indications of good mixing are uniformity of colour and the absence of unmixed powders in the mass. With a little experience it should be possible to arrive at the optimum mixing time.

Regulation of feeding the mixed mass to the pre and final plodders is important in order to avoid a build up of the mass in the system.

It is also necessary to regulate the temperature of the extruded bar within the range of 50°—55°C. Higher temperatures are not desirable because they affect the hardness of the bar and wrapping machine performance.

The weight of the bars must be checked and recorded at least once in an hour. Since the wear and tear of the equipments is generally higher as compared to that during the processing of soaps, the extrusion die must be checked weekly for increase in the orifice size. One corrective step is to use an adjustable die so that as the die wears out, the size can be restored by adjusting the opening of the aperture. The other more expensive alternative is to replace the orifice die from time to time.

During short breaks the plodder is kept idling without any load to prevent the worm from seizing in a stationary situation. Plodder nozzle temperatures are thermostatically controlled.

To facilitate movement of the bars along conveyors without surface damage, light liquid paraffin is used as a lubricant.

A photoelectric device helps to regulate the flow of bars to the wrapping machine. Thus when the conveyor feeding the wrapping machine is full, the belt stops and excess tablets are diverted from the line automatically for re-working. The scrap re-work conveyor also receives off-cuts from the cutting machine for recycling.

The packed stock is examined for hardness before it is marketed so as to ensure that the product meets the minimum standards of hardness. Hardness is determined using a penetrometer and standards can be established with reference to penetrometer readings.

Some Typical Formulations of Detergent Bar

The following table show some typical formulations which have been tried in the past but may be reconsidered depending on the price of the ingredients.

Table 1 : Formulations for detergent bar manufacture

Ingredient	Component % in formulation number									
	1	2	3	4	5	6	7	8	9	10
Shikakai	12.5	12.5	15	15	18	18	20	20	22	22
Soda ash	5.0	7.0	7	7	8	8	8	8	9	9
STPP(C.O)	2.5	2.5	5	5	5	5	10	15	16	16
Alk. silicate 120° Tw	5.0	7.5	5	7.5	8	8	10	10	12	12
$MgSO_4 7H_2O$	2.5	3.0	2.5	3	3	3	3	3	3	3
$Al_2(SO_4)_3$										
Calcite	30	25	20	17	14	12	5	-	10	-
China clay	15	15	10	10	12	14	12	10	-	10
Talc	15	15	15	15	10	10	10	12	10	10
Sod. sulphate (in situ)	5.0	5	6	6	6.5	6.5	6	6	6.5	6.5
Starch	-	-	5	5	5	5	5	5	-	-
TiO_2	-	-	-	-	0.1	0.1	0.1	0.1	0.2	0.2
Colour	0.1	0.1	0.1	0.1	0.1	0.1	0.1	0.1	0.1	0.1
Fluorescer	-	-	-	-	0.05	0.05	0.1	0.1	0.2	0.2
Perfume	0.1	0.1	0.1	0.1	0.1	0.1	0.1	0.1	0.1	0.1
Moisture	7.3	7.3	9.3	9.3	10.15	10.15	10.6	10.6	10.9	10.9
	100	100	100	100	100	100	100	100	100	100

PLANT & MACHINERY FOR SMALL SCALE DETERGENT

Cake Manufacture

The major equipments and machinery required for the manufacture of detergent cakes in the small scale include kneader, mixing mill, plodder, bat cutting machine, cake stamping machine and sometimes wrapping machine also.

Kneader

The primary mixing of various ingredients used in the formulation of detergent cake is done in a kneader, also known as a sigma blade-mixer and kneader mixer. The kneader is fitted with sigma shaped blades which do very good mixing of dough type materials .The generally recommended kneader is of stainless steel construction but since it is very costly, the small scale manufacturers generally use M.S. Kneader only. The kneader is jacketed to provide hot water heating of the ingredients. The stand of a kneader is usually designed with heavy-duty M.S. plates for vibrationless performance. A kneader suitable for making 200kg/hr. detergent cake is fitted with 15 H.P. motor. The discharge of the mixed material is usually carried out by means of a tilting arrangement provided on the front side for discharging purpose.

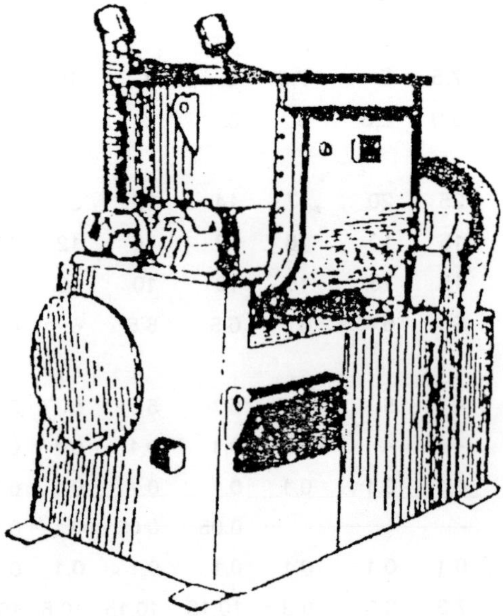

Fig. 14.4 : Kneader

Milling Machine

The milling machine is a typical two or three roll mill used for homogenizing the mass obtained in dough shape from the kneader. Here chips are formed which could be milled to the desired fineness by keeping the gap close between the rolls. Generally cold water is passed through the rolls to keep them cool.

A typical roll mill suitable for the manufacture of 200 kg./hr. detergent cake bar has 12' dia x 24' length hollow hardened chilled steel rollers suitable for water circulation. The stand is strong and sturdy, constructed from mild steel. The rollers are mounted on heavy-duty self-aligning roller bearings for absorbing lateral as well as axial thrust.

Plodder

The plodder is a very important piece of equipment in this plant. It is specifically designed with heavy-duty gear trains, breaker arms and load thrust carriers. It plods the mix and extrudes it into a bar form of desired shape. An extrusion die of distinctive design is provided on the plodder to achieve this.

In a typical plodder of detergent cakes, the plodding consists of a single worm plodding with individual drive by gear-reduction train, of spur gears supported by self-aligning bearings and thrust will be carried by heavy-

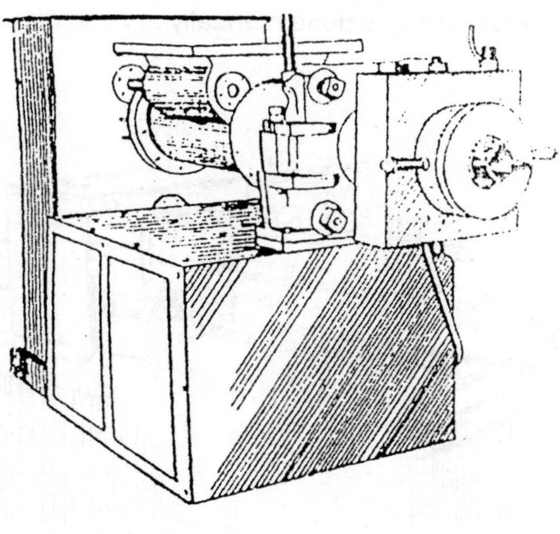

Fig. 14.5 : Plodder

duty thrust bearings. It is driven by a 15 H.P., 1440 pm motor. The main barrel is of stainless steel construction, jacketed for circulation of hot or cold water, the hopper of the plodder is of S.S. for feeding the material . It is also fitted with breaker arm to facilitate feeding. The worm is of special design and of pitch for particular detergent extrusion through special noodle plate. The worm is of aluminium silicon alloy for wear resistance. The extrusion cone and mouth piece are of stainless steel and jacketed for circulation of hot water with thermostat control.

Bar Cutter or Billet Cutter

The bar cutter or billet cutter is of the same construction as the ordinary soap-bar cutter. This cutter consists of crank linkage movement to move cutter arm to push detergent bars through adjustable piano wire fixture to cut to cake size. The top of cutter is fitted with formica sheet to facilitate bar feeding and movement. It may be hand wheel operated or fitted with a 1H.P. motor and reduction gear-bar fitted to drive crank linkage assembly.

Embossing or Stamping Machine

The embossing or stamping of cakes may be either done in ordinary soap stamping machine or in roller embossing machine. Roller embossing is found to be most effective for embossing the cake with respective cake trade name; and this has been achieved by two bronze rollers engraved to particular trade name of cake.

In roller embossing, the billets are cut into cakes after embossing. The operation of embossing is done manually and the output is about 100 cakes per minute.

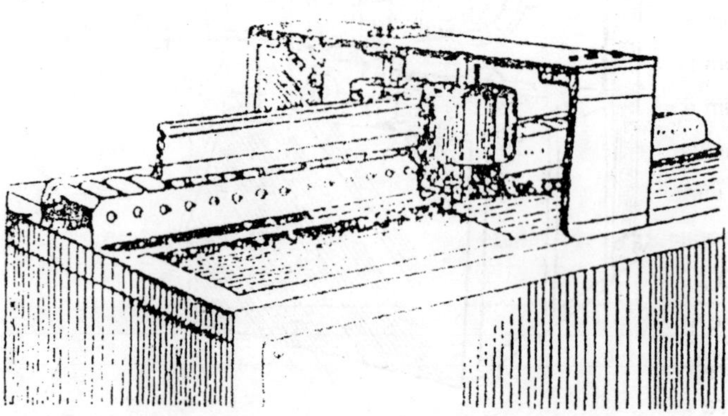

Fig. 14.6 : Roller Embossing Machine

Pulverizer

Sometimes, some of the material like soda ash, STPP etc. are required to be ground to a fine mesh size before charging into the kneader because they have tendency to cake on absorption of moisture during storage. Although lumps of soda ash can be broken up in the kneader itself, STPP forms very hard lumps which can be broken up only in a pulverizer. The pulverizer is generally fitted with suction and cyclone collector with tripled stand, driving and driven pulleys, cyclone collector base plate and tension device and 440 volts 3 phase motor of adequate capacity.

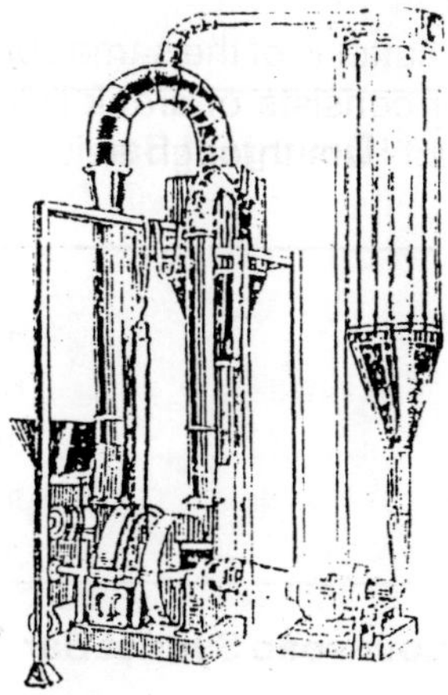

Fig. 14.7 : Pulverizer

Formulations of detergent cakes

Formulae	1	2	3
Sodium Stearyl isethionate (cottonseed oil)	65	65	27
Sodium lauryl isethionate (cottonseed oil)	-	20	27
Sodium dodecyl benzene sulfonate	445	65	6
Sodium lauryl sulfate	-	19	-
Corn strach	104	455	5
Tetrasodium pyrophosphate	13	13	-
$Al_2(SO_4)_3$	13	13	-
Total dry weight	**650**	**650**	**65**

The ingredients are placed in a mixer, 15-20% water is added and the temperature is maintained at 80-100°C until the mix is a uniformed, fused slurry and the water has been reduced to 5 per cent. It is then removed to be formed into bars.

Soap-Surfactant Combination

Formula 4

Sodium dodecyl benzene sulfonate	41.3
Sodium lauryl sulfate (cottonseed oil)	15.0
Sodium cocoate (80:20)	30.0
Calcium stearate	6.0
Titanium dioxide	1.5
Polyethylene oxide gum	2.0
Water	4.0
Perfume	0.2

Detergent Bar

Formula 5

Shikakai	68.0
Stearate from cottonseed oil	9.7
Stearyl alcohol	6.3
Cetyl alcohol	3.4
Paraffin wax (M.P. 131°F)	9.7
Water	2.9

Low-soap Syndet Bar

Formula 6

Shikakai	25.0
STPP and TSP	35.0
Soda ash	5.0
Sodium sulfate	10.0
Soap chips	2.5
CMC	2.0
Prussian blue pigment	0.5
Water	15.0

Formula 7

Shikakai	20.0
Di-isopropyl naphthalene sulfonate (55%)	20.0
Diamyl sulfosuccinate	10
Sodium tallow soap	47.0
Carboxy methyl cellulose	2.0
Colour & perfume	1.0

Soap-Synthetic All-purpose Bar

Formula 8

Shikakai	20
Isopropyl naphthalene sulfonate	20
Diamyl sulfosuccinate	10
Calcium stearate	45
Vegetable gum	5

Formula 9

Shikakai	20-30
Soap	30-40
Sodium tripolyphosphate	30-40
Sodium sulfate	5-10
Corn starch binder	5-10
CMC colour and perfume	2-3

Formula 10

Shikakai	20-30
Cottonseed soapstock	30-50
Glycols and glycol ethers	20-25
CMC	2-3
Colour and perfume	q.s.

All Syndet Bar

Formula 11

Shikakai	20-30
STPP	40-50
Sodium sulfate	5-10
Corn starch and talc	10-20
CMC	1-3
Lecithin	q.s.
Perfume and colour	q.s.

Alkyl-Sulfate Syndet Bar

Formula 12

Shikakai	40-70
Plasticizer from Castor oil	20-25
Binders	5-30
Sodium sulfate	5-10
Water	5-10

Formulae	13	14
Shikakai	70	40
Superfatting plasticizer	20	20
Binding and softening complex		30
Water and mineral salts (Sod. sulfate)	10	10

Proctor & Gamble's Soap Syndet Formulation

Formula 15

Sodium coconut glyceryl ether sulfonate	19.0
Sodium coconut soap	31.0
Sodium tallow soap	23.0
Disodium alphasulfonated castor fatty acids	2.5
Coconut and tallow fatty acids (50:50)	10.0
Alkali metal inorganic salts	6.5
Other additives	3.0
Water, colour and perfume	5.0

Proctor and Gamble's Syndet Laundry Bar

Formula 16

Shikakai	25.0
STPP	30.0
Sodium bicarbonate	30.0
Sodium silicate	7.3
Sodium CMC	1.0
Coconut monoethanolamide	2.0
Water, perfume and colour	4.7

Formula 17

Shikakai	20
STPP	46
Urea	10
Sodium silicate, powder	7
CMC	2
Sodium sulfate (anhyd.)	15
Optical brightening agent.	q.s.

Formula 18

Shikakai	10-20
Linseed fatty acid	20-50
Water soluble sodium metasilicates	20-50
Water, perfume, colour and CMC	15-35

Formula 19

Shikakai	35
STPP	35
Silicate based on L.O.	5
Sodium perborate	5
Soda ash	5
Perfume, colour and water	5
CMC	2
Soap flakes	3
Fillers	5

Formulation-1

	parts
Shikakai	4.5
Sodium Stearoyl Isothionate (linseed oil)	60.0
Corn starch	10.5
Tetrasodium pyrophosphate	15.0
Aluminium sulphate	10.0

Formulation-2

	parts
Shikakai	72
Castor oil	8
Sodium silicate, 44 percent solution	20

Chapter 9

HERBAL LIQUID AND PASTE DETERGENTS

The detergents discussed so far are powders or bars. Herbal liquid detergents are becoming increasingly popular for washing of all kinds because of their convenience, ease of dispensation and dispersion in water. From the manufacturing angle, liquid detergents can be manufactured using relatively simple equipments such as a stainless steel or an FRP tank fitted with a slow-speed stirrer. The quality of the products can be controlled with the help of a pH meter, viscometer and basic analytical facilities. Liquid detergents are of various types designed to satisfy particular needs and a few examples are :

1. Heavy duty liquid detergents for regular washing
2. Light duty liquid detergents for washing of fines
3. Liquid shampoo and
4. Dish washing liquids

There are many other liquid cleaning agents for which reference may be made to the bibliography listed in the book.

Requisites of surfactants for formulating liquid detergents

A. High solubility

B. High cleansing power

C. Stable foaming

D. Less irritative

E. Easily biodegradable

Surfactants Most Commonly Used

(a) Ammonium and organic amine salts of cottonseed oil $[(OHC_2H_4)_3NOS(O)_2OC_{12}H_{25}]$.

It is a foaming surfactant. This type of surfactants are widely used for liquid detergent formulations as well as in the preparation of shampoos.

(b) Triethanol amine salts and ammonium salt of linear alkyl benzene sulphonic acid (LABS) is effective and cheaper and extensively used for the formulation of household liquid detergents and shampoos.

(c) Alkyl phenol ethylene oxide condensates are also widely used. Apart from their good detergency they are also very mild to human skin. But they tend to produce unstable foam.

(d) Fatty alkyl and fatty acyl radicals derived from coconut oil, sulphated and neutralized with sodium or triethanol amine base are also used in good amount in formulating foaming shampoos.

A great number of synthetic surfactants are proposed for liquid composition. In selecting surfactant high solubility is considered its primary requisiteness. Ammonium or triethanol amine salts of anionic detergents are preferred to sodium salts (mentioned before). Solubility can also be increased by addition of small proportion of alcohol or glycerol ether to the aqueous solvent. Table-1 gives a general idea from the consumption figure of various surfactants used in formulating liquid as well as powdered detergents.

Table-1

Consumption of Surfactants in Detergents (in kilotons)

	Powders	Liquids
Anionics		
Alkyl Benzene Sulphonate	143	43
Alcohol Ethoxy Sulphates	45	small
Alcohol Sulphates	23	—
Nonionics		
Alcohol Ethoxylates	45	41
Alkyl Phenol Ethoxylates	5	5
Amines, Amine Oxides	5	5

Builders

Ethylene diamine tetra-acetic acid (EDTA) being completely stable in aqueous solution, it is a satisfactory builder for liquid detergent formulations. Small amount of EDTA is usually used in liquid soaps, detergents for household use and liquid shampoos to clarify and stabiles the solution by sequestration.

Potassium pyrophosphate is used as builder in formulating most of the liquid detergents. This is also a sequestering agent.

Sodium carboxy methyl cellous is also incorporated in liquid detergents as soil pending agent.

Viscosity Controllers

Liquid detergents deserve close viscosity control for its use in various handling devices. Polyethoxy nonionics and fatty alkyloamides of ninol type are effective viscosity control ingredients. These compounds possess additinally surface activity and detergency power.

Other Ingredients

PVM/MA (Polyveny) methyl ether maleic anhydride) as mentioned before, is used as foam stabilizer. Other chemicals, as used in liquid soaps preparations are also applicable in liquid detergents.

HOUSEHOLD LIQUID DETERGENTS FOR LAUNDERING

Heavy Duty

Surfactants need some amount of builders as mentioned before, for attaining good detergency in its use as laundering formulations. Making a solution for liquid detergent with just enough quantity of various builders as well as surfactants having good clarity and stability is under limited liberty. But the proper identification of various aider compounds, formulations of liquid detergents for specific services are made marketed with good acceptability. Generally concentration of active surfactants are kept in the range of 12 to 25 percent, it may be raised up to 35 to 40 percent.

Manufacture of Paste Detergents

In certain parts of the world, detergents are used in a finished or semi-finished form as pastes of varying concentrations. Certain detergent raw materials such as the sodium salt of lauryl alcohol sulfate are sold in a concentrated form without any addition of inorganic fillers as pastes. Alkylbenzene sulfonic acid can be very easily used for the manufacture of paste detergents, either from the 100 per cent or 90 per cent varieties, depending upon availability.

The manufacture of the paste can be done in a soap crutcher, or in a specially built neutralizer, equipped with a cooling jacket. The neutralizing vessel should preferably be built of stainless steel, but if precautions are taken so that the pH of the paste does not fall below 7 during the process of manufacture, a mild steel vessel can be used.

Because sodium alkyl benzene sulfonates are not completely miscible with water, various materials must be used to prevent separation into two phases. This can be done by the use of hydrotropes; small proportions of CMC alkylolamides. However, hydrotropes will tend to produce thinner pastes and this will mean adding inorganic salts to make them stiffer again. In general, dodecyl benzene sulfonate will produce a paste of medium consistency and the bio-degradable linear alkylbenzene sulfonates, a thinner paste. Consistency can again be varied by the addition of on organic salts.

Sodium chloride, sodium sulfate, tetrasodium pyrophosphate or sodium silicate may be used to the extent of not above 3 per cent, in general, to obtain a stiff paste. Sodium chloride is the cheapest; and gives the greatest stiffening effect, but is corrosive to iron or steel. Sodium sulfate and tetrasodium pyrophosphate suffer from the disadvantage that in cold weather they might crystallize out from the paste into needle like crystals, while both the tetrasodium pyrophosphate and the sodium silicate raise the pH of the paste, but add to the detergency. The high pH can be regulated by using some of the sulfonic acid to neutralize a portion of the alkalinity of these two materials.

If CMC is to be included in the formulation, it is necessary to dissolve it separately. If a separate mixing vessel with a slow speed stirrer is available, water to the amounts of ten times the weight of the CMC is charged into the container and the CMC poured in slowly with stirring. The stirring is continued until all the lumps of CMC are dispersed, concurrently with the process of the manufacture of the paste. If a mixing vessel is not available, the solution can be made in the same way in a 45 gallon drum and the CMC added while stirring with a hand crutcher. This dispersion is best prepared the day before it is required and left to swell and dissolve by itself overnight.

The CMC dispersion, if in contact with iron or steel, will tend to corrode the vessel and also will become discoloured by the rust formed. It is, therefore, essential to produce this dispersion steel clad with plastic or rubber. The stirrer itself should also be non-corrodible.

If a mild steel neturalizing vessel is being used for the manufacture of the paste, all the remaining water called for in the formula (all the water if no CMC is to be added) and the requisite amount of caustic soda solution, with inorganic salts if they are to be used, are run into the vessel. Mixing and cooling is started and the sulfonic acid added at such a rate that the temperature does not rise above 65°C. If 100 percent sulfonic acid is used the heat of reaction is low and the temperature will not rise very high, provided that an efficient cooling coil or jacket is available. If 90% acid is used, the heat of reaction is considerably higher and the rate of addition of the sulfonic acid must be adjusted.

When about 80 per cent of the sulfonic acid has been taken up and the paste is still distinctly alkaline, the requisite amount of sodium hypochlorite solution is added and mixed in. The balance of the sulfonic acid is now added, taking care that the pH of the paste does not fall below 7. Mixing is continued until the paste is uniform and the CMC solution (if called for) is added, or, if an alkylolamide is to be used, this can now be put in. If a hydrotrope is employed, this can be added with the sulfonic acid.

When a stainless steel neutralizing vessel is being used, the procedure is similar, except that the sodium hypochlorite can be put in at the beginning with the water and caustic soda and no special precautions need be taken about not passing to the acid pH. If an acid pH is reached, the desired pH of 7.5-8 can be achieved by the addition of a litre or two of caustic soda solution.

Aslight variation of this procedure occurs when a highly concentrated liquid is required. This is done by neutralizing the sulfonic acid with an ethanolamine. In this instance, the requisite water which depends on the final concentration desired and the ethanolamine, are charged into the vessel. The sulfonic acid is added slowly with intermittent stirring so as not to generate foam. The reaction is instantaneous. The only precautions that need be observed are to avoid the production of foam and to keep the temperature from rising above 60°C.

Formulations of Liquid and Paste Detergents

The first requirement processing alkylbenzene sulfonic acid to form liquid detergents is to remove as much spent sulfuric acid as possible from the alkylbenzene sulfonic acid before neutralization. By close supervision of the washing process after sulfonation, material containing a ratio of sodium sulfate to sodium alkylbenzene sulfonate at best as low as 1:9 can be produced. Milwidsky recommends that the 90% sulfonic acid obtained by oleum or sulfuric acid, sulfonation and subsequent decantation of acid, can be again washed once or twice with not more than 10% by weight of water at a time, settling and discarding the bottom layer by this method some more sulfuric acid may be removed. The methods of formulation fall into two classes, according to whether sodium alkylbenzene sulfonate is used with additional solubilizing agents, or alternative alkalies to caustic soda are used entirely or in part to obtain a more soluble salt. Combinations of the two methods can also be used.

Adjuvants which have been used as solubilizing agents are urea, dicyandiamide, alcohol, non-ionic surface active agents etc. The main alkalies used as alternatives to caustic soda for neturalization are ammonia, triethanolamine etc. Using these agents in various combinations, formulations have been designed for three grades of liquid detergents *viz.*, a cheap grade containing about 12% active agent, a normal grade containing 25% active agent, and a highly viscous concentrated grade containing about 40% active agent for these applications where it is desirable to have the minimum water present.

The active agent is considered to be the total weight of salt of alkylbenzene sulfonic acid, together with the nonionic surface active agent where present, in the formulation. The following formulations are suggested for making general purpose liquid detergents. The proportions given are by weight.

HEAVY DUTY LIQUID DETERGENTS

A Few Formulations are Listed in Table-2

Table - 2

	Formula No.				
Ingredients	1 %	2 %	3 %	4 %	5 %
CNO fatty acids	8.0	—	—	—	—
KOH (40%)	5.0	—	—	—	—
Shikakai	10.0	10.0	20.0	9.0	12.0
Di-ethanolamine	—	3.6	7.2	3.3	4.0
Non-ionic (100%)	—	2.0	—	3.0	—
Polyvinyl pyrolidone	—	0.7	—	—	0.7
Potassium pyrophosphate	12.0	12.0	12.0	10.0	—
Potassium silicate (100%)	4.0	4.0	3.0	4.0	—
Mono ethanolamine	2.3	—	—	—	3.0
EDTA	—	—	—	—	5.0
CMC 100%	2.0	—	1.0	1.0	—
Potassium xylene sulphonate	5.0	5.0	5.0	4.0	4.0
Optical brightener	0.2	0.1	0.1	0.1	0.1
Water	Bal.	Bal.	Bal.	Bal.	Bal.
	100	100	100	100	100

Of these formulations the first one is the low foaming type, designed for washing machines. Alpha olefin sulphonate (AOS) may replace 40% of LABS in the above formulations but trials are necessary for achieving a cost effective and acceptable product.

In the above formulations CMC can be replaced by PVP (Polyvinyl pyrolidone) to obtain a clearer solution. The AD from alkyl benzene should preferably by derived from sulphonation by the SO_3 gas process for reducing in organics and hence the cloud point of the liquid.

Light Duty Detergents

Light duty liquid detergents are used for washing delicate fabrics such as wool, silk, nylon etc. The active detergent should preferably be derived from the sulphonation of the alkylate by sulphur trioxide gas for minimising the inorganic content of the liquid. One formulation is given below :

	%
Alpha olefin sulphonate	2.0
Shikakai	9.0
Tri-ethanolamine	1.8
Caustic soda (45% soln.)	1.6
Sodium hypochlorite (10% Soln)	0.5
Lauric acid di-ethanolamide	1.0
Water	84.1
	100.0

It is claimed that an 18% solution of alpha olefin sulphonate in demineralised water is an equally good light duty detergent for fine washes. AOS has a good fabric-softening effect on wool, silk and acrylics.

Liquid Shampoo

Shampoos are toilet preparations that need to be formulated with special care for dermatological acceptance. The main active matter used is sodium lauryl ether sulphate or tri-ethanolamine lauryl sulphate along with lather boosters. AOS is also claimed to be an active matter suitable for incorporation in shampoo. A few formulations are listed in Table-3.

Table - 3

Liquid Shampoo Formulation

Ingredient	1 %	2 %	3 %
AOS (40%)	—	—	8.0
Tri-ethanolamine lauryl sulphate 100%	—	15.00	—
Shikakai	12.00	—	5.0
Ethoxilated coconut monoethanolamide	1.00	1.00	1.00
Formalin preservative	0.05	0.05	0.05
Sodium chloride	0.50	1.00	qs
EDTA	0.03	0.03	0.03
Orthophosphoric acid	1.00	1.00	1.00
Colour, perfume, water	qs	qs	qs
	100.00	100.00	100.00

Typical Formulations

No. 1

	Parts
Shikakai	10.00
Lemon juice	.50

Amla	2.00
Ritha for clarification	0.80
Baheda	12.00
Potassium silicate (50 percent)	8.00
Potassium xylene sulphonate (stabilizer)	4.50
Optical brightening agent	0.05
Perfume	0.15
Water (demineralized)	58.00

Opaque Viscous Solution

No. 2

	Parts
Shikakai	10.00
Lemon Juice	4.50
Distilled coconut of fatty acids (higher acids only)	6.00
Potassium hydroxide (40 percent solution)	4.00
Potassium xylene sulphonate	5.00
Tetrapotassium pyro phosphate	14.00
Potassium silicate (40 percent solution)	8.00
Carboxy methyle cellulose	1.50
Optical brightner	0.20
Perfume	0.05
Water (D.M.)	46.75

Procedure

First 1.5 parts of carboxy methyle cellulose is dissolved in 15 parts of water with stirring in a separate vessel. Then 6 parts of coconut oil fatty acids are put in the mixing pan and 20 parts of water is added to it. It is then neutralized with 4 parts of previously prepared 40 percent potassium hydroxide solution with constant agitation and warming. Agitation is continued until a clear homogenous solution is made.

Then all the remaining ingredients are added in order of their position in the list above, with stirring.

Then the carboxy methyl cellulose solution as prepared first is added to the whole mass and agitation continued with addition of balance quantity of water. The finished product is ready for packing.

Light Duty : (for silk, wool etc.)

Light duty household liquid detergents used for washing silk, wool and other synthetic fabrics are best formulated using a combination of LAB sulphonic acid amine or ammonium salt with a relatively high percentage of nonionic alkyloamide giving good foam stability and high detergency.

TYPICAL FORMULATIONS

No. 1

	Parts
Shikakai	15.°C
Monoethanol amine	3.5
Urad ki Dal	8.0
Potassium dichloroisocyanurate, (59 percent available chlorine)	0.4
Potassium sulphate	1.0
Alcohol	5.0
Perfume	0.1
Water (demineralized)	67.0

Procedure

LAB sulphonic acid, potassium sulphate and water being taken in to the mixing pan or neutralizer, potassium dichloroisocyanurate is added and stirred for half an hour in order to complete bleaching. Then 8 parts of lauric acid monoethanol amide together with 3.5 parts of monoethanol amine is melted by heating to liquid form in a separate pan and then added to the whole mass in the neutralizer.

After complete neutralization and formation of homogeneous solution, perfume and alcohol are added with aviation. The product is ready to be packed.

The product contains 25 percent active matter.

No. 2

	Parts
Shikakai	17.0
Multani Mitti	9.0
Aqueous ammonia (25 percent)	4.7
Sodium lauryl sulphate (30 percent solution)	35.0
EDTA	1.2
Alcohol	15.0
Perfume	0.1
Water (demineralized)	18.0

After complete neutralization EDTA is added. The product contains 37 percent active matter and its cloud point is below O°C.

Shampoos

Shampoos based on synthetic detergents are dealt in chapter-4 along with soap shampoos.

Rug Cleaning Liquid Detergent Formulations

Cleaning of rug is carried out on the floor itself where it is placed.

The detergent formulations contain very little or not at all any other soluble additives.

The process of rug cleaning consists of spreading the viscous solution of detergent on the rug and ten it is made to work through the superficial layers by means of a brush. Brushing action also swiftly moves out the foam which carries much of the removed dust. The foam is then sucked by vacuum cleaner or squcczed from the rough surface.

The detergent formulation is such that, after drying, the residue left, tends to be powdery and easily removable by vacuum cleaner.

A solution of sulphated or sulphonated anionic surfactant thickened with sodium stearate to make more viscous and compounded with foam stabilizer, gives excellent result and is widely used in rug cleaning.

A Recommended Formulation

	Parts
Shikakai	18.0
Sodium stearate	7.5
Honey	2.5
Water (demineralized)	72.0

Formula 1

	Parts
Shikakai	12
Industrial methylated spirit	8
Water, to make 100	

Formula 2

Shikakai	8
Triethanolamine alkylbenzene sulfonate	4
Water, to make 100	

Formula 3

Shikakai	25
Industrial methylated spirit	12
Water, to make 100	

Formula 4

Shikakai	25
Urea	15
Water, to make 100	

Formula 5

Shikakai	25
Urea	15
Lauryl isopropanolamide	3
Industrial methylated spirit	3
Water, to make 100	

Formula 6

Shikakai	12.5
Triethanolamine alkylbenzene sulfonate	12.5
Water, to make 100	

Formula 7

Triethanolamine alkylbenzene sulfonate	40
Water, to make 100	

The cloud points of these formulation when tried in laboratory were all bellow 5°C. If the product is required to have a could point slightly higher or lower than that obtained, then a slight decrease or increase in the amount of solubilizing agent should be tried. For these reasons, the foregoing formulations are suggested as guides only, and do not exclude different combinations, for instance, a formulation based on amonium or triethanolamine alkylbenzene sulfonate and containing a fatty alkanolamide. When using mixtures of alkalies to neutralize the alkylbenzene sulfonic acid, the replacement of one alkali by an other should be made on the basis of their equivalent weight.

Heavy-duty Liquid Detergents

Formulae	8	9	10	11
Shikakai	10	20	9	12
Diethanolamine	3.6	7.2	3.3	4
Non-ionic (100 per cent)	2	—	3	—
PVP (100 per cent)	0.7	—	—	0.7
$K_4P_2O_7$ (100 per cent)	12	12	10	—

Potassium silicate (100 per cent)	4	3	4	—
Monoethanolamine	—	—	—	3
EDTA	—	—	—	5
CMC (100%)	—	1	1	—
Potassium xylene sulfonate	5	5	4	4
Optical brightening agent	0.1	0.1	0.1	0.1
Water, to make 100				

Formula 12

Heavy-duty Liquid Detergent with 'Controlled Foam'

CMC (66%)	2
Water	18
Distilled coconut oil fatty acid	8
Water	25
Caustic potash (40% soln)	5
Monoethanolamine	2.3
Shikakai	10
Potassium xylene sulfonate	5
Tetrapotassium pyrophosphate (100%)	12
Potassium silicate (40% soln)	10
Optical brightening agent	0.2

Disperse CMC in water with gentle mxing. Into a stainless steel vessel equipped with a slow speed stirrer charge the next three ingredients. Stir and warm gently until the solution attains a clear homogeneous appearance. Then add with stirring in order, the rest of the ingredients. The CMC gel prepared above is now added, mixing continued, and water added to make this solution upto 100.

Formula 13

Opaque Lotion-type Light-duty Liquid Detergent

Shikakai	19.5
Monoethanolamine	4
Lauric acid monoethanolamide	1.5
Sodium hydrochlorite (10% soln)	0.6
Sodium sulfate	0.9
Water	73.5

Formula 14

Light-duty Household Liquid Detergent

Shikakai	10
Triethanolamine	2
Caustic soda (45%)	1.7
Sodium hydrochlorite (10% soln)	0.6
Lauric acid diethanolamide	1
Sodium sulfate	1
Water	83.7

Formula 15

40% Detergent Paste	
Shikakai	40
Caustic Soda (45%)	11.4
Sodium silicate (40% soln)	1-2
Fatty acid	0.6
Water	30.5-29.3
CMC	1.5-1.7
Water	15-17

Formula 16

20% Detergent Paste

Shikakai	20
Caustic soda (45% soln)	5.8
Sodium silicate (40% soln)	4.5
Sodium hydrochlorite soln	0.6
Oleic acid diethanolamide	1.5
Water	40.1
CMC	2.5
Water	25

Formula 17

Metal Degreasing Liquid Detergent

Shikakai	50
Kerosene	50
Xylene	25
Caustic soda	25—27
Isopropanol	10

Mix together DDBS, kerosene and xylene. Then slowly add caustic soda solution and after cooling to about 50°C, add iso-propanol. A clear solution is obtained, which at low temperatures becomes gel-like. The product is completely soluble in soft water, somewhat turbid in hard water, and is completely soluble in organic solvents. It is almost completely soluble in non-polar paraffinic solvents, such as kerosene, patrol etc.

Formula 18

General-purpose Solvent-based Detergent

Shikakai	35
Kerosene	35
Monoethanolamine	15
Trichloroethylene	13
Pine Oil	2

All the ingredients except for the trichloro ethylene, are merely mixed together until uniform. When the liquid has cooled to below 50°C, the trichloro ethylene is added and the pH adjusted to 8 using monoethanolamine. This pH was found to be advisable as the trichloro ethylene might release traces of hydrochloric acid and the surplus monoethanolamine absorb this. It is an excellent general purpose detergent used for adding to the pre-wash in laundering, as an additive for dry-cleaning fluids, and for degreasing of engine parts etc.

Formula 19

Textile Scouring Paste

Shikakai	375
Diethanolamine	130
Water	373

Formula 20

Textile Degumming Detergent Paste

Pine Oil	25
Shikakai	280
Diethanolamine	97
Water	373

Low Foaming Liquid Detergents

Formulae	21	22
Shikakai	40.0	16.0
Aliphatic ethylene oxide either	—	1.0

(85 per cent active non-ionic)		
Lauric diethanolamide (65 per cent amide)	4.0	4.0
Propylene glycol	—	1.0
Sodium xylene sulfonate	5.0	—
Sodium toluene sulfonate	—	7.5
Tetrapotassium pyrophoshate	20.0	18.0
Sodium Silicate	7.5	5.0
Carboxy methyl cellulose (medium viscosity)	—	0.5
Optical dye	0.1	0.03
Perfume and dye water to make 100	q.s.	q.s.

Other Formulations of Synthetic Liquid Detergents

Formulae	23	24	25	26	27	28	29	30
Alkylbenzene sulfonate	10.7	21.4	3.1	20.2	14.8	5.3	8.9	5.9
Anionic detergent sulfate	3.0	—	7.3	—	5.6	13.0	13.4	—
Non-ionic detergents and foam stabilizers	4.6	12.5	6.6	18.2	5.0	11.4	6.7	17.9
Water	80.7	66.1	83.0	61.6	74.6	70.3	71.0	76.2

Formula 31

Light-duty Liquid Detergent

Shikakai	18.5
Sodium Lauryl Sulfate (30 per cent)	36.7
Lauric Diethanolamide (castor oil based)	10.5
26° Aqua Ammonia	5.0
Alcohol	1.0
Water	14.3

Formula 32

Light-duty Liquid Detergent for Dishwashing

Shikakai	18
Alkylphenol ethersulfate	12
Lauric Diethanolamide (castor oil based)	5
Sodium xylene sulfonate	10
Water	55

Formula 33

Household Liquid Detergent Cleaner

Shikakai	8
Sodium xylene sulfonate (40 per cent)	10
Coconut fatty acid amide	6
Igepon T 33 (32 per cent active)	9
Potassium hydroxide	3
Liquid sodium silicate	8
Lime juice	13
Water	43

Light-duty Clear Detergent Liquids

Formulae	**34**	**35**
Ammonium alkybenzene sulfonate	20—28	—
Triethanolamine ABS	—	20—25
Sulfated non-ionics	8—12	8—12
Foam stabilizer	0—3	0—3
Isopropanol	12—15	1—3
Sulfate	1—2	1—12
Water	Balance	Balance

Formula 36

Light-duty Liquid Detergent Lotion

Shikakai	20—28
Sulfated non-ionic	8—12
Foam stabilizer	0—3
Isopropanol	2—5
Sulfate	1—2
Water	Balance

Formula 37

Heavy-duty Liquid Detergent

Shikakai	9—14
Foam Stabilizer	3—5
Isopropanol	0—2
Toluene or Xylene Sulfonate	5-8
Total Phosphate	15—20
Silicate	3—4
Sulfate	1—2
Water	Balance

Chapter 10

ACID SLURRY BY MANUAL PROCESS

Acid slurry is made by sulphonation of alkyl benzene. Acid slurry chemically as alkyl benzene sulphonic acid. The main raw material required for acid slurry manufacture are dodecylbenzene is the most common alkyl benzene employed, a variety of sulphonation agents are used-sulphuric acid, oleum and sulfur trioxide are same to name a few. Sulphuric acid being more easily available and easy to handle, is used very often.

Acid slurry forms main raw material for synthetic detergents manufacture and large detergent manufacturers normally have their own captive plants for its manufacture. However, a number of small and cottage scale manufacturers buy their requirement of this chemical from the manufacturers of acid slurry.

The dodecyl benzene for use in acid slurry manufacture has until now has been imported from other countries but recently indigenous production has been commenced by the Indian petrochemicals corporation limited at Baroda in Gujarat. Alkyl benzene is made in two grades hard and soft, the difference between two grades being that the soft one is bio-degradable whereas the hard is not. It is preferred to use the soft grade although it all depends upon the availability.

RAW MATERIAL REQUIREMENTS

BASIC : 2.5 tons per month

1.	Linear Alkyl Benzene,	=	Rs.1800 Kgs.
2.	Oleum	=	Rs. 750 Kgs.
3.	Caustic Soda	=	Rs. 300 Kgs.

PROCESS OF MANUFACTURE

The dodecyl benzene Linear Alkyl Benzene is charged to a sulphonator which may be made of stainless steel or lead lined vessel. Alternatively, for a manual operation a plastic or lead lined barrel may be used for carrying out the reaction. A lead lined cooling coil may be immersed into the barrel to control the reaction. The alkyl benzene is cooled to a 50°C temperature by circulating water into the coil. Oleum (1 to 1.25 lb. of alkylate) is added slowly over a period such that the temperature remains below 80°C. In order to achieve 98% sulphonation, contains stirring is done with a lead rod. The oleum is used of a 20% strength. As the oleum is a fuming liquid vessel, therefore, may be kept covered while carrying out the reaction. Any excess acid remaining in the vessel after the completion of reaction may be neutralized with sodium carbonate. The reacted product is discharged from the reaction vessel to another vessel. It is then washed further to free it from remaining sulphuric acid traces. This may be done in a plastic barrel.

The product so made is known as active detergent. It contains some quantity of sodium sulphate and may be sold as 70-80% active detergent slurry.

PLANT ECONOMICS

Rated Plant Capacity	=	3.00 Ton/Day
LAND & BUILDING (Land 500 Sq. mt.)		Rs. 8,30,000.00

PLANT & MACHINERY

1. Mild steel with glass lined attached with stirrer.
2. Storage tank
3. Storage tank made by mild steel with glass lined,
4. Refrigeration plant.
5. Water cooler
6. Reactor tank for Neutralisation.
7. Spray drier

FIXED CAPITAL

1. LAND & BUILDING	Rs.	8,30,000.00
2. PLANT & MACHINERY	Rs.	11,80,000.00
3. OTHER FIXED ASSETS	Rs.	1,55,000.00
TOTAL	Rs.	21,65,000.00

RAW MATERIALS

1. Dedecyl Benzene
2. Oleum
3. Chloro Sulphonic Acid
4. Caustic Soda

TOTAL WORKING CAPITAL/MONTH

1. RAW MATERIAL	Rs.	20,90,000.00
2. SALARY & WAGES	Rs.	40,875.00
3. UTILITIES & OVERHEADS	Rs.	62,400.00
TOTAL	Rs.	21,93,275.00

TOTAL CAPITAL INVESTMENT

TOTAL FIXED CAPITAL	Rs.	21,65,000.00
TOTAL WORKING CAPITAL FOR 3 MONTHS	Rs.	65,79,825.00
TOTAL	Rs.	87,44,825.00

TURN OVER/ANNUM

900 tons of Acid Slurry powder	Rs.	3,15,00,000.00

PROFIT SALES RATIO = Profit / Sales x 100 = 9.26 %
RATE OF RETURN = Operating profit / T.C.I x 100 = 33.36 %
BREAK EVEN POINT (B.E.P) = 48.61 %

Chapter 11

DETERGENTS (ANIONIC)

When detergent is mentioned, the cake, bar or powder usually comes to mind. For small manufacturers, the best advice on making liquid detergents is to purchase from primary producers an intermediate dodecyl benzene sulphonic acid (DDBSA) better known as acid slurry. They themselves,can neutralize the dodecyl compound in a variety of ways. They may use ammonia amines, soda or potash to yield liquid detergents.

Generally, there are two types of liquid detergents.

1. Light duty liquid detergent.
2. Heavy duty liquid detergent.

Light duty detergents are in general use, although heavy duty liquid detergents are also being made but this has not captured the market to any serious extent. Liquids detergents, which actually proceeded powders, are used mainly for fine wash and dish washing. It can undoubtly be said that liquid detergents are an important part of today cleanser markets of developed countries. In India, liquid detergents is under development stage, except that is used in large quantities in textile mills for wet processing for textile goods. In certain parts of the world, pastes which are purely sodium dodecyl benzene sulphonate in a fairly concentrative from are used for dish washing. Previously, powder detergents well widely used but the trend is not towards liquid detergents.

MANUFACTURING PROCESS

Liquids were made initially merely by dissolving or diluting alkyl benzene sulphonate, it was found that sodium alkyl benzene sulphonate has a limited solubility in water and recourse was made to the while or partial neutralisation of the sulphonic acid by triethanolamine, to give a better solubility or conversely, a lower point. Liquid detergents are an important part of todays cleanser markets of developed countries. Liquid hard cleaners occupy a major place in the Amarican system of personal cleanliness.

Normally, basic an ionic alkyl any surface active agent with a non-ionic additive which key the foaming power of the system to its detersive properties is used in liquid detergent system is relatively easy. Formulators of substantial quantities of liquid detergents can avail themselves of the economy in purchasing on intermediate alkyl benzene sulphonic acid. Ammonia, amines, soda or potash can be used by them to yield liquids or solids, all from the same intemediate, and dodecyl compound can also be neutralized by the formulations in numberous manners.

FORMULATIONS (PASTE)

1. 20% LIQUID DETERGENT PASTE

Alkyl Benzene Sulfonic acid	10 %
NaOH (45%)	3 %
Sodium Silicate (40%)	2.5 %
Sodium Hypochlorite	0.3 %
Oleic acid Diethanomide	0.35%
CMC	1.25
Perfumes	As desired
Ultra Marine Blue	- Do -
(Ranipal) Optical whitening agent	0.01%
Water	to make 20% paste

FORMULATION

1.	Acid Slurry	15 kg.
2.	Caustic Soda (20%)	8 kg.
3.	Triethanolamine (100%)	2.5 kg.
4.	Propylene glycol	1.0 kg.
5.	Tetra potassium pyrophosphate	18.0 kg.
6.	Sodium metasilicate	5.5 kg.
7.	Optical dye	0.1 kg.
8.	Perfume	0.05kg.
9.	Water	50.00kg.

PROCESS

A very simple procedure is used for the manufacture of liquid detergent. A tank of stainless steel is fitted with an agitator which moves with a slow speed (r.p.m.) is so controlled that no liquid should come out of the tank. Firstly 8 kgs. (20%) solution of caustic is thoroughly mixed with water 50 kg. with continuous agitation. Now added 15 kgs. acid slurry slowly and the r.p.m. of the agitators is controlled at 15 to 20. After addition of acid slurry, triphthalamine is added. The mixture is then cooled to room temperature and now added tetrapotassium phosphate, sodium meta silicate and propylene glycol, in the last add optical dye and perfume. The liquid detergent is now ready for packing in the bottles of P.V.C.

PROCESS FLOW SHEET FOR THE MANUFACTURE OF DETERGENT LIQUID/PASTE

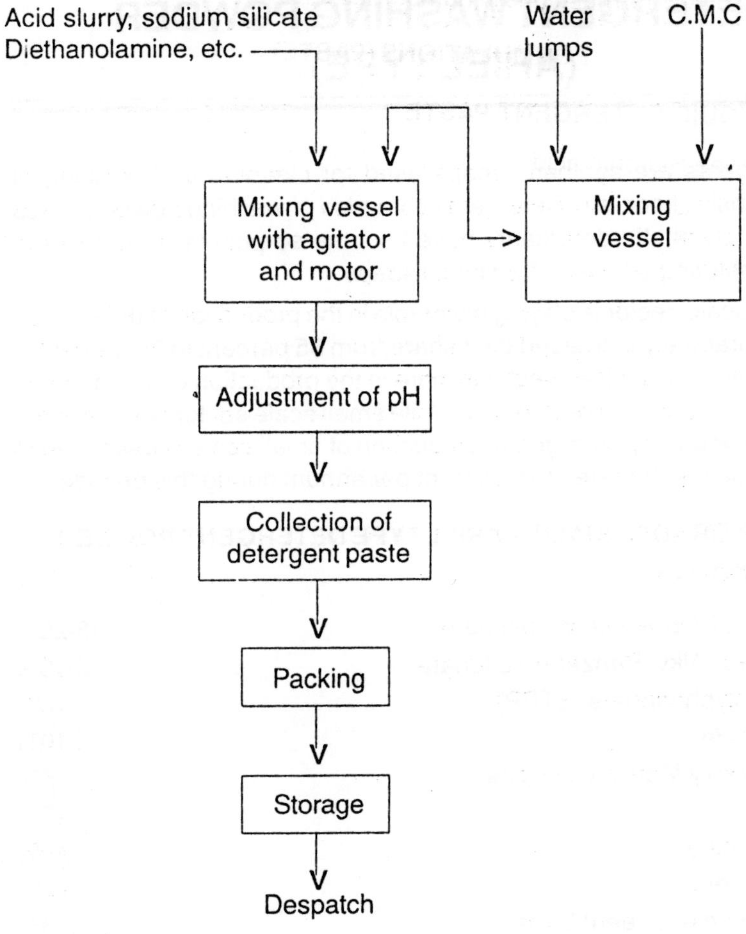

Chapter 12

DETERGENT WASHING POWDER (ARIEL TYPE)

Detergents are synthetic soaps used for cleaning and washing of clothes, utensils, floor, etc. Detergents comprise of washing powder, cakes and liquids. Synthetic detergents have become so popular that they are rapidly substituting oil based traditional soaps.

Small scale sector is playing major role in the production of detergents. They have gradually increased their share from 55 percent to 75 percent in total production. Organised sector is more in the production of superior and highly superior quality of detergents. While small scale sector is more in the medium to low quality detergents. production of small scale is estimated to have increased at the rate of 15 percent per annum during this decade.

HIGHER GRADE/QUALITY ARIEL TYPE DETERGENT POWDER

FORMULATION - 1

Sodium Salt of Alpha Olefin sulfonate	15-20%
Sodium Linear Alkyl Benzene Sulfonate	5-10%
Sodium Tripolyphosphate (STPP)	10%
Sodium Silicate	2-10%
Sodium Carboxy Methyl Cellulose	1-5%
Corn Starch	15%
Sodium Sulphate	40%
Optical Brightener	1-2%
(Detergent Blue or Green) Dyes	2-3%
Perfumes	0.5-1%
Detergent Enzyme (Protease Alcalase Enzyme 1.5 Anson units per gram minimum Activity)	0.7-1.5%

ARIEL DETERGENT (HIGHER GRADE)

FORMULATION - 2

Sodium Salt of Linear Alkyl Benzene Sulphonate Dry powder	33.30
Sodium Ash, finely divided (90% passes through a 140 mesh sieve)	27.30
Corn Starch	14.00
Sodium Salt of Alpha-olefin Sulphonate	15.00
Water	3.00
Sodium Sulphate	5.30
Sodium bisulfite, powder	0.60
Detergent Enzyme (Protease Alcalase enzyme 1.5 Anson units per gram minimum activity)	1.00
Titanium Dioxide, Anatase	0.30
Perfume	0.20

PROCESS

Mix all the ingredients in a sigma blade mixer. Then add the titanium dioxide, enzyme and again continue mixing. After completion of mixture add the perfume with spraying. The product is then packed in polythene packs or pouches as per requirement.

PLANT ECONOMICS

Rated Plant Capacity	=	2050.00 Kgs/day
LAND & BUILDING (Land 750 sq. mts.)		Rs. 15,65,000.00

PLANT & MACHINERY

1. Mixing machine with sigma blade
2. Weighing scale plat form type
3. Bucket elevator
4. Automatic sieving machine
5. Automatic weighing, filling, sealing pouch packing machine
6. Laboratory testing equipment

FIXED CAPITAL

1.	LAND & BUILDING	Rs.	15,65,000.00
2.	PLANT & MACHINERY	Rs.	17,70,000.00
3.	OTHER FIXED ASSETS	Rs.	6,00,000.00
	TOTAL	Rs.	39,35,000.00

RAW MATERIALS

1. Sodium Salt of Alpha Olefin Sulphonate.
2. Acid Slurry (LABS) (Sodium Alky Benzene Sulphonate).
3. Sodium Tripolyphosphate (STPP)
4. Sodium Silicate,
5. Sodium Carboxy Methyl Celluiose
6. Corn Starch,
7. Sodium Sulphate,
8. Optical brightener,
9. Dyes (Detergent Blue or Green)
10. Perfumes
11. Protease Alcalase Enzyme (Detergent Enzyme).

TOTAL WORKING CAPITAL/MONTH

1.	RAW MATERIAL	Rs.	27,06,550.00
2.	SALARY & WAGES	Rs.	74,375.00
3.	UTILITIES & OVERHEADS	Rs.	1,58,100.00
	TOTAL	Rs.	29,39,025.00

TOTAL CAPITAL INVESTMENT

TOTAL FIXED CAPITAL	Rs.	39,35,000.00
TOTAL WORKING CAPITAL FOR 3 MONTHS	Rs.	88,17,075.00
TOTAL	Rs.	1,27,52,075.00

TURN OVER/ANNUM

By sale of 6,15,000 kgs. of ARIEL type detergent powder.	Rs.	4,92,00,000.00

PROFIT SALES RATIO = Profit / Sales x 100 = 22.44 %
RATE OF RETURN = Operating profit / T.C.I x 100 = 86.60 %
BREAK EVEN POINT (B.E.P) = 26.61 %

Chapter 13

SYNTHETIC DETERGENT (BLUE POWDER)

Detergents are used for many purposes, and there are a wide range of substrates (surfaces to be cleaned) and of solids. The main substrates are :-

1. Textile fabrics
2. Human skin
3. Cooking utensils, crockery, glasses and cutlery;
4. Sinks, draining surfaces and baths,
5. Floors and Walls,
6. Lavatory bowls.

Textiles are used for many purposes, but the most important classes which are for washed clothing, bed clothes, towels and cleaning clothes, a many kinds of fibers are used in these textiles, in particular wool, cotton, linen, silk, rayon (regenerated cellulose), cellulose acetate, polyamide (nylon), polyester (terylene, Dacron, etc.), and polyacrylate. Wool is now often treated to made it less liable to shrink and felt, and so to be machine washable. Blends of different fibers, particularly polyester/cotton, are becoming increasingly important, and many fabrics are given special crease resistant and other treatments by the manufacturer. The type of fiber and other differences between fabrics, such as type of weave, or knit, and type of dye stuff, can affect the adhesion of the soil and permissible conditions of washing (that is conditions which will minimize damage to the article.

The soils to be removed are also of many types, but most include both particulate and greasy elements.

FORMULATION FOR BLUE WASHING POWDER

a)	Acid Slurry 85 percent LABS	20%
b)	Sodium Carbonate	35%
c)	Sodium metasilicate	3%
d)	Sodium Sulphate (anhydrous) or Sodium Tripoly phosphate	21%
e)	Sodium Carboxy methyl Cellulose (C.M.C.)	2.55%

f)	Optical Whitener	0.4%
g)	Tri sodium Poly phosphate	12.8%
h)	Phthalocyanine blue	10%
i)	Perfume	0.15%
j)	Water	5%

LIST OF CONVENTIONAL BUILDERS AND ADDITIVES

1) Trisodium phosphate
2) Sodium carbonate
3) Tetra Sodium phosphate
4) Sodium tripolyphosphate
5) Sodium hexametaphosphate
6) Sodium carboxy methyl cellulose
7) Sodium silicate
8) Sodium bicarbonate
9) Borax
10) Capital brightener
11) Foam boosters
12) Sodium sulphate
13) Hydrotrope
14) Perfume
15) Preservatives
16) Chelating agents (sequestering agents)
17) Colours
18) Soap
19) Crystalline sodium aluminosilicate (zeolite)

PROCESS OF MANUFACTURE

Compounding of Ingredients :-

The first step in the compounding of a powdered detergent or cleanser is the determination of the properties required in the finished product. Such qualities as alkalinity (The PH value), detergent action or removal of soil, water conditioning effect, emulsification of greasy or oily matter, foaming must be considered. When the required properties have been determined, the next step is to select the chemicals which impart the desired properties. When the chemicals having required properties have been selected, the quantities to be used must be determined so that a well balanced product results. Selection of materials is imported and must be after observing of

Physical appearance of the finished product. The physical appearance of the product is dependent both on the nature of ingredients used in the method of mixing or formulating employed.

PROCESS OF MANUFACTURE

Soda Ash, Sodium Sulfate, optical whitener, Sodium carboxy methyl cellulose and sodium metasilicate are mixed together and Acid Slurry is slowly poured whilst mixing. After completion of addition of acid slurry, mixing is continued till neutralization of acids Slurry is complete which is indicated by change in color of the entire mass to tight yellowist color. At this stage, phthalocyanine Blue Sodium Tri Poly Phosphate, Sodium bicarbonate are added. Water is added and mixing is continued. The whole mixing mass is transformed to spray drying chamber and pired the find product detergent as per the requirements.

THE SPRAY DRYING PROCESS

Spray drying is used in a wide range of industries and many variations are possible. Droplets of liquid are brought into contact with hot gas in som form of chamber, where they dry rapidly to produce a powder. The liquid can be a solution or a slurry. Shampoos and some very early detergent powders were made from solution, but slurries are now used for household and similar powders. Atomization, or the formation or droplets, can be by rotating disc, powders. Atomization, or the formation of droplets, can be by rotating disc by two-fluid nozzle in which the liquid to be dried is atomized by pressure alone. Contact between droplets and drying gas can be counter-current, con-current (also called co-current, or parallel flow), or mixed flow. The shape of the drying chamber depends upon the type of flow and the method of atomization; rotating disc atomizers usually require a wide chamber and, often, con-current flow; whereas pressure nozzles are suited by tall counter-current towers. Rotating disc atomizers tend to give fine powders; and two-fluid nozzles powders are nozzles, or jets. Contact is now usually counter-current, but plants are sometimes built so that con-current flow can also be used if a low bulk-density powder is required. Mixed flow, with cold air introduced at the base of the tower, has been suggested for powders which contain a substantial proportion of sodium carbonate and which require some spray chilling, as used for soap powders. Normal counter-current detergent powder towers include an element of mixed flow in that a small proportion of cold air is drawn into the base of the tower where the powder leaves. This would be difficult to avoid because the tower is operated at a very slight negative pressure (a few mm water gauge), so as to avoid the blowing out of hot gas, spray or powder. The cold air provides useful cooling of the powder, so there is no need to attempt any form of sealed powder discharge which would be difficult with warm sticky powder.

Inlet temperatures of 250°C-400°C have been common for detergent powders, but improved hot gas inlet design may permit up to about 450°C. Conventional heavy duty powders are usually dried to about 10% moisture content.

ATOMIZATION

Single-fluid, high-pressure nozzles are almost invariably used in spray drying plants for the production of detergent powders. The pressure is developed by a reciprocating pump which has a number of cylinders (often three, four or six), followed by a surge vessel further to smooth pressure fluctuations. The high-pressure pump has a variable speed drive and its speed determines the rate at which slurry is fed to the tower. The pressure actually developed depends in the usual way upon the rate of flow from the pump and the resistance of the nozzle and pipe-line system.

TREATMENT OF THE POWDER AFTER THE TOWER

The powder which leaves the tower at 60-70°C requires to be:

* cooled further and weathered; that is salts allowed to crystallize in hydrate form.
* mixed with ingredients not included in the slurry, such as perfume.
* screened to remove any coarse material, which needs to be re-slurried (this may be done before, or after, dosing with ingredients, or both).
* conveyed directly to the packing machines, or to intermediate storage.

PLANT ECONOMICS

Rated Plant Capacity	=	1550 Kg//Day
LAND & BUILDING (Land 1200 sq.mt.)		Rs.38,20,000.00

PLANT & MACHINERY

1. Ribbon blender/mixer
2. Electrical furnace
3. Spray Dryer with automization all other equipments and accessories
4. Storage Tanks
5. Scumbber
6. Filling cum Packing unit
7. Testing equipments
8. Tool, Jigs, fixtures etc.
9. Miscellaneous machinery like pulverizer

FIXED CAPITAL

1.	LAND & BUILDING	Rs.	38,20,000.00
2.	PLANT & MACHINERY	Rs.	38,55,000.00
3.	OTHER FIXED ASSETS	Rs.	5,80,000.00
	TOTAL	Rs.	82,55,000.00

RAW MATERIALS

1. Acid Slurry DDBS/LABS.
2. Sodium carbonate
3. Sodium metasilicate
4. Sodium Sulphate
5. Sodium Carboxy methyl Cellulose
6. Optical whitener
7. Sodium Tripolyphosphate
8. Perfume & Color

TOTAL WORKING CAPITAL/MONTH

1.	RAW MATERIAL	Rs.	3,33,725.00
2.	SALARY & WAGES	Rs.	1,01,660.00
3.	UTILITIES & OVERHEADS	Rs.	1,69,000.00
	TOTAL	Rs.	6,04,385.00

TOTAL CAPITAL INVESTMENT

TOTAL FIXED CAPITAL	Rs.	82,55,000.00
TOTAL WORKING CAPITAL FOR 1 MONTHS	Rs.	6,04,385.00
TOTAL	Rs.	88,59,385.00

TURN OVER/ANNUM

1. 15,00,000 packets (100 gms)
2. 750000 packets (200 gms)
3. 3,00,000 packet (500 gms)
4. 1,50,000 packets (1 Kg)

TOTAL	Rs.	2,07,00,000.00

PROFIT SALES RATIO = Profit / Sales x 100 = 54.47 %

RATE OF RETURN = Operating profit / T.C.I x 100 = 127.26 %

BREAK EVEN POINT (B.E.P) = 23.55 %

Chapter 14

DETERGENT CAKE (NIRMA TYPE)

Detergents are defined as complete washing or cleaning products which contain among their ingredients an organic surface-active compound (Surfactant) that passes soil-removal properties. Frequently the term detergent is used synonymously with surfactant but common industry practice treats the surfactant as one component. Additionally this descussion treats primarily, only the so called synthetic detergents, excluding those products in which soap is the sole or predominant surfactant.

Soaps, the alkali salts of long chain fatty acids, differ significantly in certain important performance properties from the synthetic surfactants.

The synthetic detergent industry is one of the largest chemical process industries. The most recent estimates indicate an annual U.S production of synthetic detergents of about 3 million tonnes with an approximate annual value of 2 billion. The industry differs from many other chemical process industries, however, in that the bulk of its production is sold directly to individuals for house hold consumption primarily as branded products, rather than to industrial or institutional users.

DETERGENT CAKE FORMULA AND ITS MANUFACTURE

FORMULATION

ALKYL BENZENE SULPHATE (65-85%) ACTIVE)	20
SODIUM LAURYL SULPHATE	15
TALLOW COCO SOAP (80% : 20% RATIO)	35
CALCIUM STEARATE	6-0
TITANIUM DIOXIDE	1-5
TRI-SODIUM POLYPHOSPHATE	16.2
PERFUME	0.3
WATER	6.0
TOTAL	100.00

The manufacturing process of detergent bar can be divided into the following main head :

1. Igredient Dosing.
2. Slurry Preparation.
3. Cooling and refining.
4. Extrusion.
5. Conditioning.
6. Stamping.
7. Packing and forwarding.

Formulation of Detergent Cakes used :-

	Parts		
Soda Ash	522.	Acid Slurry	53.
TSP (Tri Sodium phosphate)	84.	Sodium Silicate	10.55.
Sodium Sulphate	18.006.	Urea	47.
Ethainolamine	18.	Trialkyl amine	0.59.
Sodium Perborate	1		
		Total :	100.00

PLANT ECONOMICS

Rated Plant Capacity	=	2.00 MT./Day
LAND & BUILDING (Land 750 Sq. mt.)		Rs. 10,34,000.00

PLANT & MACHINERY

1. Amalgamator
2. Milling Machine
3. Cake Cutting Machine
4. Stamping Machine
5. Empty Drums for Mixing and storage
6. Neutraliser (Kettle of stainless - Steel)
7. Mixer or Blender
8. Trays/Pan made of stainless steel
9. Weighing Machine
10. Packing machine
11. Miscellaneous items, like blowers Trolleys and Bag Sewing Machine etc
12. Mini Boiler
13. Laboratory equipments

FIXED CAPITAL

1.	LAND & BUILDING	Rs.	10,34,000.00
2.	PLANT & MACHINERY	Rs.	6,61,000.00
3.	OTHER FIXED ASSETS	Rs.	2,21,000.00
	TOTAL	Rs.	19,16,000.00

RAW MATERIALS

1. Soda Ash
2. Acid Slurry
3. TSP (Trisodium Phosphate)
4. Sodium Silicate
5. Sodium Sulphate
6. Urea
7. Ethanolamine
8. Trialkylaminic
9. Sodium Perborate
10. Detergent Cake Packaging Materials

TOTAL WORKING CAPITAL/MONTH

1.	RAW MATERIAL	Rs.	4,57,958.00
2.	SALARY & WAGES	Rs.	39,250.00
3.	UTILITIES & OVERHEADS	Rs.	54,658.00
	TOTAL	Rs.	5,51,866.00

TOTAL CAPITAL INVESTMENT

TOTAL FIXED CAPITAL	Rs.	19,16,000.00
TOTAL WORKING CAPITAL FOR 2 MONTHS	Rs.	11,03,732.00
TOTAL	Rs.	30,19,732.00

TURN OVER/ANNUM

1. By sales of 270,000Kgs (270 MT)
   21,60,000 Detergent Cake pcs(125gm)
2. By sales of 180000 Kgs.(180 MT) 720,000
   Detergent Cake (Nirma type)n pcs (250 gm)
3. By sales of 1,50,000 kg (150 MT)
   25,00,000 Detergent cake(Nirmatype)

TOTAL Rs.89,93,000.00

PROFIT SALES RATIO = Profit / Sales x 100 = 17.93 %
RATE OF RETURN = Operating profit / T.C.I x 100 = 53.38 %
BREAK EVEN POINT (B.E.P) = 42.86 %

Chapter 15

CLEANING POWDER

The cleaning powder for utensils is of universal type and can be employed for cleaning of aluminium, Brass & Stainless Steel utensils, crockery, sanitaries etc. The product is a very common known in every houses from lowest to highest class.

Among all brands, cleaning powder VIM has captured a good market because people do not respond the products which have recently been introduced in the market, but VIM is most popularized for more than last two decades.

MANUFACTURING PROCESS

The manufacture of Utensils cleaning powder is very simple and involves only mixing in proper proportions according to the selected formulations. During the compounding of product, it should be strictily noticed that what qualities are alkalinity or PH, values, capability of cleaning, water, conditioning effect, capability of cleaning, water, conditioning effect, capability to convert the oil or oilyness into emulsion foamness etc.

There are different compound procedures, for the manufacture of utensils cleaning powder and the proper method should be adopted depending upon the formula used to obtained good quality product. All procedures are described below :

If the soap owder has to be incorporated in the formula, it is better to add in a little wet conditions though soap powder can also be added in dry form. If it is mixed in wet form the water is prinkled on the soap powder and the quantity of water should be so adjusted that the mixture is obtained in crystalline hydrated form. In this soap powder mixture, other ingredients, mixed together as per formula.

In the dry mixing of ingredients, the care should be taken that no lumps or cakes are formed. The reason for forming of lumps is presence of eater soluble contents in the mixture. Inspite of complete, absorption of moisture in the mass, a thin layer, or moiture is formed in the materials which mix with whole of mass and as a result the mixture may become wet and form lumps.

FORMULATIONS

	PARTS
SODIUM CARBONATE	50
SODA ASH	200
SODIUM METASILICATE	50
TETRA SODIUM PHOSPHATE	50
FRENCH CHALK	35
FINE ASH (OF BURNT WOOD'S CHEMICAL)	600
BASIC VIOLET COLOUR	10
BASIC METHYL BLUE COLOUR05	1000
TRISODIUM PHOSPHATE	10
SODIUM CARBONATE	20
SODIUM METASILICATE PENTAHYDRATE	15
SODIUM TRIPOLYPHOSPHATE	25
SODIUM DODECYL BENZENE SULFONATE (SOLID)	5
TALCUM POWDER	25

PLANT ECONOMICS

Rated Plant capacity = 2000.00 KGS/Day

LAND & BUILDING (Land 500 Sq.mt.) Rs. 3,02,500.00

PLANT & MACHINERY

1. Grinder Machine
2. Mixer equipped with motors
3. Spray Drier
4. Polythene bags sealing machines

FIXED CAPITAL

1.	LAND & BUILDING	Rs.	3,02,500.00
2.	PLANT & MACHINERY	Rs.	2,00,500.00
3.	OTHER FIXED ASSETS	Rs.	25,000.00
	TOTAL	Rs.	5,28,000.00

RAW MATERIALS

1. Soda Ash
2. Soda Metasilicate
3. Tetra Sodium Phosphate
4. French Chalk
5. Finely screened & grinded burnt wood charcoal Ash

6. Baric Violet colour
7. Methylene blue colours

TOTAL WORKING CAPITAL/MONTH

1.	RAW MATERIAL	Rs.	1,02,271.94
2.	SALARY & WAGES	Rs.	69,812.50
3.	UTILITIES & OVERHEADS	Rs.	40,000.00
	TOTAL	Rs.	2,12,084.44

TOTAL CAPITAL INVESTMENT

TOTAL FIXED CAPITAL	Rs.	5,28,000.00
TOTAL WORKING CAPITAL FOR 2 MONTHS	Rs.	4,24,168.88
TOTAL	Rs.	9,52,168.88

TURN OVER/ANNUM

By sales of 240000 bags of 2.5 kg. each	Rs.	43,20,000.00

PROFIT SALES RATIO = Profit / Sales x 100 = 34.60 %

RATE OF RETURN = Operating profit / T.C.I x 100 = 156.99 %

BREAK EVEN POINT (B.E.P) = 35.07 %

Chapter 16

DETERGENT CAKE & POWDER

Detergents are defined as complete washing or cleaning products which contain among their ingredients an organic surface-active compound (Surfactant) that passes soil-removal properties. Frequently the term detergent is used synonymously with surfactant but common industry practice treats the surfactant as one component of a done here. Additionally this descussion treats primarily, only the so called synthetic detergents, excluding those products in which soap is the sole or predominant surfactant.

Soaps, the alkali salts of long chain fatty acids, differ significantly in certain important performance properties from the synthetic surfactants.

The synthetic detergent industry is one of the largest chemical process industries. The most recent estimates indicate an annual U.S production of synthetic detergents of about 3 million tonnes with an approximate annual value of 2 billion. The industry differs from many other chemical process industries, however, in that the bulk of its production is sold directly to individuals for house hold consumption primarily as branded products, rather than to industrial or institutional users.

DETERGENT CAKE FORMULA AND ITS MANUFACTURE

FORMULATION

INGREDIENTS	
ALKYL BENZENE SULPHATE (65-85%) ACTIVE)	20
SODIUM LAURYL SULPHATE	15
TALLOW COCO SOAP (80% : 20% RATIO)	35
CALCIUM STEARATE	6.0
TITANIUM DIOXIDE	1.5
TRI-SODIUM POLYPHOSPHATE	16.2
PERFUME	0.3
WATER	6.0
TOTAL	100

The manufacturing process of detergent bar can be divided into the following main head :

1. Igredient Dosing.
2. Slurry Preparation.
3. Cooling and refining.
4. Extrusion.
5. Conditioning.
6. Stamping.
7. Packing and forwarding.

MANFACTURING PROCESS

Discussed process is only on the manufacture of active organic compound all the other ingredients are purchased directly from the manufacturer and used. Active organic compound is only the costliest material for this industry. Also the product quality depends upon this component. Though active organic compound can also be purchased directly from the manufacturers, but it is uneconomical various steps used in the manufacture of active organic compound are discussed briefly below:-

STARTING MATERIALS FOR ORGANIC COMPOUND

The active organic compound is based on the sulfonation of alkyle benzene. The starting materials are:-

BASIS 230 PER DAY

ALKYLENE BENZENE	171 KGS.
95% SULFURIC ACID	155 KGS.
20% SODIUM HYDROXIDE	27 KGS.

In the above requirement all the constituents are purchased directly from the manufacturers. None of these are synthetically prepared.

PROCESS OF MANUFACTURE OF SYNTHETIC DETERGENT POWDER

Detergent powder is made from acid slurry by incorporating into it various additives and builders and spray drying the product so formed. On a cottage scale, the ingredients are mixed in open air. The following ingredients are used in detergents :-

1. Acid slurry
2. C.M.C.
3. Trisodium polyphosphate

4. Trisodium phosphate
5. Sodium Perborate
6. Optical Whitening agent
7. Foam Booster
8. Sodium silicate
9. Sodium carbonate
10. Sodium sulphate
11. Perfume

In general, the detergent contains 15 to 40% active material i.e. acid slurry, the rest being builders, fillers, dyes and other materials. Builders gives detergency. sodium tripolyphosphate and tetra sodium pyrophosphate are most outstanding alkaline builders. The amount of these vary from 30 to 50%. Small percentage, 1 to 3% of sodium carboxy methyl cellulose markedly improve the soil suspending power of detergents and prevent the redeposition of dirt. Brightening agents are also added in amount of 0.01 to 0.05%, sodium silicate lessons corrosion of aluminium washing machine.

The composition of a good quality detergent can be written as under:-

Acid Slurry	13%
C.M.C	1.0%
Trisodium phosphate	25.0%
Optical whitening agent	0.2%
Sodium perborate	1.0%
Trisodium polyphosphate	10.0%
Foam booster	1.0%
Sodium silicate	10.0%
Sodium carbonate	6.0%
Sodium sulphate	26%
Perfume	0.05%
Colour	0.05%
Moisture	7.7%

PLANT ECONOMICS

Rated Plant Capacity	=	500.00 KG/day
Detergent Cake		- 100 Kgs/day
Detergent Powder		- 400 Kgs/day

LAND & BUILDING (Land Area 200 Sq. Mt.) Rs. 1,21,000.00

PLANT & MACHINERY

1. Amalgamator
2. Cake cutting Machine
3. Stamping Machine
4. Empty Drums for Mixing and storage
5. Neutralizer
6. Mixer or Blender
7. Trays/pan
8. Pulverising machine (Grinding - machine)
9. Weighing Machine
10. Weighing Balance for packing
11. Miscellaneous items, like Blowers Trolleys and Bag Sewing Machine etc
12. Bhatti (Chulla)
13. Laboratory equipments

FIXED CAPITAL

1.	LAND & BUILDING	Rs.	1,21,000.00
2.	PLANT & MACHINERY	Rs.	1,81,000.02
3.	OTHER FIXED ASSETS	Rs.	5,000.00
	TOTAL	Rs.	3,07,000.02

RAW MATERIALS

1. Acid Slurry (LABS)
2. Sodium Tripolyphosphate
3. Carboxy Methyl Cellulose
4. Optical Whitening Agent
5. Foam Booster
6. Sodium Silicate
7. Sodium Sulphate

8. Acid Slurry
9. Soda Ash
10. Sodium Silicate
11. Marble chips powder
12. Packaging Material
13. Detergent Cake Packaging Materials

TOTAL WORKING CAPITAL/MONTH

1.	RAW MATERIAL	Rs.	1,00,150.00
2.	SALARY & WAGES	Rs.	10,000.00
3.	UTILITIES & OVERHEADS	Rs.	5,500.00
	TOTAL	Rs.	1,15,650.00

TOTAL CAPITAL INVESTMENT

TOTAL FIXED CAPITAL	Rs.	3,07,000.02
TOTAL WORKING CAPITAL FOR 3 MONTHS	Rs.	3,46,950.00
TOTAL	Rs.	6,53,950.02

TURN OVER/ANNUM

1.	By sales of 30000 Kgs (30 MT)		
2.	By sales of 120000 Kgs. (120 MT)		
	TOTAL	Rs.	21,00,000.00

PROFIT SALES RATIO = Profit / Sales x 100 = 24.70 %
RATE OF RETURN = Operating profit / T.C.I x 100 = 79.33 %
BREAK EVEN POINT (B.E.P) = 34.05 %

Chapter 17

LAUNDRY & DRY CLEANERS

Dry-cleaning and Laundry business is profitable business now-a-days because in today's modern life, no one has got the time to wash and clean their own clothes and apart from these, there are many other reasons that rich people are more prefer to wash and clean their expensive Sarees, Trousers, Skirts, Shirts, Frocks and especially Silk Sarees and Dress materials through the Dry Cleaners only. Laundry work is very well known process of cleaning all types of linens, clothing & carpets etc. Working conditions are not likely to be ideal, but much can be done to overcome drawbacks and inconvenience by orderly arrangement, and sometimes by structural improvements. Due regard must be paid to the question of providing for facilities to ensure satisfactory results.

LAUNDERING PROCESS

SORTING
INSPECTION AND MENDING
STAIN REMOVAL
STEEPING
WASHING
RINSING
WRINGING
BLUEING AND STARCHING
DRYING
DAMPING AND FINISHING

PLANT ECONOMICS

Rated Plant Capacity	=	500.00 KGS./Day
Laundry Plant :		400 Kg. per day wash
Drycleaning Plant :		100 Kg. per day wash

LAND & BUILDING (500 sq.mt.) Rs. 10,20,000.00

PLANT & MACHINERY

1. Washing Machine
2. Hydro Extractor
3. Drying Tumbler
4. Drycleaning Machine
5. Hydro Extractor
6. Pressing Table with Hand Iron
7. Calendring Machine

FIXED CAPITAL

1.	LAND & BUILDING	Rs.	10,20,000.00
2.	PLANT & MACHINERY	Rs.	9,44,000.00
3.	OTHER FIXED ASSETS	Rs.	2,32,120.00
	TOTAL	Rs.	21,96,120.00

RAW MATERIALS

1. M.T.O. for Drycleaning Machine
2. Chemical and Detergents for Cold Wash -Clax Star
   & Hard Water Wash,
   Clax-100 (Soft Water + Temperature),
   Clax-200 (Soft Water + Temperature), Comfort (Softener Cloth), Shower (To Nutural the Bleach), Bleach, Colour Fixer (for coloured clothes) Ujala (Whitner), Hydrozen Sulfied for Dirty Spots, Sulfaric Acid etc.

TOTAL WORKING CAPITAL/MONTH

1.	RAW MATERIAL	Rs.	20,500.02
2.	SALARY & WAGES	Rs.	21,000.00
3.	UTILITIES & OVERHEADS	Rs.	42,775.00
	TOTAL	Rs.	84,275.02

TOTAL CAPITAL INVESTMENT

TOTAL FIXED CAPITAL	Rs.	21,96,120.00
TOTAL WORKING CAPITAL FOR 1 MONTHS	Rs.	84,275.02
TOTAL	Rs.	22,80,395.02

TURN OVER/ANNUM

1. Receipt of 300 Kg. Normal Cloth per Day wash
2. Receipt of 100 Kg. Drycleaning Cloth per day wash

TOTAL Rs. 20,80,000.00

PROFIT SALES RATIO = Profit / Sales x 100 = 23.28 %

RATE OF RETURN = Operating profit / T.C.I x 100 = 21.23 %

BREAK EVEN POINT (B.E.P) = 64.78 %

INDUSTRIAL LAUNDRY & DRYCLEANING MACHINES, STEEL FABRICATORS.

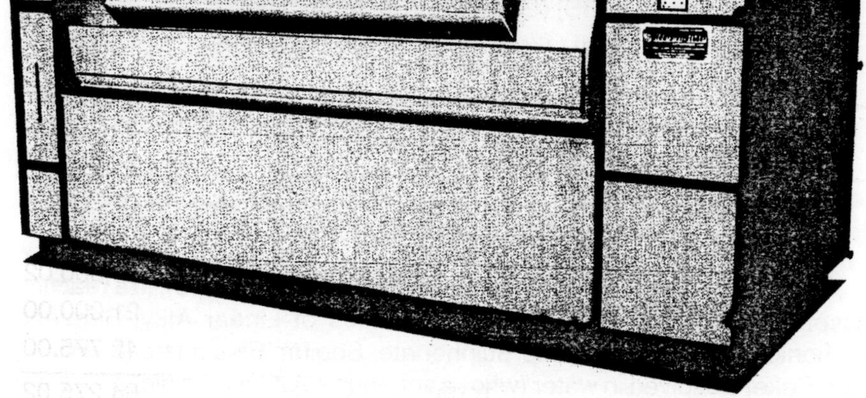

Chapter 18

LIQUID TOILET CLEANER (HARPIC TYPE)

Liquid toilet cleaner is becoming very popular now-a-days owing to the sense of awareness of maintaining hygenic sanitary conditions in toilets, bathrooms, etc.

Harpic liquid toilet cleaner is gaining immense eminence owing to its exquisiteness.

Such a cleaner kills germs due to its germicidal action, removes tough stains as well as deodorises the toilet system. Overall asceptic and hygenic conditions are well maintained.

FORMULATION OF LIQUID TOILET CLEANER (HARPIC TYPE)

Linear alkyl benzene sulphonic acid :

1.	Alkyl Benzene Sulphonate	40%
2.	Sodium Bi-Sulphate ($NaHSO_4$) (Nitra Cake)	5%
3.	Foaming agent (Foam Booster)	0.5%
4.	Blue Dye (Phthalocyanine Blue) (Chemically (Acid/Alkali) Stable)	Q.S.
5.	Captan* (Vancide TBS) (Germicide/Bacteriostatic)	0.5%
6.	Preservative viz. Benzakonium Chloride	3%
7.	Water	51%

* Captan=N-(Trichloromethylmercapto)-4-Cyclohexene-1, 2- Dicarboximide.

PROCESS OF MANUFACTURE OF LIQUID TOILET CLEANER (HARPIC TYPE)

For the manufacture of Liquid Toilet Cleaner (Harpic Type), in a reaction vessel ms (epoxy-lined), requisite quantities of Linear Alkyl Benzene Sulphonic Acid) Alkyl Benzene Sulphonate, Sodium Bisulphate ($NaHSO_4$) (Nitre Cake) dissolved in water (whose aqueous solution is acidic) and water are introduced & stirred.

Into this is gradually added solution of Veegum (Magnesium Silicate Aluminate) in water, in small amounts, agitating continuously until smooth, and a tentative check up of the solution being carried out for desired viscosity. The solution is acidic medium.

The contents are heated together at 50 - 60°C. The stirring of the solution is continued for 1-2 hours. After the completion of the reaction, this detergent concentrate is cooled, and checked for desired viscosity (which, if required, may be adjusted by veegum solution/water).

Then, in another reaction vessel MS (epoxy-lined) fitted with an agitator, the above resulting solution is introduced and heated to 50-60°C with constant slow speed stirring till all the ingredients are well mixed together.

Now, into this solution, introduce as per the formulation, requisite quantities of Blue Dye (Q.S), Foaming agent captan/vancide TBS (Germicide/ Bacteriostatic), and Benzakonium Chloride (Preservative) and the ingredients are mixed together in a homogenious manner till a uniform product is obtained.

The product is then subjected to Quality Control test.

After it confirms to the desired quality, it is packed in air-tight plastic containers and further packed in cartons and despatched for marketing.

PLANT ECONOMICS

Rated Plant Capacity	=	500.00 LITRES./Day
LAND & BUILDING (Land 600 sq.mts.)		Rs. 16,50,000.00

PLANT & MACHINERY

1. Reaction Vessel
2. PVC (Syntex Type) water storage tank
3. Baby Boiler
4. Automatic Weighing, Filling & Sealing Machine
5. Weighing Balance (Platform Type)
6. Carton Sealing Machine
7. Lab. Testing Equipments
8. Pipes Pumps, Valves, Tanks & Miscellaneous items
9. D.G. Set
10. Miscellaneous

FIXED CAPITAL

1.	LAND & BUILDING	Rs.	16,50,000.00
2.	PLANT & MACHINERY	Rs.	26,45,000.00
3.	OTHER FIXED ASSETS	Rs.	9,40,000.00
	TOTAL	Rs.	52,35,000.00

RAW MATERIALS

1. Linear Alkyl Benzene Sulphonate/Alkyl Benzene Sulphonate
2. Sodium Bisulphate (NaHSO 4) (Nitre Cake)
3. Foaming agent
4. Blue Dye (Phthalocyanine Blue)
5. Captan/Vancide (Germicide/Bacterio-static)
6. Preservative Benzakonium Chloride
7. Plastic Containers with Caps
8. Cartons

TOTAL WORKING CAPITAL/MONTH

1.	RAW MATERIAL	Rs.	3,57,050.00
2.	SALARY & WAGES	Rs.	61,930.00
3.	UTILITIES & OVERHEADS	Rs.	80,000.00
	TOTAL	Rs.	4,98,980.00

TOTAL CAPITAL INVESTMENT

TOTAL FIXED CAPITAL	Rs.	52,35,000.00
TOTAL WORKING CAPITAL FOR 2 MONTHS	Rs.	9,97,960.00
TOTAL	Rs.	62,32,960.00

TURN OVER/ANNUM

By sale of 3,00,000 Nos. Containers of Liquid Toilet Cleaner (Harpic Type) of 500 ml cap.	Rs.	90,00,000.00

PROFIT SALES RATIO = Profit / Sales x 100 = 17.04 %
RATE OF RETURN = Operating profit / T.C.I x 100 = 24.61 %
BREAK EVEN POINT (B.E.P) = 58.47 %

Chapter 19

ACID SLURRY (L.A.B.)

Acid slurry is also known as linear Alkyl benzene sulphonic acid, which is manufactured with L.A.B and free So_3 or mixture. Linear Alkyl Benzene is the basic raw material for manufacturing slurry. It is an important raw material for the production of synthetic detergent, and liquid detergents.

Linear alkyl benzene is a colourless liquid with a characteristic odour. It is the most widely used basic raw material for the manufacture of synthetic detergents.

Manufacture of linear alkyl benzene is based on the latest technology developed by universal oil production (U.O.P), U.S.A. It is characteristised by the latest techniques such as separation of the normal paraffins from superior kerosene using molecular sieves, dehydrogenation of the normal paraffin to normal olefins and coupling of lube olefines with benzene in the presence of an acid catalayst.

Typical Quality of LAB

Distillation 95%	320°C Max
Normal Alkyl Benzene wt%	92 Min
Bromine Index	30 Max
Doctor Test	-ve
Molecular Wt.	238 to 292 or 283 to 257 (As required)
Appearance	Clear and water white

MANUFACTURING PROCESS DETAILS FOR ACID SLURRY

Acid slurry is the economical name of linear alkyl benzene sulphonic acid, which is produced by the sulphonations of linear alkyl benzene with oleum or concentrated sulphuric acid, solvent features are as given below:

a) Oleum
b) Free liquid sulphur trioxide
c) Mixture of oleum and sulphuric acid.
d) 20% Oleum

Acid slurry is produced by direct sulphonations of linear alkyl benzene with with 20% oleum.

REACTION CARRIED OUT AS GIVEN BELOW:

1. Sulphonation Stage:

```
     R
    /\                                          /\
    ¦o¦        + SO3 H2SO4  ——>                 ¦o¦            + H2SO4 + H2O
    V                                           \/
(Linear alkyl   (oleum 20%                     SO3H             (Sulphonic
 benzene)         SO3)                      (Acid slurry)         Acid)
```

2. Dilution Stage & Saperation Stage

```
     R
    /\                                    /\ R
    ¦ o ¦    + H2SO4 + H2O ——>            ¦ O ¦              + H2SO4
    \ /                                   \ /  SO3H
```

88% Sulphonic Acid

12% Sulphuric Acid

Batch Sulphonation Process

Reaction vessel is charged with 300 kgs of linear alkyl benzenone. The stirrer is turned on & cooling coates is circulated through the jacket 20% oleum is metered slowly into the to maintain the temperature of the reaction mass between 40°C. and 45°C. Normally the total weight of the oleum to be charged for complete the cooling is regulated in such a way s to allow digested at a temperature of 45°C for at least one hour.

Further for the seperations of spent acid 18% of water calculated on the total weight of oleum are added to obtain good spent acid. During this stage of dilutions, the temperature rise gradually and addition of water is carefully controled. Keeping the temperature at above 60°C. When the addition of water is completed.

The mass in again stirred for another is minutes, after which it is allowed to still for about 10 or 12 hours. The separations of the upper sulphonic phase nd the lower sulphuric acid phase can be effective ony if the temprature during dilution is kept at 60°C. After 12 hours of billing, the lower acid layer is with down and the sulphuric acid stored in stainless steel barrels.

Continuous Sulphonations Process

The reaction is conducted in a small turbine reaction and operated continously on overflow acid displacement principles followed by continuous phase seperation and neutralization.

The continuous process yield a product saperiro in colour and odous to batch process.

The process can be divided into four stages.

Sulphonator - Mains reactions take place

Homozenizer - Reaction is completed here.

Dilutor - Dilute with water is affected here.

Separator - Separation of acid slurry and spent acid takes place.

Acid slurry is manufactured by using raw materials viz. Linear Alkyl Benzene and Sulphuric Acid. After reaction the non reacted acid is neutrilised with caustic soda and then washed to remove unreacted parts.

PLANT ECONOMICS

Rated Plant capacity	=	2.00 TON./day
LAND & BUILDING (215 sq. mts.)		Rs. 3,55,464.00

PLANT & MACHINERY

1. Sulphonator
2. Homogenizer
3. Dilution vessel
4. Separator
5. Storage Tank
6. Storage vessel for L.A.B. (MS. body, SS. lining)
7. Storage vessel for Acid Slurry
8. Miscellaneous (Rotameter, pipe line and pumps)
9. Water, cooler & Control

FIXED CAPITAL

1.	LAND & BUILDING	Rs.	3,55,464.00
2.	PLANT & MACHINERY	Rs.	11,40,000.00
3.	OTHER FIXED ASSETS	Rs.	1,70,000.00
	TOTAL	Rs.	16,65,464.00

RAW MATERIALS

1. Linear Alkyl Benzene
2. Sulphuric Acid

TOTAL WORKING CAPITAL/MONTH

1.	RAW MATERIAL	Rs.	14,58,120.00
2.	SALARY & WAGES	Rs.	18,720.00
3.	UTILITIES & OVERHEADS	Rs.	52,600.00
	TOTAL	Rs.	15,29,440.00

TOTAL CAPITAL INVESTMENT

TOTAL FIXED CAPITAL	Rs.	16,65,464.00
TOTAL WORKING CAPITAL FOR 2 MONTHS	Rs.	30,58,880.00
TOTAL	Rs.	47,24,344.00

TURN OVER/ANNUM

600 tons of acid slurry Rs. 2,28,00,000.00

PROFIT SALES RATIO = Profit / Sales x 100 = 14.01 %
RATE OF RETURN = Operating profit / T.C.I x 100 = 67.59 %
BREAK EVEN POINT (B.E.P) = 33.32 %

Chapter 20

NEROL LAUNDRY SOAP

Laundry soaps are available in various types in the form of bars, cakes, chips, flakes, powders etc. Genuine soaps in the form of bars contain about 30 per cent moisture and not less than 67 per cent anhydrous soap. Powders may not contain more than 2 per cent moisture. The anhydrous soap content of built soaps will be around 50 per cent while that of filled soaps between 30 and 50 per cent. Two main types of laundry soaps are white and yellow. White laundry soap is usually a full boiled product made from 25 - 40 per cent coconut oil and 65-75 per cent tallow, hydrogenated fish oil etc. It is always prepared with sodium silicate or other soap builders in sufficient amount to reduce the anhydrous soap content tc about 50 per cent. Such soaps are never milled. Yellow laundry soap is similar to white laundry soap except that it contains a substantial proportion of rosin. The rosin imparts a distinctive yellow colour to the bar. Rosin soap is relatively soft and sticky and hence, yellow soaps cannot be prepared with as much builder as white soaps. Its anhydrous soap content is usually over 50 per cent. It is also usual to employ less coconut oil in yellow than in white laundry soap because of the greater solubility of rosin soaps.

Laundry soaps are among household soaps which comprise various types of soaps available in difficult forms. Household chipped or flaked soaps used for laundry purpose are generally a little lower in moisture content than the corresponding bar soaps. a representative composition is moisture 10-20%; soap 50-60; tetrasodium pyropheesphate-15%; sodium metasilicate -7%; and soda ash 8 per cent.

LAUNDRYSOAPS V/S MIXED SOAP DETERGENT LAUNDRY BAR

Consideration has been given during recent years to mixtures of soaps and synthetic detergents designated with the idea of overcoming the major disadvantage of soap, namely its poor resistance to hard water. The earlier detergent bars suffered disadvantages such as a tendency to defat the skin, causing a feeling of clamminess after use, irritancy and drying out of the skin, bringing in its train skin allergies to persons with sensitive skins. Apart from this the bar was highly priced compared with its bar soap equivalent cracked badly, dissolved away too rapidly in use and further more was difficult to process on modern high speed soap machinery.

FORMULATION

(IN KGS.)

1.	MAHUA OIL	4
2.	RICE BRAN OIL	4
3.	WATER	7.5
4.	STARCH	4
5.	COMMON SALT	1
6.	SODA ASH	0.5
7.	CAUSTIC SODA LYE 35°Be	5

(IN KGS.)

1.	COCONUT OIL	25
2.	MAHUA OIL	20
3.	ROSIN	10
4.	SOAP STONE (TALE)	27
5.	WATER	50
6.	SILICA OF SODA	10
7.	SODA ASH	5
8.	CAUSTIC SODALYE 25°Be	57

(IN KGS.)

1.	COCONUT OIL	5
2.	MAHUA OIL	15
3.	RICE BRAN OIL	4
4.	CASTOR OIL	6
5.	SODA CAUSTIC LYE 36°Be	15
6.	SOAP STONE POWDER	10
7.	SODIUM SILICATE	10

MANUFACTURING PROCESS OF LAUNDRY SOAP FROM SOAP FLAKES

The process employed for this purpose is called full boiled process. The various steps involved in this process are :

1. The first brine charge
2. Thes second brine charge

3. The finish
4. Crutching and filling
5. Cooling frame
6. Slabbing & cutting
7. Drying and packing

1. THE FIRST BRINE CHANGE

In a reaction kettle the soap flakes and little quantity caustic soda solution (20° Be) is added. It is boiledwith addition of little water.

The boiling requires approximately four hours. Salt is than added,.allowed to dissolve and the continued until the soap has separated. The steam is shut off and the boil is allowed to settle.

2. THE SECOND BRINE CHANGE

The spent lye is now drained off through a valve at the bottom of the kettle. Steam is again admitted and water is sprayed. This thins the soap to the conditions usually known as closed. Caustic soda lye is again added followed by same procedure as in first brine charge.

3. THE FINISH

After the cattle has settled and the lyes have been drawn off there are usually two layers of soap of different appearances and fatty acid contents. The object of this operation is to obtain the highest possible yield of neat base soap and to obtain optimum quantity of higher. The finish operation requires several days because the setting must be thorough.

4. CRUTCHING AND FILLING

Various builders,fillers and other additives (i.e., sodium silicate, colour etc.) are added to the liquid heat soap in the crutchor. The crutcher operation requires only ten to fifteen minutes. The soap should be at a temp. between 140-150°F for best result in the crutcher.

5. COOLING FRAMES

The soap is drained from the crutcher into the frames. These frames are usually 13" wide x 56" long x 41" high and when filled will hold 1000 to 1200 lbs of soap. The frame box is a four wheeled dolly which facilitates the soap for subsequent operations.

Framed soap usually requires 3-5 days to cool and solidify. When the block has solifified, frame sides are stipped and the block cleared preparatory to slabing.

6. SLABBING AND CUTTING

Slabbing reduces the blocks of soap to slabs and cutting reduces it to bars. The block of soap is wheeled in the fram dolly into position under the soabber. This machine may be power or hand operated.

The dolly wheels are blocked to prevent movement of the block during the operation. The slabbing is performed by putting a series of tal piano wires, mounted in a strong angle ironframe, through the solid block of soap.

7. DRYING AND PACKING

The Bars cakes of washing soap are separated and stacked in racks air dry for two days or more and subsequently packed in cartons and are ready for storage and shipping.

PLANT ECONOMICS

Rated Plant Capacity	=	1.00 Mt/Day
LAND & BUILDING (Land 500 Sq.mts.)	Rs.	7,30,000.00

PLANT & MACHINERY

1. Cauldron for Mixing, Cooking at various stages.
2. Moulds.
3. Coal Fired open hearths.
4. Automatic Soap Cake Cutting Machine
5. Soap Stamping Machine.
6. Miscellaneous viz. Weighing Slabe, Testing Equipment, Fire Fighting Equipment etc.

FIXED CAPITAL

1.	LAND & BUILDING	Rs.	7,30,000.00
2.	PLANT & MACHINERY	Rs.	1,29,000.00
3.	OTHER FIXED ASSETS	Rs.	67,000.00
	TOTAL	Rs.	9,26,000.00

RAW MATERIALS

1. Sedimeats of Ground nut (or Ground Nut cake),
2. Caustic Soda Flakes (for making 36 degree Be lye or 45 % Solution),
3. Rice Bran

4. Neem Oil
5. Salt
6. Packaging Material.
7. Miscellaneous.

TOTAL WORKING CAPITAL/MONTH

1.	RAW MATERIAI	Rs.	2,27,910.00
2.	SALARY & WAGES	Rs.	95,040.00
3.	UTILITIES & OVERHEADS	Rs.	1,60,450.00
	TOTAL	Rs.	4,83,400.00

TOTAL CAPITAL INVESTMENT

TOTAL FIXED CAPITAL	Rs.	9,26,000.00
TOTAL WORKING CAPITAL FOR 3 MONTHS	Rs.	14,50,200.00
TOTAL	Rs.	23,76,200.00

TURN OVER/ANNUM

By Sale of Nerol Laundry Soap, 300 M.T.	Rs.	66,00,000.00

PROFIT SALES RATIO = Profit / Sales x 100 = 4.81 %
RATE OF RETURN = Operating profit / T.C.I x 100 = 13.35 %
BREAK EVEN POINT (B.E.P) = 84.34 %

Chapter 21

LIQUID DETERGENTS FOR WOOL

The detergents are divided into several classes e.g.

a. Anionic

b. Cationic

c. Non-ionic

d. Amphoteric.

Each type acts differently in aqueous solutions.

When detergent is mentioned, the cake, bar or powder usually comes to mind. For small manufacturers, the best advice on making liquid detergents is to purchase from primary producers an intermediate dodecyl benzene sulphonic acid (DDBSA) better known as acid slurry. They themselves,can neutrilize the doecyl compound in a variety of ways. They may use ammonia amines, soda or potash to yield liquid detergents.

Generally, there are two types of liquid detergents.

1. Light duty liquid detergent.
2. Heavy duty liquid detergent.

Light duty detergents are in general use, although heavy duty liquid detergents are also being made but this has not captured the market to any serious extent. Liquid detergents, which actually proceeded powders, are used mainly for fine wash and dish washing. It can undoubtly be said that liquid detergents are an important part of today cleanser markets of developed countries. In India, liquid detergents is under development stage, except that is used in large quantities in textile mills for wet processing for textile goods. In certain parts of the world, pastes which are purely sodium dodecyl benzene sulphonate in a fairly concentrative from are used for dish washing. Previously, powder detergents well widely used but the trend is not towards liquid detergents.

MANUFACTURING PROCESS

Liquids were made initially merely by dissolving or diluting dodecyl benzene sulphonate, it was found that sodium alkyl benzene sulphonate has a limited solubility in water and recourse was made to the while or partial neutralisation of the sulphonic acid by triethanolamine, to give a better solubility or conversely, a lower point. Liquid detergents are an important part of todays cleanser markets of developed countries. Liquid hard cleaners occupy a major place in the Amarican system of personal cleanliness.

Normally, basic an ionic alkyl any surface active agent with a non-ionic additive which key the foaming power of the system to its detersive properties is used in liquid detergent system is relatively easy. Formulators of substantial quantities of liquid detergents can avail themselves of the economy in purchasing on intermediate dedecyl benzene sulphonic acid. Ammonia, amines, soda or potash can be used by them to yield liquids or solids, all from the same intemediate, and dodecyl compound can also be neutralized by the formulations in numberous manners.

FORMULATIONS FOR LIQUID DETERGENT FOR WOOL, COLD WATER WOOL DETERGENTS

I

	%/Wt
Sodaphos	30.0
STPP	10.0
Anionic (85%)	25.0
Salt Cake	34.5
CMC	0.5

Proc : Mix all ingredients together until uniform.

II

	%/Wt
STPP	45.7
$NaHSO_4$	7.3
Anionic	25.0
CMC	0.5
Salt Cake	Balance

Proc: (For I and II) mix ingredients together until unifor.

Salt Coke = Sodium Sulphate

CMC = Carboxy Methyl Cellulose

Sodaphos = Sodium Phosphate

Anionic Components,
Athyl arge sulphonate
Dodecyl Benzene,
Sulphorate
Dodecyl Benzene Sulphuric acid (DDBSA) (known as Acid Slurry)
Sodium lauryl sulphate (SLS)

PLANT ECONOMICS

Rated Plant capacity of liquid detergent	=	150000 litres
LAND & BUILDING (400 sqmt.)		Rs. 5,00,000.00

PLANT & MACHINERY

1. Mixing/Blending vessel
2. Storage Tank
3. Storage Tank Cap: 3000 ltr.
4. Pading & filling machine (Semi-Automatic).
5. Weighing machine
6. Other Miscellaneous item viz. pipe fittings, pumps, motors etc.

FIXED CAPITAL

1.	LAND & BUILDING	Rs.	5,00,000.00
2.	PLANT & MACHINERY	Rs.	4,40,000.00
3.	OTHER FIXED ASSETS	Rs.	1,59,000.00
	TOTAL	Rs.	10,99,000.00

RAW MATERIALS

1. Dodecyl Benzene Sulphonate (Anionic)
2. Sodium Tripolyphosphate
3. Salt Coke (Sodium Sulphate)
4. $NaHSO_4$
5. CMC (Carboxy Methyl Cellulose)
6. Packaging Material

TOTAL WORKING CAPITAL/MONTH

1.	RAW MATERIAL	Rs.	2,04,406.25
2.	SALARY & WAGES	Rs.	26,000.00
3.	UTILITIES & OVERHEADS	Rs.	40,000.00
	TOTAL	Rs.	2,70,406.25

TOTAL CAPITAL INVESTMENT

TOTAL FIXED CAPITAL		10,99,000.00
TOTAL WORKING CAPITAL FOR 2 MONTHS		5,40,812.50
TOTAL	Rs.	16,39,812.50

TURN OVER/ANNUM

By sale of 150000 litres of liquid detergent	42,00,000.00

PROFIT SALES RATIO = Profit / Sales x 100 = 14.25 %

RATE OF RETURN = Operating profit / T.C.I x 100 = 36.51 %

BREAK EVEN POINT (B.E.P) = 52.93 %

Chapter 22

LAUNDRY FOR CLOTHES WASHING

Laundry work is very well known process of cleaning all types of linens, clothing & carpets etc. Working conditions are not likely to be ideal, but much can be done to overcome drawbacks and inconvenience by orderly arrangement, and sometimes by structural improvements. Due regard must be paid to the question of providing for facilities to ensure satisfactory results.

Some most important utilities can be as under:

1. Light & Ventilation.
2. Supply of gas & electricity.
3. Hot water supply.
4. Storage accomodation. and
5. Ideal equipments.

LAUNDERING PROCESS

SORTING

The sorting process is for the purpose of grouping articles according to their use and subsequent washing, consideration being paid to fabric and colour. It enables the worker to wash the cleaner articles first, so that water, detergents, and labour may be economized. At the same time, it guards against wrong treatment of different types of fabric, and the loosening, fading, or transfer of colour where this is not fast.

House hold articles, such as table linen, bed-linen, and cloths of all sorts, are separated from articles of personal wear. Woolens, silks, and rayons are separated from cottons and linens, and loose colours, known or suspected, are set apart.

INSPECTION AND MENDING

Articles are looked over so that attention may be given to those that need mending, or any other special attention. For example, pockets should be brushed out, and any pins or metal buttons likely to rust should be removed.

Unless articles in need of repair are particularly soiled, mending is carried out before the wash to prevent further tearing. Otherwise, when time does not permit, a hole is drawn together by the fish-bone stitch before the wash, and patched before the finishing process is started. It is often wiser to replace fastenings after the wash, to prevent damage. Very soiled articles are mended after the wash.

STAIN REMOVAL

1. Try to ascertain nature of stain.
2. Remove immediately, or as soon as possible.
3. Note the material to be treated.
4. Try simplest methods first, i.e. washing land open-air bleaching.
5. Treat area covering stain rather than the whole article.
6. Repeated applications are better than one strong one.
7. Test use of any strong agent on corner of article before use.
8. Neutralize acidic substance after use, and rinse in four changes of water.
9. Wash and boil article, if possible, after use of chemicals.
10. If nature of stain is uncertain, treat in the following way until it is removed: (a) with cold water; (b) with warm water; (c) with open-air bleach if necessary; (d) in an alkaline solution, and rinse; (e) in an acidic solution, and rinse; (f) bleach by artificial means; (g) repeat processes as above; (h) try solvents, on dry material.

STEEPING

This process is of great importance, and its value is often underestimated. Soft water is essential to obtain maximum results, and enough time (as fabric permits) must be allowed. The containers used should be sufficiently large, and must be clean to avoid fresh stains, and free from rust to prevent iron mould.

WASHING

Soiling matter which has been loosened in the steep is absorbed by the washing solution and held in suspension, and grease still in the fabric is emulsified. A synthetic detergent solution emulsified more effectively than soap, but is likely to be less capable of holding matter in suspension. When the use of a synthetic detergent is desirable, the fact that it is less cleansing than soap can be overcome, when washing very soiled articles, by steeping in synthetic detergent solution, and washing with soap first, and then synthetic detergent. Particularly soiled parts can be treated by applying the synthetic detergent, in powder or concentrated liquid form, to the damp fabric, and applying friction suitable to the fabric.

RINSING

After washing with soap, lime curd will be deposited in fabrics if hard water is used for rinsing, and will cause gray discoloration of white articles. In the case of wool, there may also be clogging with subsequent apparent shrinkage. The rinsing out of soap, therefore, should be done in soft water to prevent lime curd deposit. The last rinse, however, should be in hard water to prevent galling, the appearance of brown streaks in drying. If soft water is not available, or as an alternative to softening with soda, a very small quantity of synthetic detergent in the first rinsing water will reduce the risk of discoloration through lime curd.

WRINGING

This process is carried out by hand, or by means of a machine wringer, worked by hand or electricity. Both methods are suitable for cotton and linen. Delicate cotton, woolen, silk and rayon fabrics are squeezed by hand, in place of wringing, followed by squeezing or machine wringing in a towel to absorb the water. One or other of these processes is essential to speed up the drying process, and , in the case of indoor drying, to prevent dripping.

BLUEING AND STARCHING

Blueing is a method of treating white articles to obtain an apparent improvement of colour, the blue counteracting yellow discoloration from soap.

DRYING

The purpose of drying is to evaporate moisture, and, whenever possible, to bleach at the same time by carrying out the process in the open air. When drying has to be done indoors, the use of a drying cabinet is ideal; if this is not available articles are placed on racks worked on pulleys from the top of the room, on lines, or on clothes-horses placed in front of a fire. Articles can be taken down when ready for finishing, and rolled up, to avoid necessity for damping, and to equalize the moisture unless, in the case of open-air drying, longer time is required for bleaching.

DAMPING AND FINISHING

Damping gives back to the dried fabric sufficient moisture for good finishing.

The finishing process is carried out by means of a mangle, an electric rotary ironer, or a hand iron. The mangle gives finish by means of moisture and pressure, but, if article are not well folded, results will be unsatisfactory. The use of the electric rotary ironer is similar, but heat takes the place of heavy pressure. Hand ironing is carried out by means of moisture, heat, and pressure, and the best results can be obtained by this method, especially with skilled manipulation.

Airing is needed (1) to retain the good finish of the work, (2) to prevent the possibility of mildew forming, and (3) to safeguard health.

PLANT ECONOMICS

Rated Plant Capacity	=	500.00 KGS/Day
LAND & BUILDING (500 sq.mt)	Rs.	11,00,000.00

PLANT & MACHINERY

1. Industrial washing machine
2. Hydro extractor
3. Drying tumbler (steam heated)
4. Flat bed press (steam heated)
5. Vacuum finishing table
6. Steam generator
7. Installation kit complete with pedestral,steam and return lines,insulation, fittings, cables, mountings
8. Auxiliary equipment wash room trolley,
9. Ironing table
10. Shelf trolley
11. Mobile table with stainless steel top

FIXED CAPITAL

1.	LAND & BUILDING	Rs.	11,00,000.00
2.	PLANT & MACHINERY	Rs.	7,46,500.00
3.	OTHER FIXED ASSETS	Rs.	3,75,000.00
	TOTAL	Rs.	22,21,500.00

RAW MATERIALS

1. Soap solution,
2. Miscellaneous consumables, as starch, blue and other

TOTAL WORKING CAPITAL/MONTH

1.	RAW MATERIAL	Rs.	35,000.00
2.	SALARY & WAGES	Rs.	66,375.00
3.	UTILITIES & OVERHEADS	Rs.	41,000.00
	TOTAL	Rs.	1,42,375.00

TOTAL CAPITAL INVESTMENT

TOTAL FIXED CAPITAL	Rs.	22,21,500.00
TOTAL WORKING CAPITAL FOR 2 MONTHS	Rs.	2,84,750.00
TOTAL	Rs.	25,06,250.00

TURN OVER/ANNUM

Receipt by charging 1,50,000 kgs cloth per year	**Rs.**	37,50,000.00

PROFIT SALES RATIO = Profit / Sales x 100 = 35.83 %
RATE OF RETURN = Operating profit / T.C.I x 100 = 53.61 %
BREAK EVEN POINT (B.E.P) = 47.46 %

INDUSTRIAL LAUNDRY & DRYCLEANING MACHINES, STEEL FABRICATORS.

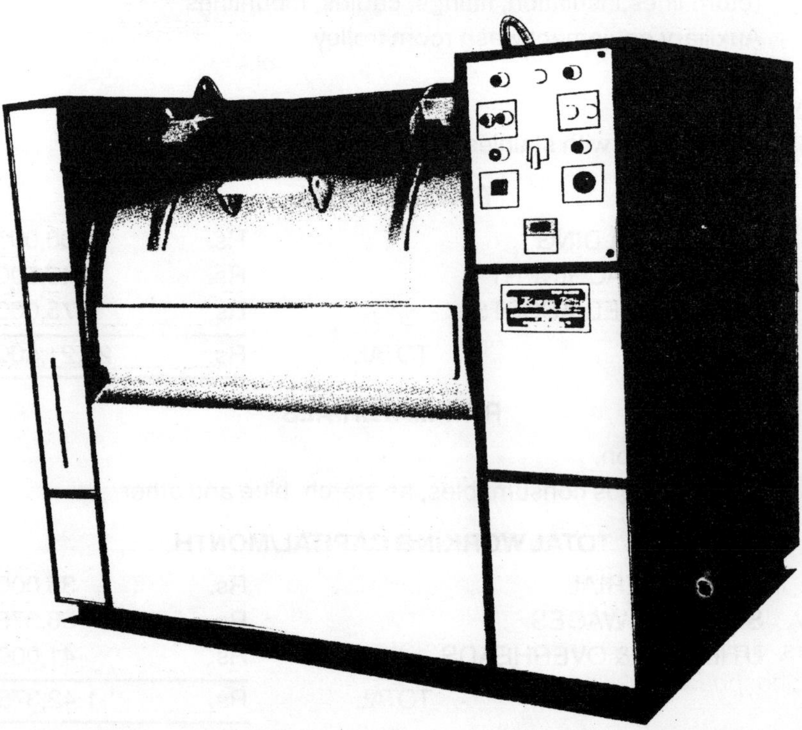

Chapter 23

NIRMA TYPE DETERGENT POWDER

The principal types of synthetic detergents are an ionic, non-ionic and employtics. Sodium dodecyle benzene sulphonate is an example of the ionic type while nylon phenol, nylone oxide obtained from ethylene oxide is the non-ionic type. The amploytic detergents like the alkyl amino propionates behave as cations in acidic solutions and like anions in alkaline solution.

Among the numerous detergent powders are available today in the market eg. Hipoline, T.Series, Areal, Surf, Sunlight, Vijay, Ketty, Nirma, Vimal, Ranjit and Bharat, Nirma detergent powder is most popular.

PROCESS OF MANUFACTURE

Detergent powder is made from acid slurry by incorporating into it various additives and builders and spray drying the product so formed. On a cottage scale, the ingredients are mixed in open air. The following ingredients are used in detergents :-

1. Acid slurry
2. C.M.C.
3. Trisodium polyphosphate
4. Trisodium phosphate
5. Sodium Perborate
6. Optical Whitening agent
7. Foam Booster
8. Sodium silicate
9. Sodium carbonate
10. Sodium sulphate
11. Perfume

In general, the detergent contains 15 to 40% active material i.e. acid slury, the rest being builders, fillers, dyes and other materials. Builders gives detergency. sodium tripolyphosphate and tetra sodium pyrophosphate are most outstanding alkaline builders. The amount of these vary from 30 to 50%. Small percentage, 1 to 3% of sodium carboxy methyl cellulose markedly improve the soil suspending power of detergents and prevent the redeposition of dirt. Brightening agents are also added in amount of 0.01 to 0.05%, sodium silicate lessons corrosion of aluminium washing machine.

The composition of a good quality detergent can be written as under:-

Acid Slurry	13%
C.M.C	1.0%
Trisodium phosphate	25.0%
Optical whitening agent	0.2%
Sodium perborate	1.0%
Trisodium polyphosphate	10.0%
Foam booster	1.0%
Sodium silicate	10.0%
Sodium carbonate	6.0%
Sodium sulphate	26%
Perfume	0.05%
Colour	0.05%
Moisture	7.7%

PLANT ECONOMICS

Rated Plant Capacity	=	500.00 KGS/Day
LAND & BUILDING (200 sq.mt)	Rs.	4,00,000.00

PLANT & MACHINERY

1. Mixer/Blender
2. Trays/Pan made of stainless steel
3. Grinding Machine
4. Weighing Machine
5. Weighing balance for packing
6. Miscellaneous like Gloves, Bag seaving machine

FIXED CAPITAL

1.	LAND & BUILDING	Rs.	4,00,000.00
2.	PLANT & MACHINERY	Rs.	65,000.00
3.	OTHER FIXED ASSETS	Rs.	52,500.00
	TOTAL	Rs.	5,17,500.00

RAW MATERIALS

1. Soda ash
2. Acid slurry
3. T.S.P.
4. Sodium Silicate
5. Sodium Sulfate
6. Urea
7. Ethanolamine
8. Trialkylamine
9. Sodium perborate

TOTAL WORKING CAPITAL/MONTH

1.	RAW MATERIAL	Rs.	72,765.63
2.	SALARY & WAGES	Rs.	23,250.00
3.	UTILITIES & OVERHEADS	Rs.	28,900.00
	TOTAL	Rs.	1,24,915.63

TOTAL CAPITAL INVESTMENT

TOTAL FIXED CAPITAL	Rs.	5,17,500.00
TOTAL WORKING CAPITAL FOR 3 MONTHS	Rs.	3,74,746.89
TOTAL	Rs.	8,92,246.89

TURN OVER/ANNUM

By sale of 1,50,000 kg Nirma Type Washing Powder Rs. 22,50,000.00

PROFIT SALES RATIO = Profit / Sales x 100 = 22.68 %
RATE OF RETURN = Operating profit / T.C.I x 100 = 57.19 %
BREAK EVEN POINT (B.E.P) = 49.04 %

Chapter 24

NON-IONIC LIQUID DETERGENTS

1. Non-ionic detergent are condensation product of ethylene oxide with a hydrophobe. The hydrrophobe is invariably a high molecular weight material with an active hydrogen atom.
2. The non-ionics do not ionize; but acquire their hydrophilic character from an oxidizenated side chain, usually polyoxethylene.
3. The oil soluble portion may be derived from fatty acids, alcohols, amides or amines.

FORMULATION

Various formulations for non-ionic liquid detergent are below:

Formula 1:

Heavy Duty Liquid Detergent:	
Linear alkyl benzene sulphonic acid	10 parts
Diethanotamine	3.6 parts
Non-ionic (100%)	2.0 parts
Poly-vinyl-pyrrolidone (PVP) (100%)	0.7 parts
$K_4P_2O_7$ (100%)	12 parts
Potassium xylene sulphonate	5.0 parts
Potassium silicate (100%)	4.0 parts
Water to make	100 parts

Formula no.2

Heavy duty Liquid Detergent	
Dodecyl benzene sulphonic acid	20.0 parts
Diaethanolamine	7.2 parts
$K_4P_2O_7$ (100%)	12.0 parts
Potassium xylene sulphonate	5.0 parts
Potassium silicate (100%)	3.0 parts
Water to make	100 parts

C.M.C. (100%)	1.0 parts
optical brighting agent	0.1 parts

PROCESS OF MANUFACTURE

Rapid remarkable progress in the productionof various types on non-ionics has been taking place in recent years. There are generally in phisical liquid form. The non-ionic class has non-ionizable high affinity end groups in countrast to the ionizable end groups in anionics or contionics.

The most important non-ionics detergents are obtained by reacting various hyarophopic group with ethanolamine. Ethanolamines are amino alcohols that are derived from ammonia in which at least one of the hydrogen atoms is replaced by readical 2-hydroxethyl ($-CH_3CH_2OH$). The term ehtanolamine denote in series, mono-di and tri othanolamines, generally the technical grade commercially available is rich in triethanolamine.

The procedure for compounding a 100 gal. batch (about 870lb) of liquid detergent which is to contain 35% of active surfactants. The batch will actually contaion 870x0.35 or 304 lb of sulphonates.

To prepare 304 pounds of alkyl arl sulphonate, 304/343 or 0.88 moles equal to 283 lbs of 100% sulphonic acid is required. This is equivalent at 322 pounds of sulphonic acid (88%) as supplied. The 322 of dodecyl benzene sulphonic acid contain 22 lbs. or 0.22 moels of free sulphuric acid which is to be neutralized by 0.44 moles or 17.60 lbs of sodium hydroxide. The amount of sodium hydroxide required to neutralize the dadecyl-benzene sulphuric acid is 0.88 moles or 35.2 pounds therefore, the total anyhydrous caustic soda to neutralize both free acid and sulphonic acid is 52.8 pounds.

Thus the batch requires:

Dodecycle benzene sulphoric acid	322.0 lbs
Sodium hydroxide anyhrous	52.8 lbs
Water	495.2 lbs
	870.0 lbs

The formulation may wish to include a small amount other materials and ethanol or is propanol to ensure homgeneity and control vi cosity. This formulation also lacks lauric diethanolamide, which may be included to boost suds and improve visocity. The latter isoptional as conditions may dictate.

Chapter 25

DETERGENT PASTE (TEXTILE GRADE)

Detergent paste is extensively used for soaping of textile goods in dyeing unit. It is also used for cleaning of fabric for efficacious dirt removal. Cleaning of solid cloth yarn and other textile goods can be effectively accomplished by detergent paste.

FORMULATION OF DETERGENT PASTE (TEXTILE GRADE)

1. 40 % Detergent Paste

	Parts/Wt.
Acid slurry (100 %)	40
Caustic soda (45 %)	11.4
Sodium silicate (40 %)	0.6
Sodium hypochlorite solution	0.6
C M C	1.6
Water	45

2. 20 % Detergent Paste

	Parts/Wt.
Acid slurry	20
Caustic soda (45 % solution)	5.8
Sodium silicate (40 % solution)	4.5
Sodium hypochlorite solution	0.6
Oleic acid diethanolamine	1.5
CMC	2.5
Water	2.5

MANUFACTURING PROCESS OF DETERGENT PASTE (TEXTILE GRADE)

The manufacture of detergent paste can be done in a specially built neutralizer equipped with cooling jacket. The neutralizing vessel should preferably be built of stainless steel, but if precaution are taken so that the pH value does not fall below 7 during the process of manufacture, a mild steel vessel can be used.

If CMC is to be included in the formulation, it is necessary to dissolve it separately. If a separate mixing vessel with a slow speed stirrer is available, water to the extend of 10 times the weight of CMC is charged in the container and the CMC poured in slowly with stirring. The stirring is continued until all the lumps of CMC are dispersed. The dispersion is best, prepared the day before it is required and left to swell and dissolve by itself overnight.

If a mild steel neutralizing vessel is being used for the manufacture of detergent paste. All the remaining water cooled for in the formula (all the water if no CMC is to be added) and the requisite amount of caustic soda solution with inorganic salt if they are used are run into the vessel. Mixing and cooling is started and the acid slurry added at such a rate that the temperature does not rise above 65°C.

If 100 percent acid slurry is used, the heat of the reaction is low and the temperature will not rise very high. If 90 % acid slurry is used, the heat of the reaction is considerably higher and the rate of addition of the acid must be adjusted when about 80 % of the acid slurry has been taken up and the paste is still distincting alkaline, the requisite amount of sodium lypochlorite solution is added and mixed in. The balance of acid slurry is now added, taking care that the pH of the paste does not fall below 7, mixing is continued until the paset is uniform and the CMC solution (if called for) is added, or if an alkylolamide is to added with the acid slurry.

When a stainless steel neutralising vessel is being used, the procedure is similar except that the sodium hypochlorite can be put at the begining with water and the caustic soda and no special precaution need be taken.

If an acid pH is reached, the desired pH of 7.8-8 can be achieved by the addition of a litre or two of caustic soda solution. The acid slurry is added slowly with intermitted stirring as not to generate foam. The reaction is instantaneous. The only precaution that need be observed are to avoid the production of foam and to keep the temperature from rising above 60°C.

PLANT ECONOMICS

Rated Plant capacity	=	500.00 Kgs./day
LAND & BUILDING (Land 300 Sq.Mts.)		Rs. 6,15,000.00

PLANT & MACHINERY

1. Storage tank
2. Mixing vessel equipped with agitator

3. Packing machine
4. Other miscellaneous like testing machine, weighing machines, material handling equipment

FIXED CAPITAL

1.	LAND & BUILDING	Rs.	6,15,000.00
2.	PLANT & MACHINERY	Rs.	3,55,000.00
3.	OTHER FIXED ASSETS	Rs.	85,000.00
	TOTAL	Rs.	10,55,000.00

RAW MATERIALS

1. Acid slurry
2. Di-ethanolamine
3. Potassium pyrophosphate
4. Sodium silicate
5. CMC (Carboxy methyl cellulose)
6. Potassium xylene sulphonate
7. Optical brightener
8. Packaging materials & other miscellaneous consumables.

TOTAL WORKING CAPITAL/MONTH

1.	RAW MATERIAL	Rs.	3,39,375.00
2.	SALARY & WAGES	Rs.	57,331.90
3.	UTILITIES & OVERHEADS	Rs.	35,200.00
	TOTAL	Rs.	4,31,906.90

TOTAL CAPITAL INVESTMENT

TOTAL FIXED CAPITAL	Rs.	10,55,000.00
TOTAL WORKING CAPITAL FOR 2 MON	Rs.	8,63,813.80
TOTAL	Rs.	19,18,813.80

TURN OVER/ANNUM

Receipt by sale of detergent paste (textile grade)),
150000 Kgs Rs. 64,50,000.00

PROFIT SALES RATIO = Profit / Sales x 100 = 13.07 %

Chapter 26

SPRAY DRIED DETERGENT POWDER

Detergents are used for many purposes, and there are a wide range a substrates (surface to be cleaned) and of soils. The main substrates are:

1. Textile Fabrics
2. Human Skin
3. Cooking utensils, crockery, glasses and cutlery
4. Sinks, draining surface and baths
5. Floors and walls,
6. Lavatory bowls.

The soils to be removed are of many types, but most include both particulars soils, can be general house hold dusts, or dusts of more specialised kinds (clay, coal, iron, oxide etc) depending upon the circumstances under which the article became dirty. Sebum, an exudate from the skin which contains glycerides, free fatty acids, waxes (esters) and sterols, is normally part of the soil on clothing and other articles which come into cotact with the human body, such as towels and bed clothes, soils on fabrics can also include.

FORMULATION

Formulation :

Sl. No.	Constituent	Weight %
1.	Sodium Alkyl benzene sulfonate	10-30
2.	Tallow Alcohol Sulphate	0-10 x
3.	Ethoxylated Nonyl Phenol	0-10 x
4.	Sodium Toulene Sulphonate	0- 5 xx
5.	Coconut Moncethanolamide	2- 4
6.	Sodium Tripoly phosphate	15-40
7.	Sodium Silicote (1 : 2 or 1 : 3 ration)	3-15
8.	Sodium carbonate	0-20
9.	C M C	1- 2

10.	Optical Brightening Agent	0.2-0.4
11.	SodiumPerborate	0-20
12.	Sodium suplhate and moisture	Balance

Typical Formulation Selected for the Process

S.N.	Ingredients	Weight %
1.	Sodium DDBS/Sodium LABS (50% mixture)	10
2.	Carboxy methyl cellulose	2
3.	Trisodium phosphate	20
4.	Trisodium polyphate	15
5.	Sodium perborate	0.7
6.	Optical Whitening agent (Ranipal)	0.2
7.	Foam Booster (LEA or CEA)	1
8.	Sodium silicate	15
9.	Soda ash	20
10.	Sodium sulphate	16
11.	Perfume	0.05
12.	Colour	0.05

THE SPRAY DRYING PROCESS

General

Spray drying is used in a wide range of industries and many variations are possible. Droplets of liquid are brought into contact with hot gas in some form of chamber, where they dry rapidly to produce a powder. The liquid can be a solution or a slurry. Slurries are used for household and similar powders. Atomization, or the formulation of droplets, can be by rotating disc, by two fluid nozzle in which the liquid is broken up by steam, or compressed air, by single fluid nozzle in which the liquid to be dried is atomized by pressure alone. Contact between droplete and drying gas can be counter-current, co-current or, mixed flow. The shape of the drying chamber depends upon the type of flow and the method of atomization rotating disc atomizers tend to give fine powders, and two fluid nozzles are usually used for solutions of relatively low viscosity. Granuler detergent powders are normally made in tall towders using silngle fluid pressure atomising nozzles, or jets.

Points in the choice between counter- current and con-current contact are :

Co-current contact gives light powders of bulk density about 0.08-0.15 8/ml and a mositure content of 3-8% The powder contains many hollow beads, some which tend to break to dust. Co-current contact may be useful for thermally delicate products such as powders with a very high surface ant contact with the coolest gas.

Counter-current contact gives powders of bulk density 0.15-0.45 (more usually 0.3-0.4) g/ml and a moisture content of 6-15% commonly about 10%. Beads are less fragile and less dustis usually produced. Thermal efficiency is normally higher than with co-current contact, because the gas leaves the tower after contact with wet slurry and hence can have a lower temperature and/or a higher content of water vapour. The hottest gas contacts the driest particles with consequent greater risk of thermal damages.

Chapter 27

WASHING & LAUNDRY SOAP

ADVANTAGES OF DETERGENT LAUNDRY BAR OVER TRADITIONAL LAUNDRY SOAPS

1. They do not form insoluble salts of calcium and magnesium in hard water. They can be used in hard water. They can be used in hard water with ease and they do not leave deposits on bath tubs and wash basins.
2. In comparison to laundry and hard soaps, detergent laundry bars have more powerful cleaning action. Their usage is wide spread from washing all kinds of cloth to cleaning floors, kitchen ware and anything heavily soiled with grease and oil.
3. Detergent laundry bars are cheaper and last much longer than the regular soap bars.
4. They are derived from materials unusable in food unlike edible fats used in soaps.

A 40% active matter toilet bar can compete in quality and in price with an 80% fatty acid soap but to make the bar, the 40% needs to be filled to 100% with other materials very little of which can be water. This 6% causes problems in manufacturing and alters the appearance and behaviour of the cake, but a fairly economical and very good toilet tablet has been made using a mixture of lauryl alcohol sulphates, unsulphated lauryl alochol, hydrogenated castor oil, starch and water.

FORMULATION OF WASHING SOAP

(IN KGS.)

1.	MAHUA OIL	4
2.	RICE BRAN OIL	4
3.	WATER	7.5
4.	STARCH	4
5.	COMMON SALT	1

6.	SODA ASH	0.5
7.	CAUSTIC SODA LYE 35°Be	5

		IN KGS.)
1.	COCONUT OIL	25
2.	MAHUA OIL	20
3.	ROSIN	10
4.	SOAP STONE (TALC)	27
5.	WATER	50
6.	SILICA OF SODA	10
7.	SODA ASH	5
8.	CAUSTIC SODA LYE 25°Be	57

FORMULATIONS OF LAUNDRY SOAP (COMBINATION TOILET BAR SOAP)

		%
1.	WATER AND MATTER VOLATILE AT 105°C (MAX)	12
2.	SYNTHETIC ORGANIC DETERGENT (ANHYDROUS AND SALT FREE)	25
3.	SUM OF ANHYDROUS SODIUM OR POTASSIUM SOAP AND SYNDETS (MIN)	65
4.	FREE ALKALI AS CAUSTIC SODA (MAX)	0.2
5.	FREE ACID AS OLEIC (MAX)	0.2
6.	SODIUM SILICATE Na2O : 3.25 SiO_2 (MAX) 0.2 (MIN)	2.0
7.	SODIUM CARBOXTYMETHYL CELLULOSE	0.5
8.	TOTAL WATER INSOLUBLES (MAX)	1
9.	PH5% SOLUTION (MAX)	10.3
10.	PH 5% SOLUTION (MIN)	0.5

MANUFACTURING PROCESS OF WASHING SOAP

The process employed for this purpose is called full boiled process. The various charges involved in this process are :

1. The first brine charge
2. These second brine charge
3. The strong charge
4. The finish
5. Crutching and filling
6. Cooling frame
7. Slabbing & cutting
8. Drying and packing

PLANT ECONOMICS

Rated Plant Capacity 600000 KGS/YEAR
1500000 BARS OF 200 GM./YR.

LAND & BUILDING (1250 sq.mt.) Rs. 18,25,000.00

PLANT & MACHINERY

1. WASHING SOAP : Iron pan
2. Kettle
3. Baby Boiler
4. Soap cutting machine
5. Soap Stamping machine
6. Soap dies and moulds (wooden)
7. LAUNDRY SOAP : Amalgamator (with mixing sys.-5 H.P motor (made of AISI 316 St.Steel.)
8. Milling machine
9. Twin Worm duplex Vacuum machine (Bitra-slab type)
10. Vertical cooling tunnel (TRV-Duplo type)
11. Wrapping machine

FIXED CAPITAL

1.	LAND & BUILDING	Rs.	18,25,000.00
2.	PLANT & MACHINERY	Rs.	3,18,500.00
3.	OTHER FIXED ASSETS	Rs.	1,00,950.00
	TOTAL	Rs.	22,44,450.00

RAW MATERIALS

1. WASHING SOAP : Coconut Oil
2. Mahua Oil
3. Rosin
4. Soapstone
5. Sodium silicate
6. Soda ash
7. Caustic Soda lye
8. LAUNDRY SOAP: Alkayl Benzene sulphonate
9. Sodium luryl sulphate
10. Calcium Stearate
11. Titanium di oxide
12. Water

TOTAL WORKING CAPITAL/MONTH

1.	RAW MATERIAL	Rs.	7,64,328.00
2.	SALARY & WAGES	Rs.	43,250.00
3.	UTILITIES & OVERHEADS	Rs.	43,800.00
	TOTAL	Rs.	8,51,378.00

TOTAL CAPITAL INVESTMENT

TOTAL FIXED CAPITAL	Rs.	22,44,450.00
TOTAL WORKING CAPITAL FOR 2 MONTHS	Rs.	17,02,756.00
TOTAL	Rs.	39,47,206.00

TURN OVER/ANNUM

1. 6,00,000 Packets of Washing Soap of 1 Kg. each.
2. 1500000 bars of laundry soap of 200 gm. each.

TOTAL Rs. 1,68,00,000.00

PROFIT SALES RATIO = Profit / Sales x 100 = 33.06 %

RATE OF RETURN = Operating profit / T.C.I x 100 = 140.69 %

BREAK EVEN POINT (B.E.P) = 20.68 %

Chapter 28

ZEOLITE-A MANUFACTURING (DETERGENT GRADE)

Zeolites are crystalline alumino silicates containing an assemblage of SiO_4 and AlO_4 tetrahedra joined together by oxygen atoms to form a microporous solid, which has a precise pore structure. Nearly 40 distinct frame work structures have been identified to date. The versatility of zeolites lies in the fact that widely different adsorptive properties may be realized by the appropriate control of the framework structures, the silica-to-alumina ratio (Si/Al), and the cation form. Zeolite-A, has a three-dimensional isotropic channel structure constructed by an eight-membered oxygen ring. Its effective pore size can be controlled at about 0.3, 0.4, and 0.45 nm by exchanging with potassium, sodium and calcium, respectively. The potassium form, with 0.3 nm pores, is used for removing water from olefinic hydrocarbons. Sodium form can be used to efficiently remove water from non-reactive hydrocarbons, such as alkanes. The substitution of calcium can provide a pore size that will admit n-paraffins and exclude other hydrocarbons.

Zeolites are crystalline aluminosilicates of group IA and group IIA elements such as sodium, potassium, magnesium, and calcium. Chemically, they are represented by the empirical formula:

$$M_{2/n}O.Al_2O_3.ySiO_2.wH_2O$$

where y is 2 or greater, n is the cation valence, and w represents the water contained in the voids of the zeolite. Structurally, zeolites are complex, crystalline inorganic polymers based on an infinitely extending framework of AlO_4 and SiO_4 tetrahedra linked to each other by the sharing of oxygen ions. This framework structure contains channels or interconnected voids that are occupied by the cations and water molecules. The cations are mobile and ordinarily undergo ion exchange. The water may be removed reversibly, generally by the application of heat, which leaves intact a crystalline host structure permeated by micropores which may amount to 50 % of the crystals by volume. In some zeolites, dehydration may produce some perturbation of the structure such as cation movement and some degree of framework distortion.

MANUFACTURING PROCESS

The first commercial process for preparing synthetic zeolites on a large scale was based on a laboratory synthesis using amorphous hydrogels. The typical starting materials is included an aqueous solution of sodium silicate, sodium aluminate, and sodium hydroxide. Hydrogel processes are based either on homogenous gels, that is, hydrogels prepared from solutions of soluble reactants, or on heterogeneous hydrogels which are prepared from reactive alumina or silica in a solid form, for example, solid amorphous silica powder.

In gel-perform processes the reactive aluminosilicate gel is first formed into a pellet which reacts with sodium aluminate solution and caustic solution. The zeolite crystallizes in situ within an essentially self-bonded pellet, or as a component in an unconverted amorphous matrix.

A process flow sheet for the manufacture of types 4 A, as high purity crystalline zeolite powders is shown.

A typical material balance and chemical compositions are given in Table. The raw materials are metered into the makeup tanks in the proper ratios. Crystallization takes place in a separate crystallizer. An intermediate ageing step at ambient temperature may be required for the synthesis of certain high purity zeolites.

The process appears to be simple in terms of equipment and experimental conditions; however, because of the metastability of zeolite species formed from typical reactant systems, problems may arise when large-scale synthesis is attempted. Generally, the crystallization temperature is near the boiling point of water (100°C). After the digestion period, the slurry of crystals in the mother liquor is filtered in a rotary filter.

The filter cake is dried in a fluidized bed dried or tunnel dryer and then pulverized and packed in air tight packaging system.

MATERIAL BALANCE FOR ZEOLITE-A PRODUCTION (BY HYDROGEL PROCESS)

Basis: 1000 Kgs. of Zeolite-A Manufacturing

(On Dry Basis)

Raw Materials Require in Kgs.

Sodium silicate (9.4 % Na_2O; 28.4 % SiO_2)	=	1350 Kgs.
Aluminium trihydrate (65 % Al_2O_3, 35 % H_2O)	=	575 Kgs.

Caustic Soda (50 % NaOH)	=	870 Kgs.
Water	=	3135 Kgs.

Gel Composition (Mol. Ratio)

Na_2O	=	2.04
Al_2O_3	=	1.00
SiO_2	=	1.75
Water	=	70

PLANT ECONOMICS

Rated Plant Capacity	=	2.00 MT/Day
LAND & BUILDING (Land 4000 Sq. Mts.)	Rs.	99,25,000.00

PLANT & MACHINERY

1. Sodium silicate solution storage tank (S.S. rubber lined)
2. Sodium silicate melting tank
3. Alumina trihydrate storage tank
4. Aluminium trihydrate metering tank
5. Caustic soda solution preparation tank
6. PVC storage tank
7. Bucket elevator
8. Reaction vessel (S.S.vessel)
9. Gel make-up tank (S.S.tank)
10. Ambient ageing tank (S.S tank)
11. Crystallizer
12. Rotary drum filter
13. Mother liquor collection tank
14. Filter cake collection tank
15. Tunnel dryer
16. Pulveriser
17. Bags sealing machine
18. Weighing balace
19. Metering unit
20. Structurers,pumps,valves,pipes, fittings etc.
21. Boiler
22. Laboratory equipments
23. Miscellaneous equipment

FIXED CAPITAL

1.	LAND & BUILDING	Rs.	99,25,000.00
2.	PLANT & MACHINERY	Rs.	1,63,85,000.00
3.	OTHER FIXED ASSETS	Rs.	52,50,000.00
	TOTAL	Rs.	3,15,60,000.00

RAW MATERIALS

1. Sodium silicate solution
2. Alumina Trihydrate
3. Caustic soda
4. Laboratory chemicals

TOTAL WORKING CAPITAL/MONTH

1.	RAW MATERIAL	Rs.	12,29,000.00
2.	SALARY & WAGES	Rs.	4,03,250.00
3.	UTILITIES & OVERHEADS	Rs.	7,59,000.00
	TOTAL	Rs.	23,91,250.00

TOTAL CAPITAL INVESTMENT

TOTAL FIXED CAPITAL	Rs.	3,15,60,000.00
TOTAL WORKING CAPITAL FOR 2 MONTHS	Rs.	47,82,500.00
TOTAL	Rs.	3,63,42,500.00

TURN OVER/ANNUM

By sale of 600 MT Zeolite - A Rs. 5,40,00,000.00

PROFIT SALES RATIO = Profit / Sales x 100 = 27.05 %

RATE OF RETURN = Operating profit / T.C.I x 100 = 40.19 %

BREAK EVEN POINT (B.E.P) = 52.71 %

Chapter 29

DETERGENT WASHING POWDER (SURF EXCEL TYPE)

SURF EXCEL TYPE DETERGENT POWDER

FORMULATION - 1

Sodium Salt of Alpha Olefin sulfonate	:	12.50%
Sodium Linear Alkyl Benzene Sulfonate	:	10%
Sodium Tripolyphosphate (STPP)	:	10%
Sodium Meta Silicate	:	15%
Sodium Carboxy Methyl Cellulose	:	3%
Corn Starch	:	5%
Sodium Sulphate	:	10%
Zeolite-A Powder	:	30%
Optical Brightener (Tinopal or Ranipal)	:	1%
(Detergent Green) Dyes	:	2%
Perfumes (Rose, lemon, Lime Encapsulated Powder	:	0.5%
Detergent Enzyme (Protease Alcalase Enzyme 1.5 Anson units per gram minimum Activity)	:	1%
		100%

Process

Mix all the ingredients in a sigma blade mixer. Then add the enzyme and again continue mixing. After completion of

mixture add the perfume with spraying. The product is then packed in polythene packs or pouches as per requirement.

PLANT ECONOMICS

Rated Plant capacity	=	1000.00 KGS/day
LAND & BUILDING (Land 750 sq. mts.)		Rs. 17,50,000.00

PLANT & MACHINERY

1. Mixing machine
2. Weighing scale
3. Bucket elevator
4. Automatic sieving machine
5. Automatic weighing, filling, sealing pouch packing machine

FIXED CAPITAL

1.	LAND & BUILDING	Rs.	17,50,000.00
2.	PLANT & MACHINERY	Rs.	12,25,000.00
3.	OTHER FIXED ASSETS	Rs.	5,00,000.00
	TOTAL	Rs.	34,75,000.00

RAW MATERIALS

1. Sodium Salt of Alpha Olefin Sulfonate.
2. Acid Slurry
3. Sodium Tripolyphosphate
4. Sodium Meta Silicate,
5. Sodium Carboxy Methyl Cellulose
6. Corn Starch,
7. Sodium Sulphate,
8. Optical brightener,
9. Dyes (Detergent Green)
10. Perfumes
11. Protease Alcalase Enzyme (Detergent Enzyme).
12. Zedite-A Powder
13. Packaging Materials

TOTAL WORKING CAPITAL/MONTH

1.	RAW MATERIAL	Rs.	14,50,000.00
2.	SALARY & WAGES	Rs.	1,14,380.00
3.	UTILITIES & OVERHEADS	Rs.	1,53,000.00
	TOTAL	Rs.	17,17,380.00

TOTAL CAPITAL INVESTMENT

TOTAL FIXED CAPITAL	Rs.	34,75,000.00
TOTAL WORKING CAPITAL FOR 2 MONTHS	Rs.	34,34,760.00
TOTAL	Rs.	69,09,760.00

TURN OVER/ANNUM

By sale of 300,000 kgs. of SURF EXCEL type detergent powder Rs. 2,70,00,000.00

PROFIT SALES RATIO = Profit / Sales x 100 = 18.33 %

RATE OF RETURN = Operating profit /T.C.I x 100 = 71.63 %

BREAK EVEN POINT (B.E.P) = 35.51 %

Chapter 30

DETERGENT POWDER PLANTS—DRY MIX PROCESS

These plants are capable of making detergent powder of density of around 0.9 kgs/ltr.

1. MANUFACTURING PROCESS :

All the ingredients including colour and perfume are mixed in a ribbon blender till the mass is homogenized. This mass is then sieved in a vibratory sieve to obtain final required particle size, which are generally 40 to 50 meshes. Bigger particles are sent for recycling in ribbon blender.

2. BASIC RAW MATERIALS :

Raw materials are acid slurry, caustic soda, STPP, soda ash, fillers like dolomite, globber salt, talc, colour and perfume. Percentage of these materials can be fixed as per formulation or active detergency required.

3. PACKAGING :

This can be done either manually or on auto machines depending on the plant size. Packaging materials generally used are polythene bags.

4. MAN POWER REQUIRED :

1. For 50 Kgs / Hr – 5 Nos.
2. For 100 Kgs / Hr – 5 Nos.
3. For 250 Kgs / Hr – 6 Nos.
4. For 500 Kgs / Hr – 10 Nos.
5. For 1000 Kgs / Hr – 15 Nos.
6. For 2000 Kgs / Hr – 15 Nos.

5. ELECTRICITY REQUIRED :

1. 50 kgs/hr – 3 HP,
2. 100 kgs/hr – 5 HP,

3. 250 kgs/hr – 12 HP,
4. 500 kgs/hr – 20 HP,
5. 1000 kgs/hr – 25 HP,
6. 2000 kgs/hr – 30 HP,

6. AREA REQUIRED (FOR PLANT AND MACHINERY) :

1. 50 kgs/hr – 300 sq.ft.,
2. 100 kgs/hr – 500 sq.ft.,
3. 250 kgs/hr – 1000 sq.ft.,
4. 500 kgs/hr – 1200 sq.ft.,
5. 2000 kgs/hr – 2000 sq.ft.,

7. WATER REQUIRED (FOR PRODUCTION PURPOSE) :

4 % of the bath quantity.

8. EFFLUENTS :

There are no effluents in the process.

Chapter 31

LAUNDRY SOAP MANUFACTURING PLANT

1. CAPACITIES AVAILABLE :

A. 50 Kgs / Hr.,

B. 100 Kgs / Hr.,

C. 250 Kgs / Hr.,

D. 500 Kgs / Hr.,

E. 1000 Kgs / Hr.,

This plant can produce laundry soaps made from oils / soap stocks etc. of any shape, size and weight or as per requirement. Standard weights are 150 gm., 250 gms., and 400 gm.

2. MANUFACTURING PROCESS :

Basic raw material like oils / soap stocks are mixed in a crutcher with other ingredients like caustic soda, soda ash, salt etc. This mixture is boiled upto 100°C achieve complete saponification after which neat soap is formed, this neat soap is further dried either in vacuum spray drier (in case of plant 250 kgs. & more) or in cooling trays (for small plant upto 100 kg / hr.). This cutting / embossing & wrapping.

3. RAW MATERIALS REQUIRED :

Basic raw material are oil / soap stocks, caustic soda, salt, fillers like soap stone, china clay etc. These materials are readily available in India, Oil mills or vanaspati mills can manufacture laundry soap from sludge.

4. PACKING MATERIALS :

Laundry soap cakes are packed in a wax / pp coated wrappers and are then filled in cartons. Wrapping operation can be done manually for small capacity plants like 50 & 100 kgs / hr. Automatic wrapping machines are installed for capacities 250 kgs / hr. & above.

5. MANPOWER REQUIRED :

For production purpose, manpower is required as under for different capacities.

a. For 50 Kgs / Hr. – 4 Nos.
b. For 100 Kgs / Hr. – 6 Nos.
c. For 250 Kgs / Hr. – 8 Nos.
d. For 500 Kgs / Hr. – 10 Nos.
e. For 1000 Kgs / Hr. – 14 Nos.

6. WATER CONSUMPTION :

Following are the figures for water consumption for both production and non-production purpose.

a. For 50 Kgs / Hr. – 200 Ltrs / Day
b. For 100 Kgs / Hr. – 300 Ltrs / Day
c. For 250 Kgs / Hr. – 400 Ltrs / Day
d. For 500 Kgs / Hr. – 500 Ltrs / Day
e. For 1000 Kgs / Hr. – 500 Ltrs / Day

7. EFFLUENTS :

There are no effluents in the process. Very little amount of water is used and completely absorbed in the process.

8. AREA REQUIREMENT :

Following are the figures for area requirements (for machineries, raw materials and finished goods.)

a. For 50 Kgs / Hr. – 2000 Sq. Ft.
b. For 100 Kgs / Hr. – 3000 Sq. Ft.
c. For 250 Kgs / Hr. – 5000 Sq. Ft.
d. For 500 Kgs / Hr. – 10000 Sq. Ft.
e. For 1000 Kgs / Hr. – 25000 Sq. Ft.

9. ELECTRICITY REQUIRED :

Following are the figures for electricity requirement.

a. For 50 Kgs / Hr. – 12 HP.
b. For 100 Kgs / Hr. – 20 HP.
c. For 250 Kgs / Hr. – 75 HP.
d. For 500 Kgs / Hr. – 100 HP.
e. For 1000 Kgs / Hr. – 130 HP.

Chapter 32

TOILET (BATH) SOAP FINISHING LINE

1. CAPACITIES AVAILABLE

a. 50 Kgs / Hr.,
b. 100 Kgs / Hr.,
c. 250 Kgs / Hr.,
d. 500 Kgs / Hr.,
e. 1000 Kgs / Hr.,

2. PRODUCT :

This plant can produce bath soap like Lux, Dove, Cinthol, Jay etc. of any shape, and weights as per requirements. Standard weights are 75 gms., 100 gms., 125 gms., 250 gms.

3. MANUFACTURING PROCESS :

In this process ready noodles of toilet soap are purchased from outside. These noodles are mixed with colour and perfume in sigma mixer and are then passed through an extruder to extrude continuous bar which is then sent for further Cutting, Embossing & Wrapping.

4. RAW MATERIAL REQUIRED :

Since ready soap noodles are purchased, no individual raw materials are required to be stored. Only colour and perfume should be used alongwith titanium dioxide & AOS etc.

5. PACKING MATERIAL :

These soap are packed in a wax / pp coated wrappers and then filled in cartons, Wrapping is done either manually or by automatic machine.

6. MANPOWER REQUIRED :

For production purpose, manpower is required as under for different capacities.

1. For 50 Kgs / Hr – 4 Nos.
2. For 100 Kgs / Hr – 6 Nos.
3. For 250 Kgs / Hr – 8 Nos.
4. For 500 Kgs / Hr – 10 Nos.
5. For 1000 Kgs / Hr – 14 Nos.

7. WATER CONSUMPTION :

Following are the figures for water consumption for both production and non-production.

a. For 50 Kgs / Hr. – 200 Ltrs / Day
b. For 100 Kgs / Hr. – 300 Ltrs / Day
c. For 250 Kgs / Hr. – 400 Ltrs / Day
d. For 500 Kgs / Hr. – 500 Ltrs / Day
e. For 1000 Kgs / Hr. – 500 Ltrs / Day

8. EFFLUENTS :

There are no effluents in the process. Very little amount of water is used and completely absorbed in the process.

9. AREA REQUIREMENT :

Following are the figures for area requirements (for machineries, raw materials and finished goods).

a. For 50 Kgs / Hr. – 1500 Sq. Ft.
b. For 100 Kgs / Hr. – 2500 Sq. Ft.
c. For 250 Kgs / Hr. – 4000 Sq. Ft.
d. For 500 Kgs / Hr. – 8000 Sq. Ft.
e. For 1000 Kgs / Hr. – 15000 Sq. Ft.

10. ELECTRICITY REQUIREMENT :

Following are the figures for electricity requirement.

a. For 50 Kgs / Hr. – 10 HP.
b. For 100 Kgs / Hr. – 20 HP.
c. For 250 Kgs / Hr. – 70 HP.
d. For 500 Kgs / Hr. – 90 HP.
e. For 1000 Kgs / Hr. – 120 HP.

Chapter 33

DETERGENT CAKE MANUFACTURING PLANTS

1. CAPACITIES AVAILABLE

a. 50 Kgs / Hr.

b. 100 Kgs / Hr.

c. 250 Kgs / Hr.

d. 500 Kgs / Hr.

e. 1000 Kgs / Hr.

2. PRODUCT :

This plant can produce synthetic detergent cakes like Arial, Rin, Wheel, weights are 100 gms., 125 gms., 250 gms., & 400 gms.

3. MANUFACTURING PROCESS :

All the ingredients are mixed in a sigma mixer along with perfume and colour. This mixture is then passed through roll mill for homogenization. This homogenized material is then extruded in the form of a bar by extruder (producer) which is then sent for further Cutting, Embossing & Wrapping.

4. RAW MATERIAL :

Following raw materials are generally used to make detergent cake.

a. Acid Slurry (LABSA);

b. Sodium Silicate

c. Soda Ash,

d. Castle

e. Fillers like dolomite, talc, soap, stone etc.,

f. Perfume

g. Colour

h. Water

In some high quality detergent Soaps, ingredients like enzymes, zeolites, super active bases are used.

5. PACKING MATERIAL :

These detergent cakes are packed in a wax coated or polypropelene coated wrappers and are then filled in cartons. Wrapping is done either manually or by automatic machine.

6. MANPOWER REQUIRED :

For production purpose, manpower is required as under for different capacities.

1. For 50 Kgs / Hr – 4 Nos.
2. For 100 Kgs / Hr – 6 Nos.
3. For 250 Kgs / Hr – 8 Nos.
4. For 500 Kgs / Hr – 10 Nos.
5. For 1000 Kgs / Hr – 14 Nos.

7. WATER CONSUMPTION :

Following are the figures for water consumption for both production and non-production purpose.

a. For 50 Kgs / Hr. – 200 Ltrs / Day
b. For 100 Kgs / Hr. – 300 Ltrs / Day
c. For 250 Kgs / Hr. – 400 Ltrs / Day
d. For 500 Kgs / Hr. – 500 Ltrs / Day
e. For 1000 Kgs / Hr. – 500 Ltrs / Day

8. EFFLUENTS :

There are no effluents in the process. Very little amount of water is used and completely absorbed in the process.

9. AREA REQUIREMENT :

Following are the figures for area requirements (for machineries, raw materials and finished goods).

a. For 50 Kgs / Hr. – 2000 Sq. Ft.
b. For 100 Kgs / Hr. – 3000 Sq. Ft.
c. For 250 Kgs / Hr. – 5000 Sq. Ft.
d. For 500 Kgs / Hr. – 10000 Sq. Ft.
e. For 1000 Kgs / Hr. – 25000 Sq. Ft.

10. ELECTRICITY REQUIREMENT :

Following are the figures for electricity requirement.

a.	For 50 Kgs / Hr.	– 10 HP
b.	For 100 Kgs / Hr.	– 20 HP
c.	For 250 Kgs / Hr.	– 70 HP
d.	For 500 Kgs / Hr.	– 90 HP
e.	For 1000 Kgs / Hr.	– 120 HP.

(Courtesy: M/s. Chemac Equipments Pvt. Ltd., Mumbai)

Chapter - 34

MANUFACTURERS/SUPPLIERS OF DETERGENTS

Himani Detergents
Mr. Pradeep / M. S. Dhidaria (Proprietor)
Plot No. 89/ 3/ 1/ 2,
Main Salawas Road,
Village Salawas, Tehsilluni
Jodhpur - 342802,
Rajasthan, India
Mobile: +(91)-9829009895
+(91)-9414130925
Phone: +(91)-(291)-2696189

Mangalam
Mr. Keyur . / Mr. Ripal (Owner)
No. 12, Gopal Patel Estate,
Near Swaminarayan Colony,
Near C. T. M., Char Rasta,
Amraiwadi
Ahmedabad - 380001, Gujarat, India
Mobile: +(91)-9925760160,
+(91)-9898450991
+(91)-8460383778
Phone: +(91)-(79)-25855045
+(91)-(79)-27439735
Email: mangalamchemical@gmail.com
keyursheth45@yahoo.com

Polestar Polymers
Mr. Anshuman Garg (Manager)
J-195, Sector-5,
Bawana Industrial Area
New Delhi - 110039, Delhi, India
Mobile: +(91)-9999903396
+(91)-9891980983
Phone: +(91)-(11)-27043396

Juhi Marketing Company
Mr. Umesh Chandra Rao (Proprietor)
Kh. No. 56/3/3, Plot No.-4,
D-Block, Hastsal Industrial Area,
Uttam Nagar
New Delhi - 110059,
Delhi, India
Mobile: +(91)-9999312416
+(91)-9311751216
Phone: +(91)-(11)-25371645

Mahavir Chemicals
Mr. Narendra Mehta (Partner)
Shop No. 12, Govind Bhavan,
Opposite Chincholi Hanuman Temple,
S. V. Road, Malad West
Mumbai - 400064,
Maharashtra, India
Mobile: +(91)-9920427648
+(91)-9819177981
Phone: +(91)-(22)-28743924
+(91)-(22)-28741801
Fax: +(91)-(22)-28746525

Akkhin Chemicals
Mr. Manthan Shah (Proprietor)
Trinity Compound, Next To Pidilite Industries,
Near Ketyou Industrial Estate,
Kondivita Road,
Andheri (East), Mumbai - 400059,
Maharashtra, India
Mobile: +(91)-9819890091
+(91)-9920916747
Phone: +(91)-(22)-26870404
+(91)-(22)-26873337
+(91)-(22)-65342957

V- Tex Industries
Mr. Adarsh Shah (Partner)
Plot No. A/426, Road No. 28,
Opposite Emco Co.,
Wagle Estate
Thane - 400604,
Maharashtra, India
Mobile: +(91)-9821067898
Phone: +(91)-(22)-25825497

KK India Petroleum Specialities Pvt. Ltd.
Mr. Kalpesh Modi
No. 706, Palm Spring Center,
Link Road,
Malad West, Mumbai - 400064,
Maharashtra, India
Mobile: +(91)-9820083101
+(91)-9820140450
Phone: +(91)-(22)-42938012
+(91)-(22)-42938000
Fax: +(91)-(22)-42938099

Anuyog Enterprises
Mr. Yogesh Deodhar
No. 49/ A, Sahakarvind Society,
Anant Bunglow, Kothrud
Pune - 411 038, Maharashtra, India
Mobile: +(91)-9850558645
+(91)-9822617708
Phone: +(91)-(20)-32348363

Trisis Corp. (A Unit Of Chemisynth)
Mr. Sunil Jain (CEO)
F- 2, Triveni Commercial Complex,
Sheikh Sarai, Phase- 1,
New Delhi, India
Mobile: +(91)-9810461266
+(91)-9318861266
+(91)-9313413852
+(91)-8010413852
Phone: +(91)-(11)-26013852
Email: pankaj@chemisynth.in
info@trisiscorp.in

Handa Chemical Industries
Mr. Tarsem Handa (Proprietor)
1705/A, Ajeet Nagar, Baloki Road,
Haibowal Kalan, Ludhiana - 141001,
Punjab, India
Mobile: +(91)-9888729487
+(91)-8729071002
Phone: +(91)-(161)-3296852

Chemisynth
Mr. Sunil Jain (Proprietor)
F- 2, Triveni Commercial Complex,
Sheikh Sarai, Phase- 1,
New Delhi - 110017 Delhi, India
Mobile: +(91)-8010413852
+(91)-9810461266
Phone: +(91)-(11)-26013852
+(91)-(11)-26013355
+(91)-(11)-41864489
Fax: +(91)-(11)-26013859
Email: kashyap@chemisynth.in,
info@chemisynth.in
pankaj@chemisynth.in

Sunshine Home Care Product
Mr. Akil Shaikh
(General Manager)
Gat No. 468/3/5,
Nayegaon Road,
Shinde Gaon,
Nashik - 422101, Maharashtra, India
Mobile: +(91)-9766887885
+(91)-9820546429

Chapter - 35

SUPPLIERS OF PLANT AND MACHINERY (MAKING & PACKAGING)

Shachi Engineering Private Limited
Mr. Marthu Shanbhag
(Managing Director)
Plot No. 271, S. No. 38,
Mauje Bhare, Pirangut,
Tal-Mulshi, Pune - 412115,
Maharashtra, India
Mobile: +(91)-9822019088
+(91)-9689944881
+(91)-9689944889
Phone: +(91)-(20)-66546900
+(91)-(20)-66546923
+(91)-(20)-66546916
Fax: +(91)-(20)-66546915
Email: marthushanbhag@gmail.com
marketing@shachiengg.com
coordinator@shachiengg.com
detergent@shachiengg.com

DET Engineering Systems
Mr. Daulat Nighut (Director)
Sr. 128/2, Chinchwad
Pune - 411033,
Maharashtra, India
Mobile: +(91)-9527003703
+(91)-7385042255

Hardic Engineering
Mr. Hardic N. Panchal
(Marketing Manager)
C-1/77/1, Kaka Estate,
Ambica Nagar Road,
Nr. National Plastic, Odhav
Ahmedabad - 382415, Gujarat, India
Mobile: +(91)-9904201922
+(91)-9898474351
+(91)-9427417509
+(91)-9724184971
Phone: +(91)-(79)-22876114

Comp Engineering and Exports
Mr.B.B.Pol / Mr.Madhusudan Gupta / Mr.Oke
3025/8, Shreenidhi Chambers,
Senapati Bapat Road,
Pune, Maharashtra 411016 (India)
Tel: +(91)-(20)-25658205/06
Mobile: +(91)-9766640666
8698823403
Fax: +(91)-(20)-25658204
E-mail: sales@compengg.com

Mechano
Mr. Shubham Maheshwari /
Mr. A. Ansari
Plot No. 117,

Behind Yawalkar Pesticide,
Maharada Tehsil,
Uppalwadi Industrial Area,
Kamptee Road, Nagpur - 440008,
Maharashtra, India
Mobile: +(91)-9970049290
+(91)-9960151472
+(91)-9421700908

Raj Process Equipments & Systems (P) Limited
Mr. Sagar Kolhe
Jai Ganesh Vision, 3rd Floor,
B Wing,
Jai Ganesh Fame Building,
Akurdi Pune - 411035,
Maharashtra, India
Phone: +(91)-(20)-40710010
Fax: +(91)-(20)-40710009

Adhi Sakthi Projects
Mr. Senthil Kannan (CEO)
No. 40/9, Earikkarai Road, Near
Wipro Computers,
Kothapurinatham,
Thiruvandarkoil
Pondicherry - 605102, India
Mobile: +(91)-9443203221
+(91)-9442223221
+(91)-9894753715
+(91)-9789579452
Phone: +(91)-(413)-2641049
+(91)-(413)-2641059

United Detergent Engineers
Mr. Senthil Kumar C. (Proprietor)
No. 14, Bajanai Koil Street,
Uppilipalayam
Coimbatore - 641015,
Tamil Nadu, India
Mobile: +(91)-9363108587
+(91)-9843998587
Phone: +(91)-(422)-6564851

Chaudeshwari Engineering
Mr. Anil Bakkannavar (Proprietor)
B-1/4, 2nd Phase,
Near Seema Weigh Bridge
Vapi - 396195, Gujarat, India
Mobile: +(91)-9978444990
+(91)-9872661122
Phone: +(91)-(260)-2425185

Golden Heavy Engineering Company
Mr. Ramanjeet Singh (Owner)
Village Majri Kishne Wali,
Khanna Road,
Amloh, Khanna - 141402,
Punjab, India
Mobile: +(91)-8872166000
+(91)-9876063162
Phone: +(91)-(1765)-232789

Shivshiva Engineering
Mr. Mahendra Luhar / Mr. Ishwar
Bhai Luhar (Manager)
Behind Ramdev Estate,
Opposite Baroda Express Highway,
CTM Char Rasta, National Highway
No. 8, Amraiwadi
Ahmedabad - 380026, Gujarat, India
Mobile: +(91)-9428803452
+(91)-9426060156
Phone: +(91)-(79)-25854632
Fax: +(91)-(79)-25854632

Pledge International
Mr. Pragnesh Patel (Proprietor)
AF- 4, Soham Complex,
Soni Ni Chawl
Ahmedabad - 382415, Gujarat, India
Mobile: +(91)-9909538022
+(91)-9662047327
Phone: +(91)-(79)-22970077
Email: info@pledgeinternational.com
pledgeinternational@gmail.com

Rameshwar Steel Fab
Mr. Mayur Makwana / Mr. Ramesh Bhai (Proprietor)
No. 143, Kamal Estate,
Near Bombay Conductor,
GIDC, Vatva,
Ahmedabad - 382445, Gujarat, India
Mobile: +(91)-9725605639
+(91)-9427109533
+(91)-9426405639
Phone: +(91)-(79)-25830827
Email: rameshwarsteel@gmail.com
info@rameshwar.co.in
d24mayur@gmail.com

Super Metal & Company
Mr. Mukesh Sablok (Proprietor)
No. 3/33, L.I.G. Colony, L
.I.G. Chouraha,
Behind Maya Medical Store,
A. B. Road
Indore - 452008,
Madhya Pradesh, India
Mobile: +(91)-9827212950
+(91)-9406630066
Phone: +(91)-(731)-2554272
+(91)-(731)-2557517
Email: india@supermetalcompany.com
info@omshrisaiseva.org

Varsha Machines
No. 112, Talab Road,
Near Government Primary School,
Mujessar, NIT Faridabad - 121005,
Haryana, India
Mobile: +(91)-9990575712

Rising Industries
Mr. Asim Kuila
Teghoria Loknath Mandir, Jhowtala,
Ghosh Dutta Para, Tanushree Apartment
Kolkata - 700157, West Bengal, India
Mobile: +(91)-9830260440
+(91)-9804212381
+(91)-9733037425
Phone: +(91)-(33)-25700181

Phenix Engineering
Mrs. T. Gayathiri (Managing Director)
148, Bharathiar Road,
R.K.S. Complex,
M.K. Palayam Road, Ganapathy
Coimbatore - 641006,
Tamil Nadu, India
Mobile: +(91)-9345915047
+(91)-9952550447
+(91)-9843233009
Phone: +(91)-(422)-2538444

Sakun Engineers
Mr. Hiten Bhavsar /
Mr. Bharat Bhavsar (Proprietor)
33/a New Arbuda Estate,
Near G.S.t Crossing Road Ranip
Ahmedabad - 382 470,
Gujarat, India
Mobile: +(91)-9825339820
Phone: +(91)-(79)-27523886
Email: sakunindia@yahoo.co.in

Rising Industries
Mr. A. K. Kuila (Manager)
Teghoria Loknath Mandir,
Jhowtala, Ghosh Dutta Para,
Near Honda Service Center,
Tanushree Apartment
Kolkata - 700157,
West Bengal, India
Mobile: +(91)-9804212381
+(91)-9830260440
+(91)-9733037425
Phone: +(91)-(33)-25700181
Email: mail.risingindustries@gmail.com
rising_industries@rediffmail.com

Chapter - 36

SUPPLIERS OF RAW MATERIALS FOR DETERGENTS

Aaykay Detergents & Chemicals
Mr. Anil Arora / Mr. Ajay Arora
(Proprietor)
Adjoining Raikhy Theatre,
Cinema Road
Ludhiana - 141008, Punjab, India
Mobile: +(91)-9815006964
Phone: +(91)-(161)-2721964
+(91)-(161)-2721770
+(91)-(161)-3296033
Fax: +(91)-(161)-2721770
Email: aaykaydetergents@gmail.com
info@aaykaydetergents.com
manakchem@gmail.com

Sahu Silicones & Chemicals Co.
Mr. Mahesh Chandra
(Managing Director)
A - 94/7, Wazirpur Industrial Area
New Delhi - 110052,
Delhi, India
Mobile: +(91)-9350516675
+(91)-9310516675
Phone: +(91)-(11)-47000775
Fax: +(91)-(11)-47000775
Email: sahusilicone@gmail.com
maheshchandra13@rediffmail.com

Soap, Detergent & Cosmetic Making Classes
Veena Dalwai Indus Estate, Opp
Oshiwara post office
Ajit Glass Factory Bus Stop, S.V
Road, Jogeshwari (West)
Mumbai, Maharashtra 4000102,
India
ph: 9870211067
alt: 022-26791703 / 05
Email: nagi652002@yahoo.com

Amro Chemicals Ltd.
Industrial Estate, Plaine Lauzun
Mauritius Postal Address :
P.O.Box 672, Bell Village
Mauritius
Email: info@amrochemicals.com
Phone: +230 2125300
+230 2127898/9

K. Aryan Agro Flavours India Pvt Ltd
Mr. R. K. Gupta (Managing Director)
Plot No. A - 1, Sector- A - 5, 6,
Tronica City,
Loni, Delhi - 201102, Delhi, India
Mobile: +91-9999214297
Phone: +91-11-23921790

Shree Chemicals Industries
Mr. Ajay Trivedi
197, 198, Sanjay Tower, Room No-6,
IInd Floor, Govind Nagar, Kanpur,
Uttar Pradesh - 208 006, India
Mobile: 9335029561
+91-9335029562
Phone: +91-512-3244463
Fax : +91-512-2653707
Email: info@sciindia.netMobile :
Web Site :
www.shreeexporter.comWeb
Page: www.exportersindia.com/
shrechemicals

Shree Harikrupa Industries
Mr. Jignesh Patel (Partner)
Plot No-403, Hare Krishna Complex,
4th Floor, Pritamnagar Slope,
Ellisbridge, Ahmedabad - 380006,
Gujarat, India
Mobile: +919426420428
Phone: 91-79-26578435
30023049
27912600(R)

EIRI
We Create Industrialists

MARKET SURVEY CUM DETAILED TECHNO ECONOMIC FEASIBILITY REPORTS

- To Get Loan / Finance from Banks/ Financial Institutes
- To set up your own Industry/Unit
- To have detailed & Exhausted Data on any Project

Eiri Project Reports are prepared by highly qualified & experienced consultants & Market Research and Analysis supported by a panel of experts and Computerized.

Data provided are reliable and updated collected from manufacturers/ suppliers, plant already comissioned in India

A DETAILED LIST OF READY REPORTS ARE GIVEN IN COMING PAGES

INTRODUCTION : Project Mix, Uses & Applications, Quality Control Measure & their introduction for attaining required properties Economy & productivity competence.

MARKET SURVEY : Market Position, Installed Capacity Production, Anticipated Demand, Present Manufacturers, Statistics of Imports & Exports, Estimated Demand, Demand & Supply gap (if available), LI/IL issued recently.

PROCESS OF MANUFACTURE : Inventory Controls and Tests, Comparative Study of Process for Manufacturing the product, Formulations, Process Sheet Diagram, Process Detail in Stages from raw Materials to finished products.

RAW MATERIALS : Raw material specifications, Market Codes and Raw Material Prices, Sources of Procurement of Raw Materials (Imported/Indigenous)

PLANT AND MACHINERY : Range of Machineries Required, Detailed Specification of Machines and Equipments, Prices of Machineries, Suppliers of Plant and machineries.

LAND AND BUILDING : Total land Area requirement with rates, covered area Break-up with estimated costs of construction.

PROJECT ECONOMICS : Land and Building, Plant Machinery & Other Fixed Assets, Total Capital Investment, Working Capital Assessment, Raw Material & Consumable Stores, Staff Salaries & Wages, Utilities & Overheads, Total Cost of Project, Sources of Finance/Refinance, Break Even Point Determinations.

ANNEXURES OF CHARTS/FINANCIAL ASPECTS : Repayment Schedule for 5 years., Result of Performance, Depreciation Chart for 5 years, Cash Flow Statement for 5 years., Projected Balance Sheet, Land Man Ratio etc.

For assessing Market Potential, Corporate Diversifications, Planning, Investments Decision Making to start your own setup, Entrepreneurs and industrialists are most welcome to contact EIRI at

www.eiriindia.org or www.eiri.in

EIRI Technocrats and Engineers have just prepared "Market Survey Cum Detailed Techno Economic Feasibility Reports" on lucrative products which are most viable and profitable and having bright future scope,

ALL FOLLOWING PROJECT REPORTS ARE READILY AVAILABLE

AUTOMOBILES, MECHANICAL, STEEL & IRON & METALLURGICAL

- Agricultral Equipments
- Aac & Acsr Aluminium Conductors (All Aluminium Conductors)
- Agricultral Equipments Including Threshers
- Air Brake Helical Coil
- Air Cooler
- Air Filters (For Scooter Car & Excavators Etc.)
- Aluminium & Aluminium Alloys From Aluminium Scrap To Make Utensils (Induction Furnace Melted)
- Aluminium Alloy Wheels
- Aluminium Alloys From Aluminium Scrap To Make Utensils (Induction Furnace)
- Aluminium Hot & Cold Rolling Mill
- Aluminium Conductors
- Aluminium Bottle Manufacturing (Cold Extrusion Of Aluminium)
- Aluminium/Copper Cable Lugs
- Aluminium Cans For Beer Pkgs.
- Aluminium Cans For Capacitors
- Aluminium Caps For Injection Vials
- Aluminium Extrusion
- Aluminium Furniture & Hardware
- Aluminium Sheet Rolling Mill
- Alloy Steel Casting (Foundry)
- Aluminium Utensils
- Aluminium Utensils & School Boxes
- Aluminium Wire Drawing And Super Enamelling For Winding
- Anodised Aluminium Utensils
- Anodizing Of Aluminium
- Antimony Oxide From Lead Scrap
- Anti Scale Compound For Adding In Sugar Boilers
- Arc Welding Filter Glass
- Aluminium Foil Cutting & Roll Making
- Auto Flaps For Trucks & Buses
- Automobile Workshop (Garage & Service Centre)
- Auto Bulb
- Auto Electrical Parts (Armature)
- Auto Gears
- Auto Horns
- Auto Leaf Spring
- Auto Tubes
- Auto Piston Ring
- Auto Piston
- Auto Parts (Electricla And Electronic)
- Auto Rubber Parts And Turned Components Silent Block Bush And Ceiling Fan Shaft+
- Auto Wire Outer (Outer For Auto Wire)
- Bakery And Biscuits Equipments Fabrication
- Ball Point Pen Refills
- Ball Roller & Taper Bearing
- Band Saw Blades
- Barbed Wire
- Barrels (Oil)/(Metalliic Barrels)
- Bath Fittings, Turned Components (All Type) Sheet Metal (Job Work) And Hdpe/Pp Moulded Articles
- Battery For Car (Dry)
- Battery Operated Three Wheelers
- Benefication Of Chromite Ore Processing Charge Chrome
- Bicycle Spokes
- Bicycle Assembly
- Brake Lining Asbestoes/Resin Based & Asbestoes Free
- Brass Artware/Hollow Ware Casting (With Thehelp Of Phenolic Resin)
- Brass Casting
- Brass Pipes From Brass Sheet With Longitudinally Welding
- Brass Ware By Casting Method (Brass Articles Viz. Brass Pooja Lamps And Other Casted)
- Bright Bars
- Buffing And Polishing Industry (Job Work)
- Butt Hinge (Brass Sheet)
- Carbon Brush Holder & Slip Ring
- Co Welding Wire Electrodes (Copper/Copper Alloy Coated M.S.Wire)
- Carbon Film Resistors
- Car Dealership (Hyundai)
- Carburettors
- Cast Steel Body Valve
- Cast Steel Panes For Melting Furnace
- Ceramic Coated Steel Pipes
- Chemical Etching Of Stainless Steel
- Chemical Resistant Iron & Steel
- Concast Steel Bars
- Cold Form Section Mill
- Cold Rolled Forming Of Section And Other Sections
- Cold Rolling Of Ms Strip
- Cold Twisted De-Formed Ribbed Steel
- Cold Rolling Mill
- Compressor (Hermetic) For Air Conditioners
- Compressed Natural Gas (Cng Kit) For Autovehicle
- Continuously Cast Steel Wire Rods (5 Mm)
- Continuous Casting Copper Wire Rods
- Conveyor Beltings
- Conveyor Belt, Transmission Belt & V Belts
- Cooking Ranges
- Copper/Brass Sheets,Circle & Utensils
- Copper Foil
- Copper Ingots, Rods Making & Wire Drawing
- Copper Products From Copper Scrap
- Copper Smelting Plant
- Copper Wire Rods From Copper Scrap
- Corrugated Box Making Machinery And Other Their Parts
- Cylinder Liner For Automobiles
- Disposable Plastic Razors
- Door Locks/Pad Locks
- Drill Bits & Tool Bits
- Drum Closures
- Erw Steel Pipes And Tubes
- Erw Steel Conduit Pipe
- Earth Moving Eqpt.
- Engine Valves For Automobiles
- Fabrication Of Heat Exchanger
- Fabrication Of Storage Tanks And M.S. Drum
- Ferrous Alloy Ni-Hardy I.V Casting
- Ferrous Mn Alloy Casting By Alumina Thermic Process
- Ferro Alloys
- Ferro Silicon & Ferro Manganese From Dolomite (Sms Grade)
- Fire Extinguishers
- Fire Fighting Equipments And Appliances
- Flip-Tone Cans
- Forged Conecting Rod
- Forging Unit
- Fountain Pen Nibs
- Foundry Sand
- Free Wheels, Free Wheel Bushes And Free Wheel Plates For Autorickshaws
- Fuel Briquettes From Agro Waste
- Fuel Injection System
- Fused Magnesia
- Generator Canopy
- Galvanized M.S.Strips
- Galvanizing Plant
- Galvanized Iron Wire (G.I. Wire)
- G.I. Pipes
- Gas Welding Torches And Nozzles
- Gasket Sheet
- Gate Grills & Window Frames
- Generating Set (Diesel)
- Hard Anodised Aluminium
- High Pressure Cylinder

Market Survey Cum Detailed Techno Economic Feasibility Report on all Projects are available Contact.
"ENGINEERS INDIA RESEARCH INSTITUTE". 4449, Nai Sarak (D), Main Road, Delhi-110006 (India)
Ph. : 09811437895, 91-11-23918117, 23916431, 45120361, 64727385 Fax : 91-11-23916431
E-mail : eiriprojects@gmail.com, eiribooks@yahoo.com • website: www.eiri.in, www.eiriindia.org

ALL FOLLOWING PROJECT REPORTS ARE READILY AVAILABLE

- Hollow Concrete Spun Pole
- Hospital Wares
- Hospital Furnitures
- Hot Rolling Of Stainless Steel Sheet
- Hot Dip Galvanizing
- Hot Forged Fasteners
- Hot Mix Plant
- Industrial, Petroleum And Nuclear Filter
- Ignition Coil For Automobiles
- Injection Moulded Plastic Compounds With Tool Room
- Injection Moulded Plastic Components And Metal Pipe Spinning Unit
- Investment Casting
- Iron Ore Pelletization Plant
- Iron Ore Mining And Manufacture Of Sponge Iron
- Iron/Steel Wire Gauge
- Iron Tawa
- Knives (S.S.Knives)
- Kitchen Sink (S.S.)
- Lead Tube
- Lead Alloy From Battery Scrap
- L.P.G Regulators
- Lpg Cylinder
- Lpg Stove

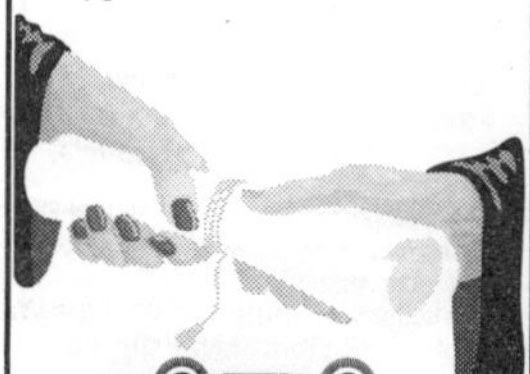

EIRI

is fully capable to prepare any Project Report of your Choice

- Lpg Bottling Plant (Gas Filling)
- M.S. Pipe (Mild Steel Pipe) - Welded
- Machine Screws & Self Tapping Screws
- Machinery For Cold Rolling Mill
- Maruti Workshop Cum Service Station
- Magnesium Ingots & Bullets Casting
- Manufacture Of Tin Containers
- Manufacture Of Storage Tanks, Pressure Vessels, Heat Exchangers
- Mark Ii Hand Pumps
- Maruti Workshop Cum - Service Station
- Mechanical Jacks
- Medical Oxygen Gas Cylinder
- Metal Cable Trays
- Metal Cutting Die Design
- Metal Cutting Of And Grinding Wheels(Abrasive Cutting Wheels)
- Metal Foundry Flux For Aluminium
- Metal Foundry Flux For Cast Iron

Casting
- Metal Hooks & Clips
- Metal Separation (Copp- Er , Tin, Lead) From Spent Wash Acid
- Metallic Ring Joints
- Metallic Gasket (Spiral Wound)
- Microvee & Absolute Filter
- Microwave Oven
- Mild Steel Ingots
- Mini Steel Plant/M.S. Ingot By Induction Furnace
- Mini Steel Plant
- Modern Vehicle Workshop
- Moped
- Mild Steel Nuts
- M.S.Hinges
- M.S.Ingot And Hr. Steel Structurals
- M.S.Ingot By Induction Furnaces
- M.S. Pipes
- M.S. Tubes And Pipes
- M.S. Welding Electrode
- Mufflers & Silencers For Three Wheelers
- Nail Cutter With Filer & Manicure
- Nichrome Wire
- Nickel Lined Screens
- Non-Ferrous Alloy Rolling
- Non-Ferrous Forging
- Non-Ferrous Foundry
- Non Pressure
- Incandescent Lamp
- Number Combination Locks For Luggages
- Nuts & Bolts
- Oxygen Lancing Pipes
- Paper Coated Aluminium And Copper Wire
- Perforated Metal Sheets
- Petromax Container Photo Etching Of Stainless Steel Plates
- Pipe Galvanizing Plant
- Piston Ring-Automobile
- Plant Protection Equipments
- Platinum Laboratory Apparatus
- Pressure Cooker & Aluminium Utensils
- Pressure Cooke(Aluminium)
- Pressure Die Casting
- Printed Aluminium Collapsible Tubes
- Printed Tin Containers
- Printing Press (Cylinder Machine)
- Pumps For Chemical Industry (Special)
- Railway Sleepers (M.S.)
- Razor Twin Blade
- R.C.C Spun Pipes
- Reconditioning Of M.S. Drums/Barrels
- Re-Rolling Copper And Brass Sheet And Rods
- Re-Rolling Mills
- Resin Coated Sand
- Resin Cored Soft Solder Wires
- Rolling Mill
- Rolling Mill (By Induction Furnace) & Manufacture Of Bars, Angles, Squares, Tubes And Others
- Roller Bearing & Forging
- Rolling Of Stainless Steel Patta
- Rollinf Mill By Tmt Technology
- Rubber Insulated Pliers (Hand Tools)

- Rubbing Compound For Automobiles
- Scientific Laboratory Equipments
- Scooter Assembling
- Secondary Lead Extraction By Scrap Battery Plates, Pipes & Sheet
- Seamless M.S. Tubes & Pipes
- Self Tapping Steel Screw
- Sewing Needles
- S.G. Iron & Alloy Steel
- Sheet Metal Products, (Ferrous/Non-Ferrous)
- Steel Drums And Barrels
- Ship/Marine Container
- Shock Absorbers
- Shoe Eyelets
- Shot And Grits By Automization Process
- Shovels
- Silico Manganese Alloys
- Silencers (Mufflers) Exhaust & Tail Pipe For All Types Of Vehicles
- Sintered Bearing
- Sintered Bushes
- Sintered Metal Products
- Soft And Hard Ferrites
- Spanners
- Spark Plugs
- Spin On Filters And Spin On Filters Components (Including Bowls)
- Sponge Iron From Iron Ore
- Steel Plant (Electric Arc Furnace Based- Eaf)
- Spheriodal Graphite Cast Iron
- Spray Dryer
- Stainless Steel Casting By Induction Furnace
- Stainless Steel Hinges
- Stainless Steel Fasteners (Nut And Bolts)
- Stainless Steel Sheet Rolling
- Stainless Steel Pipes
- Stainless Steel Patta
- Stainless Steel Sheet Rolling To Produce Stainless Steel Utensils
- Stainless Steel Utensils
- Stainless Steel Wire Drawing
- Staple Pins,Paper Pin , Gem Clips Etc.
- Steering Wheel And Connecting Rod
- Steel Castings
- Steel Chain
- Steel Foundry
- Steel Furnitures And Electrical Appliances
- Steel Furniture And Room Cooler
- Steel Nipple For Bicycles
- Steel Plant (Mini)
- Steel Re Rolling Mill
- Steel Rods And Coils From Scraps
- Steel Rolling Mill (Reinforcement Bars)
- Steel Rolling Mill
- Steel Strips (Cold Rolled) Silicon With Grain Riented For Electric Use
- Steel Tubular Poles
- Steel Transmission Line Towers & Rolling Mill To Produce Steel Section

Market Survey Cum Detailed Techno Economic Feasibility Report on all Projects are available Contact.
"ENGINEERS INDIA RESEARCH INSTITUTE". 4449, Nai Sarak (D), Main Road, Delhi-110006 (India)
Ph. : 09811437895, 91-11-23918117, 23916431, 45120361, 64727385 Fax : 91-11-23916431
E-mail : eiriprojects@gmail.com, eiribooks@yahoo.com • website: www.eiri.in, www.eiriindia.org

ALL FOLLOWING PROJECT REPORTS ARE READILY AVAILABLE

- Steel Furnitures And Electrical Appliances
- Steel Furniture And Fire Fighting Equipments
- Steel Furniture And Room Cooler
- Steel Wire Drawing And Galvanizing
- Steel Wire/Rod
- Steel Wool
- Ston Scrusher And Screening Plant
- Submerged Arc Welded Pipes
- Submersible Pump Manufacturing
- Super Enamelled Copper Wire
- Super Enamelled Copper Wire (From Copper Cathode Rod)
- Three Wheelers
- Tie-Rod Ends
- Tin Containers
- Toolroom And Sheet Metal Products
- Trolley (Shopping) For Carrying Of Stores At Super Market And Ware Houses
- Tractor Trailers
- Transmission Power Fitting
- Tubular Poles
- Tyre Retreading By Cold Process
- Super Enamelled Copper Wires
- Trolley (Shopping) For Carrying Of Stores At Super Market & Ware Houses
- Tmt Bars
- Tubular Poles For Electrical Transmission (By Fabrication Process)
- Tubular Poles Of M.S. & High Tensile Steel
- V- Belt
- Vacuum Cleaners
- Vacuum Flask (Stainless Steel)
- Valves For Refrigeration And Air-Condition
- Vehicle Welding & Painting
- Venetion Blind
- Washing Machines (Automatic & Computerised)
- Water Controller (Automatic)
- Watch Straps/Chains/ Bracelets/Belt Brass & Stainless Steel
- Water Coolers
- Welded Wire Mesh
- Welding Electrodes
- Wheel Barrow
- Wick Stoves
- Wind Mill Window Frame (Ferrous & Non-Ferrous)
- Wrist Watch

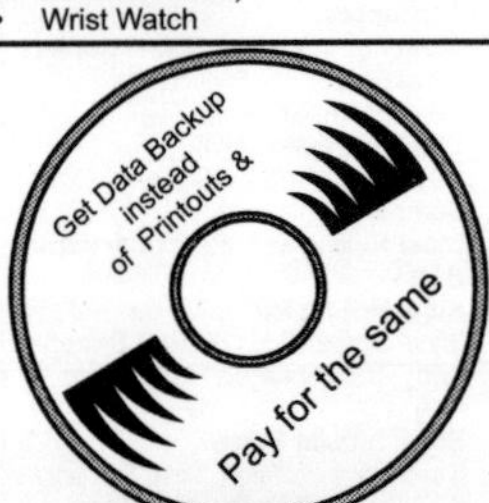

CHEMICALS (ORGANIC & INORGANIC) WITH PETROLEUM PRODUCTS

- Acetic Anhydride
- Acetic Acid (Glacial)
- Acetic Acid From Ethanol
- Acetone
- Acetylene Black
- Acetyl Chloride
- Acetylene Gas
- Acetylene Gas & Oxygen Gas (Integrated Unit)
- Acid Black Dye
- Acid Slurry
- Activated Alumina
- Activated Bleaching Earth (Activated Fullers Earth)
- Activated Carbon From Cashewnut Shell
- Activated Carbon From Rice Husk
- Activated Carbon From Rice Husk, Coconut Shell & Coconut Powder
- Activated Carbon From Wood
- Activated Carbon Powder & Granules From Coconut Shell
- Activated Carbon & Sodium Silicate From Paddy & Rice Husk
- Alcohol From Broken Rice
- Alum For Water Treatment
- Adhesive (Fevicol Type)
- Aerosol Insecticides Spray (Baygon, Hit, Mortein Type)
- Agarbatti Synthetic Perfumery Compounds
- Alcohol From Potato
- Alcohol From Rice Grains
- Alcohol From Rice Husk
- Alcohol From Molasses
- Alcohol, Beer, Starch, Liquid Glucose, Dextrose, Sorbitol, Vitamin-C,
- Alcoholic Beverages And Vinegar From Coconut Water
- Germ Oil, Cattle Feed Etc. From Maize
- Alkyd Resin
- Alkylated Phenol Likenonyl Phenol, Dodecyl Phenol
- Alum (Non Ferric)
- Alum (Ferric)
- Aluminium Chloride From Aluminium Ore
- Alum Cake
- Alum From Aluminium Hydrate
- Aluminium Ingot By Bauxite
- Aluminium Phosphide
- Aluminium Phosphate
- Aluminium Sulphate (Non Ferric Alum) 17% - 18% Alumina Content In Granules (2 Mm To 4 Mm) And Flakes
- Amines & Allied Products
- Amino Acid
- Ammonia Gas
- Ammonia Gas Bottling
- Ammonia Liquor
- Ammonium Nitrate
- Ammonium Chloride (Pure & Technical)
- Ammonium Sulphate
- Annato Seed Extraction And Processing
- Anti Corrosion Chemicals
- Anthranilic Acid From Phthalic Anhydride
- Anesthesia (All Types) Used In Hospitals
- Aniline
- Argon Gas
- Ariel Type Detergent Powder
- Anthraquinone
- Antimony Trioxide
- Atenolol
- Auramine "O"
- Azodicarbonamide
- Baking Soda From Ash
- Barium Carbonate
- Barium Compounds
- Barium Nitrate
- Barium Peroxide
- Barium-Thio-Sulphate Banzene
- Baryte Powder
- Bar Soap (All Varieties) Using Soap Noodles
- Beer Plant
- Belt Paste
- Beneficiation Of Chromite Ore Processing Charge Chrome
- Benzyl Acetate, Benzyl Benzoate, Benzyl Alcohol
- Beta Naphthol
- Bentonite Powder
- Benzoic Acid
- Benzidine
- Biofertiliser From Mother Culture
- Bio Oil For Power Generation From Coffee Husk
- Bio Gas Plant
- Bio Gas Filling In Cylinder
- Bio Tech Unit
- Bi-Chromate Of Sodium, Potassium & Ammonium
- Bi-Functional Black Mfgr.Reactive Dye (Dye From Cotton Yarn Dyeing)
- Bio-Fuel (Jatropha Cultivation And Extraction)
- Bituminous Roademulsion
- Black Phenyl
- Black Sulphur
- Bleaching Powder (Stable)
- Blue Detergent Powder
- Bone Crushing Plant
- Bone Meal (Calcined) Enrichment With Calcium & Phosphorus
- Boric Acid
- B.O.N. Acid
- Bromine Gas Plant
- Brandy
- Butanol
- Butyl Rubber For The Manufacture Of Tubes For Truck And Car Tyres
- 1,4, Butanediol
- Butyl Acetate
- Caffein From Tea Waste
- Calcined Lime (Dead Burnt Dolomite)

Market Survey Cum Detailed Techno Economic Feasibility Report on all Projects are available Contact.
"ENGINEERS INDIA RESEARCH INSTITUTE". 4449, Nai Sarak (D), Main Road, Delhi-110006 (India)
Ph. : 09811437895, 91-11-23918117, 23916431, 45120361, 64727385 Fax : 91-11-23916431
E-mail : eiriprojects@gmail.com, eiribooks@yahoo.com • website: www.eiri.in, www.eiriindia.org

ALL FOLLOWING PROJECT REPORTS ARE READILY AVAILABLE

- Calcined Petroleum Coke
- Calcining Of Magnesite & Dead Burnt Magnesite
- Calcium Aluminate
- Calcium Based Grease
- Calcium Carbide
- Calcium Carbonate
- Calcium Carbonate (Precipitated) From By Product (Lime Slurry & Carbon Dioxide)
- Calcium Carbonate (Activated & Precipitated)
- Calcium Chloride
- Calcium Gluconate
- Calcium Nitrate
- Calcium Silicate Bricks
- Calcium Stearate By Fusion Process
- Camphor Powder (Synthetic)
- Construction Chemicals (With Detailed Market Survey And Formulae Etc.)
- Carbon Dioxide
- Carbon Black From Fertilizer Waste
- Carbon Black (Petroleum Based)
- Carboxy Methyl Cellulose (Cmc)
- Casein And By Products
- Casein From Milk
- Cationic Softner (Stearic Acid Based)
- Caustic Soda
- Caustic Soda From Soda Ash By Soda Lime Process
- Caustic Soda (Liquid) By Electrolytic Process
- Caustic Soda From Trona
- Caustic Soda, Chlorine And Hydrogen Gas By Electro-Lysis Of Brine Solution
- Cellulose Acetate Moulding Powder
- Cellulose Powder & Micro Crystalline Cellulose Powder
- Cement Admixture
- Cement Colour
- Cement Water Proofing Compound
- Cement From Fly Ash & Lime
- Cement Tiles (Glazed)
- Chlorinated Paraffin Wax (Cpw)
- Citric Acid From Lemon
- Citric Acid From Molasses
- Double Firing (Heating)
- Chelated Zinc (Zn Edta)
- Chemicals From Prawn Head
- Chitin & Chitosan From Prawn Shell Waste
- Chloral Hydrate
- Chloramphenicol
- Chromic Acid (With Pollution Control)
- Chromic Acid (Oxide) & Blue Oxide
- Chlorinated Paraffin Wax (Cpw)
- Chromic Acid
- Cement Paint & Distemper
- Citric Acid From Lemon
- Citric Acid From Molasses
- Cleaning Of Cooling System And Boiler
- Coal Tar Distillation
- Coal Washing Plant
- Cobalt Octoate

- Compost For Mushroom
- Construction Chemicals
- Copper Oxychloride
- Coolant (Engine)
- Copper Phthalocyanine Blue & Green
- Correction Fluid
- Cupric Chloride
- Crude Oil Bleaching For Petroleum Jelly
- Cutting Oil
- Cyanuric Chloride
- Cyanoacrylate Adhesive
- Cutting Oil
- Defoaming Agent For Paper Industry
- De-Nickeling (Electrolytic Process)
- Detergent Cake & Powder
- Detergent Powder
- Detergent Concentrate (Idet 10)
- Dextrose Monohydrate & Dextrose Anhydrous Powder From Tapioca Starch
- Di-Basic Lead Stearate
- Di Calcium Phosphate
- Diclofenal Sodium Slow Release (Sr) Tables 100mg.
- Di Ethyl Oxalate
- Di Methyl Orthophthalate
- Di-Methyl Phthalate
- Diclofenac Gel
- Dioctyl Phthalate (Dop)
- Di Phenyl Glycerine
- Di Phenyl Oxide
- Dinitro-Chloro Benzene
- Distillery
- Distilled Water
- Dodecyl Benzene Sulphonate
- Dustless Chalk
- Edta & Its Salts
- Electroless Nickel Plating On Plastics
- Electrolyte (Like Sulphuric Acid) For Lead Acid Dry Rechargable 5.5.Ah. Battery
- Electropolishing On Gold Jewellery
- Electropolishing On Various Metals
- Endosulfan
- Enzyme Based Detergent Powder
- Ephedrine Hydrochloride
- Epoxy Resin Based Compound
- Ethanol (Biofuel)
- Ethyl Alcohol From Molasses
- Ethyl Acetate
- Ehtyl Ether
- Ethyl Alcohol (Potable Liquor)
- Ethyl Hexanol
- Extra Temperature Lubricating Grease
- Extraction Of Essential Oils By Sugar Critical Fluid (Carbon Dioxide) Method From Flowers, Herbal & Spices
- Fabric Stain Remover
- Fatty Acid
- Ferric Alum
- Ferric And Non Ferric Alum (Aluminium Sulphate)
- Ferro Chrome Ligno Sulphonate
- Ferro Manganese
- Ferro Silicone

Contact EIRI for required Project report apart from this list.

- Ferro Vanadium From Vanadium Sludge
- Ferrous Silicate
- Ferrous Sulphate
- Ferrous Sulphide
- Fertilizer From Animal Blood & Leather Waste
- Fluorescent Tube Light Powder
- Foamed Pvc Compounding & Its Products
- Formaldehyde
- Food Grade Grease Or Lubricant
- Fractional Distillation Of D.M.O (Dementholized Oil)
- Fractional Distillation Of Essential Oil & Medicinalplant Extract
- Friction Dust (Liquid & Powder) From Cnsl
- Fruit Flavours
- Furfural From Rice Husk
- Fumaric Acid
- Gas Filling Of Lpg Cylinder
- Garlic Acid
- Ginger And Garlic Paste
- Ginger Processing
- Gasket Shellac Compound
- Gear Oil
- Gibberellic Acid
- Glass Putty
- Gluconic Acid
- Glucose D- Powder
- Glycerine
- Gossypol (Poly Phenol) From Cotton Seed Oil
- Greases (Lithium Based)
- Guar Gum Powder
- Hair Fixer (Hair Gel Type)
- High Temerature Grease
- Hard Grease
- H - Acid
- Henna Paste Making
- Henna Powder Repackaging
- Heptal Dehyde
- Herbal Beer
- High Carbon Ferro Chrome
- Humid Acid
- Hydrated Calcium Silicate Brick
- Hydrated Lime From Sea Shell
- Hydrochloric Acid
- Hydro Fluoric Acid
- Hydrogen Peroxide (By Auto-Oxidation Process)
- Ice Packs (Solutions Type, White Gel Type, Violet Semi Solid Polymer Type)
- Improving Drop Point Paraffin Wax From 45-50°c To 75-80°c
- Industrial Alcohol

Market Survey Cum Detailed Techno Economic Feasibility Report on all Projects are available Contact.
"ENGINEERS INDIA RESEARCH INSTITUTE". 4449, Nai Sarak (D), Main Road, Delhi-110006 (India)
Ph. : 09811437895, 91-11-23918117, 23916431, 45120361, 64727385 Fax : 91-11-23916431
E-mail : eiriprojects@gmail.com, eiribooks@yahoo.com • website: www.eiri.in, www.eiriindia.org

ALL FOLLOWING PROJECT REPORTS ARE READILY AVAILABLE

- Integerated Complex Of Easter & Allied Products (D.O.P, D.B.P, Ethyl Acetate Wire Enamel & Cable Jelly)
- Insta Whitening System (Ujala Type)
- Imfl (Whisky) & Country Liquor
- Imfl (Whiskey) From Potato
- Iron Oxide For Making Feritte
- Iron Sulphide
- Jatropha (Biodiesel) Cultivation And Extraction
- J. Acid
- Jute Batching Oil
- Kesh Kala Tel (Hair Dye Lotion) (Vasmol 33, Black Nite Type)
- L-Lysine Monohydrochloride
- Lactic Acid From White Sugar By Fermentation Process
- Ldpe Granules From Virgin (Ldpe Resin)
- Lead Extraction From Battery Scrap
- Lead Oxide
  (A) Lead Monoxide
  (B) Lead Tetra Oxide
  (C) Greylead Oxide
- Liquid Glucose & Its By Products
- Liquid Gold (In Paste Form)
- Lemon Oil From Lemon
- Liquid Oxygen Bottling Plant
- Liquid Shoe Polish
- Liquid Floor Polish
- Lithium Based Grease
- Linear Alkyl Benzene Sulphonate
- Lube Oil Viscosity Improved For P.P.G/P.E.G.
- Lube Oil And Greases
- Lube Oil From Cnsl To Reduce Friction
- Lubricants Ashless 100% Combustion
- Maize Oil
- Magnesium Carbonate And Magnesium Bicarmonate
- Magnesium Hydroxide Powder
- Magnesium Silicate
- Magnesium Sulphate
- Malachite Green
- Maleic Acid
- Maleic Anhydride
- Manganese Sulphate
- Manufacturing Of Carbon Mono-Oxide Water Gas
- Menthol Bold Crystals From Flakes
- Menthol Crystal & Mentha Oil
- Mercuric Oxide
- Metal Pre-Treatment Chemicals
- Methyl Chloride
- Methyl Cinnamate
- Methane Gas By Sodium Acetate & Soda Lime
- Methyl Acetyl Ricinolate
- Methyl Parathion 2% Dust Powder
- Methyl Stearate
- Metol
- Metol From Hydroqui-None & Methylamine
- Micanite
- Micro Crystalline Wax
- Micro Nutrient Mixture
- Mineral Water
- Mineral Water And Pet Bottilng Plant
- Mineral Water In Bottles, Glass And Pouches
- Mini Cement Plant (By Rotary Kiln Process)
- Mixed Fertilizer
- Mosquito Repellent Vaporiser (Liquid Mosquito Destroyer)
- Mosquito & Flies Repellent Agarbatti (Incense Sticks)
- Monochloro Acetic Acid
- Monocrotophos (Technical)
- Mosquito Coil
- Mosquito Coil & Mat
- Mosquito Mat
- Mosquito Net
- Mosquito Coil Agarbatti
- Mother Tincture & Bio Chemic Medicines
- Naphthalene & Phenyl (Integrated Unit)
- Natural Mineral Water By Reverse Osmosis Process
- Nickel Plating Brightner (Primary Or Carrier Brightner & Secondary Brightner)
- Nickel Sulphate
- Nicotine From Tobacco Waste
- Nicotine Sulphate From Tobacco Waste
- Nitro Benzene
- Nitro Cellulose Sanding Sealer/Lacquer
- Nitro Musk
- Nitrogen & Oxygen Gas Plant
- Non-Ionic Surfactant (Wetting Agent)
- No-Carb Paste
- Npk Mixed Fertilizer (Molasses Based)
- N.P.K Fertilizer
- Octanol
- Oleoresin From Chilly And Ginger (Extraction)
- Oleoresins From Marigold Petals (Extraction)
- Organic Fertiliser
- Ortho Nitro Phenol
- Ortho Phthalic Polyester
- Oxalic Acid From Molasses
- Oxalic Acid From Rice Husk
- Oxalic Acid From Tree Bark
- Oxalic Acid From Waste Vegetables
- Oxygen Gas Plant
- Oxygen And Nitrogen Gas Plant
- Oxygen Gas Plant (Air Seperation Method)
- Para-Amino Benzoic Acid
- Para-Amino Phenol
- Para Toluene Sulphonic Acid
- Pectin From Raw Papaya
- Pectin From Apple Pomace
- Pectin From Mango Peel
- Pectin From Oranges
- Pectin From Citrus/Lemon
- Perfume (Lemon & Others)
- Perfume Spray Deodorant (Non-Alcoholic)
- Pest Control
- Pesticide Preparation Using Neem Fruit & Seeds (Margosa)
- Pet Bottles From Pre-Form
- Pet Granules (Dana)
- Pet Preform From Resin For Pet Bottles
- Petroleum Jelly
- Phenol
- Phenyl Acetic Acid
- Phenyl
- Phenyl (Black) In Liquid Form
- Phthalic Anhydride
- Phosphoric Acid From Rock Phosphate
- Phosphorus By Chemical Process
- Photo Emulsion For Rotary Screen Printing
- Phthalocyanine Blue
- Pigment Emulsion For Textile
- Pigment Gum
- Plant Growth Reagen Based Chlorothyltrimethyl Ammonium Chloride
- Plant Harmones Based On 2,4-Dichlorphenoxy
- Acentic Acid & Naphthalene
- Plastazote Polythylene Foam Used For Fibre Cable Joint
- Plasticine (Modelling Clay)
- Plastic Waste Reprocessing
- Plaster Of Paris Bandages
- Polyester Resin (G.P. Grade Laminate Grade, Electrical Grade)
- Polyol From Propylene Oxide
- Poly Vinyl Acetate
- Polyvinyl Acetate Emulsion
- Polyvinyl Alcohol
- Polyurethene Foam
- Potassium Dichromate/Bichromate
- Potassium Iodate
- Potassium Nitrate
- Potassium Permagnate
- Potassium Per Sulphate
- Potassium Sulphate (Fertilizer Grade)
- Potassium Per Oxy Di-Sulphide
- Potassium Silicate By Ion Exchange Process
- Potassium Silicate
- Potassium Stearate
- Processing Of Datura Stramonium Into Hyosyamina And Atropin
- Power Alcohol
- Pvc Resin From Ethyl Alcohol
- Pyridine & Its Derivatives
- Rapid Fast Dyes (Only Process)
- Reactor (Chemical)
- Resorcinol
- Reclamation Of Used Engine Oil (By Clay & Vacuum Distillation Process)
- Refinery Petrol/Diesel Etc.
- Reclamation Of Spent Bleaching Earth
- Reclamation Of Nickel Spent Catalyst From Vanaspati Industry
- Rectified Spirit From Molasses & Mahua Flowers
- Rectified Spirit From Rice Straw
- Red Oxide Paint/Primer (Anti Corrosive) Based Organic Red Pigments
- Refinery Petrol/Diesel Etc.
- Removal Of Antimony From Lead Scrap
- Resorcinol
- Rice Bran Oil (Rbo)
- Rosin Sizing Agent

Market Survey Cum Detailed Techno Economic Feasibility Report on all Projects are available Contact.
"ENGINEERS INDIA RESEARCH INSTITUTE", 4449, Nai Sarak (D), Main Road, Delhi-110006 (India)
Ph. : 09811437895, 91-11-23918117, 23916431, 45120361, 64727385 Fax : 91-11-23916431
E-mail : eiriprojects@gmail.com, eiribooks@yahoo.com • website: www.eiri.in, www.eiriindia.org

ALL FOLLOWING PROJECT REPORTS ARE READILY AVAILABLE

- Resorcinol
- Rust Prevention Lube Oil
- Saline And Injection Water
- Salicylic Acid
- Santonin
- Sennosides From Senno Leaf
- Silicone Grease
- Shoe Polish
- Silica Gel (Blue Self Indicating Process)
- Silica Ramming Mass
- Silicone Emulsion
- Silicone From Rice Husk
- Silicon From Silica (Semi Conductor Grade)
- Silicon Grease
- Silicone Resins
- Silicone Spraysilver Brazing Foil
- Silver Extraction From Waste Hypo Solution
- Silver Nitrate
- Silver Parts For Ceramic Capacitor Single Super
- Phosphate & Mixed Fertilizer (Npk)
- Single Super Phosphate (S.S.P) & Sulphuric Acid
- Soda Ash
- Soda Ash From Natron
- Soda Water Bottling Plant (Carbonated Beverage)
- Sodium Aluminate
- Odium Benzoate
- Sodium Bi-Carbonate (Baking Soda) From Soda Ash
- Sodium Chlorite
- Sodium Chromate
- Sodium Cyclamate
- Sodium Di-Chromate
- Sodium Di-Chromate & Sodium Sulphate As Bye Products
- Sodium Hexa Meta Phosphate
- Sodium Hydrosulfite
- Sodium Hypo Chloride (Bleach Liquor)
- Sodium Iso-Propyl Xanthate
- Sodium Lauryl Sulphate
- Sodium Lauryl Sulphate & Sodium Lauryl Ether Sulphate
- Sodium Nitrate
- Sodium Petroleum Sulphonate (Emulsifier)
- Sodium Silicate From Silica & Soda Ash
- Sodium Silicate From (1) Paddy Silk Husk 2) & Silica
- Sodium Silicate By Hydro Thermic Process Using Quartz And Caustic Lye
- Sodium Carbonate & Silica
- Sodium Sulphate
- Sodium Sulphide By Barium Sulphate Process
- Sodium Sulphide From Ammonia & Sodium Chloride
- Sodium Sulphite
- Sodium Tri-Poly Phosphate
- Softener (Cationic Anionic & Non-Ionic)
- Spirit From Pine Apple
- Stannous Chloride
- Stearic Acid
- Stearates Manufacture (Calcium, Zinc, Aluminium, Magnesium Stearates)
- Sulfanilic Acid In Powder Form
- Sulphur From Pyrites & Slag
- Sulphur Crystals/Lumps
- Sulphuric Acid
- Sulphuric Acid From Dcda Process
- Super Phosphate (S.S.P)
- Synthetic Iron Oxide (Yellow)
- Synthetic Red & Wellow Iron Oxide From Iron Filling & Pickle Liquor
- Synthetic Zeolite
- Tannic Acid
- Tartaric Acid
- Teflon Grease
- Textile Marker Pen/Tube
- Toilet Cleaner
- Toluene And Sbp From Crude Naphtha
- Trimethyl Ammonium Chloride
- Triphenyl Phosphite (T.P.P)
- Ultramarine Blue (Liquid)
- Urea Formaldehyde & Melamine Formaldehyde Powder
- Undecylinic Acid
- Vinyl Acetate Monomer
- Vitamin C
- Vitamin E
- Waste Water Treatment Plant For Industrial Sector In India (Only Marker Survey)
- Washing Soap And Powder
- Wall Putty
- Water Proofing Chemicals
- Water Treatment Plant
- Weedicide
- Wire Drawing Lubricants
- Wire Enamels
- Wood Polish (Non Alcoholic)
- Xanthates
- Yellow Dextrin
- Zinc Chloride
- Zinc Oxide
- Zinc Phosphating By Cold Process
- Zinc Silicate
- Zinc Stearate
- Zinc And Copper Sulphate From Brass Ash
- Zinc Sulphate
- Zinc Sulphate Monohydrate
- Acid Black
- Auramine'o'
- Azo Dyes Stuff
- Dye & Dye Intermediate
- Dye Intermediates
- Malachite Green
- Methylene Blue
- Phthalocyanine Blue
- Phthalocyanine Blue & Green
- Reactive Dyes
- Sulphur Black Dye
- Vat Dyes
- Water Chilling Plant
- Water Treatment Chemicals
- Water Treatment Plant
- Wadding Oil (100%) For Wadding Of Cotton
- Hosiery Cloth In The Dyeing Process
- White Oil
- Wax Floor Polish

ELECTRICAL, ELECTRONICS, COMPUTERS AND INFOTECH/IT PROJECTS

- Air Conditioning
- Aluminium Alloy Conductor
- Aac And Acsr Aluminium Conductors
- Aluminium Cable
- Aluminium Electroytic Capacitors
- Audio Cassette Assembling & Recording
- Audio Cassettes Duplicating Recording
- Audio Cassettes & Audio Studio
- Audio Cassettes Plane & Recorded
- Audio Magnetic Heads
- Audio Magnetic Tape
- Audio/Video Cassettes
- Auto Bulb/Lamps
- Automatic Voltage Stabilizer
- Battery Plates
- Business Process Outsourcing (Bpo)
- B/W Tv & Computer Monitor Picture Tube
- Bread Boards
- Call Centre
- Call Centre – International
- Camera (35 Mm)
- Capacitors
- Carbon Electrode Used For Battery Cell
- Carbon Potetiometers
- Ceiling Fan
- Ceiling Fan (Stainless Steel)
- Ceramic Insulator
- Children Infotech Training Institute (Rs. 10000/-)
- Choke And Patti
- Choke And Starter
- Choke Used For Fluorescent Lamps
- Colour Television
- Colour And Black & White Television
- Compact Disc
- Compact Disc Player (Audio/Video)
- Computer Education Institute
- Computer Assembly
- Computer Hardware
- Computer Keyboard
- Computer Peripherals
- Computer Printers
- Computer Ribbon
- Computer Ribbon Reinking Or Refilling
- Computer Stationery
- Computer Stationery & Imported Hardware Parts
- Computer Terminals
- Computerised Washing Machine (Automatic)
- Computer Software

Market Survey Cum Detailed Techno Economic Feasibility Report on all Projects are available Contact.
"ENGINEERS INDIA RESEARCH INSTITUTE". 4449, Nai Sarak (D), Main Road, Delhi-110006 (India)
Ph. : 09811437895, 91-11-23918117, 23916431, 45120361, 64727385 Fax : 91-11-23916431
E-mail : eiriprojects@gmail.com, eiribooks@yahoo.com • website: www.eiri.in, www.eiriindia.org

ALL FOLLOWING PROJECT REPORTS ARE READILY AVAILABLE

- Condenser For Motor Using Mpp Film
- Control Panel Board
- Cooling Coil For Air Conditioners
- Copper Strip Coil From Scrap
- Cordless Telephones
- Cyber Cafe
- Cyberkiosk
- Data Processing Centre
- D.C. Micro Motors
- D.G.Sets
- Display Systems (Led Type)
- Dish Antenna And Cable T.V. Network Equipment
- Distribution Transformers & Repairs
- Domestic Electrical Appliances-Room Cooler, Washing Machine, Water Heater, Electric Room Heater
- E-Commerce/Business
- Electric Energy Meter
- Electric Fans
- Electric Horn For Automobile
- Electric Lamp/Gls (Incandescent Lamp)
- Electric Mixer
- Electric Motors Up To 10 Hp. Rewinding Of All Types Of Motors Water Pumps
- Electric Motor Winding (For Fan, Mixies, Etc.)
- Electric Steam Iron
- Electrical Appliances
- Electrical Fixtures
- Electrical Stamping
- Electrolytic Capacitors
- Electromagnetic Relay
- Electronic Balast/Chok
- Electrical Choke
- Electronic Digital Watches
- Electronic Digital Weighing Machine
- Electronic Fire Alarm
- Electronic Gas Stove Lighters
- Electronic Phones, Dry Battery Packs And Chargers/Adapters
- Electronic Pressure Indicators, Electricals, Electronic Liquid Level Indicators, Electronic Temperature Indicator, Digital Tachometer
- Electronic Telephone Instruments
- Electronic Toys
- Electronic Watches & Clocks
- Fax Machines
- F.H.P Motors
- Floppy Diskettes
- Fluorescent Lamp Starter
- Fluorescent Tubular Lamps With Introduction To Mercury Vapour Lamp
- Franchisee Computer Education Centre (Rs. 10000)
- Gas Detector (L.P.G)
- Generator Set & Pump Sets
- Generator (Battery Operated)
- Gis Service Centre (Geographical Information Systems)
- Hardware Fitting For Transmission Line (Overhead Line Material
- Headers For Transistor Ics Semi Conductor
- H.T & L.T Insulators
- H.T & M.V Industrial Cubical Switch Board
- Information Moving Display (L.E.D Type)
- Insurance Claim Processing Centre (Eou) (Rs. 10000/-)
- Integrated Circuits
- Internet Based Stock Trading (Rs. 10000/-)
- Internet Service Provider (I.S.P.)
- Jelly Filled Telephone Cables
- Lap Top Computers
- Lead Acid Batteries
- Lead Acid Battery Plates And Assembling Of Battery
- Legal Transcription & Secretarial Services Center (Eou)(Rs. 15000/-)
- Light Emitting Diodes (L.E.D)
- Linear Ics Trainer Kit
- Loud Speaker
- L.T Transformer Repairing
- Medical Transcription Centre
- Metal Film Resistors
- Metallised Polypropylene, Polyester Film Capacitor
- Mica Base Electronic Components
- Mica Paper Waste Paper From Mica Waste
- Micro Processors Trainer Kits Based On Micro Processors
- Mini Computer (Personal Computer)
- Miniature Circuit Breaker (M.C.B)
- Miniature Watch Batteries (Button Cell)
- Mixer/Grinder (Mixi)
- Mono Chrome Computer Monitor
- Motor Start Electrolytic Capacitor
- Multi Layer P.C.B
- Multiple Relay For Low Voltage
- Neon Indicator
- Neon Sign Manufacture
- Optical Fibre Cables
- On Line Shopping Mall (Rs. 10000/-)
- Opto Mechanical & Electrical Equipments
- Photo Colour Lab
- Picture Tube (B/W)
- Plain Paper Copier
- Plastic Film Capacitors
- Polyester Capacitors
- Portable Generator Set
- Portal
- Portable Television(Tv)
- Power Capacitors

- Power Inverters
- Power Plant (Gas Based)
- Power Plant (Hydro Based)
- Power Transformers Up To 600 Kva
- Printed Circuit Board
- Pvc Wires & Cables
- Pvc Pipe And Fitting
- Re-Conditioning Of Picture Tube
- Resin Cast Ct & Pt (1 Kv)
- Semi Conductor Device
- Semi Conductors For Transistors & Diodes
- Setting Up Of A Video Studio
- Smoke Detectors
- Solar Cells
- Solar Modules
- Solar Power Plant (Energy)
- Solar Photo Voltaic System
- Solder Fluxes
- Solar Water Heating Panels
- Steel Furniture & Electrical Appliances
- Stereo Amplifiers
- Stereo Cassette Recorders/Players
- Street Light Fittings Surge Suppressor
- Tantalum Capacitors
- Teflon Coated Electric Cable
- Telemedicine (Distance Health Care) (Rs. 10000/-)
- Telephone Cord/Cable
- Telephone (Push Button Type)
- Telephone (Push Button & Cordless)
- Television (Ctv & B/W)
- Television (3-D)
- Television Deflection Components
- Television Signal Boosters
- Television Tuners
- Traction Batteries
- Training Institute Of Medical Transcription
- Transformer For B/W Tv
- Transformer For Voltage Stabilizer & E.H.T
- Transmission Power Line Fitting
- Transmission Tower Fitting
- T.V. News Channel
- Tv Audio Equipment Cabinets & Their Assembling Unit
- Un-Interrupted Power Supply (U.P.S)
- Variable Frequency
- Variable Voltage A.C. Drive
- Video Cassettes (Complete Manufacturing & Assembling)
- Video Cassettes Recorder (V.C.R)
- Video Film Studio
- Voltage Regulator For Automobiles
- Voltage Stabilizers
- Voltage Stablizer & T.V. Gain Booster
- Wax And Chemical Coated, Braided Tinsel Wire
- Website Design & E-Mail Registering
- Welding Electrodes
- Wind Energy Power Project (10 Mw)
- Wire Wound Potentiometers
- Wire Wound Resistance

Market Survey Cum Detailed Techno Economic Feasibility Report on all Projects are available Contact.
"ENGINEERS INDIA RESEARCH INSTITUTE". 4449, Nai Sarak (D), Main Road, Delhi-110006 (India)
Ph. : 09811437895, 91-11-23918117, 23916431, 45120361, 64727385 Fax : 91-11-23916431
E-mail : eiriprojects@gmail.com, eiribooks@yahoo.com • website: www.eiri.in, www.eiriindia.org

ALL FOLLOWING PROJECT REPORTS ARE READILY AVAILABLE

FOOD, AGRO FOOD, PROCESSED FOOD, AGRO PLANTATION, CULTIVATION, FARMING, DAIRY/MILK, TOBACCO/PAN MASALA, BREWERY & DISTILLERY, EDIBLE OILS, EOU FOOD PRODUCTS AND ALLIED PRODUCTS

- Alcoholic Beverages & Venegar From Coconut Water
- Alcohol Drinks From Ethyl Alcohol By Mixing Of Various Flavours
- Amla Fruit Products With Preservation Tomato Sauce, Pickles Jam And Jellies
- Anti Scale Compound For Adding Into Sugar Juice Boiling
- Apple Juice Concentrated & Dehydrated Fruit & Vegetables
- Artificial Fish Meal For Poultry Feed
- Automatic Biscuit Making Plant
- Automatic Bread Making Unit
- Baby Cereal Food And Milk Powder
- Baby Corn
- Bacteria For Cane Juice
- Baker's Yeast
- Bakery Industry
- Banana Puree
- Barley Malt
- Beer & Wine
- Beer Plant (Brewery)
- Bidi
- Bidi & Cigarette
- Biscuit Plant
- Bread (Automatic Plant)
- Black Pepper (Spices)
- Bread And Biscuits
- Breeding Farm
- Broiler Chicken
- Button Mushroom Cultivation & Processing
- Canning Of Rasagullas In Metal Cans
- Caffein From Tea Waste
- Canning Of Fruits & Vegetables
- Casein From Milk
- Casein And By-Products
- Cashew Fruit Juice From Cashew Fruit Apple
- Cashewnut Kernel Extraction From Cashewnut Fruit
- Cashewnut Shell Liquid & Kernel Processing
- Cashew Feni
- Catecheu (By Chemical Process)
- Cattle Feed From Tapioca
- Chewing & Bubble Gum
- Chicken/Sheep Meat Processing
- Chocolate (Milk)
- Cigarette And Beedies
- Cocoa Butter From Cocoa Mass
- Coconut Water (Coco Jal) - Packed
- Coconut Products & By Products Process Complex
- Cold/Soft Drinks
- Collection Of Milk And Milk Making Powder
- Collection Of Milk And Packing In Polythene Pouch (1/2 Kg.1 Kg. & 2 Kg.)
- Condensed Milk (Sweetned)
- Cold Storage
- Confectionery Industry (Toffee & Candy, Semi-Automatic Plant)
- Confectionery Unit With Toffee, Candy, Chewing Gum And Bubble Gum
- Corn Flakes
- Country Liquor From Molasses
- Custard Powder
- Cigarette
- Dairy Farm And Dairy (Milk) Products (Pasteurised Milk, Butter, Ghee, Paneer)
- Dairy Farm To Produce Milk & Packing In Pouches (50%) & Can(50%)
- Dairy For Milk Processing
- Dairy Farming (Buffalo)
- Dairy Farming (Jersey Cow)
- Dal (Pulse) Mill Unit
- Dehydration Of Carrot & Garlic
- Dehydration & Canning Of Fruits & Vegetables
- Dehydration Of Figs
- Dehydration Of Fruits And Vegetables By Vacuum Drying Method
- Dehydration Of Fruits And Vegetables By Iqf Technology
- Dehydrated Onions And Onion Powder
- Drinking Water (Packaged)
- Dry Ice By Breaking Of Air
- Drying Of Red Chillies, Haldi, Dhania, And Green Peas
- Egg Powder (40,000 Eggs Processing Per Day)
- Export Of Processed Foods And Marine Products
- Fish Canning & Pouching
- Fish Farming (Prawn & Other Marine Products)
- Fish Meal
- Flour Mill And Mustard Oil
- Flavoured Milk
- Food Colour & Orasted Groundnut Gram Peas, Etc In Pouches
- Frog Legs Processing
- Frozen Meats Processing
- Food Flavours (Whisky) Vodka, Grape, Butter Scotch)
- Food Products Complex (Dehydrated Onions, Garlic Powder & Flakes, Cattle Feed, Tomato Powder, Tomato Products, Canned Fruits & Vegetables, Tomato Pure, Ground Nut Oil, Refined Oil, Dehydrated Grapes Etc.
- Banana Powder & Waffers)
- Freeze Drying Coffee Manufacturing Unit (Processing) And Packaging In Glass Bottles
- Fruit Juice, Jam, Jellies & Allied Products
- Fruit Juice, Pickles Processing And Canning
- Fruit Juice Making & Packing In Plastic Container/Pouches
- Fruit Processing (Jam & Jellies)
- Fruit Pulp & Juice Concentrates
- Fruit & Vegetable Drying (Freeze Drying Method)
- Ginger Oil
- Ginger Paste
- Ginger And Garlic Paste
- Goat Farm
- Goat & Sheep Farming
- Gram Dall/Pulse Mill
- Grape Dehydration
- Hard Boiled Candy (Toffee & Candy)
- Herbal Cigarettes
- Honey Processing & Packaging
- Honey Coated Cashewnuts, Peanuts And Other Nuts
- Ice Cream Of Different Flavours
- Ice Cream Stabilizer
- Ice Making Plant
- Icing Sugar
- Indian Made Foreign Liquor (I.M.F.L)
- Instant Food (Idli Mix, Dosa Mix, Gulab Jamun Mix)
- Instant Food (Instant Food & Fast Food Parlour)
- Instant Noodles
- Instant Tea
- Instant Tea From Black Tea
- Integerated Starch Baking Powder/Yeast Industry
- Integrated Unit Of Dairy Farming, Milk Collection And Processing, Fish Farming, Poultry Farming And Hatchery
- Iodized Salt
- Iodized Salt (Ordinary Moisture-Less/Free Flowing In Plastic Bags And Containers)
- Jam, Jellies, Fruit Juice & Allied Products
- Katha And Cutch
- Khandsari Sugar

Market Survey Cum Detailed Techno Economic Feasibility Report on all Projects are available Contact.
"ENGINEERS INDIA RESEARCH INSTITUTE", 4449, Nai Sarak (D), Main Road, Delhi-110006 (India)
Ph. : 09811437895, 91-11-23918117, 23916431, 45120361, 64727385 Fax : 91-11-23916431
E-mail : eiriprojects@gmail.com, eiribooks@yahoo.com • website: www.eiri.in, www.eiriindia.org

ALL FOLLOWING PROJECT REPORTS ARE READILY AVAILABLE

EIRI
We Create Industrialists

- Khandsari Sugar & Imfl
- Lactic Acid From White Sugar By Fermentation Process
- Lactose & By Products Processing From Milk
- Liquid Glucose And Its Bye Products
- Macroni And Vermicilli
- Malt Extraction From Barley
- Mango Processing (Mango Pulp, Juice & Slices)
- Mayur Brand Type Chewing Tobacco
- Mineral Water
- Milk Preservation & Marketing To Whole Sellers (Inpouch Packing By Uht Technology)
- Milk Processing And Packaging Of Milk Products
- Milk Products (Casein, Lactose, Ghee & Whey Powder)
- Milk Toffee
- Mini Flour Mill
- Mini Sugar Plant
- Misri (Pearl Sugar Candies)
- Modern Rice Mill
- Murabba
- Mustard Oil Extraction & Refining
- Mutton Tallow
- Namkeen Industry (Bhujia, Chana Chur Etc.)
- Namkeen (Kurkure Type Snack Food
- Namkeen With Kurkurre Type Snack Food
- Namkeen & Sweets
- Non-Basmati Rice From Paddy
- Oleoresin, Essential Oil, Dyes & Powder Of Spices
- Oleoresin Extraction From Diptero-Carput Turminatus And Pinus Khasyana
- Oleoresin Extraction From Chilli
- Pan Masala With Packing In Pouches And Tin Cans
- Pan Masala, Tobacco, Zarda & Kimam
- Packaged Drinking Water
- Packaged Coconut Water (Coco Jal)
- Paneer From Milk
- Pappad Plant
- Papain From Papaya (Papaya Latex)
- Pectin From Mango Peel Pectin From Apple Pomace
- Phyto Tea (Herbal Tea)
- Pickles And Sauces
- Pickles Murabba Etc. (Veg. & Non. Veg.Pickles)
- Piggery Meat Process
- Pine-Apple Juice Preparation & Packaging
- Potato Chips/Waffers
- Potato Powder
- Pouch Filling & Packaging Of Edible Oil & Ghee
- Poultry Feed
- Processed Foods & Spices (Eou)
- Processed Readymade Food
- Processing Of Fruits & Vegetables
- Puree, Paste, Juice And Ketchup From Khajoor (Dates)
- Rabbit Farming
- Rasgullas Making & Canning In Metal Cans
- Ready To Eat Processed Cooked Food
- Ready To Eat Retort Packed Food
- Ready To Eat Snack Food (Crax, Roll & Ball Type)
- Rice & Corn Flakes
- Rice Noodles
- Roasted/Salted/Masala,Cashew Nuts, Almonds & Peanuts
- Roller Flour Mill (Atta, Suja And Maida)
- Salt Licks For Cattle
- Sattu
- Sausages Food Casing
- Soft Drinks (Cold Drinks)
- Soft Drinks Essences
- Soft Drinks (Non Carbonated) Mango,Licchi, Pineapple Flavours Frooti Type In Tetrapack)
- Softy Ice Cream Cones (Fully Automatic)
- Soft/Cold Drinks (Cola, Orange, Lemon Etc. Flavours)
- Soyabean Products
- Soyabean Bariyan
- Soya Milk & Paneer
- Spices/Masala With Formulae
- Spices And Namkeen (Integrated Unit)
- Snack Food (Kurkure Type)
- Starch & Allied Propduct From Broken Rice
- Strawberry Cultivation & Processing
- Sugarcane Juice Preservation
- Sugar Cubes From Cane Sugar
- Sugar Plant
- Supari (Sweet) – Betel Nut (Synthetic)
- Sweet Aroma Betel Nut
- Synthetic Tallow
- Tamarind Juice Powder
- Tamarind Juice Concentrates
- Tea & Coffee Processing & Packaging
- Toffees, Golies, Candy (Hard Boiled)
- Tomato Products
- Tomato Ketchup, Tomato Puree And Tomato Juice (Tomato Products)
- Trading Business Of Spices & Pan Masala
- Tuity Fruity
- Vermicilli (Including Roasted Vermicilli)
- Virgin Coconut Oil
- Vodka From Potatoes
- Wallnut Processing
- Wine, Brandy, Whisky &Champagne
- Wine From Dates
- Yeast From Molasses
- Zarda, Kimam No. 60,90,120,160,240,300 & 400 (Tobacco)
- Zarda Kimam And Tobacco
- Zarda-Zafrani (Babachhaptype)

GUMS AND ADHESIVES

- Acrylic Adhesive
- Adhesive (Different Types)
- Adhesive (Fevicol Type)
- Adhesive For Stickers
- Adhesive Based On Vinyl Acetate
- Adhesive Based On Polyurethane
- Adhesive For Band Aid (Johnson & Johnson Type)
- Adhesive Industries (Laminated, Sticker,Ddl & Other Types)
- Adhesive For Gasket (Liquid/Paste)
- Araldyte Type Adhesive
- Alkyd Resin
- Bopp Self Adhesive Tapes
- Cyanoacrylate Adhesive
- Ester Gums
- Fevicol Type Adhesive
- Guar Gum
- Gum Bottle (Pvc)
- Gum For Pasting Labels
- Leather To Leather Adhesive
- Liquid Adhesive For Corrugated Boxes
- Office Paste
- Poly Amide Resin
- Pressure Sensitive Adhesive
- Pvc Indulation Tapes
- Printing Gums (Guar Gum Based)
- Rubber Adhesive
- Self Adhesive Labels
- Starch And Dextrin Based Afhesive
- Surgical Adhesive Plaster
- Synthetic Rubber Adhesive
- Synthetic Adhesive For Decorative Laminate Bonding
- Tapioca Starch Adhesive
- Vinyl Ester Adhesive
- Vulcanising Adhesive Formulation Vulcanizing Rubber Solution/Cement For Automobile Tyre
- Urea Formaldehyde Resin
- Water Based Latex Adhesive

Contact EIRI
for required Project report apart from this list.

Market Survey Cum Detailed Techno Economic Feasibility Report on all Projects are available Contact.
"ENGINEERS INDIA RESEARCH INSTITUTE". 4449, Nai Sarak (D), Main Road, Delhi-110006 (India)
Ph. : 09811437895, 91-11-23918117, 23916431, 45120361, 64727385 Fax : 91-11-23916431
E-mail : eiriprojects@gmail.com, eiribooks@yahoo.com • website: www.eiri.in, www.eiriindia.org

ALL FOLLOWING PROJECT REPORTS ARE READILY AVAILABLE

LEATHER & LEATHER PRODUCTS

- Handmade Leather
- Leather Auxillaries & Chemicals
- Leather Dyes
- Leather Washers
- Leather Board From Leather Waste
- Leather For Upholstry(Sofa)
- Leather Finishing Lacquer (Nitrocellulose Lacquer For Leather)
- Leather Garments
- Leather Goods
- Leather Shoes
- Leather Shoe & Chappal
- Leather Suitcases, Briefcases & Travelling Bags
- Leather Goods And Garments
- Leather Garments, Shoe & Chappal
- Leather Pigment Used For Colouring Of Leather
- Leather Tanning
- Leather Tanning & Garments (Eou)
- Sheep Skin Pickling Plant
- Shoe Upper
- Sport Shoes (Plastic)

MISCELLANEOUS PRODUCTS

- Agarbatti (Insence Stick)
- Abrasive Paper
- Agarbatti (Mosquito Repellent)
- Agarbati Bamboo Stick
- Agarbatti Synthetic Perfumery Compound
- Air Freshner(Odonil Type)
- Air Taxi
- Amusement Park
- Anodic Aluminium Label
- Aquaculture Prawn Farming (100% Eou)
- Aqua Culture Shrimp Farming (100% Eou)
- Artificial Flowers
- Artificial Jewellery
- Asbestos Yarn
- Ash Trays For Maruti Vehicle
- Air Bubble Packaging
- Asphaltic Roofing Sheet (Metal Components)
- Automatic Book Binding
- Alkyd Resin
- Apple Juice Concentrate
- Ball Point Pen Fefills (Jotter Type)
- Bank Branch Building
- Banquet Hall
- Bio-Coal Briquettes From Agriculturalcellulose Waste
- Boot Cream/Polish
- Buffing & Polishing Compound
- Brass Badges By Etching
- Briquetted Fuel From Agro Waste
- Briquetting Of Lignite Coal
- Buffalo Horn Tip, Hoof
- Banquet Hall
- Button
- Calcined Petroleum (C.P) Coke
- Canvas Shoes
- Canvas Shoes, Jungle Boots
- Carbon Brush, Brush Holder & Slip Ring
- Cement Sheets With Coir Fibre & Other Segments
- Ceramic Tiles (Glazed) By Double Firing/Heating
- Children Recreation Centre
- Coal Briquettes
- Cold Storage & Ice
- Cold Storage For Fruits And Vegetables
- Compressor (Hermetic) For Air Conditioner
- Costume Jewellery/Imitation Jewellery
- Decorative Laminated Sheet (Sunmica)
- Dental Colleges
- Diamond Cutting & Exports
- Drinking Straw From Propylene
- Engineering College
- Engineering College, Management Institute, Cbse School, Hostel (Boys And Girls), Medical College With Hospital And Research Institute
- Electropolishing On Gold Jewellery (Gold Ornaments)
- Entertainment Club
- Fashion Technology Institute
- Fast Food Parlour
- Fast Food (Instant Food & Fast Food Parlour)
- Fire Extinguishers (Soda Acid Type)
- Fish Net
- Floriculture (Cut Flower Rose) With Green House
- Floor Covering Sheet
- Film Studio (Video)
- Flush Door, Chip Board, Wood Wool & Other Insulating Boards
- Gas Detectors Of L.P.G
- Gems Manufacturing
- Glass Bottle By Scrap
- Glass Jars Manufacturing Plant For Packaging Of 50, 100, 150, 200 Grams Coffee Packaging
- Goat & Sheep Farming
- Gold Electroplating
- Gold Jewellery (E.O.U)
- Gold Plated Silver Jewellery & Cutlery
- Granite Slab And Tiles
- Granite Mining
- Green House
- Hard Chromium Plating
- Health Club And Beauty Parlour Cum Hair
- Saloon With Sona Bath
- Health Club Cum Beauty Parlour Training Institute
- Horn Tip,Hoove Button
- Hospital

EIRI

is fully capable to prepare any Project Report of your Choice

- Hospital (100 Beds)
- Hospital (200 Beds)
- Ice Making Plant
- Imitation And Costume
- Jewellery (Necklace, Earrings Ear Top Etc.)
- Initmate Scent Chemicals From All Types Of Flavour
- Investment Casting
- Jute, Coir, Glass Rope/ Sutli
- Jute Twine
- Jute Bags From Yarn Without Spinning Process
- L.P.G Bottling Plant
- L.P.G Regulator (Domestic Purpose)
- Laminated Particle Board & Hard Board
- Laminated Safety & Toughened Glass
- Leasing & Hire Purchase
- Lichen (Charila)
- Manila Ropes
- Medical College
- Medical University
- Metal Pretreatment Chemicals Powder, Coating Chemicals
- Match Unit From Waxed Paper
- Medium Density Fibre Board
- Melamine Crockery
- Mineral Water
- Mini Cement Plant
- Mirror Silver, Golden, Pink, Black & Smokes
- Modern Advt. Agency With Dtp & Film Studio
- Motel/Small Hotel
- Multi Colour Printing
- Multi Purpose Cold Storage And Dehydration And Canning Of Fruits And Vegetables
- Multi Storey Commercial Complex Alongwith Residential And Delux Flats For Foreign Tourists & Revolving Restaurant At The Top
- Multiple Lamination Industry
- Mushroom Growing And Processing (By Deep Freezing Method)
- News Paper Printing
- Nickel Lined Industrial Screen
- Non Coking Coal To Coking Coal
- Nursing Home
- Offset Colour Printing Press (Six Colour)

Market Survey Cum Detailed Techno Economic Feasibility Report on all Projects are available Contact.
"ENGINEERS INDIA RESEARCH INSTITUTE". 4449, Nai Sarak (D), Main Road, Delhi-110006 (India)
Ph. : 09811437895, 91-11-23918117, 23916431, 45120361, 64727385 Fax : 91-11-23916431
E-mail : eiriprojects@gmail.com, eiribooks@yahoo.com • website: www.eiri.in, www.eiriindia.org

ALL FOLLOWING PROJECT REPORTS ARE READILY AVAILABLE

- Offset Printing Press
- Old Age Home
- P.C.C Electric Poles
- Photographic Developer & Fixer
- Pvc Extrusion Profile (Door & Windows)
- Pop-Corn
- Photo Etching Of S.S.
- Pre Stressed Cement Concrete Pipes
- Pilfer Proof Caps
- Pilfer Proof Caps And Crown Cap
- Pouch Making & Gravure Printing (Roto Printing)
- Poultry & Fish Farming (Integerated Unit)
- Printing Of Tin Sheets
- Radio Station
- Radio Taxi
- Readymade Garments
- Refractories With Ceramics
- Restaurant
- Rose Plantation And Rose Oil Extraction
- Rotogravure Printing
- Safety Belts
- Safety Matches
- School
- School With Hostel
- Shoe Laces
- Silk Cocoon Cultivation (Growing Of Silk Cocoon Warm)
- Silk Screen Printing Formulations For Plastic, Paper & Cloth
- Spikenard (Jatamansi)
- Stencil Coating Solution
- Sugar Candy (Misri)
- Sugar Cane Plantation
- Sugar Cane Juice Preservation
- Super Speciality Diagnosis Centre
- Surat Zari
- Synthetic Shoes & Soles
- T.V. News Channel
- Tea Packaging Industry
- Toughened Glass
- Tennis Balls
- Three Star Hotel
- Travelling Agency
- Trays, Trolleys For Hospital With Scratchless Coating
- Wax Extracts (Tanning Powder)
- Wire Rope Slings
- Wood Wool Slab
- Wooden Cane Furniture With Export Potential
- Wooden Door And Windows
- Wooden Furniture
- Wooden Panel Including Kiln Seasoning
- Wooden Furniture
- Watch Case Buffing
- Watch Dial
- Wrist Watches
- Watches (Electronic)
- Zedoary (Kachur)

Contact
EIRI
for required Project report apart from this list.

EDIBLE OILS, ESSENTIAL OILS LURICATING OILS, GREASES, VEGETABLE OILS, WAXES, CAMPHOR, PERFUMES & PERFUMERY COMPOUNDS AND REFINED OILS ETC. EDIBLE OILS, ESSENTIAL OILS, LURICATIING OILS, GREASES, VEGETABLE OILS, WAXES, CAMPHOR, PERFUMES & PERFUMERY COMPOUNDS AND REFINED OILS ETC.

- Aromatic Perfumery Compound
- Aerosol
- Agarbatti Perfumery Compound
- Bees Wax Manufacture
- Camphor
- Cardanol From Cashew Nut Shell Liquid
- Castor Oil
- Castor Oil Derivative Oleoresins
- Chilli Oil
- Citronella Oils
- Clove Oil
- Concentrate Of Rose Jasmine & Lily Etc.
- Coloured Flame Candle
- Candles (Semi-Automatic)
- Corn Oil (Maize Oil)
- Dehydrated Castor Oil
- Eugenol From Cinnamon Leaf Oil
- Extraction Of Essential Oil (Cardamon, Jeera, Ajowan, Ginger Oils Etc. & Packaging Of Ground Spices)
- Extraction Of Jasmine Essence
- Extraction Of Essential Oils By Super Critical Fluid Method From Flowers, Herbs & Spices
- Eucalyptus Oil
- Extraction Of Oil From Oil Seed Expander Extrusion Technology)
- Fat Liquor Sulphated Oil
- Flavours For Food
- Fish Oil
- Garlic Oil & Powder
- Ginger Oil, Sandalwood Oil And Nagarmotha Oil
- Ginger Oil
- Ginger Oil & Ginger Dust
- Ground Nut Oil
- Integerated Wax Complex
- Ionone From Lemon Grass Oil
- Jasmine & Lilly Flower Oil
- Lemon Grass Oil
- Liquid Paraffin
- Lube Oil & Grease

ENGINEERS INDIA RESEARCH INSTITUTE
EIRI

- Lubricating Oil
- Menthol Crystals
- Menthol Oil & Crystal
- Micro Crystalline Wax
- Mustard Oil (Edible Oil)
- Oleoresin From Spices
- Oil From Artemisia Herbs
- Palm Oil Crushing Unit
- Pan Masala
- Paraffin Wax
- Paraffin Wax From Slack Wax
- Perfume For Food Industries With Pan Masala Perfume
- Pouch For Oil And Ghee Packaging
- Refined Oil-Sun Flower Oil, Groundnut Oil, Staff Flower Oil & Cotton Seed Oil
- Refined Vegetable Oil
- Reclamation Of Used Engine Oil
- Rice Bran Oil (R.B.O)
- Rose Oil Extraction
- Smoke Less Candle
- Spice Oil & Oleoresins
- Solvent Extraction Plant (Oil Cake Based)
- Synthetic Almond Oil
- Synthetic Wax
- Synthetic Tallow
- Synthetic Ghee
- Synthetic Musk
- Turmeric Oil Oleoresin
- Vanilla Cultivation And Extraction/Processing
- Vegetable Oil Extraction & Refining
- Wadding Oil (100%) For Wadding Of Cotton Hosiery Cloth In Dyeing Process
- Wax Emulsion For Textile
- Wax Floor Polish

ELECTROPLATING, ANODIZING & ALLIED PROJECTS

- Nickel Plating Brightener
- Pcb With Garphite & Silver Coating
- Rainbow Colours On Metal
- Silver Refining By Electrolysis & By Acid
- Silver Extraction
- Silver Extraction From Waste Hypo Solution
- Silver & Gold Plating On Pvc & Nylon-6
- Tin Printing
- Titanium Jewellery Plating
- Vacuum Metallizing
- Zinc Electroplating Brightner
- Zinc Electroplating On Nut, Bolts,

Market Survey Cum Detailed Techno Economic Feasibility Report on all Projects are available Contact.
"ENGINEERS INDIA RESEARCH INSTITUTE". 4449, Nai Sarak (D), Main Road, Delhi-110006 (India)
Ph. : 09811437895, 91-11-23918117, 23916431, 45120361, 64727385 Fax : 91-11-23916431
E-mail : eiriprojects@gmail.com, eiribooks@yahoo.com • website: www.eiri.in, www.eiriindia.org

ALL FOLLOWING PROJECT REPORTS ARE READILY AVAILABLE

PAINT, ENAMEL, SOLVENTS, THINNERS, INKS & VARNISH
PAINT, ENAMEL, SOLVENTS, THINNERS, INKS & VARNISH

- Acrylic Emulsion Paints
- Acrylic Cement Paint (Dry Powder)
- Aluminium Paint
- Automobile Paints
- Ball Point Pen Refill Ink
- Bituminious Road Emulsion
- Bitumen
- Bituminious Felts For Water & Damp Proofing
- Bituminious Road Emulsion Rapid Medium & Slow Setting
- Buffing & Polishing
- Cement Paint For White & Grey Cement
- Dispersant
- Dry Distemper
- Dry Distemper & Cement Paint
- Duplicating Ink Black For Gestner Duplicator
- Emulsion Paints (Water Based)
- Hammertone Paint
- Insulating Varnish & Wire Enamel
- Iron Oxide Pigments
- Insulating Varnish (Poly Vinyl Butyral Based, Ffc Grade)
- Lime Colour (Cement Colour)
- Synthetic Red Oxide For Floorings
- Solvent & Thinners
- Marking Inks (Water Proof)
- Metal Naphthanate (As Drier For Paints)
- N.C.Putty
- Offset Printing Ink
- Oil Bound Distemper Paint
- Paint Brushes
- Paint Manufacture For Rolling Coating Of Aluminium And Steel Coil
- Paint Removers
- Paint Industry
- Paint & Varnish
- Picture Varnish
- Powder Coating Paint
- Printing Inks (Offset,Flexo & Roto Gravure)
- Primer Paint & Enamel Paint
- Putty & Water Proofing Paint
- Printing Inks (Flexo-Graphic Ink)
- Putty (Metal Casement)
- Red Oxide Primer (Anti Corrosive)
- Refrectory Paint (Graphite Based)
- Screen Printing Inks
- Silk Screen Printing Ink Formulation For Plastic, Paper, Cloth
- Stamp & Pad Ink
- Stoving Paint
- Spirit Soluble Maleic Resin
- Texture Paint
- Thinners And Its Allied Products
- Toner Ink
- Varnish Thinner (Solvent)
- Vacuum Metallizing Lacquers
- Wood Primer

PHARMACEUTICAL, DRUGS, AYURVEDIC/HERBAL COSMETICS & MEDICINES, HOMOEOPATHIC MEDICINES, HOMOEOPATHIC MEDICINES, DISPOSABLE SYRINGE, DENTAL COLLEGE & FINE CHEMICALS ETC.
MEDICINES, HOMOEOPATHIC MEDICINES, DISPOSABLE SYRINGE, DENTAL COLLEGE & FINE CHEMICALS ETC.

- Aromatic Pills
- Alumina From Bauxite
- Aspirin
- Ayurvedic Pain Balm Ointments
- Ayurvedic Churan And Tablets
- Ayurvedic Tablets (Hajmola Type)
- Ayurvedic/Herbalpharmacy
- Ayurvedic Sherbats
- Ayurvedic Products
- Bulk Drugs (E.O.U)
- Blood Bags
- Calcium Gluconate
- Capsule, Tablet & Injection With Modern Instruments
- Cashew Feni
- Chloroquinone Phosphate (Bulk Drugs)
- Clinical Thermometer
- Dental Clinic
- Dental College
- Dental Grade Eugenol
- Dextrose Monohydrate, Liquid Glucose
- Dehydrated Onion & Onion Powder
- Dextrose Powder (Anhydrous From Starch)
- Dextrose Saline Solution
- Distillery (I.M.F.L)
- Disposable Needles For Syringes
- Disprin
- Distilled Water
- Empty Hard Gelatine Capsules
- Fairness Cream
- Filling & Packing Of Capsules
- Glucose - D - Powder
- Glycerine
- Hair Colour Mate (Formulations And Process Only)
- Herbal Cosmetics
- Herbal Shampoo
- Herbal Shampoo And Cream
- Herbal Hair Oils (Ayurvedic)
- Homoe & Bio-Medicines With Mother Tincture
- Homoepathic Medicines
- Hypodermic Needles
- I.V. Fluids
- Ibuprofen
- Infusion & Transfusion Sets (I.V. Set)
- Injectable For Pharmaceuticals
- Injection Ampoules Packaging Box
- Integerated Surgical Cotton
- Ice Making Plant
- Ice & Cold Storage
- Lactose & By Products Processing From Milk
- Lichen (Jatamansi Charila)
- Liquid Glucose And Its By-Products
- L-Lysine Monohydro Chloride
- Liquid Glucose From Potatoes
- Medical College
- Methanol (Hpcl Grade)
- Nicotine From Tobacco Waste
- Ointment-Ayurvedic (Yellow & White)
- Pharmaceutical And Food Grade Gelatine
- Pharmaceutical Industry (Tablets, Capsules, Liquid, Gel, Ointment Powder Injectable)
- Pharmaceutical Unit (Eou) With Formulations, Injectables, Etc.
- Pyridine & Derivatives
- Salt (Iodized Salt)
- Saline & Injection Water
- Saline Water & Dextrose Solution (I.V.Fluid In Plastic Bottles)
- Sorbitol
- Starch (Maize)
- Surgical Adhesive Plaster
- Surgical Bandages
- Surgical Gloves
- Surgical Cotton
- Surgical Cotton And Bandage
- Synthetic Camphor Powder
- Tablets & Capsules
- Tissue Culture
- Tincture From Rectified Spirit
- Trimethopime
- Veterinary College With Hospital
- Veterenary Medicines (Only Formulations)
- Vitamin 'C', Sorbitol' Anhydrous Dextrose, Starch

Market Survey Cum Detailed Techno Economic Feasibility Report on all Projects are available Contact.
"ENGINEERS INDIA RESEARCH INSTITUTE". 4449, Nai Sarak (D), Main Road, Delhi-110006 (India)
Ph: 09811437895, 91-11-23918117, 23916431, 45120361, 64727385 Fax : 91-11-23916431
E-mail : eiriprojects@gmail.com, eiribooks@yahoo.com • website: www.eiri.in, www.eiriindia.org

ALL FOLLOWING PROJECT REPORTS ARE READILY AVAILABLE

PLASTIC, B.O.P.P. ACRYLIC, DISPOSABLE PLASTIC PRODUCTS, PET PRODUCTS, P.V.C. H.D.P.E. P.P. L.D.P.E. P.U. A.B.S. THERMOFOARMING, MASTER BATCHES & POLYMER AND RUBBER PRODUCTS, TYRE, TUBE, ADHESIVE, SHEET, COIR & MANY OTHERS

- Abs Granules From Abs Scraps
- Acrylic Beads
- Acrylic Copolymer Emulsion
- Acrylic Latex
- Acrylic Sheet
- Acrylic Sheet & Moulded Products
- Acrylic Teeth
- Air Bubble Packaging Film
- Audio Cassettes Parts By Injection Moulding
- Audio Cassettes Assembly And Recording
- Auto Tubes
- Auto Flaps For Trucks & Buses
- Auto Tyres & Tubes
- Baby Bottles (Plastic) With Whitesilicon Rubber Nipples
- B.O.P.P. Film
- B.O.P.P. Pressure Sensitive Self Adhesive Tape
- Baby Nipple (Silicon)
- Baby Nipple (Big Size)
- Ball Pen Manufacturing (Automatic Plant)
- Bath Tub (Acrylic)
- Balloon Plastic Advertising
- Blister Film Pvc
- Blister Packaging & Pouch Pakaging
- Blow Moulding Plastic Container
- Coating On Metalized Polyester Film/Metalised Paper/Aliminium Foil
- Coating On Plastic (Electrolysis) & Glass
- Coir Foam (Rubberised)
- Colour Coating On Plastics
- Colour Master Batches For Various Plastics
- Cycle Tyres And Tubes
- Discount/Credit Card
- Disposable Plastic Cups Glasses, Etc.
- Disposable Plastic Syringes & Needles
- Disposable Plastic Syringes
- Disposable Plastic Razor
- Dough Moulding Compound (D.M.C)
- Egg Trays From Plastic
- Epoxy Resin
- Expanded Polyestrene Moulding (Thermocole)
- Fibre Glass Sheet
- F.R.P Auto,Scooter Roofs & Ceilings
- Frp Pipes And Products
- F.R.P Products (Helmet, Washbasin Sheets, Roofing Sheets)
- Fibre Reinforced Plastic (High Pressure Moulding With Smc Bmc And Dmc)
- Field Rubber Converted To The 60% Latex Rubber
- Flexible P.U. Foam
- Formaldehyde Crockery & Other Items
- Formaldehyde Resin (Urea, Phenol,Melemine)
- Gasket Sheet
- Gum Bottle (Pvc)
- Glass Beads
- Helmet
- Hdpe Coated Paper Sack
- H.D.P.E. Bags
- H.D.P.E. Containers (Blow Moulding)
- H.D.P.E. Container, Poly Jars By Injection Moulding (Food Grade)
- Hdpe Fishing Net
- H.D.P.E. Jerry Cans
- Hdpe Manufacturing From Ethyl Alcohol
- H.D.P.E Pipe And Fittings
- H.D.P.E. Pipes
- H.D.P.E Printed Bags
- H.D.P.E Twines And Ropes
- H.D.P.E. & L.D.P.E Pipes And Fittings
- H.D.P.E/Pp Box Strapping
- H.D.P.E/Pp Woven Sacks Using Plain Looms
- Hologram Stickers-3d
- H.M Bag Plant With Printing Unit
- Hawai Chappals (Rubber)
- I.V Plastic Bottle
- Ice Cream Cup (Plastic)
- Injection Moulded Auto Components
- Injection & Blow Moulded Plastic Products
- Injection Moulded Plastic Products
- Integerated Complex Ester's & Allied Products (D.O.P,D.B.P, & Ethyl Acetate, Buytl Acetate, Wire Enamels, Jelly Cable Compound)
- L.D.P.E. (Low Density Poly Ethylene) Granules From Virgin (L.D.P.E. Resin)
- Integerated Surgical Rubber Goods Industry
- Injection Moulded Plastic Balls
- L.D.P.E From Ethyl Alcohol
- Ldpe Moulded Products
- Lamination Ofcoextrusion Multilayer Film In Roll Form
- Latex Rubber
- Latex Rubber Condom
- Master Batches (Coloured, P.V.C, L.D.P.E, H.D.P.E, Etc.)
- Melamine Formalhyde Resin
- Moulded Luggage
- Multi-Layer (3 Layer Bags)
- Multi-Layer (3 Layer) Film With Lamination & Printing
- Nylon Net For Giving Shade To Tea Plant In Nursery
- Oil Seal
- Pet Bottle/Containers
- Pet Bottles And Caps
- Pet Bottles From Pre Form
- Pet Bottle & Mineral Water
- Pet Granules (Dana)
- Pet Pre-Form From Pet Resin
- Pet Pre-Form Cum Pet Bottles
- Pet Pre-Form Pet Bottles Cum Mineral Waters
- Poly Carbonate Resin
- Ptfe Components
- Pu/Pvc Sole For Sport Shoe By Imported M/C.
- Pvc Battery Separator
- P.V.C Compounds (Fresh)
- P.V.C Compounds (Scrap)
- P.V.C Electrical Insulating Tape
- P.V.C. Extrusion Profiles
- Pvc Film
- P.V.C Fittings
- P.V.C Flexible Fusible Powder Heat Fusible Powder
- Pvc Footwear
- P.V.C Granules (For Insulation & Sheets Grades)
- P.V.C Granules From Pvc Scraps (With Pollution Control)
- P.V.C Hoses
- P.V.C Leather Cloth
- P.V.C Flexible Pipes
- P.V.C Pipes And Fittings
- Polythene Bags (Printed)
- Pvc Plastics Film Sheet Soft/Rigid
- Pvc Resin And Compound
- Pvc Rular
- Pvc Stablizers (Single Pack System)
- Pvc Wire And Cables
- Paper Based Phenolic Sheet For Electrical
- Phenol Formaldehyde Resin
- Phenolic Resin
- Plastic Beads From Plastic Scraps
- Plastic Buttons
- Plastic Cans
- Plastic Collapsible Tube
- Plastic Corrugated Sheet & Boxes
- Plastic Film And Sheets With Printing Flexo & Roto/Ldpe/Hdpe/Pp/Hm/Pvc
- Plastic Filter Master Batch & Other Master Batches For Various Plastics
- Plastic Doors (Sintex Type)
- Plastic Jerry Cans
- Plastic Granules Or Powder From Plastic Scrap
- Plastic Injection Moulded T.V. Cabinets
- Plastic Items Manufacture From Powder Melamine
- Plastic Goods
- Plastic Pipes & Tarpaulines
- Plastic Sheet From Scrap
- Plastic Plant (Blow Moulding & Injection Moulding)
- Plastic Products (Gold, Silver, Nickel)
- Plastic Toys
- Polyester Beading
- Polyester Film
- Polythene Bags & Automatic Printing

Market Survey Cum Detailed Techno Economic Feasibility Report on all Projects are available Contact.
"ENGINEERS INDIA RESEARCH INSTITUTE". 4449, Nai Sarak (D), Main Road, Delhi-110006 (India)
Ph. : 09811437895, 91-11-23918117, 23916431, 45120361, 64727385 Fax : 91-11-23916431
E-mail : eiriprojects@gmail.com, eiribooks@yahoo.com • website: www.eiri.in, www.eiriindia.org

ALL FOLLOWING PROJECT REPORTS ARE READILY AVAILABLE

- Polythene Printed Bags
- Polyurethane Foam And Its Products
- Propylene Film (Printed) & Bag Manufacturing
- Plastic Mats
- Pvc Wire And Cable
- Pvc Pipe And Fitting
- Polythene Shopping Bags
- Rainbow Colour On Pvc Film & Sheet
- Red Mud Pvc Pipes And Fittings
- Re-Rubberised Of Solid Type
- Resin Coated Sand Rexine
- Rexine Cloth & Allied Products
- Rubber Adhesive
- Rubber Auto Parts
- Rubber Belting
- Rubber Powder
- Rubber (And Metal Bonded) Auto Parts
- Rubber Moulding Unit Including Lining Rubber Sheeting
- Rubber Reclaiming
- Rubber Rollers For Textile Mills & Paper Industries
- Rubber & Plastic Sheets, Mats & Flaps
- Rubber Sheet And Allied Hospital Rubber Goods
- Rubberized Pvc Gasket
- Rubberised Coir
- Rubber Compound For Automobiles
- Safety Belts
- Silver And Gold Plating On Pvc And Nylon-6
- Silicone Rubber Nipples/ Teats
- Smart Card
- Spectacle Frames (Plastic)
- Spunge Rubber
- Surgical Examination Gloves
- Synthetic Pearl Coating On Polystyrene Beads
- Synthetic Rubber Adhesive
- Teflon Manufacturing
- Teflon Tape
- Teflon Tapes & Cables
- Thermocole Sheet And Moulded Products
- Expanded Polyesterene Extrusion Profiles
- Thermoformed Packaging (Blister Packaging & Pouch Packaging)
- Thermoplastic Polyurethane
- Thermoformed Cups, Plates & Glass With Hips Sheet
- Thermocole
- Thermocole Based Disposable Glass, Cups & Plates
- Tooth Brushes
- Toy Balloon, Decora Tive & Industrial Balloons
- Tread Rubber
- Tyre Retreading (Hot)
- Tyre Retreading By Cold Process
- Tyre Tubes & Flaps
- Tyre & Tubes
- Unsaturated Polyester Resin
- Unsaturated Polyester For Rexine
- V-Belt And Fan Belt
- Vinyl Asbestos & Pvc Wall Paper
- Viton (Fluoro Elastomer)

SOAP COSMETICS & PERFUMES

- Acid Slurry, Synthetic Detergent Powder
- Acid Slurry
- Agarbatti Synthetic, Perfumery Compound+
- Aromatic Perfumery Compound
- After Shave Lotion
- Antiseptic Cream
- Bath Soap (Various Types)
- Beta Ionone
- Bleaching Powder
- Blue Detergent Powder
- Cleaning Powder (Vimtype)
- Cold Cream
- Coloured Flame & Perfumed Candles (Red, Blue, Green Flame)
- Cosmetic Industry (Modern)
- Cosmetic Industry (Shampoo, Spray Perfume, Talcum Powder
- Detergent Powder (Ariel Type)
- Detergent Powder (Nirma Type) Fully Automatic Plant
- Detergent Washing Powder
- Detergent Cake And Powder
- Fairness Cream
- Fish Oil Soap
- Glycerine Transparent Soap
- Hair Removing Cream
- Herbal Cosmetics
- Herbal Shampo & Cream
- Herbal/Ayurvedic Cosmetics
- Incense Powder,Incense Sticks & Incense Cake
- Nerol Soap
- Oil Soap
- Optical Whiteners
- Rose Oil Extraction
- Shampoos (Coconut Oil Based Cold Process)
- Shaving Cream
- Sindur (Kumkum)
- Soap Coated Paper
- Spray Dried Detergent Powder
- Stain Remover
- Synthetic Detergent (Blue Powder)
- Toilet Soap And Glycerine Soap
- Toilet Soap From Soap Noodles
- Talcum Powder (Face & Toilet Powder)
- Toilet And Herbal Soap
- Tooth Paste & Powder
- Washing Detergent Powder And Washing Soap
- Washing Powder Liquid Detergents,Lotion & Shampoo

TEXTILE INDUSTRIES, READYMADE GARMENTS, COTTON, DYEING, BLEACHING, CLOTH, HOSIERY, POWER LOOM, HAND LOOM, WOOLLEN, SILK, SOCKS, SURGICAL COTTON & MANY OTHERS

- Angora Rabbit Wool
- Bed Sheet, Bed Cover, Sofa Cloth, Curtain Cloth (Home Furnishing)
- Buckram
- Canvas Shoes, Jungle Boot, Boot Rubber Knees & Boot Combat
- Carpet From Cotton Waste
- Ceramic Thread Guide
- Cotton Buds/Swabs
- Cotton From Waste Yarn
- Cotton Rolls
- Cotton Saree
- Cotton Spiders For Loud Speakers
- Denim Cloth
- Denim Cloth (Integerated Unit With Bleaching, Dyeing And Printing)
- Dispersent For Textile
- Dyeing & Bleaching
- Dyeing Of Hank Yarn
- Emulsifier For Wool Batching Oil
- Embroidery On Fabrics
- Garment Dyeing, Washing & Stitching (Jeans, Jackets, Skirts & Shirts)
- Goves Knitting
- Gunny Bags
- Hdpe/Pp Woven Sacks
- Hdpe Tarpaulins Using Plain Loom With Lamination
- Hdpe/Pp Woven Sacks Using Circular Looms
- Hosiery Cloth (Cotton) Processing (Bleaching, Dyeing, Finishing Of Cloth)
- Hosiery Industry
- Hosiery Mercerising
- Hosiery Products Like Vest, Brief, T-Shirts & Socks
- Jacquard Fabrics
- Jute Coir, Grass Rope/Sutli Making
- Jute Felt
- Jute Twines
- Knitted Fabrics
- Laminated Jute Bags
- Lamination Of Hdpe Woven Cloth (Jute,Cotton, Paper)
- Nylon Yarn Crimping, Doubling And Bleaching
- Pigment Binder For Textile Printing
- Polyester Resin For Wire Enamel

Market Survey Cum Detailed Techno Economic Feasibility Report on all Projects are available Contact.
"ENGINEERS INDIA RESEARCH INSTITUTE". 4449, Nai Sarak (D), Main Road, Delhi-110006 (India)
Ph. : 09811437895, 91-11-23918117, 23916431, 45120361, 64727385 Fax : 91-11-23916431
E-mail : eiriprojects@gmail.com, eiribooks@yahoo.com • website: www.eiri.in, www.eiriindia.org

ALL FOLLOWING PROJECT REPORTS ARE READILY AVAILABLE

- Polyester Resin
- Polyester Yarn From Waste Polyester Zip Fasteners
- Power Loom
- Printing On Saree
- Readymade Garments & Hosiery
- Readymade Garments Merchandise
- Readymade Garments & Covers
- Readymade Garments & Embroidery Of Gowns, Shirts, Blouses, T-Shirts Etc. (Only Ladies)
- Readymade Salwar Suit
- Ready Made Garments
- Recovery Of Nylon From Nylon Waste
- Rotary Printing And Dyeing On Cotton, Synthetic Textile
- Sanitary Napkins
- Screen Printing On Cotton Cloth
- Sewing Thread Reels & Balls Making Industries
- Screen Printing On Cotton, Polyester & Acrylic
- Shawls (Woollen)
- Shoe Laces
- Silk Fabrics On Handloom
- Socks Knitting
- Spinning, Doubling Dyeing, Mercerising & Bleaching Of Cotton Yarn
- Spinning & Carding Of Wool Into Yarns
- Starch Book Binding Cloth
- Surat Jari
- Surgical Cotton & Bandage
- Synthetic Textile Industry (Suiting, Shirting, Sarees) Terry Cloth
- T-Shirts
- Towels, Bed Sheet Covers
- Terry Towel
- Terry Fabrics Weaving Unit
- Textile Auxilliaries & Chemicals
- Textile Bleaching, Dyeing & Finishing & Printing Of Cotton Fabrics
- Textile And Finishing Agent
- Textile (Hosiery)
- Textile Mill
- Textile Dyeing & Printing
- Textile Printing (Job Work)
- Textile Pigment Printing Binder
- Towel (Terry)
- Velvet Cloth By Flocking Process
- Viscose Staple Fibre
- Wadding Oil (100%) For Wadding Of Cotton Hosiery Cloth In The Dyeing Process
- Weaving Of Dasuti Cloth With Printing, Dyeing, Embroidery & Finishing
- Washing Of Jeans & Other Garments
- Worsted Woollen Yarn Cloth
- Zari Glitter Salma Sitara Of Plastic Film

INFOTECH/IT, HOSPITALITY, HOSPITAL, COLLEGE, SCHOOL, MEDICAL, ENTERTAINMENT, CLUB, WARE HOUSING & REAL ESTATE PROJECTS.

- Amusement Park
- Aided School
- Amusement Park Cum Water Park
- Banquet Hall
- B.Ed And Law College
- Business Process Outsourcing (Bpo)
- Call Center (Domestic)
- Call Center (International)
- Children Recreation Centre
- Cold Storage
- Community Hall
- Community Centre
- Computer Education Institute
- Computer Software
- College
- Club
- Cyber Café
- Data Processing Centre
- Dental Clinic
- Dental College
- Diagonostic Centre
- E-Commerce/Business
- E-School (Rs. 10,000/-)
- Engineering College
- Entertainment Club
- Entertainment Club, Holiday Resort, 4 Star Hotel, Amusement Park Cum Water Park, Mushroom & Its Products, Fish Farming, Lake For Boating, Deer Park
- Fashion Technology Institute
- Fast Food Parlour
- Five Star Hotel
- Food Parlour
- Franchise Training Programme For Iit & Engineering Entrance Exams.
- Golf Course
- Health Club, Beauty Parlour
- Health Club And Fitness Center
- Health Resorts
- Holiday Resorts
- Holiday Resort Cum Entertainment Club With 4 Star Hotel
- Hospitals
- Hospital Cum Research Centre
- Hospital (400 Beds)
- Ice Cream Parlour
- Internet Service Provider (I.S.P.)
- I.T. Park (Infotech Park)
- Maternity Nursing Home
- Medical College
- Medical College, Hospital & Research Institute
- Medical Transcription Centre
- Mental Retardation Hospital & Cerebral Palsy
- Motel/Small Hotel
- Multistorey Commercial Complex

- Multistorey Residential Complex
- Multiplex Cum Entertainment Centre
- Nursery School
- Nursing School/College
- Nature Care Centre
- Nursing Home
- Old Age Home
- Online Shopping Mall (Rs. 10,000/- Report)
- Portal
- Pre-Fabricated Building
- Prenursery School
- Rehabilitation Centre For Aged & Needy Persons
- Residential Cum Commercial Complex
- Restaurant
- Restaurant With Pub
- Senior Secondary School
- Special Economic Zone (Sez)/Industrial Park
- School (Primary)
- School (Higher Secondary)
- School With Hostel
- School Of Nursing
- Three Star Hotel
- Township
- Tourist Club
- Training Institute For Medical Transcription
- Video Film Studio
- Vetenary College With Hospital
- Ware House
- Website Design & E-Mail Registering

POTATO AND POTATO BASED PRODUCTS

- Alcohol From Potatoes
- Dextrose Powder From Potatoes
- Frozen Finger Chips
- I M F L (Whisky) From Potatoes
- Liquid Glucose From Potato
- Potato Chips/Waffers
- Potato Powder (Automatic Plant)
- Potato Starch
- Potato Chips (Automatic Plant)
- Potato And Onion Flakes
- Potable Beer (Alcoholic) Based On Potato & Barley/Malt
- Potato Powder
- Sago Seeds (Saboo Dana)
- Vodka From Potatoes

Market Survey Cum Detailed Techno Economic Feasibility Report on all Projects are available Contact. "ENGINEERS INDIA RESEARCH INSTITUTE". 4449, Nai Sarak (D), Main Road, Delhi-110006 (India) Ph. : 09811437895, 91-11-23918117, 23916431, 45120361, 64727385 Fax : 91-11-23916431 E-mail : eiriprojects@gmail.com, eiribooks@yahoo.com • website: www.eiri.in, www.eiriindia.org

ALL FOLLOWING PROJECT REPORTS ARE READILY AVAILABLE

AGRO BASED INDUSTRIES

- Coal Briquettes From Agrowaste
- Furfuralfrom Ricehull
- Mushroom Cultivation & Processing (Button)
- Mushroom Growing & Processing With Air Conditioning
- Mushroom Cultivation & Processing Unit Dehydration & Packaging Of Oyster & Paddy Straw Mushrooms
- Organic Manure
- Papaya Cultivation
- Papaya & Tomato Cultivation
- Processing & Utilisation Of Coconut
- Processing Of Sheep Hair To Produce Wool
- White Oats

BAKERY CONFECTIONERY & FOOD PRODUCTS

- Agrolactor Soya Milk
- Automatic Biscuit Naking Plant
- Automatic Bread Making Plant
- Apple Fruit Juice With Canning Bottling
- Ayurvedic Sharbat
- Bakery Unit (Pastries, Bread, Buns, Cake, Toffee Etc.)
- Baking Powder
- Banana & Its By Products
- Banana Powder
- Banana Wafers
- Banana Cultivation
- Beer Industry
- Dehulling Of Jaun For Beer
- Beer & Wine
- Beer, Alcohol, Imfl
- Besen Plant
- Biscuit Plant
- Bread & Biscuit Plant
- Bottling Plant (Country Liquor) From Rectified Spirit
- Bottling Plant (Imfl And Country Liquor)
- Brandy
- Bread Rusks
- Buffalo Meat/Frozen Meat With Slaughter House
- Canned Fruits & Vegetables
- Canning & Preservation Of Meat
- Canning & Preservation Of Vegetables
- Canning Of Mango Pulp & Mango Slices
- Carbonated Beverags
- Cashew Feni
- Cashew Nut (Dried & Fried)
- Cashew Nut Shell Liquid And Kernel
- Cattle Breeding
- Cattle Breeding & Dairy Farm To Produce Milk
- Cattle Feed From Tapioca
- Chewing Ginger & Amloki
- Chewing Gum
- Chilli Sauce
- Chilli Powder
- Chicken Processing With Slaughter House
- Chocolate
- Cider Plant
- Cocoa Powder
- Cocoa Butter & Cocoa Powder
- Coconut Shell Powder
- Coconut Water
- Coconut Sweet (Watery)
- Coconut Milk Powder (Dehydrated)
- Coconut Products & By Products (Integrated Plant)
- Cold Drink
- Curry Powder
- Dairy For Milk Processing (Ghee, Butter & Paneer)
- Dairy Products
- Dairy Products Milk Packaging In Pouch (Ghee, Butter, Etc.
- Dairy Farm To Prduce Milk With Packaging (Cow)
- Dairy Farm To Prduce Milk With Packaging (Bufalloe)
- Dairy Farm & Milk Products
- Dal Moth, Chanachur & Bhujiya
- Dall Mill (Pulse)
- Dehydration Of Fruits & Vegetable
- Dehydration Of Fruits And Vegetables By Vacuum Drying Method
- Desiccated Coconut Powder From Coconuts
- Dehydration & Canning Of Fruits & Vegetables
- Dry Fruit Roasting & Packaging
- Drying Of Red Chillies, Haldi, Dhaniya, Peas & Ground Nut
- Dry Ginger (Ginger Powder)
- Egg Powder
- Fish Canning In Tin & Pouches
- Fish Dehyration (Drying Of Fish)
- Fish Meal
- Fish Processing (Beast Freezing Processes)
- Flavours For Food Industries
- Flour Mill (Roller)
- Frozen Meat
- Food Dehydration (Fruits & Vegetables)
- Fried & Roasted Ground Nut, Grams, Pear Etc.
- Fruit Juice Making & Packaging In Plastic Container
- Fruit Juice In Tetra Pack (Drinks)
- Fruit Juice, Squashes, Sauce & Ketchup, Jam, Jelly, Vinegar Etc.
- Garlic Flakes
- Garlic Powder
- Ghee & Butter
- Ginger (Pulverised)
- Ginger Glazing & Preservation
- Ginger Storage
- Ginger Processing
- Ginger Oil & Ginger Dust
- Ginger Powder (Dry) & Oleoresin
- Grape Dehydration
- Grape Cultivation
- Grape Juice
- Grape Wine
- Groundnut Processing
- Honey Processing & Packaging
- Ice Cream & Ice Candy
- Ice Cube
- Invert Sugar
- Idli Mix, Dosa Mix Sambhar Mix, Vada Mix,Gulab Jamun Mix
- Instant Coffee & Instant Tea
- Instant Noodles
- Instant Soups
- Iodized Salt From Crude Salt
- Jam Chutney Pickles & Squashes
- Katha Manufacturing
- Lecithin (Soya Based)
- Lemon & Its Products
- Macaroni Manufacturing
- Macaroni, Spaghetti, Vermicelli & Noodles
- Maize & Its By Products Malting Plant
- Mango Pappad (Aam Pappad)
- Mango Powder Ripe
- Mango Powder
- Mango Processing & Canning (Mango Pulp)
- Meat Processing (Chicken Mutton)
- Meat Processing (Buffalo)
- Menthol Bold From Menthol Flakes
- Milk Powder
- Milk Powder & Ghee
- Milk Powder, Ghee & Spices
- Milk Preservation & Marketing To Whole Sellers
- Milk Preservation & Marketing To Whole Sellers (In Pouches)
- Milk Toffee Manufactures
- Mineral Water
- Mineral Water In Pouches
- Mini Flour Mill Atta Maida, Suji & Wheat Bran
- Mithai/Halwai (Sweet & Namkeen)
- Mutton Processing
- Pan Masala (Meetha, Sada, Zarda) Making & Packing
- Pan Masala And Pouch Making
- Paneer (Cheese)
- Papad & Bariyan
- Papad Plant
- Pepsicola In Polytubes
- Petha Packaging
- Pickles
- Piggery/Meat/Chicken Processing
- Pine Apple Juice Manufacturing And Canning
- Potato & Onion Powder
- Potato & Onion Flakes
- Potato Chips
- Potato Granules
- Pouch Filling For Saunf Supari Ilaichi Etc.
- Preservation Of Raws Mango Juice
- Processed Cheese & Marine Pdts.

Market Survey Cum Detailed Techno Economic Feasibility Report on all Projects are available Contact.
"ENGINEERS INDIA RESEARCH INSTITUTE". 4449, Nai Sarak (D), Main Road, Delhi-110006 (India)
Ph. : 09811437895, 91-11-23918117, 23916431, 45120361, 64727385 Fax : 91-11-23916431
E-mail : eiriprojects@gmail.com, eiribooks@yahoo.com • website: www.eiri.in, www.eiriindia.org

ALL FOLLOWING PROJECT REPORTS ARE READILY AVAILABLE

- Pulp From Tarmarind
- Readymate Processed Food
- Rice & Corn Flakes
- Rice Basmati (Trading)
- Rice Polishing & Packaging In Pouch
- Roasted/Salted/Masala/Cashew Nuts Almonds & Pea Nut
- Roller Flour Mill
- Vanaspati Unit

INFOTECH / IT PROJECT

- Medical Transcription
- Business Process Outsource (Bpo)
- E-Commerce
- Cybercafe
- Computer Software
- Internet Service Provider (Isp)
- I.T. Park
- Computer Education Centre
- Portal (Website Design)
- Call Centre (Domestic)
- Call Centre (International)

PROFITABLE PLANTATION, CULTIVATION & FARMING PROJECTS

- Amla Plantation
- Amla Plantation, Processing & Preservation
- Bio Fertilisers
- Coffee Plantation
- Coconut Plantation
- Dairy Farming
- Eucalyptus Tree Plantation
- Floriculture - Gladiolus
- Goat Farming
- Green House
- Hybrid Seeds
- Herbs Cultivation
- Jatropha (Bio Diesel) Cultivation & Extraction
- Mushrooms
- Mushroom Growing And Processing With Air Condition
- Medicinal Plantations (Neem)
- Nursery Farms
- Organic Manure
- Papaya & Tomato Cultivation
- Papaya Cultivation
- Poplar Plantation
- Rubber Plantation
- Strawberry Cultivation & Processing
- Safed Musli Cultivation & Processing (Extract & Powder)
- Stevia Cultivation & Extraction
- Sunflower Plantation
- Sugar Cane Plantation
- Teak Plantation

- Turmeric Plantation
- Tea Plantation
- Vermi-Composting

PROFITABLE GUMS, ADHESIVES & RESINS PROJECTS

- Adhesive For Stickers
- Adhesive For Corrugation Dry Powder & Paste
- Adhesive Based On Polyure Thane
- Adhesive Industries (Laminated, Favicol,Sticker, Dda & Other Types Of Adhesives)
- Adhesive For Corrugation (Dry Powder)
- Alkyd Resins
- Adhesive Manufacturing For Joining Hdpe Pipes & Joints
- Adhesive Based On Vinyl Acetate (Fevicol Type)
- B.O.P.P Self Adhesive Tapes
- Cnsl Based Resin In Liquid & Powder Form
- D.O.P And Other Plasticizers
- Ester Gums (Food Grade)
- Epoxy Resin
- Guar Gum
- Glue Stick
- Latex Rubber Based Adhesive
- Leather Based Adhesive
- Liquid Adhesive For Corrugated Board & Boxes
- Leather To Leather Adhesive (Latex Based Adhesives)
- Melamine Formaldehyde Powder
- Office Paste
- Paper Label For Beer Bottles
- Polyester Resins
- Phenol Formaldehyde Resin
- Potato Starch
- Poly Amide Resin
- Printing Gums (Guar Gum Based)

- Rubber Adhesive
- Synthetic Adhesive For Decorative Laminates Bonding
- Starch & Dextrin Based Adhesive
- Thermosetting Adhesive
- Urea Formaldehyde Resin
- Urea Formaldehyde Moulding Powder
- Unsaturated Polyester Resins
- Water Based Latex Adhesives

TEA PLANTATION & PROCESSING BASED INDUSTRIES

- Caffeine From Tea Waste
- Decaffineated Tea
- Instant Tea And Coffee (Premixed With Sugar And Milk)
- Instant Tea From Black Tea
- Tea Bags (Dip - Dip Types)
- Tea Botique
- Tea Packaging Industry
- Tea Bags
- Tea Packaging & Distribution
- Tea Industry

ALUMINIUM AND ALUMINIUM BASED INDUSTRIES

- Aluminium Powder
- Aac & Acsr Aluminium Conductors
- Aluminium Silicate
- Aluminium Utensil
- Aluminium Wire Drawing
- Aluminium Paint
- Aluminium Ingots From Scrap
- Aluminium Alloy & Ingots
- Anodizing Of Aluminium
- Aluminium Chloride
- Aluminium Channels
- Aluminium Rolling Mill
- Aluminium Bottles
- Alumnium Foil Cutting & Roll Making
- Aluminium End Caps
- Aluminium Door And Windows
- Aluminium Collapsible Tubes
- Aluminium Phosphide
- Aluminium Ingots From Bauxite
- Aluminium Caps
- Aluminium Furniture & Hardware
- Aluminium Beverage Cans
- Aluminium Cans For Capacitors
- Aluminium & Aluminium Alloys From Aluminium Scraps To Make Utensils (Induction Furnace Melted)
- Aluminium Hot & Cold Rolling Mill (Aluminium Sheets & Circles)
- Anodic Aluminium Labels
- Aluminium Slugs & Circles

Market Survey Cum Detailed Techno Economic Feasibility Report on all Projects are available Contact.
"ENGINEERS INDIA RESEARCH INSTITUTE". 4449, Nai Sarak (D), Main Road, Delhi-110006 (India)
Ph. : 09811437895, 91-11-23918117, 23916431, 45120361, 64727385 Fax : 91-11-23916431
E-mail : eiriprojects@gmail.com, eiribooks@yahoo.com • website: www.eiri.in, www.eiriindia.org